Why Evil Exists

Charles Mathewes, Ph.D.

THE
GREAT
COURSES®

PUBLISHED BY:

THE GREAT COURSES
Corporate Headquarters
4840 Westfields Boulevard, Suite 500
Chantilly, Virginia 20151-2299
Phone: 1-800-832-2412
Fax: 703-378-3819
www.thegreatcourses.com

Charles Mathewes, Ph.D.
Associate Professor of Religious Studies
University of Virginia

Professor Charles Mathewes is Associate Professor of Religious Studies at the University of Virginia, where he teaches religious ethics, theology, and philosophy of religion. He and his wife, Jennifer Geddes, are the coprincipals of Brown College at Monroe Hill, one of the University of Virginia's residential colleges.

Professor Mathewes lived in Saudi Arabia between the ages of 8 and 15. He received his B.A. in Theology from Georgetown University, graduating Phi Beta Kappa, and his M.A. and Ph.D. in Religion from the University of Chicago. He has lived in Charlottesville, Virginia, since 1997, making it the place he has lived longest by far.

Professor Mathewes is the author of *Evil and the Augustinian Tradition* and *A Theology of Public Life*, both from Cambridge University Press; *Understanding Religious Ethics*, from Wiley-Blackwell; and *The Republic of Grace: Augustinian Thoughts for Dark Times*, from Eerdmans. He served as editor of *The Journal of the American Academy of Religion*, the flagship journal in the field of religious studies, from 2006 to 2010 and was the journal's youngest editor ever. He is also associate editor of the forthcoming third edition of the *Westminster Dictionary of Christian Ethics* and serves on the House of Bishops Theology Committee of the Episcopal Church.

Professor Mathewes has received a number of teaching awards. Every year since 1999, his classes have been named as exemplary classes for prospective students to attend during the Days on the Lawn decision period for applicants accepted into the University of Virginia. In 2007, he received a Mead Honored Faculty award—one of the university's highest teaching awards—as well as a Mead Endowment Teaching Award to fund a dream idea. He used the endowment to run a small seminar on religion and politics that culminated in a trip to Washington DC and a meeting with politicians, policy experts, and legal scholars.

When Professor Mathewes and his wife are not residing in Brown College, they live with their children outside Charlottesville, in the foothills of the Blue Ridge Mountains. ∎

Table of Contents

Table of Contents

Table of Contents

Table of Contents

Why Evil Exists

Scope:

"It is not God I do not accept," Dostoevsky grumbled, "but the world he has created." In fact, the earliest literatures grapple with a question as troubling now as it was 4,000 years ago: Why do evil and suffering exist in the world?

From the ancient Sumerian *Epic of Gilgamesh* to the terror attacks of 9/11, the problem of theodicy—explaining the existence of evil in a divinely governed or morally ordered world—has been at the heart of every major religion and many secular philosophical worldviews, as well. Charting the various formulations of this problem and the different answers people in the West have given to it are the goals of this course. These lectures examine the history of cultural definitions of the problem of evil and the "solutions" devised for living in its shadow.

The problem of evil encompasses both "natural" and "moral" evil. Certainly, human suffering due to nature—death, disease, natural disasters, and the like—is troubling enough. But human malice adds an entirely distinct kind of difficulty, for human evil comes out of humanity's distinctively moral character. The same energies of intellect and will that led mankind to cure innumerable diseases and put men on the moon led us also to poison gas and ICBMs; the capacities for emotional attachment and imaginative empathy that led to the expansion of fellow-feeling and genuine compassion for others we will never meet have led equally to our fear and hatred of those same others at other times. We will never lack for the ironic evidences of humanity's conflicted and unstable condition—the strange and, at times, terrible alloy of nobility and brutality that together define our character. What does the fact of human cruelty and malice tell us about the ultimate fate of morality and religious belief? How best should we understand such malice, and how might we best respond to its reality in our lives and the lives of those around us?

These are some of the challenges the study of evil must confront. But things are more complicated still. In fact, the questions clustered under the title "the problem of evil" are not easily reduced to a single clear and precise problem; rather, the problem is itself a problem, a "meta-problem," so to speak, a problem whose proper form is itself up for debate and dispute. When we speak of evil, are we referring to a natural force of some sort, welling up from the most primitive part of our brain? Or does evil refer to a series of willed or learned capacities into which we are trained by our elders? Or is it something else entirely?

Answers to these questions inform the response a thinker or a culture gives to the problem, because they give determinate form to the problem itself. That is to say, a particular interpretation of the problem of evil is naturally shaped by one's sense of the precise scope of the problem, and one's proposed response to evil is also in large part determined by what one thinks evil is.

Here, then, are some of the questions thinkers have asked and, thus, questions that we must ask, as well:

1. Is evil something real or merely the result of human (psychological?) confusions?

2. Is evil its own power, or is it totally parasitic on other realities, and if so, which realities?

3. Is evil naturally part of the world or (perhaps more precisely) of our innate motivations and desires, or is it something we create by our own action?

4. How is evil related to our individuality? Must we be wicked to be unique individuals?

5. Is evil inescapable for humans? How best can we resist or contain evil?

6. Can we understand evil? That is, is there a way to make evil actions totally intelligible to us? Should we want such intelligibility at all?

7. Ought we to go on using the language of "evil" at all? Or is it so connected with our troubles that we need some entirely new language with which to understand our world?

In this course, we will examine the history of cultural definitions of the problem of evil, and we will explore a wide range of proposals that have been devised for living in its shadow. Texts and writers under discussion include the ancient Sumerian Epic of Gilgamesh, the Hebrew Bible, Greek tragedies, the Christian New Testament, the Qur'an, and Jewish Rabbinic thought; traditional authorities, such as Aristotle, Augustine, Aquinas, and Plato; major writers, such as Dante and Milton; modern thinkers, including Hume, Leibniz, Voltaire, and Nietzsche; and subsequent commentators, such as Martin Buber, Reinhold Niebuhr, Hannah Arendt, Albert Camus, and Joseph Conrad. Lectures focus on historical, philosophical, and religious perspectives in tracing the history of an age-old and extremely vexing problem: our basic investigation into the inner history of evil in the world and the implications of that history for the future. In undertaking this inquiry, we hope both to gain a deeper purchase on evil's manifestations, character, and effects and to understand the challenges evil presents to life in our world. ■

The Nature and Origins of Evil
Lecture 1

Is it possible for a theory to accommodate the enormously different empirical realities that we name with the term "evil"? Can any theory account for how to connect up genocides of international scale on one side and parents who beat their children on the other; can any theory account for all that? Hard to know.

The 20th-century Polish poet Zbigniew Herbert wrote that history is a "strange teacher." It teaches us by indirection, surprise, and pain, conveying lessons that are "dense and dark," difficult to understand. Our task in this course will be to grapple with those lessons in an effort to shed light on some of the most profound questions of human history, most fundamentally, the problem of evil.

This lecture series looks at how humans, especially in the West over the past five millennia, have thought about the origins and nature of evil. Why does evil exist, and what exactly is evil? Is it a function of humans living together in society, or is it somehow superhuman? Is evil an inevitable part of the cosmos, or is it something that we created and, thus, can possibly constrain or eliminate?

Let's start by defining evil: It's something that is not just against the moral order but intentionally and willfully against that order. Evil embodies a dimension of rebellion, although this rebellion needn't be directly experienced as such by those engaged in it. People can do evil without thinking too much about the acts they are performing. In fact, people who perform evil acts—genocide, abuse of racial or ethnic minorities—often understand themselves to be obeying the moral order of their particular culture. Part of the power of evil is the way it insinuates itself intimately into people's lives.

We can identify three broad families of theories about evil. The first of these locates evil in a kind of folly, a wholly irrational eruption of chaos in an ordered world. In this tradition, some thinkers have talked about evil as privational, as depriving creation of goodness and being, depriving reality itself of some dimension or thickness or depth. This is ultimately an optimistic vision, though it also suggests a certain disturbing capacity on the part of creatures to revolt against the moral order they inhabit. This account gives us an illuminating psychological picture of humanity, but at the same time, it may be too abstract. It's not clear how the idea of evil as the absence of being could help someone when confronting evil. Further, this view doesn't seem to account for the positive power of evil, the terrible sincerity it sometimes encompasses.

Part of the power of evil is the way it insinuates itself intimately into people's lives.

A second view sees evil as fundamentally part of the cosmos, part of our natural makeup. This naturalist view helps to domesticate evil by rendering it part of our character. Evil does not appear with any satanic magnificence or any kind of alienated theological aroma; it's a part of our world. But the grim thought that evil is all too human can become the source of hope. We may not be able to defeat evil entirely—because its home is our world—but at least we are struggling with a force that is nothing other than ourselves. The difficulty with this view is that the hope it offers may ultimately seem inadequate. What is the hope a hope for—to hold off evil only for the moment?

The third account we might characterize as "evil as maturation." Here, we see the idea that to become fully adult, it may be necessary to undergo some painful separation from our too-familiar and cozy surroundings. Just as teenagers rebel against their parents to gain a sense of identity, so our moral maturation requires a rebellion against God or the moral order, a kind of wounding in order to gain wisdom. This view captures a certain dimension of evil's reality: It's true that some evil is a matter of lashing out at the world in misconstrued anger, but is it true that the purpose of all evil is our edification?

Of course, we're not only interested in theoretical insights but also with the practical advice recommended to deal with the challenge of evil in the way that challenge is construed. Whether we can test evil by direct confrontation, by trying to absorb it into ourselves as marks of our glorious martyrdom for God, by developing nonviolent practices to resist its assaults on us—these and many other practical proposals are all intimately related to particular theoretical visions of evil.

In these lectures, we'll explore humanity's thinking about evil from the ancient Near East through the 20th century. Along the way, we'll consider numerous underlying questions: Can any theoretical representation of evil capture its full reality? What is the relationship between evil and the gods or God, the absolute moral order? Is evil a matter of barbarism versus civilization, or is civilization itself complicit in evil? Most fundamentally, is any of this theoretical activity helpful in our attempts to inhabit a world filled with evil? ■

Suggested Reading

Adams and Adams, eds., *The Problem of Evil.*

Anderson, *Sin: A History.*

Bouchard, *Tragic Method and Tragic Theology.*

Bowker, *Problems of Suffering in Religions of the World.*

Larrimore, *The Problem of Evil: A Reader.*

Midgley, *Wickedness: A Philosophical Essay.*

Ricoeur, *The Symbolism of Evil.*

Russell, *The Prince of Darkness: Radical Evil and the Power of Good in History.*

Questions to Consider

1. Recall the three broad historical options presented for thinking about evil (evil as folly, evil as natural, evil as maturation). Initially, which of these options do you find most convincing and why?

2. What do you make of Herbert's assertion that *historia* is *magistra vitae* ("the teacher of life") and has provided us with "dark and dense material"? What can history teach us, and what are its limits?

The Nature and Origins of Evil
Lecture 1—Transcript

Hello, I'm Charles Mathewes. I teach at the University of Virginia, and I'm delighted to be teaching this course about how humans in the West have thought about evil.

The 20th-century Polish poet Zbigniew Herbert, survivor of the Nazis and the Soviet Union, once wrote (and I quote):

> Teachers in our high schools pound into us that history is the teacher of life. But when history crashed down on us in all its brutal glory, I understood, in the very real glow of flames above my home city, that she was a strange teacher. She gave to the people who consciously survived her, and to all who followed her, more material for thought than all the old chronicles put together. A dense and dark material. It will require the work of many consciences to shed light on it.

This is our task: to shed light on some of the most profound questions of human history; and most fundamentally, the question of the problem of evil.

Herbert was no little intellect; he was one of the most powerful poets of Polish writing; world poetry, for that matter. His poems were used as anthems for the Polish solidarity movement in the 1970s and 80s; and, in fact, we'll be looking at some of his own work later in the lecture course near the end. He's a remarkably far-seeing thinker. The passage in particular that we just read is powerfully brooding. Consider it for a second: What does it mean to call history a "strange teacher"? It means that it's cunning; that it teaches by indirection, by surprise, by pain, not by direct lessons, clearly and lucidly articulated by schoolteachers at the fronts of classrooms and readily digested by attentive students sitting neatly in rows. What does it mean to say that the material it gives us is "dense and dark"? That language suggests it's more than merely grim or merely savage; that it's something that is very difficult to understand, requiring serious effort from many people working in many different ways. Among these people are you and I; and in these lectures, this is our task: to shed light on some of the most profound questions of human history, and most fundamentally the question of the problem of evil.

Particularly in the last 100 years or so, thinkers have made repeated attempts, directly and indirectly, to come to grips with this question. Hannah Arendt, another thinker who we'll be looking at later in these lectures, once wrote that the central problem for post-World War II intellectuals will be the problem of evil. But it didn't turn out that way; thinkers of the era didn't spend much time thinking about human malice and the suffering it creates at all. Such a "head in the sand" attitude is not unique to thinkers in the post-war era; Arendt's point, after all, was an implicit criticism of those pre-war intellectuals who had not taken seriously the challenge of human evil, telling themselves that surely World War I had convinced humanity that savagery of that sort was never a suitable strategy. Of course, World War I came as a near-total surprise to thinkers as well, who had imagined that such savagery as was unleashed in that conflict had been carefully bred out of or civilized out of Europe—at least Europe, at any rate—by the long peace of the 19th century. Indeed, we don't have to look deep in the past for this pattern: The same thing was happening in the 1990s, for those of us whose memories go that far back.

The habitual avoidance of evil suggests something important about thinking about evil: namely, that it is difficult and painful work, and much of the time we would rather spend our energies avoiding thinking about this problem rather than confronting it. If we don't discipline ourselves into thinking about it, our mind will gradually drift away to reflect on other things. If discipline and focus are what we need, that is what we will get in these lectures. This lecture series looks at how humans, especially in the West over the past five millennia, have thought about the origins and the nature of evil. Why does evil exist? What exactly is evil? What is its nature? Is it something primitive in human psychology? Is it something distinctly, humanly, civilized; some dimension of human life that is, in some important way, a function of humans living together in society? Is it somehow superhuman; something that exists outside of humans but manages from time to time to take control of us in some demonic possession? Is evil necessarily part of the cosmos, an inevitable part of it; or is it somehow something that we created and thus can in some way possibly constrain, manage, reduce, slowly let wither away back to nothingness? How should we live in the shadow of evil, however we conceive of it? These are the questions we'll see these thinkers and these texts asking and attempting to answer.

To begin with, let's kind of offer a provisional definition of evil; this is complicated, so bear with me for a second here. Let's say that evil is something that's not just against the moral order, something that's not just wrong—however you construe that moral order—but intentionally and willfully against that order; that evil, that is, has a dimension of willfulness and rebellion. Let me be clear: This rebellion needn't be directly experienced as rebellion by those engaged in it. People can do evil without thinking too much about the acts that they do; indeed, often that's the worst kind. Lots of people participated in really savage forms of evil in the 20th century—genocidal oppression, horrible forms of racism, other kinds of abusive ethnic minorities—and many of those people, especially if they had been brought up in those cultures, did not understand what they were doing as violating the moral order, they understood themselves to be obeying the moral order. For those people, thinking about what they were doing as evil was not a possibility in their minds. From the outside, thinking about what they did, we see what they're doing as evil; and maybe they, later on, can see what they're doing as evil.

Albert Speer, the great architect of the Third Reich, the leading artist really of Hitler's world and also eventually the director of war munitions and supplies for the Third Reich; but a cultured, educated, and civilized man, a man who survived the war and lived for 25 years in Spandau Prison on Berlin for his part in the Holocaust and in the Third Reich's many crimes, a part he freely admitted and owned up to. At one point after the war, Speer was asked by someone, "How is it possible that you worked with Hitler and did not realize how evil what he was proposing was?" Speer said something that was very interesting—was reported to have said something—he said, "It is hard to know the devil when his hand is on your shoulder." Part of the power of evil is the way it insinuates itself intimately into people's lives. So often people don't, in fact, experience what they're doing as evil. But when we think about acts of evil considered as just that—as acts of evil—even when their perpetrators didn't recognize them as such, such acts of evil in their very essence, I propose, are attempts actively to reject the moral order, even if the people who do them don't understand themselves to be doing that.

Similarly, when we ask about the problem of human suffering, we need to narrow our focus a bit there as well. Suffering of the sort we want to investigate here strikes us as excessive or gratuitous, as not necessary. We're talking about pain that seems pointless or useless in some sense; pain that is inflicted for no point at all. One of the greatest thinkers on this character of suffering is a man named Emmanuel Levinas; we'll be talking about some of his work near the end of this course as well.

In thinking about evil and pain in this way, we can distinguish between three large families of theories about evil, each with its advantages and difficulties. Let me quickly say something about each of these, which we'll see manifest in many of the people who are coming up. First, there's the account of evil that locates it centrally in a kind of folly, as a wholly irrational, senseless eruption of chaos in an ordered world. Evil here is somehow against the order of the cosmos itself. As such, some thinkers in this tradition have talked about evil as privational, as depriving creation of goodness and being, depriving reality itself of some dimension or thickness or depth of reality; not introducing some positive evil into the world, but simply annihilating some of the good things that are there. Many thinkers have explored this vision, but for my money the most profound and far-thinking one has been Augustine, the Roman Christian bishop of the 4th and 5th centuries. This is ultimately a very optimistic and hopeful vision, though it also suggests a certain truly disturbing capacity on the part of creatures to revolt against the moral order that they inhabit.

The advantages of this account are many, but one of the most profound is that this picture is actually quite psychologically illuminating. Small children don't know why they do mean things, and in general evil deeds are always done for reasons that when we query them—when we ask about why someone did something—these reasons never quite manage to seem as intelligent or rational to us, upon reflection, as they did at the time we did them. However, this account does have its problems. One big difficulty with it is that it is perhaps too theoretical, too abstract, and because of that, possibly too escapist. After all, while it may be very metaphysically reassuring to talk about evil as the absence of being, it's not clear how that idea helps someone confronting a killer, or someone trying to think about the vast scope of evil in genocide in the century just past. The very theoretical profundity of the account, that is, may lead it to be a little distant from practical application.

This gets to a second challenge for this view; one that is experienced, one that it encountered really as a practical challenge, and then reaching out from that practical challenge to really threaten the very theoretical core of this interpretation of evil. That challenge is this: Can this picture really account for the positive power of evil; it's demonic character, the way that evil sometimes has a terrible sincerity around it? It's hard to see how you can talk about a Rwandan genocider—that is, one of the people who was involved in the genocide in Rwanda—swinging a machete or even an ordinary criminal in an alley as somehow absent of being. The problem with both, really, seems to be that they're all too present. This picture has some insights, but also has some challenges to face.

A second view does not see evil as essentially against the cosmos, opposed to the cosmos, but rather sees it as fundamentally part of the cosmos itself, part of our natural makeup. On this naturalist account, which prides itself on its cold-eyed realism, evil is simply one of the energies that we must acknowledge and reign in as best we can. Thinkers who fit roughly in this picture would include the Greek historian and political thinker Thucydides, perhaps the philosopher Aristotle, some thinkers in the Jewish rabbinic tradition, and some modern thinkers like Friedrich Nietzsche and Sigmund Freud. The insight of this view is paradoxically how it helps us to domesticate evil, as it were, precisely by rendering evil somehow part of our natural character. It does not appear here with any satanic magnificence or with any kind of alienated theological aroma; it's really a part of our world, and that very grim thought that evil is, in fact, all too human can become, if you think about it aright (these thinkers propose), the source of some real hope. For if evil cannot be defeated or driven out of our world totally, since its home is our world, at least we are facing a struggle with a force that is nothing other than ourselves; it's a force that is human-sized.

The difficulty here is that this view's hope may seem finally inadequate to some people. After all, what is the hope a hope for? That we can hold off evil for the moment? That seems unlikely to mobilize enough energy for us to do much more than resist it at the instant that we meet it. To do more, to really confront the roots of evil, it seems like we need other energies that can drive us forward. Furthermore, this account's cold-eyed realism may hide the way that it suggest to us, it insinuates to us, that evil may not be as terrible as we experience it as being. That is to say, by talking about evil as natural and by domesticating evil in this way, we are offered a comforting disillusionment of knowing that the world is not as bad as we maybe thought it was; it might be a harder world, but it's not as terrifying, these thinkers are saying. But what do we do with our experience—experience that some of us have had and all of us can imagine having—of encountering evil that seems not to be so domesticated? What can we say about the idea of a demonic force of evil? Just as the first, then, this one, too, has some insights and some challenges.

The third account may seem initially odd to you, but I think, in fact, it is more common than you might realize; and that is what we call the "evil as maturation" account. This account builds itself up around a paradox: to become fully grown up, some painful separation from our too-familiar, too-cozy original surroundings may be necessary. Just as teenagers rebel against their parents in order to gain their own sense of identity, so our moral maturation requires a kind of rebellion against God or the moral order— however one thinks about that—a kind of wounding in order to come to gain wisdom. This is a very old theory of evil: The Greek Christian bishop Irenaeus of Lyon in the 2nd century of the Common Era and the 19th-century German philosopher, Georg Wilhelm Friedrich Hegel, offered accounts of this; and I propose to you that, in fact, this account today is quite common.

The advantage of this view lies in the way it captures a certain dimension of evil's reality: Certainly it's true that some evil is clearly a matter of trying to lash out at the world in misconstrued anger at it; certainly sometimes people try to gain a sense of their identity by estranging themselves from the too-comforting confines of the world that they presently inhabit. But the disadvantage of this view lies in what we may call its partiality: It may be right that some evil turns out to be for our edification, but all evil? People who talk about this view talk about the world and the world's sufferings as a veil of soul-making; a site wherein we are taught to become human beings. But there are lots of people in the world who evil doesn't ultimately help grow up; there are lots of people in the world whom evil stops before they grow up. For those people, it seems this account is not just cold comfort, it might be actually obscene.

But we're not only interested in these theoretical insights; we're also concerned with the practical advice recommended to deal with the the challenge of evil in the way that these thinkers construe that challenge. In other words, it's not enough to know how exactly someone theoretically talks about evil; you have to see how that theoretical picture of what evil is and how it relates to humans interlocks with a set of practical proposals about how to respond to this reality. The practical and the theoretical are actually two sides of the same coin, and changes in one formulation affect the other formulations; so you have to understand both to understand either. Whether we can test evil by direct confrontation, by aggressively arming ourselves against it in some way, by trying to absorb it into ourselves as marks of our glorious martyrdom for our God; whether we develop techniques to resist its assaults on us by nonviolent practices in which we must be trained; these and many other kinds of practical proposals are all intimately related to particular theoretical visions of what evil is for each of these thinkers. That's the story that this lecture tells: The attempt of human thinking in the West to come to terms with the full reality of evil as it presents itself to us in our lived experience.

Let me say something about the overall story we'll be telling in these lectures and note some of the highlights of what's to come. Roughly, we're going to look at and tell the story of how a series of accounts challenge one another and are challenged by the realities they confront and that provoke them into thinking about evil. We're going to start 6,000 or so years ago in the Ancient Near East with some of the oldest stories we have in human history. We're going to work our way through the scriptural heritage of the Hebrew Bible, an Old Testament for Christians, and the Christian New Testament; we're going to look at Greco-Roman classical thought; attend to all three Abrahamic traditions' ideas about evil as they were formulated in those traditions in late antiquity and the Middle Ages; move into the Reformation, the Renaissance, and the Enlightenment; and culminate in the Modern Age, ending with the 20th century and our recent struggles with evil, including 9/11 and beyond. Throughout the course, we'll not only study a series of philosophers and theologians on these matters; we'll also offer many examples from history, literature, religious scriptures, and mythology in order to make clear some of the more abstract distinctions of philosophers and theologians, and also to challenge those abstract distinctions.

We study these thinkers, these texts, these traditions not just because it's interesting to know what others thought, but because it can be enormously useful. In fact, as we'll see, from the Ancient Near East on, humans have always wondered about what other people thought about these problems, and their own thinking about evil has always gone on against a backdrop of other and previous ways of thinking about it. That is to say, the activity of asking questions about these questions, the activity of inquiring into the history of thinking about evil, is as old as the activity of asking these questions itself is. In thinking about evil, then, people have always found it useful to learn what others before them have thought as well.

In thinking about these things, we'll find the following dimensions of the question worth considering. First of all, the question that I'll repeat again and again, even if only occasionally, because I think this is a really deep question for us: the question of abstraction versus concrete description; abstract thinking versus concrete narration of evils. We'll see this debate carried out through many, many people in our text: Plato and Aristotle fight it out over this in some ways; the 17th, 18th century thinkers Gottfried Leibniz and Pierre Bayle fight it out about this issue. The issue is this: Can a theoretical representation of evil capture the full reality of evil; can it capture its depth and its breadth? That is, is it possible for a theory to accommodate the enormously different empirical realities that we name with the term "evil?" Can any theory account for how to connect up genocides of international scale on one side and parents who beat their children on the other; can any theory account for all that? Hard to know.

A second challenge is the question of whether or not evil is transcendent or mundane; we saw that already. What is the relationship between evil and the gods or God, or however one construes the absolute moral order or divinity that surrounds the cosmos (or if one does at all)? Might evil be something that God plans out in advance? Might evil have a positive function in the moral structure of the cosmos? Here, there's a debate going back to, again, the Christian theologian and bishop Irenaeus and leading into the 20th century: As it possible, as very many Christians have said for a long time and as certain liturgies, certain practices of worship, in the Christian church have suggested, that the fall of humans, that evil's introduction to the cosmos is, as the Latin phrase puts it, a *felix culpa*, a "happy fault." Is there some way in which the fall itself was used by God to elevate humanity above what it would have been otherwise?

A third question is the question of whether or not evil is in some way a healthy part of our world or something that is wholly destructive and parasitic on it. Thinkers like Augustine and Nietzsche would be useful here. There's a question also about whether or not evil is natural, or a violation of nature. That's a debate that we'll see coming up with Plato and Aristotle not too far away in our lectures. Another question that's become increasingly important in the last century is whether evil is a matter of barbarism versus civilization, or whether civilization is itself in some complicated way complicit in evil; whether civilization—human civilization—might itself be in some important ways a function of evil. Remember, as early as we go back to, say, the Hebrew Bible, the Tower of Babel itself—the first genuinely human social event—is precisely designed to be a rebellion against God; and in the 20th century, lots of thinkers about the Holocaust have suggested that, in fact, the Holocaust itself could not have happened absent the conditions of modern societies and civilization.

There are lots of questions of this sort: What is the relationship between personal evil and communal evil? How can we think about individual responsibility if evil's corruption infects an entire culture, perhaps our entire species? Is the naming of evil as, itself, "evil" an achievement (someone like Camus might say it is) or an evasion (someone like Freud might say it is)? Most fundamentally of all, is any of this questioning—any of this theoretical activity—really helpful in our attempts to inhabit a world filled with evil? Or are we just sitting in our armchairs, enjoying ourselves with frivolous mental diversions?

All of these very abstract, very general questions will be silently suffusing all these lectures. I'll only mention them from time to time; but they'll always be in my mind, and so they should be in yours as well. We're not going to answer the question of why evil exists here; we're not going to choose one of these rival accounts as if this were a game show and the positions described here were contestants. What I want to do is introduce you to a range of different voices; different ways of talking and thinking about this. Some of them will sound quite familiar to you from the beginning; some of them will sound very novel, perhaps alien to you; but all of them, however distant they may seem, go into the thinking and the speaking that you do about evil. They give you many of the tools you use in coming to grips with our world's dense and dark material. Even with 36 lectures, we can't be comprehensive. There are too many people who have thought about evil, and maybe there's just too much evil to think about. Anyway, you all have your own private stocks of experiences and insights, thoughts and memories that go into your own thinking. But our thinking about evil, taken collectively, does have behind it a history of which it is tremendously edifying to be aware.

Before I end this first lecture, let me return to the passage of Herbert, which we began with, for a second. He says something very important there that I want to point out. He says that his teachers tried to teach him, but he truly learned only from seeing through his own eyes his own city on fire; and what he learned was not quite what he thought his teachers were trying to teach him, that history was a strange teacher. In doing this, Herbert suggests some profound tension between the effort at direct teaching and actual learning. This challenge between what we can call book learning and life experience is one of the deepest we have to face here. We can't forget the important suspicion that lectures like these—lectures that attempt to glean some morals, some wisdom from human history—are themselves potentially useless; a dangerous distraction, prone to make us focus on trivialities at the cost of losing the larger import of the lesson at hand. But that's a very abstract challenge; the challenge to the very possibility of a series of lectures like these, to the possibility that something useful could be communicated through them. The only real response we have to that is just to go ahead and undertake the lectures; to see something of the depth and breadth of the ways that humans from 6,000 years ago until today have developed a wide range of ways of thinking about the nature and origins of evil and attempted to discern the resources we have for dealing with that problem. That's what we'll turn to next.

Enuma Elish—Evil as Cosmic Battle
Lecture 2

> In calling these stories—the myth of the *Enuma Elish* and the *Epic of Gilgamesh*—"myths," I'm not trying to be dismissive. When I say "myth," I mean the deep structures of the cultural unconscious, the foundational narratives and the frames by which people think in these cultures.

In this lecture, we look at two of the oldest sources of human thinking about evil: the creation myth of Babylon known as the *Enuma Elish* and one of the earliest stories about a human attempting to make meaning out of death and suffering, the *Epic of Gilgamesh*. These narratives express one of the most fundamental convictions humans have had about evil: the idea that evil has a cosmic and perhaps metaphysical reality beyond human beings.

The categories of good and evil are present from the earliest civilizations of the ancient Near East. Also central to the ancient Near Eastern world is what scholars call the "combat myth," in which the cosmos is a battlefield between good and bad divine powers. This combat myth gives rise to these cultures' cosmogonies (stories of how the world and the cosmos came to be) and theogonies (stories of the creation of the gods). The creation of humanity is usually the final act in the drama that begins with the origins of these gods. In these stories, the chaos gods are confronted, defeated, and destroyed by other, often younger hero gods.

The *Enuma Elish*, the Babylonian cosmogony myth, is the oldest combat myth we have. In the story, reality begins with two primeval gods, Apsu and Tiamat; they create other gods, all of whom live in Tiamat's body because there is nothing outside the gods. Conflict arises between the original gods and the later generations they created. Ultimately, Marduk, the grandson of Tiamat, kills his grandmother and forms the earth from her corpse. By these acts, he becomes the primary god in the Babylonian pantheon.

Several aspects of this myth are key to our thinking about evil. First, the chaos god Tiamat is not represented as the source of evil per se, though she is, in fact, prior to people and, perhaps, more profoundly part of the universe than hero/ordering gods, such as Marduk. The "evil" emotions—envy, hate, fear, murderousness—mark the victorious younger gods, including Marduk, as much as they mark the older gods. Evil, then, is in some way intrinsic to reality, but it is also in inevitable conflict with the forces of order. Because the cosmos is created in a struggle and out of the old cosmos, it may bear traces or be the ongoing site of this conflict between good and evil. This explains the persistence of evil: It is literally worked into the fabric of the cosmos.

Compare this account to that of creation in the book of **Genesis,** especially Genesis 1: "In the beginning, God created the heavens and the earth." Here, there is no struggle; "the deep" (*tehom*) over which God moves at the beginning of creation is passive before God's will. God sees what God has created and deems it good.

> **Because the cosmos is created in a struggle and out of the old cosmos, it may bear traces or be the ongoing site of this conflict between good and evil. This explains the persistence of evil: It is literally worked into the fabric of the cosmos.**

Although there are important differences between the Jewish and Christian understandings of Genesis, both traditions clearly see that the impetus of this text, unlike the *Enuma Elish*, is toward a world in which one God uniformly and without resistance creates the cosmos out of passive matter.

The *Enuma Elish* explains the cosmic order, but the question remains: What's the place of humans in this order? The gods look like humans, and humans are made from the blood of a god, but one thing distinguishes the two: Humans are mortal, and the gods are not. This question motivates the *Epic of Gilgamesh*, the first recorded attempt to understand and inhabit a world in which suffering occurs and perhaps a world in which suffering is partially constitutive of what makes us human.

In the *Epic*, the king of Uruk, Gilgamesh, is plunged into grief by the death of his close companion, Enkidu. To assuage his grief, Gilgamesh undertakes a quest to find the key to immortality but is told: "The life that you are seeking you will never find. When the gods created man they allotted to him death, but life they retained in their own keeping." Gilgamesh returns to Uruk, where the sight of the city walls prompts him to praise the enduring work of human hands. Perhaps this recognition of the achievement of human effort is a sign that Gilgamesh has begun, at the end of the epic, to find a way out of utter despair: a slow turning back toward a merely human life. A parallel work or perhaps a coda to the *Epic* recounts the moment of Gilgamesh's death but suggests that it is precisely the finitude of human life that is the basis of whatever joys we can have. As we journey through life in the same way as Gilgamesh, there comes a moment when we know that death is our future, and we must decide how to live in light of that knowledge. ∎

Important Terms

Enuma Elish: Babylonian creation myth, in which the god Marduk establishes himself as king over the gods by defeating Tiamat, the chaos monster.

Genesis: First book of the Jewish and Christian Scriptures, which tells the story of God's creation of the world, the origin of evil, and the development of the people Israel.

Gilgamesh: Important surviving work from Mesopotamia in the 3rd millennium B.C.E., in which the hero, Gilgamesh, suffers as he searches for immortality and founds a city.

Suggested Reading

Dalley, *Myths from Mesopotamia: Creation, the Flood, Gilgamesh, and Others*.

Damrosch, *The Buried Book: The Loss and Rediscovery of the Great Epic of Gilgamesh*.

Forsyth, *The Old Enemy: Satan and the Combat Myth*.

Foster, *The Epic of Gilgamesh.*

Kramer, *The Sumerians: Their History, Culture, and Character.*

Mason, *Gilgamesh: A Verse Translation.*

Questions to Consider

1. The lecture suggests that "myths" need not be seen as untruths; rather, they are foundational stories that reflect the deep cultural assumptions of a civilization. In addition to the myths mentioned in the lecture, what other modern myths reflect important aspects of our culture? Do we have modern myths about evil—if so, what are they?

2. Based on the lecture's description of ancient Near Eastern culture—and the *Enuma Elish* specifically—how do you see these cultures in relation to our own? Do their beliefs about evil seem alien, or familiar, or both?

Enuma Elish—Evil as Cosmic Battle
Lecture 2—Transcript

Welcome back. In this lecture, I want to talk about two of the oldest, if not the oldest, sources of human thinking about evil: the creation myth of Babylon that we know as the *Enuma Elish*, and one of the earliest stories about a human facing the challenge of making meaning out of death and suffering, the *Epic of Gilgamesh*.

These stories go back many thousands of years, and some of their elements in all likelihood stretch back into pre-history, 10,000 years or more. Yet they still have incredible power to provoke thought and perhaps to inform us of important truths. These narratives express one of the most fundamental convictions that humans have had; not one that everyone shares, but one of the most profound ones about evil: the idea that evil is somehow larger than individual human decisions to be bad; that, somehow, evil must predate or precede human malice. They express, that is, an idea that is still powerful for many today: the idea that evil has a cosmic and perhaps metaphysical reality beyond human being; that evil is a force, or a power, or a person.

But it's an idea that need not have all of the same ethical connotations that we commonly take "evil" to possess; hence, the earliest linguistic precursor we have for our word Satan—the word that we all typically talk about as "the Devil"—the earliest version of this word, actually, in the proto-Semitic, as far down as linguistic archaeologists have been able to discover, the word is *Shatan*. It does not mean fundamentally an evil-doer, or a devil, or a demon, or anything like that; the word *Shatan* simply means "rival." God's rival is how the Devil was originally conceived of in these cultures; and we'll see today that the rivalry is in some ways at the heart of the entirety of the Ancient Near Eastern mythos of creation, a mythos that begins from the idea that humans are, in some sense, in a world composed of rival powers of good and evil.

These stories also express another fundamental conviction: that it's only experience that can really teach us about evil and its meanings. Gilgamesh, in the epic, is a very wise and brave man, but even he is tormented by the problem of evil and the fact of human suffering in ways that overcome him.

This is a hard lesson, especially for an academic like myself to bear, but even I can agree with it, at least to this extent: It's always important, when thinking about evil, to test our more grandiose and abstract claims about it against the stubborn testimony of lived human experience. The fundamental judge in all of this must be you and your own experience, but throughout these lectures I'm going to try to show how historical and fictional narratives and examples may help illuminate our situation as well.

In this lecture, we begin that effort, and in doing so we make alive again a line in the *Epic of Gilgamesh* that remains perhaps my favorite beginning of a story of all time: "It is an old story, / But one that can still be told." Think about that for a second. Imagine a small group of people on the side of the Tigris or the Euphrates River, 4–5,000 years ago. The evening is coming on, the fish are cooking on the fire, and the people have gathered again after a long day of fishing and looking in the reeds along the river for animals and for berries and fruits. They've gathered to talk and to remember the stories that they were told as children, and one of them tells the story of Gilgamesh. That's how old these stories are, and yet they can still be alive for us today; at least, that's my hope. We'll see how you think about this after the lecture is over.

But the categories of good and evil are present from the earliest civilizations of the Ancient Near East. As qualities of actions and of persons, our earliest stories talk about good deeds and bad deeds, good people and malicious people. Looking at these Ancient Near Eastern myths, it's also important to notice that this is the matrix, this is the context, out of which the Hebrew Bible itself emerges—I'll say more about that in a little bit—but we did not know much about this matrix, this context, until about 100–150 years ago when clay tablets began to appear at archaeological digs that actually told the stories of these ancient civilizations, and when they did they made us realize that the way we had been reading texts we thought we knew very well—like the book of Genesis—importantly left stuff out that we couldn't see was there precisely because they were shadowing the text of Genesis but not visible inside those texts.

In calling these stories—the myth of the *Enuma Elish* and the *Epic of Gilgamesh*—"myths," I'm not trying to be dismissive; when I say "myth,"

I mean the deep structures of the cultural unconscious, the foundational narratives and the frames by which people think in these cultures. People today have myths of similar depth—myths about individual achievement; about the justice and significance of your own nation in the world; the idea of freedom and how it is a universal desire of all people; some such ideals— these myths orient humans in all times to understand the world in certain ways, and make some things obvious to us and some things harder to believe.

Central to the Ancient Near Eastern world was what scholars have come to call the mythic pattern called the "combat myth." The combat myth was a fairly common theme across many of these cultures; Mesopotamian, Hittite, and Canaanite stories all tell the story in similar ways: the story of the cosmos, the universe as a whole, as a site of combat, a battlefield, between good and bad divine powers. This combat myth gives rise to these cultures' cosmogonies; that is, their stories of how the world and the cosmos came to be ("cosmogony" is a word that comes from "cosmo-genesis"). In this myth, the cosmos is the site, or perhaps it's the consequence, of a titanic struggle between the forces of a good god and the forces of a rival evil god. In fact, this cosmogony includes in it a theogony, a "theo-genesis," a story of the creation of the gods. The creation of humanity is normally the final act in the drama that begins with the origins of these gods. In these stories, these chaos-gods—these early chaos-gods—are confronted, defeated, and destroyed by other, often younger, up and coming hero-gods.

For our purposes, we'll focus on the *Enuma Elish*, the Babylonian cosmogony myth. Here: This is the oldest one we have, and in its deep structures, in the elements that go into its composition, it probably goes way back in prehistory. It is a classic case of this combat myth; but then it attaches an interesting coda to that about how exactly the world came to be. Let me tell the story now: Reality begins with two primeval gods, Apsu and Tiamat (those are the two gods). They create other gods, sort of their children—Ea and his siblings—all of whom live in Tiamat's body, there being nothing outside the gods. There they make such a racket, as children will, that they torment Tiamat and Apsu, and Apsu begins to be so annoyed he decides to kill the young gods. But Tiamat disagrees with this and warns Ea, her son, who then kills Apsu, the father. Ea then becomes the chief god, though he doesn't marry his mother—that's another myth; we'll get to that later—and he (Ea) has a son named Marduk, the grandson of Tiamat, who is more powerful still than Ea or, it will turn out, Tiamat.

The child Marduk is given winds to play with as a way of amusing himself, and he uses the winds to make storms, which disturb his elders, just as their frolics had once upset their parents. These gods, now the old fogies, convince Tiamat to kill Marduk. Tiamat likes this idea, but, in fact, she gets a bit too excited about it and she scares the gods, some of whom join her—they're scared into submitting to her and join her force, her team—but some of whom are scared into joining Marduk in his now outright war against her. Marduk fights and kills Tiamat and forms the earth from her corpse, slicing her in half, making her top half the heavens and her bottom half the ground and the waters. He uses the blood of her second husband, Kingu, whom he also kills—he was very thorough, Marduk—to make human beings. By the act of destroying the evil chaos-monster and, in an obscurely overlapping way, creating our new world out of her corpse, this hero-god becomes the king god, the primary god, in the Babylonian pantheon. And that's how the world in the *Enuma Elish* comes to be.

For the later career of thinking about evil, several aspects about this myth are key: First, the chaos god Tiamat is not represented as the source of evil per se, though she is, in fact, prior to people like Marduk and perhaps more profoundly part of the universe than hero-ordering gods like Marduk is. The "evil" emotions, or the attitudes of evil—envy, hate, fear, murderousness—mark the victorious younger gods such as Marduk as much as they mark the older gods. Evil, then, in some sense is an intrinsic structure of reality, part of the basic framework of the universe. Evil is natural, just part of the cosmic order. But it is also a dimension that is in inevitable conflict with the forces of order, symbolized by Marduk in some sense. Because the cosmos is created in a struggle and out of the old cosmos, the cosmos so created may bear traces of, or be the ongoing site of, this conflict between good and evil. This explains the persistence of evil for this tradition: Evil is literally worked into the fabric of the cosmos here.

Compare this account to that of the Creation in the Book of Genesis, especially in Genesis 1. Genesis 1—"In the beginning, God creates the heavens and the earth"—seems written in explicit opposition to the *Enuma*

Elish; and indeed, we now know that the Hebrew word *tehom*, which is the word that in English translations is mostly translated as "the deep," the deep over which God moves at the beginning of Creation. That word *tehom* is etymologically linked to the Babylonian word "Tiamat." But consider the difference from the beginning between these two stories: In Genesis 1, there's no struggle, there's no rival; *tehom* is there, the deep is there, but it is passive before God's absolutely commanding will, and God sees what God has created and deems it all good. There is no sense in the Genesis story that we live amidst the rubble of a long-ago cosmic war.

This is really interesting to know because, in fact, we didn't used to know this about Genesis. We only learned this about the book of Genesis because the *Enuma Elish* was discovered in the 19th century. In fact, we're not going to tell the story here, but there's a great story to tell about how the *Enuma Elish* was discovered. It was discovered by a self-taught working class Englishman named George Smith who managed in his lunch hours to go to the British Museum in London and learn Acadian and Sumerian; he literally just learned the cuneiform script and figured out what was going on in these languages. Then he convinced scholars at the British Museum to help him get over to the Near East so he could do some digs, and on those digs he turns out to have been the first person to discover both much of the *Epic of Gilgamesh* and then also the *Enuma Elish*. Before Smith and his excavations, no one had any idea that there were such texts as this.

But again, compare the *Enuma Elish* to Genesis here, and note the remarkable differences: What we see in Genesis is a wholly commanding God ordering out of the depths an ordered creation, a creation which that god then deems to be altogether good. Here's an important difference between Jewish and Christian understandings of Genesis, which will be very important to keep in mind as we go on; and this is something of a bee in my bonnet, so let me say something about this. Although we talk about the Hebrew Bible and the Christian Old Testament as if they are the same text, in very many important ways they are not actually the same text. There are some choices of text selections that differ, but more importantly it's how these two communities read the text that differs. Here, at the beginning in this Creation story (Genesis 1), there are some really important differences: Any self-respecting Jewish rabbi will tell you that there's no suggestion of what Christians call the "ex nihilo" character of creation in Genesis 1; that is, they will say although Christians want to say that God created the world out of nothing, in fact—the rabbis will say—there is something there; it's the deep, *tehom*, it's there already.

That is why this text is enormously fraught; and we'll come back to it in other moments, too, when we look at the differing ways the Jews and Christians think about the fall of Adam and Eve. In this context, though, what's important to note is that even though that is true about that text— that both Jews and Christians can fairly see that there's no obvious way to read the text in such a way that it affirms that God created everything out of nothing; which is not to say that there was a nothing before the deep, but just that the text itself doesn't say that God created things out of nothing—it is nonetheless clear that the basic trajectory, the impetus of this text, unlike the *Enuma Elish* is towards a world where there's one God who uniformly and without resistance creates the cosmos out of a passive matter. No basic metaphysical rivalry between good and evil exists here.

So the *Enuma Elish* explains the cosmic order; but then the question remains: What's the place of humans in this order? For while the gods look like humans; and while humans are made from the blood of a god—remember Kingu; Kingu's blood makes human beings—one thing distinguishes them: Humans are mortal, and the gods are not. Therein lies a tale, and that tale is the *Epic of Gilgamesh*, the first recorded human attempt to understand and inhabit a world where suffering happens, and perhaps a world where suffering is partially constitutive of what makes us human.

The Epic is, as we have it, composed in Akkadian out of much earlier Sumerian myths. The Akkadian text we have is from around 1200 B.C.E., but we have fragments of it from Sumeria that are from 2000–2400 B.C.E.; so we're talking it's an old, old text. In Akkadian, the title of the *Epic of Gilgamesh* is not, in fact, the *Epic of Gilgamesh*; it is, rather, *He Who Saw the Deep, sha nagkbu amaeru*, where "deep," where what it is to see the deep, means more than just the plumbing of a merely spatial profundity. Rather, to see the deep means to see something deep about human experience. Even in the Acadian text, people understood that the *Epic of Gilgamesh* was incredibly profound.

In this story, Gilgamesh is a hard king over the citizens of his city, Uruk, and to stop him from being so oppressive, the gods create Enkidu as Gilgamesh's equal. Enkidu is going to be Gilgamesh's friend, though he is called part-animal and part-human, where Gilgamesh is part-god and part-human. Theirs is the story of their friendship, and in a way it's the first "buddy movie" of human history. After fighting when they first meet (fighting each other), and realizing that they're well-matched, they become inseparable and they go on legendary adventures. They journey to the Cedar Mountain—somewhere probably in Lebanon—and defeat Humbaba, the ogreish guardian of the mountain. They kill the Bull of Heaven, who was sent by the goddess Ishtar to punish Gilgamesh for spurning her seduction. This murder of the Bull of Heaven doesn't go over well with any of the gods, and so they kill Enkidu as punishment.

At the death of his friend, Gilgamesh is distraught, almost mad with grief. He's also terrified by death, realizing it will come to him as it did to Enkidu. So to assuage his grief and palliate his fear, he undertakes a quest to find the key to immortality by undertaking a long and perilous journey to meet the ancient and immortal flood hero, Utnapishtim—kind of an early version of Noah—and after many difficulties, Gilgamesh finally meets this man face to face. But the old man is unwilling or unable to help, and he tells Gilgamesh, "The life that you are seeking you will never find. When the gods created man they allotted to him death, but life they retained in their own keeping." As predicted, Gilgamesh's efforts do eventually fail, and he collapses, weeping. He then returns to Uruk, his city, where the sight of its massive walls prompts him to praise this enduring work, the work solely of human hands. Perhaps this recognition of the achievement of human effort is a sign that Gilgamesh has begun, at the end of this epic, to find a way out of utter despair; a slow turning back towards a merely human life.

But even then, the old Sumerian myths of Gilgamesh do not spare him from death. There are fragments of a parallel work, or perhaps a coda to the Epic, that actually recount the moment of Gilgamesh's dying. Let me read you this, because the message is terrifically bleak. This is what is said to Gilgamesh as his life nears its end:

You must have been told that this is what being human entailed. You must have been told that this is what the cutting of your umbilical cord entailed. The darkest day of humans awaits you now. The solitary place of humans awaits you now. The unstoppable flood-wave awaits you now. The unavoidable battle awaits you now.

This is not very happy stuff, right?

The unequal struggle awaits you now. The duel from which there is no escape awaits you now.

But wait; the last line of this enormous litany of foreseen suffering:

But you should not go to the underworld with heart knotted in anger.

Even here, then, that last clause suggests that there should be some consolation. The life of humans is not entirely bleak when need not be. Another fragment of one of these poems has Enkidu, after his death, speaking to Gilgamesh from the underworld, and saying to him, "I fear you will come to hate our friendship, because it did not last forever."

Death—the finitude of human life, and the fact that this finitude makes humans vulnerable to death at any moment—this death is the great threat to all human happiness. What the *Epic of Gilgamesh* suggests, though, is that it is precisely this finitude of human life that is the basis of whatever blessings, whatever joys, we can have. It is the walls of Uruk, after all, made by human hands, which are the only things that are able to draw Gilgamesh out of his despair. No lesser animal knows that it will suffer and die. Only we do, and only we know that we are doomed to this fate; and so we are given double evils in this way, the fact of death and the prior knowledge of it. Yet we are also not yet dead, and we can choose how to live in light of death. Gilgamesh's journeys are in this way an allegory for every human's journey through life. There comes a moment when we know that death is our future, and then we must decide what to do with that knowledge. It is not a knowledge that is communicated in the sentence that "all humans are mortals." That's a sentence speakable by anybody, at any time—you can get a five-year-old to say that sentence—but very few people actually know what it means; very few people come to gain and struggle with that knowledge in a real way.

This wisdom cannot be perhaps communicated, but it is real, and it can be acquired. In this way, Gilgamesh is the first figure of a type of character we'll see again and again in these stories, in these lectures: Abraham and Job, soon; Dante, later on in the Middle Ages; even a figure like Joseph Conrad's retired sailor Charlie Marlow, who is the narrator of *Heart of Darkness*. All of these people have a kind of acquaintance with evil that has changed them, but which they cannot exactly communicate to others so that others share in their knowledge. Each person's quest is their own. What I'm saying to you now is also a failure of attempting to communicate something of Gilgamesh's story. It is, in a certain way, a futile exercise; for all of this is said about Gilgamesh's story, from the outside of the tale, as it were. I strongly urge you to read it for yourself. It is truly an old story, but one that can still be told; and one, perhaps, that still needs telling around campfires, at bedtimes, in classrooms, even recording studios, even today.

Let's wrap this up for now. What these stories give us is more than their own reflections on evil. In many ways, they set the terms on which later texts, thinkers, and writers will debate these questions. As I've already said, the *Enuma Elish* is the dualistic background against which the Genesis creation myth is written, and the dualism of the *Enuma Elish* will continue to haunt the Abrahamic faiths of Judaism, Christianity, and Islam as a shadow, a rival unspoken in their own scriptures but a rival that their own scriptures know about; a rival to their own stories of how the world began and from whence evil came. *Gilgamesh* has a more positive influence, for it exemplifies the genre of the quest story, and in particular the quest story as modeling an entire human life; the human's lifelong search for the meaning of life in the face of suffering and evil. In thinking about evil, then, these texts show us that we're using categories, and even occasionally some names, words, and titles—think about that word "Satan" again—that go back thousands of years. The afterlife of these texts, in their continued power to provoke, remains with us even today.

In the next lecture, we'll look at a rival way of thinking about evil, one that does not offer a picture of evil as so fundamentally un-human. It adds another distinctly colored thread to the tapestry we're beginning to weave of human thinking about evil. We turn to that next.

> Here, [as] in the ancient Near East, there are many gods, but the gods are more like characters in a long-running drama series, like *Dallas* or *Dynasty*. ... [They] exist, in a weird way, beyond good and evil, indulging in cruelty as easily as they take affront at it, and in neither case does it seem that their judgment or actions are beholden to any ultimately moral framework.

We turn now to Greece, where what we might call "anarchic polytheism" emerged, that is, a belief in many gods without a single organizing moral order among them. This worldview resulted in at least two approaches to the problem of evil: among the Greek tragedians, such as Sophocles and Aeschylus, the idea that sometimes, out of sheer tragic providence, the fates decree that a human must be brought down, and for Thucydides, the even more disturbing idea that evil is due, simply and terrifyingly, to luck or chance.

For the Greeks, tragic drama was a crucial structure for reflecting on evil, fate, and luck in human affairs. In *Oedipus Rex*, the king of Thebes discovers that he has unknowingly killed his father, Laius, and married his mother, Jocasta. When the truth emerges, Jocasta commits suicide, and Oedipus blinds himself and begs for exile from Thebes. The play ends ambiguously, with the chorus chanting the famous

Dover Publications.

The role of fate, chance, and luck in *Oedipus Rex* speak powerfully of the terrible paradoxes of fate and responsibility that Greek tragedy was so good at communicating.

maxim ascribed to the Greek legislator Solon: that no one should be called happy until they are dead.

The range of meanings and the role of chance in this play speak powerfully of the terrible paradoxes of fate and responsibility communicated by so much of Greek tragedy. One of the most traumatic elements of the play is that Oedipus is the vehicle for his own self-destruction; he recognizes this responsibility but also sees an unpredictable fate as guiding events. He thinks of himself as someone who has been humbled by the gods for an arrogance he did not quite see.

Sometimes, these plays seem to locate responsibility more directly in the gods themselves, to the point where humans become angry at the gods for their misfortunes. At the end of Sophocles's play *The Women of Trachis*, Hyllus attributes to the gods the cruel fate that has befallen his father, Heracles. He says, "Let the gods, their ruthlessness, their cruelty, be remembered./They take us to be their children, and call themselves Father,/and yet they well see such suffering." The moment is equivalent to a Christian or a Jew declaring the Holocaust to be, in some sense, the accomplishment of God's will.

The idea that fate has many strange twists, can turn strength against the strong, and can bring the mighty down became very pointed in the experience of the Peloponnesian War, captured in Thucydides's book on that conflict. The war was fought between Athens and Sparta, with allies on both sides, from 431 to 404 B.C. It was a devastating conflict, enabling the spread of plagues, starvation, and the ruin of the economies of the Greek world.

Thucydides's account of the war is largely an attempt to see in history a tragedy. He writes "against" the earlier historian Herodotus, who saw history and culture as natural forces that shaped character in certain ways. Thucydides, in contrast, saw people's decisions not as determined by their natural environment or cultural presuppositions but shaped by the political pressures of the moment. He believed not in determinism but in the accidental nature of things.

When he talks about the idea of motivations, Thucydides identifies an important theme that remains pertinent for us today, namely, that the human psyche in war is slowly deformed by the pressure of constant fear. Indeed, the war itself was caused by the Spartans' fear for their independence in the face of Athens's increasing hegemony over the Greek world. Once the war is started, it takes on a life of its own and begins to master the combatants. Each side hopes to exhaust the other before its own people and resources are exhausted. And neither considers the moral costs of the war—the damage and deformation it will do to their souls.

> **When he talks about the idea of motivations, Thucydides identifies an important theme that remains pertinent for us today, namely, that the human psyche in war is slowly deformed by the pressure of constant fear.**

At one point in the war, the Athenians sought the support of the small, insignificant island city of Melos against the Spartans. The Melians refused, and the Athenians responded by besieging Melos, eventually massacring the men and enslaving the women and children of the city. Afterward, the Athenians suffered a string of defeats and ultimately lost the war, yet Thucydides does not view their defeat as morally deserved because of their unnecessary cruelty to the Melians. Rather, it is, as the Athenians themselves had predicted, the wheel of fate turning; now cruelty will be done to them, not as payback but as part of the inevitable chaos and randomness of life.

For Thucydides and the Greek tragedians, there is no simple or straightforward moral order; all our moral actions are subject to dramatic reversal or deformation, and there are no guarantees that our moral sincerity will not, in fact, turn out to be destructive, perhaps even self-destructive. Further, Thucydides introduces into Western consciousness the idea of the accident, the possibility that evil and suffering may well have no cause at all. ■

Important Term

Oedipus Rex: Greek tragedy written by Sophocles, an Athenian tragedian.

Suggested Reading

Grene and Lattimore, trans. and eds., *The Complete Greek Tragedies*.

Padel, *In and Out of Mind: Greek Images of the Tragic Self*.

Thucydides, *The Landmark Thucydides*, Strassler, ed., Crawley, trans.

Thucydides, *The Peloponnesian War*, Lattimore, trans.

Williams, *Shame and Necessity*.

Questions to Consider

1. As we have seen, the Greeks added an important theme in Western thinking about evil by the introduction of the concept of tragedy. What do you see as the relationship between tragedy and evil? How are they connected, and how are they different?

2. Greek tragedians, such as Sophocles, as well as Thucydides offered varying answers to the causes of evil—is evil the result of destiny, or decision, or chance? What insights do you think these authors offer for understanding the causes of evil? What is the relationship between destiny and decision in creating evil?

Greece—Tragedy and *The Peloponnesian War*
Lecture 3—Transcript

Hello, again. So far, we've seen some of the Ancient Near Eastern roots of thinking about evil in the West; but along with the Babylonian and Acadian myths that we saw earlier were the myths, tragedians, poets, and thinkers of Ancient Greece, all of whom have shaped our thinking about evil, particularly through the concept of tragedy. So now, in this lecture, I want to turn to Greece.

As we'll now see, a dualistic language of good and evil—such as the Babylonian myth, the *Enuma Elish*, presumes—is not the inevitable shape that a culture's moral imagination has to take. We know this because in Greece, an entirely different picture emerges: what you can call an "anarchic polytheism"—that is, belief in many gods, without a single organizing moral order that the gods are all part of—dominates the moral imagination of classical Greece, and it is at the basis of Greek tragedy as well. Here, as in the Ancient Near East, there are many gods; but the gods are more like characters in a long-running drama series like *Dallas* or *Dynasty* or choose what you will, *The OC*. The struggles between them are not fundamentally enframed by a struggle between good and evil; good and evil are terms that really seem to apply more fundamentally to humans in Greece. Instead, the Greek gods in a certain way exist in a weird way beyond good and evil, indulging in cruelty as easily as they take affront at it, and in neither case does it seem that their judgment or actions are beholden to any ultimately moral framework. For all their power, that is, the gods are somehow, in themselves, completely unaccountable, and because of that, at times, the Greek poets and playwrights suggest that they are, in some important way, trivial.

This sort of ties together what was suggested separately in the *Enuma Elish* and in Gilgamesh: namely, that humans suffer, but it is the gods' doings that make humans suffer. There is something divinely governed beneath the structures often of human tragedies, this view says. Sincere actions can lead to tragic conflicts, sometimes between goods, ends, or aims of people's actions that are essentially incompatible; the sorts of things that philosophers call "incommensurable goods," goods that you cannot have at the same time.

I would love to be a professional baseball player, and I would love to be a professor; but unless I am a professor, say, of sports management, it's going to be very hard for me to dedicate my life in the right way to becoming a professional baseball player in the same time that I have to become a professional academic. They are two life paths that you cannot pursue in the same single life; those are incompatible paths in that way. For the Greek tragedians, there were times in life when humans had to confront choices between sets of goods or choices—tragic conflicts, we could call them—between rival sets of evils. Sometimes, out of sheer tragic providence, the fates decree that something must happen to bring the mighty down.

More disturbing still than the tragedians' worldview, though, is the suggestion of Thucydides, an Athenian historian and also a soldier. For whereas, the tragedians suggest, that evil is due to some mysterious but divinely ordained necessity, Thucydides suggests that evil may be due entirely and simply, and even more terrifyingly, to sheer luck and chance. Understanding the differences between the views of the tragedians (Sophocles and Aeschylus) and Thucydides will help us see two vividly different pictures of whence evil and suffering come in this world.

Let's start with tragedy. For the Greeks, tragic drama became a crucial structure for thinking about their lives in a long-standing historical development; it took place over several centuries. In the tragedies, Greeks reflected upon evil, fate, and luck in human affairs, in plays such as *Oedipus Rex*, and *The Women of Trachis*, the *Bacchae*; there's a series of these plays. It's important to know that when we think of a Greek tragedy, we think of going to the theater, maybe in an evening, and watching a play. These plays were no meant to be those sorts of things; they were not entertainments, as we think of them. The plays were part of a yearly religious ritual in Athens: the Dionysia, honoring the god Dionysius, the god of revelry and fertility; where wine and babies come together. This festival took place over five days every spring; somewhat like Mardi Gras in New Orleans, but with a more serious religious tone. The Athenians used these plays as serious venues to reflect on the political, religious, and ethical situation of their community, and the plays that survive reflect that quite well.

It's interesting to note—tragic, you could say—that the plays we have are a very, very small fragment of what was written. Sophocles wrote, we know, 123 plays, but only 7 have survived to our day. It's as if all we knew of Shakespeare was a bit of *Romeo and Juliet*, some of the history plays, and maybe *Macbeth*. We heard he wrote plays with titles such as *Hamlet*, or *King Lear*, or *Much Ado about Nothing*, or *Othello*, but nothing of those plays managed to make it to our day. That's how much of the Greeks have been lost to us.

Let's take a look at one very famous play to figure out what tragedy means in thinking about evil. Let's look at *Oedipus Rex—Oedipus the King*— perhaps one of the most popular plays for people to think about over the past 2,500 years. The plot of the play is fairly complicated, but bear with me: Oedipus is king of Thebes, Jocasta his queen, and Thebes has begun to suffer from a terrible plague, a sign, everyone thinks, of divine wrath. Oedipus is determined to find out why the plague has been sent, and he discovers through his investigations that it is due to the religious pollution caused by the fact that the previous king, Laius, was murdered but his killer never caught and punished. Oedipus then undertakes the hunt for the murderer. Through a series of inquiries, the truth emerges: It was Oedipus who killed Laius on the road to Thebes in a dispute in which the two sides did not know one another's identities. Furthermore, and more horrifying still, Oedipus is the unknown son of Laius, the king he killed, and of Laius's queen, who is Oedipus's mother, Jocasta, who is now Oedipus's wife.

Laius and Jocasta had been told by an oracle that their son would kill his father and commit incest with his mother, and so when he was born they gave him to a shepherd to kill. But the shepherd instead took pity and gave him to a Corinthian, who raised him as his own son. Jocasta, the truth fully known at last—a truth she never knew—is so overcome by shame that she hangs herself. Oedipus blinds himself by plunging her gold hairpins into his eyes and begs for exile from Thebes. The play ends ambiguously, with the chorus chanting the famous maxim ascribed to the Greek legislator Solon: that no one should be called happy until they are dead.

The range of meanings, the role of fate, chance, and luck in this play, speak powerfully of the terrible paradoxes of fate and responsibility that Greek tragedy was so good at communicating. One of the most traumatic things about the play is the way that Oedipus himself is the vehicle for his own self-destruction. As he himself puts it at one point:

> It was Apollo, friends, Apollo,
> that brought this deepest bitterness, all my sorrows to fulfillment.
> But the hand that struck me down
> was none but my own.

Oedipus both recognizes his responsibility but sees a fate as guiding things; a fate whose providential command is discernable in events, although never predictable. In a way, Oedipus begins to think of himself as someone who has been humbled by the gods for an arrogance he did not quite see.

Sometimes, though, the plays seem to locate responsibility more directly in the gods themselves to the point where humans seem to become angry at the gods or the cosmos for their misfortunes. At the end of Sophocles's play *The Women of Trachis*, we have a remarkable moment where this happens. In this play—let's not worry so much about the plot—what happens is that a father who is about to help his son get married, Heracles—the father is Heracles—is accidentally killed by the poisoning of his wife; his wife accidentally poisons him. At the end of the play Hyllus, the son of Heracles, orders his father's acid-burned body taken off stage as his father writhes in pain, as his father begs to be killed, to be burned alive because he has been killed by the gift from his wife. She thought she was giving him a love potion to keep him in love with her, but, in fact, she was unknowingly giving him a cloak drenched in acid that, of course, burned away his skin as soon as it was exposed to sunlight. When she discovers this, she commits suicide out of horror and shame at what she's done. As Heracles is being taken up and carried away from the stage, Hyllus turns to the female chorus and he says to them:

> Let the gods, their ruthlessness, their cruelty, be remembered
> They take us to be their children, and call themselves Father,
> and yet they well see such suffering.
> No one knows the future, but the present is hard,
> the present is shame for them,

and for him who bears the victimhood, the present is pain,
cruel fate.
Women [he now says, speaking directly to the Chorus], come
inside now.
You have seen many things, terrible and strange;
and there is nothing here that is not Zeus.

Imagine a Christian or a Jew standing at the end of the Second World War and saying that everything that had happened was in some sense God's will being accomplished. That would be an enormously astonishing, and for orthodox believers blasphemous, thing to say. But it was said in a Greek play in a religious festival precisely because it was a question that the Greeks were asking themselves. If we believe that the gods do govern fate, doesn't that make them in some sense responsible? What should we think about that? It's a troubling idea, but it's not incoherent, and it plays a powerful role in Greek tragedy and in much other Greek thinking.

But it's not the only point of view. The idea that fate has many strange twists and turns, and can turn strength against the strong, and bring the mighty down became very pointed in the experience of the calamitous Peloponnesian War, captured in the historian Thucydides's book on that conflict; a book that, by the way, is named *The Peloponnesian War* (useful, that). The basic story of the war is simple: It was a war between Athens and her allies, and Sparta and her allies, and it lasted almost 30 years; it lasted from 431–404. Thucydides's book doesn't cover the whole war, because it was written while the war was being fought; but it covers enough of it. The war was devastating; it enabled the spread of plagues, starvation, ruined the Greek world's economies, ruined a number of cities, and ended with the Spartans in charge of a kind of petty tyranny over much of Greece, supported by the Persians, who for the last 100 years the Greeks had allied themselves together in trying to keep out of Greece. Effectively, what this war between the Greeks did was destroy them all so much that the Persians finally were able to get control. It effectively ended the "golden age" of Greece. Imagine if the Cold War had turned hot; that's what this was like for Greece.

Thucydides's account, though it's incomplete, nonetheless bears all the marks of a work attempting to see in history a tragedy, though with some differences. Just as searching as any tragedy could be about the nature and significance of human wickedness, Thucydides took his own particular take on that wickedness. He writes in certain ways against a previous historian who it's important to understand something of in order to understand Thucydides, much as it's important—I've suggested—to understand the *Enuma Elish* to fully understand what's going on in the book of Genesis. Thucydides is arguing with the Greek historian Herodotus, who was of a previous generation and wrote, actually, about the Persian Wars; the wars that the Greeks managed to win to keep the Persians out. Herodotus saw history and culture as kinds of natural forces that shaped people's characters in certain ways, so that where you were from determined your historical behavior, your political forms, in all sorts of ways. Herodotus thought of himself as a naturalist, in a certain sense. Thucydides does not think that way. He sees people's decisions not as determined by their natural environment or their cultural presuppositions, but as importantly pressured, shaped by the political pressures of the moment. Thucydides—and this is the important thing—believes in the accidental nature of things; he does not believe in determinism. Along with this, he's completely convinced that history always repeats itself; that the fundamental conditions of human interaction, the mix of motives and modes of apprehension that together make up human nature, these don't change for him. This why, as he says at the very beginning of his book, Thucydides writes his book: to offer lessons for people who will be in the same situation as he was at some point in the future.

What's interesting about this is that Thucydides's book, even today, is taught at the Naval Academy, at West Point, at all the senior military staff colleges, and especially at the Army War College where they teach it to mid-level military officers. A number of people have drawn connections between the story of an empire gained by bravery being turned into something that becomes oppressive to some people; many military officers read this book now and they think, "Wow, this has lots to say to us and our world today." Thucydides may or may not be directly applicable to that, but one thing about his work that strikes me as very pertinent is that when he talks about the idea of states' motivations or people's motivations, he identifies one important theme that remains pertinent for us today: Namely, the human psyche in war is slowly deformed by the pressure of constant fear. Indeed, the war itself, he thought, is caused by misunderstanding and especially fear. After the Persian Wars, Athens grew increasingly powerful, eventually gaining hegemony over most of the rest of Greece. The Spartans feared for their own independence, and the growing tension between Athens's hegemony and Sparta's fear led eventually to the war. Once the war is started, like all wars, it takes on a life of its own and it begins to master the combatants. Both sides expected a quick victory, but neither gets it. Both bear with the war, however, hoping it will exhaust the other side before it exhausts their own. Neither considers the moral costs of the war—the damage and deformation it will do to their souls—though Thucydides himself does, and in some ways this is the greatest moment of his work.

The classic case of this is the famous story—famous among a fairly narrow set of relatively nerdy individuals like myself—of the "Melian Dialogue" at the end of Book 5 of *The Peloponnesian War*. Melos was—and is, you can visit it today—a tiny island of no strategic importance in the middle of the Aegean Sea. It's a neutral in the war. A military group of Athenians come to it and meet with the leaders of Melos in private. They ask to have control of the island, and for the Melians to ally themselves with Athens. Here's the Athenians view why this should happen: If we don't take control of your island and city, others will see our not doing so as a sign of our weakness. Indeed, if you simply declare yourselves neutral between us and Sparta, others will say, "The Athenians couldn't get them on their side, so they must be weaker than we thought; therefore, we should try to resist the Athenians more." Because we don't want that, because we want to forestall that possibility, you must become our allies, though you don't really want to be and we don't really need you to be.

The Melians, facing this, see that they cannot appeal to the Athenians's sense of justice—the Athenians are clearly far beyond that—so they appeal instead to setting a good example; they say to the Athenians, don't mistreat us because, after all, what goes around comes around, and if you mistreat us, so it will be done in turn to you. The Athenians reply: That's our belief, too, but there's no way to avoid this fate; no number of good examples will teach humans out of this kinds of deep pessimism about human behavior. The key for us—the Athenians, that is—is that might outweighs right. God is not fundamentally the arbiter of justice, but rather God is the "patterner of power applied," a very curious phrase that Thucydides uses. God seems to be the structure of power that actually is imposed in the world. Force, they say, is its own law, and the law—famously, the Athenians say to the Melians—is what the strong impose and what the weak must acquiesce to. After Thucydides's report of this dialogue, he very quickly tells the story of what happened. The Melians refuse the Athenians's offer. The Athenians besiege the Melians and eventually take the city. When they do, they massacre all the men and take the women and the children off to slavery. Eventually, several years later, they replace all those people on the island with a colony of Athenians.

After this event in Thucydides's story, things begin to go really bad for the Athenians, and they suffer a string of disastrous defeats and eventually lose the war. Thucydides's book doesn't record the end of the war, though he clearly foresees that a calamity is heading Athens's way. But he does something very important: Other people who wrote about the war read the Athenians's defeat as in some sense morally deserved by what they had done during the war. Thucydides does not. In no way does he suggest that their defeat is because of their cruelty to the Melians; rather, it is that, as they predicted, the wheel of fate and chance is turning around, and now cruelty will be done to them, not as payback, but as the inevitable chaos and randomness of life.

Is evil or cruelty wholly a matter of circumstance and accident? The Athenians in civilian life would never have imagined that one day they would effectively exterminate an entire island's population, not because of any strategic importance but only because of the fear of what other people would think if they didn't do it. Yet, that's just what they did. Thucydides doesn't read this as revealing some dark stain in the Athenian soul or revealing some sort of absolute brutality at the heart of all humans that's finally unleashed in situations of war. That's not his point; his point is that people in certain contexts will behave in certain ways. Character has little to do with it; but the necessity of a context seems, over time, to outweigh the noble sentiments of moral character.

In a way, this is the grimmest sort of fatalism; this is the fatalism you might see in a foot-soldier in a war who sees only random death and persistent, soul-drubbing cruelty. Those who are best are rendered more vulnerable by their virtues, or put in more danger by their courage, and so they die or are maimed more quickly in combat. In war, it is the cowardly and the cunning who stand the best chance of surviving. Thucydides himself knew this, because he was a general in the Peloponnesian War. He fought in various engagements and finally was exiled from Athens for his inability, finally, to lift a siege of a crucial outpost before the outpost surrendered. Thucydides, in telling the story of that event, doesn't make it a large part of the war; he makes it a very passing mention in his book. He talks about himself in the third person: "Thucydides the Athenian was sent out to do this. He traveled as quickly as he could; it was winter and cold. But his ships did not get there in time, and after that he was exiled." It's an astonishing revelation that if you don't look for it in the book you won't realize is there because the book is so clearly not the kind of book that politicians or generals today write that is mostly about justifying themselves; Thucydides was actually interested in trying to tell the story of this war.

For him, for the Greek tragedians, the key here, when it comes to thinking about evil, is that there is no simple or straightforward moral order; all of our moral actions are subject to dramatic reversal or deformation, and there are no guarantees that the human's moral sincerity will not in fact turn out to be destructive, perhaps even self-destructive. Furthermore, Thucydides, I think, introduces into Western consciousness the idea of the accident; the possibility, that is, that evil and suffering, whenever they happen, may well have no cause at all, at least no cause that we can recognize as an intentional purposeful act, whether of a human being or of some callous divinity off in some paradise somewhere.

Thucydides and the Greek tragedians are only two of the voices that the Greek world offers us. In our next lecture, we'll look at a rival view to both of them in Greek thought: that of the philosophers Socrates, Plato, and Aristotle—who came after the tragedians and Thucydides—and those inspired by these philosophers, who argue that the myths and the tragedies significantly misunderstood the nature of our situation and the nature of the cosmos.

Greek Philosophy—Human Evil and Malice
Lecture 4

The disagreements between [Plato and Aristotle] and their mutual opposition to tragedy echo down through the rest of the Western philosophical and religious traditions. The debates these guys had in a small corner of Greece 1,500–2,500 years ago have really, incredibly, shaped everything that came after that.

T he Greek tragic tradition met a kind of internal resistance in the Greek philosophical tradition. The philosophers of Greece certainly took reality and history seriously, but they were also interested in assessing the strengths and weaknesses of people's views of reality in order to determine how best to think about evil and tragedy.

We begin with **Plato**, whose thinking about evil developed significantly over time. In his early dialogues, he seems to have thought that evil is a consequence of ignorance, that no one goes against a well-formed judgment, and that such judgment can never be truly evil. Evil here is a matter of "miseducation," which can be corrected by better information. Today, we, too, often believe that evil is simply a matter of ignorance that could be eliminated if people were properly educated.

As time went on, Plato's views darkened. By the middle of his life, he understood "evil" in a more profound and troubling way, and his depiction of the differences between good and bad people became far more radical. The character Thrasymachus in Plato's *Republic*, for example, represents a crucial problem for social order and harmony.

© Photos.com/Thinkstock.

Plato (428–347 B.C.E.) was a disciple of Socrates and the teacher of Aristotle.

Thrasymachus is a Sophist, a teacher of political rhetoric, and he argues with Socrates that justice is nothing more than the interest of the stronger. When he can't intimidate Socrates into agreeing with him, Thrasymachus withdraws into surly silence. Despite Plato's earlier idea that evil is, in some sense, ignorance, we can see that no amount of new information will help this character. He doesn't want to change or learn; he wants only to dominate. For Plato, goodness remains the properly intelligible thing to do, but unintelligibility—the irrationality of evil—has become more profound and radical in the human character.

Thrasymachus represents a terrifying challenge to Plato—and remember, it was people like Thrasymachus who would order Socrates to be killed. Plato confronts us with a frightening question: How should we live in a world that is often governed by people like Thrasymachus, those who are not on the way to becoming intelligible creatures? Can we bring the wholly irrational into the realm of reason, and if not, can we improve the social order so that the wholly irrational is not so prevalent in the future? Evil is not so easily captured here in descriptions of ignorance; it seems more tenaciously part of our world, more difficult to correct, and requiring far more fundamental changes for us to be unsusceptible to its attractions than the mere delivery of information to those caught in its clutches.

Plato also sees evil as a failure to be properly aligned with the moral order and, thus, with the good. Thrasymachus represents the person caught in a tyrannical soul—a disordered soul. And a tyrant, for Plato, tyrannizes himself before anyone else. He revolts against the conditions of his own creation. That's the mature picture of evil that Plato offers: one in which evil is a form of revolt against the conditions of our own creation and one that spreads evil through human society by infecting others with a misorientation to the good through erroneous cultural standards.

Aristotle, in contrast, explores the nature of evil in a far more "mundane" way through his discussion of *akrasia*, weakness of will. As Plato did, Aristotle thought that people could be wrongly habituated, but Aristotle saw neither good nor bad habits as rational. Humans are not simply aligned to the good, and evil is not a rupture of that relationship; humans are as much flesh as they are mind, and the flesh shapes a good deal of human behavior. For Aristotle, the goal is to find a happy medium in which the mind and the body interact responsibly, with distinct, harmonious interests and ends.

Evil here is not a radical rejection of intellect for flesh; it's more mundane than that. It's not an absolute revolt against nature but a misordering, a jumbling of our natural drives. Because Aristotle has a more moderate picture of humans than Plato, his picture of evil is also less dramatic. For Aristotle, humans exist on a continuum, which means that not all people can be made better. In this, he can be seen as offering a kind of "medicalizing" of evil, treating it as an unfortunate pathology. Nonetheless, both Aristotle and Plato are united in their skepticism about the possibility for radical human change after childhood.

Aristotle (384–322 B.C.E.) has a more moderate picture of what humans are, and therefore his picture of evil is less dramatic than Plato's.

As we'll see, the struggle between the Platonist and the Aristotelian views of the ultimate nature of evil—between evil as a kind of metaphysical revolt and evil as a mundane challenge—will echo across the rest of this lecture series. ∎

Names to Know

Aristotle (384–322 B.C.E.). Born in Stageira as a member of the aristocracy. Eventually, Aristotle made his way to Athens, became a disciple of Plato, and studied at Plato's Academy for almost 20 years.

Plato (428–347 B.C.E.). Born in Athens, the son of Ariston, a prominent aristocrat. As a young man, Plato seems to have traveled extensively before returning to Athens, with ambitions to be a poet; there, he became a disciple of Socrates.

akrasia: An ancient Greek term that Aristotle uses for "weakness of will." Suggests an explanation for evil as a pathology of moral motivation, a divided, incoherent, or "weak" will.

Suggested Reading

Aristotle, *Nichomachean Ethics*, Irwin, trans.

Aristotle, *Poetics*, Janko, trans.

Nussbaum, *The Fragility of Goodness: Moral Luck in Greek Tragedy and Philosophy*.

Plato, *Gorgias, Menexenus, Protagoras*, Schofield, ed., Griffith, trans.

Plato, *The Republic*, Grube and Reeve, trans.

Questions to Consider

1. Plato and Aristotle had different views concerning the nature of evil and its relation to human life. How do you see Plato's and Aristotle's views reflected today? Do people tend to see evil as a radical challenge or a mundane one?

2. For the early Plato, evil was primarily a matter of ignorance rather than malice. What do you see as the relationship between evil and knowledge? Can we tell good and evil apart clearly? Can evil be combated through education, or is the problem more pervasive?

Greek Philosophy—Human Evil and Malice
Lecture 4—Transcript

Hello again. So far in these lectures, we've looked primarily at events, and at people thinking about events; now we're going to begin to look at people who are reflecting on just that: reflecting on how people think about events. This is, in some ways, one classic definition of what a philosopher does.

The Greek tragic tradition met a certain kind of internal resistance within the Greek context—within Greece itself—in the form of the tradition of philosophy, which deserves its own distinct attention; that's what we'll give it in this lecture. These philosophers certainly take reality and history seriously, but they're also seriously interested in assessing the strengths and weaknesses of people's views of reality in order to determine how best to think about these matters. Here, we'll study how Plato and Aristotle thought about evil, human malice, and tragedy, both as allies together against the view of the Greek tragedians and Thucydides, and also as themselves—Plato and Aristotle—offering two rival accounts of the nature of the human condition and the human fault. The disagreements between them and their mutual opposition to tragedy echo down through the rest of the Western philosophical and religious traditions. The debates these guys had in a small corner of Greece 1,500–2,500 years ago have really, incredibly, shaped everything that came after that.

Let me start with Plato first. Plato's dates—we're pretty confident of them—Plato was born around 428 B.C.E. and died in 347 B.C.E. He was an Athenian; he was a disciple of Socrates; he was the teacher of Aristotle. We know that Plato wrote not just the dialogues we have, but a number of lectures that were also compiled into books and were available in the ancient world. We've lost those; but we do have the dialogues. These dialogues purport to tell stories of events in Socrates's life; in other words, Socrates is more or less pretty commonly always the main character in these dialogues. The earliest dialogues have a pretty historical reporting of actual events in Socrates's life, especially the ones around the death of Socrates. Those seem to be almost journalistic reports of what actually happened; maybe a little sanding of the edges or something like that, but by and large Plato is really trying to tell the story of Socrates's life.

But over time, in the dialogues, the character Socrates becomes less and less historical—less and less rooted in the actual historical figure—and more and more a literary figure that Plato uses to convey the story he wants to tell. That's not to say that you can just identify Plato's views with the views of the character in his dialogues named Socrates. Indeed, the older Plato gets, the more he's his own person, his own thinker, and not just Socrates's student, Socrates's disciple. The more fictional the character Socrates gets in Plato's dialogues—and that means the more Plato uses this figure in combination with the others in his dialogues to promote the idea that Plato's thoughts are in some sense arising from the conversation itself—Plato's thoughts are, in some sense, in between the various figures of the dialogue. Plato—who people think of as someone who really hates art or despises or suspects poetry—has always been a remarkable artist and a fantastic writer; never, ever forget that, it's an important thing about his own work to keep in mind.

Plato's thinking about evil developed really significantly over time. Initially, in his early dialogues and for the first few years of his own kind of free-thinking on things, he seems to have thought—or at least reported that Socrates thought and young Plato believed him—that evil is a consequence of ignorance; that no one goes against their well-formed judgment, and that such judgment—such a well-formed judgment—can never be truly evil. This is the view that's expressed, for example, his early dialogue, the *Protagoras*. In this dialogue, ignorance of the most serious kind, truly dangerous ignorance, is the basis of all wrong action. In this passage I'm about to read to you, notice how fundamentally evil is connected with the fact that the evil-doer on the character Socrates's account here must simply not be thinking right. This is Socrates: "No one willingly pursues evil, or at least what he takes to be evil; human nature forbids that; furthermore, faced with the choice of two evils," that is, faced in a way that a person will know that he or she faces a choice of two evils (back to Socrates here), "no one will choose the greater if he can choose the lesser."

On one level, this is all pretty good common sense, right; that if you're confronted with something you know is evil, you're going to avoid it? Plato's idea—at least as presented by Socrates here—is that because virtue is teachable, because we can be informed and made better by the possibility of people giving us new information or data about our situation; and because the process of teaching is the informing of the person with knowledge that they did not have before (where this is informing is a pretty deep concept; it's not actually simply just giving people data, it's also, in a way, shaping their soul to receive that data properly); and because fault can usually be corrected in our ordinary experience (Plato/Socrates seems to think here) by giving someone more articulate help in seeing the full character of the situation, the full dimensions of it, by giving them more information; therefore, evil (he thinks) is a matter fundamentally of not being in the right situation to know what to do. Evil is a matter of "miseducation," and this can be corrected by better information.

There's a lot to be said for this view, right? For us today, we do often believe that a lot of the evil we face in the world is simply a matter of ignorance; it's bigotry; it's shallow aims that would be enriched, deepened, and altered if we were properly educated; we talk about people being badly brought up. It's not just a matter of our opinions, we have data about this: We actually think that a lot of people make bad choices in their lives precisely because they don't know any better. There's a lot of power in this view, and we shouldn't just dismiss it. The ancients certainly didn't. Many people, who disagreed profoundly with Plato on other things, do, in fact, agree with him on this (agree with the early Plato on this). A great example of this tradition is found in later philosophers, even Stoics, who are far from being followers of Plato. Consider this example from Marcus Aurelius in his *Meditations*, another wonderful book. The *Meditations* is Aurelius's actual private diaries, the only private diary we have of an emperor. It's an astonishing book. Just to pause for a second on that: Imagine if a president were to write a book entirely for his own or her own purposes—a book of her own thinking, her own dreams, her hopes, her discipline about how she lives her days in office—and then that book goes missing and is discovered 100 years, 200 years later. That's the sort of thing that the *Meditations* are; fantastic, incredible work of a truly brilliant philosopher.

This is Aurelius in the *Meditations*:

> When you wake up in the morning, tell yourself: The people I deal with today will be meddling, ungrateful, arrogant, dishonest, jealous, and surly. They are like this because they can't tell good from evil.

That's Aurelius. One interesting thing just to note about that is it's amazing to imagine a Roman emperor trying to confront these people and saying, "You know, I'm just dealing with some surly people here." Any other emperor apart from Aurelius probably would have just taken these people outside and had them killed. Someone is surly to the emperor? This is not a good idea. It's a fascinating clue about Aurelius's character as a person: that he doesn't want to kill them, he just tries to understand who they are and negotiate the way around their difficulties in dealing with them. Anyway, that's just about Aurelius. What's crucial about this for our purposes here, though, is that the picture here Aurelius offers—which reinforces Plato's picture—suggests that people are pretty much the same inside, except that some people just have one set of skills better developed and a little bit more information than other people. If every other person had the ability to tell right from wrong in this way, they wouldn't be so bad; and if they had more information, they'd be able to make better judgments. In some important ways, this is a pretty optimistic picture of evil, right?

So far so good; but as time went on for Plato, his views darkened, became more sober. By the middle of his life, Plato understands "evil" in a more profound, complicated, and troubling way, and his depiction of the differences between good and bad people has become far more radical. This is probably seen best in his discussion of the dangers of the "irrational," most famously represented in the character Thrasymachus in the *Republic*; in Plato's fabulous, fabulous dialogue, the *Republic*. Thrasymachus is an interesting figure who really only features in the first book of the *Republic*; the *Republic* has 10 books, he's really in the first book. He pops up a couple times later in the dialogue as the evening of the conversation goes on, but it's really only in the first one where he and Socrates have a very fierce debate about the nature of justice. Thrasymachus is a Sophist. A Sophist is someone who teaches people the arts of political rhetoric. For people like Plato, he's a combination of both a spin doctor and a lobbyist in a certain way, or a consultant to a lobbyist; he's not a very favored person in Plato's world.

In the first book of this dialogue, he claims, to try to defend—and Socrates and he talk about this—Thrasymachus claims that justice is just the interest of the stronger. Interestingly, as it comes out in the conversation, this isn't really even a definition of justice; it's kind of a use of words meant to bully others into submission by Thrasymachus. What does it mean to say that justice is the interest of the stronger? That's in some ways itself not a definition as the attempt to refuse the point of giving a definition precisely because the point of that idea of what justice is, and the point of Thrasymachus's own words, are in some sense basically just to use force where people would actually like to have understanding. Thrasymachus debates Socrates, that is, really effectively just to get submission from Socrates, not to get understanding or cognitive agreement. In fact, Thrasymachus's name in Greek actually means "fierce or terrible fighter"—*thrasymachus*; *machus* is a warrior—and he's presented in this first book especially as roaring, sweating, shaking, loud, and blustery. He blushes at times, he's not fully in control of his body or his emotions, which, in fact, the emotions are really just an aspect of his body for Plato and the Greeks; in a certain way, his body is in control of him, but his body isn't coherent, it's a series of passions and desires. What Thrasymachus wants most of all is just to get his own way, to intimidate other people; but what his own way is, is just what his body is telling him it wants. He is a kind of a tyrant, but he is himself also tyrannized by the bodily components that go into him. When Thrasymachus can't intimidate the other people in the conversation, especially Socrates, into agreeing with him, or at least being silent—which he would think of as almost as acceptable— he withdraws into a kind of surly silence of his own for most of the rest of the dialogue.

It's hard to give an account of what Thrasymachus is doing here in cognitive terms, in language, precisely because that's exactly the challenge Thrasymachus presents in the dialogue. He represents, for Plato, a really crucial problem for social order and for harmony: He can't really be engaged in an intellectually serious manner. Thrasymachus is more of a symptom of a world gone mad; a symptom that must be diagnosed and for which a cure must be found and prescribed. But let's face it: Considering the first idea Plato had of evil, that evil is in some sense ignorance, no amount of new information is going to help Thrasymachus. For starters, he's not really interested in changing; indeed, he's not really interested in information. He doesn't want to learn; he doesn't want to talk to people really; he just wants to dominate, at least as he understands domination.

Here, then, in the *Republic*, this great classic middle dialogue of Plato's, Plato has deepened his sense of the connection between goodness and intelligibility. Goodness remains the properly intelligible thing to do, as in his younger view; but now unintelligibility, the irrationality of evil, has become more profound and radical in the human character, especially in those characters who are not, in some sense, on the road to intelligibility, on the road to rationality. Thrasymachus is not just incapacitated in his knowledge of good and evil a la Marcus Aurelius; he's incapacitated in his larger intellectual grip on the world as a whole. Indeed, he has no intellectual grip on the world; his response to reality, to the world, is more, really, a matter of irritable appetitive reactions to not fully understood stimuli. This is not a properly thoughtful human response; indeed, Plato suggests, in an important way, it's not properly human at all.

Thrasymachus, then, represents a terrifying challenge to Plato; and remember that it was people like Thrasymachus who, in a few years, would end up offering to kill, ordering Socrates to be killed. This is an important thing about this dialogue: Socrates's death shadows, is looming, over the whole dialogue; is looming over all of Plato's dialogues. It's a strange but really important fact to realize that in the history of Western literature there are really only two characters that in everything we have written about them have already experienced their own death. In other words, the characters may not give evidence of having experienced their own death, but the authors writing about them know the destiny of these two characters. The two characters are Socrates and Jesus. Everything we have about Socrates and about Jesus are all written in the shadow of what ultimately is their fate. The worry about Thrasymachus with Plato is not just that he's silly or harmless or stupid or he'll just go off in a corner and brood on his own; the worry is that we live in a world where Thrasymachuses also live, and the world that we live in is often one governed by people who are like Thrasymachus.

What should we do about that? That is, in some ways, after the first book of the dialogue, the fundamental question of the rest of the *Republic*: How should we live in a world governed by people who are not really on the way to being intelligible creatures? That's a terrifying question, actually; and in a way, Plato must ask two important questions here, two distinct questions: First, how far can the wholly irrational—what Plato calls the *alogon*, the completely arational—be brought into the realm of logos, the realm of reason, of discourse, of conversation; the realm of human intelligibility? How far can Thrasymachus be brought into the conversation of the *Republic*, and what does his being brought into it look like? Second, if we can't finally bring this *alogon* into the realm of logos, if we can't finally bring the figure of Thrasymachus into the realm of intelligibility, how can we improve the social order, our political world, our world in general so that there are fewer Thrasymachuses in the future? Evil is here not so easily captured in descriptions of accident and ignorance; here, evil seems more tenaciously part of our world, more difficult to correct, and requiring far more fundamental changes for us to be unsusceptible to its attractions than the mere delivery of more information to those caught in its clutches.

Questions such as these prompted Plato to explore the nature of human malice and malady in a new way, a way that no one had ever done it before. He saw something that people before him had not seen, or had not seen in the same way and with the same power: namely, that the cultural context in which everyone lived was powerfully shaping our sense of what is right and what is wrong; indeed, it is misshaping that. This is why Plato, and after him in a different way Aristotle, both critique the tragedians and Thucydides. He's also accused of hating poetry and any form of creative fictional expression. This is an odd accusation given the fact that his works are all artful dialogues. In fact, in one of them—I think it's the last one, the "Laws"—he actually says that the city that they are composing, the city that they are imagining, is the best kind of tragedy available. The problem for Plato is not with the idea of tragedy or the idea of creative thinking, abstract thinking, utopian thinking, imagining a rival city, a perfect city; the problem is how people have represented what would go into that perfect city, what goes into their pictures of what is normative about the world. It's not that he hates the form of poetry; he hates the content of poetry. Plato is in this way really usefully understood as kind of the first critic of the mass media.

For Plato, evil is seen as an importantly "political" fact; a reality whose continued flourishing—or continued toleration, anyway, by us humans—is due to the way the human world is organized. Culturally, we teach our children these stories, and these stories slowly mislead us, they mis-educate us in important ways, about how the world is, in fact, really determined. Remember the end of the *Women of Trachis*: There is nothing here that is not Zeus; there is nothing in this tragic scene that the gods did not order. Plato thinks that's incredibly dangerous to teach children; and so Plato offers what really amounts to the first truly radical critique of the way humans ordinarily live and organize their lives. In doing this, Plato is attempting to suggest that the kind of inquiry he undertakes is actually an enormously courageous inquiry.

One of the most interesting things about the *Republic*, this dialogue the *Republic*, is precisely the way that Plato takes a language in there of courage, bravery, fortitude, fear, anxiety, danger, all these terms that are originally militarily organized terms—they are terms originally used for combat and battle in Greek—and he continually suggests that the proper way to understand the real meaning of these worlds, where real courage lies, is actually in the kind of inquiry that he and his friends are undertaking. He's doing this not to kind of mock soldiers, because Plato and his friends were the military of Athens; every citizen of Athens would fight in the army when there was a battle. It's not like he's saying that in some sense, "We're better than those soldiers"; Plato and his friends were the soldiers, he's just saying instead, "Real courage is manifest by us, not so much on the battlefield," not so much there, "but rather real courage is manifest by us when we ask these fundamental questions about the nature and structure of our world."

Let me go on then: In this sense, evil for Plato is a cultural and political fact; but it's also, he comes to see, interestingly a kind of quasi-theological fact: It's a failure to be properly aligned with the moral order, and thus with the god, for Plato. Here's the first time we begin to see develop outside of the Hebrew Bible—a theme we'll see there as well—a crucial theme: the idea that evil is not simply a moral violation, a break in the horizontal human world, but is in some sense a rupture of a vertical relation we are supposed to have with God; it's a kind of a metaphysical revolt.

Consider how anarchic Thrasymachus seems; how jumbled he is. Plato depicts him this way at the beginning of the *Republic*, and by the end of that *Republic* he has given us an abstract philosophical description of the sort of person whom Thrasymachus is meant to represent: that is, the person caught in a kind of tyrannical soul. A tyrant is, for Plato, first and foremost a disordered soul, one who tyrannizes himself before anyone else. Why is the tyrant tyrannizing himself? Because the tyrant is revolting against the conditions of his own creation. That's the mature picture of evil that Plato offers; one where evil is far more radically a form of revolt against the conditions of our own creation, and one that spreads that evil through human society by infecting other people with a misorientation to the good through giving them bad cultural standards to try to live up to. That is, in some ways, the ultimate representation of evil for Plato.

In contrast, Aristotle, his student, explores the nature of evil in a far more "mundane" or worldly way through the discussion of a term that he makes famous: *akrasia*, or weakness of will. It's too simple, and inaccurate and misleading, to say that evil is a matter of sheer ignorance. Aristotle buys that. Why? Because sometimes you know the good but you do the bad anyway. Anyone who has tried to go on a diet knows all about that. Often it's the case that, in fact, the weakness of will that we suffer from that makes us do things that our minds tell us we shouldn't do. Clearly Aristotle rejects the early Plato's idea that information is in some sense the crucial ingredient that evil people are lacking. But he also thinks that the later Plato remained both in a way too rationalist and too theological about the nature of evil. People can be wrongly habituated for Aristotle, just like Plato; but neither good nor bad habits are rational, not in the way that Plato thought good habits are. Humans, that is, are not simply aligned just to the god as Plato thought they would be, and evil is not a rupture of that relationship; humans are as much flesh as they are mind, and the flesh part of humans for Aristotle matters as much, shapes a good deal of human behavior in fundamental ways. Plato seemed to think that our bodies would eventually become wholly subservient to our minds; that in some ways they would become offshoots of the mind. Aristotle wants to say that's not true; the point here is to find a happy medium where the mind and the bodies interact in a responsible way, with their distinct—though not ideally conflicting—interests and ends, and how they work together to accomplish everything.

This also means that evil has to be rethought for Aristotle. It's not a matter of a radical rejection of intellect for flesh; it's a more mundane problem than that. It's not really a matter of absolute revolt against nature, but a mis-ordering, a jumbling of our natural drives. Aristotle has no patience for Plato's idea that humans can radically revolt against their natural makeup, the conditions of their existence; we're not that transcendent. This is interesting: Plato's picture of evil is far more dramatic and radical than Aristotle's, but that's also because Plato has a far more elevated picture of what humans should be. Aristotle has a more moderate picture of what humans are, and therefore his picture of evil is also less dramatic. Humans exist by and large for Aristotle on a continuum between roughly coherent people and people for whom moral integrity of any sort is a pipe-dream; people such as addicts, or certain kinds of psychopaths. This means, of course, that for Aristotle, not all people can be made better; much like the representation of Thrasymachus, Aristotle has a picture where some people are just not really worth saving, they can't be saved in a way.

Aristotle, then, can be seen to be offering a kind of "medicalizing" evil, treating it not in very dramatic terms, but rather as seeing it as a certain kind of unfortunate pathology, towards which individuals in certain circumstances are prone. This does work against our tendency to over-dramatize evil, even to melodramatize it, like Plato perhaps did; it helps us resist any temptation to make evil seem something with a certain demonic grandeur or magnificence. It also asks us to see in evil a certain set of clinical symptoms that we, with proper philosophical detachment, may be able to address. Aristotle's is a much more moderate, a much more sober picture of evil than Plato's; but possibly also more hopeful, at least moderately hopeful, for the possibilities of some improvement for most of us.

But both Plato and Aristotle are united in one thing that makes them different from some of the other thinkers that we'll see a little later: They are very skeptical of the possibility of radical human change after childhood. Aristotle and Plato—unlike, say, the Christian accounts like Saint Paul's— are not really hopeful about human abilities to change. This is just a general question I want to put to you: Is it really possible for people, once they are more or less properly morally formed—age 10, 12, 15, however you think—

to change much? That's a deep question, and it's one that's worth pondering throughout all these lectures.

But anyway: The struggle between the Platonist and the Aristotelian views of the ultimate nature of evil echoes across the rest of this lecture series. Here, in quick compass, is a summary of these two views: First, Plato's view sees in evil a more radical and perhaps even theological challenge, a sign of a kind of a metaphysical revolt. But he also sees humans as in some ways quite elevated because of this and evil as something that is possibly fixable in some ultimate way; because if we can design our societies so that they are not rendering us susceptible to evil, perhaps evil will go away. Aristotle's view sees evil as a fairly mundane challenge, a matter of how to organize our relatively messed-up natures, and is always at best a sloppily designed, sloppily put together society populated by sloppily put together people. This is paired for Aristotle both with a more moderate picture of human nature—one where humans are mind and flesh in some combination of those two things—and not as theologically ambitious as Plato's, so it's more modest about humans. But it's also less dramatic—and, as I said, possibly melodramatic about evil—because evil is natural; it might not be really amenable to much social engineering of the sort that Plato says, and because of that, Aristotle can be seen as more cautious than Plato is, both in assessing the threat of evil and in prescribing a remedy to it. As I said, the debate between these two views will be long-standing; permanent thorough our lectures, really.

Alright, let me wrap this up. We've now seen two major bodies of literature on evil: the texts of the Ancient Near East, which talk about evil as part of a cosmic struggle of the gods; and now the work of the Ancient Greeks, which differ quite a bit among themselves but collectively talk not so much about a cosmic battle in which humans are innocent bystanders, but rather a conflict between humans and the ordering—or sometimes, as for the tragedians, the dis-ordering—principles of the cosmos. I want to turn next to some texts in the Hebrew Bible, and the Christian Old Testament as well, before moving on to the Christian New Testament. These sources begin to bring together the two streams of thought about evil we've seen begun in these last four lectures, but also they add their own little extra stuff as well.

The Hebrew Bible—Human Rivalry with God
Lecture 5

> One of the ways we keep these texts at a safe distance from ourselves is by imagining that they were written down by people in a time of unimaginable strangeness compared to our own, unimaginably distant from ours. ... But if we believe that, we insulate ourselves from the possibility that these texts were written down by people like us and have something directly to say to us about our common human condition, and I think they do.

In this lecture, we turn to the Scriptures of the people Israel, in which we see a vision of evil as fundamentally a form of rebellion against a single, good, sovereign God. Further, the origins of evil are intertwined with a particular kind of human ambition that is first named here: the ambition to rival God.

The story of Adam and Eve follows a recounting of the creation that seems set against the combat myth paradigm of the ancient Near East. In Genesis, the world is wholly good, is seen as such, and is governed as such by a wholly good God. But for the ancient Israelites, we must note that the Fall did not represent the entry of evil into the world in a completely unanticipated way. Adam and Eve did not create evil out of nothing, as Christians believe God created the cosmos; rather, they are the first to actualize the potential for evil, which was part of the cosmic structure that God had created from the beginning. Despite the overall resistance of the text to the Babylonian combat myth, the Genesis account still suggests that evil and temptation were a potential presence in the world.

The language we get of Eve "seeing that the fruit was good to eat" suggests a perverted vision, a parody of God's seeing that the world is good. Eve's temptation is a temptation to behave as God does, the temptation to judge for herself, a temptation, that is, to theological sovereignty. As the serpent says, "You will be like God, knowing good and evil."

This raises a question: What exactly is the sin here? Is it the experience of temptation or the sheer disobedience of the will that prompts the act? And what

Adam and Eve do not create evil out of nothing. Rather, they are the first to actualize the potential for evil, which was part of the cosmic structure that God had created from the beginning. Theirs is only, as it were, the first failing, not the origin of all fault in the cosmos.

is it about the knowledge of good and evil that is so destructive for humans? The Hebrew root of the word "knowing" suggests an intimate experience more than a merely intellectual acquaintance. Such knowledge gives its knower a certain set of skills and a certain kind of maturity perhaps, but the Bible suggests that it is a flawed maturity. This knowledge is both accomplishment and burden, blessing and curse. The story seems to tell us that perhaps all such human maturity is accidental and reluctant; perhaps any real wisdom contains within itself a certain ambivalence about the cost incurred to gain that wisdom.

The nature of evil in Genesis is clearly a form of rebellion—a kind of rivalry against God—perhaps initially inadvertent, but then it compounds itself in Adam and Eve's flight and hiding from God. There seems to be a longing for rivalry with God, but at no point are humans actually able to rival God. Evil and rebellion have a fundamentally futile character in this story that the combat myth never contains. The fact that Adam also took the fruit suggests a strange community to evil. Once they have both eaten the fruit and their eyes are open, Adam and Eve work together. Evil is not simply an individual act; it is compounded and deepened by communality.

The story seems to tell us that perhaps all such human maturity is accidental and reluctant; perhaps any real wisdom contains within itself a certain ambivalence about the cost incurred to gain that wisdom.

With Adam and Eve's children, **Cain** and **Abel**, we see the pattern of rebellion continue, but this time, the rebellion has direct inter-human implications. Cain and Abel's story is about the dangers of resentment: Cain resents God's choice of Abel's sacrifice over his own and kills his brother. Such resentment warps our vision of what is important and comes to "master" us, just as God says sin will master us in the exchange with Cain about Abel's whereabouts. Cain's reply to God is an angry retort— "Am I my brother's keeper?"—suggesting that sin is now, outside of the garden, perpetually part of our lives, and we are engaged in a grim struggle against it.

Another biblical story, that of the Tower of **Babel**, exemplifies rebellion in an explicitly political way. Humans here are working in concert against God, to build "a tower whose top will reach into heaven." God's response is to render the world fractured among many different languages and people. A suspicion emerges here that carries forward even to today: the problematic unity of all mankind against God. Because it is so powerful, God fears the community of humans when it is separate from the right worship of God and from obedience to God.

In the Hebrew Bible, we see a relatively coherent picture of a God whose plans for humanity are straightforward and easy to manage, yet those plans are, in some completely inexplicable way, rejected by humans entirely. This tradition secures the goodness and sovereignty of God and the goodness and stability of the moral order as a whole, but at the cost of rendering the root motive for human evil thoroughly mysterious. ∎

Important Terms

Babel: In the book of Genesis, the site where humanity attempts to construct a tower to heaven; often associated with Mesopotamian Babylon.

Cain and **Abel**: Sons of Adam and Eve in Genesis. The story recounts the murder of Abel by his brother, Cain, after God shows favor to Abel. Suggests that evil is now a permanent feature of human life that must be struggled against.

Suggested Reading

Anderson, *The Genesis of Perfection: Adam and Eve in Jewish and Christian Imagination.*

Levenson, *Creation and the Persistence of Evil.*

Questions to Consider

1. What is your response to this lecture's reading of the Genesis story? Is this a different telling of the Fall than you have heard before? Do you agree that the story suggests that Adam and Eve *actualize* (rather than create) evil in the world?

2. How do you see the Genesis account in comparison to others we have examined so far? Does the concept of rebellion against God presented throughout the Genesis stories add important dimension to the idea of evil? In what ways do you see the stories of Genesis continuing to exert influence on our conceptions of evil?

The Hebrew Bible—Human Rivalry with God
Lecture 5—Transcript

Welcome back. We're turning back now from Greece to the Ancient Near East, but now to the Scriptures of the people Israel. In the early episodes from the Book of Genesis, we see a vision of evil fully on display, one that suggests evil is fundamentally a form of rebellion against a single, good, sovereign God. The origins of human evil here, in this account, are intertwined with a particular kind of human ambition that is really first named here: a human ambition to rival God. Evil in this tradition thus has an ineliminable theological dimension—much like I said with Plato—prompted, though, by psychological motivations of resentment and rivalry; and God here, in this account, seems both a guard against evil for humans and also, indirectly, in advertently, a goad towards it.

Before we begin by looking at Genesis, a side note is really in order. As I suggested when we were talking about the *Enuma Elish*, we by and large have a habit of thinking that the Bible was written in almost complete isolation from the rest of the world and from the rest of history, as if it were written, as it were, in a vacuum. Clearly now we can tell from the *Enuma Elish* that that is not so, and it helps us to know what the Bible—what any biblical text—is saying "no" to, in order to understand what it is affirming. But it's not just that the books of the Bible came out of a world already filled, swarming, with stories from other cultures; that world also had physical remains, ruins of long-abandoned cities from earlier cultures. Consider this: The earliest known written records that we have in human history go back to about 3000 B.C.E. or so. But, in fact, civilization was already about 2,000 or more years old then; as long ago, that is, as the Roman Empire and the first Christians are to us today. The people of that time, 3000 B.C.E., already lived amidst rubble and beside ruins. Theirs was already an old world. People came to written self-awareness in mythology already with a deep past. The human has always had a historical self-consciousness about coming late in the world; humans have always come late in their history.

This is important for this lecture, because one of the ways we keep these texts at a safe distance from ourselves is by imagining that they were written down by people in a time of unimaginable strangeness compared to our own, unimaginably distant from ours. Somehow, these texts seem to us completely alien in some way; unaffiliated with the history we inhabit. But if we believe that, we insulate ourselves from the possibility that these texts were written down by people like us and have something directly to say to us about our common human condition; and I think they do. Let's see what that is.

Let's look first at the story of Adam and Eve, a story of rebellion in perfection; but not, perhaps, the story that many people think they know. Recall, first of all, the *Enuma Elish* here for a second: The story of Adam and Eve follows a recounting of the creation which seems resolutely, though again silently, to set its face against the combat myth paradigm of the Ancient Near East. In the *Enuma Elish*, remember, there was a cosmic struggle: Forces of order, forces of chaos; finally, the forces of order win, but they use the forces of chaos as a basis on which to build the cosmos; order and chaos, good and evil, coexist in a world that no one is really in charge of. But in Genesis, this is not the case; in Genesis, there's no struggle: God commands and it is done. Yes, there are traces of this earlier story. We saw: The Face of God moves across the waters of the deep; *tehom*, in Ancient Hebrew, which is, again, lexically related to Tiamat—the Sumerian chaos-goddess; the one killed by Marduk; the one who the world was made out of her corpse—but the traces in Genesis of the earlier myth really serve only to reinforce the distance between this vision of the world and that of the combat myth. Here, the world is wholly good and seen as such, and governed as such, by a wholly good God.

But we have to be careful: The story of Genesis, as it would have been read by the ancient Israelites who first put it on paper, is in very fundamental ways not the story most people today read, especially Christians, when they read the story of Adam and Eve in Genesis. We read the story today as the story that Saint Paul tells, in fact, in his New Testament letters of Adam and Eve and of Genesis, the larger story; or at least what later readers took to be Paul's story. Here, Satan in the guise of a serpent creates all evil in the world in a context in which God creates a totally good, totally ordered cosmos out of nothing. Adam and Eve are not just the first people to fall in the world; they, in some sense, inaugurate the history of evil itself. This is a Christian, indeed a very Christologically-informed reading of the Genesis text—that is, a reading that is profoundly informed by another experience of Jesus Christ, which has shaped Christian accounts—but we don't want to go that way; we want to look at the text in a more archaeological sense, in terms of how it was most likely to have been read by its earliest audience. Just as an example of that, almost all of us assume that the fruit in the Garden of Eden, of course, is what? Is it a pomegranate? No, it's an apple; but, in fact, the story of the apple as the fruit in the Garden of Eden is actually a late medieval version of the story. In the Genesis account itself, it only says "fruit."

In this reading of the story—how the people at the time it was written down would have understood it—the Fall does not represent the entry of evil into the world in a wholly unanticipated way; instead, the Fall is more representative than constitutive of the reality of evil in the world. Adam and Eve do not create evil out of nothing, as Christians believe God created the cosmos; rather, they are the first to actualize the potential for evil, which was part of the cosmic structure that God had created from the beginning. Theirs is only, as it were, the first failing, not the origin of all fault in the cosmos. Despite the overall resistance of the text to the Babylonian combat myth, all these Ancient Near Eastern stories, the Genesis account still suggests that evil and temptation were a potential presence in the world, and one bound to have some impact in the history of the world.

Also, just as an aside on this story, what exactly is the nature of Eve's temptation? The language that we get of Eve "seeing that the fruit was good to eat"—which recalls, by the way, God's seeing of creation as good— suggests a perverted vision, a parody of God's seeing that the world is good. Something deep is being said here about temptation. Eve's temptation here is, in some ways, a temptation to behave as God does; the temptation to judge, to judge for herself; a temptation that is to theological sovereignty. As the serpent says, "You will be like God, knowing good and evil."

This raises another question: When exactly does sin begin? When exactly is the moment of sin? Where does the fall start? Where is their first step off the precipice? With the act of eating the apple; with the seeing of it as good to eat? With the serpent's question; with Eve's first answer to the serpent? This is enormously rich for the later theological traditions that comment on these texts, Jewish and Christian alike, because it bears importantly on what exactly is the sin? Is it an external act? Is it the experience of temptation? Is it the sheer disobedience of the will that prompts the act? Is it the simple eating of the fruit, as if there were some poison in it, as in Snow White's apple in the story of Snow White? Why, after all, is the tree there in the garden at all? What was God thinking; and why is it that the knowledge of good and evil is the crucial thing here? What it is about the knowledge that's so destructive for humans? This knowledge appears four times in the story, and it seems to mean a kind of knowledge that encompasses all things; not just the meaning of these two terms, "good" and "evil," but more like "from alpha to omega" or "from soup to nuts." Yet the term still seems loaded with a meaning that is both ominous and opaque. Why is it the knowledge of good and evil that is the problem; and of all the forms of knowledge that could cause a fall from happiness, why would it be the knowledge of good and evil?

One clue here may be in the term "knowing" that is used. The Hebrew root of this word is *yd'* or *yada*. This is not simply an abstract conceptual knowledge, not knowing math or knowing how to drive a car, really (well, maybe a little bit more like knowing how to drive a car); but the "knowing" in this sense is the same word that is used in the Bible with a sexual connotation. It designates an intimate experience, more than a merely intellectual acquaintance. Such knowledge gives its knower a certain set of skills and a certain kind of maturity perhaps; but, the Bible suggests, it is a flawed maturity. This knowledge is both accomplishment and burden, blessing and curse; but mostly curse. Perhaps, the story of Adam and Eve is telling us, all such human maturity is accidental and reluctant; perhaps any real wisdom contains within itself a certain ambivalence about the cost incurred to gain that wisdom. Very few are the 20-year-olds who want to be 80; but very many 80-year-olds are at least sometimes interested in being 20 again. Innocence doesn't look so bad from the side of experience.

The nature of evil here is interesting: It's clearly a form of rebellion—a kind of rivalry against God, to be like God—perhaps initially inadvertent, but then it compounds itself in Adam and Eve's flight and hiding from God. There's a longing for rivalry with God, but at no point are humans actually able to rival God. There's a fundamentally futile character to evil and rebellion in this story that the combat myth never contains. There's another thing about this story that is really interesting to think about: Adam took the fruit as well, in a way of an act of solidarity with Eve. There's a weird community suggested to evil here. Once they have both eaten of the fruit, then their eyes were open, and they worked together. Evil, that is, is not simply an individual act; it is compounded and enriched and deepened by the communality that comes with evil as well. We'll see this in a minute when we look at the Tower of Babel as well.

Once this evasion has happened and God begins to lift the kinds of punishments that will ensue because of it, this litany of maledictions seems endless: effort, pain, labor, enmity, and nature. The litany is endless, in fact; and this is, ironically perhaps, truly the real fruit of tree of the knowledge of good and evil. So Adam and Eve—and that's how you say it, "Adam"; we can say "Adam," but "Adam" and Eve—are exiled from Eden as a consequence of their sins. The gates of paradise are closed to them, and to all who follow them. All of us now live, as it were, East of Eden.

Interestingly, there's a long-standing controversy in Christian theology—we won't get into it here, but I just want to mention it to you—as to whether redemption is a matter of our sheer restoration to the Edenic state, or is a matter of something even greater: an elevation in Jesus Christ to a new status. For Christians, that is, the relationship between Adam and Christ—who is sometimes called the "second Adam" or the "new Adam is complicated. Is redemption a return to innocence, or is it something else, a greater wisdom acquired through the loss of innocence but movement into another kind of mature moral state? Anyway, I want to mention that only to say that it's a topic for another lecture series.

Turning from the Fall now to Cain and Abel, Adam and Eve's children, we see the pattern of rebellion continue; but this time the rebellion begins to have direct inter-human implications, not simply implications for the divine human interaction. The basic story here is simple: The surprising choice of one brother over another by God in their mutual offers to God of sacrifices provokes wrath in passed-over brother, and this wrath leads the passed-over brother (Cain) to murder so that Cain kills Abel, whose blood then cries from the ground to God. God discovers Cain's crime and exiles him, making him what the scriptures call a "restless wanderer" over the face of the earth (leading to any number of pretty good country-Western songs). This is in some ways a story about the dangers of resentment. As God says to Cain in their exchange about where Abel is: "If you do well, you can hold up your head; but if not, sin is crouching at your door; it seeks to master you, but you must master it." It's a very, very famous, very famous, text. It begins to be very important for all later Jewish epics, and especially rabbinic epics as well.

The danger of resentment here as a motivator is quite clear: It warps our vision of what is important and, in fact, comes to "master" us. Ironically, this is visible in Cain's very reply to God when God asks him where Abel is. Cain says, famously, "Am I my brother's keeper?" What you might not have realized, though, is that Abel as a shepherd and Cain as a farmer, Abel is the one who is a "keeper"; the word "keeper" is also the word for "shepherd" here. Cain is saying, "I'm a farmer, I'm not a shepherd; I shouldn't care about my brother's place." There's a very interesting kind of angry retort to God there; it's not just a naive question on Cain's part. The lesson here—and we'll see this taken up in later lectures as well—is that sin is now, East of Eden, perpetually part of our lives, and humans are engaged in a grim twilight struggle against it; and much of the time we will fail. Cain gives in to his sin and suffers the consequences.

This story of the rival brothers is repeated perpetually throughout the Bible, as the mysterious election of some by God over others leads the non-elected others repeatedly to envy and to do violence to the elect. But God repeatedly also turns the evil against itself and creates good. You can even see this in the Christian New Testament: Paul plays on this when he talks about the surprising way that Jesus is the cunning messiah who has won through dying. There's always a matter of sibling rivalry. Jesus sets himself up against the Temple authorities, and thus, in a way, turns out for Paul to be the younger brother who is favored by God.

Eventually, Cain's wandering comes to a sort of an end, and he settles down and he founds a city; in fact, he founds the first city in history (at least as people read the Bible). Think about that: The first murderer is also the first founder of a city. A figure we'll look at later, Saint Augustine, makes a lot of hay about this because he compares Cain and Abel to Romulus and Remus, the founders of Rome (well, Romulus founds Rome and he kills Remus at the same time). Because of this—because of this connection between cities and sin, even here in Genesis—we're going to turn to cities as sites of rebellion against God now, and the classic case of this, of course, is the Tower of Babel.

The Tower of Babel exemplifies rebellion in an explicitly political way. Remember the logic of the decision to build the tower; this is in the 11th chapter of Genesis:

> The people say, 'Come, let us build for ourselves a city, and a tower whose top will reach into heaven, and let us make for ourselves a name; lest we be scattered abroad over the face of the whole earth.'

Here, rebellion against God is now overt and collaborative; this is political rebellion. Humans are now working together in concert—which in itself is a good thing—they're singing "We Are the World" or something, but "We Are the World" against God. God's response to this, of course, is to render the world fractured among many different languages, many different people. There's a deep thought here about sin and politics, and a profound suspicion that begins to emerge here that carries forward even to today: The problematic unity of all mankind against God, the idea that all of humanity could be joined together in a rivalry with God, is explicitly named as a danger by God. God sees what they're doing and he says:

> Behold, the people is one, and they have all one language; and this they begin to do; and now nothing will be restrained from them, which they have imagined to do.

God fears the community of humans when it is separate from the right worship of God and from obedience to God precisely because it is so powerful. Human communities, human peoples working in communities, turn out to be an exceptionally problematic thing in the early book of the Hebrew Bible.

Interestingly, there's no report of the tower's toppling in the text. The suggestion is that the people simply stopped working on it and walked away. This made for an especially vivid moment in the Bible, because, as I said at the beginning of this lecture, by the time this text is written, civilization in the Ancient Near East was already millennia old, and so the ruin of the tower might have been something that one would have expected to see, somewhere out there on the far horizon, as you were herding your sheep somewhere on the plain of Shinar, somewhere like that.

Also, calling this tower "Babel" is not simply a matter of referring to Babylon; it refers also to *babel*, to a language of chaos and incoherence. It suggests that the fracture of humans into multiple languages and cultures is itself a sign of the human decline, so that in two different ways, two large-scale memories come out of this story: on the one hand, the idea that humans working together is something that is feared by unless they are working under God's control; on the other, the idea that the plurality of cultures and languages in the world, our "multitudinousness" in this world, is itself a further sign of sin. But, of course, the fundamental point here is that "Babel" is also a place where many peoples try to live; if not together, at least in proximity to one another. This is one of the first moments when vast cosmopolitan human political organizations—the sorts of things we call "empires"—begin to be associated in the Jewish and then Christian traditions in a particular way with human depravity and corruption. We'll see this again when we get to the Christian New Testament in the Book of Revelations. There's a complicated ambivalence, and possibly hostility, to large-scale human endeavors; a certain kind of concern about cities and empires emerges here. When people talk about, say, a big city like New York as a "Babylon," there's actually a deep psychological resonance that goes way back in the tradition echoing this.

The set of stories that we've looked at in these texts share some common traits: They suggest that evil is real and palpable, and works sometimes to divide humans, sometimes to bring them together, sometimes to set them at odd and with blades against one another, but always to set them up in rivalry with God. This is crucial: Evil in these accounts has an inescapably theological dimension, a dimension of rebellion, whether of a broken relationship such as a violation of the Covenant—we'll talk about the Covenant in the next lecture—or a rupture of the harmony that is the natural order, or the formation of a human community, an empire, to rival God's rule. Part of the consequence, the punishment, for evil is precisely God's retribution for that rebellion. By thinking of it as rebellion, it immediately means that God is in an important way innocent of evil, for after all God can't be held responsible for those who go against God. In other words, God cannot be the kind of person who creates a world and sets up creates who will, in some important way, revolt against that God. So unlike, say, the Ancient Near East stories where you have the role of human community as revolting against God only because some other gods support it; or against the Greek tragedians, where you have an account where the gods seem in some complicated way to undergird multiple patterns of theological and political revolt against the deities and also against human order.

In the Hebrew Bible, what we see is a relatively coherent picture of a God whose plans for humanity are straightforward and easy to manage, and yet those plans are in some completely inexplicable and curious way rejected by humans entirely. That might be the core curiosity of this tradition, because this tradition in a certain way secures the goodness and sovereignty of God, and the goodness and the stability of the moral order as a whole, but only at the cost—and it's a large cost—of rendering the root motive of human evil in some important way thoroughly mysterious. Why is it that when Eve looks at the fruit of the three of the knowledge of good and evil she sees that it is good to eat? Why does she want that? That's a question that thinkers, theologians, priests, rabbis have wondered about for 3,000 years. Why, when you had everything in the world, would you want more?

But there is another tradition, a rival story in the Bible alongside this original story, which seems to suggest that God is not wholly or at least not in any simple way simply good; that God has a murkier and altogether more sinister dimension. We will turn to that dimension, that rival story, next.

The Hebrew Bible—Wisdom and the Fear of God
Lecture 6

> Interestingly, the story of Job, the figure of Job, seems outside of the major narrative of the people Israel in the Hebrew Bible. ... There's something important about Job here, something about the universality of his condition. He is not marked out as a member of the people Israel; he's simply a human.

One major strand of the Hebrew Bible sees evil as fundamentally a rebellion against God and God's good order. But another strand talks about evil and suffering in disquietingly different terms: as things perhaps willed directly by God. This strand raises questions about the nature of God's governance of human life, the mystery of God's dispensing of both good and evil to humanity, and humanity's proper response to a God who acts in such mysterious ways.

We begin with **Abraham** and the covenant. A covenant is not a contract because it is open-ended; it doesn't completely define the boundaries of the ethical relationship it creates. In many ways, a covenant is an act of faith and hope. Abraham's covenant with God gives him his life, but it is not a life without darkness.

When God tells Abraham that God is going to destroy

The story of Sodom and Gomorrah is a story about judgment and justice.

Dover Pictorial Archive Series.

Sodom and Gomorrah, Abraham begs God to spare the innocent, which God does. This crucial moment reveals that God and Abraham are not in a covenant of power but an ethical covenant. God makes known that God can be appealed to as a force for justice. But then God asks Abraham to kill his son. To sacrifice Isaac means effectively that Abraham must leave his family behind, just as God had asked him to leave his family in Chaldea and to leave behind his original name and identity. In many ways, the call to sacrifice Isaac is a call for Abraham to sacrifice himself.

This story tells us that God is far more foreign to our notions of right and wrong than we might at first realize. At times, God seems intent on destroying us, and we cannot complain

The warning of Abraham's life—that God's ways are not our own—is made much more explicit still in the Book of Job.

because everything we are—our names, our identities, our children—is from God. Abraham's silence in the face of God's command seems somehow inhuman, as if there is something enormously profound in Abraham, but he knows he cannot communicate it. That is, he has some wisdom about life and God's expectations for us that we perceive in his silence precisely because he can't share it.

The warning of Abraham's life—that God's ways are not our own—is made much more explicit in the Book of Job. As we know, God allows Satan to inflict terrible suffering on Job, who then refuses the consolations of his friends and is ultimately told to curse God and die. In the end, God answers Job's complaints by telling him that he cannot know God's ways. Job's story seems to tell us that we shouldn't try to investigate evil, but it also raises important questions: If Satan is doing God's work, then is God allowing evil to happen or is God actively doing evil? And is there any real difference between the two?

Job's comforters give a voice to the readers of the Book of Job, both groups attempting to bring the apparent irrationality of Job's punishment into the realm of the intelligible. And Job's rhetorical duels with the comforters are the most important parts of the Book of Job because those duels establish his faithfulness. But does the story of Job's suffering offer us wisdom, or is it helpful only to those who have already suffered? One of the great puzzles of many of these texts is that it's not clear that the people who most need to hear the lessons they seek to convey are able to apprehend those lessons. It may be that we can't understand what such texts are trying to communicate until we have undergone similar experiences. If we think of Job as a "wisdom text," perhaps it is saying that real wisdom may be acquired only through intimate, first-person experience.

> **Job's comforters give a voice to the readers of the Book of Job, both groups attempting to bring the apparent irrationality of Job's punishment into the realm of the intelligible.**

The stories of Abraham and Job serve as puzzles and goads for the rest of the tradition in two distinct ways: First, they disturb the faithful's confidence that God's plans for humanity are wholly intelligible and entirely in agreement with our own wishes and aims. Second, they force us to question how a recognition of God's terrible mysteriousness might be achieved by us short of the trials put upon Abraham or the sufferings inflicted on Job.

The prophets of ancient Israel struggled with such questions. How can we be present in the world before God when we don't know how God will act toward us? As with Abraham and Job, the prophet Isaiah tells us that we can have no clear and certain knowledge; we can know only that the obedience called for will not necessarily be easy. A fearful reverence before God is probably the wisest course to take but also a course taken only by the wise. ∎

Abraham: Early patriarch of Israel whose story is recounted in Genesis. He makes a covenant with God and obediently follows God's command to sacrifice his son, Isaac, though God intervenes at the final moment.

Suggested Reading

Brueggeman, *The Prophetic Imagination.*

Heschel, *The Prophets.*

Kierkegaard, *Fear and Trembling*, Hong and Hong, eds. and trans.

Mitchell, *The Book of Job.*

Newsom, *The Book of Job: A Contest of Moral Imaginations.*

Scheindlin, *The Book of Job.*

Questions to Consider

1. The stories of Abraham, Job, and the Prophets presented a new development in thinking about evil—namely, the idea that evil may actually be an instrument of God's providence. What is your response to this? Can evil be a tool used by God to accomplish God's own purposes?

2. Is Abraham's obedience to God best seen as a contrast to Adam and Eve's rebellion? And should it disturb us that Abraham's obedience is proved by God commanding what seems to be an "evil" act?

The Hebrew Bible—Wisdom and the Fear of God
Lecture 6—Transcript

Welcome back. One major strand of the Hebrew Bible—the one we looked at in our last lecture—talks about evil as fundamentally a rebellion against God and God's good order. But there's another strand, one that talks about evil and suffering in disquietingly different terms: as things perhaps willed directly by God, in the sovereign darkness of God's mysterious governance of human life. This strand of the Bible raises questions about the nature of God's governance of human life, and about the mystery of God's dispensing of both good and evil to humanity.

All this raises the question of humanity's proper response to a God who acts in such mysterious ways; and it raises the question of how that response in turn shapes human beings in their overall life. The figures that we'll treat of here are considered very wise and faithful figures in the Bible; but as Job says in his book, "Where shall wisdom be found?" Is it, as the Book of Proverbs says, true that "fear of the Lord is the beginning of wisdom"? Is that the right way to think about these traditions? Is this dimension of the Bible attempting to tell us that in order to properly inhabit a world governed by a good God, a certain kind of humility and perhaps even a certain kind of fearfulness is required?

To look at this question more fully and begin to think about how the Bible may be trying to answer it, I want to look at a series of stories in the Hebrew Bible—what Christians will also call the Old Testament—a series of stories very important for this tradition, but in a different way also constitute a sort of minority report about what's going on in the tradition's message about God and about the people Israel and God's governance of history. I want to look especially at the stories of Abraham, of Job, and then think about how the prophets used those stories to think about the meaning of history and the purpose of God's plans for humanity in their own time. The upshot of this story is that indeed there is something in what Proverbs says: that a fearful reverence before this God is probably the wisest course to take, but also only a course taken by the wise.

Let's begin with Abraham and the Covenant. This language of covenant is very important and it will behoove us to spend just a little bit of time thinking about what makes a covenant and why it is so important in this tradition. While there were proto-covenants—kind of early, preliminary covenants of a sort—made with Adam and Eve and then with Noah, in fact, the Covenant in this tradition is made between God and Abram (that's Abraham's first name, Abram). Abram, as a condition of this Covenant—one of its formulations, anyway—changes his name to Abraham, which is the "father of many nations." Abraham's identity, that is, his very name, is given to him in accepting the Covenant.

A covenant is not a contract, it's very different. Most basically it's not because it is open-ended; it doesn't completely define the boundaries of the ethical relationship that it creates. Like a marriage—which is often talked about as a covenant—a covenant talks about sharing in a journey for better or worse. It is powerfully committing for both sides—perhaps more powerfully committing than a contract, precisely because of its open-endedness—but it is disquietingly uncertain about where this will go (again, much like a marriage). With a contract you know what you're getting into—if you buy a car, you're able to return it under certain conditions—with a covenant, not so much. The meaning of the covenant, the meaning of what it binds together, emerges only over and through the history of the relationship itself. A covenant, that is, is an act of faith and hope.

As for Abraham, in Abraham's covenant with God, the covenant he affirms gives him his life. Insofar as it is a good covenant, it means he accepts and affirms the life it gives him, which he seems to do. But that life is not without its darkness, either. Abraham exemplifies a certain faithfulness precisely because he seems to live into that covenant in ways that are unpredictable, and he responds to God's surprises in that covenant in ways that are unpredictable as well. His story has multiple moments, and here I just want to focus on three. First, the story of Sodom and Gomorrah: This is a story about judgment and justice. God wants to destroy these towns because they are so full of sinners, and he tells Abraham this: "Hey, I'm going to go and flatten these towns." Abraham begs God to let the innocent be spared, and he asks God again and again, "Shall not the judge of all the earth do right?" Indeed, God allows the innocent, Lot and his family, to be spared. This is a really crucial moment: God and Abraham are revealed to be not just in a covenant of power, but an importantly ethical covenant; God has revealed in this behavior that God can be appealed to as a force for justice. This is a very important thing: Abraham now understands this God not just to be a good God for him but also a good God for the cosmos.

But then God goes and does something new: He asks Abraham to kill his son. This is the famous Akedah, "binding," the sacrifice of Isaac. Probably of the three Abrahamic faiths, this event is the one that both binds them all together and also torments each one of them individually, precisely because of the many confusing dimensions of this story. Right now in my world, in religious studies, we like to talk about the Abrahamic faiths—all three of them: Judaism, Christianity, Islam—as the "Children of Abraham"; this is the big phrase. I like the phrase; it's a nice phrase. But what we don't notice a lot, and what would be important to notice if we were to continue with this, is that God tells Abraham to kill his child. So what does that mean?

Consider some of the details of this story: God asks Abraham to sacrifice Isaac; and not just Isaac, he says, "Isaac, your son, your only son, whom you love." Those are formulaic statements on God's part, but they are also packing into what Abraham is being asked to do a certain density of drama that suggests that God knows what he's asking Abraham to do. To sacrifice Isaac means effectively to leave his family behind, just as God had first asked Abraham to leave behind his family in Chaldea (that's where Abraham came from); and just as God asked Abram to leave behind his name and his identity and become Abraham. Indeed, because God had established the covenant with Abraham through Isaac, and not through Ishmael (Abraham's other son, who he has shunned at this point), the call to sacrifice Isaac meant that Abraham is being asked to sacrifice not just his name—after all "Abraham" is glossed as meaning "the father of many nations"—but in some important way to sacrifice his own identity; to sacrifice Isaac is to sacrifice himself. Abraham seems willing to obey this, but of course God's messenger stops him before the sacrifice is made, the angel of God. "Angel," of course, in Greek is the word *angelos*, which just means "messenger"; so the messenger of God stops Abraham here.

Scholars read the story as, at its base, a rejection of the practice of child sacrifice, which was widespread in the Ancient Near East. But I think that is too shallow a reading; it seems deeper than that. The lesson seems to be: This God is far more foreign to our notions of right and wrong than we at first took this God to be. Sometimes this God will act in ways that may seem intended to destroy us, and we can have no complaint about this, it seems, because everything we are—our name, our identity, our children, our family, everything—is from this God; God possesses us all, in some ways before we possess ourselves. Our response to these moments, when God does a terrible thing, will reveal how we understand the covenant. Indeed, recall that just before the Akedah, just before the near-sacrifice of Isaac, what happens is the story of Sodom and Gomorrah; so it's precisely this ethical covenant that's been established that now is, right after this, challenged in the event of the request to sacrifice Isaac. In fact, it is in the threat of Sodom and Gomorrah, right after that, which Abraham learns that he will have a son, that God will grant him a son, whom he will name Isaac. This is a very dense moment here.

After the events of the near-sacrifice, the Akedah, Abraham does not return to his first wife, and Isaac's mother, Sarah at her encampment at Hebron. He goes on instead to his second wife, Keturah's, encampment at Beersheba; perhaps that's understandable. Abraham and Sarah are not reported to speak again, nor are Abraham and Isaac. After this, Abraham's life rapidly moves towards its end. First, he secures a wife for Isaac, in the story of his servant and Rachel at the well, thus securing the future of his family. Then Sarah dies, and he secures a burial place for her in the cave of Machpelah near Mamre. Then Abraham himself dies. The division that had happened between his two sons, Isaac and Ishmael, is apparently resolved now, at least provisionally, when they bury Abraham in the same cave where Abraham buried Sarah, thus, in a way, bringing the two brothers together and returning husband and wife together.

People wonder about the silence of Abraham in the face of the Akedah; in the face of God's command. There's no reported argument between him and Isaac, nor between him and Sarah, nor really between Abraham and God; Abraham doesn't suggest any resentment of God's command. There's something inhuman about this silence; there's something enormously profound that is present in Abraham, but that Abraham seems to know he cannot communicate. That is, he has some wisdom about this life and God's expectations for us in this life that precisely because he can't share it, the rest of us can perceive it in that silence. What can we learn of this?

One way to think more about this is to see a situation where words are used—plenty of words, in fact—but to very little effect; and that is the story of the Book of Job. The warning of Abraham's life—that God's ways are not our own—is made much more explicit still in the Book of Job. The Book of Job is an interesting book because the proportion of action to dialogue is almost as skewed as it is in a kind of very strange art film; very little happens in the book, but a lot of words are said (maybe it's like Congress or something). But here's the basic story: Satan returns to God's court; Satan, in the Book of Job, is seen as an angel who is used at times by God for certain activities. He tells God, "I have been up and down and to and fro upon the Earth." God says, "Did you see my wonderful servant Job who's fantastic?" Satan said, "Of course I saw him, but there's no way in the world Job would be so nice if you made him suffer." God says, "You are crazy; go and try." So Satan goes down and inflicts a series of sufferings on Job; that's the prompting of the book. Job then sits, basically, having lost his children, having lost his industry, his wealth, his home, in his silence and then his friends come and try to console him; and then, after their consolations fail, after he refuses their consolations, he is told by his friends and his wife to curse God and die. He refuses, but he still complains to God; and finally, out of the whirlwind, God speaks to Job and tells him effectively "my ways are not your ways," you cannot know and it is better just to accept what has happened.

Interestingly, the story of Job, the figure of Job, seems outside of the major narrative of the people Israel in the Hebrew Bible. He's not a descendent of Abraham, anyway; some ancient rabbis thought Job was a literary figment actually—1,500 or 1,800 years ago, certain scholars were saying, "This is clearly a literary device that we have in our scriptures here"; that's a pretty remarkable thing for people 1,800 years ago to say—but others thought that Job was a wise man whom the Pharaohs would consult. But all the Book of Job itself says of him is that he was "a man in the land of Uz," who was "was blameless, upright, fearing God and turning away from evil"; that's Job 1:1. There's something important about Job here; something about the universality of his condition. He is not marked out as a member of the people Israel; he's simply a human. What's interesting about the book in general is that in some important ways, it seems to be a story about why you shouldn't try to solve evil; why you shouldn't try to investigate why these things happen to you. It's not that there aren't important questions to ask; some of the questions you might want to ask are: Consider the relationship between God and Satan; if Satan is doing God's work, then is God letting evil happen or is God actively doing it? If God merely lets it happen anyway, isn't it that the same as if God did it directly, since God is the ruler of the universe entirely?

Questions like this raise a larger philosophical puzzle about what Job is about that the role of the comforter, the figure of the comforters, actually bring up as well. The comforters who come to help Job—it's not clear whether they're there to help Job or rather to help themselves—play a huge role in the story, and what they are trying to do in a sense is find some explanation for Job's suffering. In a way, what the comforters are doing is standing in the role of the readers themselves of the Book of Job, because the readers are almost certain to want to offer some kind of explanation for why this has happened to Job. What the comforters do is give the readers a voice in the book, and what they're trying to do is find some way to bring the apparent irrationality of the punishment into the realm of the intelligible, perhaps even the justifiable; in any event, they think, more endurable. So much of the Book of Job is consumed by their words and Job's replies to them, so much so that people sometimes actually ignore those words; they think that they're just getting in the way. They're clouding the action of the Book of Job because they think that nothing happens there; that's just people talking; that's not very important. You have to go back to the action; the Bible's an action movie, so you have to see where the action is going on. Not so: The action is happening in those words; in some important way, it is precisely Job's rhetorical duels with the comforters that are the most important part of the Book of Job, for those duels establish Job's faithfulness; his refusal to accept glib fake explanations.

In this, the Book of Job, in my experience, maybe in yours, actually speaks to a pretty common experience that people can have. If bad things happen to you—if you lose a loved one; a parent, or God forbid a child, or just a loved one, a spouse—a lot of people feel an enormous pressure when they talk to you to find some consolation that will actively remove the pain and the loss and the suffering you feel. I know I feel that pressure myself when I'm encountering people in the midst of enormous suffering. Sometimes that can be useful, but a lot of times it seems to me—and I think I'm backed up by the Book of Job here, which is, you know, not a bad backup—that sometimes those attempts at consolation are much more about making the consoler feel comfortable in the situation. The person devastated is devastated, there's no quick fix for them. They have no answers; they're going to have to go on with their life and, over time, find a way of living. But there's no quick trick that can make things better for them. The Book of Job is, in important ways, the first time in the Bible where the human predilection to offer words where no words are going to be useful is brought to the surface and examined and found wanting.

Is Job a useful story, one that has wisdom we can pass on? Or is the story of Job's suffering only helpful to those who have already suffered, as Abraham has? One of the great puzzles of a lot of these texts—let me just stop for a second and say this—and I've sort of said this with Aristotle's *Ethics* in an earlier lecture, is that it's not clear that the people who most need to hear them, to hear the lessons they want to convey, are able to actually apprehend them. It might only be after the experiences have happened that you can finally understand what the text was trying to communicate to you in the first place. If we think of Job as a "wisdom text," perhaps it is saying that real wisdom—at least some forms of it; some of the most important forms—may only be acquired through intimate, first-personal experience, particularly in terms of suffering; that there is no easy way to learn of reality except through suffering it. Maybe that suggests, as I suggested with the knowledge of good and evil, that some forms of wisdom carry with them the question of whether the very wisdom we get is worth the cost we pay to get it.

The stories of Abraham and Job serve as puzzles and goads for the rest of the tradition in two distinct ways: First of all, they disturb the faithful's confidence that God's plans for humanity are wholly intelligible and entirely in agreement with our own wishes and aims. They insist that believers recognize a terrible mysteriousness in God's providential governance of the world. Second, they put to us the question of how such a recognition might be achieved by us short of the trials put upon Abraham or the terrible sufferings inflicted upon Job. Is there a way to gain the wisdom of faith, to feel the fear of the Lord that these texts insist is the beginning of wisdom, without suffering the actual pain that these figures encounter? Again, as we've seen before and we'll see again, the question here is more general than that for us: Can armchair theoretical reflection get us useful knowledge about suffering and evil? Or, as with the fruit of the tree of the knowledge of good and evil that Adam and Eve tasted, does such knowledge always and only come at the cost of real pain?

These are the questions that the prophets of Ancient Israel struggle with. The prophetic tradition is one of deepening self-awareness over the course of the prophet's lives and over the course of the series of prophets about the power of God's governance over history and God's perpetual doing of a "New Thing" in history. Even though the prophets are compiled in the scriptures and thus seem to be on the same plane with Abraham, the Book of Job, or all that stuff, in a certain way they are Ancient Israel's philosophers; they are the ones who offer a second order reflection on their faith. They are the first theologians, as it were; the first to take the deposit of faith and try to figure out with that deposit: What is God doing now? The basic question they asked, again and again, is: Why do bad things happen to the good people Israel? Well, they say, these people are not so good, for starters; they've abandoned the covenant. They've also ultimately violated God's law in many ways. Prophets like Amos will say this; Amos, of course, is famous for preaching repentance and demanding that justice roll down in a mighty stream. Amos thought, quite clearly, that in fact the problem that the people of Israel were facing was not due to some fundamental mysteriousness in God's providence; the rules were very clear, and they were simply not following the rules. By the time of the prophet Jeremiah, things had gotten more complicated. There was clearly a way in which history was being seen now as what is called "theophanic"; that is, "revealing of God's will." A "theophany" is a showing of God; "theo-," "-phany." History is a medium whereby just as we can in the scriptures, Jeremiah seems to be saying, we can read about what God is doing and interpret those events to show us how God stands vis-a-vis us right now; and unless we do better, Jeremiah says to the people Israel, we will continue to be punished by God.

Irrespective of whether or not the people Israel did any better, sufferings continued to come their way. By what we call Second Isaiah—by the second prophet in the Book of Isaiah—a new and perhaps profounder kind of wisdom is being preached by the prophets. It deepens Jeremiah's interpretation in seeing history itself as theologically rich, but now it sees history in a kind of eschatological and messianic way. What I mean by those terms is somewhat technical, but I can explain it pretty easily: To talk about history as eschatological means to read history from a coming end of history. Second Isaiah is famous for prophesying deliverance for the people Israel as a light unto the nation, revealing through the salvation of Israel that all of the world will be redeemed. Second Isaiah has a profoundly optimistic picture of Israel, but it is also profoundly somber about what happens in the meantime. There's a kind of sovereignty to God that puts God in a way beyond good and evil here. As Second Isaiah says—this is chapter 45 of the Book of Isaiah—"I form light and create darkness, I make weal and create war, I am the Lord, who does all these things."

This sets up the question of how to be present in the world before God, even though you don't know how God will act towards you. That's behind a lot of Isaiah's prophecy here: Knowing we have this hope coming out, how should we behave now? As with Abraham, and Job, Isaiah says we can have no clear and certain knowledge; we can only know that the obedience called for before the apotheosis of the people Israel, before its revelation and sanctification of all the nations, the obedience called for will not necessarily be easy but that keeping faith is close to the center of who we are in our very identity.

The prophets then end with a terrible and awe-filled humanity; that is who we should be, and that is why the fear of the Lord, the prophets affirm, is indeed the beginning of wisdom. Following the example of Abraham, inspired by the story of Job, a fearful reverence before this God is probably the wisest course to take, but also only a course taken by the wise. The prophets, thus, are really not so much predictors of the future as reflectors on the past; historians who tell their people where they have come from in order better to see where they are going. Their basic question is not what will happen as much as what is God doing now?

Let me conclude here a bit: So far, we've seen the cosmic battle of the *Enuma Elish*, the Greek tragedians, the historian Thucydides, the philosophers Plato and Aristotle, and now the Hebrew Bible. Much separates all these, but they share some interesting things in common. The differences should be pretty visible. Whether or not you see the cosmos as a battlefield, whether or not you see humans as rebelling against the unitary God—how these things work—the differences are widespread. For Plato and Aristotle, for example, humans are dependent on the context in which they develop in important ways; and now with the Bible, humans are dependent upon, but in revolt against, a good God.

The range of views is pretty broad, but one thing seems common that's worth noting: In all these approaches, the vulnerability of humans to terrible suffering is pretty clear. That, I think, should strike us; for we don't today have that sense of vulnerability. We're pretty unique in that. Historically, in most of the world apart from really the current First World today, suffering and death are pretty common. It wasn't that long ago that even the children of wealthy parents died with some regularity. In July of 1924, Calvin Coolidge, Jr. died in the White House where his father was President. Imagine the child of an American President dying today. Yet at the time it was sad, but not unbearable. What we see, in other words, is one important fact that separates us from all these accounts: our relative invulnerability compared to them as regards suffering. We'll think more about that later.

With all these texts, we see something of the breadth of the religious inheritance of Ancient Israel, an inheritance passed into both Rabbinic Judaism and into the Christian churches, though transformed in different ways by both of them. We turn to the Christian New Testament next.

Christian Scripture—Apocalypse and Original Sin
Lecture 7

> Somehow in the last century or so, lots of Christian churches have just simply ignored [the book of Revelation], like it's an unpleasant, smelly, aggressive relative who shows up to family gatherings but no one wants to talk to. This is a big mistake; this is a shame, because, in fact, the embarrassment of Christians to talk about this text ... makes them especially susceptible to ignoring a crucial dimension of the Christian message here.

Early Christian communities are often presented as small groups of gentle people living in the nooks and crannies of the Roman Empire, practicing their faith as far as possible from the centers of power. But far from being wholly pacifistic, early Christians saw themselves as bit players in a cosmic struggle between God and Christ, on the one hand, and the principalities and powers commanded by Satan, on the other. This "cosmic war" motif is visible in Paul's letters and comes to full fruition in the book of **Revelation**.

The early Christian tradition seemed to think that evil had declared war against God and the forces of goodness. Here, Christianity is developing the rebellion motif we saw in the Hebrew Bible, but it is now applied to angelic powers, as well as humans. The Gospel texts especially have a strong sense of the demonic powers as a vivid presence in the world. Recall that Jesus, at the beginning of his mission in the Gospel of Mark, is tempted by Satan in the desert, and many of his miracles are reported to have come at the expense of bad spirits. Indeed, a sense of a coming final battle with these evil spirits seems to lurk behind many stories in the Gospels. The fact that Jesus "set his face to go to Jerusalem" (Luke) tells us that a final confrontation with the satanic powers seems to have been inevitable to Jesus.

Later, Paul understood the churches to be caught in a struggle between God and Satan, with the outcome already decided, perhaps, by the Crucifixion and the Resurrection. Note here what Christian theologians refer to as the "already and not yet" motif. In Jesus's life, death, and Resurrection,

Christians believe that Satan has already been defeated and the world is already saved, though it has not yet come to its full salvation. The powers of evil are still afoot and can still fight back, and because of this, the faithful must equip themselves spiritually for a struggle.

In Revelation, the theme of a battle against supernatural powers is even more pronounced. An apocalyptic text, like the book of Revelation, speaks of the

© Dover Publications, Inc.

In the Gospels, Jesus seems alert to the presence of the demonic spirits, as in the Gospel of Mark, when Jesus is tempted by Satan in the desert.

end of the world and seeks to offer its readers a skeleton key to decipher the signs of the times. More basically, Revelation also aims to teach people how to live in this world in the end times. More than a collection of predictions about the end of the world, it is about the present world. The theme of combat again pervades this text, crystallized around the metaphor of combat between the "dragon"—an embodied force of evil—and a good God.

> **The powers of evil are still afoot and can still fight back, and because of this, the faithful must equip themselves spiritually for a struggle.**

Another dimension of the New Testament's heritage about evil is the idea of **original sin**. This doctrine seems to have gotten its start in the early Christian apprehension of the significance of the goodness of Jesus Christ. The earliest Christians clearly had a sense that the person—not the message—of Jesus Christ was, in some important way, theologically revelatory. For Jesus to be as good as Christians thought he was, the world must be pretty bad; for Jesus to be as powerful as they experienced Jesus as being, the enemies arrayed against him must be strong. Early Christians, thus, depicted the human condition more darkly and represented the powers of evil more dramatically than did others of their time. The sense of spiritual combat that already existed made evil more palpably and determinately part of creation itself.

The magnitude of God's activity that Christians perceived in Jesus's life, death, and Resurrection demanded a powerful opponent over whom to triumph, and that opponent had to be the force of evil insinuating its way into human history. Saint Paul, in his letters, looked back through the history of evil and found its beginnings in the story of Adam and Eve. For Paul, the story of Adam and Eve is not simply the first instance of a failure that had always been possible; it is the radical introduction of some new substance of malice and power that had not existed in the world before.

It's important to note that the notion of original sin doesn't mean that nature itself is evil; it's that we have appropriated our natures in a way that makes them evil. When God's kingdom comes to earth, Christ and everyone will be resurrected in the flesh. Salvation is not a matter of escaping the flesh but of properly inhabiting it. ■

Important Terms

original sin: Christian doctrine that stresses evil as dramatic, powerful, and endemic to the human condition.

Revelation: Apocalyptic text contained in the New Testament that describes the final cosmic battle between God and the forces of evil.

Suggested Reading

Kovacs and Rowland, *Revelation: The Apocalypse of Jesus Christ.*

Questions to Consider

1. Why do you think the concept of an apocalyptic cosmic struggle was so important to early Christian thought about evil? Is this concept still applicable or useful today?

2. In these New Testament texts, thinking about evil becomes amplified through Paul's understanding of original sin. Do you see Paul's reinterpretation of the Genesis story as a helpful Christian contribution or a deviation from the story's "true" meaning?

3. How is the contemporary Christian picture of the world similar to these early Christian texts? How is it different?

Christian Scripture—Apocalypse and Original Sin
Lecture 7—Transcript

Welcome back. From the stories of the Hebrew Bible, we now turn to a set of texts that presented themselves as essentially in continuity with those earlier texts. In some ways, they were and are; but in other ways they suggest a significant break with those earlier works, or at least certain construals of those earlier works. We've seen some big themes: dualism versus monotheism; providence or fate versus accident; evil as mundane or this-worldly versus evil as theological or other-worldly. We've looked at two large wellsprings of Western thought about evil: namely, the Ancient Near Eastern world, both Babylonian and then the early texts of the Hebrew Bible, and the world of classical Greece. Now, with this lecture, we'll see the first body of literature in which those two worlds begin to commingle.

There are two ways that evil is addressed in Christian Scriptures: first, in the demonic representation of evil in some of the more apocalyptic dimensions of the Christian scriptures, culminating in the Book of Revelation; and then second, in the development of the earliest moments of what comes later to be known as the doctrine of original sin, particularly in the letters of Paul. The first is reflected from older traditions; the other is a distinctly Christian development, it seems to me, based upon an important re-reading of the Adam and Eve story in light of the early Christian community's experience of Jesus Christ.

Much of the time, early Christian communities are presented as kind of pacifist quietists, small groups of gentle people living in the corners and the nooks and crannies of the Roman Empire, wanting to live out their deeply interior faith as far as possible from the centers of power and ways of violence in the Roman Empire; kind of weak, marginal people crouching in the shadows as the legionnaires and the muscular people of Rome walk by. Certainly, the Christians of the first couple hundred years after Christ were pretty marginal and weak groups in the Roman Empire, although they were getting stronger after about 100 or so C.E. But the received picture misses an important dimension of their thought, which will come to be very important as the tradition develops. For far from being wholly pacifistic, early Christians saw themselves really as kind of bit players in a cosmic struggle that dwarfs our capacity to imagine it; a cosmic struggle between God and maybe Christ on the one hand and the principalities and powers commanded by Satan on the other. This "cosmic battlefield" metaphor is clearly derived from earlier Ancient Near Eastern traditions, and it emerges in a context of 1st century Palestine that was itself suffused with apocalyptic imagery and expectations. Many people in the Palestine of the 1st century of the Common Era were, in fact, expecting the end of the world or a coming messiah. But the Christian account is in some ways complicated and in some ways rendered distance and unique because of the way it reads that struggle through ancient Israel's vision of the unquestioned, though sometimes hidden, sovereignty of the one God.

The "cosmic war" motif that we're talking about here is really visible, especially in the Gospels; it has a little bit in Paul's letters; and then comes to full fruition in some ways in the Book of Revelation. Let's talk about those in turn: Early Christians clearly imagined the cosmos to be a battlefield; they talked about evil as real all the time, these texts always do. In Paul, you have Paul talking about the "principalities and powers"—that's in his Letter to the Ephesians—the idea that Satan seems to be behind the forces of the principalities and powers at work in this world. Furthermore, the tradition seems to think that evil has quite clearly declared war against God and the forces of goodness; indeed, evil just is this declaration of war. Here, Christianity is developing the "rebellion" motif we saw in the Hebrew Bible; but now applies it not just to humans but to angelic powers. Certainly in the past few centuries before the Christian New Testament emerges, ancient Jewish thinking had developed more of a notion of rebellious angels or spiritual powers that walked the Earth in some complicated, hidden way against the power of God; so there was this notion of rebellious angels or demons that was in the air that the ancient Christians breathed. But they really took it in a new and more systematic and rigorous way, really making that much more serious.

The Gospel texts especially, while they differ in many ways, seem to have a strong sense of the demonic powers as a vivid presence in the world. It's not always apparent that they're represented as part of a Satan-centered conspiracy; sometimes the powers are diverse and multifarious and they don't seem to be working in concert in any important way. But the presence of a struggle with demonic powers that humans are in some sense caught up in—even though the main combatant is God against the demonic power; Satan in some texts, Lucifer in others—this motif is a repeated presence throughout these texts; demonic spirits are perpetually present in and throughout the Gospels.

Just think about some of the examples: At the beginning of his mission in the Gospel of Mark, Jesus is tempted by Satan in the desert. At different times in the Gospels, Jesus seems alert to the presence of, as he puts it in Matthew, "the devil and his angels"; and many of Jesus's miracles, especially exorcisms, are reported to have come at the expense of bad spirits (the Gadarene swine in Mark; the swine who run off the cliff). In Luke, after Jesus has sent out his disciples for their first kind of apostolic missions, they return and he says to them, "I saw Satan fall like lightning from heaven"; and throughout the Gospels, there is a coming final battle with these evil spirits that seems to lurk behind a lot of the stories in the Gospels. Finally, of course, John reports in the Gospel of John that in Gethsemane—that is, the garden where Jesus is finally arrested by the authorities, and in some ways his worldly mission comes to its fruition—Jesus's plans in that garden are represented as climaxing in his triumph over the "prince of this world." He says in John 12: "Now is the judgment of the world; now shall the prince of this world be cast out."

In fact, it's quite clear that the Gospels think that Jesus knew that this struggle with Satan was inevitable; after all, the Gospel of Luke says quite early on that Jesus "set his face to go to Jerusalem." That's an interesting and powerful metaphor. At a certain point it became inevitable to Jesus, and he was determined to move inexorably towards a final confrontation battle with the satanic powers that Jesus seems to have known—this is what Luke suggests—that this confrontation would result in his own death. That text, one of the most interesting and theologically rich texts actually in the entirety of the Christian New Testament—Jesus "set his face to go to Jerusalem"— and for the past 1,900 years anyway, Christian theologians, in thinking about the degree to which Jesus understood the mission in which he was engaged in, have thought centrally through that text, what does it mean to set your face to go to Jerusalem?

In all these ways, then, the presence of demonic powers engaged in struggle with God and God's angels, and with Jesus, Jesus's disciples, and all humanity is a powerful theme in the Gospels; and it's also powerful in Paul. Paul understood the churches to be caught in a struggle between God and Satan, with the outcome decided already in some important way, perhaps for Paul by the Cross and the Resurrection. As Romans says at one point, "The God of peace will soon crush Satan under your feet." This is important; let me stop here for a second and say this: This temptation, this tendency, to think about the Christian message in terms of what Christian theologians talk about as a motif of "already and not yet" plays itself out both positively in terms of the redemption of humanity or the salvation of the world from evil; in Jesus's life, death, and resurrection, Christians believe, the world is already saved though it has not yet come to its full salvation. There's still some tension between the current state of being slowly redeemed, which is painful, and the final consummation of that redemption. That's a positive way this theme works itself out. But it works itself out negatively, too, because in principle the crucifixion and resurrection of Christ, theologians after Paul— and I think it's fair to call Paul the first theologian like this—Paul and those after him believe that the crucifixion and resurrection of Christ in principle defeats Satan, defeats the powers of evil and darkness. But those powers are still real, and they are still vivid and afoot and at loose in the world that we live in; and so even though in principle they have been defeated, in fact, they still walk up and down and to and fro upon the Earth as Satan did in the Book of Job.

That's Paul sense there: In some important ways the battle is over, but in another way we're still involved in a kind of mop-up operation of evil. Evil can fight back, and it does fight back; even though its back has been broken, nonetheless, it has the ability to punch back hard. Because of this, the faithful must equip themselves spiritually for this struggle, and Paul uses a remarkable range of military metaphors for this process of equipping. Consider the central passage of this sort; this is in Ephesians 6:10–18:

> Finally, be strong in the Lord, and in the strength of his might. [Listen to the armament and weapon metaphors here.] Put on the whole armor of God, that you may be able to stand against the schemes of the devil. For we wrestle not against flesh and blood,

but against the rulers, against the authorities, against the cosmic powers over this present darkness, against the spiritual forces of evil in the heavenly places.

Therefore take up the whole armor of God, that you may be able to withstand in the evil day, and having done all, to stand firm. Stand therefore [check this out; check out this list of metaphors], having fastened on the belt of truth, and having put on the breastplate of righteousness; and as shoes for your feet, having put on the readiness given by the gospel of peace [the gospel of peace; in the middle of these military metaphors, the gospel of peace pops up]. In all circumstances take up the shield of faith, with which you can extinguish all the flaming darts of the evil one; and take the helmet of salvation, and the sword of the Spirit, which is the word of God, praying always in the Spirit, with all prayer and supplication.

Sometimes we look at the Bible and we miss the forest for the trees; it's so familiar to us, we don't actually see what's right there on its surface. Paul is quite clear in this passage that there's a struggle Christians have to engage in; but we, in thinking about this text, whether we're Christians or not, seem to miss that, we seem to not notice that. Paul did, and the communities that Paul wrote to did, and they saw the life of the disciples of Christ as an ongoing struggle, not against humans fundamentally, but against supernatural powers.

In Revelation, this theme is even more pronounced. Revelation, of course, is probably the most famous of the apocalyptic texts of early Christianity, though interpretive attention to it in our world seems to have been by and large abandoned by many churches today. It's rare that you would go into a Christian church—many Christian churches, I would say—and actually read as one of the scripture readings on a Sunday an excerpt of the Book of Revelation; it would be a really fun reading on a Christmas morning or something like that (that could be kind of fun, to shake things up a little bit). But what's interesting is the Book of Revelation, which is a pretty big text—I mean, physically it's quite large—and it's a very important text over the history of Christian thought, somehow in the last century or so lots of Christian churches have just simply ignored, like it's an unpleasant, smelly, aggressive relative who shows up to family gatherings but no one wants to talk to.

This is a big mistake; this is a shame, because, in fact, the embarrassment of Christians to talk about this text for fear of being associated with more apocalyptic tendencies in their culture makes them especially susceptible to ignoring a crucial dimension of Christian message here. Too much of the time, Christians are ignoring this crucial dimension of their religious heritage, and it misshapes the story they tell and the story they understand about their faith in important ways; two different ways it misshapes that story. Let me pause here for a second and say this: The first way it misshapes the story is that it ignores the fact that in popular culture today, the Book of Revelation is still incredibly powerful. Up until the Harry Potter series of novels, the best-selling collection of novels in the history of I think American publishing, possibly world publishing, was the Left Behind series. Whatever your views about the Left Behind series, the fact that very few churches even tried to think about what those books were telling people about the meaning of Christianity is an astonishing failure on the part of the churches. That's one thing: Even if the churches don't want to think about the Book of Revelation and the apocalyptic message it might contain, nonetheless, they will be the ones who are in some sense going to be accountable for dealing with people coming into these churches and trying to think about what these texts mean for them; that's one thing. The second thing is by ignoring the Book of Revelation, Christians are, it seems to me, trying to avoid a certain complicated historic prophetic interpretation of history that relates them in complicated ways to the faith of Judaism and also to a richer understanding of the texts of the Old Testament, which Christians ought to be attending to as importantly as they do the New Testament. I'll say more about that as we go on in this course, but one of the big problems, it seems to me, is precisely that Christians have preselected—Christians today, maybe let's say, in the West—a body of scriptures that, for them, tell a certain story of Christianity, but it renders it hard for them to see that story as in as rich continuity with the Jewish faith as it should be.

Let's look at the Book of Revelation very concretely. It's an apocalyptic text. By "apocalyptic," I mean something quite technical, but worth your knowing. An apocalyptic text is a text that talks about the last things and speaks of the end of the world, and seeks to offer its readers a skeleton key to decipher the signs of the times. Certainly a lot of Revelation is about that; but this raises a deep question about the point of the book: Is the Book of Revelation really just a kind of skeleton key to the end of the world? Is it really just to help people look out for the end of the cosmos? Is it a kind of eschatological meteorology guide to determine the theological weather? Or was it also—and maybe more basically—about teaching them how to live in this world in the end times? That's what I think it was doing. Here's one of the greatest challenges to the continued use of the book of Revelation by churches today; and perhaps this might be a major reason why many Christians today find this part of their Scriptural heritage so hard to understand, because they can't see this text as anything more than a collection of kind of predictions of the end of the world. But I think it's actually more than that: It's about the present world, whatever its prophesies about the world to come.

To see this, note how the theme of combat—just as it did in Paul and in the Gospels—pervades this text, especially crystallized around the metaphor of combat with the "dragon"; the combat between the dragon, an embodied force of evil, and a good God. Examples of this are not hard to come by: Consider that at certain points the imperial beast of Satan is represented, and there is a war between Satan and the angels as well. But the most dramatic example of this motif in Revelation is probably the war between the archangel Michael and the angels on one side, and the dragon and his angels on the other:

> Now war arose in heaven, Michael and his angels fighting against the dragon; and the dragon and his angels fought, but they were defeated and there was no longer any place for them in heaven. And the great dragon was thrown down, that ancient serpent, who is called the Devil and Satan, the deceiver of the whole world—he was thrown down to the earth, and his angels were thrown down with him.

Clearly, the "dragon" here turns out to have a long history, both in the later thinking about evil—both as itself, the terror people had of mythological demons—and also as an interesting metaphor; because from the earliest reception of the Book of Revelation, the other meaning of the dragon:

people understood it to be the Roman Empire. Just as I said in the lecture on the Tower of Babel, human organizations that are in some sense separate from God in both the Jewish and the Christian scriptures take on a kind of patina of illegitimacy and theological disrespect fairly early on. Christianity was significantly marked by being formed in a period where it was radically outside of the structures of worldly power, and in important ways those structures were arrayed against it. Both in Palestine and the larger Mediterranean world, Christians did not have friends in high places. This has, I think, shaped the way Christians have thought about evil and thought about worldly power in profound and potentially very long-lasting ways. I'll just leave that out there; we'll talk about that more.

But the story of the dragon still asks us a question: How does this cosmic struggle map onto our experience here, in this life? What does it mean that—and again, the Book of Revelation is very clear about this—humans witness this struggle in Heaven? Humans are not the ones fighting—we're not taking up weapons against these angels; that's the archangel Michael and the good angels doing that—we're kind of innocent bystanders; we're villagers, where two air forces are fighting high above us in the sky. What do we do here? Here the other dimension of the New Testament's heritage about evil becomes important, and that is the idea of "original sin." After all, along with this cosmic apocalypticism, the other great theme on evil in the Christian New Testament is the beginning—just the beginning—of the development of the Christian doctrine of original sin, particularly in Paul's letters.

The development of this doctrine is a very interesting thing; and I want to propose to you that, in fact, it gets its start not in a direct apprehension of people's nastiness, it actually gets its start in a dawning Christian apprehension of the significance of the goodness of Jesus Christ. It was precisely the combination of the early Christians's apprehension that Jesus Christ was in some really, really significant way a theological revelation of God. However that gets worked out in the later tradition in terms of talking about Christ as one of the three persons of God, the earliest Christians clearly had a sense that Jesus Christ—not just Jesus's message but Jesus's person—is in some important way theologically revelatory. This means that for Jesus to be as good as Christians thought he was, the world must be pretty bad; for Jesus to be as powerful as they experience Jesus is being, Jesus needs to be that powerful because the enemies arrayed against Jesus are that strong. This means that Christians, by backing into it sort of, depicted the human condition more darkly than others of their kind, and they represented the power of evil dramatically perhaps than others did in their time. This sense of spiritual combat that they had already—we talk about this with Revelation—made evil more cosmic as apocalypticism makes evil more palpably and determinately part of creation itself; that is, evil begins to be both more profound and more intimate at the same time. The profundity, of course, is captured in that notion of the dragon; the intimacy gets captured in the notion of original sin.

The magnitude of God's activity that Christians perceived in Jesus's life, death, and resurrection demanded a powerful opponent over whom to triumph, and that opponent had to be the force of evil insinuating its way, snaking its way, through human history; and Saint Paul, in his letters, looked back through the history of evil and found in the story of Adam and Eve the beginnings of that evil. As I said, at its time, speaking archaeologically, the story of Adam and Eve is not about the origins of evil, it's about the first time that evil happens. But Paul doesn't see it that way: Paul sees the story of Adam and Eve as talking about the beachhead of evil in creation; it is a cosmic calamity for Paul. It is not simply the first instance of a failure that had always been possible; it is, rather, a new thing, and a real and radical introduction of some new substance of malice and new power into the world that had not been there before.

There will be more to say about this and the complicated relationship this sets up between Judaism and Christianity later. It's true that these two traditions share a lot of the same texts, but what's interesting is they're kind of like to traditions that are separated by a common scripture. In looking at the texts as they do, both sides see very different things in the same exact passages. This is an important thing to take away from now because we'll come back to this. When we think about the Christian conceptions of evil, following on in Irenaeus, Augustine and others; and when we thinking about the Jewish conceptions of evil, thinking about rabbinic understandings of evil, thinking about Jewish responses to the Shoah, the Holocaust, in the 20th century; we will find that their understandings of evil root themselves in the same texts but in very different ways, and that's going to be very important for us.

But for now, when it comes to the Christian account, we can say that the development of this Christian conception of evil includes a dramatic depiction of sin and a representation of evil as powerful, active, and seeking humanity's downfall. It is profoundly—this picture of evil; ironically, perhaps—tied up with the radical hopefulness, even optimism, in Christian faith as the early Christians experienced it of God's saving work in defeating the Devil and sending Jesus to save all of humanity and create a "New Covenant" with all of humanity. This is the consequence in some ways—in fact, it's the material, the cause, as well—of the parting of the ways between Judaism and Christianity, but it is more consequence than cause. This is a large and dramatic break that we will come back to later. In fact, in just a few lectures, we'll talk about Rabbinic Judaism, and we'll see it then as well.

Nevertheless, despite all I've said, neither the Book of Revelation nor the New Testament corpus as a whole expresses any complete and total hostility towards the world, or any absolute desire to flee from it. It's the cosmos's current structure that is the problem, not the fact of our existence in it. This is important: Like the Hebrew Bible, and unlike, say, Greek views of the tragedians, for example, the notion of original sin doesn't mean that nature itself is evil, it's that we have appropriated our natures in a way that makes them evil. The aim of Revelation and of the New Testament as a whole is to teach patience and endurance in a time of trial for the churches. The sense of a cosmic struggle is inescapable here, but note that in the Book of Revelation the dualism that is set up between good and evil is temporary and provisional. At the end of the Book of Revelation, the "New Jerusalem," the new kingdom of God, comes down to earth from heaven. Humans are not raptured from Earth up to Heaven; God's kingdom comes to earth. Furthermore, the idea of the resurrection of the body—which is a very early Christian metaphor, early Christian belief—is very important here: Christ and everyone will one day be resurrected in the flesh. Salvation is not a matter of escaping the flesh, that is, but of properly inhabiting it.

Next, we're going to turn to how this view gets worked out in complicate and diverse ways in the thinking of some major Christian theologians, especially Irenaeus and Augustine.

The Inevitability of Evil—Irenaeus
Lecture 8

It would have been possible, for example, for someone not well versed in philosophy, not as able to speak philosophically and abstractly as Irenaeus was, to have first explained and given an account of Christianity, and in that case, the future of Christian thinking would have been very, very different.

Christian theology has a tradition of offering what are known as theodicies: theories of evil that make it intelligible and attempt to explain how we can affirm the existence of a good, all-powerful God in the face of the reality of evil. Two of these theodicies in particular have been quite powerful: that of Augustine, which we will explore in the next lecture, and that of Irenaeus.

Christian theology is relatively unique in comparison to other world religions in its fixation on the problem of evil. Indeed, according to Christianity, the world is far more profoundly mired in evil than our ordinary experience suggests it might be. As we said in the last lecture, with the growing recognition of the magnitude and power of Christ's saving work in the world, the early Christian community was required to revisit its assessment of worldly corruption, and in doing so, rethink and deepen its sense of the sinfulness of the world.

Among the earliest thinkers who began to systematize the Christian account of good and evil was **Irenaeus of Lyon**, generally considered to be the first truly great church father. His greatest work is *Against Heresies*, written in opposition to Gnosticism, a pseudo-philosophical movement popular among elites in the ancient Mediterranean world. Gnosticism argued that the materiality of the world is the source of evil and that humans in their true essence contain a spark of innocence that must be unlocked from the cage of flesh and allowed to escape. The Gnostics ultimately began to claim Christianity as a form of Gnosticism, but for that to be true, Christianity had to be understood as a radical renunciation of the Jewish story.

For someone like Irenaeus, Gnosticism threatened the Christians' vision of how they should live in the world, who their ancestors were, and who their rivals were in the present world. Irenaeus and the mainstream of orthodox theology in the Christian world argued that Christianity was a part of the story of the people Israel, although it offered a new version of that story. This view ensures that the Old Testament is read as an authentic story of God's dealing with humanity.

According to Irenaeus, humanity must succumb to sin, fall into sin, and receive its punishment, namely suffering and death. He offers the story of Jonah in the belly of the whale as an allegory for the human fall.

Irenaeus posits a picture of evil as an inevitable and necessary component of the development of the human race. He explains this by interpreting the story of Jonah in the belly of the whale as an allegory for the human Fall. Just as Jonah had to be swallowed by the whale, so must humanity succumb to sin and receive its punishment, namely, suffering and death. Then, God will raise the dead, and having passed through this evil journey, humanity will have learned by experience what evil truly is and how mercifully God has acted in redeeming humanity from it.

But humans need, over time, to grow and mature, not only in their individual lives but over the course of human history, in order to become fit for the destiny that God intends, which is union with the divine.

In Irenaeus's view, God initially created Adam and Eve as immature and childlike in their innocence. But humans need, over time, to grow and mature, not only in their individual lives but over the course of human history, in order to become fit for the destiny that God intends, which is union with the divine. This maturation is a complicated matter of transforming our desires from immediate material desires for base, natural ends to a desire for genuine union and communion with God. Humanity's rebellion against God and descent into sin are essential for the fulfillment of this destiny.

Irenaeus is the first thinker in the Christian tradition to offer an account that divides evil into two groups: natural evil, such as earthquakes, plagues, and so on, and moral evil, that is caused by intentional human will. For Irenaeus, moral evil hurts us as much as the people whom we hurt, but in doing so, it causes us to recognize suffering in our world and, ultimately, choose to turn to God. God will not compel us in this; God will simply continue to offer us salvation, and the deeper we get into despair, the more attractive that offer of redemption will seem.

Two points here require further reflection: First, is it true that to be blessed, one must know what it is to be damned? And second, does this account trivialize the reality of evil and suffering? What about those who suffer horrendous evil without having a chance to learn from it? What about an evil such as the Holocaust, which seems wholly out of proportion to any kind of lesson it could communicate to us? How could we gaze into the eyes of the 12 million people who died in the Holocaust and say that their suffering improved their lives? ■

Name to Know

Irenaeus of Lyon (c. 150–c. 202 C.E.). Irenaeus was probably born in Smyrna and raised by Christian parents. During the persecution of Christians by Marcus Aurelius, Irenaeus was imprisoned for his faith, and he eventually became the second bishop of Lyon.

Suggested Reading

Hick, *Evil and the God of Love.*

Irenaeus, "Against Heresies," in *Ante-Nicene Fathers*, vol. 1, *Apostolic Fathers, Justin Martyr, Irenaeus*, Roberts and Donaldson, eds.

Questions to Consider

1. What do you make of Irenaeus's distinction between natural and moral evil? Was Irenaeus correct to describe certain aspects of our existence, such as hunger or pain, as "evil"? And is it important to differentiate between the evil humans cause and the evil we experience independent of human willing?

2. Is it true that Irenaeus's account of evil risks downplaying or trivializing suffering and evil? Can it be true that evil is a necessary step on the way to greater good?

The Inevitability of Evil—Irenaeus
Lecture 8—Transcript

Hello again. So far, with the exception of Plato and Aristotle, we've mostly looked in this lecture series at approaches to understanding and thinking about and responding to evil that are less directly theoretical and more concrete, more literary, more mythological, more scriptural. With this lecture, we're going to move into a series of attempts by thinkers to offer a distinct interpretation, each of them offering their own account more or less, of what the meaning of evil is, where it comes from, and what humans can do about it.

Christian theology in particular has a tradition of attempting to offer what have come to be known as "theodicies": theories of evil, accounts of evil, which make it intelligible, make it understandable, how we can affirm the existence of a good all-powerful God in the face of the reality of evil. This word "theodicy"—let me say something about this for second here—actually is not invented early on in the tradition; the word itself comes very late, it comes with Gottfried Leibniz in the late 17th century. We'll look at him and his work later. But from the coining of the term by Leibniz, people began to see that much earlier in the tradition of especially Christian thought a lot of thinkers had been generating things that looked roughly like theodicies. In fact, in the history of Christian thought, there have been several distinct—you could call them—"families" of such theodicies; lots of versions of basic prototypes of certain kinds of theodicies. Two in particular have been very, very powerful: the Augustinian tradition of theodicy, thinking about evil; and the Irenaean tradition of theodicy. In this lecture, we're going to look at the Irenaean theory, the Irenaean theodicy; in the next lecture, we'll look at the Augustinian.

Why is it that Christian theology in particular has generated this kind of intellectual practice? Christian theology is relatively unique not just in the West, not just in comparison to Islamic or Jewish thought on evil, in fact, it's pretty unique all around the world; there's not a lot of direct and serious philosophical thought in Buddhist thinking, in Hindu thinking, in Shinto or Confucian thinking about the nature and origin of evil. There's thinking about it in all those traditions, it really is; but nonetheless, none of them seem to have the same fixation on returning to the problem of evil.

For none of them, that is, the problem of evil is quite as problematic as it is for Christians.

I think there are two reasons for this in the basic Christian narrative that it's worth our while keeping in mind: First of all, Christians, like Jews—basically because they come out of the tree of Jewish tradition here—say God is wholly in charge of the world; the world is cosmically under God's sovereign control. That's one thing that Christians really affirm with Jews and actually with many other traditions; many other traditions affirm a basic moral order to the cosmos. But what make Christians distinct from Jews and other people, and in some ways unique—we'll see Nietzsche complains about this a lot at some point in the future, one of our future lectures—what makes Christians distinct is that they say that the world is really much, much worse than we might initially think it is; that is, the world that we live in is really far more profoundly sunk in evil than our ordinary experience of the world suggests that it might be.

That's an anomalous thing to say—let me stop and pause on this for a second, too—because one of the things you'll hear Christians saying is that, famously Reinhold Niebuhr (someone we'll talk about later) said that the doctrine of original sin is the only empirically confirmable doctrine in Christian thought. In other words, it's the only doctrine among the many things Christians are supposed to believe—about the unity of God, the trinity of God, the godliness of Jesus as the Son of God; the various things that Christians are supposed to believe—the one thing, Niebuhr said, that everyone can basically see by looking around them is that humans are really screwed up. Actually—and I love Reinhold Niebuhr really—there's a much more complicated story here: In fact, it seems, Christians really cultivate a certain perception of sinfulness, evil, and corruption in the world and they need to do that. Why? Again, I think it goes back to what I was saying about the New Testament in the last lecture: What's going on in this text is that as the experience of Christ is processed by the early Christian community, the growing recognition of the magnitude of Christ's saving work is so powerful that it actually requires us to revisit our assessment of the corruption of the world; and in doing that, it allows us to rethink and deepen our sense of the sinfulness of the world as we see it.

Among the most important of the thinkers, the earliest thinkers—in fact, in some important ways the earliest thinker—to really begin to systematize Christian thinking about good and evil and, in fact, the whole Christian narrative is the great early Greek-speaking and Greek-writing Christian theologian Irenaeus of Lyon (Lyon in France). Irenaeus offered a remarkable and profoundly influential discussion of the nature of evil, sin, and the ultimate vindication of God's goodness in the last judgment. But as I said, Irenaeus was a Greek-speaker who lived in Lyon in Roman France. That's an interesting story; and he does have an interesting story: In fact, he was born in Smyrna on the Aegean coast of Turkey, the city that's now known as Izmir in Turkey, into a Christian family, probably between 120 and 140 A.D., roughly speaking, and died—he was not martyred, he died, which is relatively unusual for a bishop of this time—as Bishop of Lyons around 200 A.D. We roughly know his dates; he's certainly a historical figure.

He seems to have heard and seen Polycarp, a disciple of John the Evangelist, before Polycarp was martyred, and so Irenaeus is understood as a kind of link in the chain to the apostolic era; that is, he saw someone and heard someone who was one of the disciples of John the Evangelist, which is a pretty impressive thing (that's pretty high "street cred" for a theologian). He's the earliest recorded witness we have to the canonicity of the four Gospels; that is, to the idea that the four Gospels—Matthew, Mark, Luke, and John—and only those four Gospels that the Christian churches in the East and in the West now recognize as canonical are, in fact, the four authoritative tellings of the life, death, and resurrection of Jesus. As he published his writings, they were immediately recognized to be foundational to the Christian faith and used throughout the Mediterranean world and even into the East, because at this point actually much of Christianity in Irenaeus's time was east of the Mediterranean in the Palestinian coastal areas, Syria, Jordan, Iraq, even into Iran; there were early Christians in India. It's only after the Islamic eruption of the 7th and 8th centuries that you get Christianity moving more westward. But anyway, Irenaeus is generally thought to be the first truly great Church Father; the first great patristic (that's the term for him).

His greatest work is called the *Against Heresies*, and it's the first really vast and ambitious Christian theological account of the universe and God, and the humans' place in the universe before God. In all sorts of ways, it has set the terms of later Christian speculative theology far more profoundly than it is easy for any of us to realize. It would have been possible, for example, for someone not well-versed in philosophy, not as able to speak philosophically and abstractly as Irenaeus was, to have first explained and given an account of Christianity; and in that case, the future of Christian thinking would have been very, very different. He's also important because as part of this first attempt to articulate the logic of Christianity in a systematic way, it's an attempt that is proposed, like the title of the book suggests, against. There was an opponent he was worried about, and the opponent is a shadow of orthodox Christianity—of what becomes known, let's say, as orthodox Christianity—and that shadow is Gnosticism.

Gnosticism deserves its own lecture series, and it's an enormously complicated and powerful system of thought in its own way. Here, for the perspective of these lectures, let me just say very briefly a couple things about it. Gnosticism was, in important ways, a kind of pseudo-philosophical movement; a very popular movement, especially amount elites in the ancient Mediterranean, late antique Mediterranean world. It argued in important ways that materiality, the materiality of the world, is the source of evil and that humans in their true essence are actually inner spirits that need to be unlocked from their cages of flesh and allowed to escape. This is an interesting account, right? Gnosticism, then, seems to suggest a couple different, important things: First of all, it seems to suggest that the true human essence is an innocent speck of purity inside a cage of flesh. The materiality that surrounds us—that is, evil—is in some ways hurting us; the true essence of humans is not to be a wicked person or an evildoer but in some sense to be victims. Second, it suggests the solution to this problem is, in fact, to escape materiality, to get out of the world; and certain radical Gnostics, in fact, simply became what were called "enlightened people" and starved themselves to death.

Irenaeus was if not the earliest, one of the earliest and certainly the most profound of the realist Christians to argue that Gnosticism was, in fact, a profoundly mistaken way of being a human; and, as the 1st and 2nd centuries moved on and Christianity became more of a live option for people in the Mediterranean, the Gnostics began to say, "Our interpretation of Christianity is the right one; Christianity is actually a kind of Gnosticism." The Gnostics could do that only on one important condition: that Christianity had to be understood as not a continuation of the Jewish story but as a radical renunciation of it in several different ways. First of all, the God of Genesis clearly says that creation is good; so the Gnostics had to say that was not a real God; that was, in fact, Satan masquerading as a God. Second, the Gnostics have to say that Jesus did not, in fact, suffer and die on the cross; Jesus in some sense faked his own death. The Gnostics were the first kind of conspirator theorists; they were the 1st and 2nd century version of the JFK conspiracy theorists and stuff like that. Jesus wasn't really killed up there, he faked it.

For someone like Irenaeus, the threat of the Gnostics is profound in several different ways: First of all, it's profound in how it threatens the Christians' vision of how they should live in the world. Second, it threatens the Christians' vision of who their ancestors were and who their rivals are in this world now. Irenaeus and the mainstream of orthodox theology in the Christian world basically said, "We are part of the story of the people Israel; we may offer a new version of that story." Irenaeus can be fairly accused of a bit of supersessionism, of saying that the Christians are proper inheritors of God's favor because the Jews have rejected Jesus; that's what's called "supersessionism," and Irenaeus seems to be an example of that, at least an early example. But that's not his main point; he says that sort of thing because, it seems to me anyway and to other scholars now, he's more fundamentally philo-Judaic; that is, he's more fundamentally trying to identify himself and his traditions with the history of the people Israel and thus allow that what the Christians call the Old Testament is, in fact, an authentic story of God's dealing with humanity. Remembering that the Gnostics had actually said that the entirely of what the Christians call the Old Testament, the entirely of the Hebrew Bible, the Torah, was not, in fact, a divinely-inspired text but a demonically-inspired text, imagine what would have happened if Gnosticism had become the orthodox version of Christianity. The bloodiness of that picture, the ugliness of the anti-Semitism would be astonishing.

Irenaeus, in general, posits a picture of evil as an inevitable and necessary component of the development of the human race. He explains this, in fact, by offering one of the first theological interpretations of scripture by telling the story of humanity as the story of Jonah in the belly of the whale as an allegory for the human fall: Just as Jonah had to be swallowed by the whale, so must humanity succumb to sin, fall into sin, and receive its punishment, namely suffering and death. Then God will raise the dead, and having passed through this evil journey, humanity will have learned by experience what evil truly is, how horrible it is, and how mercifully and blessedly God has acted in redeeming humanity from it. To be blessed, that is, Irenaeus suggests, one must know what it is to be damned. As Dante will suggest later, you have to go through Hell to get to Heaven.

More theoretically, Irenaeus's picture is relatively simple: First of all, in Eden, Adam and Eve were not fully mature creatures; God initially created them as immature, childlike in their innocence. The human needs, over time, to grow and mature, not only over their individual lives but over the course of human history, in order to become fit for the destiny that God intends, which is union with the divine, communion with God, and growth into the "perfect likeness" of God. This is a matter in complicated ways of transforming our desires from immediate material desires for base, natural ends to a desire for genuine union and communion with God. That transformation may sound like Irenaeus is giving something to the Gnostics, but he's not actually; he's saying that we would eat, we would feast, in paradise but it would be spiritual pleasures that are central to our lives. What happens is that humanity's rebellion against God and descent into sin and evil turn out to be crucial, so to speak, essential, for the fulfillment of this destiny. We learn what it means to be transformed by experiencing the pains we inflict upon ourselves by trying to be sated, by trying to be happy, wholly with the goods of this world. That's what Adam and Eve effectively did: They were not wrong in thinking they could be like God, but they thought they could be like God simply by eating material things; that was their mistake.

It's important to notice that Irenaeus is really the first thinker, at least in the Christian tradition, to offer an account of evil that divides evil into two groups; and this will be really important for us as this tradition goes forward and moves into a more philosophical vernacular as well. There's natural evil; those evils that are caused by nature, by accidents of nature: mudslides, earthquakes, plagues, things like that. Then there's distinctly moral evil; evils caused by intentional human will, even if that intentional human will is manifest in some accidental way. A person who is trained in their driving to be talking on the cell phone all the time and accidentally hits someone because of that bad habituation in the talking on the cell phone has done a morally evil thing; it's not a pure accident, right? They had to discipline themselves in certain ways to not care about being so attentive to the road. Those of us who drive on highways know about these dangers very much. The experience of moral evil is in some ways the centerpiece of what we take to be human malice. It's what humans cause one another through their freely-willed actions, whether directly through their freely-willed actions or indirectly through habituation in certain ways. Malice, jealousy, hatred, partiality, pride; these sorts of dispositions and the behaviors that spring from them are moral evil.

Irenaeus wants to say that the moral evils we fall into after the Fall hurt us as much as those people that we hurt; and in doing that, they slowly cause us to realize the suffering world that we are under and eventually, he thinks, we will freely choose to turn to God and find our end in the Divine. God will not compel us in this; God will simply continue to offer us salvation and the deeper we get into despair, the more attractive the offer of redemption will come to seem to us. Despite the fact that we do our damndest (literally) to condemn ourselves to Hell, Irenaeus strongly insinuates we will nonetheless finally find God's mercy so powerfully attractive as to be impossible to resist.

Adam and Eve's sin, then, lay in their attempt to grasp more than they were ready for in Eden; it was a sin, really, of impatience. But it was foreseeable because, after all, youth is impatient; age and wisdom are patient. It's only after you have hurt yourself by being impatient that you learn the wisdom of patience. By experiencing life outside of God's plan, humanity then comes to grow and appreciate what God has in store for it. At one point I talked about this as something like the rebellious teenager theory of evil. It's not clear, but certainly in some sense Irenaeus had enough experience with children—it's not clear if he had children of his own, but he had enough experience with children—to know what was going on in their rebellions. On this account, the world is a veil of soul-making. Natural evil has a purpose in this picture; it trains us to feel compassion and to help one another. The death that is part of natural evil, the death that is part of our mortality in this fallen world, is a good thing because it ends the suffering and puts us to sleep so we can be resurrected by God.

This is a powerful, powerful vision; but there are two things about it that need more reflection. First, consider the deepest insight I think this account has; I said it before: To be blessed, one must know what it is to be damned. Is that true? I don't know if it's true; I think it hearkens back to a very old pattern we've seen already in Job and others that suggests that suffering is in some important way the core experience that teaches us the kind of wisdom that enables us to be in the right position to be redeemed by God in this tradition. But is that true? I don't know. It can sound like a bad consolation to some people, especially in certain situations where suffering may be just too great for them. This account, which seems to begin with Job, can very quickly move into being one of Job's consolers again. You can imagine Irenaeus sort of saying to Job, "You're on the way to learning all the good things that God has in store for you by suffering in this way." I don't think Job would like that.

That touches on the second challenge. Consider one deep question this account struggles to answer: Does it trivialize the reality of evil and suffering, or force all evil and suffering to seem like it's ultimately for our good? Is this true to our experience of evil? What about those who suffer horrendous evil without (at least in this life) seeming to have a chance to learn from it? Some kinds of natural evil may, in fact, teach us not to care about the world in problematic ways. We've all known people who, in the midst of horrible life-ending illnesses, have become more gentle, more loving, more susceptible of receiving kindness and able to give it; many of us have been fortunate to know those people. But first of all, that's a very fortunate experience for those who are dying in that way and for us who are there around them, and there's no way we can say that they ought to be that way, or that they need to be that way, or that if they're suffering they should be that way; that's not, it seems, fair to me at all. That's a gratuitous and a gracious response by people in situations of extreme evil; but we can't say that it's, in some sense, the standard response of people in extreme evil. Lots of people suffer horribly and die without becoming intrinsically better people from that suffering, at least as far as we can tell. Also, lots of people suffer horribly and die without being able to develop into the kind of people who are like that. Irenaeus, it seems to me, never went into a child's cancer ward; never thought much of the difficulties of infant suffering in this situation.

Furthermore, alongside all this, some kinds of evil seem wholly out of proportion to any kind of lesson they could communicate to us; any kind of moral upbuilding that they could enable for us. The classic example of this in the 20th century has been, of course, the Holocaust. Can you imagine how an Irenaean theodicy would account for such gratuitous suffering as 12 million people, a majority of them very aged or very young; those 12 million people dying in death camps? How is that improving their lives in any fundamental way? How can we say with any kind of straight face, any kind of straight gaze into the eyes of the damned or the dead, that it could be a good thing for them?

Let's conclude for now: Irenaeus's overall thought had really foundational important for all of Christendom, both Latin and Greek Christianities. His thought about evil has not seemed to have a very powerful influence in Western Christianity. Pretty soon after Irenaeus was alive, only about 200 years later, Augustine's work began to eclipse his vision really quite dramatically, and for most of the history of Western Christianity most people when thinking about evil have been by and large Augustinian. But Irenaeus's thought was not forgotten; it lay in wait between the covers of books for more than 1,600 years. Some people found it and formulated ideas from it once in a while, but then it emerged again in modified and powerful form in the thought of Hegel and Marx. Indeed, even today, insofar as we ourselves think about our history as progressive, as a school in which we can experiment with certain efforts and see what works and what doesn't, a school that teaches us lessons that we can permanently learn; in short, insofar as we can learn from our mistakes and take tutelage from our suffering and thus be grateful for the wounds we have suffered, we are in a distant way heirs of Irenaeus.

But fully seeing those connections is a task that we will take on many, many lectures from now. Right now, what I want to do is turn to that other great ancient Christian thinker on evil, one of enormous power and influence as well: Saint Augustine.

Creation, Evil, and the Fall—Augustine
Lecture 9

In doing evil, I have damaged the web of human relations and affections in ways that have weakened that web, made it thinner, more fragile; I have deprived that web of human relations and affections of being. I have also lessened the soul of that poor child, and also, Augustine will say, ... I have lessened my own soul, as well.

Augustine of Hippo is sometimes called the second founder of the Christian faith, and he is also one of the greatest thinkers in the West of any religious or philosophical persuasion on evil. Augustine was born in North Africa to a Christian mother and a non-Christian father. At the age of 32, he converted to Christianity and later became bishop of the city of Hippo and rose to prominence as a theologian.

Much of the tradition of African Christianity in the late 4th and early 5th centuries is captured in the work of the theologian Tertullian. Tertullian placed responsibility for evil squarely on humans, who were created entirely free to choose good or evil. Along with this simple responsibility comes a simple punishment: After the Fall, humanity suffers evils. Augustine's story of evil is very different. In his view, the Fall is a mystery; punishment in this life is universal but obscurely distributed; and ultimately, God's justice and mercy will be revealed in salvation. Until then, the relationship between the suffering we experience in this life and the reason we deserve that suffering is completely obscure.

In the background of Augustine's thought was his own youthful attachment to a Gnostic popular

Augustine of Hippo (354–430 C.E.) is best known as the great theorist of human interiority.

religion called Manicheanism. This dualist faith embodied a combat-myth picture of the universe: Matter is evil, and spirit is good. In contrast to this view, Augustine, in later life, insisted that matter is good because a good God created all. Here, he affirms the Hebrew Bible as part of the true revelation of God. Good and evil are not metaphysical rivals for Augustine; all that is, insofar as it exists, is good.

To articulate his view, Augustine makes two fundamental claims about sin and evil. The first is that evil is essentially privational, meaning that evil is an irrational swerving from a wholly good creation that deprives that creation of some quality of being. Evil is, ultimately, a "nothing," a nihilation, essentially nothing more than the privation of some fundamentally good reality. The evil of an act is simply how that act lessens existence in some way. There is no "metaphysical substantiality" to evil; there's no rival metaphysical center of power named "evil" that works against God. Augustine believed in demons, but he understood those demons and Satan as rival spirits rebelling against God, though nonetheless under God's sovereign control.

The second claim Augustine makes is sometimes called the perversion theme. If evil is nothing, then sinful people are perverted toward wanting nothing; they are turned away from what they should want and aim their lives at wanting things that are empty, meaningless. Here, sin is the perversion of an originally wholly good human nature. But perversion—human wickedness— ironically always bears the appearance of an intelligible good. For Augustine, any human act has a reason, and he believes it is impossible for someone to want to do evil precisely because it is evil—a radical nihilation.

Despite its dark psychology, Augustine's is a relatively optimistic picture of human behavior. Its sin is merely a perversion of humanity's originally good nature, although that makes it more difficult to eliminate, because those who are caught in the grip of sin often cannot see that what they're doing is bad. But it also means, ironically, that humans have not completely gone astray from the good path because they still think about what they're doing in terms of a good end. Note that evil is not mere "appearance" on this account. In fact, the logic of perversion functions to secure the reality of evil.

In *The Confessions*, Augustine offers an interesting comparison of an evil act he once performed and the crimes of the Roman tyrant Sulla. He says that his own act of stealing pears from a neighbor's tree is worse than the cruelty and savagery of Sulla because his act lacked even the appearance of rationality. Sulla, at least, had material aims—power, wealth—while Augustine merely sought to destroy another's property. This story marks an important moment in the history of thinking about evil: the radical interiorization of evil, the suggestion that the outward manifestation of evil may be somehow less important than what evil does to one's soul. Perhaps even more frightening is the thought that some people don't even try to make sense of the evil they do. Augustine sees a mysterious parallel between that kind of anarchic evil—evil without a beginning, without a rationale—and God's providence. Again, the cost of securing God from responsibility for human evil is to make that evil mysterious. Further, because Augustine focuses on inner evil—the corruption of the inner self as the root of outward misbehavior—he makes evil even more mysterious and, perhaps, more remarkable—as it should be. ∎

> Despite its dark psychology, Augustine's is a relatively optimistic picture of human behavior.

Name to Know

Augustine of Hippo (354–430 C.E.). Sometimes called the "second founder of the faith," Augustine is commonly recognized as one of the most important figures in Western Christianity. He was born in Thagasate, a Roman city in North Africa.

Suggested Reading

Augustine, *City of God*, Dyson, ed. and trans.

Augustine, *Confessions*, Boulding, trans.

Brown, *Augustine of Hippo: A Biography*.

Evans, *Augustine on Evil*.

1. Do you find Augustine's claim that evil is "privation" convincing? What could it mean to say that evil has no metaphysical reality but is instead a "lessening" or "lack" of reality? Does this view contradict or compliment the early Christian emphasis on apocalyptic conflict?

2. How ought we to assess Augustine's claim that evil is a perversion of a wholly good world? Is evil something alien to the world's true being or something implicit in the world from the very beginning?

3. Does Augustine's story of the pear tree strike you as insightful or exaggerated? Is there such a thing as unmotivated evil?

Creation, Evil, and the Fall—Augustine
Lecture 9—Transcript

Welcome back. As I said at the beginning of the last lecture, there are two major strands, two major traditions, of thinking about evil, theodicy, in Christianity. Irenaeus inaugurates one strand and is, in many ways, the most important thinker in that group. The primary instigator of the other and far more influential strand is Saint Augustine of Hippo, philosopher, rhetorician, theologian, bishop, public official; if not the greatest Latin writer ever, at least, as the Church historian Jaroslav Pelikan once put it, "the greatest man ever to write Latin."

Augustine is known for many, many things; probably he's perhaps best well-known as the great theorist of human interiority. He introduces the idea that in some important way motiveless evil is worse than evil that seems to have a rationale, and also that the true locus of evil's "badness" lies not in the effects evil has in the world, but in the derangement of the will that it effects on the person who does it. In this lecture, especially, even though it may not be clear right away, we are talking about a view that you already know a great deal about; a view that you are already quite familiar with precisely because Augustine has been such a profound, shaping influence for the way that people in the West anyway think about themselves, the world, history, and the nature of evil and sin.

Saint Augustine is sometimes called the second founder of the Christian faith, and for good reason. For Western Christianity, Augustine's influence has been profound, though never without its critics, especially in the past century or so. But nonetheless, he's one of the greatest thinkers in the West of any religious or philosophical persuasion you may care to mention on evil, and with good reason, for his eye saw its own share of evil. He was born in 354 in a backwater town of North Africa to a Christian mother and a non-Christian father (as far as we can tell his father was non-Christian anyway). He was primed from an early age by his parents to use his education and his brainpower, which was clearly substantial, to raise his social standing; and raise it he did: He was trained as a rhetorician—a teacher or professor of rhetoric—and he eventually became a professor of rhetoric and taught first in Rome and then in the imperial capital of the late Roman Empire of Milan, where he once actually gave a speech praising the emperor in the emperor's presence; a command performance, a sort of very high-status thing to do. But he found this way of life increasingly unsatisfactory, and he was drawn increasingly to his mother's Christianity.

He marked his own conversion at the age of 32 and after that he quit his job, he quit his teaching post, pretty quickly and retired with his friends first to a patron's estate outside of the city of Milan, and then he went back to Africa to set up a sort of lay monastery and think tank where he and his friends would live celibate lives together, eat, pray, work, read, and talk. But after a few years of this very happy retirement, he was forced to accept a sort of vice bishopric, a vice bishop role, in the city of Hippo on the North African coast. He was visiting the city and he was in a church for a church service that day and the bishop of the city pointed Augustine out in a crowd and said to the crowd, "Don't let that man leave. We know who he is, he's Augustine from Thagaste"—the place where he had his monastery—"don't let him leave until he agrees to become my assistant and then eventually my replacement." In fact, that's what the crowd did: They compelled him to stay until he consented to first become a priest and then become their coadjutor bishop, the vice bishop, and then the main bishop of the city of Hippo for almost 40 years, until he died.

In that position, he rose to prominence first in North Africa, then across the Latin West, to the point that he was known as the major Latin-speaking theologian that the church in the Greek East had to respect. Never without controversy, he debated fiercely a number of rival views throughout his career. He wrote enormously influential books: the *Confessions*, the massive *City of God*, a huge book on the Trinity, essays, and innumerable commentaries on books in the Bible. He regularly gave sermon after sermon, some of them lasting hours, and he could apparently keep the people pretty captivated; the sermons are pretty good, I must admit. We only have a few hundred of these, though we know he gave thousands over the course of his almost 40 years as a preaching bishop. He also wrote very influential letters. Interestingly, Augustine's letters and sermons—not his texts, but the letters and sermons—are still occasionally discovered today. Just in the spring of 2008, in fact, a new series of I think four or five sermons were found collected in an old manuscript book of "Great Sermons You Can Use" complied from medieval preachers in Germany. It's an astonishing thought to think that this man who was so profoundly influential, all of his works were read avidly, there are still things out there that are yet to be found, yet to be known, and that might still be waiting in some monastery somewhere.

To understand Augustine's views, it will help to contextualize them in their setting, to put them in the setting in which they were first formulated and for which he formulated them; that is, African Christianity in the late 4th and early 5th centuries. Much of this tradition is readily captured in an earlier African theologian, Tertullian; and in particular, his vision of evil is on that, in a complicated way, again, shadows Augustine's. You have to understand Tertullian's views in order to see where Augustine is coming from in his thinking. There are other shadows behind Augustine, and we'll talk about them later—again, like Irenaeus, he's shadowed by the Gnostics in a certain way—but look at Tertullian first.

First of all, Tertullian thought that the human is confronted with the bare fact of their responsibility for evil. Adam's fall is his own fault alone, for humans were created entirely free to choose good or evil. Along with this simple responsibility becomes a simple punishment: After the fall, humanity does suffer evils, of course, but they are all well-merited, and clearly so for Tertullian. Most interestingly—and this is the part of Tertullian's work that has gotten him in most trouble—Tertullian has a very troubling vision of the ultimate punishment of evil. It's a vision that's deeply disturbing in lots of ways, and was famously assaulted by Friedrich Nietzsche almost 1,600 years after Tertullian wrote it. Tertullian, in the midst of critiquing the "spectacles" of Rome—that is, the shows, the plays, the gladiatorial contests that amused people in Rome of his time, including the visual displayed martyrdom of Christians that pagan Rome repeatedly engaged in; famously, the Christians thrown to the lions in the floor of the Coliseum or what have you—Tertullian suggests that Hell will be the true spectacle, and one that all true Christians will find themselves delighted to see; when those on the floor of the stadium will be the sinners who have caused Christians to suffer in this life, now they, the sinners, will be suffering on the floor of the stadium while the blessed sit on the stands and watch and enjoy the suffering of the damned, of the sinners. In fact, the watching of the suffering of the damned, for Tertullian, constitutes—or so it seems—a significant part of the happiness of those who are blessed. In other words—and it seems to me Nietzsche was right to notice a kind of theological inconsistency about this—Tertullian wants to say that the whole point of Hell in a way is to be a spectacle for the blessed who will be able to delight in the sufferings of the damned. This is, as Nietzsche pointed out, a view of good and evil that is incredibly laced with resentment about those who are causing suffering to Christians in that day. It's also profoundly punitive, and really quite psychologically disturbing.

In contrast to this, Augustine offered another very influential, very different story of evil; one that rendered it much more obscure. On his view, the fall is a mystery, punishment in this life is universal but obscurely distributed, and ultimately God's justice and mercy will be revealed in salvation; but until then, the obscurity of the relationship between the suffering we experience in this life and the reason we have deserved the suffering, that is completely obscure and Augustine doesn't want us to try to interpret too much how the things of this life communicate some status we have before God.

Tertullian and North African Christianity is one background out of which Augustine is coming. The other context, out of which Augustine himself emerges and that is always there in the background of his thought, is his own youthful attachment to a certain kind of Gnostic popular religion called Manicheanism. We don't need to worry about the details of Manichaeism, but let me just say this: It was, like many of the other Ancient Near Eastern stories, a combat myth picture of the universe. There was a dualist faith: Matter is evil, spirit is good; the universe that we know was created out of this battle. In fact, the world that we inhabit and all matter that we feel is composed—in the myths of the Manichean creation myth—out of the skins of the corpses of the archons of darkness; such a great line, "the archons of darkness," it sounds like a rock band or something. In contrast to this view that Augustine had himself dallied with as a young man, Augustine insisted that, in fact, matter is good because a good God created all. Augustine again affirms the Hebrew Bible as part of the true revelation of the real God. Good and evil are not metaphysical rivals for Augustine; but all that is, insofar as it exists, is good. It's just that things exist on a continuum of levels of being. Rocks do not have the same quality of existence as plants do; and therefore, they are not as good, in some metaphysical way, as plants. But that doesn't mean that they're bad, it just means that they're of a lower level of being.

To articulate his own view, Augustine makes two fundamental claims about sin and evil. Let's talk about them both in turn. The first claim is that evil is essentially privational. That's a weird word; it means it is an irrational swerving from a wholly good creation that deprives that creation of some quality of being. Evil, that is, is ultimately a "nothing," a nihilation, wholly lacking being; essentially nothing more than the privation of some fundamentally good reality. Evil of an act is simply how the act lessens existence in some way. If I hit a child, the consequence of my act is that the child will mistrust people more; maybe begin to feel that if adults use violence in this way then the child can use violence in this way, too, beating up her or his classmates. Thus I have damaged the web of human relations and affections in ways that have weakened that web, made it thinner, more fragile; I have deprived that web of human relations and affections of being. I have also lessened the soul of that poor child; and also, Augustine will say—and we'll see why in a little while—I have lessened my own soul as well.

A similar thing will happen if I lie. A lie undiscovered misleads people and so loosens their grip on reality, making them less effective in the world, less able to bring the world's goodness to fruition. If the lie is discovered, of course, then their trust in me is lessened, I have seemed to them less reliable as a person, and again, the web of human affairs has been damaged. Furthermore, when I tell a lie, even if it's believed only for a moment, my trust in the reliability of the world is by extension also damaged because if I can fool people then they can fool me, too. In all of this, Augustine wants to insist, there is no "metaphysical substantiality" to evil; there's no rival metaphysical center of power and gravity named "evil" over against God. Augustine clearly believed in demons; he clearly believed that Satan is a power and a force; but he understood those demons and Satan as rival spirits that are rebelling against God but still, nonetheless, under God's sovereign control, in this moment as well as ultimately.

This all goes back, of course, through Augustine to the first chapter of Genesis and to the idea that this is a God who simply orders the world to be created and it is created. Augustine, in fact, is one of the first major Christian thinkers to develop this Genesis account into the Christian account of what's called the "Creation ex nihilo," a "Creation out of nothing." He does this to oppose the more pessimistic Manichean view that, in fact, the Creation is, again, "made out of the corpses of the defeated enemies of light"; but, of course, the irony is that he also creates a situation where there begins to be a differing Christian and Jewish conception of what Genesis looks like, how that first creation myth goes.

For Augustine, Satan is not fundamentally a rival deity to God; Satan is God's rebellious servant, who still in some mysterious way serves God's sovereign providence. Just as God created all and called it good, as God is source of all, there can be nothing—not even Satan, even in Satan's original being, in Satan's good being—that is not in some sense good in God's eyes. Is—being itself, that is; the character of being—and goodness, for Augustine, are the same thing. He's not saying here that everything that is, is nothing but good—he recognizes that lions are not good to the prey that they fall upon— but the reality of existence itself is a very, very good thing for Augustine. That's the first, most basic affirmation, and because the reality of existence itself is fundamentally good, evil has to be nothing; has to be an attempt to annihilate that goodness.

The second claim he makes, along with the privation theme, is sometimes called the perversion theme: For Augustine, if evil is nothing, sinful people are still perverted towards wanting nothing; they are turned away from what they should want, and aim their lives at wanting things that are empty, meaningless, finally, ultimately, nothing. Sin, then, is the perversion of an originally wholly good human nature. As we saw, in Judaism, the possibility of human temptation and failure is built in the human nature from Creation forward; Adam and Eve do not originate evil, they are just the first examples of a pattern that human history will show again and again. Augustine follows Paul: Any mark of human weakness or frailty is a consequence of the primordial calamity of the Fall of Adam and Eve. As perversion, then, human wickedness ironically always bears the appearance of an intelligible good.

This is really important, and I actually think this is one of the most philosophically difficult and deep statements that Augustine makes and, in fact, probably anybody makes. The crucial psychological point here is this: For a human to do something, an act must have a reason. If it's not just a hiccup or a reflex, like kicking a knee up when a doctor taps it with a hammer, the doer of the deed must have some justification. No one thinks of himself or herself as bad and acting from bad motives. The great pre–World War II French Movie called *The Rules of the Game* made by the writer and artist Jean Renoir; and in that movie, the character that Renoir plays says to someone else a wonderful and very Augustinian line; he says, "The truly terrible thing about this life, monsieur, is that everyone has their own reasons." I'm not saying that people need a perfect justification for what they do, a complete one, one that anyone would endorse; but we need an account that gives us at least the appearance on its surface of a momentarily plausible rationale for doing what we do. This is why one of the most common, and in some ways one of the most psychologically illuminating, statements humans can make is the statement, "It seemed like a good idea at the time." Everything we do seems like a good idea at the time.

Augustine thinks this is very deep because it is impossible, he thinks, for someone to want to do evil just because it is evil; radical nihilism of this sort is ruled out. This is important, because we'll see later on certain figures in the tradition—especially Satan as represented by John Milton—do try to say things like, "Evil be thou my good"; Satan actually says that in Milton's *Paradise Lost*. But Milton's point is actually very Augustinian: The reason Satan says that is precisely because he wants to be as far from God as possible; so he's trying still to affirm himself by saying, "Evil be thou my good." That is on Milton's Augustinian reading of Satan: By using those words, Satan is saying, "I am the most important person in the world, and I value me very highly because of it."

Another much more mundane example: Consider a lover and his or her beloved. A lover can be jealous of his or her beloved's other friends, and envy and begrudge every other person any time that they spend with the beloved. From the lover's perspective, this isn't a problem, right? This attention doesn't seem bad; it's genuine love for the beloved person. But from an outside observer's perspective, possibly also the beloved's own point of view, it is bad; it's an excess of attention that is destructive, maybe obsessive. Maybe it's scaring the beloved; you know, "Why are you so around me all the time?" But it is, in fact, Augustine would say, an excess of a real good, the good of caring. Sure, that real good is warped in certain ways; it's perverted in certain ways; but from the perspective of the lover, the fact that they see a real good being affirmed in their attention here is what makes it so hard for someone in the grip of such a perversion to see it as bad, because for them it looks like they can give a good account for what they're doing. "I just love you," right? This is why police are terrified to get involved in domestic conflict situations because they know that it's people who understand themselves to be loving each other the most who are going to be the most dangerous in situations of violence.

Ironically, this picture really does mean, despite its kind of dark psychology in some ways, that Augustine has a relatively optimistic picture of human behavior. Its sin is merely a perversion of humanity's originally good nature. That makes it more difficult to eliminate, more difficult to fix because those who are caught in the grip of sin often cannot see that what they're doing is bad; but it also means that, ironically, humans are not completely gone astray from the good path because at least in terms of how they think about what they're doing, they still have to think about it in terms of a good end. This concept lies behind Augustine's profoundly ironic view of human history. Particularly in his, again, vast text *The City of God*, history turns out to be a story of humanity who are trying or are being taught to unlearn their efforts to be their own god, their own rulers; which is why, for Augustine—as with the Book of Revelation and going back to the Tower of Babel—empires figure so large in human history. Empires for Augustine, just like this earlier tradition, are really ultimate expressions of human rebellion precisely because they are devices we use to avoid imagining that we need to be dependent upon God.

Let's be clear: Evil is not mere "appearance" on this account. The logic of perversion functions, in a way, to secure the reality of evil. Evil, though, in its effects is simply the lessening of being, its diminution; evil is simply the name we give to the diminishing force that attacks being itself. The devils, for Augustine, turn themselves into small and puny creatures compared to the great and powerful angels they were initially. The great example of this, in fact, is the famous "Pear-Tree Incident" in Augustine's autobiographical book *The Confessions*. In this story—which is recounted in Book 2 of that very, very famous book—Augustine compares the crimes of he and his friends, in stealing pears from a neighbor's tree, to the great crimes of Roman history, especially the terrible crimes of the tyrant Sulla. Sulla, in

Roman history, is basically as bad as it gets. Sulla was the evil tyrant who, once he had taken control of the city of Rome, sent his gangs through the city picking up people they didn't like, killing them, killing their families, and taking their property. How is it possible that Augustine and his friends sneaking into a neighbor's garden and stealing pears that he himself says were about to fall from the tree—they were in some ways overripe pears—and not necessarily eating them but just tossing them on the ground; how is that worse than a tyrant terrorizing the city of Rome?

This is the audacity of Augustine's account. He and his friends' evil was even worse than Sulla's because their wickedness lacked even the appearance that Sulla's did of rationality. Sulla at least had material aims—he wanted power, he wanted wealth, he wanted to defeat potential enemies—that motivated his cruelty, his savagery. Sulla, that is, is a demon that is in some ways comfortingly intelligible to us. Augustine and his friends just went into the garden to destroy; they didn't have any aims beyond the mere destruction of another person's property. Augustine reads this as the epitome of human evil. He does think that there was a positive account—he spends a few moments thinking about this—he does think, finally, there's a positive way he can account for what they did: They did it out of love for each other. They did it out of a kind of desire to be a gang together; by doing something bad they joined in a kind of tighter fellow feeling, which, again, is a psychologically acute insight about teenage depredation and crime. But more importantly, Augustine thinks what was going on was a crime that really didn't have much motive, and that's what made it so terrifying. Some of the pears they took and bit, some of them they just threw away. By the way, what might Augustine be alluding to with the story of his friends and him taking someone else's fruit from a tree?

This raises a question for us; Augustine's story, and his insistence that he and his friends were worse than Sulla: Is motiveless evil worse than motivated evil? But within what register is this evil worse? Augustine's story here marks a very important moment in the history of thinking about evil: It marks what we can call the radical interiorization of evil; for Augustine is the first person, I seems to me to really suggest that the outward manifestation of evil—what the consequences of the evil are; Sulla's slaughter of Romans versus their taking of pears that were about to fall away anyway—may somehow be less important than what evil does to one's soul. Perhaps, in fact, the outward manifestation may be of completely low importance, minimum importance, maybe no importance at all.

What does it mean to say that evil is truly a matter of what happens inside the soul? What does it mean to say that unmotivated evil, an evil that lacks any obvious material cause, is in some ways the most terrifying kind of evil? Again, you can go back to the early myths that Christians and Jews had— it's not quite in Scripture—about the fall of Satan. You can connect it up with the story of Thrasymachus in Plato's *Republic*. These sorts of figures seem not fully coherent. Satan's fall seems utterly incoherent to us; it doesn't make any sense at all. That's the real scary thing for Augustine: The real scary thing is when people don't even try to make sense of the evil that they do. But if this is so, a question that haunts a lot of Augustine's writings, a lot of his thought, is that there seems to be some mysterious parallel between that kind of completely anarchic evil—an evil without a beginning, without a rationale—and God's mysterious providence as well. Maybe, in fact, human evil is a parallel way, a parallel that imitates God's mysterious providence in history.

So Augustine explains that the fundamental principles of the cosmos are not to blame for evil; but what I pointed out about the story of Adam and Eve is also true about Augustine, even more so: The cost of securing God from responsibility for human evil is to make that evil profoundly mysterious. Furthermore, because he focuses on inner evil, the corruption of the inner self as the root of outward misbehavior, he makes evil even more mysterious and perhaps more remarkable. It's not too far to say, in fact, that evil is remarkable for Augustine in unprecedented ways. Indeed in one way, often unappreciated by people who read him, part of his aim is precisely to make evil more remarkable. As he says in *The City of God*: "The difficult task we face is how to learn how not to know the reason for evil."

What does he mean by that? He means that in our world, it is all too easy to understand evil actions where understanding means not finding them at all remarkable; explaining them, giving an account of them, and in some ways explaining them away; not finding them astounding. But Augustine wants us to find evil actions remarkable because he thinks they are remarkable; they are astounding; they are a remarkable, mysterious fact about us, and not a good fact. All too often we find good acts in need of explanation, but not evil ones. That, for Augustine, just shows the extent of our sickness. In a decent world, we would find good actions natural, logical, and a wholly reasonable and cruel or indifferent actions astonishing. The extent to which we do not, the extent to which we are callous to evil and astonished by goodness, just reveals the depth of sin in which we are sunk for him.

Let me conclude: The epistemological optimism of this view—that is, the hope that we can, in fact, know the rationales of our actions, and yet also we can know that evil is in some fundamental way mysterious, completely empty of meaning—is complemented by a certain kind of anthropological pessimism; that is, a picture of the human that insists that human nature now, after the Fall, can't by itself be good. Furthermore, the interiority of the self on Augustine's picture is very, very profound and amplified. He is, in some ways—and this sense in many other ways—the master of interiority. The question for Augustine is really about whether we are the sorts of people who have, or can have, a mysterious sort of depth.

In the next two lectures, we'll look at two rival pictures of evil: one developed by the Jewish rabbis in the same time roughly that Augustine and Irenaeus are writing, and one developed by Islamic thinkers a few centuries later; two accounts that offer really quite profound contrasts to these works. Let's turn to those next.

Rabbinic Judaism—The Evil Impulse
Lecture 10

I think that there's a deep insight being communicated in especially the Rabbinic tradition's focus on the minutiae of life, the small things around life, simple decency rather than moral heroism. The rabbis' resistance to more theologically radical pictures of evil—like the Christian Satan, for example— ... makes evil an intrinsic part of humans' natural makeup in a certain sense.

The mainstream view in Jewish traditions over the past two millennia is that of **Rabbinic Judaism**. This form of Jewish fai+th and practice arose in the 1st century in the wake of the destruction of the Temple in Jerusalem and the Diaspora and flourished from the 3rd century until the 20th. Rabbinic Judaism offers a powerful but subtly nuanced picture of evil in wholly mundane terms, one that resists the cosmic drama of sin and redemption found in Christianity.

Much of the discussion in the Rabbinic tradition centers on the "evil" and the "good" impulses in the human heart. The rabbis saw God creating in humans two different and rival sources of energy, with humans caught in a contest between these two competing energies. The Jewish conception of these two impulses suggests an entirely different picture from the Christian one of how the human is organized and what sort of motives and struggles go on inside us.

The good impulse is something like what we would call conscience; it's an inner sense that alerts us when we are considering violating God's law. This impulse develops around age 12 or 13, when Jewish youth first begin to struggle with God's word in Torah and the observance of the Commandments. In contrast, the evil impulse is innate in humans from the womb. This impulse, however, is not demonic; it's not an unnatural expression of some sort of anarchic hostility to God's creation. It seems rooted, rather, in a kind of paranoid self-interest, an expression of the idea that we naturally take special interest in our own well-being and, in many cases, view the world as a threatening place.

Jewish thought seems influenced by a desire to distinguish itself from Christian thinking in its resistance to the overdramatization of evil. For example, it turns out that the "bad" impulse is what enables humans to build houses, to marry, to have children, and to engage in business. It is the source of self-interest, even self-interest properly construed. The danger, of course, is that self-interest can become excessive and overmaster us.

Evil is something we meet in our hearts and our lives every day. It is a challenge and a gift sent by God to bring humans to maturity.

The implication of this psychology for understanding the human condition is that humans are caught up not so much in a vast metaphysical melodrama as they are in trying to handle temptations encountered every day. For the rabbis, evil is not supernatural but derived from our naturally created being; it is something that happens to us because of our impulses. Unlike many popular Christian accounts—in which the devil is a powerful presence in the world, seducing humans—in this account, evil's origins are sought in the exercise of the human will.

This view doesn't trivialize evil because when it is left uncountered by other parts of our nature, the evil impulse can lead us astray and cause great damage. The Rabbinic view recognizes this impulse as powerful; it's a life force, but it can warp us in ways that are against life. Its power is related to its initial appearance as small; it moves in subtle ways. As the Talmud puts it, "At first the evil impulse is called a 'wayfarer,' then it is called a 'guest,' then finally it is called a 'master.'" In this account, evil is not so much an abstract philosophical problem as it is a practical challenge confronting those afflicted by it. It is something we meet in our hearts and our lives every day. It is a challenge and a gift sent by God to bring humans to maturity. This is part of a larger understanding of the nature of Jewish suffering: Evil serves as a challenge but not one that will overwhelm the people Israel.

The Rabbinic account is a profound challenge to an overly Christianized conception of evil in light of sin. Indeed, this picture is so different from Christian notions of evil that some Jewish scholars consider it a picture of "badness" rather than "evil." This tradition emphasizes human responsibility and struggle, especially the struggle to live in accordance with Jewish law.

This account is not, however, without its problems, especially for Jews living since the Holocaust, the **Shoah** ("catastrophe"). Is this picture of evil too mundane and too ordinary to handle the Shoah? Ironically, the Shoah may threaten any account of evil that is *not* vastly dramatic. The evil for the rabbis is about greed, jealously, envy; it's a happy and relatively small-scale picture of evil. This picture seems not to be continuous with the evil that was experienced in the Holocaust—evil completely out of proportion to the character of everyday moral challenges. When the Holocaust occurred, many believed that the longstanding covenant between God and God's people had fallen apart. God let the Holocaust happen, and since that time, Jews have been struggling to understand the meaning of the Shoah. ■

Important Terms

Rabbinic Judaism: Form of Jewish faith and practice that flourished from the 3rd century C.E., the era of the composition of the Talmud, to the present.

Shoah: Hebrew word meaning "catastrophe," now often used to describe the Holocaust.

Suggested Reading

Urbach, *The Sages: The World and Wisdom of the Rabbis of the Talmud*, Abrahams, trans.

Questions to Consider

1. What advantages does the more mundane understanding of evil in Judaism hold over the Christian view? What are its drawbacks?

2. How do you assess the rabbis' understanding of *yetzer ha ra* (the bad impulse) and *vetzer ha tov* (the good impulse)? Do human beings naturally possess both good and evil impulses? Or, perhaps, is *yetzer ha ra* even a necessary part of human flourishing?

Rabbinic Judaism—The Evil Impulse
Lecture 10—Transcript

Welcome back. From Augustine now, we're turning to a profoundly different, though not entirely unrelated, alternative view about evil; the mainstream view, in fact, in the Jewish traditions over the past two millennia: the view of Rabbinic Judaism. "Rabbinic Judaism" is that form of Jewish faith and practice that arose after the fall of Jerusalem in the 1st century and the Diaspora, or the scattering of Jews, across the Mediterranean and Near East in the following couple hundred years. It really flourishes from the 3rd century of the Common Era—that's effectively the era of the composition of the Talmud; the Talmud is the body of literature that comments upon the Torah, Jewish religious law, in general—to effectively the 20th century, and in some ways it's still flourishing today. This tradition takes the Talmud—that body of commentary on Jewish law—to be a text of near-scriptural authority for interpreting the Torah; indeed, the Talmud is the textual fixing in this tradition of the "Oral Law" in [comparison] to the "Written Law" of the Torah.

The rabbis were the community's teachers and ministers, scholars who knew the Torah and knew the debates surrounding the Torah in the Talmud so well that they were effectively walking repositories of the tradition. They understood the height of their religious duty to be the study of Torah and Talmud, the enormously complicated sets of argumentative commentaries that previous rabbis had created in order to understand how to live faithfully as Jews in this very complicated world. Rabbinic Judaism offers a powerful but subtly nuanced picture of evil in wholly mundane, fairly everyday terms; one that resists the overly dramatic, perhaps even melodramatic, cosmic drama of sin and redemption found in Christianity (Book of Revelations, Irenaeus, Augustine).

In the wake of the Shoah or Holocaust, there's been a huge wave of Jewish rethinking of the faith; but, in fact, there have been analogies, events of similar existential crisis, in Judaism at different moments in Jewish history. One of them is the famous Babylonian Captivity where the remnants of Israel, or a large part of them, were exiled to Babylon in the 6th century B.C.E. Rabbinic Judaism emerges out of another one of these, the destruction of the

Temple in Jerusalem and the Diaspora, and this was a revolution in Jewish thinking on a scale with the effect that the Shoah has had, the Holocaust has had, and is having. In the Diaspora, the Jews effectively lost the Promised Land, and they lost the central ritual place of worshipping God (namely the Temple in Jerusalem), and they did not return to Israel as a people—they did not return to the land—for almost 2,000 years. A new kind of religion had to be built out of the rubble and the ashes of the old, and that's what the rabbis really centrally did.

In terms of evil in particular, the rabbis explored a series of alternative moral psychologies of human malice; but much of their discussion—and it really became the canonical view—centered around the "evil" and the "good" impulses in the human heart. The evil impulse is called the *yetzer ha ra* and the good impulse is called the *yetzer ha tov*. Adam and Eve ate of the tree of the knowledge of *tov* and *ra*; good and evil. The rabbis saw God creating in humans two different and rival sources of energy; inclinations or "impulses" (this is where this word *yetzer* comes from). In fact, for the rabbis—who, as I suggested, are very textually-minded scholars; they're really committed to finding the evidence of what they want, what they want to see, what they are arguing for, in the text of scripture especially—the condition of the human, as driven by these two impulses, is signified, in fact, in the scriptures themselves. In Genesis 2:7, the Bible states that God "formed the human"; *vayyitzer* is the word. The spelling of this word is unusual because it uses two Yods, the "y" sound in *vayyitzer*. There's also a doubled consonant as well in *l'vav'kha* in Deuteronomy where it says, "You shall love the Lord your God with all your heart." The two Yods suggest a dualism in the self, and the idea that the whole heart, which suggests that there's more than one piece of the heart as well as the doubling of the consonants in that word, both suggested to the rabbis, or they used that as evidence for the idea that humans are caught in a contest between two competing energies.

Let me stop for a second and think about this, because this is already beginning to be an interestingly different way of thinking about good and evil than the Christian account we've just been looking at. This account seems to me rooted in the idea that the behavior of good or evil is anchored in basic impulses in the human that are there basically from creation. Again, consider this in light of the large Christian context in which many of these Jews are now living: In these narratives, the Christian narratives, evil is seen as a kind of unnatural calamity; and again, that's related to the Christians' conceptions of Christ as so, so good. For Christ to have been so good, something must have been pretty bad for Christ to remedy it. The Jewish conception of these two impulses suggests an entirely different picture of how the human is organized and what sort of motives and what sort of struggles go on inside the human.

The *yetzer ha tov*, the good impulse, is something like what we would call "conscience"; it's an inner sense that alerts you when you are considering violating God's law. It warns you; and it really develops, the rabbis think, around age 12 or 13, when the young Jewish boy—or today we would also say girl—first begins to become an adult, at a boy's Bar Mitzvah or a girl's Bat Mitzvah for example, when the child first begins to struggle with God's word in Torah and the observance of the Commandments that, for the rabbis, is the true mark of a maturing Jew. In contrast to the *yetzer ha tov*, the *yetzer ha ra*—what we're translating here as "the evil impulse"—is a far more murky concept. It does not really get introduced when you're 12 or 13; it's part of the humans' creative nature, innate in the human from the womb. Genesis, for example, says, "The yetzer of the human heart is ra from youth"; "The impulse of the human heart is bad from youth" (that's Genesis 8:21).

But this impulse is not demonic; it's not an utterly unnatural violation of creation expressing some sort of anarchic hostility to God's creation; it seems rooted, rather, in a kind of self-interest, in a protectiveness of the infant, of the young child, an expression of the idea that creatures will naturally take special interest in their own well-being. The rabbis note, though, that this is a kind of paranoid kind of self-interest; and they say that the young child or the infant sees the world as a threatening place, a dangerous place. You know, honestly, if you think about how small children react when their parents introduce them to you, often they'll hide behind their parents' legs or something like that; in other words, the rabbis have a great deal of empirical evidence they can point to here. Children are terrified of strangers (sometimes) and they are scared of the bigger world; and this seems accurate to how children behave in the world, at least part of the time. It's also a psychologically acute assessment of how a great deal of human aggression is related to perceptions of danger. Even today, psychologists—who sometimes can seem to be specializing in reinventing the wheel—will tell us that if you feel fearful, you are more prone to lash out violently against those around you. Fear turns out to be one of the most powerful motivations towards aggression and wickedness.

Some hear an allusion to the *yetzer ha-ra*, the evil impulse, in the command to have "no other gods" in Exodus, in the Commandments; that is, there's a tacit recognition, some rabbis think, that the *yetzer ha-ra*, this evil impulse, is a personified agency of a sort. But nonetheless, none of the rabbis suggested that this was actually any sort of rival to God; that would make it more like the Satan of the pre-Genesis Ancient Near East and, again, appeal to a kind of combat myth or metaphysical dualism. But that's not the aim; again, the rabbis and the Jewish tradition in general are always shadowed by that resistance to those Ancient Near Eastern combat myths. But now, we're also beginning to see that Jewish thought is silently influenced, silently inflected by a desire to distinguish itself also from Christian thinking; so even as it resists a kind of metaphysical dualism of the combat myth, this Jewish tradition is going to begin to try to figure out ways to resist an over-dramatization of evil as well.

Here's one way, because it turns out that this evil impulse, the *yetzer ha-ra*—sometimes we should call it a bad impulse—is actually not so bad after all in some dimensions. The *yetzer ha-ra* is the impulse in the human that enables humans to build a house, to marry, to have children, to engage in business; the evil impulse, in some ways, seems to be at times the source of self-interest, even self-interest properly construed. It's a part of life, that is; it actually supports life, it enables life; but it can be excessively partial and caught up in self-interest and greed. That's the danger of the *yetzer ha-ra*; not its bare existence, but when it comes to overmaster you. In the same way, you can imagine this playing out in the story of Cain and Abel when God says, "Sin is crouching at your door; it seeks to master you, but you must master it." What the rabbis read that as for the *yetzer ha-ra* is precisely the struggle; not to eliminate the *yetzer ha-ra*, not to send it off like Cain (a restless wanderer), but rather to make it a fruitful part of your ordinary life.

Classical Rabbinic understandings of these categories still profoundly influence Jewish thought about evil today. The implications of this psychology for the rabbis' understanding of the human makes the human less caught in a kind of vast, metaphysical melodrama (a la Christianity) and more a matter of the handling of the everyday temptations that we encounter all around us. This focus on everyday temptations is really important; it's not simply a momentary thing about evil in the Jewish tradition. Some critics of Judaism will argue that Judaism in some ways is too focused on the mundane commandments to do one thing or another. One of the most interesting contemporary Jewish thinkers, Arthur Waskow, has made this argument that in a way these critics are complaining that Judaism is a religion of pots and pans. I think that there's a deep insight being communicated in especially the Rabbinic tradition's focus on the minutiae of life; the small things around life; simple decency rather than moral heroism. The rabbis' resistance to more theologically radical pictures of evil—like the Christian Satan, for example—and their similar resistance to depictions of the history of human evil in terms of calamities like the Christian notion of the Fall, makes evil an intrinsic part of humans' natural makeup in a certain sense.

But that's a good thing; the rabbis, that is, make evil not supernatural but really derived from our naturally created being. That is, in some important way, evil is something that happens to us because of the impulses of ourselves; and if that's the case, then we are, in important ways, able to handle those impulses, we can learn to deal with them. That's not to say that in this account evil must be understood in reductively human and naturalistic terms, there's no necessary dimension of this that says evil is not a big thing at all; but unlike many popular Christian accounts where the Devil is a really powerful presence seducing and captivating humans, in this account evil's origins are to be sought in the exercise of the human will, not as an external force overmastering my human will. I can't blame anybody else if I go to the bad; if I go to the bad, I only have myself to look at in the mirror. I look at myself in the mirror and I say, "I am that man."

This does not trivialize evil at all, however, because when left un-countered by other parts of our nature, the evil impulse, the rabbis think, will lead us astray and cause great damage; again, going back to Cain and Abel: "It seeks to master you, so you must master it." The rabbis recognize this impulse as powerful; it's a life force but it can warp us in ways that are very against our life, destructive of our life, and destructive of other's lives. But its power is in significant ways related to its initial appearance as small; it moves in subtle ways. As the Talmud puts it, "at first the evil impulse is called a 'wayfarer,' then it is called a 'guest,' then finally it is called a 'master.'" This goes back to the idea, the rabbis' idea, that in some important way you need to focus on the minutiae of life, the smaller, minor things, the things that don't look very dramatic; those are the moments when you can actually resist evil successfully. By the time you are standing outside your neighbors' house with a gun in your hand, if you're deciding at that moment whether or not to go in and shoot them, already evil is too far in your house, too far in your life; it has moved from wayfarer to guest to now master. You want to stop it at the wayfarer stage.

Evil, then, on this account is not so much an abstract philosophical problem as it is a practical challenge confronting those afflicted by it. Evil is something we meet in our hearts and our lives every day. We meet it on the road when we're driving to work and someone cuts us off; we meet it on the roads when we're driving to work and we think about cutting someone else off. Evil should be faced as a challenge whose successful overcoming on a daily basis will strengthen and deepen the person in their wisdom and their faith. The conviction the rabbis had, and that governed this whole picture, is that evil in this sense was a challenge and a gift sent by God to mature humans in certain ways, not entirely unlike Irenaeus. This is part of a larger understanding of the nature of Jewish suffering that the rabbis held to. Evil would serve as a challenge to people, but it would not overwhelm the people Israel. In particular, the Jewish people would suffer repeated persecutions— the rabbis at the time they were writing knew that persecutions had been in the people Israel's past and they would certainly be in the people Israel's future—but, they thought, such persecutions would never become so extreme as to threaten that people's existence.

In seeing all this, we are really seeing one rich and profound challenge to an over-Christianized conception of evil in light of sin. Even secular people today, it seems to me, have a fairly thoroughly Christian conception of evil and sin; but they don't have to, there are other accounts out there that are viable and plausible. And there are interestingly non-Christian, non-religious ways of conceiving of evil; ways that make evil less melodramatic and more ordinary in a way parallel to the Rabbinic account as well. But this Rabbinic tradition offers a very sober religious view of malice. It's again, profoundly non-dramatic; it doesn't play into any attempt on our part to over-dramatize the struggles we have, which would, in a certain way, maybe reinforce our own egotism, this tradition might think. "Oh, my struggles against evil are so magnificently vast; I am part of a cosmic war." The rabbis are like, "No, you're trying to grow up; that's what you're trying to do. Deal with that." Second, evil, even though it is not dramatic, is a powerful reality. It's a mundane reality, it's a worldly reality—there's no "Satan" of any kind of vast metaphysical density here—but nonetheless, there's a realism about how evil can, over time, come to shape and grip and warp someone's inner soul in a powerful way.

Indeed, this is so different from many Christian notions of evil that some Jewish scholars think it's inappropriate to call this a picture of "evil" at all. These thinkers argue that Rabbinic Judaism doesn't have a picture of "evil," it just has a picture of "badness." The category of "evil" itself, they say, already rhetorically gives the game away to Christianity. Instead, you should think about the *ra*, the *yetzer ha-ra*, as an impulse to badness, not an impulse to evil. This tradition emphasizes human responsibility and struggle, and especially struggle in living according to the Halakha, to Jewish law, in order to govern your behavior so that you don't flip out of your control. But you are responsible for this; you are responsible for you, no one else. In this halakhic view, suffering, then, is kept within human dimensions. Jewish law teaches, the rabbis believe, that suffering and evil is a human issue; a challenge that humans are set and that humans must struggle to overcome. Again, this is in contrast to Christianity where suffering always threatens to overwhelm a creature's capacities to resist it; suffering always threatens to become, that is, a theological problem, a divine reality. From a Rabbinic Jewish perspective, evil in Christianity always threatens to become melodrama, and it always seems to want to escape individual responsibility; not I, but Christ in me, is the one who's doing all this. Rabbinic Judaism thinks that's a very large-scale way of evading the real moral challenges that we face. Admittedly, they say, not all evil may thus be understandable—sometimes psychopaths happen—but in general, the shape of human evil is such, the rabbis thought, that it can be confronted through the practices of Halakha and the behavior of tradition Jewish religious practice.

But this account is not without its own problems, especially, it seems, for Jews living today after the Holocaust, the Shoah. The problem here is simply put: Is this picture of evil too mundane and too ordinary to handle the Shoah? Ironically, the Shoah may seem to be something—the Shoah is what the traditional Jewish sense of the Holocaust is; "Shoah" means "catastrophe"— that threatens any account of evil that is not vastly dramatic. How could it be otherwise? How could an account of evil that is not enormously dramatic and satanic capture the evil of the Shoah? The evil for the rabbis is about greed, jealously, envy; this is a happy and relatively small-scale picture of evil. It's a picture of evil based on a context of nasty, brutal people but not really continuous, we think, with the evil that was experienced in the Holocaust, in the Shoah. That kind of evil seems completely out of proportion to the character of the moral challenges that an ordinary person in an ordinary town in the 8th century somewhere in Mesopotamia, somewhere in Palestine, somewhere in North Africa, any of the diasporic Jewish communities; any of them would have faced a challenge, but not the challenge for the kind of industrialized slaughter represented by the Holocaust, the Shoah.

When that happened, it seemed to many people that traditional Jewish understandings of evil were really quite radically challenged. Here, it seemed, that the old agreement with God, the longest standing covenant between God and God's people, had fallen apart; and that the persecution of the Jews had reached beyond traditional pogroms, traditional massacres, to become metaphysically eliminationist in character. Somehow, God had let it happen that a people, the Germans, got it in their minds completely to annihilate the entire ethos, the entire people, of Israel. Post-Holocaust Jewish thought, post-Shoah Jewish thought, has struggled mightily with this challenge, and the struggle shows no signs of ceasing anytime soon. Indeed, you can say that the attempt to understand the meaning of the Shoah has been one of the most powerful inducements to Jewish thought since 1945; but we'll talk about that in several later lectures in this course.

For now, in thinking about this Rabbinic understanding of evil, I hope we've seen that it stands in a distinct place, again shadowed by these Ancient

Near Eastern combat myths, now also shadowed by the developing very dramatic and metaphysical Christian conceptions of evil, but bearing within itself a certain level of psychological and moral acuity and self-knowledge about the challenges and the quality of the difficulties that meet ordinary humans in their ordinary life every day. Next, I want to turn to another different account: the Islamic account of the Fall of Satan and the character of Satan as the epitome of evil; and we will find some interesting views there as well.

Islam—Iblis the Failed, Once-Glorious Being
Lecture 11

The Qur'an is unique among the Scriptures of the Abrahamic faiths in explicitly rendering the episode of the origin of evil in creation by recounting the rebellion of Iblis, the rebellious spirit. Some Islamic thinkers call Iblis an angel; some call Iblis a genie. Iblis is the one who becomes Ash Shaitan, the primordial rebel against God.

Islamic conceptions are relevant to a Western understanding of evil for a number of reasons, not least of which is that Islam serves, in a way, like Rabbinic Judaism: as a kind of internal critic of mainstream Western thinking about evil.

The **Qur'an** is the sacred text of Islam, but it is not, per se, the Muslim Bible. In a way that is different from the Torah and the Christian New and Old Testaments, the Qur'an itself is sacramental, a material means of holiness, a way of participating in God. It is, in some sense, more akin to the Christian Eucharist than to the Christian Bible or the Jewish Torah. Further, in Islam, there is no distance between the content of God's message and the poetic and linguistic form in which it exists in the Qur'an. This recitation is exactly what God meant to give God's people.

The Qur'an tells the story of **Iblis**, the rebellious spirit, who is asked by God to "bow down to Adam." But Iblis refuses to do so, and God is angered. Iblis tells God, "I will lay in wait for them, everywhere, on Your straight path." God replies, "You who were once high, now I am casting you down low."

The main traditions of interpreting this story cast light on Islamic understandings of evil and the relation between religious piety and moral rectitude. Augustine would point out that Iblis has motives for his refusal of God: It seems inappropriate that he should lower himself below Adam, who is made of clay, given that Iblis was made of fire. Note, too, that Iblis does not act; he refuses to act. Then, in his description of why he will now lay in wait for the good people of God, Iblis says, "Because you, God, brought me low." It seems that evil can be both something that is done by people and something that happens to them, and in fact, many people who have done evil acts report their deeds as things they were compelled to do. The action looks ambivalently as if it was done and as if it happened, as if it didn't really have an agent.

Further, in the Islamic tradition, Satan himself is only ambiguously a personal agent. Sometimes Iblis appears as an agent, a person, with desires and designs on humanity, but at other times Iblis seems more like an impersonal force, a power in the cosmos that humans experience as preying on their weaknesses and seducing them. But is it they who convince themselves that they are seduced, much in the way that Iblis convinced himself that it was God who cast him down? Such questions of responsibility are enormously complicated. The idea here seems to be that evil is both personal and impersonal at once—both something you do and something you watch yourself doing.

The Qur'an is the revelation according to Muhammad. It was written in pieces during Muhammad's life. Then it was compiled, organized, and fixed textually after his death.

This also helps us think about Iblis as saturating all dimensions of human existence. Satan is potentially everywhere and anywhere, in all of our deficiencies, large and small. But most fundamental of all in this account is the fact that Iblis doesn't do anything. He is committed in the most literal way to nothing.

The majority tradition in Islamic thought thus gives us a powerful and stark depiction of Iblis as a failed creature, a once-glorious being now fallen into a darkness of the soul. But another tradition, one represented by a number of Sufi mystics, suggests that Iblis was, in a certain way, the perfect monotheist, the one angel who would not bow down and worship Adam when God created him. These writers suggest that even monotheism can be taken too far, that it can become a kind of idolatry, and that the believer can become, in a certain sense, holier than thou. Judaism and Christianity, too, recognize that it is always possible to misappropriate the faith. Simply being a believer is no guarantee of moral rectitude; in fact, the appearance of belief can itself be one of the best disguises for evil.

For the Sufis and those who follow them, this interpretation of Iblis is part of a larger mystical worldview in which all is in God's hands. God's will for Iblis is not violated by Iblis's refusal to bow before humanity but fulfilled by it. This interpretation insinuates a complication into the main story that offers an even deeper insight into the nature of evil. Evil's origin is not completely irrational, nor simply a matter of excessive self-love or a sense of pride; evil is due to a misplaced but plausible sense of right value. This leads us to think about the ways in which our own traditions might not just enable but perhaps aggravate or amplify evil. ∎

Important Terms

Iblis: Rebellious angel in the Qur'an, later associated with Satan.

Qur'an: Sacred text of Islam, literally meaning the "recitation." Contains the revelation according to Muhammad, transmitted to him by Gabriel.

Suggested Reading

Awn, *Satan's Tragedy and Redemption: Iblis in Sufi Psychology*.

Questions to Consider

1. Recall the concluding question of this lecture in light of the discussion of Iblis in Islamic thought: Might evil itself be, at least sometimes, prompted by a genuine good? What do you think the answer to this is?

2. Does the understanding of Iblis offered by Sufism present Satan too sympathetically? Or are we right to see evil as, in some sense, more of a tragic mistake than a malicious occurrence?

How does the Islamic account of Iblis illuminate Jewish and Christian conceptions of Satan and evil? Does the contrast make the unique aspects of each tradition more striking?

Islam—Iblis the Failed, Once-Glorious Being
Lecture 11—Transcript

Hello, again. This lecture is on Islamic conceptions of evil, especially as they emerge out of the Islamic scriptures of the Qur'an.

50 years ago, it might have been a pretty curious thing to have a lecture on Islamic conceptions of evil in a course like this. Why, one might have wondered, would you want to talk about Islam? How relevant is that to a Western understanding of evil? In the past 50 years, we've come to realize that Islam is an intrinsic part of the history of Western thinking on evil in complicated ways. First of all, Islamic thought was deeply influenced by earlier Greek, Jewish, and Christian thinkers; and so to understand Islamic thought reveals things about those earlier traditions that might otherwise go missing. We might not be able to see as well in them as we can by seeing them through the prism of Islamic thought. Second, Islam was itself the source of the transmission of much pre-Christian literature and philosophy, especially Greek philosophy, to Western Christendom, which also picked up a good bit of insight on a series of important topics from the Islamic philosophers and lawyers themselves. Third, Islam serves in a way like Rabbinic Judaism as a kind of internal critic of the mainstream of Western thinking about evil; a critic who is both within and without this mainstream. It serves as a useful contrastive option to the main line of thinking that these lectures follow, but also it serves as a vital account that has its own integrity, even if it is somewhat oblique to that mainstream. Because of this, you could almost call this class, this lecture, an exercise in "comparative satanologies."

Let me start by mentioning some uniqueness's about the Islamic account that are really important for this lecture. The Qur'an is unique among the scriptures of the Abrahamic faiths in explicitly rendering the episode of the origin of evil in Creation by recounting the rebellion of Iblis, the rebellious spirit. Some Islamic thinkers call Iblis an angel, some call Iblis a genie; Iblis is the one who becomes Ash Shaitan, the primordial rebel against God. Before I get going into the details of this story, though, it's important to say just a little bit about the background of the Qur'an, because it's a very complicated and very fraught topic intellectually and theoretically today.

The Qur'an is the sacred text of Islam, but one should be careful about how one frames that. The Qur'an is not, per se, the Muslim Bible. Yes, it's roughly as long as the Christian New Testament and it's similarly divided into sections. There are 114 *suras* (chapters) in the Qur'an and each of those *suras* is composed of verses called *ayahs*, which is also translated as the word "sign." Each of the verses, thus, of each of the *suras* of the Qur'an is a sign of God's providence and love towards humanity. So far so good; it looks like another holy book. But the similarities can mislead in some important ways, much as the Christian New Testament is not the Christian Bible as opposed to the Jewish Bible of the Hebrew scriptures. The New Testament stands in complicated relationship to the Hebrew Bible, which is more or less identical with what Christians call the Old Testament.

Similarly, the Qur'an is complicatedly related to both Torah and the Christian Bible, New Testament and Old Testament. First of all, Islam respects the sacred books of both the Jewish and Christian positions; suggests—it claims, in fact, overtly claims—that those books themselves contain significant dimensions of God's revelation through the sending of the prophets of God; and Islam incorporates significant segments of the narratives of both the Hebrew Bible and the Christian New Testament into its teachings; and, at times, the story themselves appear, slightly differently told, in the Qur'an. Second, the Qur'an is not quite the same thing as a "bible." A bible literally comes from the Greek word "the book"; the Qur'an literally means "the recitation." The Quran is the revelation accorded to Muhammad, transmitted to him by the angel Gabriel; and Muhammad, then, would go recite it to his followers and to rivals and other people interested in the towns. It was written down actually only in bits and pieces during Muhammad's life, and then it was only compiled, collected, organized, and fixed textually after his death and canonized in the form that we have it, it seems to be, by Uthman, the third Caliph, who ruled about 20 or so years after Muhammad's death.

The vast majority of Muslims across the centuries have believed the Qur'an to be the perfect record of what the archangel Gabriel recited to Muhammad as God told him to recite. The Qur'an is composed entirely of exceptionally powerful lyric poetry, some of the most beautiful Arabic poetry ever written. In a way that's different from the Torah and the Christian New Testament and Old Testament, the Qur'an itself is sacramental; a material means of holiness; a way of participating in God; in some sense, more akin to the Christian Eucharist—the ritual of Communion, the Lord's Supper—than to the Christian Bible or the Jewish Torah. The Qur'an is the word of God for Muslims, but in this case it is somewhat akin to how Jesus is the word of God for Christians because the Qur'an was recited by God to Gabriel in Arabic. In other words, there's no distance whatsoever between the content of God's message and the linguistic form in which it exists in the Qur'an. We know for a fact that Jesus didn't speak Koine Greek, and yet the New Testament that we have is in Koine Greek; in other words, the language of Jesus already had to be translated, so not even Jesus's sayings do we have exactly as they were said in the day that they were. At no point does Judaism or Christianity suggest that God is speaking in the language of the people who are writing down the texts; that's not the way these traditions think about God's revelations. But in Islam, it's very clear that the poetic form and the linguistic form of the Qur'an are exactly what God meant to give his people. At one point in the Qur'an God says, "I have given you an Arabic Qur'an, an Arabic recitation"; and that means that this language and this recitation, these poems, are intrinsically very, very theologically rich and dense.

Many people, in the West, perhaps—also many Muslims, I think—think that the Qur'an is a rigorously legal text; but, in fact, it is literally an assemblage of poetic verses that shape the soul and inform sthe mind as much as guide the will, direct the will, of the believer. Of the roughly 6,000 verses in the Qur'an, only around 500 have the form of law, directly commanding or forbidding believers to do something or other. Indeed, the entire Qur'an has only about 200 verses directly commanding believers to pray, but 600 verses commanding believers to reflect, to ponder, and to analyze God's magnificence in nature, in plants, in stars, and in the solar system as a whole. This will, I hope, help us understand something of the context out of which the Iblis story emerges in the Qur'an; and it's important because the Qur'an will sometimes tell stories at different moments, repeatedly tell the same story, in order to uncover different nuances of the story for a particular larger message it wants to tell. The Qur'an, in fact, tells the story of Iblis several different times, each time offering different facets of the story. My favorite version, the version I think is most relevant for our purposes, is in the seventh *sura*. Let me read you this; this is God speaking first:

We created you, We formed you; and then We commanded the angels, "bow down before Adam," and they bowed. But not Iblis; he refused to be one of those who bow.

God said: "What prevented you from bowing down as I commanded you?" And he [Iblis] said: "I am better than he: You created me from fire and him from clay."

God said: "Get down from here! Here is no place for your arrogance, Get out! You are the lowest of creatures!"

but Iblis said, "Give me respite until the day they are raised."

and God said, "You have respite."

And then Iblis said, "Because you have put me in the wrong, I shall lie in wait for them on Your straight path; I will assault them from the front and the back, from their right and their left; nor will you find that most of them are grateful."

God said, "Get out! You are disgraced and expelled! I swear I shall fill Hell with you and all who follow you."

That's a long quote; let me give you a little commentary on it, let me tell you a little about it. In the Qur'anic stories, Iblis is asked by God to "bow down"; all the angels, all the spirits, are told to "bow down to Adam." The words "bow down" here in Arabic is the word *sujud*. That word is also the word used for the ritual prostration in Islamic prayer. In other words, at least on one meaning of the term, God is telling the angels to worship Adam. Iblis refuses to recognize Adam's theological supremacy. Iblis doesn't do anything—this is important, too, we'll come back to this—he doesn't do something, he simply doesn't bow; and in that act, he becomes the accuser, the rebel, the opponent, Ash Shaitan, Satan, and from this rebellious refusal all evil proceeds. He says, "I will lay in wait for them, everywhere, on Your straight path," and God says, "You who were once high, now I am casting you down low." It is precisely because Iblis is so high that he doesn't want to get lower than Adam; he doesn't want to lower himself in that way. Instead, what happens is because he is too high for God, God casts him down; you see the kind of poetic paradoxes here.

Understanding this event and understanding how the Qur'an describes it and the main traditions of interpreting these stories really casts a lot of light, interesting light, on Islamic understandings of evil and the relation between religious piety and moral rectitude. Think about Iblis's fall; again, a little bit like Augustine: it has its reasons; Iblis has his motives. It seems inappropriate to Iblis that he should lower himself below something that was made of clay since he was made of fire. Furthermore, another picture, another dimension, of evil here: Iblis does not, per se, act; Iblis refuses to act. He does not bow down. Then, in his description of why he will now lay in wait for the good people of God, Iblis says, "Because you, God, brought me low"; that is, Iblis blames God for making him go bad.

This gets at a couple different dimensions of evil in Islamic accounts that are worth noting. First of all, one paradoxical dimension of it: Evil is clearly something that is done by people, but it also can be seen as something that happens to them; at least, many evil people, people who have done evil acts, often report their deeds as effectively things they had to do, they were compelled to do it. It's not their fault; they didn't mean to; or they meant to but they only meant it in the best description of the act. Effectively, then, action of this sort looks ambivalently like it was done but also like it happened, like it didn't really have an agent. Furthermore, in the tradition, Satan himself—in the Islamic tradition—is only ambiguously a personal agent for Islamic thought. Sometimes Iblis appears as an agent, a person, with desires and designs on humanity; the Qur'anic story we gave tells that perfectly. But at other times, Iblis, the satanic energies, seems more like an impersonal force; a power in the cosmos that humans experience as preying on their weakness and seducing them. But is it they who convince themselves that they are seduced, much in the same way that Iblis convinced himself in that fall that it was God who sent him down? Or do they seduce themselves into believing in their own seduction? Again, questions of responsibility are enormously complicated here, but they seem inescapable in these traditions.

The idea here seems to be that Satan's character as ambiguously personal and the nature of satanic action, evil action, as ambiguously done or happening to a person reveals something really deep about the nature of evil: that evil is both personal and impersonal at once; intimate to you, something you do, and also something that you watch yourself doing, something that happens outside of you. Not to be too psychological about this, but it seems to me that in a lot of accounts of people engaging in atrocities—people who were killing other people; people who were involved in genocides; people who were involved in murders—often what the perpetrators of these acts report is a kind of experience of a double consciousness: an awareness that they are doing these things and an awareness a part of their mind is fully engaged in the act of doing it, but another part of their mind is watching them do it; there's some kind of strange splitting that happens, at least in some really dramatic instances of truly horrific violence, as if we can't bear fully to be ourselves in those moments. This notion of Iblis's ambiguous agency and ambiguous personhood, it seems to me, get right at that in an important way.

Furthermore, this helps us think about Iblis as saturating all dimensions of human existence. Satan is potentially everywhere and anywhere, in all of our deficiencies, large and small; Satan urges us to wash ourselves hastily and to ignore the cries of those being murdered. That's a Qur'anic example: that Satan is behind those moments when you feel impatient in engaging in the ritual ablutions you should undertake before prayer, the ritual washing you should undertake before prayer; Satan is there, and Satan is also there when you ignore the cries of those you hear being murdered outside your house. That's an attempt to talk about a category of evil that in some ways captures both Rabbinic concerns with the minutiae of ordinary life and also the kind of metaphysical concerns of some of the more dramatic pictures of Christianity. But most fundamental of all on this account, remember Iblis doesn't do anything. At no point, actually, does Iblis doing anything until at the end when he says, "This is what I'm going to do; I'm going to ruin things for you, God." Iblis is fundamentally and finally merely destructive, against God's creation, committed in the most literal way to nothing.

The majority tradition in Islamic thought thus gives us a powerful and stark depiction of Iblis as a failed creature, a once-glorious being now fallen into the uttermost darkness, darkness of soul. This is a catastrophe of a creature now, who now seeks desperately to drag others down into that same catastrophe, not so much for company there, not so much because it will be more pleasant when more people are in the pit, but in some sense to master them; to convince himself that he is able to master these fools. We'll see this desire for company in Hell appear again in later thinkers—Christian thinkers like Anselm, Aquinas, and Dante, again and again—the idea of a communality to evil that is a false communality, a false community. Furthermore, this picture of evil wants to avoid any sense of imagining, recognizing that this agent can serve God as a tempter. In other words, Satan on this count, Iblis, doesn't want to think that Satan is still working on God's team. In all these ways, this is not far from Christian understandings of Satan, though the explicit attention to the idea of evil as having its own reasons, which we've seen here, this explicit elaboration in the scriptures of the fall of Satan as motivated, is not present in Christian scriptures.

But that's the majority view, that's the orthodox, mainstream view in Islamic thought; but there is another tradition in Islamic thought on Iblis. We can call this the minority report; one represented by a number of Sufi mystics. These are some people who are very, very serious in their faith but they manifested their faith in different ways than the mainstream of the orthodoxy found appropriate; and these mystics developed this different interpretation of these events and their interpretation was carried forward as well by other, later thinkers. These writers suggest that Iblis was, or perhaps is, in a certain way the perfect monotheist; the one angel who would not bow down and worship Adam when God created him. This sounds crazy, especially in Islamic terms. Remember that in Islam there is no god but God; monotheism is the first and foremost virtue of the faithful. How could Satan be the perfect monotheist? Isn't being a monotheist good? Isn't it good especially in Islam? That's all true; but the Sufi's suggest that there's a way that monotheism can be taken too far; that it can become a kind of idolatry, and that the believer can become, in a certain sense, holier than thou. On one description of this account, then, Iblis could seem a tragic figure and a cautionary tale for those who value their own personal piety above all.

Interestingly, in Judaism actually, there are similar structures that can function as well. The law above all other laws is to preserve life. You can break the Sabbath, you can break the fast on Yom Kippur, you can break any number of rules in order to secure life in Jewish law. Securing the life of the world is a fundamental good. The Sufi's are sort of saying that there's a way of appropriating Islamic law that denies the goodness of life, and that is, they say, deeply un-Islamic, but it is nonetheless a danger on this religious tradition. Similarly, in Christianity, of course, one of the most popular lines in the Reformation is the fact that, "Even the Devil knows scripture." In other words, for all three of these traditions in different ways, the Sufi interpretation is paradigmatic of a particular moment. It is always possible; the traditions have to recognize, to misappropriate the faith. Simply being a believer is no guarantee of moral rectitude; in fact, the appearance of belief can itself be one of the best disguises for evil. Perhaps the best believer turns out to be Satan. That's a disquieting thought.

For the Sufi's, and for those who follow them in the Islamic tradition, this interpretation of Iblis is part of a larger mystical worldview where all is in God's hands. God's will for Iblis is not violated by Iblis's refusal to bow before humanity; God's will is rather fulfilled by it. This interpretation insinuates, that is, a complication into the main story that offers an even deeper insight into the nature of evil as the faith professes it. Evil's origin here is not completely irrational, nor simply a matter of excessive self-love or a rude sense of pride; evil is due to a misplaced but plausible sense of right value. Iblis, on this account, cannot worship what is below him, or what is other than God; and he is offended that God has commanded spiritual beings to prostrate themselves, to worship, material ones, and that God has commanded anyone to worship anything other than God. It's precisely Iblis's prim theological propriety that is the problem. Iblis is driven by a set of motives that we can see at least on their first look to be noble and worthy. This is not irrational, this is not rebellion; it's grounded on a reasonable, though misplaced it turns out, assessment of the right order of values.

It's pretty clear that the Sufi's were led to this view by some difficulties that they had living among the more orthodox believers of either the Sunni or Shia variety. (Sunni and Shia are the two main branches of Islam, much as Christians have Protestants, Catholics, and Eastern Orthodox.) The Sufi's were often terribly persecuted, and so had good reason to grow to resent the more orthodox, the more theologically self-righteous. The Sufi's, after all, would, in their ecstasies, engage in some relatively wild theological speculations of the sort that others would find troubling; so certainly their views of Iblis and their interpretation of the story were shaped by what they saw as the demonic suffering they suffered at the hands of their more orthodox neighbors.

But I think there's a real insight here for all three Abrahamic faiths on evil; it's something of what I said before: The insight is that you have to think of a way in which your own tradition could not just enable but maybe aggravate, amplify evil. It is precisely the story of Iblis as a believer who has gone wrong because of his belief that is the most powerful thing about that counter story, and the thing I think that all three traditions could benefit from enormously.

As with the discussion of Rabbinic Judaism's thought about evil, this account of Iblis—the orthodox account and the minority report—offer significantly different pictures of evil from what we have so far, in our mostly Christian account, seen. Here, evil appears to be a moral choice, a decision for one good over another, not a completely irrational rebellion; not the sort of thing that Augustine talks about as lacking all reason. It raises this question— especially the Sufi minority report interpretation—might evil itself be, at least sometimes, prompted by genuine, real good? That's the question that we should end this lecture on. We'll turn next to some Christian scholastics who think about these questions in deep, again though silent, conversation with some of the Rabbinic and Islamic views we've thought about from within the stream of thinking inaugurated by Augustine. We'll turn to those next.

On Self-Deception in Evil—Scholasticism
Lecture 12

> What does evil feel like, or more accurately, what does it think like, from inside? This is a profound and interesting effort at empathy toward something that we really shouldn't feel empathy toward, not because Augustine and those who followed him, like Aquinas, wanted to feel pity for wicked-doers, but rather, because they wanted to get as clear as possible about the inner logic of evil's rationales.

This lecture shifts us back from Islamic to Christian thinking, in particular, the Scholasticism that emerged in Western monastic schools starting soon after the end of the 1st millennium. This style of teaching and learning involved mastering a huge body of traditional theological information, developing the ability to summarize that information and articulate it in potent expressions, and debating the various tensions and conflicts that emerged from within that body of knowledge. This focus on debating the details of Christian theology demanded a precise and intricate kind of reasoning. Two of the greatest thinkers in the Scholastic tradition were Anselm of Lyon and **Thomas Aquinas**, both of whom chose to concentrate their study of the nature of evil on the fallen angels—the devil and his minions—rather than humans. In this lecture, we'll look at the "logic" of Satan's rebellion through the thought of Anselm and what we might call the "moral psychology" of the devil and communal evil through the works of Aquinas.

In his very brief treatise "On the Fall of the Devil," Anselm explores the nature of Satan's motivation for rebelling against

Thomas Aquinas (1225–1274) is often considered the greatest mind in the Scholastic age.

God's providential order, unpacks the multiple dimensions of misery that befell Satan because of that rebellion, and offers a picture of the relationship between good and evil in the cosmos. Much of the treatise in general can be summarized in the pithy statement of Anselm that Satan wanted everything and got nothing, while the good angels sought nothing and received everything.

Aquinas's description illuminates the nature of human evil and the curious collegiality it can provoke in its adherents.

For Anselm, the pursuit of one's own good without reliance on God or anyone else is both radically self-deceptive about one's identity as a creature of God and about one's true good, namely, loving dependence and relation, a sharing in God's community. God created the universe and gave all the creatures within it a will to participate in the universe, but Anselm says, each of the creatures must actualize that will—inhabit and endorse it. The mystery of the devil is that he inexplicably chooses not to accept that will and seeks something more; what that "more" is can't be specified. The devil's desire is bottomless; because it can never be specified, it can never be sated, and the fact of this longing is what makes Satan miserable.

The work of Aquinas offers, perhaps, a less dense picture of the mindset of an evildoer. What does a wicked person's mind report to itself when it is doing evil? Aquinas gives us a wonderful description of what he thinks it was like for Satan to have convinced himself that he was going to succeed in rebelling against God. Aquinas believed that Satan wanted to be like God, not because he wanted to be separate from God—that would be the same as saying that he didn't want to exist—but because he desired "something he could attain by the virtue of his own nature, turning his appetite away from the supernatural beatitude which is obtained by God's grace." Satan believes it's possible, in other words, to keep the end of ultimate happiness in his mind as an ideal that he will try to attain, but he also convinces himself that he can get it by his own efforts, rather than receiving it as a gift from God.

In this, Aquinas explains Satan's motivations for rebelling against God: There's a resentment that God is higher than Satan and a desire to be like

God, both slathered over with self-deception, the ability of Satan to convince himself that he can get to what God is. This also explains the nature of the allegiance the infernal creatures make with one another. The fallen angels work together, but each pursues his own solitary ends; each one wants to be his own God. Aquinas's description illuminates the nature of human evil and the curious collegiality it can provoke in its adherents.

For Augustine, Anselm, and Aquinas, evil is, most of all, privative; it deprives reality of being in some ways, and it does this by shrinking back from connection to the rest of reality. Evil is an attempt to be private, and for Aquinas and these other thinkers, that notion of radical solitude is theologically problematic. This idea is interesting in comparison to our world, where we value privacy deeply. Nonetheless, Anselm and Aquinas give us deep, realistic, and profound pictures of the role of self-deception in the exercise and agency of evil. ■

Name to Know

Aquinas, Thomas (1225–1274 C.E.). Born to a prominent family in Aquino in southern Italy. At the age of 19, Aquinas expressed a desire to join the monastic order of the Dominicans, but his family opposed this decision and locked him in a castle for two years.

Suggested Reading

Anselm, *Anselm of Canterbury: The Major Works*, Davies and Evans, eds.

Aquinas, *On Evil*, Davies, ed., Regan, trans.

———, *Summa Theologiae*, Fathers of the American Dominican Province, trans.

1. What do you make of the Scholastic attempt to understand evil by dwelling on the fall of Satan and the angels? Does this approach seem clarifying or obscuring?

2. Is Aquinas right to suggest that evil may often involve self-deception and the desire to attain something that one simply cannot possess? What are some examples of this kind of self-deception common in our world?

On Self-Deception in Evil—Scholasticism
Lecture 12—Transcript

Welcome back. To shift from Islamic thoughts and reflections on Iblis, which was the topic of our last lecture, to Christian scholasticism of the High Middle Ages may seem like a recipe for some sort of intellectual whiplash, but as I tried to say last time, in fact, the later history of Christian thought is pretty impossible without Islamic thought. In the past half-century or so, scholars have really come to appreciate the vast intellectual debt that Europe owes to Islam. It wasn't in fact, as the book title suggests, the Irish that saved civilization, it was in fact Islam. When western Europe was trying to put itself back together again after the collapse of the Roman Empire, it was Islam that secured civilized life in the Mediterranean, and also secured the transmission of Greco-Roman classical antiquity to the Latin west—largely through the gathering together of these texts in their Greek and Latin forms and their translation in Islamic Arabic-speaking centers of learning in Baghdad, Cairo, Damascus, in places like that.

At that point, once that western heritage had been secured by Islam and then began to be transmitted back to the Latin-speaking west—it was really the Latin-speaking west that needed contact with these literatures again—the intellectual discipline that begins to be known as Christian Scholasticism emerges. Soon after the end of the 1st millennium, Christian intellectual culture in the west began to mature institutionally and intellectually. Theologians began to teach in cathedral schools, in schools associated with particular cathedrals. In fact, they created these schools associated with the cathedrals. Various religious leaders—leaders of monasteries, bishops, religious intellectuals of a sort who developed followers in the west—became important thinkers in their own right. There was a large-scale renaissance of monastic intellectualism at this time. As this went on, pre-Christian Greek and Roman thinkers were rediscovered, and more attention was also paid to Jewish and Islamic thought as well. Much of this work served to develop and systematize Christian thought beyond the achievement of Augustine—still considered by all these intellectuals the great Christian Latin thinker, the greatest thinker of the west. For them, because of the painful severing of ties with the Greek Christian east, for mostly political reasons, it began to be almost entirely a Latin Christianity that people in the west understood to be the central conveyor of the Christian heritage.

As the intellectual conversation expanded in those first couple centuries of the new millennium—from 1000 to 1100 or 1200—very slowly, a network of medieval thinktanks and schools developed. First associated again, with cathedral schools and then monasteries, and then slowly as kind of free-standing institutions of learning modeled importantly, it seems to be the case now, on Islamic centers of learning in Cairo and Baghdad and elsewhere—centers of learning that were understood to be the kind of proto-universities of the world. The intellectual and institutional context that emerged in these universities—the style of teaching and learning that emerged there—is something that we have come to call Scholasticism: the thought of the schools.

Before I go on, let me just give you a taste of how scholastic teaching and learning went forward. Scholastic teaching and learning was really mostly about the development of skills in public debate. This is an interesting fact. Most of the learning was not really contained in books, per se—the books were repositories, records of debates that were held in public before the students, and that students could be involved in by asking questions—but effectively what Scholastic learning was was the mastering of a huge body of traditional information, the development of the skill of summarizing that body of information, and being able to articulate it in its most potent expressions, and then the ability to take that body of information, kind of like an intellectual juggling act, and learning how to debate the various sets of tensions and conflicts that emerged from within that body of knowledge. One of the most important texts of medieval Scholasticism—one of its earliest, in fact, one of its most prompting texts—is a book by Abelard, an early and very controversial medieval scholastic intellectual. He wrote a book called *Sic et Non* in Latin, that is "Yes and No." He effectively simply gathered together the entire tradition of Christian thought that he could get his hands on, and demonstrated that very respected, very important authorities—ecclesiastical authorities, intellectual authorities, philosophers, theologians, bishops, councils, the scriptures—at different times every one of these authorities could be heard to be saying something on both sides of an opinion. Abelard was like the nightmare YouTube of his day; he recorded everything he found. When he did, he created enormous tensions—intellectual tensions—in the world of western Christianity because he pointed out that the entire system was incredibly filled with what looked like contradictions. In a way, Abelard's provocation of the tradition really effectively generated the history of Scholasticism because it began to be a system to figure out how to make sense of the fact that very intellectually serious, very authoritative people were able to take seriously and with sincere truthfulness claims that were effectively contradictory, and the tradition had to figure out how to make sense of those claims.

One of the things that this focus on a particular body of knowledge requires and the form of intellectual debate demands is a very, very precise, at times very abstract, but always extremely intricate kind of reasoning. Scholasticism in this way is sort of like the work that you would expect an intellectual jeweler to do. It's still today, by philosophers and theologians, recognized as enormously philosophically impressive work. Some people still think it was the worst kind of mere academic gamesmanship, debates about how many angels can fit on the head of a pin or something like that; but when you look at the debates and what they're debating in the context of the moment, they were, in fact, enormously impressive in the seriousness of the matters that were handled and the precision of the debates that were undertaken. I think it took until at least the 20th century to rival these thinkers for the sheer brain power and the care that they did with their work.

Two of the greatest of the thinkers of this tradition were unarguably Anselm, who also became the Archbishop of Canterbury, and Thomas Aquinas. Anselm is not exactly a scholastic—he's a bit too early for the full maturity of Scholasticism, and he himself was never per se a university teacher—but his thought served as one of the main ingredients of mature scholastic theology. Aquinas is often considered the greatest mind in the scholastic age, and not without reason, though he himself was, we can say, fairly idiosyncratic. For our purposes, though, they both most importantly developed interesting and powerful analyses of evil, deriving from Augustine's work in some important ways, but influenced by other philosophical currents; and they used these philosophical analyses to ask some deep and abiding questions about the origins and nature of evil. They each offer, then, searching discussions that pertain directly to the matter of our course: what an "evil act" is, how it is intelligible as an evil act, and how it is also not ultimately intelligible.

Most centrally, they investigate the mystery of wickedness by exploring the study of the fall of the Devil and the nature of what Aquinas will end up calling the Infernal compact, the agreement among the demons to work together; not centrally by addressing the experience of human malice. This is a deliberate decision on both of their parts. By treating of their discussions of the fall of the angels, the fall of the Devil, we'll be able to look at their understandings of agency in what we can call a relatively hydroponic manner; that is, we'll be able to look at their discussion of the roots of agency as we would be able to study the roots of a plant that is growing in water, with no soil clouding your view.

Both Aquinas and Anselm deliberately focused a lot of their attention on the nature of the evil will on the fallen angels, the Devil and the Devil's minions, precisely because for them it seems to be a cleaner study of how agency can go wrong than looking at embodied humans. Embodied humans have lots of motivations that can obstruct and obscure things; I mean, most of them thought about the nature of the human fall. But to figure out the core essence of what happens to a free agent when it freely chooses evil, they both thought that looking at a disembodied angel and the disembodied angel's rebellion and fall would be a cleaner and crisper analysis of this. I think they were right. In this lecture, we're going to explore first the "logic" of Satan's rebellion through the thought of Anselm and especially one of Anselm's most influential treatises called "On the Fall of the Devil"; and then second, we're also going to look at what we could call the "moral psychology" of the Devil and of communal evil via a series of works by Aquinas.

Anselm in his very brief treatise "On the Fall of the Devil"—it's really only about 25–30 pages in an ordinary paperback book size; when I teach this in my classes, though, we spend normally three weeks reading those roughly 30 pages, 10 pages a week, because it is extremely dense stuff—explores the nature of Satan's motivation for rebelling against God's providential order; it unpacks the multiple dimensions of misery that befell Satan because of that rebellion; and all of this is in the purpose of summarizing a picture of the relationship between good and evil and the good and evil creatures, and the longings and desires of good and evil creatures, in the cosmos. Much of the treatise in general can be summarized in a very pithy statement that Anselm offers during it: He says that Satan basically wanted everything and got nothing, while the good angels sought nothing and received everything. Let me quote this for you, because Anselm's Latin is really quite tremendous: "The angels are separated between those who, adhering to justice"—that is, those who stay with God; stay with what is due them—"enjoy all the goods they wish and those who, having abandoned justice (those who have rebelled) lack any good they desire."

The pursuit of one's own good on one's own—that is, without reliance on God or your colleagues, your neighbors, your friends and relatives—is both radically self-deceptive about who one is, most fundamentally because one is a creature of God thus one needs God's assistance in being at all; and secondly is radically self-deceptive about what one's true good is: namely, it is loving dependence and relation, sharing in God's community, not solitary self-mastery. For Anselm, God creates the whole universe and gives all the angels, all the creatures within it—but he's focusing on angels here, remember—a good will; a will to participate in the universe. But, Anselm says, each of the angels must on their own actualize that will; they must make it their own; they must inhabit the will, endorse it. The mystery of the Devil for Anselm is that the Devil inexplicably chooses not to accept that will, but instead seeks something more. The "moreness" of this more is a really interesting puzzle, and Anselm is quite psychologically acute about this. What is the nature of the "more" the Devil speaks? In a sense, it can't be specified, because any particular specification would be obviously insane; the Devil only wants more, a generous but incompletely general and vague ambition.

When I teach this with my students I love to use an analogy to a movie they've never seen, but hopefully some of you will have seen this or if not, go and watch this movie: It's the old classic movie *Key Largo* with Lauren Bacall and Humphrey Bogart. There's a wonderful scene when Bogart and Bacall are facing some gangsters, and Bogart says of the gangster leader, Johnny Rocco, "I know what Johnny wants; Johnny, you know what you want?" and Rocco says, "What?" and Bogart says, "You want more" and Rocco says, "Yeah, that's right, I want more," and it's left completely unspecified what it is. Then Rocco turns to Bogart and says, "What do you want?" and Bogart says, "I want a world where there are fewer Johnny Rocco's."

That's a very Anselmian moment, because the problem with a figure like Rocco—the problem with a figure like the Devil—is precisely that the ambition that they have is so vague and so general it can never actually specify in any particular way about the world they live in. The Devil's desire—evil desire, Anselm is saying—is endless and bottomless just because it is impossible; just because it can never be specified and thus can never be sated. An analogy here is useful; the analogy would be with lies: It's easy to tell one lie, but the activity of lying is effectively bottomless because there's no proper place to end lying. At any moment when you're lying, it always can seem to make more sense to tell just one more little lie; but each small, minute lie makes you that much worse and in that much worse of a situation. Yet by the time you get into lying, you're so far into it that the psychological cost to you—in my experience anyway; check this with your own experience—of owning up to your lies, each one of which is maybe the size of a small grain of sand, but the psychological cost is the cost of the whole pile of sand, the whole amount of lies; so it always feels easier to tell just one more lie. That's Satan's problem: It always seems easier for Satan, on Anselm's account, effectively to try again to imagine a world where the vague desire he wants could be sated, even though the very fact of longing for this world is precisely what makes Satan miserable. Remember the good angels accepted what they got and they were happy about it. Satan actually makes himself miserable precisely because of his ambition.

All this is, it seems to me, a relatively dense but quite philosophically profound picture. It's also, though, for Anselm, as I said, 30 pages; this is a very pithy argument. Could we get a more unpacked, less dense picture of this? I think we can, actually, in the work of Thomas Aquinas. Aquinas lived about two centuries after Anselm, a century and a half let's say, and he is probably the greatest intellectual that the West has known in between I would say Augustine and pick your modern hero (for some people Kant, for some people Hegel, who knows; Picasso). Aquinas, though, is an enormously intellect and he was famous for being able to do the activity of scholastic intellectual juggling more effectively than anyone else. There are famous stories of Aquinas actually literally writing four or five books at once, like one of those chess grand masters who you'll find sometimes in parks in New York City or elsewhere who can play 10 games at once against 10 different opponents. Aquinas would sit in a room or stand in a room and he would have five or six scribes around him, and he would dictate a sentence to one scribe about one of the books he was writing, and then dictate the next sentence to another scribe for another book he was writing, and while those scribes were finishing their sentences he would go over here and dictate other parts of other books.

We actually know this is true because we have records, and there's a really fascinating way that we can tell: He was actually commenting on a series of Aristotle's philosophical ethics texts at the same time that he was writing in his *Summa Theologiae*, this vast work, the questions—the chapters; they're questions, really—the part of that work that is on ethics, on the virtue; and, at the same time he's doing that (writing a commentary on Aristotle; writing the *Summa Theologiae* on virtue) he's also writing a commentary on Paul's Letter to the Romans. In other words, he's doing multiple books; and not like an hour on one book, an hour on the other book, an hour on the third book, he's literally writing them sentence by sentence simultaneously. That kind of intellectual juggling requires a certain kind of mind and a certain sort of skills that are acquired by training that are pretty much lost to our world today. Aquinas was an enormously impressive guy.

For anyone following in a broadly Augustinian line on evil as Aquinas was, the difficulty is, as Anselm showed us, how do you present the mindset of an evildoer? What does a wicked person's mind report to itself that it is doing when it is doing evil? Remember we talked about for Augustine, the nature of willing evil is the kind of absence of reasons in some important way, and yet the appearance of those reasons to the person who's doing them. But this raises this real puzzle: What does evil feel like, or more accurately what does it think like, from inside? This is a profound and interesting effort at empathy towards something that we really shouldn't feel empathy towards, not because Augustine and those who followed him, like Aquinas, wanted to feel pity for wicked-doers, but rather because they wanted to get as clear as possible about the inner logic of evil's rationales, not least to help ourselves avoid thinking in this way when we are tempted so to do; to help ourselves from becoming such rationalizers of evil.

Consider Aquinas's representation of the satanic psychology; he has a wonderful description of what he thinks it was like for Satan to have convinced himself that he was going to get somewhere in rebelling against God. This is mostly around Aquinas's glossing of the idea that Satan wanted to be like God. What is it mean to be like God for Satan? Let me read you this passage here: "One may desire to be like God in a way that is not natural to one"—not natural in the sense of not appropriate, not fitting for one—"as if one were to desire to create heaven and earth, which is proper to God." There is sin in this sort of desire. What's interesting here, what's in the background here, is that Aquinas has to agree that there would have been a way to want to be like God that is appropriate; and why is that? Because all rational creatures are supposed to imitate God in some way, at least in the exercise of their reason. The idea that humans and angels are supposed to be like God is not in itself a terrible idea; the problem is how they are going to be like God.

I continue here: "It was in this way that the devil desired to be like God," this bad way, "Not"—now here's Aquinas making a very crucial distinction—"that the Devil desired to resemble God by being subject to no one else but himself absolutely"; that's not what the Devil did. Why didn't the Devil do that? "For in that case, he would be desiring his own 'not-being'; since no creature can exist except by holding its existence under God," receiving its existence under God. In other words, here he's saying the psychology of the Devil can't be that nuts to desire that directly and self-consciously you want to be separate from God is to mean that you would say to yourself in a very explicit way, "God is the source of being. I want to resist God. I want to resist the source of my being. I want to die." On some description of what rebellion against God is, Aquinas is saying, if you actually think it through properly, you will come to the conclusion that this kind of rebellion is nothing more than a longing for suicide, which is precisely why Satan doesn't want to come to that conclusion. That's where direct desire is impossible for Satan; he can't form that thought in a coherent way.

So we continue with Aquinas:

> But rather it was in another way that Satan desired to be like God—by desiring, as his ultimate end of beatitude, something that he could attain by the power of his own nature, desiring as his ultimate happiness something that Satan could get on his own, turning his appetite way from the supernatural beatitude that is obtained by God's grace.

That is, so instead of thinking, "Well, I want to die," the Devil re-described the end he was seeking so that he could now imagine achieving it on his own. That's one possibility for what the Devil was doing. If you won't make me lunch, then I will go outside and I will just eat the grass, and I will be happy with that because you won't do what I want you to do, or you won't let me do what I want to do. That's one option for what the devil was doing; but Aquinas gives him another. Or, if he desired as his ultimate end that likeness of God that is bestowed by grace, if he still desired beatification and likeness of God, rivalry of God in some sense; if, that is, Satan wanted to live in a world where the combat myth was true; he thought to acquire that likeness by the power of his own nature and not from divine aid as God ordained. This, again, is really important: Here, Aquinas is saying, it's possible for the Devil to keep the end of ultimate happiness in his head as an idea that he will still try to attain, but now he will convince himself that he can get it by his own efforts, rather than receiving it from God as a gift; that he would reach out and grab it rather than accepting it as a gift.

All this, it seems to me, explains the nature of evil as a kind of desire; one kind of desiring to be like God and not another. It explains the character of Satan's motivations in rebelling against God: There's a resentment that God is higher than Satan, an envy at that superiority; and a deserve to be like God; all of that slathered over with a kind of self-deception, an ability by Satan to convince himself that he, in fact, can get to what God is. This explains for Aquinas also the nature of the allegiance the infernal creatures with one another; that is, this helps us understand the moral psychology of communal evil. All of the fallen angels work together in a way, but each one for their own, private good; each one pursues their own solitary end; each one wants to be their own God. It's a kind of alliance of egotists, which makes it a very unstable alliance. All of this is interesting in itself in Aquinas; but it also—and he means it to do this—illuminates the nature of human evil and the curious kind of "collegiality" it can provoke in its adherents; for there is a certain kind of collegiality among the damned. Aquinas is in no doubt about this, that the collegiality, the false community, of the damned is only the false community of those who each individually are seeking their own private and wholly individual, wholly solitary good.

This is an important moment because here we touch on a metaphysical conviction of the premodern world—one really beginning with Augustine but having many roots before that—about the nature of evil, which it will be very differently seen in the modern world; and that is the connection between the Latin term *privatzio* and evil and its relationship to the category of privacy in our world. For the Latin theologians, the word *privatzio*—and there were other words in other languages that could do this, too, but let's focus on them right now: Augustine, Anselm, and Aquinas, all the people in the Latin-speaking West—evil is most of all privative, like depriving reality of being in some ways; but it does this by shrinking back from being connected to the rest of reality. In other words, evil is an attempt to be private, to be alone and on your own. For Augustine and Aquinas, these people thought that the notion of radical privacy, radical solitude, or radical self-possession and possession of our own property, is actually theologically problematic. Augustine's monastery was a monastery where no one held anything privately; everyone held all goods in common. Aquinas, in being a Dominican, lived in an order that was committed to poverty and to refusing the goods of the world insofar as those goods were to be held by them as possessions of their own. Both of them thought that the notion of private poverty or private being were ways of participating in a certain kind of practice that inevitably leads to evil.

This is really interesting in comparison to our world, and it identifies, I think, a pretty profound tension between the premodern world and the modern world because we believe deeply in privacy; we believe deeply that each person is an individual who should be left in some fundamental way alone or should be allowed to be alone. We believe, that is, in a picture of the ideal character of the human that Anselm, Aquinas, Augustine, a lot of these premoderns—we'll see Dante saying something similar in a little bit—

would have thought sounded a lot more like the satanic psychology than it did anything appropriately Christian or normative. I put that out there just as a thought to keep in mind as we go forward here. There is, in fact, a really profound way that these earlier thinkers really challenge not just some of our beliefs but the very way we've organized our society, politically, socially, culturally. For them, the society itself looks like it's a society in a strange way that Satan designed. I like our society, by the way, I'm not suggesting that we need to be rejecting it; I just think there's a really profound tension between this picture and our own.

Let me wrap up here: The Scholastics were always dense and elusive; all their thought is hard and needs time to unpack. But we begin to see what Aquinas and Anselm were about in untangling the sorts of semi-plausible pictures of human motivation, pictures of desire, that are not immediately and obviously absurd—even if they are absurd in their ultimate incoherence—from ideas that would be patently absurd, obviously absurd, even to falling angels. Anselm and Aquinas, for all of their scholastic abstruseness, for all of their scholastic intricacy and difficultly, give us some of the deepest, most realistic, and most profound pictures of the role of self-deception and the illusion in the exercise and the agency of evil that we have yet encountered.

Next, we're going to turn to a figure who offers an even richer and more vivid account of evil, working with the thought of Anselm and Aquinas but on a far, far grander canvas: Dante.

Dante—Hell and the Abandonment of Hope
Lecture 13

The most direct historical implication of this passage is very disquieting, and that is, of course, that the gate to Auschwitz in the Holocaust had over it a sign, as well, and that sign said, *"Arbeit macht frei,"* "Work will make you free." Clearly, that sign was modeled on Dante's *Inferno* sign.

Dante Alighieri's vision of hell in his epic poem the *Inferno* has probably done more to shape Western imaginations of hell, the devil, and punishment than any other work. In this lecture, we'll look at three themes in the poem: the overall logic of hell; the paradoxical logic of what Dante calls the ***contrapasso,*** the "counter-penalty," on which the nature of punishment in hell is based; and the ultimate irony that is at the heart of the poem.

The *Inferno* is the first part of Dante's *Divine Comedy*, a story of a man who is facing a crisis of faith and identity and is taught the true nature of reality in guided tours of hell, purgatory, and paradise. Most people read the *Inferno* for its depiction of hell, but the real story of the poem is the moral and spiritual development of the character Dante, who is reported as growing in wisdom throughout the *Divine Comedy*. We see, for example, his changing

Dante Alighieri (c. 1265–1321) is one of the most powerful describers of evil in the Christian tradition.

understanding of the word *pietá*, which means both "piety" and "pity." Dante meets adulterers, deceivers, murderers, and others on his journey; the details of their crimes differ, but they all share one thing in common: They never owned up to what they had done or what they had become. True piety in this situation is to have no pity for the damned; it is to see and judge the damned as God sees and judges them.

To understand what Dante learns in the course of his journey, we have to understand the nature of infernal punishment and the logic of *contrapasso*, "counter-punishment": the way in which each person's punishment perfectly fits his or her defining crime. Indeed, each punishment is a kind of cryptogram that must be decoded by Dante—and us—in order to see the moral reality it represents.

> **Each punishment is a kind of cryptogram that must be decoded by Dante—and us—in order to see the moral reality it represents.**

The most famous lines in the poem are those on the sign above the gates of hell: "Before me nothing was created / that was not eternal, and I endure eternally. / Abandon every hope, you who enter." It's interesting to consider Satan's position with regard to these lines. He is trapped in the ice in a frozen lake at the bottom of hell, but when Dante and Virgil climb out of hell after observing Satan, we find that, in fact, hell is upside down from the perspective of the rest of reality. From the soles of Satan's feet, Dante and Virgil look up and see the Mount of Paradise, on top of which rests God. In other words, Satan is locked in the ice, and he's not just trying to escape the ice; he's still trying to get away from God. In some sense, he is condemning himself to hell by his own activity.

Hell is not extrinsic to the crimes for which the damned are sent there. When Dante saw the adulterous lovers in hell, he felt pity for them. But in refusing to own up to what they had done, the lovers are saying that they don't want to be around God; they don't want to be around the truth. Hell is an extension of the crimes of the damned, their full flowering. Hell is what evil wants to be.

Satan wants more than anything else not to serve God. But everything that is, including Satan, is part of God's system. Thus, Satan's real desire is, in some way, not to be at all. Still, because Satan is a creature of God and finds his own being good, he cannot but want to persevere in that being. Satan's most essential desire—not to be a part of God's creation—conflicts with the foundations of his own essential being; he wants to be and not be at the same time.

Remember that every punishment is a cryptogram of the sin that it punishes. What was the real sin of Satan? His desire to escape God's service. The thing that would turn that sin against itself is to serve as the lynchpin of hell, to become the vehicle whereby God makes hell. Satan's sin is to desire not to serve God, and his punishment is precisely to become one of God's greatest servants. We can go one step further and note that it is the beating of his own wings that keeps Satan trapped in the ice. This reveals the irony in the sign above the gate at the entrance. "Abandon all hope, you who enter" doesn't mean "Just give up now"; it means get over your false hopes, leave your "spin" behind, and you might be able to leave. If you want out of hell, all you have to do is give up hope of getting yourself out. Hell is ultimately self-made and self-inflicted; it's chosen by the damned themselves. ■

Name to Know

Alighieri, Dante (c. 1265–1321 C.E.). Born in Florence, Italy, to a prominent family. Like many of his contemporaries, Dante was thoroughly involved in the controversy between the Guelphs and the Ghibellines, two factions associated with the papacy and the Holy Roman Empire in a struggle for political prominence.

Important Term

contrapasso: Theme in Dante's *Inferno* that emphasizes the continuity between sin and punishment in hell.

Suggested Reading

Dante, *Inferno*, Hollander and Hollander, trans.

Hawkins, *Dante: A Brief History*.

1. Was Dante right in his assertion that we ought not pity the damned? Does true piety also entail a refusal to pity those who are punished for their evil deeds?

2. How would you respond to Dante's suggestion that hell may be an intrinsic (rather than extrinsic) punishment? Is it true that evil often does contain its own punishment and that perhaps hell is the fullest expression of this?

Dante—Hell and the Abandonment of Hope
Lecture 13—Transcript

Welcome back. In the last lecture, we looked at some theoretical formulations, philosophical accounts, of the problem of evil that were very, very abstract; but as I tried to say, they have some very, very powerful and fundamental real-world implications about thinking about the nature of evil and the inner psychology of evil. Now I want to look at a different genre entirely, an epic poem on these topics, which is beautiful and on its surface amazing, but also incredibly profound about the philosophical and theological depths of the problem of evil.

Dante Alighieri certainly deserves to be counted as among the most powerful expositive theological minds of the history of Christianity; that is, one of the most powerful describers of what this tradition has thought about evil, and also about goodness and blessedness, too, in his *Paradiso*, he's fantastic on that. But here we're going to stay entirely in Hell. Dante's vision of Hell in his epic poem the *Inferno* has probably done more to shape Western imaginations of Hell, demons, the Devil, and punishment than any other work. In this lecture, I want to look at three themes in this poem: First of all, the overall logic of Hell, the conceptual architecture of it as it were; the paradoxical logic of what he calls the *contrapasso,* the "counter-penalty," which is at the heart of the nature of punishment in Hell for Dante; and then, last but certainly not least, the ultimate irony and I would say in some important ways the joke, the joke on the Devil, that is at the heart of the whole poem and that many people, perhaps understandably, miss.

Let me give you something of Dante's background here. He lived from 1265–1321 thereabouts—in other words, he overlapped with Aquinas for about 10 years, because Aquinas dies in 1275—and Dante was a Florentine. He was politically engaged, interested in keeping Florence free from outside influence, he served in its army as all young men would, and when he was 9 years old, of course, he met and fell in love with Beatrice Portinari. She was actually younger than 9, so this was like a 9 year old and a 7 year old. Imagine a 9 year old's love for a 7 year old provoking what turns out to be this incredible *Divine Comedy*; the three incredible poems of the *Inferno, Purgatorio,* and *Paradiso*. Beatrice turns out to be the inspiration, the emotional and in some ways intellectual inspiration, for Dante's entire life, although he never actually really gets to know her very well. Eventually, in his life as an active citizen of Florence, the intrigues of the city went against him, and in 1301, on a mission in Rome, Florence fell to a strong group of pro-Papacy Florentines. Dante was not among them; he was in Rome. Dante never set foot in his home city again. Interestingly, the City Council of Florence finally rescinded the punishment of exile on pain of torture and death if he returned to Dante; they finally got him off the hook on that. But do you know when they did it? In 2008. Dante fled to Northern Italy and lived in a series of cities; he eventually died and was buried in Ravenna, an exile, where his tomb remains, even today, guarded by the police of Ravenna who are afraid that some Florentines will try to come and steal his bones back.

The *Inferno* is part of the *Commedia*, the *Divina Commedia*, the *Divine Comedy*—although that's not a term Dante seems to have given it; he just called it the *Commedia*—a story of how a man "at the midpoint of our life's journey," around 35 years old (just before, for Dante, he was exiled) seems to be facing a crisis of faith, of identity, some sort of massive psychological crisis and he is shown mercy by an old love, Beatrice, who is now in Heaven, and is shown that mercy by being taught the true nature of reality in guided tours of Hell, Purgatory, and Paradise. The *Inferno* begins this larger story. It turns out you really do need to go through Hell to get to Heaven; that is, to understand the proper nature of the cosmos and your place in it, you must understand it from where everything ends up, from everything's ultimate destiny, and some things don't end well.

First, let's look at Dante's understanding in the *Inferno* of the meaning and legitimacy of Hell, and its overall logic. It's important to know that even though Hell is the reason most people read the *Inferno*, the real story of the poem itself is, in fact, the moral and spiritual development of the character "Dante" in the poem. The character "Dante" in the poem is reported as growing in wisdom throughout all three poems, but for our purposes really in Hell. The maturation of this character is really what the poem is about. People should see that the great imaginative achievement of the poem is not, then, the pictorial representation of Hell it offers, but the depending appreciation for the meaning of reality that the character "Dante" undergoes.

This is important because by noticing the way that certain language changes for him in significance over the length of the poem, we begin to see how that maturation happens. One important way it does is by noticing the way that Dante changes his understanding of the meaning and the true significance of the word *pietá*. In Italian, especially in late medieval Italian, *pietá* means both "piety" and "pity." What does it mean that piety, a religious sensitivity, and pity, a this-worldly, affective sensitivity, a sensibility to other people's suffering, are lexically identical for Dante? That suggests a tight connection between religious rectitude, religious propriety, and proper emotional responses to situations. Dante agrees with that, but whereas you and I might think that it means that our religious responses must become as sensitive to reality as our emotional ones, Dante proposes that things should go in the opposite direction; that is, that we have to correct our emotional responses, our affective responses to situations in order to have them align to the proper religious ones. That means centrally that in Hell we should not to be nice to the damned.

There's a great example of this early in the poem, in Canto 5, in the fifth song in the fifth chapter. There's the famous story of Paulo and Francesca. These are adulterers who have a sexual affair prompted by their reading together a medieval romance, and they do that by reading their lives into the book they are reading. In other words, there begins to be a confusion for them between the fictional story of the romance and their own interpersonal story at the time that they're reading it. It's a dangerous allegory for Dante of the power of reading in general, especially the power of reading problematically fictive books; it's about Plato worrying about tragedy here. Paolo and Francesca, though, are caught in flagrante, in flagrant sexual intercourse, in bed together by her husband—who is also, by the way, Paolo's brother—and they are killed by him in a fit of fury. They end up in Hell. Dante knows their story in life, and so in the tour of Hell he finds them there. There, in Hell, they are condemned to run in a circle trying to catch each other endlessly, and they never are able properly to actually realize their consummation.

What's interesting about this story, when they tell it to Dante, is that they both blame the book that they were reading for their affair; that is, they don't take responsibility themselves. Dante hears their story, and just as they were overwhelmed by the passions of the book, Dante is overwhelmed by pity for them—by *pietá* for them—and at the end of their story, he faints. In this episode, hearing Dante is just as vulnerable as they are to passion and sympathy, we discover that, in fact, Dante has not yet understood that he is, in fact, responsible for his emotional responses to situations. He doesn't see the sympathy that he has is dangerous in the situation. At the beginning of the *Inferno*, that is, Dante suffers from a kind of theological Stockholm syndrome, an infernal Stockholm syndrome, where it's easy for him to feel pity for people even in situations where pity is properly inappropriate. Virgil, his guide in the *Inferno*, is trying to tell him this throughout, but the only way he learns is by beginning to see over time by meeting and interviewing the damned again and again, by beginning to see they are damned for a reason. Adulterers, deceivers, murderers, cannibals, traitors; the details of all their crimes differ, but they all share one thing in common: they never owned up to what they had done, or what they had thereby become. They never came to terms with what they had done; and in refusing to acknowledge that, in indulging in that kind of self-deception, each person's soul has been warped in some particular way, and that warping now, after their deaths, cannot be undone. Interestingly, part of what it means for their warping to not be able to be undone is that none of the damned in Hell wishes that warping to be undone; none of them want to leave. You hear no true repentance in Hell. There's much grief, and many requests for pity, but no repentance; none of them actually want to get out. We know this from the beginning, although we don't really realize it, because as they walk through Hell they realize the gates of Hell have been smashed down and broken open by Jesus Christ's descent into Hell to rescue those who really want to leave. In other words, Hell is a prison whose gate is open.

True piety, then, before this situation, is to have no pity for the damned because pity for the damned is impious. As Virgil teaches Dante in a famous line: "Here pietá lives when it is quite dead." In other words—and there's a play on "pity" and "piety" in that one—here piety lives when pity is quite dead, that's the crucial thing; and pity lives only when piety is quite dead. True piety for the real Dante, as Dante comes to see over the course of the poem, is thus to see and judge the damned as God sees and judges them. He, in fact, develops a kind of maturity and ability to see properly over the course of the whole book. Near the end of the book, he interviews one of the people who are trapped in ice near the bottom of Hell—the bottom of

Hell, by the way, is not flames, it's ice, which is interesting in itself—but in interviewing this person, the person says, "Will you help me by alleviating the pain from my eyes by wiping the ice away from my eyes?" Dante says, "If I refuse to do that, let me go to the bottom of the ice," which, of course, is where he's going because he's going to go see Satan at the bottom of the ice. He's kind of lying to the damned person, but of course the damned person doesn't know that; so the damned person thinks he's made a promise to do this. Then when Dante refuses to after he's interviewed him, Dante says to us, the audience: "To be rude to him was *cortesia*," was courtesy; to be *villano* to him, to be a villain to him, was to be courteous. To be a villain to the damned is the right thing to do.

What is it that Dante comes to know in this journey that shapes his perceptions in this way? To understand this, you have to understand the nature of infernal punishment itself, which means understanding the meaning of the logic of this term in Italian, *contrapasso*, "counter-punishment": the way that in Hell each person's punishment perfectly fits their defining crime, the crime that defines the particular subspecies of malice that they most determinately indulged in. Indeed each punishment, in a way, is a kind of cryptogram, a coded message that needs to be decoded by us who see it—Dante who sees it, and through Dante's eyes we the audience—in order to see the moral reality it represents. This accounts for all the punishments, including the ultimate punishment reserved for Satan at the very bottom of Hell itself. Each one of these punishments raise all sorts of deep and interesting questions about the moral psychology of evildoers, and in particular about whether they can ever really wholly and purely, without any second thoughts, genuinely will the evil that they do, or whether their conscience inevitably tells against them. This is because of the crucial thing about all of these people: in some sense, they all like their punishments; they all seem to endorse them in some important way. They don't want to leave, they complain about them; but it's like characters in the TV show *Seinfeld*, they just never change. Nothing about them ever changes, including the fact that even though they moan and whine about the punishments, nonetheless there's something about them that they don't seem to mind; the punishments seem what they wanted all along.

This gets us back to the most famous lines in the poem; the lines that have regrettably had the most immediate impact in human history. Let me read them for you, and then I'll say something about that impact. These are, of course, the words on the sign above the broken gates of Hell. Everyone knows the last line, but you have to understand there are nine lines of verse—it's a big sign—above this gate and each of them is enormously important:

> Through me the way to the city of woe,
> through me the way to eternal pain,
> through me the way among the lost people.

Listen to this part:

> Justice moved my most high maker [OK, justice, we can
>   accept that];
> what made me was divine power [certainly, power],
> the highest wisdom, and the primal love.
> Before me nothing was created
> that was not eternal, and I endure eternally.
> Abandon every hope, you who enter.

There's a lot to think about in this passage; most disquietingly and, as I said before, the most direct historical implication of this passage is very disquieting, and that is, of course, that the gate to Auschwitz in the Holocaust had over it a sign as well, and that sign said, "Arbeit macht frei," "Work will make you free," and clearly that sign was modeled on Dante's *Inferno*'s sign. In other words, the diabolical minds—very cultured, but very diabolical— who designed the death camp of Auschwitz actually quoted a fictional text about Hell in an elusive way, but nonetheless there's a clear allusion there, to Dante in designing their death camp. That's an extremely disquieting historical thought; we'll come back to other dimensions of the Holocaust later, but for now, let's go back to Dante and that remarkable nine-line series on what Hell is.

Think about this for Dante; don't think about the abandoned hope yet, you'll have to think about that later. That's a much different line than you think it is. Think about this: Hell was made not just by God's justice, that makes complete sense, but by God's love; the "primal love" is what makes Hell. What does it mean for the highest love to create a Hell? That is, in some important ways, the biggest question at the heart of Dante's picture of Hell; and when Dante comes to see the meaning of that, Dante can then come to understand why, in fact, piety lives here when pity is quite dead. Consider Satan for a second, the last of the damned they see, the king of the dammed, the mayor of Hell; but also in some important way the first inmate of hell. Look at his condition: He's half-sunk in the frozen ice lake at the bottom of Hell; his wings are beating furiously as he is trying apparently to escape the ice; but he also has in his three mouths—the mouths are themselves a parody of the Trinity—the three greatest traitors of human history: Brutus and Cassius, two Roman traitors, and then Judas Iscariot. He's chewing them; he's desperately trying to chew them out of his mouths so that he could, I don't know, breathe, talk, do anything. But, of course, their bodies are continually being reintegrated by God's grace in such a way that they are inevitably needing to be chewed more. Satan is kind of being force fed the greatest traitors of all of reality.

In this situation, which is interesting in so many ways, of course Dante and Virgil, his guide, can't speak to Satan—Satan has these traitors in his mouths—but there's no attempt to communicate with Satan at all; they only watch, they only see. In some sense, there's no way to communicate with this epitome of evil; all you can do is observe it. What is it that they observe? Let's think about Satan's position for a minute. Why is he trapped in this lake of ice? Because the ice is frozen and he's half-sunk in it. But why is the ice frozen? It's because his own wings are beating; that is, his very attempt to escape the ice is what is locking him ever more firmly in the ice. Why is he here at the bottom of Hell; what is this about? Why is he down here; why isn't he in some castle in the center of Hell? Again, he's really not the "Mayor of Hell," he's really Hell's first inmate. Hell itself is a vast crater created by Satan's plummeting fall from Heaven; and at the bottom of that crater, at the dead center of damnation, is where Satan has come to rest. But again, why is Satan resting there? Is he resting? I don't think so. I don't think there's any rest involved for Satan; he's desperate to flee. But what is it exactly he's fleeing? What exactly is he trying to do, just get out of the ice?

It turns out it's more complicated than that: As Dante and Virgil climb out of Hell, they go over to Satan's body and then climb down his legs out of Hell. It turns out that as they climb down, they have to turn around and start climbing up again, not up his body, but directionality itself reverses on Satan; it turns out, in other words, that Hell itself has all been upside down. As they get out, crawling off of Satan's I think it's his feet, that's when they get outside and they first see the stars, and it's Easter morning. That's the great allegory of this is that it starts on Good Friday when they enter Hell and they get out of Hell on Easter morning, following Jesus. But the crucial thing here is that Satan is upside down in the ice from the perspective of the rest of reality. What does that mean? From the soles of Satan's feet, they can look up, and there is the mount of paradise on top of which is God. In other words, Satan is locked in the ice, and he's not just trying to escape the ice, he's still trying to get away from God.

Here's the astonishing thought: Satan is in some sense condemning himself to be in Hell by his own activity. As I've said, people are in Hell in some sense because they want to be there. Only in the 20th century, I think, in C.S. Lewis's wonderful little allegory *The Great Divorce* do we come across a similar view of what Hell is. The upshot of all of this is that Hell is not essentially an extrinsic punishment for people who have been bad; Hell is in some important way intrinsic to their sins themselves. An [extrinsic] punishment is getting a spanking for taking your sister's candy. The spanking is extrinsic to the act of taking the candy; it's outside of that act, it's not necessarily part of the act of robbery. It is a separate thing that happens to you as a kind of consequence by your parents of you stealing the candy. An intrinsic punishment is what happens to you when you get violently sick after you've crammed down your gullet all of your sister's candy. Then, the sickness is very consequentially related to the eating of the candy and to its theft.

Hell is not extrinsic to the crimes for which the damned are sent there. That was Dante's problem with Paolo and Francesca; he thought, "Oh, these poor people just fell in love, who can really blame them for that?" It wasn't so much the falling in love, it was the falling in love, committing adultery, and then refusing to own up to what they had done; and in doing those things, the point is for Dante, these people, in refusing to own up for what they have done, are already saying they don't want to be around God. They don't want to be around the truth; they want to live in a kind of duplicitous place. Hell, for Dante, is that place; Hell is just the extension of the damned's crimes, their full flowering. Hell is what evil has wanted to be, for Dante, all along.

Consider all the damned: They have profoundly mixed desires; they have ambivalent longings. Think about Satan again: On the one hand, Satan wants more than anything else not to serve God, not to work in God's system, not to be a part of God's great plan; Satan's motto could be, "I will not service," *Non serviam*, in Latin. But here's the catch (think back to Aquinas or Anselm on this): Everything that is, including Satan in Satan's very being, is part of God's system. Thus Satan's real desire is, in some way, not to be at all. Think back to Aquinas: Dante actually slightly disagrees with Aquinas here; he says even though Satan might not be able to say this to himself that is actually Satan's real longing. Satan's rebellion, Satan's sin, is not actually an imposition against God, it is most basically a form of flight; a form of flight that longs to take the ultimate flying out of the way as possible: the ultimate metaphysical form, which is self-annihilation. But Satan, just because Satan is a being, a creature of God and finds his own being good, also cannot but want to persevere that being; to continue in existence. So Satan's most essential desire—not to be a part of God's creation—conflicts with the foundations of Satan's own essential being; and Satan wants to be and not be at the same time (much like a teenager in this way).

Satan has created the crater, we saw, that's at the bottom of Hell, and Satan is at the bottom of that crater, sunk in that frozen lake—a lake frozen and kept frozen by the furious beating of Satan's own wings—but his desire is not simply to flee that lake; remember that his desire is to keep going this way because down that way he's realized he's upside down, down that way is God. In other words, Satan's own captivity is not only imposed by Satan on himself, but is imposed by Satan on himself by God in the background as a way of stopping Satan's flight. All of this is a tremendous symbol of Satan's confusion.

But what is the *contrapasso* here for Satan? What is the real punishment that Satan is enduring? Is it just being frozen in a lake and being forced to eat bad people? That doesn't seem like much. I mean, we've seen people split from head to toe, cut in two; we've seen people eating each other earlier in the *Inferno*. Remember, every punishment is a cryptogram of the sin that it punishes. What was the real sin of Satan? The real sin of Satan was his desire to escape God, escape God's service. I really think that Satan on Satan's business cards has, "Satan, Non Serviam," "I do not serve"; that's Satan's motto, that's his corporate logo. If that's Satan's sin, not to want to serve, what is the quintessential punishment, the thing that would turn that sin against itself? Of course, it is to serve as the absolute lynchpin of Hell itself; to become the vehicle whereby God makes Hell, and to be the instrument of the darkest punishment of the lowest of the traitors at the base of Hell. Satan's sin is to desire not to serve God, and Satan's punishment is precisely to become one of the greatest servants of God one could be.

Think about this just one more step: What would stop Satan from being trapped here? Why, nothing more than stopping beating his own wings. It's they, after all, that freeze his body into the lake. Why doesn't he just do that? This reveals the incredible irony in the sign above the gate at the entry to Hell. On that sign, that last line, "Abandon all hope you who enter here" can sound like a "Just give up now, you better just give up all hope"; in fact, it also means something else: It means get over your false hopes, leave your spin behind, and you might be able to leave. If you want out of Hell, all you have to do is give up hope of getting yourself out of Hell and then you can just walk out. Above the gates of Hell are the instructions for escaping Hell.

So Satan is truly punished precisely because he wants to not serve the good by serving the good. But is that punishment? Who doesn't want to serve the good? Only insane people would do that, perhaps. Is Satan insane? In a way maybe; he wants to die, as thoroughly as anyone can genuinely want that end. But that's not a perfect and whole-hearted desire, because no creature can desire that whole-heartedly; so Satan is, again, most fundamentally confused, ambivalent. God lets Satan have Satan's way as far as possible; God lets Satan do what Satan wants. But still Satan's actual desire can't finally make sense, and Satan can't get outside of being God's creature. Hell, then, is self-made and self-inflicted; it's chosen in some profound but utterly mysterious way by the damned. They don't just get what they deserve, that is, they get what, in some utterly mysterious way, they actually want.

Dante's picture of evil is not properly understood here as direct advice about how to deal with the realities of evil and suffering in this life; that's not his aim in this poem. His aim is really indirectly useful for that, but its central purpose is the spiritual and ethical reeducation of one soul in our life, a soul who has lost his way; personified in the character Dante in the poem, but really referring to all of us in this life, wandering as we all are in our own dark woods, sometimes, and for some of us, more dark than others. The poem, then, is really an effort to help us resist the enormous tidal power of the habituated sin of our world, sin in which we more or less all heartily participate, and to teach us to replace that habituated sinful vision with a new vision of good and evil. Remember here Augustine saying he wanted to teach us how not to know what we should not know. Only insofar as the poem does that, only insofar as it teaches us to see through evil's spurious self-presentation, can it have any practical effects on our world. This is the lesson about evil that Dante most desperately wants to teach.

From Dante now we're going to move to a very different context; the one that is in important ways not entirely disanalogous to Dante's own: the Reformation.

The Reformation—The Power of Evil Within
Lecture 14

> The proper theological term for what Calvin believed in and affirmed is a "super-lapsarian double predestination." That's a pretty impressive thing; it sounds like, again, something you'd expect an Olympic gymnast to do or something.

In this lecture, we move into the Reformation and the boundaries of the modern world. The two thinkers we'll encounter, **Martin Luther** and **Jean Calvin**, are influenced by the past but also profoundly innovative and, in some ways, set the terms for much that will come.

The Reformation emerged amid increasing concern about the stability of the created order. Massive social change—the beginnings of an industrial revolution and a booming economy—had occurred in the wake of the devastation of the Black Death. Intellectually, people were beginning to develop new ways to understand and organize society and the cosmos.

The thinking of Martin Luther grew out of anxieties related to the individual's relationship to God in this age of social change. For Luther, the church was a secondary expression of this relationship. He believed that God is absolutely powerful and completely sovereign but mysteriously hidden from us. All we have is the God visible in the Scriptures and in Jesus Christ. The distance between the human Christ and the all-powerful God is the space in which the devil plays with us. The devil, for Luther, is an inner power, able to corrupt faith. He is immaterial, but he obstructs and mystifies humans into making terrible choices. And he is most interested in striking at those who are serious about being good Christians.

One of the most important concepts in Luther's thinking is "works righteousness"; this is the idea that we are made good by what we do, that in some sense, we have to earn or deserve our salvation. The devil loves this idea, insofar as he can insinuate it into our minds: that we would have anything to do with our salvation and, thus, could claim any credit for our salvation. For Luther, the response we should use when confronted with the temptation to think this way is simple: Instead of trying to fight the devil ourselves, we must appeal to Christ to protect us.

The picture of evil that Luther offers is not one of threat or immediate danger; it is, rather, of deception and obscurity. To counteract evil, Luther insists on the absolute governance of the world by a sovereign and providential deity. God's providential mastery over creation is so important to Luther that he's willing to ascribe a responsibility for evil to God. To explain this responsibility, he appeals to the idea of the inscrutability of divine providence, the lives of Abraham and Job, and the prophetic tradition's interpretation of the travails of ancient Israel. Any attempt to master God's providential control over history on our part will fail. Direct, immediate resistance to evil is a collapse into evil itself, because it returns us to relying on ourselves.

Martin Luther (1483–1546) was a trained medieval Scholastic, versed in the thought of Aquinas and Anselm.

The thinking of Jean Calvin presents a very different picture. Calvin is famous for his ideas of predestination and the total depravity of humanity. He believed that the blessed are predestined to heaven and the damned are predestined to hell, and they are both predestined in those ways from before the Fall. In other words, before humans fell, God foreknew and preordained—not just knew but determined—that some would be blessed and some would be damned. This doctrine of election means that everything about you is outside of your immediate control. This is good news for Calvin precisely because of the doctrine of total depravity.

Calvin believes that human nature was changed—deranged—in the Fall, but it's not evil. Humans are trapped in sin, but they are not actually compelled to sin; our desires are so warped that we actually want to sin. This means that without God's providential control over our lives, we are certain to send ourselves to hell. It is only the mysterious, gracious providence of God's love that allows any of us to be corrected from our own completely idolatrous ways to move toward salvation. For Calvin, unlike Luther, there's very little active place for Satan in this thinking. The human mind itself does more than enough to make evil happen in the world.

What happens in the Christian life to resist Calvin's picture of drowning in sin is sanctification. This is the practice whereby those Christians who have been saved come ever more fully to live their lives as holy people. Evil resists sanctification because evil is slothful, narcissistic, and inward-turning; sanctification is an increasing direction of our energy outward to one another and to God. We must not do anything but understand ourselves as redeemed by God, and part of that redemption is a renunciation of our own perpetual efforts to hide from our reality. Christians are not free from sin for Calvin; in fact, they are never more sensible of sin, their own and others, than when they have been saved. ∎

Names to Know

Calvin, Jean (1509–1564 C.E.). Calvin was born in France and studied philosophy and law. He was strongly influenced by French humanism and was eventually forced to flee France because of his call for Catholic reforms.

Luther, Martin (1483–1546 C.E.). Born in Eisleben, Germany, a city that was then part of the Holy Roman Empire. Luther briefly studied law but became a monk in the Augustinian order after making a vow during a lightning storm.

Suggested Reading

Calvin, *Institutes of the Christian Religion*, McNeill, ed., Battles, trans.

Gordon, *Calvin*.

Luther, *Basic Theological Writings*, Lull, Russell, and Pelikan, eds.

Obermann, *Luther: Man between God and the Devil*, Walliser-Schwarzbart, trans.

1. As noted in the lecture, the thinkers of the Reformation did not emerge out of thin air; rather, their innovations concerning the nature of evil were thoroughly related to their historical experience of dislocation, disease, and change. What analogous historical or cultural experiences are shaping our current conceptions of evil?

2. For Luther, the devil was profoundly powerful, though utterly immaterial. Do you agree with Luther that evil is always tempting but never compelling? Can the devil ever "make" someone do anything?

3. Calvin famously argued that all aspects of creation—including evil itself—exist under God's providential governance. Does this emphasis on governance risk making God too complicit in evil? How can God allow but not endorse evil?

The Reformation—The Power of Evil Within
Lecture 14—Transcript

Hello again. In this lecture, I want to shift from the medieval world into the early modern world, especially focusing on the high reformers, Martin Luther and Jean Calvin.

Before we go on, I want to pause a little bit here to kind of sum up where we've been. In some ways, in moving into the Reformation we're moving into the edge of the modern world. These thinkers begin to be people who are remarkably like us in our thoughts and our patterns of belief and behavior, and many of the assumptions that they have or they begin to formulate are assumptions that we have as well. To understand this, it will be useful to remind us of something of where we've been up until now. We've seen some very early Ancient Near Eastern accounts of the combat myth; we saw the heritage of classical Greek, both tragic and philosophical in its dimensions; we saw the initial formulations of the Hebrew Bible and the Christian New Testament, and then Rabbinic Judaism and a series of Christian views and Islamic views, culminating in some ways for us in the classical formulations of these things in the high Middle Ages. Now, at the threshold of the "modern world," we come to two thinkers who are profoundly influenced by the past but also profoundly innovative, and in some ways set the terms for much that will come precisely in the ways that they play with and resist the inheritance they received from the past.

We'll see in different ways that Martin Luther, a trained medieval scholastic, someone who was deeply versed in the thought of Aquinas and Anselm among others, understands evil in a particular way; and we'll see in a second that he in interesting ways sees the Devil as in some significant ways like a theologian. Calvin, on the other hand, is not a classically trained theologian or philosopher, he's not a scholastic; he, in fact, was a trained Renaissance humanist lawyer. It's interesting to think about Jean Calvin, who we think of in some ways the classic theologian, is actually trained as a lawyer and as a humanist, someone who was interested in literature and literary text. Calvin, where Luther sees and in some ways plays up this metaphor of the Devil as a kind of theological, Calvin sees the challenge of evil to lie in the endlessly inventive character of the human imagination; the interiority of the human.

Something that other Renaissance figures—again, the world he was trained in—identified and praised in humans, Calvin sees as precisely the locus of the problem of evil.

In the Reformation, thinkers took up with new seriousness the possibility that there was a genuine positivity to Satan's power that was in some ways at odds with traditional Augustinian and Scholastic understandings of evil out of which these thinkers had sprung. This was, in important ways, because of the context out of which the Reformation itself came. The Reformation emerged in a world where there was an increasing, slowly-growing concern about the stability of the created order. There had been massive social change, the beginnings of an industrial revolution were happening, and a booming economy. All of this happened in the wake of probably the greatest catastrophe that the West has known in the last 4,000 years: the Black Death.

In the one year of 1348, from the port city of Caffa in the Black Sea stretching all the way into Scotland and to Portugal, the plague that became known as the Black Death—what we think of now, we think it was the bubonic plague—swept across Western Europe and killed an enormous swath of the population. Fully somewhere between a third and a half of the population died from this plague. If you caught the plague, from the first showing of the symptoms—from the beginning of welts on your arms, maybe a light fever—you had about four or five days to live, and roughly four out of five people who caught the plague did not survive. Thus, 1348: At the end of that year, fully between one-half and one-third of the population of Europe was gone, and gone in a heartbeat. Imagine if at this time next week you woke up and half of your family was dead; that's the kind of trauma that's put on the entirety of Western European civilization.

After the Black Plague, there were enormous social changes. First of all, labor had begun to be much rarer, and so peasants were actually able to agitate for more rights and more wealth; so you get the beginnings of an actual shifting of wealth in Europe away from the old model of serfdom more towards an attempt to actually generate a peasant class that had some property of its own. About 100 years after this, in 1453, Constantinople, the last vestige that Western Europe sees of the Roman Empire, the last direct connection to the classical past, falls to the Ottoman Turks. Apart from Russia and a few sovereigns in the East, all of Christendom, all of Christianity—at least as the West understands it—is now contained within the boundaries of Europe itself. At about this time, Europeans, having recovered from the Black Death, begin to send out their tendrils of exploration and trade on ships that go all the way around the world. Remember that Columbus discovers the New World, he discovers the Americas, in 1492; so the discovery and exploration of the Americas is happening at exactly the same time that the Reformation is happening.

Furthermore, the capacity of humans to know what is going on in this changing social order—intellectually developing ideas of new ways of understanding and organizing society and new ways of understanding and organizing the cosmos—are growing as well. There's a sense that knowledge of the world and of our past was outstripping the capacity of medieval scholastic modes of knowing to accommodate it. The Late Middle Ages also, though, were a deeply fraught time, full of dynamism, change and reaction, plague—we've seen that already—wars, rumors of wars, and powerful currents of religious energy. Luther may have been the very, very most famous reformer of this period, but almost a century before Luther another reformer had appeared, Jan Hus, who, had he survived, might very well have had a reformation of his own in that day, but he was caught and executed at the Council of Constance in the early 15th century.

Sometimes, to some people, it can seem as if Luther and the whole Reformation appeared like a comet streaking across the sky; but, in fact, the world of his time was crowded with just the sorts of energies that enabled the Reformation to take root and grow. There were profound anxieties about the apocalypse and particularly about the idea of the antichrist; the idea of a figure that comes and seems promisingly messianic but is actually evil cloaked in goodness, corruption hidden in glorious magnificence. There was a deep spiritual and intellectual paranoia abroad in the land in the late Middle Ages. All this is manifest in the late medieval theology, especially in its renewed emphasis—this is the generation's before Luther—on the revolutionary power of God and the utter unknowable abyss of God's absolute power and will. In different ways, Luther and Calvin will eventually take up this heritage and use this emphasis on the power and sovereignty of God in ways that are revolutionary.

Let me say something about Luther first: Martin Luther started off his career (we can say) as a monk and a professor. He ended as a preacher, a hymnodist (writer of hymns), and a husband and father of six. He and his wife, Katalina—who was a former nun herself—had six children, four of whom survived to adulthood. He lived from 1483–1546. Luther worked out of anxieties, as I've said, that were abroad in his day; larger concerns about one's personal relation to God and the identity of the person in an age of increasing wealth and social change, particularly when people were growing increasingly impatient with the corruptions of the church. For Luther, in some important ways, the church is a secondary expression of the relationship between God and the human; and this is very much in opposition to church thinking of his time, which wanted to put the church between God and the individual. For Luther, God is absolutely powerful and completely sovereign. But this omnipotent God—complete, sovereign God—is mysteriously hidden from us; all we have in this life is the God visible in the scriptures in Jesus Christ. The distance between the human Christ, who teaches and preaches and dies on the cross and is raised again, is the space in which the Devil plays with us; that distance between the all-powerful God and the human Christ.

Satan, for Luther, is a powerful, powerful figure, but in an interesting and subtle way. He's not a monster or a bogeyman, Satan is an inner power, able to corrupt faith. Satan is immaterial; Satan does not touch you; Satan has no physical menace to you. The Devil, rather, for Luther, is a tempter and a deceiver; a deluding agent who would obstruct, trick, and mystify humans into making terrible choices. The Devil attempts to mislead you, to corrupt and deflect you, in order to get you to hurt yourself. The Devil works, that is, by seducing you into bad thinking. The Devil can, and most definitely does, quote Scripture. The Devil is a theologian.

Certainly some of Luther's depiction of the Devil comes out of his own conflicts with other Christian intellectuals and leaders of the churches at that time; certainly some of it comes out of Luther's own intellectual anxieties and paranoia; but something there is also extremely, I think, psychologically acute, for this Devil's power does not come through sheer muscular strength, but rather through how he can work to disrupt your own proper reasoning. This Satan may not be very terrifying at first, but what he lacks for Luther in

191

grandeur, he more than makes up for in subtlety. The devil comes to people who are serious about being good Christians, who are trying to be sincere; that's who the devil strikes. The people who are just happy to eat, drink, and be merry because they don't care about the fate of their immortal souls, the Devil already has those; he doesn't' have to worry about those people. He's not interested in them; he's trying to get the people who he doesn't have yet. Those are the people who the Devil is most interested in.

In Luther's own experience—he reports this in a number of sermons and also treatises—he says, "I encounter the Devil most immediately and most frequently just at those moments when I am tempted to rely on myself." In other words, the Devil is the insinuation that maybe I should be the one to figure this thing out; maybe I can do this on my own; maybe I don't need the help of God; maybe I don't have to pray for Christ's grace in accomplishing this task. Go back to Eve in the Garden, at least as Paul—and after Paul, Augustine and Luther himself—will interpret that: What happens to Eve when she sees the fruit? Again, she's like God; she feels that she can make this judgment. Just as God saw that creation as good, now Eve sees the fruit as good. For Luther, this is a paradigmatic example of how the Devil gets inside peoples' minds who are, in some sense, trying to be good people, but manages to warp them in disastrous ways.

This gets to one of the most important phrases of Luther's work, and that is "works-righteousness"; the Devil is all about "works-righteousness." What is that? Works-righteousness is the idea that we are made good by what we do, by what we accomplish; that in some sense we have to earn or deserve our salvation. The Devil is all about this idea; the Devil loves the idea, insofar as he can insinuate it into our minds, that we would have anything to do with our salvation and thus could claim any credit for our salvation and for what Luther calls the "theology of glory," a theology that is all about glorifying ourselves, talking about ourselves as achievers, people who have accomplished something. For Luther, the response to evil that we should employ when we are confronted with these temptations is simple: You can't engage the Devil; you can't resist the Devil. That's not what you should do; you should not see this temptation and say, "I will fight that." That is, in fact, already playing the Devil's game, because now you are trying to fight the

Devil on your own. Instead, Luther thinks, you have to appeal to Christ to protect you from the Devil.

In this way, Luther's big innovation really is the kind of remarkable character that Satan is in his writings; and in recent years, many scholars have emphasized the reality of Satan for Luther. But, in fact, the Satan that is real for Luther is a Satan who is really quite immaterial; who works wholly by means of messing with human subjectivity, with messing with our interiority, with our pride and with our thought. For Luther, this Devil is external, able to affect only thinking and our way of seeing the world. This Devil is not a muscular threat to us. Instead, the picture of evil that Luther is offering us here is not one of threat, of immediate danger, of peril; it is, rather, of deception and obscurity. Evil doesn't only lurk in uncertainty and confusion—that's a classic line about Luther's thought, that for Luther uncertainty is, in fact, a sign of sin; that might be true, but it's not quite exact—evil actually is uncertainty and confusion. To counteract this picture of evil, then, Luther insists on the absolute governance of the world by a sovereign and providential deity. We may not know how that God is governing the world, but nonetheless we know that God is in charge. In fact, God's providential mastery over creation is so important to Luther that he's willing to ascribe a responsibility for evil, even evil, to this God.

As early as his quite early work, *On the Bondage of the Will*—one he writes only a couple years after he writes his famous "95 Theses"—Luther emphasizes that God's providential control is over all aspects of our lives, even the evil aspects. How? This is a mystery for Luther; and here he appeals to the idea of the inscrutability of divine providence, the lives of Abraham and Job, and the prophetic tradition's interpretation of the travails of Ancient Israel. But what Luther knows is that any attempt to master God's providential control over history on our part will fail; all we must do and all we can do is appeal to Christ as our savior in this situation. Direct, immediate resistance to evil turns out to be, for Luther, a kind of collapse into evil itself; because, once again, we would be trying to rely on ourselves.

With the thinker of Jean Calvin, we have a very different picture. Calvin is about 25 years or so younger than Luther; he's born in 1509 and he dies in 1564. He's trained in a very different world. He's trained as a French humanist, trained as a lawyer, and in those roles his background and his expectations about what happens in the world are very different from a medieval scholastic monk's, which is what Luther was. Calvin, though, became the second great Reformer after Luther, and he eventually settled and lived out most of his life in Geneva, which he made the headquarters of the international Reformation. Calvin's, unlike Luther's in interesting ways, was a reformation of refugees; it was a cosmopolitan reformation of fugitives. First of all, political fugitives: Many of the people who came to Geneva, and Calvin himself, were actually there because they had fled from other places, fled from persecution elsewhere; and then they went out from Geneva to the rest of the world preaching the Gospel in new ways, but always alert to the fact that they had been at one point refugees. Not just literal refugees, but more profoundly for Calvin theologically, refugees from Satan on the roads of the earth. In fact, it's interesting to think about how often Calvin's examples, his theological stories, include travelers on the roads. Luther's, in contrast, often take place with people sitting down at tables drinking beer (Luther loved beer), or desks, writing (Luther loved nothing more than writing with beer beside him), or in bed (Luther did love sleeping). Calvin, on the other hand, always talks about Christians as being on the road. This is a Reformation that is emphasizing the exodus character of the Christian life; the idea that everyone is a pilgrim in this world.

Famously, Calvin, of course, you think about Calvin you think about what? You think about predestination and the idea of the total depravity of humanity. These are two important things that we need to take a little time to explain. First of all, let's be as up front as possible about Calvin's understanding of predestination. He was pretty serious about it. In fact, and this sounds like something the Harlem Globetrotters would do, but the proper theological term for what Calvin believed in and affirmed is a super-lapsarian double predestination. That's a pretty impressive thing; it sounds like, again, something you'd expect an Olympic gymnast to do or something. What it means is that Calvin believes that the blessed are predestined to Heaven and the damned are predestined to Hell, and they are both predestined in those ways—that's a double predestination—from before the Fall; "super lapsos," "before the lapse," "before the Fall." Calvin thinks that before humans fell, God foreknew and preordained—not just knew but determined, ordered, willed—that some would be blessed and some would be damned.

That's an astonishing thought; how does he get there? How does Calvin think this is a useful theological thought? Because, in fact, he does. What's interesting about the discussion of providence in his masterwork, the *Institutes of the Christian Religion*, is that Calvin takes it as a crucial thing that God's providential control is over all aspects of our lives, even the evil aspects. In fact, Calvin took the doctrine of election as itself a kind of doctrine of comfort. We used to joke that when we send students out to the job market in academia that it's only when you're trying to figure out where you will be working in the next year, where you'll get an academic job, and you realize you have no control over the market, no control over who interviews you, who picks up your resume, who doesn't; when you realize the utter lack of control you have over your life, it's only at that point that Calvin's doctrine of election truly becomes a doctrine of comfort for you. What the doctrine of election means is really quite simple: It means that, in fact, everything about you is outside of your immediate control. Again, Calvin thinks this is a good thing; this is good news for Calvin. Why? This gets us to the second point: Calvin's doctrine of total depravity.

Total depravity here—his assessment of the human as totally depraved—is not nihilism; the human is not utterly evil, just thoroughly corrupted. The human's nature has been changed, deranged in the Fall; but it's not, per se, evil. The sinful human is perverted, but because the human is essentially creative—again, this is a residue of Calvin's renaissance humanism here— this is the mind is an unceasingly laboring "factory of idols." For Calvin, the mind is a fertile ground for evil, lustful and ever-changing. Humans are trapped in sin, but they are not actually compelled to do this; rather, it is the way their psychologies are set up that they want to sin. Their desires are so warped that they actually want to sin; they desire to make idols of things. This means that absent God's providential control over your life, you are yourself certain to send yourself to Hell. It is only the mysterious gracious providence of God's generous love that allows any of us to be corrected from our own completely idolatrous, own personal ways to move towards salvation in any solid way.

For Calvin, unlike Luther for example, there's very little really active place for Satan in his thinking; there's no need for a powerful Satan. The human mind does more than enough good duty for Calvin in making evil happen in the world. Calvin's renaissance humanism, as it were, allows for the idea that the human has a great deal of power; but, of course, what that does is turn the humans' capacity for power directly to evil. Interestingly, for Calvin, the metaphoric seduction into evil is not a big one as it was for Luther; instead, what you get is a metaphor of drowning. Evil, sin, death, indirectly the Devil; these things always threaten to drown you for Calvin, and the drowning is a falling back into your own self, a falling back into your own ego. That's the thing for Calvin that Hell is; it's not so much an assertion of pride as it is a collapse back into the self.

What happens in the Christian life to resist this for Calvin—and this is the other huge development that Calvin offers the rest of modernity and definitely the rest of Protestant Christianity—is sanctification. The practice of sanctification is the practice whereby those Christians who have been saved come ever more fully to live into their lives as sanctified and holy people. Evil resists sanctification because evil is slothful and narcissistic, and turned inward; sanctification is a growing deepening of our energy and a growing deepening of our turning outward to one another and to God. Sanctification explains why, for Calvin and for all who came after him— the Reformed tradition of Protestant Presbyterianism that came after him— why discipline is so important. Discipline is the central immediate strategy to counteract evil. If evil wants us to lounge around in our self, to wallow narcissistically in ourselves, to drown ourselves in ourselves, the remedy to all of this is to practice discipline and to be disciplined about what we do in every day, and by doing this to come to see ourselves aright; to see your sins, which are hidden from us and which our mind continually tries to distract us from by luring us to think about other things, and to be able in seeing our sins to see them as things that God has saved us from.

What you must do, then, is not do anything but understand yourself as redeemed by God; and part of that redemption is a renunciation of your own perpetual effort to hide from your reality. When you give that up, when you give up that duplicity, that self-deception, you come to see that, in fact, you're completely screwed up; again, nature is deranged for Calvin. Grace, and through grace the reading of the Bible—which functions as a kind of set of "spectacles" for Calvin in seeing the world aright—helps you come to see the world as properly a place of sin. This is very important for Calvin, and something that is often forgotten both by critics of Calvin and sometimes by Calvin's heirs: Christians are not free from sin for Calvin; in a way, they are on the way to being free from sin, but in another way they are never more sensible of sin, their own and others, than when they have been saved. In fact, in the process of sanctification, after they have been justified, that is the only time they are able genuinely to see the sins they have been caught up in. Knowledge of sin, then, is, in a way, a sign of election and it is also a sign of retrospection; it's a sign of reflection on your history that makes sense of your history in a new kind of world. This is important. A later Calvinist—someone we'll look at later in this lecture series, actually—Karl Barth, famously said (famously to people like myself) "only Christians can sin." What he meant by that is interesting: He means that it is only from within the condition of attempting to live out a genuinely Christian life, only from within the Christian story, can a person come to see who they have been and who they still all-too much are, namely, a sinner.

To solve the problem of evil, then, it's arguable that in certain ways both Luther and Calvin kind of incorporated evil more immediately into God than anyone else we've seen so far, or at least seen recently. Luther and Calvin both understood themselves to be challenging traditional medieval notions of good and evil, whereas evil in the form of Satan had been admitted earlier to be under God's final control. By the late Middle Ages anyway, Christian understandings of Satan had again begun to slip away from under God's sovereignty, so that Lucifer seemed to a lot of late medieval thinkers and believers a rival independent force to God that humans had to contend with on their own. That's a fairly anxiety-inducing thought.

Luther and Calvin both responded to this, paradoxically perhaps, by diminishing human power and strengthening Satan's subtlety and wiles, but only because that would make humans more likely to despair of their own power and appeal instead to God's infinite power. But the effect of this is to further the interiorization of evil; its deepening in our inner selves, its representation as inside of us. Essentially for both Luther and Calvin, the struggle with evil takes place in the human soul, not in the cosmos (as in the Book of Revelation) or in human history (as with Saint Augustine), but rather in the lonely and individual.

Innovation is not necessarily a bad thing; it's possible to revolutionize understandings of evil and not be condemned for it. We see how far and how quickly this went with our next figure: Niccolò Machiavelli.

Dark Politics—Machiavelli on How to Be Bad
Lecture 15

The central aim is stability, but you have to understand people's psychologies—how they resent things and how to quiet those resentments—not because you want them to like you, but because you don't want them to render the political community unstable.

With this lecture, we move into more secular approaches to the question of evil. Here, God looks very far away at best, and morality may be real but only a small part of the world that we inhabit.

Niccolo Machiavelli is a famous figure but often misunderstood. He notoriously said, "The prince must love his city more than his soul" and, in order to love his city correctly, must learn how not to be good. Machiavelli seems to be the first person to think that the reality of evil in politics is inescapable and that the prince, instead of trying to resist it, should, at certain points and in certain ways, work with the grain of politics rather than against it in favor of a larger moral aim.

Machiavelli is often thought of as a relativist, a nihilist, a man who counseled mendacity, duplicity, skulduggery, and a bloody-minded malfeasance to politicians. Although Machiavelli himself would not have been entirely displeased to have his works become camouflaged by that reputation, for those who read him carefully, another and more profound meaning emerges. His basic idea is that goodness and virtue are real but that moral perfection cannot provide any simple guidelines for the governance of our world, especially in politics. This is why the prince or any political ruler must learn how not to be good.

Machiavelli believes that a prince is wise to punish rebels against the realm even after they have surrendered, primarily because their punishment will deter others from undertaking similar rebellions. Fear is an important political motivator. Even more controversially, Machiavelli recommends the use of proxies for especially unpleasant deeds, proxies whom the prince can later turn on and punish for performing those very deeds. This approach defuses the resentments of the citizenry by directing them to a suitable target, who can then be properly punished, avoiding future instability in the realm. The integrity of a political agenda is, for Machiavelli, the absolute baseline for a successful political regime.

This line of thinking represents a significant change from earlier political treatises, which first and foremost, exhorted rulers to be good and moral. For Machiavelli, this is simply unrealistic, both in terms of what is possible for political rulers and because it mistakes the cause and effect of certain actions in the polity. A nice and decent ruler may seem weak to some people; a just ruler may be unable to defuse the resentment of those who were against his getting into power. Thus, a simple moralism in politics may be against the good of the polis.

Machiavelli believes that people are governed by two broad categories of motivation in politics: their loves and their fears—and primarily the latter.

The central political anxiety for Machiavelli is instability. We must be able to ensure stability in the world for any of the other goods of politics or private life to go forward. This means that the stability of the political order must come before the ethical happiness of that order. Politics is extremely complicated. How can we anticipate that morality will result in some useful system with which to govern the lives of the citizens when we can't ensure that everyone agrees about what's right and wrong? In fact, we know that politics inevitably generates different judgments from different people. Simply telling people that they ought to be good sets politicians up to lose.

Machiavelli believes that people are governed by two broad categories of motivation in politics: their loves and their fears—and primarily the latter. Rulers, he says, can rely on the idea that people are much more likely to do things if they are frightened by concrete threats than if they are offered vague hopes of good things in the future. Machiavelli also believes that *fortuna*, "fortune" or "luck," plays a significant role in politics. In this realm, luck or accident might take the form of an economic crisis or a military threat. Such events are not in the ruler's control, yet he is responsible for facing them, and at times, he may have to take unpleasant actions to secure the good of the community. Much of this is read as strategies for being a wicked ruler, but Machiavelli is not trying to teach people how to be evil. Rather, he says that the most powerful medicine against the prince's corruption is his ability to control situations where unpleasant actions must be undertaken. Machiavelli wants to teach rulers how to be evil in a cold-blooded way so that the evil doesn't infect them and make them entirely hot-blooded evildoers. This is why being a prince is so difficult; a prince must make a stone of his heart.

Machiavelli advocates a certain cold-eyed realism about the political world, but his thinking also speaks to us of the need to resist pretty ideas. For Machiavelli, politics is the art of the possible, not the art of the ideal. ■

Name to Know

Machiavelli, Niccolo (1469–1527 C.E.). Born in Florence, Italy, where he received a classical education and training in service to the Florentine state.

Suggested Reading

Machiavelli, *The Portable Machiavelli*, Bonadella and Musa, eds.

Skinner, *Machiavelli: A Very Brief Introduction*.

Questions to Consider

1. Do we expect our rulers to be "bad" for the sake of our polity? Was Machiavelli right to insist that a ruler ought not be good but, rather, be willing to do wrong for the sake of his or her country?

2. Do you read Machiavelli's position as a "realistic" or a pessimistic one? Should we expect that virtue and politics go well together or not?

3. How do we see Machiavelli's ideas at work in the contemporary world of politics?

Dark Politics—Machiavelli on How to Be Bad
Lecture 15—Transcript

Welcome back. After the Reformation, we're going to be moving into some more frankly secular approaches. We'll come back to some religious approaches in a little while, too; but at this point, now the possibility of a wholly secular picture of evil begins to be possible in Europe in a way that it wasn't, apparently, before. On these pictures: God looks very far away at best, and morality becomes something quite different for these thinkers. The difference can be shown by a simple question: Does the end justify the means? For earlier thinkers like Augustine or Aquinas, that's a hard thought even to conceive of. Some ancient thinkers would have rejected justice as a coherent idea; someone like Thrasymachus, or Thucydides's representation of the Athenians on the island of Melos. Others would say that justice does not need worldly justification. It's only with Niccolò Machiavelli that we begin to get the idea that some things may be made good by what they accomplish; that, in other words, morality may be real but only a small part of the world that we inhabit.

Machiavelli is a famous figure, but often misunderstood. He was born in Florence in 1469, he died in 1527, and he was Secretary and Second Chancellor to the government; that is, he was very involved in foreign affairs and European affairs in an age of profound political turbulence, violence, and political skullduggery. In 1512, Machiavelli's faction, his party, was driven from power in Florence. Machiavelli was first exiled to private life, then he imprisoned, then tortured. When he was released, he was compelled to retire to the Florentine countryside, outside the city. It was there on his estate that he wrote his great works.

For Machiavelli, notoriously "the prince must love his city more than his own soul." Furthermore, the prince, in order to love his city aright, must "learn how not to be good." Those two quotes of Machiavelli, really famous quotes, are actually quite not only significant but obscure. Understanding what they mean, and why Machiavelli thought that understanding them demanded that a prince had to undergo a new kind of education before he could be an effective prince, is the main aim of this lecture. It's a lecture in a way about the nature of political evil. Machiavelli seems to be the first person to think that the reality of evil in politics is in some important way inescapable; and that the prince, instead of trying to resist it everywhere, should at certain points and in certain ways work with the grain of politics rather than attempt to resist it for a larger, genuinely moral aim at the end of his efforts. Machiavelli is often accused of being a complete nihilist or a relativist, and that's not really fair. We only get that picture if we read *The Prince*, the one book that people often read of his. In fact, he wrote a major Renaissance political treatise called the *Discourses on Livy*, on Livy's history of the early Roman state, which is still probably his greatest work. It's an amazing work of philosophical and political acuity. But for good or ill, that's not what he's really known for. His last and his most notorious work is *Il Principe (The Prince)*, which was only published in 1532, five years after he had died.

No book, it seems to me, has been more publicly vilified and privately read. Shakespeare, in his plays, speaks of "the Murderous Machiavelli," and yet Shakespeare's sovereign, Queen Elizabeth I of England, read Machiavelli quite avidly. She was, in fact, quite a learned sovereign, quite an educated woman, and adept at translations, especially of classical historians, so she had read Machiavelli first on Livy; but then she found *The Prince* and fell in love with that as well. In fact, she kept one book under lock and key in her bedchamber in her palace, and that was a French translation of Machiavelli's *The Prince*. More publicly vilified, more privately read; probably Machiavelli would have approved of that fate for his work.

He sometimes is called "the first modern political man" because of his cold-eyed vision of what is at stake in politics and what must be done. You will have heard that Machiavelli is a relativist, a nihilist, a man who counseled mendacity, duplicity, skullduggery, and a bloody-minded maleficence to politicians. Again, while Machiavelli himself would not have been entirely displeased to have his works become camouflaged by that reputation, for those who care to read him, another and more profound—and for that very reason, more complicated, shadowy, and disquieting—meaning emerges. His basic idea—it's partially visible in *The Prince*, more visible elsewhere, but *The Prince* makes sense with this idea—is that goodness is real and virtue is real, but that moral perfection cannot provide any simple guidelines for the governance of our world, especially in politics. This is why the prince, or any political ruler, or anyone involved in politics for that matter, must learn, as Machiavelli puts it, "how not to be good."

Here are two examples of what I mean: First, a Prince, Machiavelli thinks, is wise to punish with unremitting fierceness rebels against the realm even after they have surrendered; not most centrally because they truly deserve that punishment, but rather because when they are seen to be so punished, it will deter others from undertaking similar rebellions, and thus further secure the stability of the realm. Fear—and we'll come back to this in a minute—turns out to be very important as a political motivator for Machiavelli. More controversially still, Machiavelli recommends the use of proxies for especially unpleasant deeds; proxies whom the Prince can later turn on and punish for performing those very deeds. In other words, a lot of the dirty work of politics should not be done by you, it should be done by someone else who can then be stained with the nastiness of it and then you can distance yourself from them. Machiavelli recommends this not, note, so that the Prince himself can "get away with" these crimes—Machiavelli's not interested in the Prince getting away with the crimes—but because that way the dirty work that needs to be done to keep the community moderately safe and stable manages to get done while the resentments of the citizenry, reasonable resentments, about that dirty work, resentments that, Machiavelli clearly notes, could themselves be sources for more instability in the future, unless they are defused; while those resentments find a suitable target who is seen to be properly punished in a way that dissipates those resentments, or at least lowers them to a level that the realm can safely endure.

Just note for a second: That whole long thing I just said, it's like a paragraph, that's one sentence, and it's a very Machiavellian sentence. It's an attempt to accommodate in one thought the multiple dimensions of politics that Machiavelli says a ruler, a politician, needs to keep in mind at all times. There is a good, there is a bad. The central aim is stability, but you have to understand people's psychologies, how they resent things, and how to quiet those resentments, not because you want them to like you but because you don't want them to render the political community unstable.

In Machiavelli's time, one of the greatest enemies of liberty and freedom in his world was the family of the Borgia's; and, in fact, perhaps the greatest and most rough of the Borgia's was Cesare Borgia. Machiavelli actually admires Borgia's ruthlessness, not because he worships bloody-mindedness—Machiavelli's not that kind of person—but because Borgia, for Machiavelli, exhibited a unity and coherence of purpose and intents that was good for the polity. People under his rule, people inside his community knew what he was about, and people outside his community knew what he was about. There was never any uncertainty about what he would do at any moment unless he wanted to surprise people. In other words, the integrity of a political agenda, its predictability, is for Machiavelli the absolute baseline for a successful political regime. To be chaotic, to be unpredictable, to be unstable is not a recipe for success; it's not a recipe for a happy polity. Though, again, you want to be able to surprise people from time to time, you nonetheless also want to be able to be a predictable and stable place for them.

In all of this, and even in his praise of Cesare Borgia, this is an enormous change from earlier political treatises, a genre of political writing called the "mirror of the prince," which was a very popular genre of medieval political writing. In these treatises, the writer talked again and again about the first and foremost thing that the ruler has to be is good; the ruler has to be ordered, the ruler has to be moral, the ruler has to be right. Machiavelli rips all of that away; he says it's simply unrealistic. It's unrealistic in two different ways: First of all, it's unrealistic about what actually is possible for political rulers. Many of them are not going to be good people, not essentially. Second, though, he thinks that it is deeply unrealistic precisely because it mistakes the cause and effect of certain actions in the polity. A nice and decent ruler may seem weak to some people; a kind and generous and merciful ruler may let rebels go when he should not do that; a just ruler may generate resentment among those people who supported his getting into power and yet not be able to defuse the resentment of those people who were against his getting into power about the fact that he got into power. In other words, a simple moralism in politics for Machiavelli is anti-realistic and so anti-political; it is against the good of the polis. To talk about people being good as the first virtue of politics is actually bad for politics, morally bad. The whole point of his argument was to care for the polis, for the polity, and the rhetoric—not just the arguments of the Prince, his work—are meant to do just that. Essentially he is preaching a kind of realism, sort of like

Thucydides. Machiavelli makes the claim throughout that text to see the world as it is, not how we would like it to be.

Let me stop here for a second: The central political anxiety that Machiavelli has is instability. He's seen too much anarchy, too much chaos in his world and he realizes that in important ways we have to be able to ensure stability in our world for any of the other goods of politics or private life to go forward. This means, then, that for Machiavelli, the stability of the political order has to come before the ethical happiness of that order; and this raises profound questions, and Machiavelli is really the first one to raise them, about the continuity of political life with our ordinary, everyday, day to day interpersonal, ethical lives. This is a huge thing, and we'll see it come up again and again. In different ways, thinkers throughout the rest of this course are going to be asking this question: Politics is a complicated, complicated thing; how can we anticipate that, in fact, morality will be some useful or stable predictable system that we can use to govern our mutual life when we can't insure that everyone is on the same page about what's right and wrong, and, in fact, when we know that politics inevitably generates judgments on different people's minds that actually disagree about what's right and wrong. How can we expect, then, that simply telling people that they ought to be good, or they ought to be kind, or my God they ought to be nice is going to be an effective way of being in politics? In fact, you set yourself up to lose; and not just to lose personally, but to harm the political causes that you support. And not just the personal political causes that you support, but to harm your very political community itself.

Understanding that basic claim of Machiavelli is important to seeing how he thinks people ought properly to understand the world. That unlocks a whole political psychology for him; because once you get away from the idea that basically you ought to be good, you can then look around and see how people act, especially in politics. He has an interesting point to make about politics. He says in politics people are governed by two large bodies of motivation, two large families of motivation: They're governed by their loves, and they're governed by their fears; but by and large, they're really governed by their fears. Occasionally love will help, occasionally love will manifest itself in some good thing; but by and large, you can rely on the thought that people are going to be able to do things more if you scare them with certain concrete threats than if you offer them certain vague hopes of good things in the future. This is why the police don't drive around streets offering people rewards for driving under the speed limit, even though actually they would be less busy in some streets, in some highways, if they did try to actually reward people who were going under the speed limit because most of us go over the speed limit most of the time.

That's one fact, this interesting political psychology for Machiavelli that people are really driven more by their fears, and that's a fact that we have to acknowledge. The other fact is another very crucial word for him: *fortuna*, "fortune." *Fortuna*, for Machiavelli, plays a huge role in politics. *Fortuna* is accident, luck; all sorts of stuff that happens that you have no control over. Perhaps you become the ruler of a country that faces immediate economic crisis, and your agenda for changing the country's way has to take second place to dealing with that economic crisis. Perhaps there are enormous military threats on your border from an unstable regime that has collapsed; suddenly, your polity has to be organized to defend itself against that unstable regime (people who weren't reading Machiavelli, right?) Again and again, Machiavelli says, a ruler has to be bad because at times they will find that the events they have to face are not in their control; and yet, nonetheless, they are responsible for facing those events.

There's a famous, famous line about Napoleon, the French emperor who did read Machiavelli. When Napoleon crowned himself emperor of France, a quite interesting satanic moment, he apparently then said to the surrounding audience, "I now hereby take on myself the responsibilities for all that France has done since Louis I"; since 600 or 700 years before him. What did he mean by that? He meant that, in fact, any ruler of a country, the moment they step into office is from that moment forward is responsible for everything that has happened and that might happen. You can complain about, "This isn't my fault," "This happened before we were there," "It's not fair"; it's not going to be useful for you, Machiavelli says. The truth is, you're going to have to come to terms with the thought that you are, in fact, responsible for this polity and that means no one but you is going to be able to control what goes on; and that means sometimes you may have to do some stuff that is relatively unpleasant in order to secure the good of the community.

A lot of this presents itself, or is read as, being strategies about being wicked, being a nasty person, being a naughty prince; but the basic point Machiavelli is trying to make here is not about teaching people how to be evil—my God, anybody who's been in politics knows that most people know how to be bad already—the point for Machiavelli is that you need to teach the Prince in these ways how not to be good precisely in order that they not become in a complete and total way evil. Machiavelli, that is, is trying to say that the most powerful medicine against the Prince's corruption is precisely the ability to learn how to control those situations where dirty hands have to happen; dirty acts, dirty deeds have to be done. In that situation, it will always be easy for a Prince to feel like they are in some sense staining their souls. Machiavelli wants to give them an account of how they may have to do certain acts that everyone would agree are evil, but nonetheless in a way that enables them to understand the necessity of doing those acts for the good of the state as a whole. Machiavelli wants to teach rulers how to be evil in a cold-blooded way so that the evil doesn't infect them and make them an entirely hot-blooded evildoer.

One interesting and important challenge to Machiavelli is that actually a lot of evil, maybe even in political terms, is not actually very cold-blooded. A lot of the evil we experience in our world and we experience in ourselves is not a matter of cold and calculated rational deliberation. It's hard to imagine, that is—a critic of Machiavelli could say—how someone can properly use all of evil in this cold-blooded way. Isn't Machiavelli asking for a level of psychological distance, frostiness, and alienation from those around you on the level for the Prince in a way that is impossible for at least almost every human being? Can Princes be expected to be self-mutilating in this way? Machiavelli might reply that may be so; but that's why being a Prince is so hard. In a way you have to become inhuman, you have to make a stone of your heart; and the reality of princedom is that stony-heartedness. For Machiavelli, it's unwise to try to disguise that, to coat it in the sickly-sweet perfume of pretty rhetoric, like a perfume covering over an over-ripe chamber-pot; it's better to recognize the realities of what being a Prince entails before you begin that task when you have time to prepare and consider. This is why, along with saying a Prince must learn how not to be good, he also says a Prince must love his city more than his own soul;

because, for Machiavelli, in undertaking the necessary evils, the regrettable wickedness's that he has to do, he is most likely to lose that soul.

In all of these ways, Machiavelli serves not just in his own right to speak to us of a certain cold-eyed realism about the political world, he also serves to speak to us about a certain kind of rhetorical pattern of resisting nice ideas, of resisting pretty thoughts, and saying instead that politics is actually the art of the possible, not the art of the ideal. In this, Machiavelli, even though he is largely I think identified with an extreme nihilism and cynicism about politics, still remains—perhaps especially in the way he thinks about evil and how the Prince should engage in evil—in modern politics the central political thinker that people still use, even if they don't recognize it.

Machiavelli's work is profound, dark, and filled with allusive and cryptic thoughts. We're going to turn in our next lecture to a rigorously systematic thinker who had some of the same thoughts and used them in interestingly similar ways, and that is Thomas Hobbes.

Hobbes—Evil as a Social Construct
Lecture 16

> Given ... that moral norms arise from peoples' cooperation to affirm laws and rules—whether explicit rules about right and wrong in the form of political laws, traffic laws, etc., or tacit rules about what is good or bad behavior in the form of cultural standards— ... the state of humans in the state of nature means, for Hobbes, that in nature itself, there are no such standards; there are no such laws.

Thomas Hobbes is generally considered to be the first truly modern philosopher in Western history. His great work *Leviathan* is relevant for us in two important ways: First, in his overall picture of humans in a state of nature, he seems to suggest that evil is the human's natural state. Second, he insists that good and evil are not metaphysically natural categories; they're not descriptions of reality but essentially constituted by the constructed political community in which we live.

The "state of nature" is a complicated condition that Hobbes uses to imagine what people would be like outside of civilization. In this condition, humans are roughly equal in strength and intelligence, that is, in their hope of being able to get what they want. They are also roughly equal in fear. Humans in a state of nature seek to fulfill their basic needs and are naturally fearful of others because they know that each one of them could kill another. For Hobbes, this results in a permanent state of semi-conflict: the "war of all against all." No one in this situation can be trusted because there is no way of holding another to account if trust is violated. These conditions engender a spiraling paranoia in humans: There is always good reason to harm someone else, even if you have no evidence that he is going to harm you, because he could harm you at some point in the future. For Hobbes, if we want to put in place a stable system of government, we can't begin from a sense of humanity's decency or kindness; we must acknowledge this savagery.

Hobbes is not saying that humans are naturally evil; in fact, outside of some preset social order, he believes there is no way to talk about good and evil at all. The savagery of humans when left to their devices suggests that morality has no reality as a metaphysical standard or a natural motivator for humans. In the state of nature, there are no moral norms. "The Desires," Hobbes writes, "are in themselves no Sin. No more are the Actions ... till they know a law that forbids them: which till lawes be made they cannot know." Without laws, people don't know or care if they're doing right or wrong; they're doing what is, strictly speaking, in their own interest.

To counteract this state of complete moral anarchy and amoralism, humans collectively agree to work together. Most of what we know of life, including our apprehension of good and evil, derives from this decision to live in communities. For Hobbes, good and evil literally have no reference beyond our agreement on these categories. Morality has no basis in our natures but is merely something we construct socially.

Absent that strong ruler and a very narrow range of principles, human life will devolve again into being "solitary, poor, nasty, brutish, and short."

In their readings of Thucydides, Hobbes and his contemporaries realized that language itself has the ability to be mobile across meanings and that sometimes changes in language may be the result of changing political circumstances. Hobbes goes even further than this: Not only can language be perverted by politics, but absent politics, language loses its sense altogether.

Nonetheless, human flourishing relies on successful human communities and use of language, and the conditions under which such communities can be founded and can continue through time are very narrow. Typically for Hobbes, these conditions involve a powerful, almost tyrannical, executive power to ensure obedience. Absent that strong ruler and a very narrow range of principles, human life will devolve again into being "solitary, poor, nasty, brutish, and short." In all of this, Hobbes is merely describing the conditions of humans, not endorsing the view that morality is just convention. He certainly thought that any ethical system, once established, ought to be obeyed to avoid reverting to the state of nature.

Many people have challenged Hobbes's views, both about the nature of human motivation in a state of nature and about whether morality exists outside of social conventions. Joseph Butler, an Anglican bishop, challenged the core premise of Hobbes's picture of moral psychology by pointing to the phenomenology of moral experience—the experience a person has when he or she is doing something good or bad. Butler argued that humans act out of two different senses of self-interest: the desire to accomplish our own aims and the desire to express genuine caring for others. Butler's assertion that Hobbes misunderstood human moral psychology is still debated today, and Hobbes's picture of rational self-interest has influenced modern game theory in its aim to apply mathematical models to the interactions of people and nations. ∎

Name to Know

Hobbes, Thomas (1588–1679 C.E.). Born in Wiltshire, England—supposedly when his mother heard news of the first sighting of the Spanish Armada—and educated at Oxford.

Suggested Reading

Hobbes, *Leviathan*, Tuck, ed.

Hobbes, trans., *The Peloponnesian War*, Grene, ed.

Martinich, *Hobbes: A Biography*.

Questions to Consider

1. For Hobbes, talking about evil only made sense in a social context—good and evil are culturally constructed, not "naturally" present in the world. What role does communal agreement play in identifying what is good and evil? Are good and evil primarily categories that humans create in communities or essences naturally present in the world?

2. What is human existence like in the "state of nature"? Is a strong centralized authority necessary to defend humans against chaos?

Hobbes—Evil as a Social Construct
Lecture 16—Transcript

Welcome back. In this lecture, I want to talk about someone who most of us consider to be the first truly modern philosopher of Western history: the English philosopher, Thomas Hobbes. Hobbes was born in 1588 and he died in 1679; that is, he basically spanned the entire century between Calvin and Sir Isaac Newton. His birth was prompted, he said, by reports of the Spanish Armada's sighting off the coast of England, an event that many English thought presaged their imminent invasion and subjugation by a foreign king, Philip II of Spain. This was one of the most traumatic moments of English history, even though the attempted invasion, of course, failed, and Hobbes always said afterwards, "My mother gave birth to twins: myself and fear." Many of his contemporaries, and those who came after him, would most certainly agree that Thomas Hobbes is one of the greatest thinkers of fear in the world.

He was educated pretty well at Oxford University—pretty well by those standards; pretty good by ours—but was always more of a self-taught person than taught by others. He was very much a product of a Renaissance humanist training, and in 1629 his first major work came out, and it was the first translation into English from the original Greek of Thucydides's *The Peloponnesian War*; already we're seeing some connections with previous lectures in our series here. That translation was universally acclaimed and it won Hobbes a great deal of fame and respect. In the coming decade, he continued to think philosophically and politically about the nature of the human community and the proper shape of human organizational structure, and he began to be more and more involved in English politics, as intellectuals of the time frequently were. During the English Civil War, Hobbes fled from all sides, ending up in France. Eventually, after the war and his masterpiece *Leviathan* was completed, he fled back to England, for the royalists had determined that his work was inimical to faith in the king, and the king at this point was, of course, back in France.

Hobbes's work in the *Leviathan* is relevant for us in two important ways: First of all, in his famous overall picture of the human in the state of nature and the basic human motivation set, which Hobbes insists is quite savage, he seems to suggest—and he comes very close to saying, though he never quite says it—that evil is the human's natural state. Second of all—and this is why he never quite says it, he only almost says that humans are naturally evil—in his discussion of the nature of good and evil itself, the terms we use, the categories we employ in thinking, he insists they are not metaphysically natural categories at all; they're not descriptions of realities that are part of the fabric of the cosmos, but they are essentially categories constituted by the constructed political community we live in. This claim, that the very foundations of the moral language we employ is, in fact, a construction—something that humans have to agree to and does not exist before that agreement—is very influential for all later writers on good and evil, whether they affirm it and build on it or react violently against it and argue against it. As one might expect, this view, and the larger worldview behind it, has profound and interesting similarities with the thought of Thucydides and Machiavelli.

Let's talk a little bit first about the basic picture of the human and of human nature in what Hobbes calls the "state of nature"; this is the condition that, of course, in his summative judgment he says, in the state of nature, "the life of man, nasty, brutish and short." The state of nature is a complicated condition that Hobbes uses to imagine what people would be like outside of civilization; but effectively, imagine people who didn't have any prior attachments or affiliations to one another kind of living in the same area, living in caves or beneath trees or whatever. A few facts about humans would become prominent in how they interact with each other. First of all, humans are roughly equal in strength and intelligence, roughly equal; and what Hobbes means by "equal" is we all have equal hope of being able to get what we want, and we all have equal hope of being able to kill somebody else in a conflict over what we want. In fact, Hobbes would add a third thing to that in some ways, he would say we all have equal fear of being killed by another person in a contest over what we want.

Because, even in a state of nature—outside of government, outside of society, outside of any coherent system of ordering ourselves—even in this situation, people still have to get certain things (food, cover to sleep under, security for themselves), inevitably human desires overlap on various objects or various locations or various ends and they rest on identical things;

so a problem arises over the conflict of the scarcity of goods. Furthermore, this immediate conflict over the scarcity of goods is "complexified" by the fact that, as Hobbes points out, humans are not only interested in certain things being given to them or being acquired by them, they're also interested in certain things not happening to them: most basically, we don't want to die. Thus, humans not only go around this state of nature seeking out various things and looking for people who might be trying to seek them as well in order to elbow them out of way, they also go around the state of nature terrified of one another because they know that each one can kill any other. Again, and in this way like Machiavelli and in some ways like Thucydides, Hobbes thought that fear was, in fact, at least as deep if not deeper a motive for human behavior than any other, including love and desire.

Therefore, in this state of nature, in this condition, Hobbes says, a strange, permanent state of semi-conflict arises; a state of what he calls the "war of all against all." In this "war of all against all," no one can be trusted; no one can be relied upon; because you effectively have no way of holding each other to account if you, in fact, violate each other's trust. Furthermore, Hobbes thinks, the basic conditions for generating a stable human language would be lacking from this. A language requires a community of some political order to be in place, Hobbes thinks; so not even really is there a real language in this condition, nonetheless, despite all this Hobbes thinks in an important way humans can imagine themselves into this state. Even though it is not fully a human life, not one that we would recognize as a suitable for people to live in, nonetheless, it's one we could imagine to be our condition.

Hobbes says this teaches us something very important about how humans are taken on their own, taken outside of society, taken outside of civilization: Humans are originally animals; they're originally beasts. They seek ends, and if they see others they will hurt and kill them if they can so that they can get the things they want without interference from those others; and they will hurt and kill them for fear that those other people would hurt and kill them before they hurt and kill the other people. In other words, there's a spiraling paranoia built into the psychology of Hobbes, and in this paranoia—which will become very important later in his thinking and in people who descend from him intellectually—there is always a good reason to, in fact, harm another person, even if you have no evidence whatsoever that they're about to harm you, because they could harm you at some point in the future. Therefore, killing them now is removing a potential future enemy.

Hobbes is not saying this is a good state, he doesn't approve of this state. He wants to say this is simply a fact that he notes; a reality of our condition; that absent society, absent civilization. We are these kinds of beasts. For Hobbes, the savagery of humans in settings where they can get away with it is simply a fact from which you have to begin; and—and this is very important for him, and makes him sound a little bit more like Machiavelli (but if you think about it, I think anyway, far more ruthlessly amoral than Machiavelli was)— if you want to have a stable system of government or morals, you won't begin from a sense of human's decency or kindness, you won't begin from a sense that human have the moral law in them, you will begin from the premise, for it is only by assuming that humans are savage and showing how even the most savage human can come to see the wisdom for their own self-interest of joining in associations to build societies; it is only by accepting that premise, Hobbes thinks, that you will actually generate a rationale for a social order that everybody in society can affirm.

Let's be very clear here: Hobbes is not saying that humans are naturally evil; that would mistake his point of view completely. Humans are not naturally evil, nor are they naturally good; nor are they, in some sense as they should be—we will see in a future lecture for Friedrich Nietzsche—"beyond good and evil." Hobbes is not saying we need to get "beyond good and evil"; rather, Hobbes is saying that in a certain way humans in a state of nature are beneath or before good and evil. For—and this is the other shocking part of Hobbes's argument; this is the second large factor in it and the part that over time was equally astonishing to his contemporaries and those who came after—outside of some preset social order, there is no way to talk about good and evil at all; there is no such language of good and evil for Hobbes. The savagery of humans, when left to their individual devices outside of the social order, suggests, he thinks, something very dark about the reality of morality as a metaphysical standard or a natural motivator in human beings' natural constitution. It means, Hobbes thinks, that morality has no reality in that sense.

Centrally—and for our purposes, this is really crucial—the failure of human society to capture these kinds of phenomena, the inability of human society to fully describe the forms of behavior that humans take outside of that society, means that in this extra-social situation, in the state of nature, there are, in fact, no moral norms: "The Desires," he says, "are in themselves no Sin." Let me quote you this passage here, because this is a very important passage; very controversial passage: "The Desires ... are in themselves no Sin. No more are the Actions ... till they know a law that forbids them: which till lawes be made they cannot know." In other words, without laws, without explicit agreement among people, there is no standard by which an action can be known as bad or good." "Nor can any law be made, till they have agreed upon the person that can make it."

What does that mean? That means that laws need a social system of governors, a ruler or a legislator of some sort. Absent that legislator, there is no way for laws to exist, Hobbes says; and absent laws existence, there is no way for people to know if they're doing right or wrong. In fact, they don't even care if they're doing right or wrong; they're doing what is strictly speaking in their interest. That's the law, if we want to call it that, that they will follow. Given, that is, that moral norms arise from peoples' cooperation to affirm laws and rules, whether explicit rules about right and wrong in the form of political laws, traffic laws, etc., or tacit rules about what is good or bad behavior in the form of cultural standards, given this assumption, the state of humans in the state of nature means for Hobbes that in nature itself there are no such standards; there are no such laws.

This is very important, so let's take a second to think about the state of nature a little bit more thoroughly here, and how humans get out of this state of nature. To counteract or rise above this state of complete moral anarchy and complete not immoralism but amoralism—a condition of being without morality—humans collectively agree to work together; and Hobbes is, in this, generally recognized as the first social contract theorist. Most of what we know of life derives from this collective decision, Hobbes thinks, to live in communities, including, he says, our "moral sense," our apprehension of good and evil. For Hobbes, good and evil literally have no reference beyond what we agree are good things and evil things. This is because since our knowledge of good and evil depends on our having words with stable meanings which to talk about them, when such words do not exist, we have no ideas of good or evil at all.

This is huge; and it was immediately recognized, or almost immediately recognized, as being an astonishing claim on Hobbes's part. Most people, when the *Leviathan* was originally produced, were astonished by his depiction of the state of nature and the idea that humans are in their being fundamentally bestial. But a few thinkers very quickly, and more and more people as time went on, realized that in some ways even more troubling than that is Hobbes's basic idea that the language of good and evil doesn't apply in nature itself. Hobbes turns out to be not only the first social contract theorist—that person who talks about how societies form on their view by contracting together by consenting to a series of laws—he's also what philosophers today call the first full-fledged social constructivist; that is, he is the first person to say that morality has no basis in our natures but is merely something we construct socially, entirely in some important way contingently as a matter of explicit decisions, possibly even shallow preferences, it is sometimes implied. There may be some ancient parallels with parts of this view. The figure Thrasymachus in Plato's dialogue the *Republic* we saw seems to suggest in some important way that morality is merely what the strong can get away; and, of course, Thucydides seems to suggest that the Athenians on the island of Melos say something similar. But Hobbes is really the first truly clear example of someone stating this overtly and following out its consequences to their end.

Interestingly, though, the idea seems to be something that Hobbes and his contemporaries had glimpsed in their own readings of Thucydides. Thucydides tells stories in the Peloponnesian War that seem to suggest some real dark truths about the nature of human order. Let me read you a passage that Hobbes translated; a passage that was very widely recognized in the Renaissance as a moment of revelation not just about Thucydides's world, but about the world that the people of the Renaissance, of the 16th and 17th centuries especially, were living in. What happens when political instability creates cultural anarchy? Hobbes is talking about a particular rebellion that happens in the city of Corcyra, and during the revolution he says:

The received value of names imposed for signification of things [that is, the definitions that names had, the way that names referred to things], was changed into arbitrary [this is Thucydides in Hobbes's translation, remember]. For inconsiderate boldness was counted true-hearted manliness; provident deliberation, a handsome fear; modesty, the cloak of cowardice; to be wise in everything, to be lazy in everything. A furious suddenness was reputed a point of valor.

Thus, Hobbes. Hobbes, in recognizing the idea that language can float, that language has an ability to be mobile across meanings of words so that a word at one point can mean one thing and then in another context entirely another, and that sometimes these changes in language can be due to changing political circumstances, was not even the last person to make this point. Of course, in our century, thinkers studying the way that the Third Reich thought about language have talked about this, and also most famously perhaps, the English essayist and writer George Orwell, in a number of writings, has talked about the possibility that language itself can be perverted by politics.

Hobbes goes further than this, though, in some way, because what he says is that language can not only be perverted by politics, but absent politics, language loses its sense altogether. Hobbes and his contemporaries saw Thucydides's lesson as not only revealing something about their own time, but revealing something that, in fact, in their world was shocking about the nature of human moral order in general. Theirs was a world where patriotism at one moment meant the support of the king, at the next moment it meant a desire to exile the king, and the moment after that a desire to kill the king. On Tuesday, virtue meant scholastic ethical submission to a religious community; but then on Wednesday, it would mean republican independence from a tyrant. At one time fidelity meant one thing, and then in the next moment its opposite. The revolutions in politics that these people survived, Hobbes and his contemporaries, were nothing compared to the revolutions in language and meaning and culture that they had to endure on a daily basis.

None of this is to say that for Hobbes everything is equally likely to be successful in human linguistic endeavors; far from it. Human flourishing relies on successful human communities knowing words properly and being founded, and the conditions under which they can be founded and can continue through time, are very narrow and typically for him involve a powerful, almost tyrannical, executive power to ensure, to compel all, to obey the rules. Absent that very strong ruler founded on a very narrow range of principles, human life will devolve again into a condition of being solitary, poor, nasty, brutish, and short. But Hobbes thinks that he's not proposing this; he's merely describing the conditions of humans, not evaluating them. In this he's like Machiavelli: I'm not telling you how things should be, I'm telling you how things are. Surely we can say that some conditions are evil and some things are bad and some things are good, and we might think that Hobbes's teaching is evil or we might think it's good; but from Hobbes's perspective, we can really only say that they are evil from where we stand. We can't actually say any more than when we say "good" or "evil," we are saying something we promote, or something we abhor. Those are his two huge points: First, the human is a beast; second, the bestiality of human means that language is, in some important way, a social construct.

The responses to Hobbes from the moment of the *Leviathan*'s publication were immediate and vehement. Many called him an atheist or an immoralist. Interestingly, they really couldn't call him a relativist, because they didn't have a language to talk about that charge in; there really wasn't much of a way to talk about Hobbes as a relativist at the time. Of course, at the same time and for the century after he wrote, many of the people who attacked him were also borrowing from his views, using his arguments in support of their own ends or at least simply responding to his charges on the terms of debate that he had established. But Hobbes wasn't trying to endorse the view that morality was everywhere and always nothing more than convention; he was simply saying that this was what would happen if people descended into a state of barbarism. There is no net of "natural virtue" or a "basically good human nature" that would stop people from becoming beasts. As the old Latin saying had it, *Homo Homini Lupus*; "to the human is a wolf," "man is wolf to man."

Hobbes certainly thought that any ethical system, once established, ought to be obeyed, the people inside it ought to obey it, not because of any kind of absolute moral command, because if they didn't obey it eventually that society would revert back into a state of nature, and that's much worse than almost any moral system you inhabit. If anything, Hobbes has appeared as the centuries have gone on not as a relativist or an immoralist but really more of a tyrant, a defender of absolute power. But there, lurking at the heart of those views—those arguments for an absolute centralized power—is the first formulation of something that we can call relativism. That suggests that for Hobbes he thought in some important way our understanding of evil is a social construct.

Since Hobbes, many people have challenged his views, both about the nature of human motivation in a state of nature, whether or not they are so ruthlessly self-interested; and also about whether or not morality has any purchase outside of social conventions. Among the most important and profound challengers was an Anglican bishop, Joseph Butler, who lived soon after Hobbes. Hobbes had tried, Butler understood, to reestablish moral order out of sheer individual self-interest, and part of his argument, Hobbes's argument, was the claim that all moral actions would reduce to self-interest anyway, even if we don't know that they do. Butler's challenge was to this claim: He challenged the core premise of Hobbes's picture of moral psychology, of the moral reasoning of the human; and he challenged it by talking about what philosophers call the moral phenomenology of moral experience, the experience that the person has when they are doing something good or bad. Butler thought that Hobbes's view meant that humans always only acted out of self-interest, and that even when they thought they were being kind to somebody because they should be kind to that person, because that person needed kindness, they were doing it out of self-interest, was Hobbes's argument. Butler thought that this rejection of a natural morality only worked if self-interest is one thing.

But for Butler, it doesn't work, because there are two senses of self-interest. I'm talking about this now, and I want to talk about this a little bit more, not just because it's interesting about the Butler-Hobbes debate, but because the kinds of arguments Hobbes makes about humans being founded entirely on self-interest are still quite abroad in our culture today; and understanding them, and understanding the counterarguments to them, whichever of those views you take, will help you understand something more of their depth. For Butler, two senses of self-interest: The first is the ordinary sense of self-interest in which I am interested in having my will fulfilled in the world. If

I want a drink I want a drink; if I want to get the drink. If I want my child to get a particular teacher in school, that too is something I want to happen. If I want to give ten thousand dollars anonymously to charity, I want that gift to happen in the way I want it to happen as well. All of those things are forms of self-interest; in some sense, they're all forms of me wanting my will fulfilled.

But there's a second sense of self-interest, in which that last example of giving ten thousand dollars anonymously to charity, is not obviously in my material self-interest, and Butler thinks that Hobbes confuses those two senses. Of course I do, in fact, want my altruism to be carried out—that's the first sense of self-interest—I want my aim to be accomplished. But only, Butler says, someone morally tone-deaf would miss how my desire to see my interests accomplished in that case does not equate to sheer selfishness. I can genuinely care for other people, Butler says, and the fact that the care is genuinely my care doesn't mean that it is not genuinely also for other people. Hobbes's elision of that distinction, his confusion of those two categories, Butler thought, means that he actually misunderstands human moral psychology in very important ways. Anyway, that's a crucial debate that's still going on today since Hobbes has had such profound influence in a number of academic disciplines as well as in our culture as a whole.

Hobbes's thought, and that thought of his various intellectual descendents, has had enormous influence in our society, mostly around this idea that Butler took on that humans are self-interested thoroughly in the ways that Hobbes proposes. But there's been another dimension or a specification of this dimension in the 20th century that became very important, and I just want to mention for a second before we go on: game theory. Hobbes's picture of the human as rooting everything they do in the structures of rational self-interest has been taken by a series of very, very sophisticated mathematical models, and taken up and redefined as the practice of what's called game theoretical understandings of how people and possibly international states should interact. In this picture, game theorists will sometimes argue that you can imagine one nation attacking another nation before the second nation attacks the first entirely out of fear that the second nation will attack it. That is, the first nation might be rational on a Hobbesian, game theoretical reading, it might be rational in striking another nation and destroying its military capacities—perhaps even its industrial base—in order to secure itself from the threat, the potential, possibly even merely hypothetical threat, of that other nation. In offering that picture, Hobbes's thought has had a profound influence on international politics and also on, interestingly, nuclear strategy. While you might think that a scholar who lived in a pretty quiet corner of the world during a pretty turbulent time—that is, England and France in the era of the 17th century and the English Civil War—wouldn't necessarily have a lot of application to our world today, in fact, his thought is shaping our world every day.

We'll next move on to other great Renaissance thinkers, and then into the Enlightenment's skepticism about the naturalness of traditional moral categories as well. But in Hobbes, I hope you see that the profound challenges he puts to us, both about our received understandings of right and wrong and about the typical ways we think about how to be or not be good and how to avoid doing evil, stay with us even today.

Montaigne and Pascal—Evil and the Self
Lecture 17

A lot of these people coming out of the Renaissance focus on this Renaissance theme of the creativity, … but whereas other Renaissance thinkers seem to think that is an unremittingly positive thing about the human, thinkers that we've been looking at—Calvin, Montaigne, Pascal—they all identify the turbulence of the mind as one of the most profound modern innovations when it comes to thinking about the roots of evil.

Our thinkers in this lecture, Montaigne and Pascal, engage in a debate about the intricate connections among religious belief, the self, and the self's performance of its beliefs in the world. Most centrally for both thinkers, the main question is about the dangers of zealotry (Montaigne) or the dangers of a lack of zealotry (Pascal).

Michel de Montaigne was a profound student of the effects of our beliefs on others, particularly how our beliefs may cause others to suffer great evil. He lived in an age of hyper-zealotry, though he did not share in that zealotry. His book *Essais* was the product of 10 years of near-total isolation from his family and others. One theme that emerges throughout the *Essais* is the tension between the vehemence of one's beliefs and the reality of the world's apparent indifference to those beliefs and the way those beliefs can lead to horrific suffering on the part of others.

In the *Essais*, Montaigne focuses on the banalities of everyday life, an activity that he thinks teaches us more than attention to abstract dogmas or doctrines of philosophical theories. Through these banalities, we discover how we actually behave, and we learn that humans are completely ramshackle assemblages of desires, interests, and thoughts; more or less coherent but fundamentally misaligned within ourselves. To try to fix this messiness, Montaigne suggests, leads inevitably to evil, although our inherent creativity often results in anti-humane, anti-worldly beliefs and behaviors.

In a number of essays, Montaigne analyzes the ways in which zealous, hyper-sincere piety can be destructive on its own or can curdle into a kind of hatred that is even more evil than its direct expression would be. In an essay titled "Of Virtue," he cites a number of gruesome stories— of self-mutilation, suicide, and martyrdom—all connected by the thread of extremity. In another essay, "Of Moderation," Montaigne asserts that nature, including human nature, is moderate, but the human mind need not be moderate. This is our glory and our tragedy: Our imagination is so fertile that we are prone to thoughts that can lead to annihilation of ourselves and others. We have this tendency because we prefer simple answers and final solutions to our own messiness.

For Michel de Montaigne (1533–1592), the main question is about the danger of zealotry, of serious religious belief.

Another voice in this conversation is that of the mathematician and scientist Blaise Pascal. In philosophy, Pascal is most well known for his *Pensées*, "*Thoughts*." This is a collection of aphorisms that he hoped to organize into an argument for the truth of Christianity. In the *Pensées*, Pascal proves himself to be a great anatomist of the dimensions of self-deception that are pervasive in evil.

Pascal on evil is classically Augustinian. He is most interested in the cruelty we do to ourselves by not thinking about our religious beliefs. He disagreed with Montaigne profoundly about the relationship between serious religious belief and moral sanity. Where Montaigne saw zealotry as dangerous, for Pascal, anything less than zealotry would be an evasion of the realities confronting us.

Like Montaigne, Pascal saw humans as muddied, but he believed that we were not meant to be in this state. Pascal said that we are "neither an angel nor a beast"; we're filled with "astonishing contradictions"; and we posses "no truth which is either abiding or fully satisfactory." We are moving constantly, both in our minds and in the world, trying to make sense of things and finding no stable resting place. The endlessness of our own perversity teaches us something about the infinitude of our longing: It can be sated only by the presence of God in our lives.

The first step in our healing is a recognition that our lives our riddled with sin and an acknowledgment of the emptiness of so much of what we do. Only with this recognition will the infinite abyss of longing in our hearts be filled by the infinite gift of God. We face difficulty in this because of two warring instincts: We want an end, but we don't want to reflect on ourselves wanting that end. We want to actively avoid thinking about ourselves. Pascal diagnoses this active ignorance with a single devastating word: *divertissements*, "diversions." Our lives are a series of diversions, endless rounds of empty frivolities, that add up to avoidance of confrontation with the basic realities of our existence, most centrally, the fact of our inevitable death. Great evil, Pascal thinks, can come from such trivialities. Pascal believes that people must finally confront the question of whether or not they will believe in God and follow God's commands for them; *divertissement* allows us to avoid this. This is why zealotry is so necessary for Pascal and why he opposes Montaigne's suspicion of it: We must be serious, because in the end, life will come for us and so will death. ■

Important Term

divertissements: Term meaning "diversions" used by Blaise Pascal to describe a way of being in the world aimed at avoiding the facts of one's existence, especially the fact of death.

Suggested Reading

Connor, *Pascal's Wager: The Man Who Played Dice with God.*

Friedrich, *Montaigne*, Eng, trans., Desan, ed.

Montaigne, *The Complete Essays*, Screech, ed. and trans.

Pascal, *Pensées and Other Writings*, Krailsheimer, ed. and trans.

1. In many ways, Montaigne and Pascal represent two significantly different perspectives on the nature of human existence and the nature of evil. Is diversity and incoherence simply part of human life, or is this itself a product of evil?

2. How would you assess Pascal's observation "It is being miserable to know that one is miserable; but it is also being great to know that one is miserable"? How could knowing one's misery be both debasing and glorifying?

3. Do you agree with Pascal that *divertissement* represents a significant temptation in human life? Can we avoid "wagering" in Pascal's sense or not?

Montaigne and Pascal—Evil and the Self
Lecture 17—Transcript

Welcome back. To move from Machiavelli and Hobbes to Montaigne and Pascal, as we do in this lecture, is to change not just writers but really whole experiences of reading. The France of Montaigne and Pascal was simply far richer and more ornate, and significantly less existentially fraught, than either Machiavelli's Italy or Hobbes's England. Furthermore, moving from Machiavelli and Hobbes to Montaigne and Pascal is a matter of changing styles and approaches and topics as well. Machiavelli and Hobbes are both resolutely public writers; their work, even *The Prince*, is meant to be read as if it were spoken speaking in the midst of the prince's court or the floor of Parliament. Montaigne and Pascal are profoundly private writers, deeply focused on anatomizing the weather of their own souls, and apparently indifferent to the vast geopolitical scale that Hobbes and Machiavelli write at. We'll see, of course, that their apparent indifference to these larger themes is more of a mask than a reality; but nonetheless, at least on their surface, they're quite different in that way.

Yet for all those differences, they too have a profound interest in the nature and character of human malice and suffering, and the lessons that they draw from it are as much political as they are personal. Most centrally, Montaigne and Pascal have a debate about the complicated and intricate connections between religious belief, the self, and the self's performance of its beliefs in the world. Most centrally for both Montaigne and Pascal, the main question is about the dangers of zealotry, of serious, serious religious belief (as it is for Montaigne) or the dangers of the lack of zealotry (as it is for Pascal).

The questions they both ask are of a more interior, personal, and brooding nature; and yet there are some powerful resonances between them nonetheless. They never met, of course, but Pascal was an enormous admirer of Montaigne's writing; disagreed with him profoundly, but nonetheless understood what he was about and took him on, on his own terms, in a very interesting way. For both of them lived in a world that was not so much politically turbulent—there was a bit of political turbulence for Montaigne, but not so much—but more religiously pluralistic; their France was more religiously pluralistic than it would be until maybe today. France in the late 16th/early 17th century was one of the main areas where Protestants and Catholics tried to get along, and among the people who tried to help them get along, Michel de Montaigne is one of the greatest.

Montaigne is one of the most profound students of the effects of our beliefs on others, particularly how our beliefs may cause others to suffer great evil. He lived in an age of hyper-zealotry, though he did not himself share in that zealotry. He had a really interesting upbringing. He was born in 1533 to a very wealthy merchant family that had sort of bought into the French nobility. Immediately after his birth, he was sent by his father to live with a peasant family, where he lived until he was three years old. His father wanted to make him acclimated to peasant life; to make him appreciate peasant life. Then he was brought back to his father's house where he was raised by his father entirely in Latin and Greek, his father never spoke French to him; in fact, even the servants were required to speak only Latin to him. (Things are pretty different now; it's pretty hard, actually, to find a good Latin-speaking butler these days.) But inevitably with an upbringing like this he was not only strange, he was very precocious. He was a lawyer in his teens; he was a Counselor to a Count; and then ultimately a Courtier to the French King Charles IX, all before he was 30. He was marked out for remarkable advancement and prestige in the French noble world.

Then, when he was 30, suddenly, without any expectation, his closest friend, Etienne de la Boétie, died. It was devastating for Montaigne, who thought of Boétie as a second self. He never fully recovered his public presence. He married soon after the death; and then, in 1571 at the age of 38, after slowly over the course of several years extricating himself from public affairs, he retired fully from public life, literally locking himself in a tower on his estate, out of which he emerged, even for his family, only very rarely, and even then only with the greatest reluctance. After almost 10 years of near-total isolation, he published the first edition of his book *Essais*. Paradoxically, for so determined a recluse, the *Essais* by Montaigne is the first work of genuinely revelatory exploration of a private self written for public reading. Just think about that for a second; it's a very weird paradox. This is a guy who basically spent 10 years locked in a tower on his own with books and paper, and what does he do in those 10 years? He produces a book that is all about his inner life. We can understand that if you're locked alone for 10 years you're not going to have much else to think about; but still, why would you then publish it? It's a pretty odd thing that someone so private in person could be so self-revelatory between the covers of a book. In a way Montaigne, modernity's first reclusive artist in any genre—painter, musician, writer, what have you; the first truly reclusive artist—is also the modern world's first truly literary confessionalist.

After the publication of the first edition of the *Essais*, Montaigne travelled for a couple years for his health; he was understandably after 10 years in a tower somewhat ill. Then he was unwillingly elected the Mayor of Bordeaux, the town outside of which he lived, and he served in that post as a moderate trying to balance the demands and the needs of his own Roman Catholic community and the Protestant Huguenot community from 1581–585, when he retired again to his tower to continue his own writing and rewriting of the *Essais*. He died in 1592.

Montaigne's work takes up remarkably contemporary topics like religious extremism and terrorism. Much like Machiavelli, he saw himself as a realist who sees what is; but he's much more of a self-focused realist, a miniaturist of the soul so to speak, than Machiavelli ever was. One theme that emerges throughout the *Essais* is the tension between the vehemence of one's beliefs and the reality of the world's apparent indifference to those beliefs, and the way that those vehement beliefs can lead to horrific suffering on the part of others. In thinking about how he made this argument, you have to understand something of the genre in which he's writing. He writes essays; in fact, he's really the first person to coin this phrase, to write in this genre. These are not treatises like Hobbes or a brief programmatic book like Machiavelli's *Prince*. Essays are truly efforts whose profundity and whose ultimate punch is really actually masked at first anyway by an apparent casualness, an easiness of flitting from one topic to another, so that people are led through some complicated and quite profound matters by feeling like they're in the midst of a loose and wandering conversation; an after-dinner conversation about a number of things. "Oh, I've heard of this"; "I've heard of that"; "That makes me think of this." Montaigne, in fact, coined the term "essays"—in French, it means "attempts" or "efforts"—and effectively remains one of the greatest masters of the genre.

In fact, his style matters very much to the point he's trying to make. Attention to the banalities of everyday life, the accretion of experience, attention to the details of how we dress every morning, what we wear, how we walk; when we start walking, do we start with our right foot or our left foot? When I scratch my head, how hard do I scratch? These are sorts of things that Montaigne talks about. Attention to these banalities, Montaigne thinks, teaches us much; much more, in fact, than attention to abstract dogmas or doctrines of philosophical theories, because through these banalities, we will discover how we actually behave and that's crucial for him. Essays are focused on the ordinary aspects of our lives, and they can track this behavior very well.

What do we see when we do this, when we track our behavior? We see, above all, this: Humans are messy and jumbled; completely more or less ramshackle assemblages, desires, interests, thoughts, more or less coherent but fundamentally not very aligned properly in ourselves. To deny our messiness, to try to fix it, Montaigne suggests, leads inevitably to mutilation and evil. But—and here Montaigne is a child of the Renaissance, as much as Calvin, his fellow Frenchman whom Montaigne read with interest though not assent, was—for Montaigne the human mind far outreaches the body, and is in a constant turmoil of invention and creativity. Again, much like Calvin, though from a very different angle, Montaigne worries about the turbulent creativity of the human imagination; for it can and does lead us to profoundly anti-humane, anti-worldly, evil beliefs and behaviors.

In a series of essays within the larger *Essais*, two of which I want to pick out in particular, Montaigne analyzes the ways in which our zealous, hyper sincere piety, our vehemently held beliefs, can at times be destructive on their own or curdle into a kind of hatred that is even more evil than their direct expression would be. In one essay, for example—an essay titled innocently "Of Virtue"—Montaigne tells the story of the amazing things he knows people can do. He starts with some interesting examples of strength and stuff, and then he seems to veer off topic and he talks about a series of increasingly outlandish behaviors he has heard of: a man who is nagged by his wife so much because she is so jealous of his leaving their house and talking to other women that eventually one day he has enough and takes a knife and cuts off his own penis and gives it to her; Montaigne is astonished by this. But then he says, "Oh but wait, I've heard another story": a man who disappointed his mistress in bed and went home in shame, and decided that the way to solve this problem is, again, to cut off his own penis and mail it to her.

Montaigne goes from that to think: What about widows who throw themselves, in India, on the pyres of their husbands? What about those among us who have been willing to die for our beliefs in horrible ways in our own pyres of fire? Do you notice how he's shifted from outlandish stories of what happened in the neighborhood? Now he's talking about religious zealotry in his own area. Then he says, "Oh, and then I've heard of this man, the first man to actually manage to kill William the Silent," who's a Dutch leader; a Catholic managed to kill this guy, this Protestant leader, and instead of trying to run away he stood there and waited to be captured. Montaigne says, "There must be a kind of virtue in this, although I suspect that, in fact, we would all find it somewhat troubling." What's happened? He's now identified a person who, for the Roman Catholic world, is a remarkable martyr and a hero; this guy who goes and kills a political leader and then stands there and is willing to be tortured and killed for his beliefs. He's connected that with an angry peasant who cuts off his own penis when he's nagged by his wife, and he suggests that these two people are connected by a common thread: the thread of extremity. Perhaps, he's suggesting in this essay, the extremities of our lives are less attractive when we think about them in a careful way then they seem to be in abstraction.

In a second essay, building on this in some ways, called "Of Moderation," he reflects on a saying he's heard. The saying is, "The archer who shoots too far misses, just like one who shoots too close"; in other words, it is just as possible to go extreme and miss your target as it is to not be ambitious enough and miss your target. Nature, he says, including human nature, is moderate; but the human mind need not be moderate. This is our glory and our tragedy, he thinks; and our imagination is so fertile that we are prone to bouts of thought that can lead to self-annihilation and other-annihilation as well. We need to be reminded again and again that even though our mind is in some sense limitless, our bodies and our world are not; and we need to keep things under control in moderate ranges, not to go extreme, because when we go extreme we annihilate ourselves and we annihilate others.

This self- and other-annihilation, this tendency humans have to a vehement, zealous destructiveness, horrifies and intrigues Montaigne. Why are we like this, he wonders? Most basically, he thinks, we are like this because we hate messiness; we hate our messiness, our muddiness, and we love purity, we love extremity, we love simple answers and final solutions. Humans are messy in a messy world, but we hate it. We want tidiness; we want things to be neat and orderly; we want things to be black or white, simple and straightforward. Many of us, he thinks, would rather castrate ourselves or kill ourselves, many of us would definitely kill others, than accept the messiness of our world. That's an astonishing fact, that we are so extreme that we cannot, in fact, tolerate complexity, even when that complexity is itself extreme complexity. That's the complicated facts of our lives. We are people who live moderate lives but we want to live on the extremes.

In all this, Montaigne is the pioneer of a certain kind of moderation and a certain kind of skepticism about zealotry of any sort and extremism of any sort—political, religious, athletic—any kind of monomaniacal focus on anything is the kind of thing that Montaigne worries about; and he is the pioneer of this. Others came after him and others are still working today, worrying in some ways that religious extremism, for example, is the philosophical and psychological source of a lot of the evils in our world; there's clearly something to that. Perhaps Montaigne's most famous and remarkable intellectual followers in this way is a person who those of us who live in the United States don't know much about, the famous French diplomat Charles de Talleyrand-Périgord, who astonishingly served and survived as Secretary of State in France under Louis XVI, then the Revolutionary regime, then Napoleon, then finally the restored Bourbon Monarchy. Talleyrand's famous house motto, "sûrtout, pas trop de zèle"—"above all, not too much zeal"—is in some ways a perfect epitome of Montaigne's view; and Talleyrand's efforts throughout his life to create a stable European order in the midst of a revolutionary era would be exactly the sort of thing that Montaigne would have approved of. Would that we had Talleyrand's today in our world.

But along with Montaigne, another and I would say personally equally necessary voice in this conversation on the other side, is Blaise Pascal, one of the greatest intellects of European history. He was a brilliant mathematician and scientist. Born in 1623, and he died when he was only 39, in 1662. Like a lot of these people, Pascal died when he was younger than I am today; I can hardly deal with that. He was a renowned child prodigy; he became famous for science and mathematics. He invented, in fact, the very first calculating machine. At 23, in 1646, he became associated with the Jansenists, a very hyper-Augustinian religious movement within the Roman Catholic church, but one that was in deep conflict with the Jesuits who at that time had the King's ear in France; so Pascal began to be on the outs with the French establishment, intellectual as well as political.

In 1654, on November 23rd of that year—as a matter of fact, between 10:30 p.m. and a half-past midnight—he had a radically powerful religious conversion. We know about this, and we know with such precision about the time of this conversion, because it seems the very next day, or maybe that night, he wrote out a note about it, and dated it, then sewed it into his doublet, the vest respectable 17th-century gentlemen wore, where it was discovered after his death. Pascal is most well known today for his *Pensées*, his *Book of Thoughts*; that's what *pensée* means in French. It's a collection of aphorisms that are more or less jumbled that Pascal was working on when he died. He had meant eventually to organize them into an argument for the truth of Christianity; an argument that he hoped would turn some of his readers anyway back to God in repentance and inspire in them a desire for a truly Christian life. In the *Pensées*, he appears to be and proves himself to be one of the greatest anatomists of the dimensions of self-deception that are so pervasive in evil. There, in that work—in the small excerpts that would one day have gone into that work had he lived—we see human self-deception analyzed with the most acuity, I think, that anyone has ever shown.

Pascal on evil is classically Augustinian; I mean, in some ways he's kind of hyper-Augustinian. For him, he's not so much focused on the topic that interests Montaigne, the idea that religious belief manifests itself in cruelty to others; Pascal is interested more in the cruelty we show ourselves by not thinking about our religious beliefs. As I had said, he read Montaigne very closely, and he disagreed with him quite radically even as he admired him. Montaigne actually would not have found this disappointing; he would have liked it, because he knew (Montaigne did) that each author's words must be digested and modified in the guts of the living reader for them to become vital again. But most profoundly, Pascal disagreed with Montaigne about the relationship between serious religious belief and moral sanity, rectitude. Where Montaigne saw zealotry as dangerous, for Pascal anything less than zealotry, anything less than what Montaigne would call zealotry, would be mere evasion of the realities confronting us.

Pascal's anthropology explains this a little bit. Remember I said that for Montaigne, humans are muddied but they hate that about themselves. For Pascal, something about that is true, but the problem is that the muddiness is something we're not supposed to be. Humans are weak, frail, folly-filled creatures for Pascal, shadows of what they were meant to be. We are, he says famously, "neither an angel nor a beast," we're filled with "astonishing contradictions" and we posses "no truth which is either abiding or fully satisfactory." We're moving constantly, turbulently in our minds; constantly, turbulently in the world; trying to make sense of our world and finding no stable resting place within it. In this he's not just like Montaigne; he's very much like Calvin as well. A lot of these people coming out of the Renaissance focus on this Renaissance theme of the creativity, the endless creativity, of the human mind; but whereas other Renaissance thinkers seem to think that is an unremittingly positive thing about the human, thinkers that we've been looking at—Calvin, Montaigne, Pascal—they all identify the turbulence of the mind as one of the most profound modern innovations when it comes to thinking about the roots of evil.

The very magnitude of our lusts, for Pascal, the endlessness of our perversity, teaches us something about the infinitude of our longing; it's a longing that can only be sated—this is very Augustinian—by the presence of God in our lives. As he famously said, "I have discovered that all of mankind's evils come from one thing: that they do not know how to sit quietly in their own room." The key here is the human is an incoherent tangle, at least incoherent from the point of view of what we call the natural world, the order of creation, from where we stand. We desire truth and happiness but are incapable of them. This desire, Pascal says, is left to us as much as punishment for our fall as for a reminder of from whence we have fallen. This is not just a bad thing about us; not just a sign of our misery, it's also a sign importantly about grandeur. As Pascal says, "To know that one is miserable is to be miserable"—of course—"but to know that one is miserable is also to be great." That is to say, to have the ability to not just experience yourself but to kind of step back and experience yourself experiencing yourself in that way; to actually have a sort of sideways-on view of yourself; to be able to reflect on yourself in the moment is a gift of human beings and a feature of our creation that is distinctive about us and truly magnificent, Pascal thinks.

Our lives are riddled with sin, governed by our sinful refusal to recognize that sinfulness, and the first step, therefore, in our healing must be that recognition of our sinfulness, our vanity; the emptiness of so much of what we do. Only then will the infinite abyss of longing that we have in our heart, only then will it be filled by the infinite gift of God. Until then, we will seek trying to fill it with other, bad ends, bad happiness's. No natural science will understand the human, something beyond nature is needed; a theological insight, he thinks. To understand ourselves, we need to "listen to God," then.

The difficulty is, we find listening to God or listening to ourselves horrible. We find self-reflection incredibly painful and distasteful. We don't want rest; we don't want to contemplate; we have two secret instincts at war with one another: We want an end, but we don't want to reflect on ourselves wanting that end. We want to actively avoid thinking about ourselves; and it is in the study of this active ignorance, this active desire we have—unconscious, preconscious, what have you—that Pascal makes what I think his most distinctive, most significant, and most abiding contribution to thinking about evil. For he diagnosed this active ignorance, this dynamic avoidance of ourselves, with a single, devastating word: divertissement.

Divertissement is "Diversions"; these are diversions. We engage in our lives in a series of diversions, a series of tricks, that add up to a whole way of being in the world by way of avoiding confronting the basic facts, conditions, realities of our existence, particularly and most centrally the fact of our inevitable death. Divertissement, for Pascal, is a certain culturally-specific way for him of talking about how humans can lead a life fundamentally organized around avoiding what they should be doing. It is another language for describing the condition of humans caught in Original Sin; one, this language, highlighting the active character of the endless round of empty frivolities we indulge in, in order to not think about what we should be thinking about. Pascal uses this word very intentionally. It's a word of some common use in his France as it would be today; "diversions," it sounds light and harmless. But it needn't be so: Great evil, he thinks, can and does come from trivial causes. Dueling and murder, he says in the *Pensées*, both come from ennui, from boredom; and thus, Pascal thinks, the magnitude of the horrors that we produce are out of all proportion to the triviality of the cause; divertissement.

It should be clear that this is a direct critique of Montaigne's view, for being too forgiving and blind towards these trivial things. Pascal says it's precisely the trivial things you should worry about; at that level you may be able to control it perhaps (just perhaps, because even there it's going to be hard). But by the time you get to things where we already recognize real crimes, or real catastrophes—mutilation, amputation, castration, murder, suicide, self-immolation—it's far too late to stop people from driving themselves straight to Hell. So for Pascal, the issue is that people must finally confront the question of whether or not they will believe in God and confront God's commands for them, and it is only by being caught up in divertissement that we continue to avoid this. This is why zealotry is so necessary for Pascal, and why he opposes Montaigne's suspicion of it: because we have to be serious, because in the end, life will come for us and so will death.

Pascal, then, lives after Montaigne in several senses. Where Montaigne is about diversity and acceptable incoherence and the messiness of human life, and for whom evil is an effect of denying that diversity and incoherence, Pascal thinks that human incoherence is itself an effect of human evil and fallenness. They directly disagree. In thinking about this disagreement, though, I urge you to keep both views alive, because it seems to me that both people have a good bit of evidence on their side.

Next, I want to turn back to England and consider another Renaissance thinker, one who is enormously influential but one whose influence is often not fully seen by us because we think of him fundamentally as just a poet: John Milton.

Milton—Epic Evil
Lecture 18

> Satan is both simultaneously a rebel and a person who knows rebellion is futile, and the amplitude and magnitude of his verbal rebellion, and the magnificence of it, are paralleled in Milton's representation by a brilliant representation of Satan as also, behind that verbal pomposity, completely despairing about the futility of this whole exercise.

O ne thinker who potentially rivals Dante for the depth of the influence of his literary work on our thinking about the nature of evil is **John Milton**. The work for which he is best known is *Paradise Lost*, written, as the poem says, "to justify the ways of God to man." The epic provides us with a powerful depiction of both the character of temptation and the descent into sin and corruption.

Dante wrote about an ordinary person coming to see evil for what it is. In contrast, Milton wrote about evil's self-understanding. And to do that, he bends metaphors in complicated ways, famously describing hell, for example, as "darkness visible." With these paradoxical metaphors, Milton recalls the medieval Christian concept of *felix culpa*, the "happy fault," the view that the Fall of humans was, in some ways, fortuitous because it brought Christ as the savior.

The poem quickly establishes that Satan's sin is rebellion against God, but Satan sees his rebellion as prompted by God and is unwilling to own up to his responsibility. Interestingly, the poem depicts Satan as a master of possibilities, of hypotheticals, but never able to settle on any of them. His language reveals him to be a sinuous thinker. It's also true that Satan oscillates wildly on the question of choice. When he thinks about his own condition, he blames God, but when he thinks about his ambitions, he believes himself to be wholly unsponsored. Satan sees Adam and Eve as innocents, caught up in the war between God and himself. He believes that he is using the tree of the knowledge of good and evil as bait for Adam and Eve, but of course, that turns out not to be the case. One of the other angels points out that rather than be in a lower state than he thinks he deserves, Satan would prefer not to be at all.

It's also interesting to note that Satan can never be sincerely satanic; he realizes, somehow, the foundations of his own being: the futility of sin. At the deepest level, Satan represents the unavoidability of truth. He frequently breaks down in the poem, and he's continually paranoid that, in fact, everything is still God's plan—his fall, the temptation of Adam and Eve, and their eventual redemption. Of course, Satan's paranoia turns out to be right. The tree, which Satan believed was his bait for Adam and Eve, turns out to be God's bait for Satan; God uses Satan's temptation to pave the way for Christ's redemption and elevation of humanity.

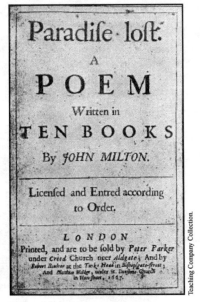

Although they are perfected humans, Adam and Eve are innocent of sin, and that innocence complicates their relationship to the events that unfold within and around them. They are warned about sin by the angel Rafael, but they don't quite understand what it is they are being warned about; thus, the warning is not particularly useful. Eve's sin is more a matter of careless folly, vanity, and pride than of deliberate, satanic evil. Adam's decision to eat the apple after Eve has done so is both a

Milton's best known work, *Paradise Lost*, is an epic poem deeply learned in Calvinist and Puritan theology.

sign of his love for her and of the misordering of his loves. If he had properly loved God, he would have rejected Eve. The fact that Adam takes full responsibility before God reveals the difference between satanic and human sin: Satanic sin is often just about itself; human sin often ropes in others.

The Fall does not defeat God's plan. As Satan suspected, God foreknows the Fall and foreknows its certainty of happening, but God does not preordain it. The difference between God knowing that something will happen and commanding that thing to happen is God's participation in time from the perspective of eternity. From any perspective within time, God's knowledge of future events will look like foreknowledge. But from God's eternal presence to all moments of time, everything has already happened, so God knows everything before history even begins. God also knows that God will use the Fall to create an even greater story: that of Christ and redemption.

Many have wondered whether Milton's representation of Satan is too powerful. Satan's psychic agony and his paranoia about God conspire to present a remarkably seductive picture of evil: vivid, vigorous, terrifically driven. In contrast, God, Christ, the good angels, and even Adam and Eve seem pale and tepid. But Milton's depiction of evil in its purest satanic form is not an elevation of Satan. When we consider the motives and rationales of Satan and Adam, if there is any tragedy in the poem, it lies in Adam's choice of Eve, not in Satan's choice of himself. ■

Name to Know

Milton, John (1608–1674 C.E.). Born in London and received an elite education with help from his wealthy father. Milton enrolled at Christ's College, Cambridge, where he received his M.A. but continued his learning far beyond his university education.

Important Term

Paradise Lost: Epic poem composed by John Milton, an English poet in the 17th century.

Suggested Reading

Beer, *Milton: Poet, Pamphleteer, and Patriot*.

Milton, *Paradise Lost*, Teskey, ed.

1. Is Milton's Satan too intriguing, or does Milton's sympathetic portrait instead offer us a nice meditation on the intelligibility and seductiveness of evil?

2. How should we understand Satan's worry over divine providence in Milton's poem? Could Satan's fall, and the origin of evil itself, in fact be part of God's plan all along?

Milton—Epic Evil
Lecture 18—Transcript

Hello again. In this lecture, I want to talk about the one thinker who potentially rivals Dante for the range and depth of his influence through his literary work on our thinking about the nature of evil; and that is, as it has to be, John Milton. Milton is arguably the greatest poetic genius of the English language. He's rivaled really only by Shakespeare for his literary import. He was born in 1608 and he died in 1674, so he stretches across the turbulence of the 17th century of England. He was remarkably well-educated, even by the elite standards of his time. He took a B.A. and then a M.A. at Cambridge, and then spent, after his university time, six years in semi-seclusion at his father's country house reading everything important. When I say everything, I am not joking: Some people think that Milton may have been the last person alive in Europe to have effectively read every book of import, or almost every book he could find, just before printing made the actual mastery of the entire body of knowledge impossible. But as for languages alone, he not only knew Latin and Greek, of course, and Hebrew naturally, and French and Italian, of course, but Spanish, Dutch, and Old English as well. He was accomplished in some Chaldean, which is an early version of what happens to be some of the Ancient Near Eastern languages that become Aramaic and things like that, and he knew a little bit of Arabic as well.

He was not just a literary figure, but a controversialist and polemicist against the Catholic-sympathizing King Charles I and became eventually a major player in the Commonwealth Government of Oliver Cromwell after the deposition and then execution of the king. At the royal Restoration in 1660 of the executed king's son, he was condemned and his writings were burnt, but he went into hiding and survived until a general amnesty was pronounced. When he reemerged, he was jailed briefly for a time but then released. As this was going on, his personal life was in some turbulence, too: He lost two wives early on and then had found a happiness with his third wife only in the 1660s. But he was also going slowly blind; and after his time in power he began the composition of the work that he is best known for, *Paradise Lost*, but he was completely blind the entire time he wrote it.

He began writing it in the waning days of the Commonwealth, when it was increasingly clear that the government would not survive, and moving into the domestic semi-exile he suffered in the Restoration era. He would compose the verses in silence in his mind during the day, and then recite them in the evening aloud for his daughters or for an amanuensis, a secretary he had, who would write them down word for word as he gave them verbally to them. He was a rebel himself, and then one who helped to govern, and then saw that rebellion and that government collapse. He was caught in fierce conflict that rivened England throughout the 17th century between Calvinist republicans and Catholic monarchists. He offers a picture of evil that is profoundly Augustinian, but emphasizing, as a Calvinist and a republican, the individual's responsibility and by extension dignity by focusing on a rebellion gone terribly awry, and a leader horribly mutilated by his own revolt.

Before I go any further, I've used this word "republican" a couple times; I really ought to just be very clear and say when I'm talking about "republican" I'm not talking about a present-day political party, I'm talking about a political thinker of today or anytime in roughly the last five centuries or so who believed that the proper shape of a human governance is actually to be one of self-governance by the people who are being governed. A republican is someone who believes that the people as a whole have to govern themselves, not be governed by a king.

Milton's overall work is obsessed with the question of evil. His writings on education, on liberty of speech, his anti-monarch writings, even his arguments about divorce all revolve around how to avoid or limit our own corruption by evil. His epic poem *Paradise Lost*, which is deeply learned in Calvinist and Puritan theology, was written, as he says early on in the poem, "to justify the ways of God to man"; to demonstrate that while the Fall was real and evil—he's not trying to whitewash the Fall or say it was for a larger good or a necessary thing; he's not an Irenaean theodicist in that sense— nonetheless, while the Fall was real, we still live in a fundamentally good universe and we must be grateful to the God who governs this universe. This poem provides one of the most powerful and vivid depictions of the nature of evil, both of the character of temptation and the slow (or fast) descent into sin and corruption. Milton's vision of the nature of metaphysical evil considered in itself is represented best really in the figure of Satan, and the character of humans when they come in contact with it is, of course, the study of what happens with Adam and Eve. Here, I want to look at the representation of the decay of Satan over the course of the poem; and then as well the corruption but residual nobility of Adam and Eve in the epic's dramatic action; before finally saying some stuff about God as the provident orderer of this poem and of the cosmos.

Before we do that, though, stop for a second and think about a difficulty that Milton had that Dante did not: the difficulty of writing directly about evil. Dante didn't do that; Dante wrote about an ordinary person, one like us, coming to see evil for what it is. He did not write about evil's self-understanding in itself. Because of the challenge that the structure of his poem sets him, Milton has to write about evil in itself. To do that, he has to really bend metaphors in complicated ways, not just in thinking about Satan and Satan's inner life, but even in his descriptions of Hell; so that famously Milton describes Hell as a kind of "darkness visible." More importantly, though, these metaphors he's using rest back on a history of paradoxical metaphors used to think about evil, many of which rely on this very early pattern formulated first in Latin and a practice that enters into medieval Christian rituals, and then begins to be something that both Roman Catholics and Protestants use: the category of what's called in Latin the *felix culpa*— I've said this before—the "happy fault." If you think about Hell as a kind of visible darkness, which is what Milton wants to talk about it as, it's possible also to talk about evil in the context of Christian theology as a happy fault, because it turns out that it's only because the humans fell that Christ comes to save everybody—at least this is the view of much orthodox Christian theology—so it was of a necessity for humans to fall so that Christ would come, which is a great blessing; that's the argument anyway.

The difficulty of talking directly about evil in these ways is far more profound then you might first realize, and much more difficult than it may at first appear. We'll see thinkers later on trying to do this as well, when we talk about evil not just in realistic philosophical descriptions but also in literary descriptions, especially in the 19th and 20th century. But let's start with Satan now. What exactly is Satan's sin? Pretty early on it's established: It's rebellion against God. But why? What for? How does Satan see the rebellion? In fact, Satan sees the rebellion as prompted by God. He sees himself as tempted; tempted by God. As Satan says in the first book, God "tempted our attempt, and wrought our fall"; God made Satan so great that it was easy for Satan, inevitable perhaps, Satan thinks, for him to be tempted; at least that's Satan's idea.

So Satan admits he's a rebel, but as with the Islamic accounts of Iblis, and with the medieval scholastics like Anselm and Aquinas, he has an excuse: from his perspective, God was behind his fall. Satan, then, is not really willing to own up to his own responsibility in this; he wants to figure out a way to make it someone else's fault. This, it seems to me, is related to another fact about Satan in the poem, a fact that is interesting for thinking about evil today. Among his many other gifts, Satan is a master of possibilities, of hypotheticals, but never able to settle on any of them. It matters a lot that Satan's first spoken word in the whole poem is "if" when he first, at the bottom of the pit—they've all fallen to the bottom of the pit and they're laying there, him and the fallen angels—and they're stunned and he looks over like this and he sees another angel there (it's Beelzebub, who was another high angel) and he says, "if thou be'est he; but O how fallen!"

This wonderful first line of Satan's, which is wonderful both for its content—if that's you, but oh how disastrous your fall has been—and "if" is the first word, it's a hypothetical, and notice how the hypothetical starts a sentence that doesn't end right away. Right away, Satan stops, he looks at the fallen Beelzebub, and he goes off on another tangent about how fallen Beelzebub is. Somewhere, the "if thou be'est he," that part of the sentence, has an ending part of the sentence, but it hasn't come yet; in fact, it won't come for Milton for very many lines. Satan is a sinuous thinker; he doesn't just end up as a serpent, he thinks sinuously. He has a hard time making straight declarative sentences. Typically they come only at the end of vast, wandering lines, paragraphs, which are enormously rhetorically powerful; but when considered outside of the rationalizations that led up to them, can sound enormously dubious. So, for example, Satan says, "The mind is its own place, and in itself / Can make a Heaven of Hell, a Hell of Heaven." In other words, here in Hell, I can be in Heaven; this can be my Heaven. Or most famously, "Better to reign in Hell, than serve in Heaven." If we can understand the psychology behind these lines, we will grasp the core of Milton's picture of satanic evil.

I guess one question is about whether or not choice itself, freedom, is about having lots of possibilities? Does Satan think he had a choice, or does he think he was set up? He seems to oscillate wildly between two of these things here, these two extremes: When he thinks about his own condition, he blames God—"God set me up for this"—but when he thinks about his own ambitions, he thinks of himself as doing it himself, as wholly unsponsored. Think about Satan in comparison to Iblis: In Iblis's case, his fall—the fall of Satan in the Islamic text—is caused by Iblis not doing something, by not acting; and again, we've seen that there's at least a semi-reputable ethical or spiritual rationale for Iblis's resistance on some readings of Iblis. But in Satan's case for Milton, this is not so; Satan's rebellion is clearly wholly self-willed, wholly committed to the idea—more extreme even than Aquinas or Anselm or Dante, too—that Satan should be his own god. In a way that Anselm and Aquinas thought wasn't really possible for Satan, Milton says Satan can actually formulate this thought; and Milton tries in his poetry to represent Satan's thinking as he does this.

How can Satan do this? What's the motive for Satan's sinning? What is Satan's inner life like? We get some of this when Satan tries to talk to other people, to the other fallen devils and especially sometimes to, say, Adam and Eve. In fact, Satan's vision of Adam and Eve sees them in a way as sort of like the Athenians see the Melians in Thucydides. He's looking at them, and he sees them and he says, "Oh, you poor creatures. You are going to suffer for what God has done to me. God's the one who's causing me to cause you to suffer. It's not really your fault; you're caught up in a much larger war between superpowers—myself and God—that treat you like a plaything." Satan thinks he's using the tree of the knowledge of good and evil as a bait for them, luring them out; although, of course as we'll see in a little while, it's not clear for whom the tree of the knowledge of good and evil turns out to be a bait at all. To himself at times, Satan seems to think of himself as someone who, as one of the other angels says, would "rather than be less / cared not to be at all" (this explains the "better to reign in Hell than serve in Heaven"). In other words, rather than be at a lower state than he thinks he deserves, he would rather not be at all. Again, Satan in some sense resents the conditions of his own existence. That's one part of Satan's reality.

The other part that's complicating this whole story is that Satan can never be sincerely satanic; he can never fully believe the story about himself that he's trying to tell. For he knows, and somehow realizes, the foundations of his own being: the futility of sin. At the deepest level, Satan represents in a way the unavoidability of truth. He frequently breaks down in the poem; he frequently despairs. He's continually paranoid that, in fact, everything is still God's plan—that his fall is God's plan, that the temptation of Adam and Eve in the garden is God's plan, that their eventual redemption and elevation (to Satan's former spot in Heaven's court, by the way; they're going to get his apartment), but that's God's plan, too—that the whole plan is God's, not Satan's, and that Satan is thus still a bit player in God's drama. Of course in all this, Satan's paranoia turns out to be right; in fact, the tree, which Satan thought was his bait for Adam and Eve, turns out to be God's bait for Satan. God uses Satan's temptation to pave the way for Christ's redemption and elevation of humanity as it is foreseen and prophesized by the end of the poem. This is the *felix culpa*. So Satan is both simultaneously a rebel and a person who knows rebellion is futile; and the amplitude and magnitude of his verbal rebellion, and the magnificence of it, is paralleled in Milton's representation by a brilliant representation of Satan as also behind that verbal pomposity completely despairing about the futility of this whole exercise.

Think about Adam and Eve now: In comparison to Satan, Adam and Eve are far more, well, they're relatively simple. They are pretty clueless of sin; they don't really understand what it is. This is not to say that they're stupid or that their state is not to be envied; they are perfected humans—they're strong, lucid, extremely intelligent, emotionally astute, serene; they're simultaneously supermodels, celebrities, and Nobel Prize winners—they're basically everything that you and I are not. But one thing that they are that we are not, they are innocent; and that innocence complicates their relationship to the events that unfold within and around them. In fact, Adam is warned, just as in Genesis, in this poem not to eat of the tree by Raphael, one of the angels.

Raphael says to Adam (this is Book 7):

> …but of the Tree
> Which tasted works knowledge of Good and Evil,
> Thou maist not [that is, you shouldn't eat]; in the day thou eat'st,
>   thou die'st;
> Death is the penaltie imposed, beware,
> And govern well thy appetite, least sin
> Surprise thee, and her black attendant Death.

This knowledge that Rafael offers, this warning he gives Adam who them communicates it as well to Eve, can this be useful to them? It's unclear. As the title of a very famous book about this poem puts it, Eve and Adam are "surprised by sin"; that is, they are warned about sin, but they cannot quite understand what it is that is the "it" that they are being warned about. Once again, we come back to the question of the relationship, the very puzzling and mysterious relationship, between innocence and experience here. If Adam and Eve had been warned in a way that acquainted them with sin, in a way they would have had to fall into sin to be able to understand what it was; but absent that immediate acquaintance, any kind of warning is going to be finally not all that useful for them. And inevitably, when Adam and Eve do sin, the sin of Eve—the first one to sin, off on her own gardening—is more of a matter of careless folly, vanity, and pride than of deliberate, monstrous, satanic evil.

Of course, part of the lesson here is that careless folly, vanity, and pride are shown to be disastrous; Milton is not sanding off the sharp edges here. but more interestingly, Adam's decision to eat the apple along with Eve, after she's done it, is itself both a sign of his love for her and also a sign of, and in a way the very event of, the mis-ordering of his own loves; for if he had been properly loving God, he would have eschewed Eve, he would have rejected her at that moment, turned her into God. She would have died, and God would have given him another wife to start a still-perfect human race with. Eve's frivolous sin is one thing; but Adam—some people think Eve is blamed for the whole thing here; it's not true, Eve's frivolous sin is one thing—takes full responsibility because he cannot bear to lose Eve. This is the difference between satanic and human sin. Satanic sin is often just about itself; human sin often complicatedly ropes in other people, or we are roped into sin by other people. Adam falls because he "falls in love"; Adam falls in love in, for, and because of love for Eve.

Think about God: Does the Fall defeat God's plan? Not at all. As Satan suspected, God foreknows this fall, and foreknows its certainty of happening; but God does not preordain it, nor does God create Adam and Eve merely as setups, as "Fall guys." As Milton has God say early on in the poem, God made Adam "Sufficient to have stood, though free to fall." God knows with certainly that it will happen, and God makes God's plans accordingly in the poem. In fact, God says this in the poem, talking about the reason they cannot blame him. God says they cannot blame:

> Their maker, or their making, or their fate,
> As if predestination overruled
> Their will, disposed by absolute decree
> Or high foreknowledge; they themselves decreed
> Their own revolt, not I: if I foreknew,
> Foreknowlege had no influence on their fault [I'm not to blame],
> Which had no less proved certain unforeknown.

That is, had I, God, not foreknown this, it still would have happened.

There's an important thing that Milton is doing here that's very important to see. You have to understand the difference between God, in the philosophical tradition that Milton is coming out of, the difference between God for knowing that something will happen and God commanding that the thing happen. The difference is related to God's participation in time from the perspective of eternity. Eternity does not mean a parallel extension of time running alongside the moments of history; that's not how eternity works. Eternity is a single instant of the fullness of time; and in that instant of the fullness of time, all moments of time are equally present to eternity. In a sense, God in eternity foreknows nothing, because everything is known simultaneously in the present for God in eternity. From any perspective of time, God's knowledge of future events in time will look like foreknowledge; but that's only because we are thinking about it from within time itself. From God's eternal presence to all moments of time, everything has already happened;

so God knows everything before history even, from our perspective, begins. That's why God can foreknow things without compelling them to happen for Milton. God's eternity allows that knowledge to happen for him.

The second thing that God does, or God can say, is not just that God foreknows this, but God will use this Fall to create a greater story still: the story of Jesus Christ and redemption. Gabriel points this out when Adam and Eve and their descendants eventually come to inhabit all the virtues once again, especially love; then they will, he says, "possess / A paradise within thee, happier far." So Satan's plan is, as ever, vexed and turned against him. Remember again Dante's story here; remember the overall story of Christianity: However great evil is, however real it is, it is always going to be enframed by a larger and happier narrative; a narrative whose ultimate ending is guaranteed to be happy. It's an interesting fact about Christianity: For Christianity, the end of the world is already in its own important way scripted in the Book of Revelation; therefore, Christians always are convinced of a happy ending to the world, at least for them.

Let's try to bring together some of these themes. For Milton, human evil is a kind of folly, radically absurd; but it's also a kind of satanic rebellion, which is far more dramatic and dark than we might initially think. But it also is ultimately futile; again, a matter of folly. But God is able to use human evil, and even for Milton satanic evil, as a device for the improvement of the world and potentially as a strategy for human maturation. Many have wondered over time, over centuries, whether Milton's representation of Satan is in some ways too powerful, too vivid, too seductive. The vision of him in his psychic agony, the tortured nature of his motives, and his self-torture at his destiny, his knowledge and his paranoia of what God is doing all conspire to present a remarkably seductive picture of evil: vivid, vigorous, terrifically driven. Satan looks to be the most lively of fictional characters. In contrast, many people have found God, God's son Christ, the good angels, and even Adam and Eve wan, pale, tepid, particularly by comparison to Satan.

Some have even suggested that this was perhaps a deliberate plan of Milton's; that, in fact, Satan turns out to be the most interesting and lively figure not just in *Paradise Lost* but in English literature altogether and Satan appears so purposefully. Indeed, the late 18th century poet and philosophical prophet of sorts—a pretty amazing guy—William Blake famously wrote that, "The reason Milton wrote in fetters when he wrote of Angels & God" (that is, Milton wrote in chains when he wrote of angels and God), "and at liberty when of Devils & Hell," he wrote with his full powers unrestrained when he was talking about the Devils and Hell), "is because he was a true Poet and of the Devil's party without knowing it." That's an astonishing claim, that, in fact, two different ways true poets have to be of the Devil's party in some sense—this is part of what is being suggested here—because they are creating, and to be a creator is to be a rival to God, and that's what the Devil most basically is on this charge anyway.

But I actually think that's wrong; I think Milton knew very well what he was on about. I think his depiction of evil in its purest satanic form is not in fact an elevation of Satan, except in the sense that a specimen is raised up to us so that we may look at it more closely. When one considers the motives and rationales of Satan and Adam, if there is any tragedy in the poem it lies in Adam's choice of Eve, not in Satan's choice of himself; and this explains a bit, I think, the rebel Milton's decision to write an epic where the rebellion was satanic. He had to figure out why he could say sincerely that the English Civil War was not, in fact, a satanic conspiracy; because many people thought it was. In the composition of *Paradise Lost*, Milton manages to make that claim; but more than that, he manages to present what still remains, I think, the unrivaled imaginative representation of probably the full range of human experience that English literature has yet produced.

Next, we'll see the context of another setting, another world in thinking about good and evil; one that is complicatedly related to Milton, but also in some important ways very different: the world of the late 17th and early 18th century Enlightenment.

The Enlightenment and Its Discontents
Lecture 19

Leibniz thinks God has chosen to create a world with free beings who were able to sin and probably would sin, because freedom, even if it was infected and defected by sin—made defective—is still a better thing considered on its own than if we had no freedom in the world at all.

The 17th-century Enlightenment suggested that humans should now, in our full maturity, attempt to address by reason what we had earlier taken on faith and accepted with resignation, namely, that evil could be comprehended and would eventually be conquered. In this lecture, we'll look at three crucial moments in this challenge: the debate between Pierre Bayle and Gottfried Leibniz, the debate between Voltaire and Rousseau, and the amalgamation of these debates in the thinking of David Hume.

Our first debate, that between Bayle and Leibniz, focuses on the question of the proper ambition of the human intellect. Bayle was a fideist, someone who is skeptical about reason's powers to determine most things. He believed that people's deepest convictions are effectively immune from rational assessment and that debate and philosophical analysis are particularly pointless when it comes to religious belief, because people's choices are simply too idiosyncratic in this arena. He famously wrote, "Evil is a problem that reduces all philosophy to hopelessness." Bayle also argued that Manicheanism—the view that proclaimed a metaphysical dualism of rival substances of good and evil in the basic fabric of the cosmos—was the most straightforward philosophical account of evil, considered without appeal to Christian revelation.

Leibniz possessed the most acute philosophical mind of his age. His most famous work, the *Theodicy*, is an extended defense of abstract philosophizing about evil that does not presume any of the assumptions of the Christian faith. Here, Leibniz asserts that the world we inhabit can be proved to be the work of a just and perfectly good God who creates only the best. God is constrained by nothing but logical possibility. Before God begins creating, God intends pure good in its simplest form; then, once creation is underway,

God does the best that can be done with the matter at hand, within the constraints of logic. Thus, we live in "the best of all possible worlds"; it has, Leibniz thinks, the minimal possible evil for the maximal possible good.

Almost a century later, in the wake of the devastating Lisbon earthquake, Voltaire and Rousseau carried on a second version of the Leibniz/Bayle debate. The earthquake stood as the epitome of the problem of natural evil and prompted philosophers to try to make sense of it. Voltaire criticized the optimistic theodicies of Leibniz and others from the basis of the reality of the earthquake. He argued that justifications of these sorts of events are inevitably useless, distracting us from our practical obligations with theoretical questions. For Voltaire, to ask theoretical questions when confronted with practical evil is a profound misconstrual of our own moral and intellectual obligations. Voltaire's hostility to theodicy seems to emerge from his overall skepticism about intellectual efforts; they are simply not grounded in reality.

> **[Rousseau] further suggests that optimism itself—the tendency humans have to look for signs of hope—is a philosophically significant fact about the human condition.**

Rousseau believed that Voltaire's critique of optimistic theodicies was anti-intellectual and cruel. Evil presents us with important concerns on both a practical and an intellectual level. Even if we don't like some formulation of the intellectual effort to address these concerns, to simply turn off our brains is an anti-human thing to do. He further suggests that optimism itself—the tendency humans have to look for signs of hope—is a philosophically significant fact about the human condition. Humans are hopeful, intelligent, meaning-seeking creatures; our optimism suggests that in the face of evil, we can well rely on a kind of supra-rational hope as a mode of response. The source of evil is the same energies that are the wellspring of human hope; evil stems from the misuse of free will and the misappropriation of our optimism.

Hume offers a kind of synthesis of these various views. He believes that theory can lead us in unpleasant directions, writing: "Is [God] willing to prevent evil, but not able? Then is he impotent. Is [God] able, but not willing? Then is he malevolent." But Hume thinks the real problem is that theory gets us nowhere in understanding the place of evil in rational religion; the world is simply too open to offer much in the way of clarity about religious beliefs. Nonetheless, humans do want order to exist, and we do want to care for one another. We are naturally moral and hopeful. Evil and suffering exist, but so do goodness and decency. These facts leave us with a kind of bemused uncertainty about how to formulate theoretical beliefs. But for Hume, this is not a bad thing; we ought to be less concerned with abstract beliefs and more with helping those in need and living our lives to the fullest. ■

Suggested Reading

Antognazza, *Leibniz: An Intellectual Biography.*

Hume, *Dialogues Concerning Natural Religion.*

Leibniz, *Theodicy: Essays on the Goodness of God, the Freedom of Man, and the Origin of Evil,* Huggard, trans.

Neiman, *Evil in Modern Thought: An Alternative History of Philosophy.*

Questions to Consider

1. The Enlightenment thinkers returned in a powerfully new way to the connection between evil and ignorance, this time with an optimistic twist. Is evil merely a name for good that has not yet been understood?

2. What do you think of Voltaire's insistence that justifications and theorizing about evil are useless distractions? Does philosophical reflection on evil do any good at all?

3. Is the case for Manicheanism as compelling as the thinking of such Enlightenment figures as Hume and Bayle? Is the belief in an equally strong power opposing God the most plausible explanation for the existence of evil?

The Enlightenment and Its Discontents
Lecture 19—Transcript

Hello again. The spiritual crisis of the Reformation, the intellectual crisis of the Renaissance, the Political crisis of the early modern rise of the centralized military-industrial state, all lead to a general sense of crisis by the end of the 17th century. There's a general sense of the inadequacy of received forms in learning, in politics, in society, in values and faith, the rise of the new individualism; all these things are happening, and together they come to provoke what we come to know as the Enlightenment. Our lecture today is about how a series of enlightened thinkers thought about the problem of evil.

In the setting of the Enlightenment, holdovers that are in some important way from before the Enlightenment—especially, say, churches and monarchies—are hostile to innovation, almost inevitably seeing the new movements around them as a threat. There will be a structural tension built into the Enlightenment's own thinking of a hostility to traditional forms of thinking because the Enlightenment sees those traditional forms of thinking as in some important way associated with those pre-Enlightenment social structures. It's important right away to say that the Enlightenment is not one thing, there are several different Enlightenments; historians today talk about three or four. For our purposes, that's not that important; what's important, though, is that there are several themes or research agendas, lines of thinking, in the Enlightenment that are all about evil and that all stand in some pretty profound tension with each other. For our purposes, most basic here is a tension between an Enlightenment founded on the idea of turning all of human knowledge into a form of knowledge that is modeled on that of the natural sciences, an Enlightenment of the sciences, versus an Enlightenment that is more humanistic and potentially skeptical of the prospects for that scientific transformation of all knowledge.

Most centrally, however, beyond that—beyond those tensions, though—the Enlightenment itself is in a certain way an argument, and much of that argument centered around the problem of evil. How should we understand evil? What is it? Is it a natural thing; is it a socially constructed thing; is it related to certain social conditions? Is it something that wells up in people unless they are properly trained? Is it something that wells up in people when they are improperly trained? How should we respond to evil? Should we adjust our societies? Should we rethink the way that we teach people about the past? Is there nothing we can do? These are profound and abiding questions for the Enlightenment.

In general, when confronted with the many difficulties it took itself to confront, the Enlightenment innovated by suggesting that humans should now attempt at last, now in our full maturity, to address by our own reason and our own human effort what we had earlier taken on faith and accepted with resignation; namely, that evil could be comprehended and would eventually be conquered. Instead of believing that evil was an ultimate mystery and that it would always be with us, the Enlightenment demanded of people that they try to understand the roots of evil—that's kind of the scientific dimension of the Enlightenment—and that they try in some way to come to terms with and defeat it; to fix the world; to stop the suffering in the world. There are, of course, lots of different ways of going about this. For our purposes, I want to focus on three crucial moments, three big steps or debates, in the Enlightenment: the first one between Pierre Bayle and Gottfried Leibniz; the second one between Voltaire and Rousseau; and the third, a kind of amalgamation of some dimensions of all of those other debates, the Scottish Enlightenment's most famous thinker David Hume and his views about evil.

First, let me talk, though, about the prospects for reason and the hope for what reason would provide for the Enlightenment itself. Much modern thought about evil can be traced back to certain provocations. In thinking about the proper scope of reason's applicability to struggling with the problem of evil, probably the provocation that strikes us most profoundly is this first debate, a debate about the proper ambition of the human intellect; a debate carried out centrally in the work of Pierre Bayle and Gottfried Leibniz. These are two very different people, and they have very interestingly different biographies. Bayle was a persecuted Calvinist, a religious minority from France. He had fled from France to live in the capital of tolerance, Holland. Leibniz was the son of a university professor who became a cosmopolitan diplomat, used to dealing with complicated international issues through deliberation and reason, talking to the authorities of any number of different religious beliefs or political affiliations. These two people come from very different worlds, and they offer different understandings of what it means to be enlightened.

Bayle offered a series of profound and troubling arguments about evil. Most famous of his many works was a book that was known as the *Historical and Critical Dictionary*, a massive text that was, in fact, a dictionary offering definitions of a number of important words; but the definitions themselves were loaded with philosophical arguments in interesting ways. Bayle was what we would call a "fideist"; that is, he's someone who skeptical about reason's powers to determine most things, and relies on faith—in Latin, *fides*—really for his most important convictions. Bayle thought that people's deepest religious convictions and other convictions were effectively immune from rational assessment and critique, and that debate and philosophical analysis are particularly pointless when it comes to religious belief, because people's choices are simply too individually-colored, too idiosyncratic; judgment calls wherein subjective perspective, personal history, and sheer individual taste combine to make it impossible to bring people's views out onto the surface and figure out ways of deciding which are the best and which are the worst.

Because of Bayle's skepticism about reason's power to do this—because of Bayle's fideism, that is—while he was a pessimist about reason, he was interestingly a stout defender of religious toleration. He thought that people should be allowed to have their own beliefs. But in terms of philosophy, he thought that philosophy had a far smaller scope, a far narrower compass, than many of the more optimistic rationalists of his time thought. He famously argued in the dictionary that "Evil is a problem that reduces all philosophy to hopelessness"; and in defining the word "Manichaeism"—that's the view, remember, that Augustine disputed; the view that proclaimed a metaphysical dualism of rival and antithetical substances of good and evil in the basic fabric of the cosmos—he argued that Manicheanism was the most straightforward philosophical account of evil, considered without appeal to Christian revelation. His sly suggestion in his definition of the Manichean view is that a Manichean view "would be rather difficult to refute if it were maintained by pagan philosophers skilled in disputing." This provocation served as a goad to much later modern rationalist metaphysics. To those who thought that the world was clearly morally ordered, both traditional Scholastics and more optimistic Renaissance humanists, Bayle's suggestion is a direct challenge to show how the world is clearly morally ordered; how it's not more obviously caught between rival good and evil metaphysical sources, rival good and evil gods. To all speculatively interested or philosophically-inclined thinkers, Bayle is offering an indirect challenge as well: to show the legitimacy and fruitfulness of abstract philosophical speculation itself.

Among all the people who were provoked by Bayle, almost certainly the most far-seeing and insightful, the most acute philosophical mind of his age, Gottfried Wilhelm Leibniz. Leibniz, who overlapped with Bayle a bit—he lived from 1646–1716—was a brilliant polymath. He was an epoch-making mathematician and rival actually to Newton—both Newton and Leibniz separately invented the mathematical structures we know as calculus today—and a philosopher who as philosopher knew no rival, though he published very little in his life. Leibniz's most famous work is, in fact, called the *Theodicy*—it was published in 1710—and it's the first use of that word in any language because Leibniz invents the word. "Theodicy" means "the justice of God," and the book is an extended defense of abstract philosophizing about evil that does not presume any of the assumptions that Christian faith allows believers to work from without demonstrating them.

The *Theodicy* is a defense of the idea that the world that we inhabit can be seen to be, can be proved to be, the work of a just and perfectly good God who creates only the best. The crucial thing for Leibniz here in showing this—and you could have a whole lecture series just on this book; it's an incredible book—is that God is constrained by nothing but logical possibility; so God does the best God can within the constraints of creation. "God wills," Leibniz says, "antecedently the good and consequently the best." That means that before God begins creating, God intends the pure good in its most simple form. But then, once God's creation gets underway, all God can do is do the best possible with the substances, the matter, at hand within the constraints of logic. This means that our world is, in some important way, the "the best of all possible worlds"; that is, it has, Leibniz thinks, the minimal possible evil for the maximal possible good.

That's a very complicated mathematical formulation there. What he's actually trying to say is that Leibniz thinks God has chosen to create a world with free beings who were able to sin, and probably would sin, because freedom, even if it was infected and defected by sin, made defective, it is still a better thing considered on its own then if we had no freedom in the world at all; if the world were entirely a matter of rocks, plants, and animals that were really responding to sensible stimuli and were not actually free. Even with sin, a world with freedom is better than a world that does not have any freedom and also lacks sin. That's Leibniz's argument.

The poet Alexander Pope, an English poet, offers one vivid Leibnizian picture of how Enlightenment optimism at its most lively could depict this picture; perhaps also it's Enlightenment optimism at its most self-satisfied. In his "Essay on Man," which is actually a poem entitled the "Essay on Man," Pope writes, and let me quote this directly here if I may:

> All Nature is but Art, unknown to thee [divine governance; art];
> All Chance, Direction, which thou canst not see;
> All Discord, Harmony, not understood;
> All partial Evil, universal Good;
> And, spite of Pride and erring Reason's spite,
> One truth is clear, 'Whatever IS, is RIGHT.'

"Whatever is, is right"; Pope's picture of the world offers a powerful argument: that the problem of evil is often simply a matter of flawed perspective, either the perspective of the observer who fails to see the larger context that explains the necessity and possibly ultimate goodness of an evil—thus making of a partial evil a universal good, in Pope's terms—or the perspective of an actor who fails to see that the apparent reasonableness of their wickedness is only "reasonable" from a flawed and partial perspective.

All of this suggests that, in fact, again, here we're touching on the basis of two rival approaches to the Enlightenment. One is quite skeptical of theoretical approaches and wants to emphasize the empirical facts of the matter; this is Bayle. Reason can't access ultimate reality, and so it's best for us to leave be. In some ways, this is like Machiavelli, it might be like Hobbes, it's definitely like Montaigne, and it anticipates some later strands of modern thought, perhaps especially some forms of Romanticism culminating maybe in Nietzsche, on the incommunicability of individual experience. The other—and this is Leibniz's view—is more rationalist, it's more confident of the power of the human mind to make clear the structure of reality even when such intellect seems at a remarkable distance from our everyday perceptions of reality. Much of this theory is not so much known by direct knowledge of reality, by immediate acquaintance, as it is by a form of knowledge or conviction that the theory, as it were, backs into sort of by derivation or implication or deduction of other aspects of the theory. In the same way that where we see smoke rising in a forest we anticipate that there is fire at the basis of that pillar of smoke, a lot of the thinking of a thinker like Leibniz is not a matter of simply pointing and seeing in the world about where reality is, but rather saying that if reality is this way, we have to deduce that standing behind it is this other fact about reality. We'll see this kind of reasoning come up very powerfully in the thought of the philosopher Immanuel Kant in a later lecture.

But let me move on here from the Leibniz/Bayle debate, which really kind of set the term for the question of the limits of reason especially when dealing with evil, to a kind of second iteration, a second version, of that debate carried on almost a century later between Voltaire and Rousseau. Some thinkers had been raising, outside of Bayle's own work, fundamental questions about the scope of reason's capacity to establish a clear and unquestioned moral order in the universe. Some of these thinkers thought that the world should not be as confidently displayed as Pope's poetry suggested it could be. They were skeptical of the optimism and the hopefulness about reason that some thinkers had, and they began to worry more and more as the 18th century went on that, in fact, something important had been missed. The crucial event of this whole era that really shapes the entire thinking of the Enlightenment in ways that it's hard for us to see—again, in the same way that Ancient Near Eastern mythological traditions shadow the Hebrew Bible's understandings of good and evil—the Enlightenment's understanding of evil is shadowed by this event that effects everything that comes after it: the Lisbon Earthquake of November 1, 1775.

In a recent book, a philosopher, Susan Neiman, says that what Auschwitz is to the 20th century, Lisbon was to the 18th. It is the epitome of the problem of evil. Interestingly, Lisbon, of course, is the epitome of the problem not of moral evil, not of an evil caused by obviously human hands, but of natural evil, a problem caused by nature itself. What happened on the morning of November 1, 1755, is that there was a very big earthquake in Lisbon. It was devastating; it ruined buildings and started fires. But 40 minutes later, things got far, far worse: The Bay of Lisbon emptied out, and a tsunami rolled in and washed away the rubble, the burning fires, and a large number of the people. 85 % of the buildings were destroyed or heavily damaged, and about 40,000 or 50,000 people of the capital city of Portugal, Lisbon, simply disappeared, washed out to sea. After this, Portugal, which had been declining as a power but still had significant power especially overseas, was never a power in Europe again.

This event made philosophers across the continent extremely curious to think about how an ordered world could make sense of an event like the Lisbon Earthquake. François-Marie Arouet, who became known as Voltaire, criticized the optimistic theodicies of Leibniz and Pope and those who came after them from the basis of the reality of the Lisbon Earthquake. After the earthquake, in essays and poems, he argued that justifications of these sorts of events are inevitably uselessly theoretical; that is, they are empty of a helpful meaning. They distract us from fundamental philosophical implications, asking the question of we can imagine that somehow a God could create a world where a decent moral order would allow horrific events like this to happen, but why not ask more basic questions about what kind of God is more obviously in charge of a world where this happens, or is a God more obviously in charge of the world where this happens? Second, these theoretical questions distract us from the practical obligations that the reality of evil presents to us. It's quite possible to see someone being mugged on the side of the road and say, "Now what kind of world is it where someone can get mugged on the side of the road?" But they're lying there; you should go help them. That's Voltaire's point: To ask theoretical questions when confronted with practical evil is a profound misconstrual of your own not only moral but intellectual obligations.

This vision of Voltaire's is especially explored in his brilliant book *Candide: A Novel*, which offers a wonderful story of a man who has many misfortunes that happen to him, but then at the end of the novel he finally says, "In the end, we all have to retreat back to our own lives and cultivate our own gardens." In some sense, he's lost his hopefulness about the intellectual ambitions of his youth, and he's come to see that it's much happier to live a quiet and happy life in your own garden.

Voltaire's hostility to theodicy seems to emerge from his overall skepticism about intellectual efforts, theory, abstract reasoning per se; his suspicion there is that it's simply not grounded in reality. He was skeptical about traditional thinking too—traditional Catholic theology was not on Voltaire's top 10 list of things to be reading—but he didn't take it as seriously as he did the thinking of his Enlightenment colleagues who were more optimistic about reason.

In response to Voltaire, others such as Jean-Jacques Rousseau took the problems presented by history and reflection on human evil in a slightly less angry way than Voltaire did. Consider Rousseau's recoil from Voltaire's critique of optimistic theodicies: Effectively, he thinks Voltaire is just making fun of these theodicies. He says in a letter to Voltaire that your critique of them offers no positive contribution, it only offers scorn. There's something, he suggests, profoundly misanthropic and anti-intellectual to Voltaire's hostility to the intellectual effort of theodicy here.

Second, Rousseau says, Voltaire's rejection of theoretical questions about evil is also cruel. There's something important that evil presents to us not just on the practical level, there's something important it presents to us on the intellectual level. Even children who want to know why their parents are suffering from an illness don't necessarily only have practical questions about how to help their parents, they're also able to ask very abstract questions: What does it mean that mommy or daddy is sick like this? What does it mean about the world I'm living in? They may not be able to put it in those words, Rousseau says, but everybody, no matter how young, is an incipient philosopher and can ask these questions. Rousseau's disquiet here foreshadows the work of Immanuel Kant, to whom we will turn in a future lecture as well. Much as Leibniz's first construction of this theodicy did, Rousseau is modifying the inspiration here to say: You may not like some formulation of the intellectual effort, but to suggest that you simply have to turn off your brain on these issues is a profoundly anti-human thing to do, Voltaire.

Third, Rousseau suggests—and here again he is in important ways pre-shadowing Kant, foreshadowing Kant—that optimism is itself, the tendency humans have to look for signs of hope, is a fact about the human condition that must be acknowledged and has to be a philosophically significant fact. Rousseau is no naïve traditionalist—he was no more fond of the Roman Catholic hierarchy in France than Voltaire was—but he values the evidence of the past enough to suspect that the traditional insistence on the world as a morally ordered place gets at something deep, some deep intuition and conviction that humans have. It's an intuition that we have perhaps historically mis-expressed in various ways over the course of human history to be sure, Rousseau says. We have many flawed and faulty dogmas—this conviction we have has become formulated in many different ways over the course of human history—but if you look at all these religions and all these philosophies, again and again we see behind their dogmas some intuition of the moral order of the universe. That intuition is what we cannot simply jettison, as you, Monsieur Voltaire, would have us do.

Rousseau thinks humans are hopeful and intelligent, meaning-seeking creatures; our optimism is inexpugnable from our being and our interest in philosophically respectable justifications for that optimism is a permanent fact about us; it's not one that merits scorn. The optimism itself suggests that in the face of evil we can well rely on a kind of supra-rational hope as a mode of response to it. We may not be able rationally to formulate that hope, but nonetheless we can never attempt to suffocate that light, extinguish that candle of hope. Rousseau thinks that it's also the case that a lot of human evil itself comes out of the misuse of human free will and the misappropriation of this optimism we have, an optimism perhaps that's more locally identified with our own self-interest in some ways. But more mercifully than some of his antecedents, Rousseau did not think that this perversion that was pervasive in human free will was in any traditional way related to a doctrine of original sin; it was not a willful misuse, he thought. It was rather a result from unintended consequences of free decisions taken in response to actions early on in our lives. For him, the source of evil comes out of the same energies that are the wellspring of human hope; and even as that hope always springs again anew into our hearts, we are going to have to confront its perpetual struggle with our misappropriation of that hope and our misappropriation of that freedom in our evil actions. But you cannot deny the hope by recognizing the evil actions alone.

After in some ways in conversation with Voltaire and Rousseau, David Hume, working out of Edinburg—though he knew Paris; he knew the French world quite well—differs from both of them but shares similar concerns with both about optimism; and in a way offers a kind of synthesis of these various views. Philosophically, of course, Hume is known as a skeptic, and a kind of a naturalist; someone who wants to understand human motivation and human thinking as different dimensions of the human as a natural animal. His work offers the most powerful restatement of the problem of evil as that problem presents itself to religious belief. He well understood the words of Epicurus, and he quotes them in his famous *Dialogues Concerning Natural Religion* very well. He says: "Is [God] willing to prevent evil, but not able? Then is he impotent. Is [God] able, but not willing? Then is he malevolent. Is he both able and willing? Whence then is evil?" Hume has a way with pithy statements, and that is probably one of his most pithy and most wonderful statements. Effectively he's saying, if God wants to help us with evil but can't, then God is not fully as powerful as we think he is; if God can help us with evil but doesn't want to, then God is not as good as we thought he is; and those are our options unless you can think of a third one. Hume says, "I can't think of a third one."

For Hume, that is, theory may lead us in unpleasant directions if we use it too far; but actually, he thinks, the real problem is using theory where we really shouldn't, because in this, he's a little bit like Pierre Bayle. Theory gets us nowhere in understanding the place of evil for rational religion. The fact of evil suggests the cosmos' indifference towards humanity, and evil offers evidence to support some forms of Manichaeism. But Hume is no fideist like Bayle was. He wants to be a mild skeptic, someone dubious of pretty much every religious account because the evidence that we can garner from our observations of the world will inevitably be insufficient to support any account over almost any other account. The world is simply too open to offer much in the way of clarity about religious beliefs.

But part of the evidence that Hume reads in the world is Rousseauean in nature: Humans do want there to be order, and we do want to care for one another. We are naturally moral, naturally hopeful. Evil and suffering exist for Hume, of course, but so does goodness and decency. Because of that, Hume's skepticism extends even to atheism. He thinks even atheism is significantly under-supported by the evidence of our lives. We're left instead with a kind of bemused uncertainty about how to formulate our theoretical beliefs, at least to the level of specificity that many of us have thought that we needed to formulate them to. But for Hume—and here he's a bit like Montaigne—this is not a bad thing; we ought to be less concerned with our abstract beliefs and more with helping those in need and living, for our lives, a happy and flourishing life.

In general, in all of these debates and for all of these thinkers, there are two large themes about thinking about evil that will come up again and again, that have been formulated here in some way or other: First is the question of the more abstract versus the more concrete modes of thinking about evil. The second is the question of the metaphysical plausibility of the dualism of evil and good; or, if you don't want to frame it that way, the more general question of the proper understanding of the proportions of good and evil in the cosmos. Optimists of a certain sort thought that the world was largely good, but then events like Lisbon raised the question for some people.

In the next lecture, we will see that the work of Immanuel Kant offers his own innovative attempt to bring all these tensions to a resolution in a single philosophical system.

Kant—Evil at the Root of Human Agency
Lecture 20

> Throughout his mature work, Kant tried to show that human reason has real power but also real limit and that the best exercise of that reason is to use it to chart the limits of human thinking and, thereby, to deduce as clearly as possible without direct knowledge what it cannot properly know.

Immanuel Kant is, simply, the most revolutionary and foundational thinker of the modern world. Yet for all his intellectual power, he led quite a pedestrian life. He was born, lived, and worked his entire life in the town of Königsberg in East Prussia. With the publication of the massive *Critique of Pure Reason*, he effectively accomplished a Copernican revolution in philosophy, shifting the focus of philosophical attention from objects—the outside world—to the subject—the human being and the puzzle of how we can know our world.

In the *Critique of Pure Reason*, Kant suggested that metaphysical theodicies, such as that offered by Leibniz, cannot accomplish what they set out to prove. Like Hume, Kant thought that the evidence of the world was simply indeterminate on the question of the goodness of God. Furthermore, that indeterminacy extends so far as to make any explicitly theoretical claims in this realm of thinking finally not confident enough to be defended. Kant believed that something more is required of us than sheer speculative cognition if we are

Immanuel Kant (1724–1804) shifted the focus of philosophical attention from objects to the subject, to the knowing and acting subject.

to find a satisfactory response to the problem of evil, and that something was what he called practical reason. Given that theory can't help us intellectually solve the problem of evil, what we need to do is investigate why evil is a problem for us at all. When we undertake this investigation, we discover that we have another source of quasi-knowledge inside us, apart from reason, in the persistent urging of our will toward resisting evil and working to repair it where we can. In short, it is our will that tells us what is evil and makes us experience it as evil. This experience of the will's opposition to evil is the basis of what Kant calls practical reason properly understood.

For our study, Kant's most important work is *Religion within the Limits of Bare Reason*. It is an exploration of "rational religion," which is all we can know about religion from the perspective of human reason. This is an assessment of the core rational principles on which any religion must be founded, stripped of the historical trappings imposed by particular faiths.

> **Kant's language of radical evil means to be a sober acknowledgment of the profundity of human corruption, while also insisting that humans have brought this condition on themselves.**

Kant insisted that Christian dogmas of original sin get at the universal truth that **radical evil** operates at the base of the human will. Kant locates radical evil in a fundamental disposition of the will to privilege itself over the general good. It is a corruption of our core "moral maxim," prompting us to act out of a "maxim of sensible self-interest"; we treat others as instruments in a drama that is all about our own self-glorification. But this corruption can never be total; we must admit that other people exist, and we know that on some level, they matter beyond our own self-interest. That means that evil is always partial and always builds on a kind of irrationality. Nonetheless, for Kant, this corruption of our moral maxim is so deep that it requires a radical transformation of our overall character, an awakening to the reality that there are other people in the world who have as much moral import as we do.

To many of his readers, Kant's views on radical evil seemed to return to the old superstitions that intellectuals had fought so hard to escape. But for Kant, the language of radical evil was meant to capture the truth latent in traditional religious understandings, namely, that evil's elimination from our lives is not easy or straightforward and is not entirely describable in terms of rational, self-willed human action. His language of radical evil means to be a sober acknowledgment of the profundity of human corruption, while also insisting that humans have brought this condition on themselves.

Kant pioneered a method known as "demythologizing," in which the resolution to a problem we face is recognized to go beyond mere cognition to an appreciation of the power and wisdom of myth; nevertheless, this myth still admits itself to some kind of analysis. The demythologizer is suspicious of the idea that an individual, simply thinking through problems alone, will come to suitable answers. Myth (religion) has a profundity of meaning and a density of symbolic reference beyond the ability of any philosophical system to fully articulate. With this approach, Kant gave us an intellectual style of thinking about evil that has grown increasingly popular over the centuries, that is, not simply to dismiss the past as irrelevant but to appreciate it and, at the same time, to handle it with gloves made entirely of reason. ∎

Name to Know

Kant, Immanuel (1724–1804 C.E.). Born in Königsberg, Prussia, where he lived all his life. A student at the University of Königsberg, Kant made several important contributions to astronomy in his early career before turning increasingly to philosophy.

Important Term

radical evil: The term used by Immanuel Kant to describe the fundamental disposition of the will to privilege itself over the general good.

Suggested Reading

Kant, *Religion within the Boundaries of Mere Reason and Other Writings*, Wood and di Giovanni, trans.

1. Does Kant's concept of radical evil accurately reflect what earlier Christians meant by original sin?

2. Do all human beings actually possess a fundamental disposition of the will to privilege itself over the general good?

3. Was Kant correct to argue (against previous Enlightenment thinkers) that the problem of evil cannot finally be answered by theoretical reason alone?

Kant—Evil at the Root of Human Agency
Lecture 20—Transcript

Welcome back. In this lecture, I want to talk about the thought of Immanuel Kant, the great German philosopher, on evil. While there have been several significant philosophers in the past few centuries—majorly significant philosophers; Leibniz and Hegel also come to mind—it's hard to imagine that anyone would seriously contest Kant's claim to be the most revolutionary and most foundational thinker of the modern world. His thought is as fundamental and far-reaching as Plato's, or Aristotle's, or Aquinas's, or Augustine's, or Descartes's. It's simply impossible to imagine putting another modern philosopher into that group of people.

Kant had, for all his revolutionary intellectual power, a quite pedestrian life. He was born in 1724 in the town of Königsberg in East Prussia. It was his hometown throughout his childhood; and, in fact, he never in his entire life travelled more than 110 miles from Königsberg. He had offers to move to other universities eventually; he never took them. He was raised in a very strict Pietist family and that background stuck with him his whole life, long after he stopped being a Pietist himself as a young adult. Pietism was a form of German Protestantism that was very rigorous and very, very focused on having the proper emotional response to the scriptures and to one's experience of religious salvation, and also it was a very moralistic kind of religion. He enrolled at the University of Königsberg in his hometown in 1740, and he would remain there at the university as a student and then a professor for basically the rest of his life.

Initially, actually, Kant was a scientist who made significant discoveries, really made his name in a way, in kind of planetary physics. He discovered some interesting discrepancies in the velocity of the earth's rotation due to tidal variations, believe it or not; and these discrepancies, what he discovered, have actually of really substantial importance for planetary science. People recognized its interest and insight in the 18th century, but it was not fully appreciated for what it meant for understanding how worlds move and things like that until the 19th century. But in 1755, at the age of 31, he became a lecturer at the university—it was his first real job—and he was assigned to teach on metaphysics; so he began doing lectures on metaphysics and on the philosophy of nature. Fifteen years after that, after many attempts to get other jobs, better jobs—again, in Königsberg or at the university, but never really outside of it—he was appointed the professor of logic and metaphysics in 1770.

Being a professor in a German university gives you a certain level of stability and financial safety, but it comes with a significant amount—then as now—of labor. Kant taught, by contract, by his legal obligations, at 7 am four days a week, and then did private teaching—tutorials, reviews, things like that who paid him extra or just came for his office hours—every day, but all of his duties would end by lunchtime, which was always a really substantial meal for Kant. Actually at that meal he famously always kept an open invitation to any sailor who appeared in the harbor of Königsberg—assuming that they were of relatively decent character—to come and share his meal, and tell him what they had seen of the world. Though he didn't himself apparently want to or at least feel the need to travel far, he was perpetually extremely interested in the outside world; he used to give lectures on world geography and things like that. He was very interested in the world. He basically keeps this schedule for the rest of this life, and the good people of Königsberg famously used to say that you could set your watch by Professor Kant's walk after his lunch. The one day he failed to take his walk is when he received in the mail from the 18th-century version of Amazon.com his copy of Rousseau's novel *Emile*, which he basically apparently read in one day avidly. Rousseau will come up later as one of Kant's enormous influences.

The other great influence for Kant, of course, is one he discovered it seems in 1771, when he first encountered the work of David Hume, whose work he ever after credited for "awakening" him, he said, from his "dogmatic slumber." Having appreciated the work of Hume, Kant effectively went into a kind of intellectual seclusion and reeducation, reconsidering the foundations of human knowledge and the basic structure of the world. For the next 10 years he published nothing. The authorities at the university must have been quite upset at this: They had just appointed this guy professor, he is clearly a very prominent guy, and yet now once he gets the job he suddenly stops publishing things.

First of all, it's astonishing—we should note this—how many of the people that we've been looking at in these lectures have had these longstanding periods of intensely private research. We saw it with Milton, we saw it with Hobbes, we saw it with Montaigne, now we see it with Kant. If we had the ability to know biographically more about people deeper in the past—Plato, Aristotle, Augustine, Aquinas—we would probably find similar intense periods of really radical interiorization in their lives, where they're really burrowing deep down into themselves and into their scholarship in a way that seems to make no sense to people outside of them. Second—and I say this as an academic—this silent period is a pretty strong argument for sort of tenure that Kant himself had. Had Kant not been assured of permanent employment, he probably would not have been able to take, to enjoy, the peace and quiet required to undertake the massive project that he did. In those 10 years, he wasn't just being an aimless, pointless dilly-dallier; he was rethinking the basic structures of human existence and knowledge themselves.

In 1781, he broke his silence with the massive—800 pages in the German—first edition of the *Critique of Pure Reason*. It was so vast, and precisely because he had been so deep down inside himself inside his own thinking on this, it was so difficult to attach Kant's project to the fashionable questions, concerns, and formulations of his age in the scholarly world, that the work actually was largely ignored on first publication. It took about 10 years, another edition of the *Critique*, and some heavy efforts at explanation, revision, and publicity on the part of Kant and some of his friends and early followers, people who grasped what he was trying to do—which was not easy to do, especially in that first edition; it's hard to understand Kant now, but it was especially hard to understand Kant in that first edition—it took about 10 years for people to being to understand the impact of what he was doing; and when that happened, the philosophical world changed.

Kant had effectively accomplished what peopled called of his work a "Copernican revolution" in philosophy; he shifted the focus of philosophical attention from objects to the subject, to the knowing and acting subject. Before Kant, it's not entirely unfair to say that philosophers were caught in the naïve assumption that the human knower can be taken for granted and that the puzzle is about how the outside world can be known. How it is that the world itself can be known to us is a puzzle really about objects in the world for earlier thinkers than Kant in some way. After Kant, it becomes clear that the puzzle of knowledge is not first and foremost a puzzle about how the world can be known, but about how we can know our world and in what, precisely, that knowledge consists.

Kant, after the first critique—which you might guess, because we call it the "first critique"—kept publishing works of enormous impact. He published two other very important critiques: the *Critique of Practical Reason*, which is kind of his *Ethics*, and then the *Critique of Judgment*, which is a study of aesthetics and the theory of beauty and the understanding of the meaning of art; how people experience beauty in the world. And he always taught rigorously, up until 1796, fully 56 years after he had entered the University of Königsberg as a young student. He died in 1804.

Kant's work can be understood as an attempt overall to retain something of the theoretical and intellectual ambition of Leibniz while reckoning seriously with the challenge of other thinkers, especially Hume and Rousseau. His work is important for all aspects of later philosophy and political theory; modern life in general. His understanding of the human and of the human's predicament, thinking how it experiences the world, has shaped all aspects of our life. I won't go into it here, his larger philosophy, which is a lecture series entirely on its own; but let me just say that throughout his mature work, Kant tried to show that human reason has real power but also real limits, and that the best exercise of that reason is to use it to chart the limits of human thinking, and thereby to deduce as clearly as possible without direct knowledge what it cannot properly know. Kant actually famously said he denied reason to make room for faith; and not just religious faith, but faith in certain realities outside of our minds, certain moral truths that we cannot empirically prove.

In his other critiques, and especially in the *Critique of Pure Reason*, Kant suggested that metaphysical theodicies cannot accomplish what they set out to prove; theodicies of the sort that Leibniz offered. Here he had learned a lot from Hume. Like Hume, he thought that the evidence of the world was simply indeterminate between there being a good god and there being no such deity, and even whether there is a bad god. Furthermore, he thought that the indeterminacy extended so far as to make any explicitly theoretical claims in this realm of thinking finally not confident enough to be defended. That is, Kant argued that arguments for and against the goodness of an omnipotent God in the face of the reality of evil are, in fact, interminable, they're unending; and that this fact, that we can show that these arguments for the goodness of God and against the goodness of God both can continue without being radically refuted but also will continue ad infinitum without being finally completely evidenced, completely proven, shows us (he thought) that sheer reason cannot answer our questions in this area. In fact, he thought, something more is required of us than sheer speculative cognition if we are to find a satisfactory response to the problem of evil; and what that is, is what Kant calls "practical reason."

Practical reason is the topic of his second critique, the *Critique of Practical Reason*; we don't need to go into that very much here. But we can say on this stuff, if he is understanding himself as appreciating the lessons of Hume on theodicy, here he's appreciating the lessons of Rousseau in response to Voltaire, especially about hope. If theory can't help us intellectually solve our problem with the problem of evil, what we need to do, then, is investigate why the problem is for us at all? That is, we need to problematize, to identify as a puzzle, and to begin to be curious about the fact that evil bugs us. Deer are not troubled by the fact that lions hunt, stalk, and eat them. Antelope do not generate seminars about the problem of the wolf. Humans are the only creatures who seem to have this puzzle about why bad things happen to us. When we do this, when we investigate this experience we have, we discover that, in fact, we have another source of a kind of quasi-knowledge inside us apart from reason in the persistent urging of our will itself towards resisting evil, expressing outrage at it, and working to repair evil where we can. In short, we discover that it is our will that tells us what is evil and makes us experience it as evil. This experience of the will's opposition to evil is the basis of what Kant calls practical reason properly understood.

Practical reason properly understood; let me stop here for a second and think about this. What he wants to say is that if you understand why you are so outraged at this, this intuition about outrage at evil and wrongness actually can serve as a kind of foundation for understanding how you should act in the world. If the world doesn't rationally give evidence for good or evil, nonetheless the fact that we seek evidence for good is itself, for Kant, the source of the motive for us for doing good. It's a brilliant move on his part. In other words, the morality of the world turns out to be not a fact about the world out there in itself, but again it's a fact about how we can only live with ourselves, Kant thought, in some basic way—although people can clearly go wrong—how we can only live with ourselves or best live with ourselves if we live in a world where the intuitions that drive the basis of our action, those intuitions that we should live in a just world, are allowed to have their fullest extent in shaping our action and shaping the way that we through our action shape the world.

Kant's philosophical metaphysics, his epistemology; these have been enormously influential. His moral theory has been profoundly influential as well. But surprisingly, his thinking about evil itself has not often been studied or appreciated as much. Most philosophers, actually, will read the *Critique of Pure Reason*, the *Critique of Practical Reason*; the really esoteric and "beturtlenecked" philosophers might go ahead and read the aesthetics of the *Critique of Judgment*; but much of the time scholarly attention stops there. But the fourth of these books, the four big books he wrote, *Religion within the Limits of Bare Reason*, hardly anyone looks at this book. Yet for our purposes, this is, in fact, the important book, which he publishes in 1793 and is in some ways the last of the great works of Kant.

The book's title itself is very important for its argument. The book is an attempt to talk about "rational religion," which is all we can know about religion from the perspective of human reason. He suggests that actual historical religions function as clothes for this "rational religion," with each historical religion more or less adequately clothing the rational religion. We can look at an historical religion—Christianity, Judaism, Hinduism, what have you—and assess how properly it captures, it clothes, that rational religion, the core of religious belief that Kant thought was universal, and that's how we can assess the adequacy of these historical pictures. The book, then, means to talk about and wants to talk about religion naked of the historical trappings that any particular religious faith has put upon it. It wants to lay out the criteria for assessing any actual religious faith by looking at the core rational principles on which any religion, Kant thinks, has to be founded.

I have doubts—I study religion and I have my doubts—about whether such a thing as rational religion exists, at least in the way that Kant thought it exists. It seems to assume, Kant seems to assume, a unified core of basic religious beliefs common to all traditions, and yet that core doesn't seem there when you consider those many things that humans count as religions around the world; that we would count as religions around the world, whoever "we" are. But let's leave that alone for right now, and let's go on to think about what Kant is talking about here in terms of radical evil; for that's what's important in this book for us.

Kant insisted that Christian dogmas of "original sin" get at the universal truth, meaningful even for those outside the Christian faith; that something he called "radical evil" can be seen to operate at the base of the human will. Talk about radical even can seem maybe a bit mythological; it can seem too melodramatic a picture. We'll see that many of Kant's own readers in his own time thought of that worry and raised it with Kant, and many reviews complained about it. But Kant is not trying to be mythological; he's trying to be as precise as possible about the source of evil. He locates it, radical evil, in a fundamental disposition of the will to privilege itself over the general good; that is, "radical evil" is a defect in the human at the root of human agency. That's what "radical" means in Latin; *radius*, it means "at the root." Radical evil is a corruption of our core moral maxim—that's what Kant calls the core moral disposition out of which we act—and it corrupts it so that we do not act out of the maxim that we should treat everyone as we would want to be treated, but instead we act out of some form of what Kant calls a maxim of sensible self-interest, where we treat everyone else in some way or other as instruments in a drama that is all about our own self-glorification; we treat everyone else as if they were bit players in a movie where we were the sole star.

Interestingly, by talking about radical evil as corruption here—and Kant is very clear about this—he aligns himself with a certain strand of thinking we've seen already, what we can call broadly the Augustinian strand on evil. We'll see Kant descending from Augustine in some ways in a minute, but on this he's very Augustinian, because the corruption as corruption can never be total. We cannot but in some sense admit, Kant thinks, that other people exist, and so we know that we are compelled on some level to admit that they matter beyond our own self-interest. Thus, when we are selfish, Kant thinks, we are rationally contradicting ourselves; we are incoherent; we are not as fully rational as we should be. That means that evil—and again, going back to Augustine—is always partial and always builds on a kind of irrationality that is at the heart of human malfeasance in the world for this tradition.

Nonetheless, for Kant—as we saw for Augustine, but let's focus on Kant here—this corruption of our moral maxim is so radical, is so deep in us, that it requires itself a radical transformation of our overall character. For Kant, the change is a matter of a revolution inside the self, a waking up to the reality that there are other people in the world who have as much moral import as you do, and that this transformation of the root disposition—the "maxim" by which we guide our actions—is actually profoundly altering of our whole being. Kant says this is what early Christians talked about, about conversion, about metanoia, a change of one's whole being. How does this happen? Kant actually doesn't really say, apart from saying that it is in some important way our decision; but because it's a decision at so fundamental a level of our being as to be in some sense a decision about how we are to decide things—it's about how we act in general, so how do we decide to change the principle of how we decide?; it's mysterious—it seems to come for us, anyway, in our experience of it, also from in some sense outside of us as a kind of magic, or perhaps grace. Such changes as these—these radical transformations—are of the sort of things, Kant thinks, which only religious language has ever really adequately described.

Kant's views on radical evil were scandalous for many of his readers. They saw Kant as one of the great figures of Enlightenment, of the idea that a human mind, unfettered at last from the tight shackles of tradition, daring, as Kant himself once put it, to think for itself at last; that this mind could on its own confront and overcome the age-old difficulties that had long vexed humanity throughout its history. For him now to be talking about "radical evil" seemed to bring back all the old superstitions and intellectual canards that they had fought so hard to escape. Some thought Kant had sold out to the emerging Prussian police state, which looked smilingly—as police states often do—on traditional religious practice. Others thought he had just become massively reactionary in his old age; rumors even began to spread that he might be senile, going a little dotty in his dotage. But Kant knew better;

and what he knew was that the language of radical evil meant to precisely capture the truth latent in traditional religious understandings: namely, that evil's elimination from our lives is not easy or straightforward, and is not entirely describable in terms of rational human action that is entirely self-willed. He meant to say that the idea is important without collapsing into or falling back to traditional notions of original sin, because Kant thought those notions failed adequately to capture the individual person's responsibility for their wickedness. His language of radical evil means to be a sober acknowledgment of the profundity of human corruption while also insisting that this is a condition that the human has brought upon him or herself; it's not an illness, it's a self-inflicted wound.

Those who read him carefully realized he had aligned himself, in his discussion of the nature of human moral action, more with those heretical Christians who insisted that humans and not Christ, not grace, were fundamentally responsible for their own moral perfection. Once Kant was understood to be not so much defending traditional Christianity by his more extreme Enlightenment followers but actually still endorsing a kind of Christian heresy, he became more tolerable to them. But nonetheless, the crucial thing he had done, which shadows which had been done before but he was the first person really to do it, and which only became clear over time in the method he used, was to inaugurate or pioneer a method we can call "demythologizing."

Demythologizing, demythological demythologizing accounts, often suggest—essentially suggest, I would say—that a resolution to a problem we face must go beyond mere cognition, mere thinking about the problem, and the explicit formulations of rational intelligence, and appreciate the power and wisdom of myth. Nonetheless, these approaches—a demythologizing approach—insists there's positive wisdom and insight in them; but this myth is something that only partially gets at the truth of the point, the demythologizer will say, so philosophical analysis or some kind of clear analysis, conceptual clarity, must be applied in order to clarify and systematize the truth of the matter. To do this, you have to recognize the obscure profundity, the demythologizer says, of traditional religion; how it suggests that sheer human experience processed over many generations has a level of insight that the simple activity of one person thinking on their own cannot provide.

Again here, we see the tension, the conflict, which comes out in a lot of these people we've been thinking about: the tension between the wisdom of experience versus the capacities of individual intellectual effort, of theory. The demythologizing, even though it's a very intellectually ambitious practice, is also profoundly suspicious of the idea that an individual, simply acting on their own to think through these problems, is going to come to the right, or profound, or suitable answers. Myth has a profundity of meaning, demythologizers will say, and a density of symbolic reference beyond the ability of any philosophical system to articulate in a full way; and the account says all this even as it does not affirm such religious stories or mythologies as literally true. It seeks instead within them to find a deep though incompletely formulated truth about the human. It demythologizes in this way in taking out a myth and looking at it, and identifying it, and reformulating it in something that it thinks of in a clearer and more precise language of rational human cognition.

This is a very controversial strategy in thinking about human life in general and especially maybe in thinking about evil. There are a couple worries about it you can have: First of all, can it be completed? Is there some way that you can actually completely demythologize a myth and render it intelligible and acceptable for intellectual digestion without any remainder? Lots of people have tried, and as far as I know, so far no one has actually succeeded in that. Another way of framing this question is to ask rather directly: Does such an attempt distort the mysterious mythological message at the heart of a story and render it so rational and articulate as to be flatfooted? It's possible, I imagine, to talk about *Moby Dick* as a story about a fish. It's possible to talk about *Hamlet* as a story about an insecure prince. It's possible to talk about the *Epic of Gilgamesh* as a story about a guy who feels really sad that he lost his friends. But in each of these formulations, something really important gets lost.

Those are worries about this approach, but it's only fair to say that in important ways we all in different ways undertake this approach all the time. Whenever you hear anyone talking about the profundity of ancient ways of thinking about evil, and how they almost got things right but now we know better, you're hearing the echo of Kant. You might have heard some of that in what I've said in previous lectures in this class as well. Also, whenever you hear anyone talking about the problem of humans being basically that they are selfish, and implying that they have to make themselves better on their own, they are also echoing, unknowingly, Kant. Kant turns out, that is, to be behind both the intellectual style of thinking about evil that has grown increasingly popular in the past several centuries—that is, not simply to dismiss the past as irrelevant but to appreciate it, but at the same time handle it with gloves made entirely of reason so that you try to discern in the muddy past a kind of rational essential message that we can extract; that's one way he's been influential—and the other is by focusing our attention essentially on the idea that at the heart of the human is a selfish will whose struggle to become better is a struggle that ultimately only the self can accomplish on his or her own.

From Kant now I want to look at someone who disagreed with him but also drew on him profoundly for a very different picture of evil, and a picture of evil that we've seen echoed in a distant past in our lectures before in the thought of the theologian Irenaeus: that is, here I want to turn to the thought of the German philosopher Hegel.

Hegel—The Slaughter Block of History
Lecture 21

The U.S. Civil War, for example, is itself not just a dumb event; it is, in a complicated way, an intellectual event. It is an attempt in part by the two sides, the two bodies of competence, to understand the meaning of the American Revolution, as people on both sides of that war recognized. The Civil War was an intellectual struggle as much as it was a military struggle.

In this lecture, we'll look at two aspects of the work of Georg Wilhelm **Friedrich Hegel**: first, his construal of the meaning of original sin and the nature of evil for humans and, second, his assessment of the overall place of evil and the role it plays in history.

The Enlightenment rejected the doctrine of original sin as primitive and unscientific, but Hegel saw it as a consequence of human reflexivity, the ability of humans to step back and think about themselves as they are doing something. Thinking naturally estranges us from our immediate situation; we become self-conscious, which is a form of sin for Hegel. To render ourselves as available as objects of thought is, in some sense, to lose our original organic integrity.

Further, Hegel sees that humanity is clearly at odds with the world and its true nature. The doctrine of original sin, in any of the various religious formulas it's offered, may be stale or mythological, but the insight being communicated is profound: We do, in fact, exist in a state of inevitable and seemingly inescapable estrangement from the world and ourselves. The Fall is the rupture of pure unself-conscious identity into a split awareness. That's formulated as evil, but it brings with it an awareness of the lost status as one that was good. Sin is not only an experience we experience in itself, but it also gives us a kind of nostalgia for an endemic earlier state. Hegel thinks this condition is necessary for our maturation into complete self-consciousness, which somehow entails a return to a complete absorption in the context in which we find ourselves, something like a master musician performing his or her craft.

For Hegel, the story of history is, on one level, about the human intellect coming into maturity through its reflection on history and its struggle to understand the story of its own development. This picture assumes that history actually means something that we can understand and render intelligible to ourselves. History is an activity or a process, but it is in part a process driven forward by people attempting to discern just what that process means. The very activity of questioning shapes the events that come afterwards.

> **For Hegel, reality is essentially rational, and the core of history is an intelligible story of how both the human and the "World Spirit" are coming to know themselves.**

It's true that we attempt to make history intelligible all the time, but Hegel extends this claim audaciously: History is not only the human mind coming to understand itself, but in fact, the mind is involved in a much larger working out of something far more vast than merely the human, namely, God's unfolding self-understanding. For Hegel, reality is essentially rational, and the core of history is an intelligible story of how both the human and the "World Spirit" are coming to know themselves. Having chosen, over many thousands of years, this course of history—however filled with evil and mysterious suffering it may be—the World Spirit chooses this history as the story of its own realization of its power. This representation of God means that God is using the whole of history—and human attempts to understand history—to make sense of God. We are, thus, bit players in a history far greater than we can currently comprehend.

In Hegel's view, then, history has a certain telling that makes sense, and that telling is, in some sense, a rational telling. Consider the phenomenon of the Black Death. It killed about half of Europe, but it also created the conditions for the Reformation. A thing that can devastate a civilization at one moment may, in fact, turn out to enable that civilization to survive and prosper in other ways in the future. This is what Hegel calls the "cunning of reason." Still, we can't always, at the moment, tell just what reason is meaning to do; all we know is that, in the end, it will make sense. Thus, history can be said to be providentially governed, and the true philosophy of history is a theodicy, a justification of all the suffering that has happened.

Hegel's theodicy is not, however, the mechanical and static kind that Leibniz offered. Hegel has a more organic and developmental understanding of evil. He begins with the idea of divine providence, but once he adopts a view of God as immanent in human history, the only conclusion left is that events that are real are justified precisely because they are necessary. The Lisbon earthquake, devastating as it was, was a necessary part of the World Spirit's coming to know itself. Further, Hegel doesn't attempt to reconcile humans to the existence of evil. In his view, concrete evils happen as part of the unfolding of the logic of history, but they are ultimately justified by the course of history, and in that justification, they turn out never to have been evils at all. ∎

Name to Know

Hegel, G. W. F. (1770–1831 C.E.). Born in Stuttgart, Germany. When he was 13, his mother died of fever, which Hegel and his father both caught and barely survived. After completing his early education, Hegel enrolled at the seminary in Tübingen, where he became friends with Friedrich Schelling, later a well-known philosopher.

Suggested Reading

Hegel, *Phenomenology of Spirit*, Miller, trans.

Pinkard, *Hegel: A Biography*.

Questions to Consider

1. What do you think of Hegel's view of original sin? Can it be that the fact of human thinking itself is the origin of sin and evil? What do you think of Hegel's claim that "human beings are not what they ought to be"?

2. Does history truly have a meaning and spirit behind it, as Hegel claimed? Or, as is often asserted, is history merely one damned thing after another?

3. Can Hegel's account of history take evil seriously enough? If all is necessary, can evil really be anything more than disguised good?

Hegel—The Slaughter Block of History
Lecture 21—Transcript

Hello again. Georg Wilhelm Friedrich Hegel is the greatest intellectual descendant of Immanuel Kant; but that's not to say that he was in any way the earlier philosopher's supine follower. He took over and appropriated thoughts and themes in Kant's work while giving them his own distinct spin, which was really quite revolutionary in its day, and were it to be understood today, in ours. Hegel is the consummate philosophical systematizer. He thought, in fact, that the cosmos itself, all of reality, was identical in some important way with the proper—that is, his own—philosophical system.

Occasionally in the history of thought, it happens that what seems to be an acute case of megalomania turns out to be a very important philosophical insight, and in Hegel's case, this very well may be true. I won't go much into his larger system; here in this lecture I really want to focus on two crucial aspects of his thought that are of really direct pertinence for us: First, his understanding of the origin of evil for the individual and what he saw as its mythological formulation in concepts such as original sin (much as Kant did); and then second—far more revolutionary and quite different from Kant, actually—his assessment of the overall place of evil and role it plays in history considered as a whole. When we think about Hegel, we think about him as someone who takes a very philosophically dense take, construal, of history; and, in fact, we will see that it is precisely around the problem of evil that Hegel's historical philosophizing is most profound.

Hegel was born in 1770 and died in 1831; so he didn't live as long as Kant and he was a young man when Kant was at his magisterial prime. In his student days, he was very close friends with the poet Friedrich Hölderlin and the philosopher Friedrich Schelling; in fact, they were roommates together, I believe in Tubingen in Germany. As a professor at the University of Jena (which is a city in Germany) in 1806, he was finishing up his first and in some ways most important masterpiece called the *Phenomenology of Spirit*, and it was in Jena in 1806 that Napoleon was about to fight an enormous battle with a series of royal armies that were aligned against him. Famously, Hegel, sitting in his study in Jena doing some final edits and corrections on the manuscript of *Phenomenology of Spirit*, at one point looks out his window down to the street below and sees Napoleon riding by with his retinue; and he had a thought that he reports to a friend in a letter later. He says, "I saw the world spirit outside my window."

It's an incredible moment. Hegel thought that the writing of *Phenomenology of Spirit* was an event not just of philosophical importance for the world, it was a moment in which the world would come to understand itself in a new and far more profound way; and thus in his writing of this, he was rendering intelligible the meaning of the world through the story of its history up to that moment. For Hegel in some sense, the point of the world was to come to self-consciousness—we'll see about this in a second—and to come to self-consciousness is to understand what it has been trying to become all along. Hegel, at his desk there looking out the window, sees what he takes to be the world spirit; that is, the central place in the material world, the axis, the spot in matter—namely the person of Napoleon—where the world spirit is most acutely working itself out, creating the conditions for its own self-realization as time goes on. Yet Hegel also says, "I, writing at my desk, am the one who knows what's actually going on there." Hegel actually thinks of himself, in the activity of writing the *Phenomenology of Spirit*, as more important for the history of humanity and the world than Napoleon, because Napoleon is only acting; it is Hegel who will eventually provide the understanding of what Napoleon's actions mean.

That's what I mean about megalomania; but it's also, again, very, very acute because Hegel wasn't entirely wrong. He, in fact, did have a kind of understanding that would be important in ways that definitely, you could argue, rivaled Napoleon's importance over the history of the next several centuries. Eventually Hegel becomes the professor of philosophy at the University of Berlin, which is the central German university of the age. He enormously influences a generation of students and creates rival schools of Hegelianisms, Counter-Hegelianisms, Quasi-Hegelianisms; and he dies there during a cholera epidemic, though we don't think was cholera itself, in 1831.

Again, there are a lot of different and important things to talk about when it comes to Hegel; I just want to talk about two here: one is his construal of the meaning of original sin and the nature of evil for humans; the other is how he understands the course of history to be a working out of a certain solution to the problem of evil. Let me focus on the first here, Hegel on the doctrine of original sin, both because of its interest in itself, and also because of how it shows us something important about Hegel's understanding of how to think about philosophical concepts.

The Enlightenment rejects the doctrine of original sin—we saw this with the hostility to Kant on radical evil—because it finds, Hegel thinks, the form in which the doctrine is taught incredible, literally unbelievable. It's presented, Hegel says, as an external force outside of the self, infecting the self (from Satan via the apple) and also hereditary (a biological transmission in some sense); so the Enlightenment thinks of this as primitive, naïve, unscientific, and simply not true. But Hegel, following Kant, insists that there is something to the doctrine, something the doctrine captures, even as it has been traditionally misunderstood. For him, the true meaning of the doctrine is missed in the confusions on its surface. The reality is that—and he thinks this is really important—the fact of human thinking itself, human subjective self-consciousness, is the origin of the knowledge of good and evil and thus of original sin. Original sin, then, is a consequence of human reflection; human reflexivity. What does that mean?

Human reflexivity is the ability humans have to step back and think about themselves as they are doing something. After all, all thinking is, in some sense, is a form of stepping back from a situation and reflecting upon it from a sufficient distance to not be caught up in its immediate imminent tumult; thinking, that is, naturally estranges us from our immediate situation. We become self-conscious, and self-consciousness is kind of a form of self-estrangement for Hegel; it's kind of a form of sin. It is this way because humans, in being self-conscious, are effectively rendering themselves available to themselves as objects of thought. To so render yourself available to yourself as an object of thought is in some sense to lose your original organic integrity. That's all Hegel means there: The loss of that original organic integrity, the loss of the ability to be in the moment is, for Hegel, sin.

That's not the only part of this: It's also the case that Hegel says the doctrine of original sin says that humans are in some sense by nature evil; that is, it somehow is constitutive of the structures of human existence as a whole, at least as we find them. Many thinkers in the Enlightenment dismiss this view by suggesting that it's far too pessimistic; and Hegel agrees, if we think of nature as fundamentally static. But the deep insight of the statement—that humans are constitutively sunk in evil in some sense—Hegel thinks is that, in fact, and as all should be able to recognize, "human beings are not what they ought to be," he says. Humanity is clearly at odds with the world and its true nature. The formulation of original sin, in any of the various religious formulas it's offered in, may be stale or mythological, but the insight being communicated, Hegel thinks, is quite profound; for we do, in fact, exist in a state of inevitable and, at present, inescapable estrangement from the world and from ourselves.

We know this because we are all able to watch ourselves act in the world; again, we have reflexivity. We all have the experience of not being fully in a moment, both being in it and not in it, just because when we see ourselves acting in that moment, just to the extent that we are watching ourselves, we are not in that moment. In fact, you can sometimes have the experience of noticing yourself not being in the moment; that is, you can sometimes have the experience of noticing yourself noticing yourself as you try to exist in the moment. You're not only a double self then; you have somehow segmented yourself off again and are now watching yourself watching yourself. In fact, that's bottomless; that kind of radical self-consciousness for humans, Hegel thinks, is bottomless, and that is a crucial fact about us as creatures and it's a crucial intuition that the doctrine of original sin is trying to convey. The fall is the rupture of pure unselfconscious identity into a split awareness, however multiply split that awareness may be; a sense of alienation and loss. That's formulated as evil, but also and simultaneously it brings with itself as its necessary consequence an awareness of the lost status as a one that was good. Sin is not only an experience we experience in itself, it also gives us a kind of nostalgia for an endemic earlier state. That's original sin.

Yet, Hegel thinks, this is a kind of *felix culpa*, a happy fault; for it is a necessary fact for our maturation as self-conscious agents, an inevitable stage—again, call it the awkward, self-conscious teenager stage—in our progress towards what Hegel sees as our final situation of complete self-consciousness, which is somehow also returned to a complete absorption in the context in which we find ourselves. What this endpoint is, is tremendously obscure in Hegel; it involves the complete harmony of the person and the activity they are involved in, but all of that taken back into the mind so that the mind is fully aware of what's going on, and in some sense the mind appreciates what's going on even as it's engaged in it.

The only examples that I can point to, and I thought about this a lot—it's hard to actually imagine, as it should be because we're all caught in this now, Hegel thinks; except for a few very graceful moments, we're all caught in this alienation—the only examples I can think of here that even gesture at what Hegel is trying to get at, it seems to me, are the examples of certain masters of particular skills: athletes, musicians, racecar drivers, dancers or actors, maybe novelists when they are actively writing and typing furiously on the computer or the keyboard. They're people whose actions are both completely automatic and natural, and thoroughly saturated with a serious thinking-through of the situation. This gives us a glimpse of what Hegel means, but only a glimpse. Again, we can't fully know what this condition of reconciled harmony will be like from outside of it, because it's like attempting to describe what our lives will be like when they have been so reconciled, which they manifestly have not been yet. The individual subject's will—the subject's capacity to assert itself; it's capacity for freedom, that is—is both the problem and the potential for the problem's ultimate what Hegel calls "sublation"; that is, the problem's ultimate resolution in a higher synthesis. That gives us some intuition of what Hegel's own vision of history is about, and how history is itself, Hegel will say, the working out of the meaning of the problem of evil in time.

The story of history for Hegel on one level is about the human intellect coming over many generations into its maturity through its struggle to understand history, to understand the story of its own development. (There's another level we'll get to in a minute, a more theological level; but focus on this one here.) In other words, the human comes to grow up as a species—not just an individual, but as a species—precisely by reflecting on history and coming to see what it means. This picture is more philosophically contested than it may at first appear. It assumes that history itself is rational; that is, that history actually means something that we can understand and render intelligible to ourselves and to one another. History is an activity or a process, but it is in part a process driven forward itself by people attempting to discern just what that process means. History, that is, considered as a whole, is an ongoing intellectual inquiry into the shape of the meaning of what it is to be human through interpreting the events that we undertake and the things that happen to us as an ongoing practice of questioning and finding answers for what this means.

This means that the very activity of questioning itself attempt shapes the events that come after that questioning in certain ways. The U.S. Civil War, for example, is itself not just a dumb event, it is in a complicated way an intellectual event; it is an attempt in part by the two sides, the two bodies of competence, to understand the meaning of the American Revolution, as people on both sides of that war recognized. The Civil War was an intellectual struggle as much as it was a military struggle, and that's why someone like Abraham Lincoln could write in, I don't know, 600 or 700 words in the "Gettysburg Address" a speech—again, of 600 or 700 words—that was probably more powerful for determining the outcome of that war than any numbers of battles would have been. History unfolds, and the mind matures—this is kind of the basic philosophical presumption of the story here—in a dialectical relationship. Each new event in history shapes our minds in a new way, and our minds, so newly shaped, in turn shape the new history in new ways as well. It's like a dance in which each partner's next step is new, but responds to the other partner's immediately previous step. History and the human intellect play a game of back and forth where each in turn sharpens and focuses the picture that they are coming mutually to represent.

This may sound kind of crazy; it may seem odd to call history "intelligible." Something so vast and complicated; how can it be intelligible? The truth about Hegel is that Hegel sometimes can make things sound really profound that on one level are actually really obvious; on another level, on Hegel's level, they are really profound, but on a basic level actually what he's saying is really obvious. Every time we try to understand history, every time we try to make sense of history, every time we tell a story about what happened and we leave some things out and keep some things in, highlight some things, downplay other things, we are implying that there is some real story, there is some sense to be made, about our past. On one level, then, Hegel is clearly right; anthropologically, ethnographically, we do this all the time; we do believe history is intelligible. Others might challenge our confidence or conviction about this, but their challenge is far deeper than it may at first appear; it's not a challenge to an abstruse philosophical idea that history must be somehow meaningful; it's a challenge to the very idea that when we tell stories about history we are finding meaning in it. In other words, Hegel is offering as a very philosophically significant point, something that actually on some level looks like a common place. I'm not saying this as a criticism of Hegel; I'm saying that in some important way he's grabbed onto something philosophically very profound that we do all the time, that we never noticed how profound it was. That in itself would make Hegel a really worthwhile philosopher to think about.

But then Hegel goes on to make a more audacious claim even than that, and one that it is significantly easier for us to dissent from; many people have dissented from it without much trauma intellectually, other than Hegel. He says that history is not only the human mind coming to understand itself; more than that, more deeply than that, more truly than that, the human mind itself is involved in a much larger working out of something far more vast than merely the human: namely, what Hegel thinks of as God's unfolding self-understanding. That is to say, for Hegel, reality itself is essentially rational, and the core of history is an intelligible story not just of how the human is coming to know itself, but how the World-spirit is coming to know itself, and know itself as free; that is, as having chosen over many thousands of years this course of history, however filled with evil and mysterious suffering (mysterious at the time) that it may be. The spirit chooses this history as the story of its own slow realization of its own power.

This representation of God—this story of what Hegel calls the World-Spirit—means that God is actually using the whole of history, and human attempts to understand history, to make sense of itself, of this God. History, then, is the dialectical process—again, the back and forth process—of Spirit coming to full self-awareness, working out the explicit knowledge of what it had potentially had been all along in the material events of the history of the human race and the history of the world as a whole. Hegel's first book, which was called the *Phenomenology of Spirit*, that's why it's called that, because it's about the structures of the logic of history understood as the working out of the thinking of Sprit, absolute Spirit, in history.

This may sound very abstract—in fact, I know it sounds very abstract; it sounds very abstract to me—but what Hegel is trying to get at is really something important here: Most fundamentally, we are bit players in Hegel's view in a history far greater than we can presently properly comprehend (well, a history that most of us can't presently properly comprehend; I mean, Hegel seems to be able to comprehend it pretty well). That may sound presumptuous and I'm sorry for being a little snarky there; but Hegel actually means it quite seriously, and he takes as his model the individual human's maturation and uses that to explain what he's talking about. When you were a child, you acted in certain ways and certain things happened to you, and you didn't quite understand what was going on. But as an adult, you can look back on your childhood and you can now see it as a process, only dimly understood at the time that it was happening, of your coming to a mature self-conscious possession of yourself as an adult (or maybe at least what we hope to be mature self-conscious possessions of ourselves; I mean, for most of us I think that's more of an aspirational ideal than a concretized, realized goal).

But in some sense, the story of our childhood into adulthood is a story of our growing ability to understand ourselves, to decide for ourselves what we want to do, and to be able freely and responsibly to decide not just what we want to do but who we want, in some sense, to be. Hegel thinks the world itself is also in this process of maturation. In fact, Hegel thinks it's quite near its completion. One of the signs that we are getting near the completion of this process is that the intellect of Hegel has come along to help us see that the final stages are beginning to be set. This all means that in Hegel's view, history has a certain telling that makes sense; and that telling is in some sense a rational telling, it's an intelligible telling. History in its most real is intelligible. As Hegel famously says, "what is rational is actual and what is actual is rational."

That doesn't mean that everything that is, is right—Pope's line—at least it doesn't mean that in a sense that everything that is must be at all times approved of, that resistance to anything is always wrong. That's not what Hegel means. History's course is necessary in some sense for Hegel, though it's not a terrifically narrow sense of necessity. The future is not now and will never be absolutely predictable, as if we had a really good sort of "meteorology of the Spirit." Hegel and astrologers such as Nostradamus are doing very different things in their work. Our resistance to what we don't want to happen in history, Hegel says, is as much a part of history's rationality as the things that we don't want to happen are. Disease is a part of history and it's real, but inoculations are a part of history, too; and in some ways perhaps, the disease is more real only insofar as it prompts the inoculations. Indeed sometimes, in fact what looks like resistance to inevitability actually has the future on its side. Sometimes adversity turns out to strengthen the weak and make them ultimately come out on top. Consider one historical phenomenon: The Black Death that, as we saw, may have killed half of Europe, created the conditions—as I suggested also—for the Reformation 200 years later. A thing that can devastate a culture, a civilization, at one moment may, in fact, surprisingly turn out to enable that culture to survive and prosper in other ways in the future. This is what Hegel calls the "cunning of reason"; reason is cunning, it's crafty, it surprises us all the time.

But still, Hegel thinks, even though reason is cunning, it can only be so cunning; and there is the possibility of discerning a shape and purpose to history—at least Hegel thinks so—and reason's aims will inevitably be accomplished no matter what. But we can't always, at the moment, tell just what reason is meaning to do; all we know is that in the end it will make sense. In fact, it will make the only sense there could be. All this means that in some sense things that are not as central to the story that it ultimately means to be telling, those things will not have the big role in history that they may seem to at the moment that we experience them. History, thus, can be said to be providentially governed, and the true philosophy of history will be, for Hegel, also and simultaneously, as he says, a theodicy; a justification of all the suffering that has happened. Because evil is so deeply irrational, we must figure out why there is evil in the world; and Hegel thinks his philosophy of history is an account of why.

In fact, he says very frankly that his count is "a theodicy, a justification of the ways of God." But this is not the kind of theodicy that Leibniz offered or that Pope poeticized, which was mechanical and static; saying that all was as harmonious as a well-functioning watch. Hegel has a more organic and developmental understanding of evil. He begins with the idea of divine providence, but once he adopts a view of God as immanent in human history, as directly governing the forces of human history and in some ways coming to understand itself in human history, the only conclusion left is that events that are real are justified precisely because they are necessary. The Lisbon Earthquake, devastating as it was, was a necessary part of the World-Spirit's coming to know itself; the World-Spirit's advance towards full and complete self-consciousness. In this case, in part, because of the corrective prompt it gave to overly-simple optimistic thought about evil in the Enlightenment. The people who died in the earthquake were just kind of the unfortunate byproducts of that; but the true meaning of the event was to shock thinkers about evil on some reading of Hegel anyway.

Furthermore, whereas previous attempts to develop a philosophical theodicy aimed at reconciling humans to the existence of evil, Hegel doesn't do that. He believes that there cannot be any absurd "remainder" to reality, any kind of postulated body of evil stuff that exists alongside the real story, so he has to show that evil is not really ultimately evil at all. In fact, he has to show that the world is as it ought to be in all its essential rational details. "Concrete evils" happen, that is, as part of the unfolding of the logic of history; but they are finally justified by the course of history, and in that justification they turn out never to have been evils at all.

All this should be vaguely reminiscent of Irenaeus; Irenaeus of Lyon, remember, the early Christian theologian who we heard about in another lecture. As we saw, Hegel himself recognized that it is a theodicy, and a theodicy that justifies evil by claiming it is necessary and productive of a better future for us. In some readings of Hegel, some people accuse him of being conservative, or even authoritarian. I don't think the problem with Hegel is that he's an authoritarian; in important ways, he's not. He's a progressive; he's in certain ways a kind of modern political individualist in some ways. The problem with Hegel, at least as I read him, is that he is inescapably and inevitably parochial. Does the method demand that anyone who employs it be parochial? In other words, if you actually think that you've unlocked the key to history, does your understanding inevitably reveal your understanding itself to be narrow and not able to see the whole story? Because Hegel himself would assume that there could have been other people who had some of the thoughts he had at previous moments in history who were just wrong, because they hadn't seen the whole history. Perhaps the same thing could be said of Hegel himself. In any event, Hegel offers us no powerful counterexample to this charge.

Hegel is also criticized for being sometimes "overly optimistic," but this is only because he takes our ambition to understand with mortal seriousness, and I think that's an ambition that we must prove in the end to be correct. Hegel's account, that is, suggests that if we cannot "understand" evil, we will find that we are not the thinking creatures we take ourselves to be, and that history is not the intelligible process that we take it to be.

Let's just wrap this up for the moment: It's possible, after this lecture and the previous one, to offer a kind of mutual critique of Kant and Hegel. Hegel can critique Kant. By postulating only a transcendent hope, a hope that somehow is inchoate but present in the will, Kant (Hegel says), "You deflate energies we might have for improving and working on the world here and now; we need more than faith that things will ultimately be made eventually right. We need to know that we can contribute to their becoming right in history. But Kant can also critique Hegel: "Hegel," Kant would say, "by suggesting that reality is all you know, you are demanding that we accept completely everything that happens as what it means to be happening as, and that strikes me," Kant is saying to Hegel here, "as cultivating a kind of resignation that is profoundly antitethetical to what the human actually is in their free will."

We'll see this debate between one group of people arguing that evil needs to prompt us to be more active and another group of people are arguing that evil needs to prompt us to be more reflective about how we understand history itself as carrying on in the many next lectures we'll be having, because this debate carries up even to today. In the next lecture, though, I want to turn to Hegel's most influential descendent, who is indisputably Carl Marx.

Marx—Materialism and Evil
Lecture 22

> Marx did think it was a pretty shocking thing that some people had all this wealth and they wouldn't share it with other people—but he did think that talking about it as immoral was not as fully powerful a way of talking about it as simply pointing out the bare material facts. He thought that understanding those facts ... would be a more powerful motivator for effecting change than preaching to people in any way.

Karl Marx came to understand Hegel's work as offering a new philosophical vision for the shape of understanding the world and guiding human action within it. As history moved on, the world was changing, and history was changing precisely because humans were coming to self-conscious awareness of their own power and their own capacities to change the world and themselves. Hegel believed that history is a story about God coming to maturation and self-realization, while for Marx, it is about the self-realization of humanity.

Marx is not a theoretical innovator in thinking about evil; rather, he's an exemplary figure for a practical response to it. He was Hegelian in imagining that the resolution of the problem of evil is one dimension of the goal of human history. But unlike Hegel, Marx's understanding of the human is materialist, meaning that material circumstances, not ideas, determine human thought and action. Further, without the right material conditions, people can't think the thoughts that will revolutionize material conditions. Marx believed that evil is due to social conditions and material inequalities. Against Hegel, he insisted that evil is the result of these inequalities and, therefore, is contingent, not necessary; it would be overcome within history, not at its end.

For Marx, evil is a structure of unequal social relations in which some are able to gather wealth—"capital"—from others' labor and reinvest that wealth in ways that make those inequalities ever greater. Over time, enormous concentrations of wealth occur, and this wealth creates its own rationale for how the world should be run. Material wealth, for Marx, is a social force and a social reality more fundamental than political power.

Material inequalities lead to differences in other realms of human life—in education, in comfort, and in health—and these differences, Marx thought, lead people to either do or not do wicked things. If we lived in a social order of total equality, in which people were given all they needed to cultivate themselves and they gave back to the whole the fruits of their self-cultivation, evil wouldn't exist. For Marx, socialism is about self-cultivation and expression; the joy we have in our action lies in the cultivation and exercise of our talents, not in the products of our talents. This is not what came to be understood as socialism in the Eastern Bloc of communist nations governed by the Soviet Union for most of the second half of the 20th century. Marx wasn't interested in a revolution of the social order; he was interested in a revolution of human expectations and longings. He wanted us to get beyond the idea that we are in the world to acquire goods and come to see ourselves as creatures who find joy in the exercise of the gifts and skills that we have.

Karl Marx (1818–1883) believed that religion was nothing but alienated human longing, but also the most powerful reality in human history.

According to Marx, changes in social conditions and material inequalities can alter or even eliminate the big evils of human life—starvation, war, slavery— because the basic cause of these evils— disparities of wealth—would disappear. Note that Marx is not talking about a philosophical resolution of the problem of evil; he's thinking of a resolution in terms of the practical disappearance of concrete evil itself. But this vision can undergird an ethic of brutal consequentialism: Once you're convinced you know the remedy for suffering and evil, you can justify a great deal in seeking to eliminate them. Morality becomes contingent on decency, and to get to decency, anything may be necessary.

Marx raises two questions for our study, one theoretical and one practical. The theoretical question: Does the approach that Marx offers—an approach that focuses ruthlessly on a practical solution to the problem of evil—offer enough respect to theoretical questions about evil? Part of the problem here lies in Marx's understanding of history: At any moment when there is suffering in the world, we will ultimately understand that suffering to have been justified, because later events caused by the suffering will be much better than they would have been absent the suffering. In other words, every moment in history doesn't have its own integrity; its ultimate significance is only part of a larger story. Another view of history believes that each moment in history has a kind of moral sense that is determinant in itself. The moment that evil or good occurs bears its own significance, and here, no matter what the justification of suffering is in the future, the suffering of the moment still demands an answer.

> **Against Hegel, [Marx] insisted that evil is the result of these inequalities and, therefore, is contingent, not necessary; it would be overcome within history, not at its end.**

The practical question raised by Marx's approach is more immediate and direct: Is it viable to say that evil can be solved in the way Marx suggests? The history of Marxism after Marx certainly does not give us confidence that Marxism became a device for ameliorating human suffering. ■

Name to Know

Marx, Karl (1818–1883 C.E.). Born and educated in Trier, Germany. He enrolled at the University of Bonn but later transferred to the University of Berlin. There, Marx encountered the Young Hegelians, a group of thinkers who advocated for radical political proposals in conversation with Hegelian philosophy.

Suggested Reading

Marx and Engels, *The Marx-Engels Reader*, Tucker, ed.

Questions to Consider

1. In Karl Marx, we see a strongly practical approach to the problem of evil and an insistence that evil is fundamentally a problem of material conditions. Is Marx convincing in his claim that changes in social conditions can finally eradicate evil?

2. In what ways does Marx's account of evil appear more optimistic than Hegel's? In what ways does it seem less optimistic?

3. Will theoretical explanations of evil always be desired, or are they merely a symptom of material inequalities?

Marx—Materialism and Evil
Lecture 22—Transcript

Welcome back. From Hegel, now we're moving resolutely out of the realm of pure ideas and into the realm of quite palpable historical consequences. Following the "Young Hegelians" who came immediately after Hegel and as part of their crew of arguers and debaters, Marx came to understand Hegel's work as offering a new philosophical vision for the shape of understanding the world and also guiding human action within it. Following especially in the work of a Young Hegelian named Ludwig Feuerbach, Marx came to see or believe he saw that religion was nothing but alienated human longing. But that doesn't mean that Marx didn't appreciate its power; far from it. He thought that religion had been the most powerful reality in human history, precisely because it had been the consequential and structure of the way that humans thought about the problem of evil. But as history moved on, things were changing in Marx's own time, and history was changing precisely because humans were—and here Marx is a Hegelian—coming to self-conscious awareness of their own power and their own capacities to change the world and themselves.

This is the motivating point behind Marx's famous claim that "Up to now, all the philosophers have done is interpret the world." The point, however, is to change it." This is different from Hegel's "cunning of reason," which implies a kind of supra-human force working out its own self-meaning in and through human history. This is an idea that Marx could not but see as expressing human self-alienation; rather, for Marx, the crucial fact about history and its processes is that it is the working out of the species being of humanity; the yet unknown human nature whose dialectical self-unfolding is driving history itself. The important difference between Hegel and Marx, then, is that for Hegel, history is fundamentally a story told about somebody else; it's about God coming to maturation and self-realization. For Marx, it is about the self-realization of Humanity. In a way, this is a throwback to the Enlightenment's optimism of the will; the idea that in the end, sheer human effort is the one thing that will save us. But it's also the fact that force, the human will, is in fact powerful enough to do this salvation; and not just hypothetically powerful enough, but inevitably powerful enough. More so even than Hegel, Marx thought he understood in fairly concrete specificity how human history would come to its culmination over the next century or so, and what the end of history would in fact look like.

Marx is often read as somehow a 20th-century Russian thinker who accidentally lived in the 19th century; but, in fact, he was a genuinely 19th century German thinker who spent much of his adult life actually in exile in London. He himself felt the pain of the social evils his work talked about and his work struggled so fiercely and so profoundly to overcome. The details of his life are relatively simple: He was born in 1818 in Trier, in the German Rhineland states, the palatinate states, and he died in 1883 in London. He and his wife Jenny had seven children, but only three lived to adulthood: one died at age eight, two died aged one year old, and one died at two days old, before he even had a name. Experiences like that would give you a taste for the evils of early industrialized society, particularly when you think that Marx himself was known as a very loving, warm, and generous person, especially to his family. It's not often we know the family histories of great philosophers; many of them have been effectively celibate. But with Marx at least, we have a story of someone whose very family bears the cost of his own struggles to understand what was going on in his day. Much of his income actually in his life came from two sources. One was his ally and very dear friend, Friedrich Engels, who had a certain amount of money from his industrialized family, his wealthy family of industrialists themselves working mostly in the British Midlands. Marx also was a very good and successful journalist. He wrote a number of reports about the U.S. Civil War for U.K. newspapers. He never went to the U.S., he was in England; but he nonetheless was one of the most important journalists of the 1850s, 60s, and 70s and he made a good deal of money that way.

Karl Marx is not a theoretical innovator in thinking about evil; rather, he's an exemplary figure for a certain, centrally practical response. He was Hegelian in imagining that the resolution of the problem of evil is one fundamental dimension of the goal of human history; one crucial aspect of what history intends to be. But as we saw, he differs from Hegel in some very important ways. Most immediately—and pretty importantly—his, unlike Hegel's view, was a "materialist" understanding of the human. People talk about "materialism" all the time nowadays; Marx means something very central by it. He means that not ideas, but material circumstances determine human thought and action; that is to say, ideas come from material conditions, from a cultural location, not the other way round. It was, after all, the printing press, Marx pointed out, which enabled the spread of Martin Luther's ideas and their fertilization of minds all across Europe. This is not a flat-footed claim that no one can think beyond their material conditions or that everyone is constrained by their immediate surroundings to only be able to think thoughts that are only acceptable to those people in those surroundings; it's nothing that naïve. Besides, there's no properly speaking "beyond" in any of these settings; there's no way of talking about a boundary around a culture or a particular class status, or something like that.

This is not meant to be, that is, a constraining doctrine, but simply a statement of how thinking is never totally free-floating from our material conditions, the facts of the way we live our lives. Without the right material conditions, Marx believed, people can't think the new thoughts that revolutionize those very material conditions themselves. A thinker like Isaac Newton needed a certain background, needed a certain culture of education, and needed a certain amount of wealth in order to acquire the education that enabled him to generate the thoughts that led to first of all calculus, and then to the *Principia*, his mathematical modeling of the physical basis of reality. Then that model of the physical basis of reality had to be transformed into a structure that other people could understand and appreciate; and then it had to be published; and there had to be people capable of understanding and reading it. All those things are not just ideas, those are material realities. It's quite possible for people to have great thoughts but not have ways to express them or have people who could receive them. Our thoughts are not totally unconstrained; they're shaped, formed, by what we have been taught, by what we can imagine, and by what others can receive from us. Even technical geniuses like Leonardo da Vinci or Thomas Edison can only imagine what they can imagine and what they did imagine because certain conditions were in place for them to do so, and most of us can't imagine nearly as far away from our material realities as they did.

More specifically, though, more precisely than this general issue about materialism, Marx is the founder—or the greatest formulator, we could say—of an approach to evil that we must directly confront: the idea that "evil," both what we name "evil" and whatever wickedness we do, is due to social conditions and material inequalities. Against Hegel, Marx insisted that evil is due to these inequalities, these social conditions, and therefore it is contingent, not necessary; and it would be overcome within history, not at its end. This is really important for Marx. Where Hegel offers a kind of metaphysical consolation to all the people in history that eventually history will make itself clear and everything will be seen to be for the best, Marx says that's not true; what matters, though, is that evil can be fixed now. Certain forms of evil may be necessary in the development of capital across stages sociologically and economically, but that doesn't mean that the development of capital is itself in some sense intrinsically requiring evil facts as part of its justification.

What is evil for Marx? It's a structure of unequal social relations where some are able to gather wealth—what he'll call "capital"—from others' labor and to reinvest that wealth in ways that make those inequalities ever greater. Marx doesn't think this is a new thing; he thinks this is going back thousands of years. Certainly at some point when everyone was in a tribe on land there wasn't that much capital, there wasn't that much wealth that people had. Some people had maybe more seashells than others; some people had different roles where people would give them corn or something so that they would perform certain rites for the people who gave them the corn; but nonetheless, people were roughly equal in terms of the amount of wealth they had. But over time, and especially once you get industrialism, enormous concentrations of wealth occur; and this wealth, when it is so concentrated, creates its own rationale for how the world should be run.

Naturally, those who have it, who have the wealth, learn to enjoy its comforts, become accustomed to them, and wish to keep them and grow to demand to keep them. They grow concerned that others don't have these comforts and they want to keep others away. Disparities in wealth, that is, lead to, are related to, disparities in power, and far more than the causality moves in the other direction; far more, that is, than disparities in power lead to disparities in wealth. Material wealth for Marx is a social force and a social reality more fundamental than political power itself. For Marx, political power actually is secondary to economic wealth. Political power, in fact, is nothing more than a device for securing those who have wealth to keep wealth, and ensuring that those who don't have wealth can't take it from those who do. It's not necessary that those who don't have wealth can't get it; they just can't get it from the people who have it already. Which is going to be kind of hard; how do they get wealth otherwise? Some social turbulence is possible, but realistically, Marx thought, effectively those people who have wealth are those who are likely to get more wealth in the future.

These inequalities—inequalities of wealth; basic material inequalities—lead to differences in all sorts of realms of human life: differences in education; in the cultivating of capabilities, in developing your skills, your gifts, your calling; differences in mortality rates; differences in overall life health; differences in comfort. They lead to all the differences of quality of life and cultural mode that lead people, Marx thought, to do wicked things, or not to do wicked things. Note here an interesting thing: We've been talking about evil, but ethics hasn't come in here at all. Marx wasn't necessarily someone who disagreed with people who thought that this practice was immoral— he did think it was pretty immoral; he did think it was a pretty shocking thing that some people had all this wealth and they wouldn't share it with other people—but he did think that talking about it as immoral was not as fully powerful a way of talking about it as simply pointing out the bare material facts; he thought that understanding those facts, understanding the underlying structures of the logic of history (what he thought was the logic of history), would be a more powerful motivator for effecting change than preaching to people in any way.

Furthermore, he was never really much of a normative thinker; that is, he wasn't directly or immediately interested in telling people what they should do. A little bit like Hegel, he was interested in understanding what had happened, what was going to happen in history, not to guide the dynamics, not to ride them in any way—for he thought that the dynamics of historical change were pretty much unstoppable—but in order to slightly and subtly shape them, shift their course moderately and best endure their process through our lives. But evil here is not simply just a consequence of material inequalities; as such a consequence evil also is, Marx firmly believed, strictly speaking a sheer accident. Were we in a social order of total equality where each was given all they needed to cultivate themselves and each gave back to the whole the fruits of their self-cultivation, which is what socialism is for Marx, no such evil would be real.

This, by the way, this is really important: Marx's understanding of socialism—it's something just to pause on for a second here—it's not really socialism in the way that we've come to understand it; you can't blame Marx for what came to be understood as socialism, say, in the East Bloc of the communist nations governed by the Soviet Union for most of the second half of the 20th century. For Marx, socialism—or what he thought of as true communism—is about self-cultivation and expression, and about the real joys we have in how our action lies and the delight in our action lies entirely in the cultivation and the exercise of our talents, not in the products of our talents. In our experience of socialism, in Eastern Europe and the Soviet Union especially perhaps, workers had everything taken away from them that they made by the state. This is in an important way not socialism; this is a complete monopoly of control by the state government. You may think that's a distinction without a difference, but Marx didn't. He didn't believe that true socialism would take away from people the things they cared about, but rather that the things they didn't care about would be the things the state would take away; things that they would be instead considering not as objects to be held close to their chests as possessive but things that they understood essentially as means of "sharing."

Consider the difference between someone who cooks for a living and someone who cooks for friends or for the sheer pleasure of cooking itself. When you cook for friends or pleasure, you would be scandalized if your friends left money for you; that's not the point. Marx thought that one day, money would never be the point of all of our labors; people would simply love to do the work they found themselves able to do, and delight in the exercise of their talents in doing that work. The product of the work, then, would not be where people found their value or their identity; it would be merely in the exercise of their skills. You see, Marx wasn't really interested in a revolution on the social order; he was interested in a real revolution of human expectations and longings. He wanted us to get beyond the idea that what we actually are looking for in the world are more goodies and come to see ourselves as most fundamentally creatures who find a certain joy in the exercise of a certain set of gifts and skills that we have. If we did that, Marx thought, we would no longer be as grasping as we are about material objects.

All of this is just an aside to his notion of evil here. Coming back to this, again, he wants to say that changes in social conditions and material inequalities can alter or even do away with most evil. If we get the social system right, if we get the structures right, evil will go away. If you get society organized in the right way, the transformations of human behavior that will enable us to exercise our skills in certain ways and delight in their exercise, those individual anthropological changes, those dispositional changes in the self, those will happen if we just get the social system right. Yeah, there will be accidents of nature—there will be earthquakes, landslides, bad weather, tornadoes, maybe even a certain range of people who are insane, pathological, a kind of crime of nature in a way; and perhaps even a minimal level of carelessness and common human thoughtlessness—but the really big evils of human life, Marx thinks, such as young people worked to death in factories or mines, plutocrats throwing away enough food from their feasts to feed the hungry mouths for months, mouths that slump unfed outside their doors, murder and killing within and between nations, criminality in the lower classes, alcoholism, drug abuse, sex slavery, all these would go away, because their basic cause, he thought, the disparity of wealth and thus the existence of a painful gap between haves and the have-nots, that would go away as well.

Note here, it's important to see that when Marx talks about a "resolution," he's not talking about a philosophical resolution; he's thinking of a resolution in terms of the practical disappearance of the concrete evil itself, not in terms of the disappearance of the cognitive problem of evil, the intellectual problem of evil. The crucial fact, he thinks, is that real concrete suffering is what must ultimately go away. The intellectual puzzle of evil is, for Marx, only a puzzle that grips us to the extent that we at least tacitly acknowledge that we cannot ourselves come to solve the practical problem. This goes back to his claim about Feuerbach, that philosophers have up until now interpreted the world, but the point is to change it. We can interpret evil as much as we want, Marx thought; the crucial thing is that small children stop dying.

This means that he thinks that evil will not be an important theoretical problem for people if the concrete problems go away; that is, that the concrete problems matter more than anything else by any means necessary—that's going to be a really crucial phrase as we go on—because it turns out that if your main goal is the removal of these concrete evils, a vision of this sort can undergird an ethic of really quite brutal consequentialism. Once you're convinced you know the remedy for suffering and evil, you can justify a great deal in doing what you must to ensure that, in fact, suffering and evil do go away, or even are simply substantially reduced. As the very, very well-known and remarkably gifted German Communist writer Berthold Brecht said, "*Erst kommt das Fressen, dann kommt die Moral*"; first comes food, then we'll worry about morality. In other words, give people enough to eat, then talk to them about right and wrong. Morality is in some important way contingent upon decency, and to get to decency, anything is necessary.

This means that, paradoxically, for Marxists—if not for Marx, but for Marxists—it may well be the case that the most ethical people ultimately are those who are least apparently ethical now; and those people who are caught up in adhering to ethics in the present, those who are caught up in believing in the proper possession of property and how it's improper for a poor person to take something that a rich person has, for Marxists that kind of ethics may, in fact, be in the long run, in the ultimate aim of ethics, itself immoral. It may be the case that it is people who look immoral now who turn out, on a Marxist view, to be properly moral in the distance. Brecht himself, the writer Berthold Brecht, had a great line about this in a poem called "To Those Born After." He said: "We, who wished to lay the foundations of peace and friendliness, / We could never be friendly ourselves." A lot is packed into that phrase "We could never be friendly ourselves." If you think about the history, say, of Marxist ideology in the 20th century, to call it "unfriendly" is probably an understatement. But in any event, this is how Marxism, which meant to remedy evil, became, ironically perhaps, one of the most powerful ideologies for doing evil that the world has ever known.

It's not entirely fair to blame Marx for all of the things done by those who said they followed him in the same way that it's, of course, not entirely fair to blame Jesus for all of the things done by those who said they followed him. Nonetheless, it's an interesting fact that some of the most frankly moralistic of visions of life, even if they don't admit that they are moralistic, are often the most quickly and dangerously corrupted. Marx himself in this way raises two very large and fundamental questions for our class, one theoretical and one practical. The theoretical question goes back to the debate between Rousseau and Voltaire: Does the approach that Marx offers—an approach again that focuses ruthlessly on the practical solution to the practical problem of evil—does this solution offer enough respect, does it give enough respect, to theoretical questions about evil that humans might have? Doesn't the sheer phenomenon of evil itself stand in need of being accounted for? Is there no theoretical worry here that will trouble people? Is a purely materialist "resolution" of all these problems adequate to meet any intellectual puzzle that people will have?

I actually don't think so; I think that this is a failure of Marx's not only political anthropology but in a way his philosophical anthropology. This is my view now, so this is not Marx. I actually think that any attempt to offer an account of the problem of evil that fails to talk about why evil happened in the first place and offer an ultimately adequate account for why that is seems to suggest that our capacity to wonder and be puzzled is far less immediately part of who we are than I think it is. In fact, I think our capacity to wonder abstractly about things is very central to we are. That's one problem with this view. The second problem with the theory lies in its understanding of history; and again, this is this theoretical question about whether or not you need a theoretical resolution to the problem of evil. Marx's understanding of the problem of evil means that at any moment when there is suffering in the world we will understand ultimately that suffering to have been justified, a la it was with Hegel, only because the later event that is caused by the suffering is much better than it would have been absent the suffering. In other words, every moment in history doesn't have its own integrity, its meaning, its ultimate significance is only part of a larger story; we can't know the meaning of any moment until the later moment. In another way, the moment of history that we are going through at this time is never something that is fully clear to us now and we can't actually know what it really means yet because history as a whole is an organic unity. That's one view of history; that's Marx's view, that's Hegel's view. Each moment of history is not possessing its own integrity; it requires a certain attention to the overall scope to see what it really means.

The other view, which is a different one and I think one that is at least more plausible initially, is the idea that each moment of history is in some important way possessive of its own integrity, its own autonomy. Each moment of history, were it to be subsumed or consumed into the totality of the whole, would possess its own integrity that would resist and protest that consummation, that consumption. Each moment of history, that is, in this rival view to Marx and Hegel, has a kind of moral sense that is determinant in itself. If you believe in the second account of history, so that at a moment the evils or the goods that happen in that moment bear their own significance and their own meaning within themselves, if you believe in that view, no matter what the justification of it is down the road, somehow the suffering of that moment still stands out as demanding some kind of answer. There must be some account of why that had to happen. And if there is no account of why it had to happen, why there was a necessity to its happening that's fine, but tell us, then, that there is no necessary justification for it; tell us, then, that the moment of suffering has as its own meaning the real suffering of the people within it, and that in some sense that suffering matters not just in that moment but eternally as the ultimate eternal meaning of that moment of suffering. In a way, I'm gesturing at the idea that there might be different meanings of God here. Remember, Hegel at least insists that God becomes identical with the World-Spirit working itself out. Marx obviously doesn't have a sense of God in that way, but Marx nonetheless thinks there's nothing outside of history. The picture I'm offering you is a picture where each moment is individually seen by a god outside of time, outside of history in eternity, who sees each moment in its integrity and sees it as an integral moment.

That's all the theoretical debate, theoretical questions around Marx. The practical questions are more immediate and direct. Most obviously, is it viable to say that evil can be solved in the way that Marx suggests it can? The history of Marxism after Marx does not give us a great deal of confidence that Marxism became on the whole a device for ameliorating human suffering, to say the least; if anything, as I said before, I'd say the consequentialism it justified provoked in people a kind of amplified level of cruelty and aggravated the suffering of the human race, at least for a century or so after Marx's own death.

Ironically, it may be that a materialist like Marx offers a solution accentuating the felt need for a theoretical explanation of evil; that is to say, a thoroughgoing materialism may make the need for an "idealist" explanation evil almost intolerably strong, because the more rigorously the materialist explanation is worked out, the more its absence feels felt in the world that we experience them offering us. Interestingly, in Marx's own time, in some of the work he himself did as a journalist as I suggested, there was, in fact, a problem of evil; a theodicy problem being "practically" worked out: the problem of American slavery climaxing in the struggles of the American Civil War.

In our next lecture, I want to turn to the story of that evil and how that evil was dealt with by two American thinkers who tried to give an account of what it was, where it came from, and what might happen to it that speaks well beyond the confines of that one particular historical event.

The American North and South—Holy War
Lecture 23

> It's a very acute psychology of how a society's vision of right and wrong can go horrendously awry, and in certain ways, it prophesies forward to what happens in the 20th century with various kinds of genocides; especially, as we'll see, the work of Hannah Arendt resonates with Twain quite powerfully on the Holocaust.

The Civil War represented a theological crisis for America, a struggle between two opposite understandings of Scripture and what God meant for the world. The central conflict, of course, was the presence of slavery in American life. In this lecture, we'll look at how two thinkers, Mark Twain and Abraham Lincoln, explored the relationship between slavery and Americans' conception of their mission in the world.

The Adventures of Huckleberry Finn is Twain's brilliant, clearly sincere protest against the kind of moral corruption that Huck both represents and is victimized by, a moral corruption that infected the whole of his society. This corruption is revealed in Huck's belief that he has committed a crime in helping his friend Jim to escape from slavery. Jim's owner, Miss Watson, has tried to make Huck a good person, but Huck believes himself to be utterly immoral—and destined for hell—because he can't obey the law and turn in Jim. Twain is telling us that the upstanding Victorian morality Huck has tried to adopt is actually a horrific, hypocritical hostility to human beings.

The conclusion here is that we ought not to let "morality"—our beliefs about what's right and wrong—float too free from ordinary human empathy. The conscience should be fed, Twain implies, both by rigorous and skeptical argument and by concrete attention to realities brought to awareness by our vital human affections. The danger is in not seeing that any one version of morality may need to be changed; if it is not changed, we may end up, like Huck, jettisoning our concern about morality altogether.

Although Twain didn't offer much of a solution to the problem he so devastatingly diagnosed, Abraham Lincoln's Second Inaugural Address serves as a hypothetical roadmap for where Lincoln would have liked the nation to go. In this speech, Lincoln frames the Civil War as God's judgment on the people of the United States, both North and South, for their collective complicity in the sin of slavery. He transforms what would have been, for many of his contemporaries, a dualism of good and evil—the South on one side, the North on the other—into two sides of a community, both of which have sinned grievously in God's eyes; now, God chooses to punish them and, thus, expiate their sins.

At this point in his political leadership, Lincoln was pivoting away from a focus on fighting the war to healing the nation, and it's interesting that he does so from a theological standpoint. Both sides of the war understood themselves to be fighting for God's cause. Lincoln suggests that we can understand the moral energies of both sides, but we must redirect them. We must recognize that both sides are fighting as penitents in a war that works out their own complicity in sin and let God decide the outcome of that war as a way of resolving that sin. Lincoln's speech is astonishing for a number of reasons: its theological register from a person who wasn't, apparently, very theological; its mercy from a leader on the verge of defeating his enemies; and its invitation for both sides to reconsider the war not as a just war against evil but as a history of just punishment that all ought to accept and reply to with humility.

> **Lincoln viewed [the evil of slavery] as one that both North and South had collaborated in producing and profited from; now, both needed to confront their complicity in this evil.**

Lincoln saw the evil that lay at the core of the war itself: the vast and dehumanizing system of slavery. But he also viewed this evil as one that both North and South had collaborated in producing and profited from; now, both needed to confront their complicity in this evil. In this, Lincoln offers a vision of how to think about evil and how to think about our own involvement in evil that might be of use beyond his own context. In suggesting that humans should defuse their tendencies toward dualism in moral conflicts, Lincoln invites us to view our enemies as fellow humans involved in a larger mutual project.

Both Twain and Lincoln were prophets well ahead of their time. Twain seems to predict the way a society can misshape its adherence to morals in ways that scholars of the Holocaust would later parallel. Twain's appreciation of how morality can conspire to reinforce racism is also at the heart of Martin Luther King's insistence that the civil rights movement was as much a struggle for white people as for black people. And Lincoln's insistence that we are all complicit and should recognize our complicity is a reminder that Americans are always one people, for good and ill, united both in our aspirations and our crimes. Further, if we can find ways of overcoming the mythology of dualism, we may find ourselves better able to live into the future. ■

Suggested Reading

Noll, *America's God: Jonathan Edwards to Abraham Lincoln.*

Twain, *The Adventures of Huckleberry Finn*, Cooley, ed.

Questions to Consider

1. Reflecting on Twain's *Huckleberry Finn*, do you think that morality can sometimes be the bearer of evil rather than evil's enemy? How can we know whether our morality may be corrupt?

2. If Lincoln were alive today, what observations might he make about America's current political, cultural, and even military conflicts? Could Lincoln's arguments in the Second Inaugural for God's providence and "malice toward none, charity for all" offer any consolation to us, or is Lincoln's time too different from our own?

The American North and South—Holy War
Lecture 23—Transcript

Hello again. In this lecture, I want to talk about two thinkers and the way that their work has been shaped by and shaped our understanding of the American Civil War as one example of how thinking about evil in a concrete situation may speak beyond that moment to a larger audience that spans generations, countries, even eras. The Civil War was the greatest war in American history—in terms of its casualties, absolute and relative, it's still the greatest war—and as Lincoln recognized in his "Gettysburg Address," it really constituted a kind of second American Revolution; a revolution of expectations and hopes and beliefs, and really argued for a revolution in the way people thought about the nation. It's one whose consequences are still being worked out and debated today. My own family actually bears some of the marks of this history. My family is half Northern and half Southern, and my father always taught us to talk about the American Civil War as the "War of Northern Aggression," which was quite a shock for us when we went to history class in school and discovered that it wasn't actually called that by many other people.

But the war itself was not just vast, it was irremediably theological. It was fought out of theological arguments about slavery and God's purposes for humans, democracy, and even the meaning of liberty. Much of the best recent work on the Civil War, by historians such as Mark Noll, point to how it was, in Noll's words, a "theological crisis," a struggle between two utterly opposed understandings of Scripture and what God meant for the world. The central problem was the presence of slavery in American life. Slavery was not an accidental reality to America, it was deeper than that; it was close to the paradoxical heart of how Americans conceived of their mission in the world; and perhaps the way Americans had been moralized into conceiving of this mission led to the Civil War in some important ways.

Here in this lecture, I want to look at how two thinkers explore this idea: one, Mark Twain, who offers a profound and searching diagnosis of this problem, though not much hope in the way of solving it; the other, Abraham Lincoln, who in a way that Twain and most of the rest of Lincoln's contemporaries failed to understand, gestured at a way that the nation might move towards some kind of healing beyond the war, and in so doing indentified a kind of resolution that may just have legs beyond the particular history of the United States. Again, this is not just a parochial moment in the history of the U.S.; it turns out, I think, to have deep implications for how many different social problems might be confronted around the world in a practical way. At least I want to propose that the problem that Twain identified and the way forward that Lincoln saw and prophesied may still be both of use today and in the future, in the U.S. and around the world. Because I want to talk about these issues in terms of the theme of American slavery, I want to talk about Twain first, as the person who formulated the problem; then turn back to Lincoln, as one who, before Twain wrote, grasped the problem and suggested how it might be fruitfully addressed. So let me talk a bit here about Mark Twain and his remarkable work, *The Adventures of Huckleberry Finn*.

Ernest Hemingway famously said that *The Adventures of Huckleberry Finn* is the greatest novel ever written in America; and most thinkers and most writers have agreed with Hemingway on that. Mark Twain is the pen name of Samuel Clemens. He was born 1835 in Florida, but he was raised in Hannibal, Missouri, a slave state; in fact it's important that Lincoln and Twain both had intimate experience of slavery growing up. Near the beginning of the Civil War, Twain went west, settling in San Francisco before moving back east in 1869. He published Huck Finn in 1885, and it was immediately recognized as his masterpiece, though he kept writing until he died in 1910.

The novel, *The Adventures of Huckleberry Finn*, is about a boy's adventures on the Mississippi River and it generally has an overall kind of indirect misanthropic tone, depicting the ways that mid-19th century America was a place full of hucksters, con artists, and people easily fooled; that is, a place just like any other place, in Twain's eyes. But at the emotional heart of the story is Twain's brilliant, clearly sincere protest against the kind of moral corruption that Huck both represents and is victimized by; a moral corruption that infected the whole of his society. His crisis that reveals this moment, this moral corruption, is easily described: Huck, who's just a white boy who lives along the river, and his friend, the slave Jim, are travelling along the Mississippi, and as they travel, it effectively means that Huck has helped Jim escape from Miss Watson, his master. After Huck does this, he comes to believe that he has "stolen" Jim, who would $ 800 worth of commodity.

What's worse, now that Jim believes he has his freedom, he means, and he tells Huck, that he will go back and help his wife and children escape, which Huck understands to be more theft. In fact, Huck says, upon hearing of Jim's plans to rescue his children from slavery, "I was sorry to hear Jim say that, it was such a lowering of him." Huck, that is, comes to believe that he has committed and enabled to be more committed still a massive crime against a person who cared for him and trusted him.

What should he do? The crucial moment of Huck's realization and the beginning of the agony of the struggle of what he could do comes in the book's Chapter 16, when he grasps that Jim's joy at being so close to his freedom means that he, Huck, must be very close to committing the final step of grand theft larceny by helping Jim. Memories of Miss Watson's many kindnesses come back to him, and how all her lessons of trying to make Huck a decent person are failing, just because he can't obey the law because he gets weak when he thinks of turning his friend, whom he loves, in to the law. What Huck takes to be his "conscience" is wracking him about this, making him think he is an utterly immoral person. Why? Because he can't turn his friend back in to a life of chattel slavery. That's the central irony there in Twain's story. The problem for Huck—and philosophers have written wonderful stuff about this—is precisely that he understands himself to be morally wrong, not just bad or weak. He thinks he knows the law—the law is you turn property—he sees Jim, and his culture has taught him to think of Jim as property; he also sees Jim, though, and sees him as a human. His sympathy for Jim wins out over his sense of the law.

Much later in the story, about Chapter 31 or so, Huck has a second chance to do what he thinks is the right thing, to turn Jim in, and he writes a note letting people on the shore know where he and Jim are; but again, he reencounters the terrible power and to his mind the anti-moral power of his affection for Jim. Only this time, and this is even more devastating in Twain's telling, he frames the decision as one about the ultimate fate of his soul, because he knows that unless he obeys the law, God will certainly condemn him to Hell for disobeying. This is from Huck Finn, Chapter 31:

> I took it up [the paper, the note he had written], and held it in my hand. I was a trembling, because I'd got to decide, forever, betwixt

two things, and I knowed it. I studied a minute, sort of holding my breath, and then says to myself:

'All right, then, I'll go to hell'- and tore it up.

It's a great moment in American literature: Huck determining, almost like Milton's Satan, that "I'll go to Hell"; but in this case, unlike Satan, Huck is doing the right thing, but he doesn't think it so he thinks he's going to Hell.

> It was awful thoughts, and awful words, but they was said. And I let them stay said; and never thought no more about reforming. I shoved the whole thing out of my head; and said I would take up wickedness again, which was in my line, being brung up to it, and the other warn't [the other being the good line, the line of being a good person]. And for a starter, I would go to work and steal Jim out of slavery again; and if I could think up anything worse, I would do that, too; because as long as I was in, and in for good, I might as well go the whole hog.

Some readings of the novel present this episode as a triumph of conscience over a wicked set of social mores, as if Huck understood himself as a heroic rebel. But that's not what he thinks; Huck understands himself to be a moral failure, a calamity for not following the moral law. The conflict here is between what Huck sees as his pre-rational, problematic, untutored sympathy, undisciplined sympathy, for Jim and the proper, upstanding, Victorian morality that Huck has been bred to or has been tried to be bred into by his society. Twain, of course, suggests this morality is actually a horrific hypocritical hostility to human beings. But Huck ends up seeing himself as weak because he takes the social norm as the only possible standard of conscience, no matter the violence it seems to do to his soul. The upshot of the situation, then, and the final twist of Twain's brilliance, is that Huck thinks he's going to Hell; and so Huck, for being good, rejects morality and becomes not so much immoral as amoral.

The moral of this story, such as it is, is more or less oblique; Twain has some suggestions for guidance, though not many. Most basically: We ought not ever to let "morality," our beliefs about what's right and wrong, float too free from ordinary human empathy, lest our agency become wholly captive to unreal abstractions at the cost of attending to the real world. Twain thinks that's what happened in Huck's world; people were taught to see other people as property, as chattel, not as real humans. He worries that any culture that can do that can go insane in very dangerous ways (apart from the fact that it enslaves human beings; it goes insane in other ways, too). The conscience should be fed, he seems to be implying, both by rigorous and skeptical argument and by concrete attention to realities brought to our awareness by our vital human affections. The danger is in not seeing that any one version of morality, our version of morality, may need to be changed; and if it is not changeable, we may end up, like Huck, jettisoning our concern about morality altogether.

Twain took this to be a story not just about Huck but also about America. The nation was so confident of its vision, so inflexible in attending to it, that it took its vision to be morally right, North and South, and it didn't leave any way to change or revise its moral imagination. This is a recipe for moral catastrophe for Twain; it leads to a completely shallow self-righteousness, which may be strong initially but is ultimately brittle, so that when it finally gives in to the facts of reality—such as the fellow-feeling you might have when you consider a friend of yours as a real human when you know (in the sense of believe) that you should see him as nothing more than someone else's property—and when it finally gives in to these facts, this morality it shatters.

It's a very acute psychology of how a society's vision of right and wrong can go horrendously awry; and in certain ways it prophesies forward to what happens in the 20th century with various kinds of genocides, especially, as we'll see, the work of Hannah Arendt resonates with Twain quite powerfully on the Holocaust. But here we don't see Twain offering much of a positive solution to the problem he so devastatingly diagnoses. His vision is in some important way too misanthropic. To see how to go forward here, we actually have to go back to Lincoln and to Lincoln's greatest speech, perhaps the greatest speech of American political history, Lincoln's "Second Inaugural Address."

Abraham Lincoln, as most people will know, lived from 1809–1865. He was raised with little education, but again, like so many others we have seen, undertook a strenuous process of self-education throughout his early adult life. He served in the militia in the Black Hawk War of 1832, and then was a lawyer and legislator in Illinois and served even a term in Congress in Washington as a Representative, where he made his first national reputation as one of the very few who opposed the Mexican-American war of 1846–1848 as an unbridled effort of human imperialism, which Lincoln thought was beneath the dignity of the American republic. His opposition to that war, of course, which went swimmingly for the United States, also cost him his seat after one term, since the people back home liked the idea of America conquering the West.

He was a surprising choice for president, first in the Republican Party and then in the general election, but became perhaps the greatest president the U.S. has yet known, his only real rivals being George Washington and Franklin Delano Roosevelt. He gave many great speeches, but none greater than his "Second Inaugural Address." This address, given in the midst of civil war in the early spring of 1865 as the war was coming to its conclusion can serve as a kind of potential hypothetical roadmap for where Lincoln would have liked the nation to go. As in so many of his speeches, it was brief and very surprising; most surprising, indeed, for its refusal to give in to the temptation to be vindictive, judgmental, or punitive to those people in the South who had resisted the war. In the Address, in fact, Lincoln offers a quite theological work: He "reads" the Civil War itself, as we'll see, as God's judgment on the people of the United States, as he says, "North and South," as punishment for their collective complicity in the sin of slavery. The point here is not to excuse the South; the point is to implicate himself and those other people who were on the side of the North. Again, this is not an attempt to whitewash Southern slavery; it's an attempt to expand the complicity to all of America.

Along with justice, then, prophets like Lincoln want to say that public life has a destiny beyond justice; a destiny that will transfigure our mundane life and not renounce it. Let me read this to you once, and then I want to go through and give you a comment on it as well. This is the crucial part of the speech:

Both read the same Bible, and pray to the same God; and each invokes His aid against the other.

It may seem strange that any men should dare to ask a just God's assistance in wringing their bread from the sweat of other men's faces; but let us judge not that we be not judged.

The prayers of both could not be answered; that of neither has been answered fully. The Almighty has his own purposes.

'Woe unto the world because of offences! for it must needs be that offences come; but woe to that man by whom the offence cometh!'

Now this is a very long sentence, the one that's coming up here. This suggests something of the difficulty of the thought being offered, and the necessity of a long time to be taken for the thoughts being worked out. Pay attention to the length here; this is an important sentence:

If we shall suppose that American Slavery [note it's not Southern slavery] is one of those offences which, in the providence of God, must needs come [it must happen by some mysterious providence; again, going back to Job], but which, having continued through His appointed time, He now wills to remove, and that He gives [note God gives] to both North and South, this terrible war, as the woe due to those by whom the offence came ...

"This terrible war." He speaks this to an audience, many of them soldiers, many of them widows or orphans of soldiers, many of them wounded in the war, all of them with intimate acquaintance of what the war has cost. A terrible war; a war so vast and so expansive that at this point the war has changed the face of America, and everyone in the crowd knows it. "This terrible war, as the woe due to those by whom the offense came"; note, both North and South.

... shall we discern therein any departure from those divine attributes which the believers in a Living God always ascribe to Him?

Think about that sentence: The whole point of that sentence is framed as a theodicy question; it's a question about whether or not we can imagine this God as just. Is this God a just God? That's the question that's being asked here; but within that asking of a question, inside of it, Lincoln frames the whole history of the war as a theological punishment to the nation as a whole, a punishment that is due to the nation as a whole for its collective sins. He has turned what would have been, what was for so many of his contemporaries, a Manichean dualism of good and evil—for the South, the good South and the evil North; for the North, the good North and the evil South—this dualism of good and evil, he has turned it into two sides of a community, both of whom have sinned grievously in God's eyes, out of God's mysterious providence, and now God chooses to punish them and thus expiate their sins through this punishment.

Note next this next very brief sentence. This sentence and then the one that's going to come immediately after that is already very long; in the middle of these two sentences this brief little moment of human longing. It rhymes, too; he clearly did this on purpose.

> Fondly do we hope—fervently do we pray—that this mighty scourge of war may speedily pass away.

That's the human hoping for this, and in a way sincerely; but the rhyming of it makes it sound a little almost too musical. Now Lincoln goes again into one of these vast periodic sentences, and it's wonderful:

> Yet, if God wills that it continue, until all the wealth piled by the bond-man's two hundred and fifty years of unrequited toil shall be sunk, and until every drop of blood drawn with the lash, shall be paid by another drawn with the sword, as was said three thousand years ago, so still it must be said "the judgments of the Lord, are true and righteous altogether."

Let me stop there for a second. First of all, in American politics today there's a lot of worries about God-language and the pervasiveness of God-language. I actually think that Abraham Lincoln's "Second Inaugural Address" is perhaps the most profound piece of theology that America as a continent has produced—I'm including Mexico and Canada here—in the last 500 years. If we talk about having religion in politics, this is about as religious as a political speech can get. He's just interpreted American history as a process of God's judgment on the people for the crime of slavery.

What's interesting about this is that he's doing this in a way that's not entirely something he always does. He's a very good writer, but Lincoln actually early on was known as someone who was a problematic free-thinker. He seems to have been someone who lots of people suspected wasn't actually very religious at all; and a lot of his earlier speeches do not speak about God in this way. Certainly this is a theme that he begins to work out over the course of the Civil War, how surprising this war has been and how it teaches us that there's a larger lesson being conveyed. But in a way, he chooses this register in the most public speech of the end of the Civil War. He really thinks at this point he's pivoting his political leadership now away from fighting this war to healing the nation; and what's interesting is he identifies the register in which to deal with this problem as a theological register. Both sides of this war were deeply, as I said, theological; both sides understood themselves to be fighting on God's cause, on God's side. What Lincoln suggests is that you can understand the moral energies of both sides, but you can redirect them; you can change their orientation and make them understand not that they are fighting in a crusade, but that they are fighting as penitents in a war that works out their own complicity in sin, and you let God decide the outcome of that war as a way of resolving that sin in some ultimate sense. This is why the end of the speech is so remarkably full of a human spirit that, after the Civil War, after Lincoln's assassination, seemed to be lacking; again, North and South, maybe lacking for another century in American history.

Think about this: A war leader at the end of the bloodiest war his nation has ever fought; a war more bloody than anyone had imagined it would be. Think about him saying this:

> With malice toward none; with charity for all; with firmness in the right, as God gives us to see the right, let us strive on to finish the work we are in [and then think about how he describes this work]; to bind up the nation's wounds; to care for him who shall have borne the battle, and for his widow, and his orphan—to do all which

may achieve and cherish a just and lasting peace, among ourselves, and with all nations.

This is a devastating speech; I actually think that all American students should be forced to memorize that speech. But it's an astonishing speech for, as I said, a number of reasons: a theological register for a person who wasn't apparently very theological, or at least the rumors were; a speech of remarkable mercy from a war leader about to defeat his enemies, mercy that no one else on his side and as far as we can tell no one on the other side would have offered at this point; but more than mercy, an astonishing invitation for both sides to reconsider what they are in, not so much as a just war against evil but as a history of punishment, a history of just punishment, providentially just, that all ought to accept and reply to with humility.

Remember again that the war itself was fought by two sides of remarkably theologically similar conviction, though profoundly opposed theological assessment of the rectitude of their two causes. They talked past each other; and in part because they both started from the same, simplistic, proof-texting approach to religion. Lincoln had it right when he said that both sides "read the same Bible, and pray to the same God; and each invokes His aid against the other." They both believed that the other side was godless and would lead the nation to godlessness, either the godlessness of an industrial technocracy where honor and extra-monetary value has no place, or the godlessness of slave drivers driving the whole nation back to a heartless feudal barbarism. They found no way to see the war as anything other than a holy war; a war of pure good against pure evil.

Lincoln saw the evil that lay at the core of the war itself: The vast and dehumanizing system of chattel slavery, which was possibly the most brutal system of human exploitation the world has known outside of intentional genocidal or mass-homicidal activities such as those performed by the Nazis, Stalinist Russia, or the Aztecs. Chattel slavery in North America before the American Civil War was a really nasty, deadly thing; don't let apologists fool you. But Lincoln saw also that this evil was one that both North and South had collaborated in producing, both North and South had profited from, and that both needed to confront their complicity in this evil. In this, Lincoln offers a vision of how to think about evil and how to think about our own involvement in evil that might be of use, might be of power, beyond his own context.

He was able not just to see what the Bible said, he was able to see how to read the Bible and to read with the signs of the times; and you can only do the former, he seems to imply, if you also do the latter. You have to understand the Bible, you have to understand your religious heritage, in light of the history you're going through; and yet you understand that history only through reading it in light of the Bible that you believe in. In doing this, Lincoln is suggesting that there's a way in which humans can come to defuse their tendencies towards dualism in vast moral conflicts and invite their enemies not simply to be their enemies, but also to be their fellow humans in a struggle far deeper than the war that they are maybe immediately involved in. In offering that picture, Lincoln offers a solution that others will pick up after him, both in the United States and beyond, whenever they reach out to their enemies: Instead of trying to polarize their enemies, they try to convince them of the rectitude of their own cause, or their understanding of a mutual project that they both can be involved in.

Both Twain and Lincoln were themselves prophets well ahead of their time. As I said, Twain seems to predict the way that a society can misshape its adherence in ways that only scholars of the Holocaust in the next century will parallel at all. His own appreciation, Twain's own appreciation, of how morality can conspire to reinforce racism is at the heart of thinkers like Martin Luther King's insistence that the Civil Rights struggle was a struggle as much for white people as for black people. And Lincoln's insistence that all would be complicit and should recognize their own complicity is always a salutary reminder that in an age such as ours of culture wars and rumors of culture wars, Americans are always one people, for good and ill, and that "we the people" are united both in our aspirations and in our crimes and must understand our common destiny, in blessing and in punishment.

But beyond America, Lincoln's lesson is powerful beyond that as well. People caught in interminable and moralistic wars can see a problem as one that many people have cooperated in producing, and thus they can come to see the solution they must deal with, they must reach, is one that all must have a hand in order to achieve it. We have been the ones to sin, Lincoln said, and for us to move beyond the sin, all of us must understand the costs we must accept. If you think about large-scale social revolutionary movements in the 20th century—Nelson Mandela and the anti-apartheid movement in South Africa; Vaclav Havel and Adam Michnik in Eastern Europe; the United States Civil Rights Movement—again and again and again the strategy is not to set up a simple opposition, or more of an opposition than was necessary, but to always welcome the other as more than just an enemy, as more than just a rival, as more than just Shaitan, the old enemy that we used to see even in the Ancient Near East. Again and again, the mythology of dualism is powerful in ways that escape merely philosophical depictions of good and evil; and again and again we find that if there are ways of resolving and overcoming that dualism we may find ourselves better able to live into the future.

Nietzsche—Considering the Language of Evil
Lecture 24

Nietzsche is hard to figure out. I don't think I understand him yet; it's not clear to me that I ever will understand him. In fact, I'm not even sure that he wanted to be understood in the sense of having his thought be perfectly transparent to another intellect. I think he wanted more to provoke and inspire, to agitate and excite, not to offer something that could ever be fully cognitively digested.

F riedrich Nietzsche's most famous claim is that "God is dead," killed by us. And once we have killed God, we have to think about how to live beyond that belief, that is, beyond the language of good and evil.

For our purposes, Nietzsche's main argument is that morality is not only incorrect, but it no longer serves any useful purpose in our world. The concepts of good and evil that we think of as naturally part of the world are not, in fact, applicable to the world as we find it. The language of good and evil, the language of truth, the assumption that we need to inquire into truth—these are all tools of our own devising that have outlived their usefulness for us. They have served a purpose in convincing us that the world is organized by these categories, but Nietzsche thinks now that the world is not.

For Nietzsche, the human is an animal that uses language and thought to make its way in the world, but the language we've developed has trapped us in an unhealthy position. Much of our ethical thinking is linguistically shaped and, in some

In *Beyond Good and Evil*, Friedrich Nietzsche (1844–1900) argues that morality is something we need to get past because it restricts our will.

ways, linguistically created. But Nietzsche says that in using language, we're always vulnerable to forgetting that the words we use are our words, and we're always tempted to impute to them a metaphysical credibility that they in no way possess.

Nietzsche further argues that the language of good and evil derives from the attempts of some humans to suppress the enthusiastic energies of others. This is the idea of slave morality, that is, the condition in which the weak in human history—the less noble—have the ability to convince the strong—the truly noble spirits of the world—that they should obey the rules the weak live by. In other words, the language of good and evil manages to keep humans ordered in a certain way, and it does so by making the central moral issue for ethics guilt and the avoidance of guilt.

Nature is an energy that seeks ever-new forms of expression; the human is a vessel for that energy, a structure that also seeks ever-new forms of expression.

Nietzsche thus proposes that the language of evil be replaced with a different language, one less freighted with heavy theological connotations. He sees the need for an evaluative framework to assess the fruitfulness of our actions, but he prefers a language for this assessment that is more authentically grounded. One powerful way of organizing that language would be around the concept of health. Here, we would assess actions by asking to what extent they are "life-promoting, life-preserving … even species-cultivating." The real problem with the dichotomy of good and evil is that it serves to keep humans stuck in patterns of behavior and constrains the development and exercise of our intellectual and physical powers.

Nietzsche also wants us to challenge what he calls the "will to truth," our unstated, almost-reflexive assumption that seeking truth as an objective reality outside of us is innately good—that if our thoughts do not generate some kind of evidence from the outside that they might be true, then they are probably false. Nietzsche argues that we need to turn the will to truth on itself and inquire into whether it is healthy for us. When we do that, we'll see that it assumes the world is composed of structures of opposites, but no such tidy oppositions exist in nature.

Nature, for Nietzsche, is a struggle, an overcoming of the moment for something greater than the moment. The human is the creature whose nature is not yet fully known and whose nature is open to the human to determine. Nature is an energy that seeks ever-new forms of expression; the human is a vessel for that energy, a structure that also seeks ever-new forms of expression. This means that the forms we have at any moment are always going to be broken apart in a new expression of the energy that is coming. This conception of nature is what Nietzsche famously called the "will to power."

Is the will to power something we're in charge of? Are we the ones discharging this will, or are we what is discharged? The psychology that Nietzsche offers understands the will to power as a fundamental force, moving through the world and challenging us, challenging our conception of ourselves as people who are in charge of us. The will to power requires us to take a radical new stance toward ourselves, with new ideas about the soul—the soul as a multiplicity of creatures, the soul as segmented in complicated ways. We will understand this new soul as not good or evil but healthy or sick. This is nothing less than a revolution in our psychologies—in how we think of ourselves and how we will live into the future. ∎

Name to Know

Nietzsche, Friedrich (1844–1900 C.E.). Born and raised in Röcken, a small town near Leipzig, the son of a Lutheran minister who died when he was 5. Nietzsche enrolled at the University of Bonn to study theology but turned to philology after losing his faith.

Suggested Reading

Nehamas, *Nietzsche: Life as Literature.*

Nietzsche, *Beyond Good and Evil,* Kaufmann, trans.

Nietzsche, *On the Genealogy of Morality: A Polemic,* Clark and Swensen, trans.

Questions to Consider

1. Nietzsche suggested that a moral revolution was necessary—one in which the language of "evil" ought to be discarded altogether. Does the language of evil serve an indispensable purpose, or would we do well to follow Nietzsche in discarding it altogether?

2. Is morality reducible to a struggle for power, as Nietzsche argued? Is any moral system always designed to empower some and suppress others?

3. Should we take Nietzsche's advice and turn our attention away from truth and toward health?

Nietzsche—Considering the Language of Evil
Lecture 24—Transcript

Welcome back. In this lecture, I want to talk about the thought of Friedrich Nietzsche, perhaps the greatest bad boy that philosophy has ever known. Nietzsche is often caricatured as a madman or a nihilist, a bushy-mustachioed proto-Nazi Bizmarckian; in any way, a kind of Teutonic horror of various sorts. But these pictures are terrible misrepresentations and they serve to keep from hearing what he has to say in an important way. What he has to say is of tremendous significance and interest for our world today, as he himself thought it would be.

Nietzsche's most famous claim perhaps is that "God is dead." It bears noting that while Nietzsche thinks this is a vastly important idea, in fact he suspects that in his time he is pretty much alone in realizing the magnitude of what has happened. In Nietzsche's telling of this story in his book *The Gay Science*, the Madman who says, "God is dead" in the square of the city is just mocked and laughed at by the people around him. He's shocked at their indifference; but then he realizes something, and in this you can see Nietzsche himself speaking:

> This prodigious event is still on its way, still wandering; it has not yet reached the ears of men. Lightning and thunder require time, the light of the stars requires time, deeds, though done, still require time to be seen and heard. This deed is still more distant from them than the most distant stars—and yet they have done it themselves.

Nietzsche thought that we had killed God ("you and I," he says), and the magnitude of the changes that are underway here because of this death are vast. But we don't yet realize what they will require of us, though we one day will. Because of all this, beneath his philosophizing, Nietzsche in some important ways thinks of himself as fundamentally a prophet, telling us what these changes will mean. Once we have killed God, once we give up the idea that morality is given to us by the world or the deity himself, then we have to think about how to live beyond that belief, beyond a belief in God, as Nietzsche will say, beyond the language of good and evil. What we need to come to is a new language of human striving, a new language of human effort, a new language in which to live, a language that is—again, as the title suggests—beyond good and evil, and especially, as we'll see, beyond the word "evil." Explaining what it means to be beyond the word "evil" is our aim here in this lecture. I want to explain what Nietzsche wants us to do in getting so beyond good and evil to suggest how he thinks we can live beyond those categories and to explain why Nietzsche thinks that so getting beyond these categories, beyond these words, beyond our captivity to these words may be the crucial next step in human evolution.

Let me give you some simple biographical information about Nietzsche. Some of this information you may have heard in some vague way, but it's useful to have it all down in one place. He was born in 1844 to a Lutheran minister father and a quite strict mother. He was a brilliant student; from an early age, he was recognized as remarkably acute and intelligent. At the age of 24—a remarkably, astonishingly young age—he was appointed full professor of classical philology at the University of Basel. He held the post for 11 years before resigning due to health problems. His was an academic career that was stifled because he simply wouldn't work within the confines of what his field decided was acceptable scholarly work. Of course, if he had done that, a few of his works might still be cited as secondary or even tertiary sources in philological scholarship; but instead, he didn't do that—he didn't stay within the confines of his discipline; he was mocked and abused for it—and his works are now some of the most assigned in college classrooms and among the most engaged in philosophical, religious, and literary studies. Maybe his aborted scholarly career was only aborted from a particular and particularly narrow point of view.

From 1879, when he resigned, until 1889, he lived the life of an independent writer and scholar, subsisting on his pension and writing furiously. Illness, which had been persistent throughout his life, became slowly worse over this time. He suffered tremendously debilitating migraine headaches, some of them lasting three or four days, and a number of other maladies that caused him never to be a fully healthy person; ironically, given the preeminence of health in his own thinking. In 1887, discovered the work of Dostoevsky, in whom he recognized a powerful intellect writing in fiction the ideas that he had been working out in nonfiction, or so he thought; just as for Dostoevsky, if there is no God, as he famously says, then everything is permitted. Dostoevsky explores that in one direction; Nietzsche appreciates the magnitude of Dostoevsky's realization of that significant fact. But he didn't have a lot of time to appreciate and explore Dostoevsky's works further, because in 1889 he went completely insane in the city of Turin, Italy, when he was only 45. He was brought back to Switzerland, hospitalized, and never wrote another word until his death in 1900.

Nietzsche is hard to figure out. I don't think I understand him yet; it's not clear to me that I ever will understand him. In fact, I'm not even sure that he wanted to be understood in the sense of having his thought be perfectly transparent to another intellect. I think he wanted more to provoke and inspire, to agitate and excite, not to offer something that could ever be fully cognitively digested. I may be wrong about that; again, I'm not sure I really understand him. But—and this is, I think, very important—the lack of understanding I feel with respect to Nietzsche is a kind of an achievement, I think. I'm not trying to be self-congratulatory here; it's just the product of some really hard work to get into the details of what he's trying to do. It's not the incomprehension of meeting Nietzsche for the first time, but of rather trying to struggle with the surface of the text, and after that struggle still being bewildered at what is going on beneath the surface of that text. I'm going to say this to you as both a kind of consolation and a goad, because understanding Nietzsche the first time is very hard. But he's well worth struggling with; just don't ever assume that the struggle will ever end.

For our purposes, Nietzsche's main argument is that morality—the system that we organize our world into to identify, name, and categorize all the possible actions we could do as either good or evil—is not only simply incorrect (he thinks that's obvious, to him anyway), but it in fact serves no useful purpose any longer in our world. As we'll see, Nietzsche's argument spills out of a kind of moral argument into psychology, and then from a proposal to rearrange human psychology it becomes a profoundly revolutionary argument across all dimensions of life, in ways that we have not yet fully come to grips with. Nietzsche once called himself and his works a destiny, the destiny of Europe; and every time we go back to read Nietzsche again, he seems more and more prescient, more and more correct, that he was, in fact, our destiny.

His work, and especially his book *Beyond Good and Evil*, argues here that morality is simply something we need now to jettison, something we need to get past. We need to get past it because it constrains us in problematic ways; restricts our will and punishes us in ways that we now need to transcend. Why is that; why does a morality of good and evil no longer serve any purpose? And how is that; how did that happen? These are the questions that in some ways Nietzsche explores really in this book. Understanding his answers to this rests on understanding his rejection of the assumptions that we take for granted, Nietzsche thinks. Most fundamentally, Nietzsche challenges us to think about the purpose of truth, the concepts of good and evil, how these concepts are all related to each other, and he suggests that all these concepts that we think of as kind of naturally part of the world are not, in fact, applicable to the world as we find it, but they are instruments of our own devising that have served the world that we have convinced ourselves we inhabit; they're tools that we use—the language of good and evil, the language of truth, the assumption we have that we need to inquire to truth—these are all tools that have now outlived their usefulness for us because now we've reached a level, a stage, of development where they are in some sense not as fruitful for us to employ. They've served a purpose for us in convincing us that the world is, in fact, organized by these categories; but he thinks now that the world is not.

He gets at this from the beginning by challenging a certain conception of what philosophy is. His book's famous first sentence: "suppose truth is a woman—what then?" That's, in fact, a really interesting philosophical and philological joke, because in Greek the word "philosophy" comes from *Philosophia*, it means "the love of wisdom." *Sophia* is a female noun. In other words, Nietzsche is saying what if we actually believe what we say we believe? What if we actually believe that philosophers are supposed to love a woman? The idea here is that we should not just be interested in getting the truth through, say, a scientific method; we have to seduce the truth, we have to seduce life, in order to get what we want. Nietzsche thinks this is the true meaning of philosophy. There is a seductive, romantic, even a sexual connotation to what philosophy really is.

This is a very "macho" way of putting this, but we can put it in a way that isn't quite as sexist as Nietzsche in his own time did: He really wants us to think about the pursuit of a meaningful life—which is what he sees as the true point of philosophy—as a seduction, a vital activity in which we are betting our hearts, not just our minds, not just our intellects; and which if we win, we win joy and love, and which if we lose, is not only an intellectual failing, in some sense, we break our hearts. The reason for emphasizing this serious engagement, this existentially gripping engagement, is really quite simple. The human is an animal, Nietzsche thinks, who uses language and thought to make its way in the world. Nietzsche's very Darwinian, he's someone who has appropriated and understood the implications, at least as he understands them, of Darwin's evolutionary view of the world and of humans; and he thinks of humans as fundamentally animals with a certain broader set of skills and a repertoire of abilities that other animals don't have, but effectively still subject to evolutionary constraints. The problem, he thinks, is that the skills and abilities we have, particularly in terms of the language we've developed, actually have trapped us in a certain unhealthy position now, and the primary surface manifestation of the problem we face is our continued captivity to the language of good and evil.

I've talked a lot about language here, and that's very important because this is a really crucial dimension of Nietzsche. In some ways a little bit like Hobbes, Nietzsche wants to say that much of our ethical thinking turns out to be linguistically shaped; not just linguistically shaped, but in some ways linguistically created. So if Hobbes was in some ways the first social constructivist, Nietzsche takes this in a really quite radical way. He wants to say that in using language, we are always vulnerable to forgetting that the words we use are our words, and we are always tempted to impute to them a spurious metaphysical credibility that they in no way actually possess. The language of good and evil is a language—and Nietzsche is a philologist here, a scholar of languages, he knows this—that emerges out of a certain cultural context, a certain background. Not everybody had a category of "evil"; we've already seen this. The category of "evil" in a certain way develops over time, over history; and Nietzsche wants to say that these categories, "good" and "evil," derive, just like other categories like "God" and "sin" and "Satan" from human efforts to live in the world, and now—this is where Nietzsche gets really interesting—centrally, the language of good and evil derives from the attempts, he thinks, of some humans to keep others in line, to kind of suppress their more enthusiastic energies. This is the famous slave morality's domination over the truly noble people of our world.

Let me step back here and explain this a little bit more: For Nietzsche, he thinks that much of human civilization is a development of people trying to figure out how to live together, and realizing that there are a few people—the truly noble souls, the noble spirits—who are so much more gifted than the ordinary run of plain humans that they're able to kind of dominate the rest of us. Nietzsche thinks that over time the weak people, the slaves, in fact end up feeling resentful about this domination and disliking it (of course they would dislike it). So over time, the slaves develop a picture of the world that allows them to say that this kind of domination is bad, this kind of domination is evil. This slave morality basically is a morality that works for people who are weak and who can't do these things. But Nietzsche thinks for noble people, there's no reason why they shouldn't try to do these things, there's no reason why if someone has a kind of excess of energy, intellectual gifts, athletic capacity, they ought not to explore and exploit those gifts to their fullest extent. The greatest achievement of human history, Nietzsche thinks, so far has been the slave morality's triumph for humans; that is, the ability of the weak in human history to convince the strong, the truly strong, that they should obey the rules that the weak live by.

There's a little irony here that's worth nothing—Nietzsche notes this, but he's not very comfortable with it so he moves on very quickly—but if the slaves actually manage to convince the strong that they really ought to obey the ethic of the slaves, are the strong really the strong? Maybe they're muscular, but they don't see very smart. Somehow there's some kind of tension here between the rhetoric Nietzsche has of the truly strong versus the weak and the fact that he has to explain that somehow the truly strong have been suckered into this in some complicated way. But leave that aside for right now; think about how, for Nietzsche, the language of good and evil— and again, especially the language of evil—manages to suppress humans, to keep them down, to keep them ordered in a certain way.

The language does this most basically by making the central moral issue for ethics guilt and the avoidance of guilt. Nietzsche thought that the main moral issue for people caught in the language of good and evil is the struggle to avoid getting blamed for things, getting evil attached to them. I think psychologically, this actually has some purchase on our lives. It's worth asking yourself: When you think about the world and you think about the ethical choices you have in the world, do you sometimes not catch yourself asking the question not "What is the good thing to do here?" or "What is the right thing to do here?" but rather "What is the thing to do here that will help me avoid blame in this situation? What is the thing that most adroitly enables me to avoid feeling guilty?" Nietzsche thinks asking those questions—asking how we are to avoid negative feelings, negative emotions, negative judgments—is in some important way unhealthy and destructive of ourselves. We should always be asking: "What is the good thing to do?" "What is the beautiful thing to do?" and "What is the truly expressive and noble thing to do?"

That's why he proposes that the language of "evil"—which again oppresses humans and confines us in a certain way on his reading of the language—be replaced with a different language, one less freighted with the heavy theological connotations that "evil" is, at least because "evil" has these connotations due to its relationship to demonic illusions, the notion of Satan, these sorts of things. Instead he wants to say, "We don't want a language of evil anymore, we want a more pragmatic language; a language of 'bad.'" In *Beyond Good and Evil*, he says, "Look, in getting beyond good and evil I don't mean to be getting beyond good and bad, I don't mean to be punting on the idea of there being an evaluative framework to assess the successfulness or the fruitfulness of our actions. We'll need that; we'll always need some way of judging whether what we're doing is wise or not. In fact, I, Nietzsche, need that in making this case at all."

But in talking about a language of good or bad, we have to find some other more authentically organic basis on which to ground that language to talk about the fruitfulness of actions for our lives. Nietzsche thinks, again following Darwin, that one very powerful way of organizing that language would be around the language of health. He asks in *Beyond Good and Evil*, he says we have to ask, "to what extent [an action] is life-promoting, life-preserving … even species-cultivating"? That's the criteria we want to use: How do we cultivate our lives? How do we cultivate our species? If we attack the fundamental metaphysical faith—the faith in opposed values such as good and evil—we can see that the real problem with that dichotomy of good and evil is that it serves to keep humans stuck in particular stale patterns, ruts of behavior, and constrains the development and the exercise of their power, their intellectual power, their physical power, in unhealthy ways. Why is that? It is unhealthy because it basically paralyzes humans; forces us not to exercise the full range of our capacities; not to ask fundamental questions because they will expose certain kinds of forbidden knowledge; not to explore certain kinds of relationships or certain kinds of actions in the world because we are terrified that in some sense by doing that we will be contaminated or corrupted in some irremediable, irredeemable way.

Nietzsche thinks this is all crazy. Humans are, more than anything else, explorers; and if we are trapped beneath the heavy weight of an external standard that has nothing necessarily to do with our own lives, where we are right now, we're never going to be able to figure out where we'll be in the future. To see how radical the change is Nietzsche wants, we have to appreciate the range of things he thinks that need to change if we want to become more healthy in this way. By changing the language of good and evil, that's a pretty substantial change on its own; but Nietzsche thinks actually there are far larger changes there as well.

Sometimes in my classes I'll talk about how philosophical or theological argument can sometimes be akin to a chess game. Making a move with one piece on one part of the board can seem like a relatively finite move on a finite kind of range of the board; if you move your knight in a certain way, certain squares become vulnerable to attack and other squares are now protected from attack. But what Nietzsche shows us, and what attention to any philosopher or theologian will show you, is that a move over on this part of the board actually affects things way over here, in ways that are not entirely immediately visible. You have to understand the whole board, the whole scope of the argument, to see what's going on. And not just at the present; you have to think about how this move might affect things on this part of the board 5, or 10, or 15, or 20 moves from now. By moving your knight up here, maybe you've exposed a bishop in a certain way; by moving your knight up here, maybe you've rendered another knight more susceptible to attack, or now you've loosed pieces that can now go and attack over here, but it will take 10 moves to get there. The same thing happens in philosophy and in theology: An argument at one place in a philosophical system, or a proposal, will actually affect things, remarkably and dramatically, elsewhere in the system. That's what Nietzsche's proposal about getting beyond good and evil actually does.

To understand the details of this argument, we have to ask four basic questions: First, what is the "will to truth"? What does Nietzsche think of nature? That's the second question. What is nature for Nietzsche? Third, what does Nietzsche think of the standard whereby we should judge things better or worse? Finally, what exactly is "the will to power"? Let's talk about challenging truth here: Nietzsche wants to challenge in a quite radical way our sense that "being true" is a naturally good thing for us to want. "Truth" is something we can interrogate to see if we believe in it anymore. We can challenge, he says, our captivity to what he calls the "will to truth," our unstated assumption at an almost-reflexive level that seeking truth as an objective reality outside of us is, in fact, innate and good; that if our thoughts do not generate some kind of evidence from the outside that they might be true that they are probably false. Nietzsche thinks that's crazy.

For Nietzsche, we need to turn on the "will to truth" itself and inquire into whether it is healthy, if it is good for us. When we do that, we will see that, as Nietzsche puts it, the problem with the "will to truth" is that it assumes the world is opposed in structures of opposites. Nietzsche thinks that no such tidy opposition exists in nature. There, in nature, sometimes what we call good is intimately related to what we call evil, and intimately related in ways that should give us cause to reflect on them more thoroughly. This is speaking of the whole range of cases that philosophers talk about as "dirty hands" cases; cases of ethical people where to do some great good, something must be done that looks evil or at least approaches evil. Even where the good thing may vastly outweigh the evil thing that needs to be done, philosophers have a lot of trouble figuring out how to justify the evil, even thought the good is done as well.

Nietzsche would have people not worry about that so much. We often do "evil" things but don't notice that we would think of them as evil in a different setting. We would think of normally sticking a child with a needle as an evil thing to do, but when we're doing it in the context of giving the child a vaccination, causing pain for their health, we think of that as a good thing. Instead of thinking of the will to truth, Nietzsche wants us to think of humans as fundamentally, again, animals. Our thinking is not the cogitation of a computer, a free-floating immaterial mind or soul; our thinking derives from our belly and our muscles, our appetites and our aversions, consciousness and our inquiries into the world. Those are the things, the existentially gripping things, which drive our thinking.

What Nietzsche uses to destabilize truth here—the lever he uses to pry it out of the floor of consciousness, the assumptions at our base that we never even question—is, in fact, this vision of health, of the human as an animal who uses language to help it make its way in the world. The question we have to ask of any actual practice humans engage in is about whether or not it is cultivating of us; we need fictions, it turns out, Nietzsche thinks, because fictions do cultivate us. We need to know how to transcend the stories we tell, and for that sometimes we need to convince ourselves of things that are not yet true; that, in fact, we are now able to build this castle, we are now able to build this tower up to God. That would not have been true, Nietzsche thinks, before we tried to build those things; but the ambition itself creates the ability, he thinks. So he says famously, "To recognize untruth as a condition of life," to imagine that you can do something and then to strive and accomplish it, that is a crucial, crucial fact. And he says, "A philosophy that risks [recognizing untruth as a condition for life] would by that token alone place itself beyond good and evil." All that is to say that we are not interested in getting the truth simply put—through, that is, using the scientific method—we have to seduce reality to get what we want, we have to seduce life to get what we want. Remember, again, supposing truth is a woman: Imagine if, in fact, philosophy is an effort of sexual seduction.

But this raises questions about what "nature" is for Nietzsche. What does it mean to live "naturally"? Nature is, in some ways, the activity that is involved in self-overcoming; again, this is very Darwinian. Nature is a struggle, a striving, an overcoming of the moment for something greater than the moment. As he says, "the human is the as yet undetermined animal"; the human is the creature whose nature is not yet fully known, is in some sense open to the human to determine. In a way, philosophy itself is the energy that can help the human determine that; philosophy itself is, as he says, the most "tyrannical drive" the human has, "the most spiritual will to power." Nature is an energy that is seeking ever-new forms of expression; the human is a vessel for that energy, a structure that is also seeking ever-new forms of expression. That means that the forms that we have at any moment are always going to be broken apart in a new expression of the energy that is coming.

"Nature," then, is a kind of endless, energetic, destructive creativity. Everything we are turns out to be a tumult of energy. The actions we engage in, Nietzsche says, are a matter of more discharge of expression of our energy more often than they are really oriented towards some finite goal that we have set in the future. We should avoid thinking that everything we do, we do with a particular end in mind. "Nature," in this way, is what Nietzsche famously called the "will to power."

Just to stop here for a second, "the will to power" is a translation of a German word *der Wille zur Macht*. The *Wille zur Macht* is really fairly translated as "the will to power"; but, in fact, it's not simply fair to call it only "the will to power." It also is in a certain way related to the will to create, to make. *Macht* is not just "power," it's also *machen*, "to make." Nietzsche actually has a Romantic edge—and I mean that the Romantic Movement, not romantic comedies or romantic novels—a focus on the human as creative that is really quite important to get in him. He's not really is a Bismarckian, interested in walking around Europe with an iron fist and smashing people; he's interested in the idea that in every dimension of life—politics, too, but every dimension of life: philosophy, science, art—there's an expressive and dynamic creativity that needs to be cultivated. In this he's a little bit like Marx; remember Marx's idea that humans are in some sense needing to find the way to find their happiness in their expression of their energies. Nietzsche, too, thinks that this expression of energy is really crucial.

This "will to power," though, has a question about it, and this gets to the basis of what we could call Nietzsche's metaphysics (if we want to call it that): Is the "will to power" something we're in charge of? Are we the ones discharging this will, or are we what is discharged? The psychology that Nietzsche offers has to understand the "will to power" as in some ways a really fundamental force moving through the world challenging us, challenging our own conception of ourselves as people who are in charge of us. We need, that is, Nietzsche thinks—if we are to get beyond good and evil—a new psychology, a new way of thinking about our own notion of autonomy here. Does Nietzsche think this "discharge" affects only our doing, or does it affect our thinking as well? Both, obviously; and this is to say something of the depth of the radical reformation of the point and purpose of our lives that this picture demands.

Getting us this far pushes us, as he himself puts it in the title of one of his works, *Towards a Genealogy of Morals*. Once we understand the need to get beyond good and evil, we have to step back and understand just what it is towards which we are going. In this way, there is a kind of anthropological revolution at the heart of Nietzsche's aims. Again, we need to rethink this notion that we are properly autonomous, separate creatures. We have to change our understanding of ourselves; not just the content of what we understand ourselves to be, but also for Nietzsche the nature of what we take to be understanding itself. We have to take a new stance towards ourselves in some radical way. Nietzsche needs new ideas about the soul—the soul as a multiplicity of creatures; the soul as segmented in complicated ways— in order to get at this new dynamism of the "will to power" that he thinks is actually motivating human agency; a soul that is most fundamentally something we can understand not as "good" or "evil," but as "healthy" or "sick." In a way, that language itself replaces—if that's the word for it—the language of good and evil.

This anthropological revolution is a revolution in our psychologies, for how we think of ourselves and how we live into the future. When we think about this, we are understanding that this rejection of good and evil for Nietzsche is a rejection merely on Darwinist grounds; but unlike Darwin—who he thought was caught in the "will to truth"; who he thought was caught in telling a story that Darwin believed was objectively true about the world— Nietzsche thinks Darwin is actually offering us a way of imagining ourselves in a new way. That's what Nietzsche wants to do; he wants to say that instead of thinking about this just as the truth, when we think about what it means to kill God, it means not just that it is true that God is dead, it means that in some sense we're beyond the very category of thinking about what's true and not true. That's how you really kill God; that's how you really get beyond good and evil; not so much by proving that these things don't exist, but by no longer caring about whether or not they exist at all.

Dostoevsky—The Demonic in Modernity
Lecture 25

Dostoevsky thinks the very genre of the novel itself is a product of Western secularity. The novel, as an imaginary story, an imaginary creation by a human author of a kind of vivid human world— Dostoevsky finds that enormously theologically problematic. It's potentially latently a rival to God's creation—any novel is—and so, potentially, a novel is intrinsically corruptive.

In this lecture, we turn to perhaps the greatest philosophical novelist of all time, **Fyodor Dostoevsky**. Dostoevsky's works repeatedly struggle with what happens to humans when they operate outside of the restraining realities of vivid and organic religious belief in conditions of a rapidly modernizing society.

Throughout his working life, Dostoevsky was obsessed with the challenge of intellectual currents coming from the West, especially with those intellectual movements that attacked traditional morality and religion. He saw the new ideas of his time as powerfully revolutionary, but unlike Nietzsche, who thought such ideas were good and exciting, Dostoevsky felt that they were nightmares that would lead to a new age of barbarism and inhumanity.

As we've seen, nihilism is the belief that there is no moral structure, no absolute framework to the cosmos. The cosmos is what we make of it. Dostoevsky found nihilism a seductive idea, but he also thought that it ultimately doesn't work with the psychology of humans. The terror for Dostoevsky is that this belief has deleterious effects on people who hold it and those around them.

In *Demons*, Dostoevsky argues that the desire of revolutionary modernists in Russia and elsewhere to improve society founders as a result of their failure to understand the nature of evil. The novelist makes use of the tradition of a multiplicity of devils in Eastern Orthodox Christianity to identify and describe the anarchic squabbling nature of evil, particularly as it is manifest in groups of revolutionaries. The problem with rebels is that we can't take them seriously from a practical standpoint, but their actions can have deadly consequences. Here, Dostoevsky is sketching a distinctly modern character: the figure of the human whose impact on reality is out of all proportion to his or her own pathetic, ludicrous reality. A tension exists between the smallness of this figure and the magnitude of the evil that he or she is able to produce.

Fyodor Dostoevsky (1821–1881) was obsessed with the challenge of the Western intellectual movements, especially those that attacked traditional morality and religion.

The story of *Demons* revolves around a group of young revolutionaries and the murder of a former member of the group, Ivan Shatov. Shatov's break with the group can be traced to his more morally supple and vivid picture of reality than that seen by the revolutionaries, one in which morality matters and humans are mired in sin. The revolutionaries, caught up in the currents of 19th-century science, rationalism, and philosophical extremism, have the view that things happen, but responsibility can't be pinned on anybody. They are creating a new world that is superior to the present one; thus, the consequences of their actions will be justified by the endpoint they achieve. In contrast, Shatov tells one of the other group members, "We are all to blame." The distinction between these two attitudes—"we are all to blame" and "no one is to blame"—is, for Dostoevsky, the driving force behind the history of the 19th century.

In *Demons*, Dostoevsky offers us a powerful account of the nature of evil in modernity that is couched primarily in political terms. He sees evil as a revolution against both the social order and the conditions of human existence in general. Further, the modern world doesn't want to acknowledge the reality of this evil. As a response to this corruption, Dostoevsky proposes the tradition of radical orthodoxy, with special focus on the drama of sin and redemption.

Where *Demons* was essentially about a collectivity of people and their collective descent into hell, *Crime and Punishment* focuses on one person: Raskolnikov, a failed graduate student who kills a pawnbroker and her sister. What's interesting to us about this book is the representation of Raskolnikov's motives. He seems to have committed the crime because it would allow him to demonstrate to himself that he is invulnerable to moral guilt or self-condemnation. Of course, in this, Raskolnikov turns out to be wrong. He is traumatized by the events and must finally confess his crimes. He believed his story was that of a liberal Western nihilist, but as Dostoevsky points out, he failed to live into that story. Dostoevsky suggests that the problem with Raskolnikov is that he's trying to usurp God's role, trying to tell his own story instead of living the story that God gives him.

For Dostoevsky, the problem of evil lies in any act of rebellion against an established order. Acquiescence to a powerful authority above us is merely one way that we observe the place in society that God has given us. ∎

Name to Know

Dostoevsky, Fyodor (1821–1881 C.E.). The son of a violent alcoholic, a former military surgeon who practiced at a hospital for the poor in Moscow.

Suggested Reading

Dostoevsky, *Crime and Punishment*, Pevear and Volkhonsky, trans.

———, *Demons*, Pevear and Volkhonsky, trans.

Frank, *Dostoevsky: A Writer in His Time*.

Questions to Consider

1. Dostoevsky's *Demons* suggests that modernity's denial of the existence of evil may, in fact, be an even more profound complicity with evil itself. Do we risk a complicity with evil by denying its existence or refusing to consider its effects?

What is the place of thinking about evil in the modern world? Has evil become passé, or does it still hold a prominent place in the modern imagination?

Dostoevsky—The Demonic in Modernity
Lecture 25—Transcript

Hello again. In this lecture, I want to talk about perhaps the greatest philosophical novelist of all time, Fyodor Dostoevsky. Dostoevsky's works are enormous and vast and incredibly dense, with plots and subplots and characters and philosophical arguments; and so you'll almost certainly have imagined reading Dostoevsky, but I'm not sure that you have read Dostoevsky. If you haven't, as with so many other things, I strongly urge you to do so as soon as you finish this lecture.

Dostoevsky's works repeatedly struggle with what happens to humans when they operate outside of the restraining realities of vivid and organic religious belief in conditions of a rapidly modernizing society, such as was the case in his world, the world of 19th-century Russia. His own experience of life imitated a great deal of his novels; and, in fact, his own life is worthy of its own novelization. He was born into a complicated family—as all really rich, complicated, and dense noble Russian families were—in 1821. His father was a violent alcoholic, though Dostoevsky and his father seemed eventually to come to a good relationship. His mother died when he was 16 and his father died when he was 18. He fell in love with literature and fell into a circle of liberal intelligentsia, young Turks in Russia who were thinking about how to engage in Western thinking and bring it into the Russian culture in the most powerful and useful way possible. In that circle, though, he became involved with some people who were on the outs with the secret police in czarist Russia, and he was arrested and sentenced to death.

Astonishingly—and imagine this happening to you—he was actually in a cell and led out with a number of other people to stand before a ditch facing a firing squad where his sentence was proclaimed and he believed sincerely that the firing squad was about to shoot. Then, his sentence was commuted to four years of exile in Siberia, and he was led away to exile. Whenever I think about that I just can't get over the thought of standing at something in his mid-20s and imagining that he's about to die, and then suddenly hearing that his life was going to go on. Clearly that would make almost anybody psychologically a more complicated figure than they had been; it did that to Dostoevsky.

Prison in Siberia was very hard, incredibly brutal; but it served to shape his views profoundly. Over time, in and out of prison—in prison first and then out afterwards—the experiences also in his life of especially addiction to alcohol and gambling gave him intimate acquaintance with obsessive-compulsive and addictive behaviors that he associated, identified really, with sin. Over the course of his life, he became increasingly a Slavophile, someone who believed that the destiny of Russia was to come back to its own organic roots and find in those roots the salvation of the whole world against the dangerous depredations of the acidic suspicions of Western European modernity. He had a profound religious experience that made his always nominal, and more than nominal in many ways, commitment to Russian Orthodoxy the absolute center of his life. The rest of his life was tumultuous—several marriages, one wife's death, again alcoholism, gambling addiction, a final remarriage and flourishing in his last decade—but his mental worldview was pretty much set by the 1860s. He died in 1881.

Throughout his working life, he was obsessed with the challenge of the intellectual currents coming from the West, and especially with those intellectual movements that attacked traditional morality and religion. Dostoevsky himself felt the powerful pull of these currents; he was drawn to them as a young man; but he found himself finally unsatisfied by them and indeed led astray by them, led down dangerous paths. His famous line in *The Brothers Karamazov*, "If there is no God, then everything is permitted" is meant to be a summary of the thoughts he often explored. In this way, we can, in fact, see him as a little bit like Nietzsche, though drawing the opposite conclusions from Nietzsche. Both saw the new ideas of their time as powerfully revolutionary, refiguring everything, shaping the way society and the human should understand themselves in completely revolutionary ways; but whereas Nietzsche thought these ideas were good and exciting and should be furthered and we should progress with them, Dostoevsky felt that the ideas were nightmares that would lead to a new age of barbarism and inhumanity, and that the most important thing he could do was identify their full meaning, diagnose their pathologies, and warn his countrymen to stay as far away from them as they could.

To understand this, it will help for a minute just to get a grip on the category of nihilism that is pervasive in a lot of Dostoevsky's work and also in some of other thinkers' work as well (Nietzsche; we'll see Albert Camus talk about this as well). "Nihilism" is the belief that in some sense there is no moral structure; and not just no moral structure, but in some ways no absolute framework to the cosmos, that the cosmos is in some important way morally and perhaps in other ways up to us, all the matter of our will. The world is what we make of it. The thing for Dostoevsky about nihilism is it's an enormously seductive idea, and it's an enormously empowering idea, but he also thinks ultimately it doesn't work with the psychology of humans to finally believe in nihilism. The terror for Dostoevsky is not that people can say they believe this, the terror is what they do when they're in the grip of this belief. You don't have to take their belief literally, he thinks, to take it seriously; whether they express it properly or not, they are in the grip of a powerful idea that has terrible deleterious effects both on them and those around them.

I want to talk about two great works he wrote, one sometimes called *The Possessed* or *The Devils*, properly really entitled *Demons*, and the other in English called *Crime and Punishment*. Together, these two books offer a powerful set of challenges to where evil is going, as Dostoevsky worries about it as the 19th century lurches to its close. Let me talk about *The Possessed* or *Demons* first. In this work, in *Demons*, Dostoevsky struggles to argue, trying to figure out a way of saying, that the desire of revolutionary modernists in Russia and elsewhere to improve society founders on their failure, their own fundamental failure, to understand the nature of evil. They fail to understand this in their own nature; in the nature of how evil manifests itself in warping their collaboration, their allegiance with other revolutionaries; and also, more basically, their failure to understand how evil is the problem that they are themselves trying to confront and overcome.

This book has a really interesting publication history actually, and its career in Russian is worth mentioning. It gets published in 1873, and it's hailed as a great novel right away. For the next 30 or 40 years, lots of Russian readers tend to it, talk about it, discuss it; a very, very popular and powerful novel. But with the Russian Revolution, of course, it effectively disappears, because lots of people in the authority structure of the Soviet Union thought of demons as basically an indictment of communism and of the revolutionaries that led to communism. There were bureaucrats within the Soviet system who disagreed with this and tried to find ways of publishing this work of Dostoevsky's, but effectively it was completely forgotten in Russia. Then in perestroika and then in the 1990s, it became widely available again and wildly popular in Russia, and now again, the Russians laud it as a great novel; though now, of course, they think, "Maybe we should have called it 'what could we have been thinking'" because it seems to prophetic to many Russians about the course of their own country in the 20th century.

Interestingly, as a background for this novel, understand that in Eastern Orthodox Christianity, and especially in Russia, there's not a lot of direct theoretical attention given to Satan, given to the Devil in the theologies; rather, what you have instead is attention to the multiplicity of devils, in the plural: local house demons, forest devils, gypsies, spirits of the swamp, that sort of thing. Dostoevsky uses this tradition—which is a theological tradition but also a folk tradition—to identify, name, and kind of describe the anarchic squabbling nature of evil, at least as it's manifest in this group of revolutionaries. Its incoherence, both in the individual in making their actions not really intelligible, most of all not to themselves; and in the group, in making their cooperation in any real way impossible—in fact, evil corrupts groups in such a way that they end up being always at war with themselves—again, Dostoevsky here is in some important ways a little like Milton.

The problem with the rebels is that we can't really practically take them with complete seriousness, but their actions have profoundly deadly consequences; and in this, Dostoevsky is sketching a character, a distinctively modern character, whose figure we will see come up again and again: the figure of the human whose consequences, whose impact on reality, are out of all proportion with their own pathetic ludicrous reality. That in some sense, there's a tension between the smallness of the figure and the magnitude of the evil that they are able to produce. Whereas in goodness, when we see someone do a great deed we're normally able to identify that person as truly a remarkable person in some sense; but with evil it doesn't seem to work that way, at least in modernity. Much of the greatest of the evils in modernity—Dostoevsky is one of the first person to suggest this— much of the magnitude of those evils is caused by people who are really in themselves kind of pipsqueaks. We'll see this especially with Hannah Arendt and her discussion of Adolf Eichmann; but understand it's operative even in someone like Dostoevsky, at least at the imaginative level.

Another thing—don't worry, we will get to the *Demons*—but another thing to know before we begin is that the very genre of the novel (this is a totally Dostoevskean, classically Russian think to do but Dostoevsky thinks the very genre of the novel itself is a product of Western secularity; the novel, as an imaginary story, an imaginary creation by a human author of a kind of vivid human world, Dostoevsky finds that enormously theologically problematic. It's potentially latently a rival to God's creation; any novel is, and so potentially a novel is intrinsically corruptive. So in *Demons*, as in all of his novels, he is anxious that the novel not seem too realistic. In this, Dostoevsky's in profound tension with his comrade Tolstoy; Tolstoy was the classic exemplar of the person who writes the great realistic novel. Dostoevsky, for theological reasons, is quite worried that the category of the novel seduces the author of the novel and the readers into a God's-eye perspective, which is deeply troubling to him. One interesting thing about Dostoevsky is he's always worried about the very genre he's writing in, that somehow it might itself be a demonic genre.

The story of *Demons* is relatively simple, as 19th century Russian novels go. Peter Verkhovensky is a wealthy, young, and idealistic revolutionary, very good with words, articulate, lucid, coming from kind of right-thinking, forward-thinking, intellectual parents, liberal parents; and Verkhovensky gathers a conspiracy of like-minded young revolutionaries about him. He convinces them that the conspiracy into which he lures them is, in fact, part of a much larger trans-Russian conspiracy, maybe an international conspiracy, but in fact the conspiracy goes no further than Verkhovensky himself; it effectively is kind of like a bridge club of secret revolutionaries. He brings into this group one by whom he is himself seduced, the most inspiring and the most seductive of all the revolutionaries, Nikolai Stavrogin. Stavrogin is a deeply charismatic figure, often an observer on the margins of events, not able to really be invested or engaged in anything, and profoundly misanthropic, someone who doesn't have a lot of fondness for humans; but also someone who is deeply tortured by his misanthropy, by his hatred of others. He does some truly horrible things in the novel, including eventually at one point paying someone to kill his mentally retarded wife Marya. He manages to convince someone else to kill her, and manages to pay them without in some sense really coming to grips what he had done, his full role in this. Dostoevsky is fantastic at representing this kind of evil that happens when we kind of back into a wickedness that we don't ever really fully acknowledge to ourselves as going on.

To solidify this group's identity, to confirm everybody in the private club of the revolutionaries, Verkhovensky kills a former conspirator—someone who was in the group but who left—whose name is Ivan Shatov, who left behind radicalism for Russian Orthodoxy. After he's killed him, Verkhovensky lets everyone in the group in on the secret. He's basically killing this guy to bond everybody in the group together; he's instrumentalizing his life for the abstract cause of the group. But the truth of the murder becomes known, the conspiracy collapses, most of the conspirators arrested by the police. Nikolai Stavrogin, in the end, is deeply aware of all of his sins including his complicity with this futile and folly-laden group of pseudo-revolutionaries; and in the end, he commits suicide in despair of his guilt at his complicity in the murder of Shatov and in the murder of his own wife, and in the whole worldview that surrounds both of these things.

As in so much of Dostoevsky, the "moral" of this novel, such as it is, doesn't emerge neatly at the end of the book; ironically, it emerges almost in the middle, in the buildup to the murder of Ivan Shatov. What finally causes the break between Shatov and the revolutionaries is that he offers a more morally supple and vivid picture of reality, one where morality matters and where humans are caught in sin. The revolutionaries don't. For the revolutionaries caught up in the currents of 19th century science, rationalism, and philosophical extremism—nihilism again—they want to say that effectively things happen, but that responsibility can't be pinned on anybody; no one is properly to blame, they want to say. All we have to do is create a new world that is in some sense far superior to this; we don't have to worry about the ethical consequences of our actions because they will be justified by the endpoint we achieve (remember Marx here).

The problem is that a figure such as Shatov, who is coming to appreciate the theological and cultural heritage of Russian Orthodoxy, realizes that it's not true that no one is to blame. He says, famously, in a confrontation with Verkhovensky: "we are all to blame"; effectively, everybody is guilty. That distinction between those who believe that "no one is to blame" and "we are all to blame" is for Dostoevsky the most fundamental and powerful distinction that drives the history as he sees it of the 19th century.

In *Demons*, Dostoevsky is offering up three important lessons: First of all, he's offering us a powerful modern account of the nature of evil in modernity. Effectively it's couched primarily in political terms—politically it's a structure of revolution against the social order—but more deeply than that, he thinks, it's psychologically about revolting against the conditions of human existence in general. The failure of modernity in the face of this evil is his second lesson. The modern world, the coming into existing modern world, simply does not want to acknowledge the reality of this evil; and it doesn't even want to acknowledge, what's more disturbing for Dostoevsky, the modern world's tacit or active complicity with it. Verkhovensky, remember, comes from a good, right-thinking family, a liberal family; tolerant, welcoming people who are open to new ideas. But their openness to these new ideas for Dostoevsky leads their son into the most grotesque and wicked nihilism imaginable. Third, as a response to this corruption, Dostoevsky proposes that the tradition of radical orthodoxy is probably the one thing that will save at least Russia, and perhaps beyond Russia all of us. The traditional cultural and religious values, and especially the drama of sin and redemption, the idea of a universal corruption as the first insight psychologically, politically, morally that would found a wise and healthy human life is for Dostoevsky essential to going forward in our context.

To turn from *Demons* to Dostoevsky's probably much more famous and certainly more widely recognized as a great novel *Crime and Punishment* is to turn from a powerful novel of political psychology to a powerful novel of psychology in general, and in fact, the powerful novelistic portrayal of what it says it is about (at least in English): a crime, and then the inner, and also a little bit of the outer, punishment that the crime entails. Whereas the *Demons* was really about a collectively of people and how they all kind of collectively led each other to Hell, *Crime and Punishment* focuses on one person: Rodion Romanovich Raskolnikov. There are a few words even in the English language that, in the 20th century and now in the 21st, have come to have a certain kind of density of meaning, and if you hear someone talk about as a real Raskolnikov they're actually not saying a very nice thing about them.

Raskolnikov is a poor, failed student in Saint Petersburg, a kind of graduate student dropout. He likes the kind of marginal life in a dingy little room, dealing with lowlifes, trying to figure out what to do with his life now that he's realized that the university's not for him. In the course of his experience of the city, he comes across a quite nasty woman who's a money-lender and a pawnbroker, quite merciless, and actually clearly who has a lot of money in her rooms. Raskolnikov decides that he will kill her, take her money, and perhaps—sometimes he seems to think this, sometimes he doesn't; the psychology is of Raskolnikov is deliciously, realistically unclear on this—he will use the money perhaps to offer some good kindnesses, some charities, some good deeds to people in the city. One day, he sneaks into her rooms and he kills her with an ax, and just as he is trying to get away, just as he is trying to sneak out, the pawnbroker's half-sister Lizaveta shows up, completely innocent, an innocent bystander, but in order to finish his crime and make sure he gets away scot free, Raskolnikov must kill her, too; and he does. After this, he's completely discombobulated, terrified, and flees with only a few small things in his hands and a small purse, leaving most of the wealth left behind. But he manages to get away entirely undetected, and unless he confesses the crime, Dostoevsky sets it up, no one will ever know. In that sense, the crime is a success.

But Raskolnikov is traumatized by it. The event of killing was much worse than he thought, and the consequences for his soul are far more drastic than he could have imagined. He wanders the city in a feverish daze. He ends up giving what little money he has left away to the family of a friend who was a drunkard but has now died; he sees him killed in the street by a cart. The daughter of the family, a young woman named Sonya, has turned to prostitution to help her family survive. Again, think of Marx; think of how brutal the 19th century was where to help a family live a daughter had to turn to prostitution. Raskolnikov and Sonya form a bond, and they talk; and Raskolnikov tells her of his crimes and the torment in his soul because of the crimes. Sonya urges him to confess. After a suitably Russian period of tormented uncertainty and plot twists, Raskolnikov agrees, he confesses, and he is sent to Siberia for punishment with Sonya following along to help him.

This is a novel of incredible density and incredible density. What's interesting about the book—a lot is interesting, but what's interesting for us—is the representation of Raskolnikov's motives throughout the book. Why did he do this? Why did he think going into someone else's room, killing her with an ax, would ever be a good idea? What could possibly have motivated that? He seems to have done it because he could, and because he imagined that by doing it he would be invulnerable to moral guilt or self-condemnation; he would show himself that he was invulnerable in this way. That is, he seems to have convinced himself that by killing someone else with an ax, he would demonstrate to himself that he is the kind of great-souled person he thinks he is. As a student, he had written a thesis entitled "On Crime," and in the thesis he suggested that, in fact, there was no such thing as evil. He compares himself in several places in the book to Napoleon, admiring Napoleon's sense of ego and will, his strength of purpose, and suggesting that he himself has the ability to make good come of this immense evil by doing good with the cash. But he turns out to be wrong. The murder is botched by the arrival of Lizaveta, and he himself is traumatized by these events to such a degree that he flees the scene without taking the money, and afterwards he can't bear himself until he finally confesses to Sonya.

Raskolnikov turns out to be quite different what he thought he was, quite different than the story he was telling himself—a story of 19th century liberal Western nihilism—and how that story he was trying to tell himself was what he wanted to live into; but as Dostoevsky points out, he failed to be able to live into that story. Again, go back to that idea that a novel is a theologically troubling thing for Dostoevsky. Just as Raskolnikov is trying to tell a story about himself, he's trying to be a novelist, Dostoevsky himself suggests the problem with Raskolnikov is precisely that he's trying to usurp God's role; he's trying to tell his story instead of having the story that God gives him be his story. Indeed, the title of the novel, *Crime and Punishment*, in English, is actually something that sounds like it focuses more on the punishment, the official punishment; but, in fact, in Russian the title is much more like *Transgressing the Limits and What Happens After*. The punishment of the novel itself focuses on Raskolnikov's own inner punishment, not the formal punishment, not the official judiciary punishment, and that's actually mostly in an afterword, in an afterthought in the novel. What really the novel's about is, first of all, Raskolnikov psyching himself up to do this deed and the enormous stories he tells himself about how he can do this, and then his inner punishment after he's done it; it's mostly a drama, that is, of Raskolnikov's own soul, absent the official judicial structure.

Both in what it says in itself and as exemplary of a distinct approach to evil in the modern world, Dostoevsky's vision is a powerful harbinger of the cataclysms that began in the 20th century and that remain with us today. As I've said, it's possible to compare Dostoevsky to many of our earlier authors, maybe especially Milton; but Milton and Dostoevsky do differ dramatically on one thing: Where Dostoevsky sees the problem of evil to lie in any act of rebellion against an established order—the act of rebellion itself is, in some ways for Dostoevsky, evil—Milton, as we saw him, makes distinctions. For him, rulers who become tyrants—and it's very easy for a ruler to become a tyrant—those rulers warrant their own overthrow. In those cases, rebellion is not evil at all; indeed, acquiescence in tyranny—whether of Satan's lordship or the king's—is itself evil. For Dostoevsky, in contrast, acquiescence in a powerful authority above you is merely one other way that you are observing the place in society that God has put you in.

For a long time, the argument in literature was about who was the greater novelist, the greater representer of reality in prose form: Tolstoy, with his vivid empiricism; or Dostoevsky, with his profound philosophical symbolism and discussions. That's a vital debate still in Russian literature, Tolstoy or Dostoevsky. But for our purposes, a similar question can be asked about who was the greatest novelist of evil? Here, there are also there are two really rival imaginative models: Dostoevsky and Joseph Conrad; you're either for one or the other. In the next lecture, we're going to turn to Conrad and assess the case made for his view as the most profound novelistic representation of evil in the modern world.

Conrad—Incomprehensible Terror
Lecture 26

Conrad really has a quite radically secular vision of evil. People just seem to fall into evil, or be lured into it, for reasons that are in some ways present to themselves; they're reasons that are not demonic or theological, but they are, in some sense, all too human.

This lecture looks at **Joseph Conrad's** vision of the fate of those who have experienced evil in the modern world. For Conrad, those who have seen the traumas of modern war and other forms of suffering may be so estranged from everyday experience that the wisdom they have acquired is incommunicable to those who might learn something from it.

In *Heart of Darkness*, Conrad asks two basic questions: first, whether the modern mind has the capacity to confront evil and, second, whether the mind can communicate the experience of evil to others. The plot of this novella is simple: It's the story of Charlie Marlow, sitting with some friends on a yacht in the Thames, attempting—and failing—to tell the story of another boat trip, one in central Africa. Marlow's experience seems completely unconnected from the experience of the men he is speaking to in the present. Conrad's vision of the "heart of darkness" is not a place where there are uncivilized, primitive people but a place where people are able to be uncivilized in a far more brutal way than those who are supposedly primitive. Marlow encounters the heart of darkness in the unintelligible figure of Kurtz. In fact, the central problem of the novel is precisely Marlow's attempt to understand Kurtz. It's important to note that Kurtz's famous line in the book, "The horror, the horror," is understood neither by those who hear it in the story nor those of us who read it.

On his return trip, Marlow reflects on his encounter with Kurtz. He believes that the phrase uttered by Kurtz must mean something, but he doesn't know what it is. Kurtz, he says, "had stepped over the edge, while I had been permitted to draw back my hesitating foot." Perhaps, Marlow thinks, this is the difference between them: "perhaps all the wisdom, and all truth, and all sincerity, are just compressed into that inappreciable moment of time in which we step over the threshold of the invisible." Kurtz, Marlow believes, possesses a terrible sincerity and vision, while his own vision is clouded.

At the end of the story, Marlow confesses that he didn't tell Kurtz's fiancée the words Kurtz spoke as he lay dying on the boat in the jungle. Although Marlow views this as a failure, Conrad makes it possible for us to judge differently: Perhaps Marlow told the truth, but the fiancée could not properly understand it. Throughout the novel, Marlow is suspicious of words, finding them untrustworthy in their ability to tell the truth. But he also knows that we need words in order to properly see our world. Marlow comes to see that his attempt to tell the story is vexed by his own incapacity to speak it and his audience's incapacity to hear it. Though "the horror" is the most famous line that Conrad ever wrote, there's no way to understand it, no way to know the horror. We are so distanced from the sources of Kurtz's experience that we cannot comprehend his cry.

Joseph Conrad (1857–1924) has a radically secular vision of evil: People just seem to fall into evil, or be lured into it.

As readers, we want there to be a clear distinction between good and evil in the story. We want Kurtz to have gone wrong and kicked away the constraints of human nature. But one reason Conrad's work is so powerful is that it challenges our belief in that easy distinction. Conrad suggests that Kurtz is beyond good and evil; he may have seen more deeply than the rest of us the reality of our world. At the conclusion of the novel, Conrad also forces us to ask a question about what Marlow tells Kurtz's fiancée. He says that the last word Kurtz spoke was her name, but what if her name is, in fact, "the horror"? Is Conrad making a statement to all of us in civilization? Is the brutality that exists at the edge of civilization actually no more brutal than that which lies at its center?

The question of the apprehensibility of evil framed by *Heart of Darkness* is carried further by Conrad's later novel *The Secret Agent*. Here, we move from evil encountered at the edge of apparent civilization to evil at the very heart of civilization—in London. Conrad forces us to wonder whether the terrorist Verloc's desire to destroy civilization as something wrong and sterile does not exist as a cancer within civilization. Perhaps the idea of civilization itself needs to be rethought; perhaps it gives us only a more subtle version of cruelty and evil. The lesson Conrad tries to teach us seems to be this: We may be able to shunt our darkness off to some faraway corner of the world for the moment, but it remains our darkness, and when we finally encounter it, we will see that it has been with us, unacknowledged, all along. ∎

Name to Know

Conrad, Joseph (1857–1924 C.E.). Born to a noble Polish family under the name of Józef Teodor Konrad Korzeniowsk. Conrad was orphaned at the age of 11, after his mother and father died of sickness.

Suggested Reading

Conrad, *Heart of Darkness*, Armstrong, ed.

Conrad, *The Secret Agent: A Simple Tale*.

Meyers, *Joseph Conrad: A Biography*.

Questions to Consider

1. Is there something incommunicable about experiences of evil, as Conrad seems to imply? Does our experience in modern civilization make us dangerously incapable of recognizing or describing evil?

2. Was Conrad right to subtly suggest that advanced civilization, despite our technological and scientific sophistication, remains incapable of escaping the "heart of darkness"?

Conrad—Incomprehensible Terror
Lecture 26—Transcript

Welcome back. In this lecture, I want to talk about the novels of Joseph Conrad as a compliment to the thought of Dostoevsky, and also in some ways an important rival and an alternative picture of how modernity can think about evil.

For as long back into my childhood as I can remember, my father never slept well. He was restless, most nights crying out or shuddering in his sleep. Sometimes he was more voluble when he was asleep than when he was awake. We all, my mother especially, got used to the idea that we might be woken up in the night by a cry of fear or anguish that would not wake him. It was just what living with my dad involved. Everyone in the family knew what was going on. He had been an infantryman in the Korean War, and like so many veterans he had never really stopped being an infantryman, even though that fact was only obvious when he was asleep. It was then in the dreams that his experiences came back to him. My father went to war and part of him never came back; I think this is true for very, very many veterans of very, very man modern wars. The experience of modern war is so extreme—the relentlessness of fear, the intensity of combat, the savagery of what combat meant; the sort of things that an machine gun bullet or an artillery shell can do to a human body—all these phenomena are common in combat and soldiers quickly acclimatize themselves to them; but once they are so acclimatized to these extreme experiences in war, afterwards many of them cannot get back to the condition they were in before. The gap between their experience of war and the experience of modern life without war is so vast, and so apparently unbridgeable, that there seems no way to move smoothly from one to the other; and so many veterans never do, simply developing a new mode of living when they come back to the world from the war, burying their experiences and the selves they became in the war deeper than they bury their uniforms and their medals.

I vaguely knew all of this as a child, in some inchoate way it was there in my experience; but it was only when I read Joseph Conrad that I realized explicitly what had been going on in my life was actually part of a larger problem faced by all that live in the modern world but know the modern world for what it is: namely far more contingent, far more complex, and far darker than the rest of us can realize. This lecture is dedicated to making sense of Conrad's vision of the fate of those who have known evil in the modern world, and making sense of Conrad's question, the troubling thought he puts in our minds: that those who know this evil, who have experienced these traumas, may stand in some fundamentally estranged way from our experience, from our lives, and from the world that we inhabit, so that the lessons they have gained and the wisdom they have acquired is completely incommunicable, untranslatable, to those who might learn something from it. Conrad, as we'll see, experienced this in his own life; and it was one of the perpetual themes of his writing: the idea that one person's experience, however desperately, urgently needing to be communicated to others, may not, in fact, be amenable to that communication.

Unlike Dostoevsky, who really roots evil in human rebellion against God in a very theological frame, Conrad really has a quite radically secular vision of evil. People just seem to fall into evil, or be lured into it, for reasons that are in some ways present to themselves; they're reasons that are not demonic or theological, but they are in some sense all too human: the horrific self-aggrandizement at the cost of those around one, in the case of Mister Kurtz, perhaps an utterly banal instrumentalization of all those around you, in the case of the Secret Agent, another figure in Conrad we'll read about. In either case, Conrad is fighting a darkening apprehension of destructiveness as offering the appearance of authenticity to those seduced by it. In that way, he's much like Dostoevsky; Dostoevsky and Conrad are both interested in the idea that extreme situations can seem to make people more real in the modern world than the ordinary experience of our modern world allows them to be. In Dostoevsky's case, the nihlist rebels are the ones who are in some ways the most real people, they think; in Conrad's case, it may be people who are anarchists, terrorists, perhaps extreme exploiters of the Congo. But extremity is in some sense for some people a virtue for Conrad, and he thinks that this is a really devastating problem.

The background of Conrad, again like Dostoevsky, almost makes a better novel than his own novels. Joseph Conrad was born a Pole and died an Englishman; in fact, died an Englishman who had just refused an offer of knighthood from the Prime Minister. His writings were hard-earned by a life lived largely as a merchant sailor for almost 20 years. He lived that career from 1874 when he was 17 to 1894. In 1889, he was the captain of a riverboat that went up the Congo, and he caught a dangerous fever and almost died on the trip. But the overall event—not just the fever but the overall event—changed him dramatically. He said in later years that "before the Congo I was a mere animal," unthinking in what he was doing. It was in seeing the savagery of what Europe, in the form of Belgium, was doing in the Congo, the kind of horrifying exploitation of human beings and complete senseless destruction of nature, that made Conrad wake up to his reflective humanity and begin to wonder why, in fact, humans are like this.

He'd always been writing, but he began writing more seriously; and over the next few years, after 1889, he began to take more seriously the idea of a career as a writer. In 1894, he leaves the sea behind for good; he will go on boats, but he won't be working on them anymore. His work as a writer took a long while to find an audience, but by 1910 or so he was beginning to make enough on his writing to live comfortably from then until the end of his life in 1924. He grew in fame over the next 14 years, but was always seen as somehow outside, outside the traditional canon of English literature, somehow not entirely proper, not entirely polite; and even now, perhaps he still is. His works are more often read not by literary theorists, but by journalists and political writers, spies and special envoys of the government; they find his work and the way it involves both large geopolitical forces and actual vivid human characters to be enormously enriching.

Conrad wrote several incredible books in order to think about the character of evil in modernity. By and large, those books are still importantly unread. The one we read most is *Heart of Darkness*; but I have to tell you that even today in my classes when I try to teach *Heart of Darkness*, the students will watch a movie like *Apocalypse Now* and think that effectively they've seen the movie version of the book and try to convince me that it's adequate to understanding what Conrad is doing. That's just not true; you really ought to read *Heart of Darkness*. The novel itself, the novella, is well worth your attention.

In it, he asks two basic questions: First, whether the modern mind has the capacity to confront evil; and second, whether the modern mind can communicate that experience to others. We understand the first question—we see that the *Heart of Darkness* is really about whether or not we can encounter the heart of darkness—but it's hard for us to see that the whole extra layer of the story, the story of Marlow's attempt to communicate the experience he had, is just as important to Conrad; so I want to play that up here. Because basically the plot of story is very simple, it's a boat trip; but be careful, don't be sent up the river by the linearity of the story. It's not just the story of a boat trip, it's the story of someone on a boat attempting, and failing, to tell the story of another boat trip. Conrad, that is, uses some very complicated techniques both in its style and its structure, and the imagery of the book, in order to communicate a very complicated moral vision. The book is effectively Charlie Marlow—who's a repeating figure in Conrad's novels—effectively it's a story that Marlow tells of his own experiences in the past in Central Africa, but he's telling it to a bunch of his friends on "The Nellie," on a yacht in the Thames, and he's trying to tell them about an experience that seems completely unconnected from the experience that they are having at that moment; though, Conrad adroitly notes, they are playing dominoes made of ivory, almost certainly from Africa.

In thinking about the complexity of this story, you have to understand that when Conrad talks about the heart of darkness, he's trying to say that it's not a place where there are uncivilized people, but where people are able to be uncivilized in a far more brutal way than the people who are supposedly the natives or the primitives there. The problem for Marlow that the book is about is the problem of his encounter with the heart of darkness in the figure Kurtz; a figure who is monstrously unintelligible, and yet enormously evocative. The problem of the novel is precisely Marlow's attempt to try to figure out how to understand Kurtz, because we all know the most famous line in the *Heart of* Darkness; we all know the famous quote, "The horror, the horror," Kurtz's famous last words. But one thing you've never probably realized is that no one in the book, not even Marlow, knows what that means. In some ways it's a perfect epitome of Conrad's point in *Heart of Darkness*. Everyone in the world, everyone in the Western world anyway, know that Joseph Conrad wrote a book called the *Heart of Darkness*, and in that book a character named Mister Kurtz says, "The horror, the horror"; but no one actually realizes that the phrase is completely unintelligible to everybody: the people who hear it, and all the rest of us.

Consider Marlow's greatest moment of self-reflection on this, thinking back on when, coming back out of the Congo after trying to encounter Mister Kurtz, he almost died of some fever; and he compares his experience of almost dying with Kurtz's. This is a long passage, but let me read it to you and think about the torment Marlow is communicating in here about what's going on and trying to understand what happened to Mister Kurtz and also what happened to Marlow in trying to understand Mister Kurtz:

> I was within a hair's breadth of the last opportunity for pronouncement, and I found with humiliation that probably I would have nothing to say [unlike Kurtz, who had something to say]. This is the reason [Conrad goes on; Marlow goes on] why I affirm that Kurtz was a remarkable man. He had something to say. He said it. Since I peeped over the edge myself, I understand better the meaning of his stare, that could not see the flame of the candle [the candle on the table beside him], but was wide enough to embrace the whole universe, piercing enough to penetrate all the hearts that beat in the darkness. He had summed up—he had judged. "The horror!" He was a remarkable man.

Think about Marlow, he comes coming back to this phrase, "The horror," he keeps repeating it; Kurtz is "a remarkable man." But he keeps clearly being befuddled by this phrase; he knows it means something, but he doesn't know what.

> After all [and this is an attempt at trying to figure out what it means], this was the expression of some sort of belief; it had candour, it had conviction, it had a vibrating note of revolt in its whisper, it had the appaling face of a glimpsed truth—the strange commingling of desire and hate. And it is not my own extremity I remember best ... No. It is his extremity that I seem to have lived through. True, he had made the last stride, he had stepped over the edge, while I had been permitted to draw back my hesitating foot.

Marlow is kind of stuck with a kind of survivor guilt here, isn't he? There's something about Kurtz that's overwhelming for Marlow, but again, completely unintelligible too. Now Marlow will try to make sense of this; he says:

> And perhaps in this is the whole difference; perhaps all the wisdom, and all truth, and all sincerity, are just compressed into that inappreciable moment of time in which we step over the threshold of the invisible. Perhaps. I like to think my summing-up would not have been a word of careless contempt. Better his cry—much better. It was an affirmation, a moral victory paid for by innumerable defeats, by abominable terrors, by abominable satisfactions.

Marlow's still trying to figure out what it was that Kurtz meant by this phrase. But he's convinced as he says:

> But it was a victory! That is why I have remained loyal to Kurtz to the last, and even beyond, when a long time after [and here he's telling us a story he's about to tell again] I heard once more, not his own voice, but the echo of his magnificent eloquence thrown to me from a soul as translucently pure as a cliff of crystal.

For Marlow, there is purity, a sincerity, a terrible sincerity in Kurtz. He's a person who can see. Marlow's vision is clouded, but he knows enough to know that Kurtz's final judgment is one that is in some important way not appropriate for everyone to hear, and especially not for Kurtz's "intended"— what a great title that is—his fiancée to hear.

At the end of the story that Marlow is telling in *Heart of Darkness*, as they're there on the yacht, "The Nellie," in the Thames, he tells how after his journey up the Congo to find Kurtz and the attempt to bring him back, on which journey back Kurtz dies, he gets back to Europe, he gets back to Belgium, and he goes to see the "intended," and Marlow tells the story of how he met her and he failed to tell her the true words that Kurtz had said as he lay dying on the boat in the jungle. In a way, the story itself turns out to be about Marlow's failure to tell the story to the "intended" at the earlier time, when it would have been appropriate in some sense for her to hear. There's a complexity here, because it's clear that it's Marlow's failure in his own eyes;

but Conrad makes it possible for us to judge differently. Perhaps, in fact, Marlow told the truth but the "intended" could not properly understand it.

To understand what I mean, think about the story itself. The basic story of the *Heart of Darkness* is a "going into the interior" and a return to civilization; but Marlow never really returns from the interior. He returns, but in a way as a failed Odysseus; someone who cannot really return, he cannot go home again. Consider how haunted Marlow is in the story by voice, by language. Kurtz, Marlow says at one point "presented himself as a voice"; and Kurtz's most famous act is speaking, "the horror! the horror!" Marlow is throughout this novel very suspicious of words; untrustworthy about their ability to tell us the truth. But he knows how much we need them in order to see our world aright, especially how much those of us who are unlike him, who have not seen the world outside of civilization, the world off of the Thames, how much they need words to understand, but also how deeply they cannot understand. Marlow, that is, comes to see that his very attempt to tell the story that he's trying to tell is vexed by his own incapacity to speak it; and also, his audience is in capacity really to hear it. Though the horror is the most famous line that Conrad ever wrote, one of the most famous lines in literature in general, there's no way of understanding it, no way of knowing the horror. Because, Conrad suggests, like Marlow's listeners on the boat, we are so distanced from the sources of that experience that we cannot comprehend Kurtz's cry. The experience itself is far beyond our experience of the world; our ordinary, normal, civilized, decent, nine-to-five experience of the day, the world. It is connected, this cry, in no real living way to the world we inhabit.

That's not to say that we're totally disconnected from those realities. Like I said, the people on the boat are playing with dominoes made in Africa. Conrad's book contains a powerfully subtle critique of the way that we live like parasites off the animals' suffering and the sweat of others. Marlow's experience of the natives in recent decades has been accused of being terribly racist and imperialist; but, in fact, he's as far from colonialist as it would be possible to be for a 19th-century European. He suggests to his friends there on the Thames that the disquieting thing about being around the natives was not their distance from him of their strangeness from him but their essential similarity; "the suspicion," he says, "of their not being inhuman," the suspicion of they and I sharing a common bond.

But Conrad's book is not really ultimately interested in rubbing our noses at our guilty complicity with criminal brutality as it is in making us confront our inability in our civilized world to say anything in response to that brutality, because our lives in modern civilizations are lived at a comfortably numbing distance from those realities, hence we remain blissfully ignorant of them. Marlowe's problem, then, as someone who has seen the extreme, comes back to the center of civilization in some sense, and tries to tell people about what the edge is like, about what the heart of darkness is like, is a problem that many people—war veterans, death camp survivors, extreme survivors of trauma—have faced in our world and find it hard to figure out how to communicate with us what they went through, what they had to endure.

When Kurtz says, "the horror," he obviously means something; but what? And what are we to say about it? We want there to be a clear distinction between good and evil in the story. Somehow, somewhere, we want Kurtz to have gone wrong and kicked off the earth; kicked away the constraints of human nature. One of the reasons Conrad's work is so powerful to us is that it directly contests the claim; it challenges our belief in the easy distinction of good and evil. Conrad in a way is a good student of Nietzsche: He suggests that Kurtz is, in some important way, beyond good and evil; he's looking at the deep source, as it were, of both of our poles of moral experience. The thought that Conrad, through Marlow, is trying to place in our minds is simply that Kurtz may well have seen more deeply than the rest of us about the reality of our world. Marlow has had some echo of that, but he finds it impossible to communicate that to us.

But there's a real question as to Marlow's status, the final ability of him to tell this truth, in the book; because maybe he can tell it, but we can't hear it. In the final scene—the interview with Kurtz's "intended" again—the final scene of the story he tells, he thinks he has walked out by lying to her about what Kurtz said. You know why? Because he says, "The last thing that Kurtz said, the last words Kurtz spoke, was your name." Marlow reads that as a lie; but what if, in fact, Conrad is playing a very nasty joke on all of us "intendeds" here in civilization? What if, in fact, despite what Marlow thinks he's saying, Conrad is making him say that the "intended's" true name, in fact, is "the horror?" What if, in fact—which is the really disquieting thought of the *Heart of Darkness*—what Marlow discovered is that the brutality that is marked out at the edge of civilization actually is no more brutal than the brutality that lies at the center of civilization.

The question of the apprehensibility of evil framed by *Heart of Darkness* is carried further by Conrad's later and astoundingly prescient novel, *The Secret Agent*. This is one of the most amazing and under-read books of the 20th century. It's really perhaps, I think, the most vivid depiction of the logic of suicide-terrorism that we have in our world, and if more people in geopolitics read this book it would be a more interesting world and possibly a safer one we lived in. The plot story is relatively simple: There's a Mister Verloc who runs a grocery in London, and he is ordered, in fact, by his masters, who are spies disguised as diplomats in a foreign embassy in London, that in order to provoke the English into arresting that foreign power's dissident exile anarchists, who have made London their favorite home for exile, Mister Verloc—who is, after all, the secret agent of this foreign power; it's never really named in the book, but it's clear it's Russia—must undertake an act of terrorism so grotesque as to compel the English to respond by basically rolling up all of the exile networks in their capital, because now those exile networks have apparently, so the English will be led to believe, the foreign power hopes, begun bombing things in London. Verloc's target to provoke this backlash will be a sign of global civilization: the Greenwich observatory; that is, the central navigational point for understanding the spatiality of the world. All longitude stretches out from Greenwich, and also all the affective hour time zones.

Verloc undertakes the mission, but accidentally, in the process of doing so, kills "Stevie," his mentally handicapped brother-in-law. Stevie wanted to spend more time with Verloc, especially on this day, and Verloc's wife prevailed upon him to take her brother on a special trip; so Verloc took Stevie with him to bomb the Greenwich Observatory. At one point he gave Stevie the bucket containing the bomb, which he was supposed to place by a tree; and Stevie was walking over there, and he tripped and fell, and the bomb blew up. In *The Secret Agent*, then, we move from evil represented as at least apparently something encountered at the edge of apparent civilization in the *Heart of Darkness*, to evil as at the heart of civilization itself, in London. The question here is whether the desire to destroy civilization, as something wrong and sterile, does not exist as a cancer at the heart of civilization itself.

Perhaps, the disquieting thought is being offered, the whole division between "uncivilized" and "civilized"—if we map it onto the division between good and evil—is simply illusory. Perhaps, in fact, the idea of civilization itself needs to be rethought; perhaps it gives us only a more subtle version of cruelty and evil.

We weren't really able to believe these stories when Conrad told them to us. We still believed that "advanced" civilization had progressed, had gotten over the cruelties and brutalities of the past; that it had been set anew on a solid, enduring foundation of intelligence, truth, decency, and beauty, and development was going to happen everywhere. War was not supposed to be a part of our world; war was not supposed to be a part of the 20th century. In a way, the 20th century has was a long, slow process of learning again and again and again the lesson that Conrad, at the end of the 19th century, tried to teach us before it was too late; and that lesson, one formulation of that lesson, is: We may be able, for the moment, to out-source our darkness; to shunt it off to some faraway corner of the world, whether the Congo, or Iraq, or the Amazon, or the East End of London (for distance is not merely geographic); but it remains our darkness, and when we finally find it out there, we will see that it in fact has been with us in here, unacknowledged, all along.

In the next lecture, we're going to turn to someone who actually has some interestingly overlapping, parallel theoretical ideas to Conrad and Dostoevsky; someone whose thinking on evil has often been represented as quite terrifying, and I think actually for very good reason. That is the psychoanalyst Sigmund Freud.

Freud—The Death Drive and the Inexplicable
Lecture 27

> Almost all the time, adults cannot expect, for [Freud], to radically change their behavior, because the dispositions that we have are too deeply habituated in us to be really significantly reformable. The best we can typically hope for is to manage our various pathologies.

Sigmund Freud's overall picture of the tensions and complexities that go into the human psyche builds on an assessment of the human and human civilization as the site of a war between rival principles of love and death. We desire love, but we also possess a **death drive**, a force or impulse that seeks annihilation. Freud also sees an ill fit between ourselves as individuals and our role in human culture and society. This tension has inadvertently generated systems of morality that we use to describe and control this ill fit. Freud's overall account is an alternative to other moral accounts, a picture of both our desires for human affiliation and civilization and the various discontents that civilization produces in us.

Freud's most basic tenet was what we call the **pleasure principle**, the idea that people want happiness, yet happiness is something we feel by contrast with normalcy. In response to this problem, humans have tried to moderate the desire for happiness in various ways, but none of these practices works perfectly. Our desire for happiness and satisfaction can be met only to a degree.

Civilization arises from our need for protection and the desire for happiness. It is rooted in social and political necessities, but it also has a more properly physiological basis in our drive toward sexual and supra-sexual union with others. This drive Freud named Eros, the principle of love. Much of psychoanalysis focuses on where this drive goes wrong, seeking to uncover how our desires obstruct our functioning as humans.

Freud notes that love itself creates resentment against civilization, because civilization restricts sexual life precisely as it expands the cultural unit. Monogamy is the price humans pay to become civilized, and that tradeoff generates resentment. As we said, there is a tension between ourselves as humans and our role in human society. This ill fit creates discontents that express themselves in self-destructive behavior or behavior that is destructive of others.

Along with our understandable resentments at the curtailing of our libidos, Freud believed that another mysterious force is at work in us, a force that actively and intentionally seeks our own destruction and that of the world. This death drive brings into the picture the potential of human nature for cruelty. Freud's account of evil, if we think of it in terms of the death drive, is a resistance to accept any form of what he saw as "consolation"—religious, moral, philosophical, romantic, even psychoanalytic—in lieu of the actual reality of the absurd presence of a destructive force in the psyche. In other words, Freud wants to say that by naming the death drive, we are doing the least consoling thing possible; we are identifying a significant problem at the heart of our being that we will never be able to solve.

> **Monogamy is the price humans pay to become civilized, and that tradeoff generates resentment.**

Freud posited the death drive when he realized that "hunger and love" alone are inadequate principles to explain "what moves the world." He decided that there must be another, contrary instinct seeking to break down those units and return them to a more fundamental state of pure potentiality. The destructiveness of the death drive is not only outwardly oriented; in fact, it's rooted in a "silent" instinct that all humans possess. It is always intertwined with the love drive and works only by warping the love drive; it never positively exists on its own.

These two drives—the love and the death drive—meet in the human soul, the psyche. It is the need of civilization to suppress the death drive, leading to its sublimation; this, in turn, results in the heavy burden of guilt felt by all people. The resentments caused by the desire to repress or sublimate the destructive energies each one of us has causes tensions in our souls. The discontents of civilization are rooted, then, in our inability to escape our instinctual aggressiveness. Civilization exacerbates the pressures of the death drive by forcing us also to sublimate the love drive, redirecting that energy into the same pool as aggressive energy.

Ultimately, Freud tells us that civilization is the result of the struggle of these two instincts in humans. He further says, ruthlessly dismissing traditional morality, "And it is this battle of the giants that our nurse-maids try to appease with their lullaby about Heaven." Traditional morality cannot make sense of the struggle between these two powerful natural drivers.

This view is remarkably pessimistic, but there is some hope. Freud suggests that Eros can gain the upper hand on the death drive, if only for a time. Still, Freud saw that in the modern world, humans possess powerful destructive abilities; the death drive has reached the possibility for its own complete consummation. ■

Name to Know

Freud, Sigmund (1856–1939 C.E.). Born in Píbor, a village in the Austro-Hungarian Empire, to poor Jewish parents, who sacrificed to provide their son with an excellent education. The family eventually moved to Vienna, where Freud studied and, later, joined the medical faculty at the University of Vienna.

Important Terms

death drive: Term used by Sigmund Freud to describe the instinct opposite to Eros in the human psyche that seeks to dissolve the world back into a primeval, inorganic state.

pleasure principle: Term coined by Sigmund Freud to describe our desire to be happy and feel pleasure, while acknowledging that happiness is not a normal state of human life.

Suggested Reading

Freud, *Civilization and Its Discontents*, Strachey, trans.

Lear, *Freud*.

Questions to Consider

1. As noted in this lecture, Freud believed that pleasure played a definitive role in human motivation and served as one of the ultimate justifications of our actions. What is the relationship between the "good" and the "pleasurable"? Is the good always pleasurable? Is the pleasurable always good? Which of these is more fundamental?

2. Are certain human actions really expressions of the desire for destruction, as Freud's concept of the death drive suggests? Is the desire for death a silent desire in human beings?

Freud—The Death Drive and the Inexplicable
Lecture 27—Transcript

Welcome back. In this lecture, I want to talk about the psychoanalyst Sigmund Freud, and talk about his overall picture of the tensions and complexities that go into the psyche and that sometimes can cause us to act in evil ways, and then also to identify and focus a bit on a particular theme in his thoughts, the theme of the death drive, which is particularly pertinent for our topic.

After Joseph Conrad's work, people began to realize that Western civilization wasn't entirely on a stable foundation. The first bit of evidence that a lot of people had that this might be the case is World War I. World War I, of course, is up until that point arguably the most devastating war in human history; devastating both in terms of absolute numbers of people killed, but also in terms of its political chaos that it created and that ensued in its wake. In many ways, World War II is really only a follow up, a second part, a second act of World War I; but in any case, as the 20th century goes on, the history of the era gets darker and darker, and in this time the work of thinkers like Conrad became more and more appreciated; and over any other influence perhaps in advanced intellectual circles the thought of Sigmund Freud was most powerful.

Freud is born in 1856 in the Austro-Hungarian Empire and he dies an exile from Nazi Austria in the beginning days of World War II in 1939. He was raised in a strict but serious family that emphasized education above almost all other things. He himself took a medical degree at the University of Vienna and was planning on studying neurology—nerve and brain science—but then psychology drew him to its charms instead. Over the 1880s and 90s he began himself to see clients and developed his famous so-called "talking cure"; that is, a method of dealing with people with certain psychological maladies that posited that people want to talk out their anxieties, and that doing so, by rendering them articulate and by bringing them into language, this activity will release the energies mis-bottled in their emotions, in their conflicts, and in their inner lives. In all of this, Freud had to not only invent this method, but then create really a language to talk about it in; and he did create that language, using ordinary German terms, which in English actually have been interestingly mangled by people who wanted to give a more scientific veneer to what Freud was talking about. The word that in English is translated as "id" is actually in German *Es* (that is, "it"), and where the English translations of Freud will often say "ego," in German Freud wrote *ich* ("I"); so, in fact, Freud in German sounds like an ordinary person, not talking about very esoteric or kind of mysterious categories (the id, the ego, the super ego) but the "it," the "I," and the "over-I," things like that.

Anyway, over time, as this language and the picture of the method that Freud developed began to spread around Europe, he developed disciples and dissidents as well. He grew famous and became a very well-known intellectual and cultural figure in Central Europe and beyond. But he finally had to flee from the Nazis in 1938 because he was Jewish and his thought was considered a degenerate form of Jewish science.

Freud's dismissal of traditional notions of good and evil, and his urging a different view on his audience, sounds a lot like Nietzsche; and there are definite overlaps, but there are some really important differences, and so it's worth getting a picture of Freud out there before we think about comparing him to other people like Nietzsche. His picture really builds on an assessment of the human and of human civilization as the site of an endless war between rival principles of love and death. First of all, we desire love; we desire union with others for causes greater than ourselves. This love can be a sexual love, but it can be familial, it can be love of a baseball team, it can be any number of things; the point is that humans long to feel identified with others in a cause and in a group that is in some sense larger than ourselves.

Along with that, he came to posit this thing that we'll come to hear as the "death drive." The death drive is a force in the human psyche that seeks the annihilation of the other and of self and of being itself out of some sort of sheer impulse towards annihilation. The basic question Freud's thought asks overall is about the strange ill-fit between ourselves as individuals and our role, our overall role, in human culture and society. The tension between these two, the ill-fit between us as individuals and the realities of our roles in society, has inadvertently generated systems of morality that we use to describe and to some degree control this ill-fit; so that morality is in a certain sense the same sort of thing that Freud's psychoanalysis is meant to be.

Freud's approach is meant to occupy as it were the same philosophical space as ethical reflection; indeed it's meant in important ways to supplant such ethics as an account of our real status, an account that uses "physiological" and "natural" analysis instead of using what Freud saw as "artificial" moral concepts to understand our situation. So Freud's account is in some important way from the beginning meant to be not so much "beyond" good and evil, although it might be, but to stand "beside" good and evil and maybe even beneath good and evil, as not just a complement to these other moral accounts, but as a kind of more adequate alternative picture of both our desires for human affiliation and civilization and the various discontents that civilization produces in us.

This is Freud's final vision of the human, one that was reached with effort and suffering after World War I where he saw that his own thinking had to go, as the title of one of his most important books put it, "beyond the pleasure principle." Through the rise of Nazism in the 1920s and 30s that would eventually drive him into exile, he saw dark forces rising across Europe that were moving in ways that were destructive in forms that his own earlier theories did not understand. Our final step in this lecture will be to look at how Freud's depiction of how he came to believe in a picture of the human that involves the death drive, what he took that picture to mean to imply about us, and why this vision offered him, he thought, the most powerful and illuminating depiction of "the struggle for life of the human species," one that illuminates what can be illuminated, and one that also leaves what cannot be understood properly in darkness.

To begin with, though, let's start with the basic Freudian picture, what we call the "pleasure principle." That was the most basic discovery Freud understood himself to have had. The pleasure principle, he thinks, is the idea that people want happiness, yet, as he said, the program of the pleasure principle "is at loggerheads with the whole world." The pleasure principle is simply our desire to be happy, to feel pleasure. We're creatures, for Freud, who by and large pursue our own individual happiness. Why does he think it's at loggerheads with the whole world? Most basically because happiness is something we feel by contrast with normalcy. We don't normally feel happy; it's an extreme moment when we feel happy, it's abnormal for us to feel more pleasant than usual. That's what happiness is: that difference in the meter where we go into the red zone a little bit. Un-happiness, on the other hand, is something we not only feel when things make us unhappy, we can actually feel unhappy by merely anticipating being unhappy later; that is—and think again of Machiavelli or Hobbes here—fear for Freud affects us more deeply than hopeful anticipation does; fear makes us presently unhappy, while hopeful anticipation definitely does not always make us presently happy. Indeed, at times, the impatience we feel at anticipation may make us unhappy now.

In response to this problem, Freud thinks, humans have tried to moderate our desire for happiness, to control it, to channel it in various ways, through individual asceticism—monastics, people who pray a lot, people study a lot; of course, people who work out a lot are also ascetics as well, they're disciplining their bodies in certain ways—through joining communities; wallowing in lower pleasures, like college boys who drink beer all weekend because they have nothing better to do; or sublimating our longings in higher desires, so that they come and find themselves partially expressed and partially satisfied in the reading of books, or perhaps the attending of or listening to lectures. But none of these practices of managing the pleasure principle, managing our insatiable desire for happiness work perfectly. There is no solution; happiness must be achieved, Freud thinks, but it cannot be. There's "no golden rule," he says, that applies to everybody; everyone must seek it on their own. So our desire for happiness and satisfaction, and the freedom that comes with that, can only be met to a degree; that is, we can only be somewhat happy, and only at the cost of repressing and/or what he calls sublimating—that is, transforming into some other kind of thing—our absolutely insatiable desire for happiness.

Civilization, then, arises from our need of protection and our desire for happiness; what he calls Eros and Ananke, "love" and "necessity" in Greek. Civilization is rooted in our social and political necessities; but it also has a more properly physiological basis in our drive towards sexual and supra-sexual union with others. This drive Freud names Eros, the principle of love, and this pulls us towards one another, towards community. Much of psychoanalysis, because of this, focuses on where that drive goes wrong, focuses on what you can call the "archaeology of the libido"; uncovering how our desires are, in buried or other covert ways, obstructing our functioning as humans. It means to be in this important way, psychoanalysis means to be, a healing science; something that helps us at least manage our longing for happiness. But Freud is very sober about the prospects for this kind of healing. Almost all the time, adults cannot expect, for him, to radically change their behavior, because the dispositions that we have are too deeply habituated in us to be really significantly reformable. The best we can typically hope for is to manage our various pathologies; and inevitably, a lot of the evil in the world comes out of the pathologies of the resentments we feel about the frustrations of our libido. But this management that Freud offers, his promise that he will help us cope with our crises, is, he thinks, the only real solution we have; even an ethical system will only also be able to manage our frustrated libido, it will not be able to solve its problem.

But the problem here is that these very energies are themselves quite destructive. Love itself creates resistance and resentment against civilization. Why is that? Again, because civilization restricts sexual life precisely as it expands the cultural unit; stable sexual lives are crucial for social stability and order, Freud thought. Monogamy is the price humans pay to become civilized; monogamy is the price you pay for Costco and Best Buy. That's why, in some important way, that tradeoff generates resentment; generates, as in the title of one of his most famous books, discontent (*Civilization and its Discontents*). There is a weird tension between us; as I said, an ill-fit between ourselves as humans and our role in human culture and society. This ill-fit creates these discontents, which express themselves both in our own self-destructive behavior and perhaps in behavior destructive of others. Were this the extent of the human condition's challenges, our lives would be difficult enough. But over the course of his career, Freud grew increasingly convinced that this was not, in fact, all; that, in fact, along with our understandable resentments at the curtailing and channeling of our libidos, another, deeper, and altogether more mysterious force was at work in us, a force that actively and intentionally sought not just our own destruction, but the destruction of the entire world. That is what Freud called the "death drive."

Contemporary psychoanalysis, and actually contemporary psychology when it attends to Freud, really typically dismisses the death drive as "mere metaphysics," as something Freud came up with that was unscientific and melodramatic. Certainly there's a lot of melodrama in the picture of the death drive that he offers; but the idea does have one advantage and I think it was an advantage Freud was very conscious of: it brings vividly into view the potential of human nature to be remarkably cruel. Freud's account of evil, if we think of it as in terms of the death drive, is not so much an account of evil as a form of principled resistance to any such account; a refusal, that is, to accept any form of what Freud sees as "consolation"—be it religious, moral, philosophical, romantic, even psychoanalytic—in lieu of the actual reality of the absurd presence of a destructive force in the psyche. In other words, Freud wants to say, by naming the death drive, we are doing the least consoling thing possible; we are identifying this huge problem at the heart of our being that we will never be able to solve. That's not to mythologize anything; that's precisely to strip away mythology and come face to face with this dark beating heart of destructiveness that wills us nothing but nil. The death drive is disconsoling in this way just because it is so clearly out of our power to manage, even in psychoanalytic terms. In a way, we are at the death drive's mercy, susceptible to it at all times. That's clearly not a comforting thought, but it's the thought that Freud had.

He came to see that he had to postulate the existence of the death drive really by kind of backing into it; he didn't actually think he could see it positively working. This is a very interesting story of how someone who effectively had a sober but in some sense confident picture of the human person comes to see that the confident picture has in some important way been shattered by the evidence of a more destructive force working in the human. Freud began the journey towards discovering the death drive—as he describes it, "discovering the death drive"—by insisting that, again, "hunger and love," necessity and love, "are what moves the world." But he decides eventually that those categories, those principles of motivation, are not adequate; there must, he thinks, be another contrary instinct seeking to break those units down, break those drivers and those people down, and bring them back to a more fundamental state of pure potentiality. He says in the *Civilization and its Discontents*: "as well as Eros there [must be] an instinct of death"; something driving against love.

Freud thinks that this destructiveness is, in fact, not just outwardly oriented, not just about outward aggression; in fact, it's rooted in a "silent" but still present instinct, he thinks, that humans, like all of nature, possess. The death drive, he says, works in silence, and is met always and only intertwined with the love drive by warping that love drive. Pause here for a second because this is really interesting: In a way, Freud starts his vision as a kind of naturalist account of evil. Remember the three big families of evil we talked about: The first was the kind of Augustinian where evil is folly, completely irrational; the second is the kind of naturalist picture of evil, where evil is somehow part of our nature, part of our organic makeup; and then the third is the developmental maturation account of evil. In a way, Freud begins with the natural account and the maturation account, but already we're beginning to see him positing something like, because he thinks of the evidences of history, a necessary, pure irrational force. What's interesting is when he says that it has to be always intertwined with the love drive; that it works only by warping the love drive in this way—it never positively exists on its own—this sounds a lot like Augustine talking about how evil is always the perversion of the good, always the corruption of the good, never its own substantial presence but always a reducing of something good that is really there. I wanted to mention that; but back to the main story.

Freud recognizes there's a worry that he could be accused of a deep pessimism and an appeal to destructiveness in nature as a way of covering over a failure of his theory; but he thinks, in fact, that it's merely an evasion strategy. He thinks he actually can say that the death drive is actually functioning; people who say it's not, who want to dismiss it or blame him for it, are trying to kill the messenger. He thinks that's not appropriate. It is part of the death drive's "silence," in fact, that pointing at it is the only thing we can do. It can't be explained at all, and that surely includes the drive's strange silence in its operations. Evil seems to include, that is, in its presence the abolition of any explanation at all; it just is, or in fact it just isn't. So Freud's notion of the death drive does seem like a sin the way Augustine talks about it in that way, as both are finally, mysteriously inexplicable.

Why it is that the aggression instinct—and not just in us; the aggression instinct is manifest of all of nature—is "inevitable" or "primal?" Again, to my mind this is another version of the same question that a lot of his critics ask: Why do you believe this? Why is it so? Why do you think it's true? While this is not, in fact, a trick question, I think answering it is very difficult. I don't know of any truly convincing answers myself that do not provoke further questions; so try, but keep in mind that you should always see if you can ask if this is a satisfactory answer or if it just raises more questions for you.

The combination of these two drives—the love and the death drive—meet in the human soul (in the psyche); it is the need of civilization to suppress the aggression instinct (the death drive), which leads to the enormous sublimation of that instinct, which in turn results, Freud thinks, in the heavy burden of guilt felt by all people. Famously, Freud said that everyone believes that at some point in the past all the sons got together to kill the father, and so all men everywhere always feel guilty about killing the primordial father. He said even if this is not historically true, it's psychoanalytically true. What he means here, the best thing we can hope he means, is that the resentments caused by the desire to repress and sublimate the destructive energies that each one of us has in our souls, this suppression of this drive causes enormous tensions in our soul. The discontents of civilization are rooted, then, in our inability, one way or another, to escape our instinctual aggressiveness and urgings towards destruction. Civilization exacerbates the pressures of the death drive by forcing us also to sublimate the love drive, by forcing us to channel it in certain ways, redirecting this energy, then, into the same pool of aggressive energy we have that we're not allowed to express.

This is a pretty kind of maybe obscure psychoanalytic picture, but basically what Freud is trying to give you is a picture of a human who is born with a desire to smash things and a desire to hug things, and the desire to smash things is completely unacceptable in civilization, so we teach the little human not to do that. But the human still has that desire; we've just not allowed the human to express the desire. Then we tell the little human, "Don't hug just anything, only hug a few things that you're allowed to hug." So a lot of the energy of the little human—I'm not saying a child here, I'm just saying little human—that would have gone into hugging all sorts of things is also not allowed to be expressed. Inevitably, this little human is going to throw some sort of massive temper tantrum. Effectively that's what Freud is talking about: He's saying that the death drive is a kind of ontological temper tantrum, a desire simply to lash out and destroy things out of frustration at not being able to destroy things when we want to.

All of this climaxes in a visionary moment in Freud's description of the death drive in his wonderful book *Civilization and its Discontents*. Let me read you this passage because it is, I think, one of the most powerful and illuminating passages for thinking about the character of the psychoanalytic picture of evil in our world:

> And now, I think [Freud says], the meaning of the evolution of civilization [this is large prey for Freud] is no longer obscure to us. It must present the struggle between Eros and Death, between the instinct of life and the instinct of destruction, as it works itself out in the human species.

Civilization is the struggle of those two instincts trying to figure out how they can relate and how they interact.

> This struggle [the struggle between these two, between life and death] is what all life essentially consists of, and the evolution of civilization may therefore be simply described as the struggle for life of the human species.

Now wait for it: This is the moment where he actually ruthlessly dismisses traditional morality, religious or philosophical.

> And it is this battle of the giants that our nurse-maids try to appease with their lullaby about Heaven.

This "battle of the giants"; this struggle, this conflict between these titanic drives in our souls, each soul of each human being; of course, Freud says, it's insane to think that any traditional morality would make sense of this in any healthy or useful way, because any traditional morality is just going to say the evil that people do is just a matter of their individual wickedness, he thinks, or it's a matter of some sort of generic human corruption, some inheritance of original sin. But Freud says no, it's not petty human wickedness, it's not inherited sin; these are powerful natural drivers that of necessity civilization can't handle so it has to repress them, but over time those drives come out anyway. Destruction, annihilation, murder are ever with humans; why? Freud thinks because that's just the kind of creatures we are. Maybe all of life, all of the cosmos is like that. We want love, but sometimes we also want death.

That's an astonishing moral view. It's one that I think hasn't been appreciated fully for the pessimism it offers. Furthermore, and from a theoretical perspective, it's a view that Freud articulates very clearly how he came to it. He didn't come to it by observing the death drive in any kind of direct observation, instead he postulates its existence by noticing the warping of people's behavior in ways that the love drive cannot make sense of. It's an interesting methodological moment, it seems to me, in the history of thinking about destructiveness, malice, and evil.

This is pessimistic, but there is some hope. Freud suggests that Eros has ultimately, or can ultimately have, the upper hand on the death drive, and it can learn to master its urgings, if only at least for a time. But Freud warns that humans now "have gained control over the forces of nature," he says, "to such an extent that with their help they would have no difficulty in exterminating one another to the last man." In other words, in the modern world, we actually begin to be so powerful in our destructiveness that it may, in fact, be the case that we can annihilate ourselves. The death drive now reaches the possibility of its full consummation.

One of Freud's interesting, errant intellectual descendents of a sort, the French philosopher Michel Foucault, famously said, "The human for millennia was what it had been for Aristotle, a natural creature whose politics have to be figured out. But in the modern world," Foucault says, "the human becomes a political creature whose politics but its natural existence into danger." I think in that Foucault is simply developing Freud's ideas.

Freud's attempt here to understand and offer some guidance for the reality of evil and wickedness suggests something that we could call hope, but it has to be far less than what we can call confidence. But it is some kind of hope; some reason to get up in the morning and struggle with the death drive. Again, think about Freud: He's interestingly straddling all three of our large families of thinking about evil. In a way, he's most basically a thinker who thinks about evil as a natural structure, but he has a notion of evil as something that's intrinsic to development across time of the individual and maybe of the species, and that we see with the death drive there's a dimension of Freud's thought that seems to inject a kind of dimension of evil as folly, as the privation of being and goodness, the perversion of good action that we saw most rigorously and profoundly worked out in a thinker like Augustine. Whether or not these three strands of Freud's thinking on evil can be put together in a proper way I don't know, but I don't think you have to worry about Freud as a systematic thinker—that's a good task—but he's a far more interesting thinker for me anyway if you think about him as suggestive and evocative. I think that, in fact, in that way Freud's work may offer one of the most profound reservoirs for thinking about evil that we have yet come across.

Now we're going to go into those thinkers who, unlike Freud, survived World War II and had to live with its consequences after. Freud offers possibly too bleak a picture of evil as a natural force perhaps; he has a hard time understanding the full complexities of the relationship between human desires for justice and human proclivities towards individual moral evil. Others may help us see that dimension of malice better, and we'll begin to turn to them, and to thinking after the calamity of the Second World War, next.

Camus—The Challenge to Take Evil Seriously
Lecture 28

Does our moral self-understanding—the way we picture the world as a whole, the shape of our lives within it—really help us come to grips with the realities that we call "evil"? This is one of Camus' most profound themes in all his writings. Is it possible, he worries, that there is something in human nature that makes it hard to take evil seriously enough?

People had thought that World War I was a terrible event for humanity, but in comparison, World War II was apocalyptic. Intellectuals believed that after the war, humans would be forced to change dramatically, but normalcy was recovered with astonishing speed. Among the responses to this recovery was that of the brilliant thinker and writer Albert Camus. Two of his books in particular have significance for our study: *The Plague* and *The Fall*.

In *The Plague*, Camus allegorizes the corruption of a society by evil through the metaphor of a plague infesting a city. The novel tracks the responses of the citizens to the various problems brought on by the plague. Of course, the plague here is not just a biological pestilence; it is an allegory for Nazi evil. Camus uses various characters in the novel, including a doctor and a priest, as devices to explore how certain sets of belief will work themselves out in confrontation with absolute evil.

One of the most interesting and thought-provoking themes in the book is the extreme resistance of humanity to coming to terms with, and bringing into focus, the problem of evil itself. Initially, many in the city are reluctant to recognize the plague as something other than an ordinary illness. As the suffering goes on, the citizens seek some cosmic explanation for the plague so that they can "fix" it. Finally, the wisest among the citizens come to realize that their questions about the causes of the plague are unanswerable and may serve as distractions from the reality of evil. The best response is not to worry about the questions but to face the plague and fight it for what it is.

When the plague is finally defeated, one of the characters comments on the astonishing speed with which people in the city return to a state of normalcy. Indeed, the citizens seem to downplay or deny the reality of the plague, perhaps because they can't process it in relation to ordinary life experience. The lesson of the novel is straightforward: Evil is real; it will confront us, and all we can do is decide how we will respond to it. There is no this-worldly solution to evil; humans will face it repeatedly. *The Plague* closes with what seems a prophetic reminder that evil can lie dormant among us for years before resurfacing.

One of the most interesting and thought-provoking themes in the book is the extreme resistance of humanity to coming to terms with, and bringing into focus, the problem of evil itself.

About eight years after *The Plague*, Camus wrote a far more ambiguous novel, *The Fall*. The narrator here, Jean-Baptiste Clamence, is a man caught in the awareness of his own sin and that of the world in a way that he recognizes but cannot quite name and cannot escape. His name translates to "John the Baptist, crying," bringing to mind a prophet, "a voice crying in the wilderness." But he also lives in the center of the ring of canals in Amsterdam, reminding us of Satan in Dante's *Inferno*.

In the novel, Clamence tells the story of his own collapse, but he does so in order to convince his audience that they are also unworthy. His strategy is seduction by narcissism, yet the seduction he employs is an incredibly self-conscious one: He realizes that the narcissism he deploys to seduce people actually governs his own life, even to the degree that his confession of his sins is an attempt to make his audience admire him.

Clamence was once a successful defense lawyer in Paris, but when he fails to come to the aid of a woman who has fallen from a bridge, his life changes dramatically. He realizes that he has hidden from his self-awareness his own selfishness and narcissism. He lives now in Amsterdam and hides in his apartment a panel from a stolen painting, *The Just Judges*. He cannot stand to have the painting on display because he now has an aversion to thinking about justice; he believes that everyone is guilty. The task for humanity is to find a way to live with our guilt, because there is no way to escape it.

At the end of the novel, we learn that Clamence has an incredible longing to be other than what he is. He doesn't want to be a sinner or a moral failure. He wants to risk his life for something greater than himself, but he lost his one chance to do so. There is no grace, no second chance; we are already and always trapped in sin.

Perhaps Camus' greatest lesson is that we have a difficult time seeing evil and recognizing it for what it is. We would rather avoid seeing it, in the world and in ourselves. But if we could see evil for what it actually is— human corruption—perhaps we could confront and resist it. For Camus, just seeing clearly is a moral victory. ■

Suggested Reading

Camus, *The Fall*, O'Brien, trans.

Camus, *The Plague*, Gilbert, trans.

Todd, *Camus: A Life*, Irvy, trans.

Questions to Consider

1. What do you think of Camus' account of evil as a plague? Is evil a permanent (though sometimes dormant) fact of human existence—an enduring condition of human life? And if Camus was right about this, how do we avoid despair and quietism? If evil is permanent, why resist?

2. The character of Jean-Baptiste Clamence suggests that evil may, in fact, lie behind our lives in more ways than we are aware. Was Camus correct in asserting that our task is not to overcome evil but to learn to live with our guilt?

Camus—The Challenge to Take Evil Seriously
Lecture 28—Transcript

Hello again. In this lecture, I want to talk about Albert Camus, the 20th century French writer and thinker.

After Freud—and after the era that Freud's death marks the end of starting in September 1939—things in the world went from bad to worse. If people had thought that World War I was a terrible event for humanity, World War II was positively apocalyptic. World War II saw the first bombings of cities where rivers in the cities boiled from the heat of the fires, boiling alive people who had jumped in the rivers. World War II saw the worldwide extermination of peoples through the use of death camps, in China of gasses; and then of course ultimately the war climaxes with suicide bombs of the kamikazes and then the atomic bombings of Hiroshima and Nagasaki, two cities left explicitly untouched by the American allied air forces so that they could be used as demonstrations of what these new weapons could do.

World War II left an enormous open space in the minds of many intellectuals. They thought that after the war, things would have to be different; things would have to change dramatically lest humanity end up destroying itself. But almost as soon as the war ended, people began again to revert again to their old ways of thinking. Among the intellectuals who dealt with the war and who worried about this, responses to the fact of this evil and then the astonishing recovery of normalcy after the war, were manifold. Some people tried to reaffirm old models of thinking; some explored wholly new ones. Albert Camus really falls more in the latter category, though he has a deep attachment to traditional ways of thinking, religious and philosophical, about evil.

Camus lived from 1913–1960, when he died tragically, actually, in an auto accident. He was a brilliant writer and thinker, deeply politically engaged but always more freethinking than his more doctrinaire compatriots such as Jean-Paul Sartre. Probably in my estimation—which is a relatively biased estimation—Camus's work will have a longer-lasting impact and a more profound impact on the way people think about how to inhabit our world than Sartre's did. His work is well known and often described as a kind of "existentialism," and indeed Camus sometimes called it "absurdism"; but in fact it's probably more profoundly useful to call it an atheistic humanism with a deep appreciation both for the spiritual impulse in humanity, and for the way that that impulse can be organized and sometimes, not infrequently, manipulated by official religions. Camus was from North Africa, he was from French colonial stock in North Africa, and was raised and educated there. His father had died before he was born actually, his father died in the First World War; and so he was brought up with his mother as a ward of the state, a hero's son. He wrote his masters' thesis, his final academic work, on Saint Augustine actually, whose own thinking on good and evil influenced him in surprising ways, in ways that I don't think people have really fully appreciated yet.

Before the war, he was a well-known writer already, having written a book that was devastating in its power called *L'Étranger*, or *The Stranger*, *The Foreigner*, *The Strange One*, about a man whose experience of the world is so distant, so buffered from emotional reality that he seems an actual kind of threat to everyone around him. During World War II, Camus was in Paris and he joined the Resistance and edited the Resistance paper, *Combat*. After the Liberation in August of 1944, he was one of the very few publicly at the end of the war to condemn the American use of the atomic bomb in Hiroshima and Nagasaki; in other words, he was already a friendly critic of those people on his own side when he thought that they were doing horrible, evil things.

In the years after the war, he and Sartre grew apart until a profound split happened in the wake of the publication of Camus's novel *The Plague* in 1948, and we'll talk about that later in this lecture. In 1957, he won the Nobel Prize for his overall work, the year after the other novel we'll talk about, *The Fall*, (*La Chute*) was published; but he died tragically—one almost successfully resists saying "absurdly"—in a car accident in 1960. He was just 47. He wrote a number of influential books, but two books in particular have had enormous impact on thinking about evil in the post-World War II era. That's not exactly true; one of them has had an enormous and well-recognized impact, and the other deserves to have that impact. The books are his two novels *The Plague* and *The Fall*. Let me talk a bit about *The Plague* here.

In *The Plague*, Camus allegorizes the corruption of a society by evil through the metaphor of a plague infesting a city. The novel chronicles the appearance, the emergence, the rise, the climax, and the defeat of the plague. It tracks the ways that a series of characters; most famously the central narrator of the novel itself and then also one of the main figures in it is a man named Doctor Rieux, a doctor. But there are others as well; importantly for our purposes one of them is Father Paneloux. The novel basically tracks the way that humans inside the city of Oran in Algiers actually try to confront and handle the various problems brought on by the plague. Of course, the plague here is not just a biological pestilence; in a way, the plague, the pestilence itself, is an allegory for Nazi evil, for an evil that possesses a society. The story is really about how humans resist that evil, but it's carried out very rigorously through the image, the allegory, of the plague itself.

Camus uses various characters in the novel as devices to explore how certain approaches to the world, certain sets of beliefs, will actually work themselves out in confrontation to absolute evil of this sort. Doctor Rieux is rigorously empirical, but he's not a narrow believer in science alone; though he does, in fact, have a broad humanistic education he still resists any kind of false consolation of the sort he thinks religion would offer. Father Paneloux, who initially offers a kind of relatively moralistic vision of the plague, delivering a sermon interpreting the plague as a sign of God's wrath at, and displeasure with, humanity; but as he lives more into the suffering of his own people and he fights the plague, he then delivers a second sermon where he preaches a response of absolute moral and spiritual commitment as the only remedy to the plague. Much like many Catholic priests that Camus knew in the Resistance, he was clearly motivated by his religion, by his spiritual faith; it was not a faith that Camus shared, but it was one that he respected enough to see that it could actually motivate powerful moral resistance to evil. Father Paneloux dies near the end of the book when he is infected.

One of the most interesting and thought-provoking themes in the book is the extreme resistance of humanity to coming to terms with and bringing into focus the plague, the problem of evil itself. Initially in the book, many are reluctant to recognize the plague for what it is—the city authorities don't want to admit it, other doctors don't want to say what it is, even the people who are suffering from it don't want to think it is what they come to realize it really is—they prefer instead to imagine that what they're dealing with here is a pretty ordinary illness. Then, as this goes on, they seek some sort of larger cosmic explanation for the plague; so Father Paneloux's first sermon is a good example of this. Somehow there's something we did; there's some explanation for this evil that we must kind of figure out so we can unlock the puzzle and come to deal with this evil by addressing it's kind of root conditions. There must be something we can do to fix this. Think about this as echoing the *Epic of Gilgamesh* in some ways, because it kind of does.

The final step for Camus—and again, this is also very "Gilgameshy," if we want to use that word—finally, the most acute and the wisest of them come to see that those ultimate cosmic questions are unanswerable; the answers we offer to the cosmos, the explanations we provide that might be useful for illuminating the problem of evil in this way, are returned unopened to the sender in a way. Our puzzles with these metaphysical questions, these cosmic questions, are often, Camus suggests, used as ways to distract us from the real facts of the case, from the reality before our faces; and that the best course of action, those who can truly see realize, the wise recognize, is to not worry about those questions but instead to face the plague for what it was, to meet it where it was, and fight it as best they could.

But then, as the plague finally ebbs away and is ultimately defeated for Camus and all returns again to normal, at the end of the novel Doctor Rieux points out: It's astonishing how quickly the plague and its terrors are forgotten; how quickly people return to a state of normality where these kinds of realities are in astonishing ways kind of forgotten, unwritten into our history. There's a story of the plague, but the real story of the plague, the real story of what happened in those events—Doctor Rieux writes, Camus suggests about the Resistance and the evil of the Nazi regime—the real story in some sense never get told, because people can't process it into their ordinary experience of life. All of the people of Oran, the city where this happened, deny the reality ultimately of what happened. They say, "Oh, it was a bad time, but things are much better now; let's eat, drink, and be merry, let's not continue to brood on the plague." In a way, this is a kind of cruel representation of the city and of ordinary people for Camus. He really does think that most people simply don't bother to worry about these things. Before the plague happens, there's a kind of "staticness" to Oran, not much happens there. When it hits, it stops business entirely; the ordinary life of the people of Oran, the way that they use their business life to distract themselves from the emptiness of their own world. This is Camus as a descendent of Pascal here and Pascal's notion of divertissement. In *The Plague*, it's not just that the plague is an experience of terror; it's also that in that plague they're thrown back on themselves in a way they find deeply discomfiting.

The lesson of this novel is straightforward: Evil is real; it will confront us, and all we can do is decide how we will respond to it. In the words of a famous Camus essay written around this time, we decide to be "neither victims nor executioners"; we must decide to be neither those who will stand and just be shot down, nor those who will do the shooting. This is especially important for Camus, because evil is not going away; it will remain a perennial problem for human beings. There is no this-worldly apocalyptic solution to evil; there's no fix to it. We're going to face these problems again and again. And as the final prophetic paragraphs of *The Plague*, *La Peste*, put it (I'm going to read you this):

> Nonetheless, he [Doctor Rieux] knew that the tale he had to tell could not be one of a final victory. It could be only the record of what had had to be done, and what assuredly would have to be done again in the never ending fight against terror and its relentless onslaughts, despite their personal afflictions, by all who, while unable to be saints but refusing to bow down to pestilences, strive their utmost to be healers.

Thinking about that, it strikes me as so prophetic, even of our own time, to those who know they have to deal with terror and fear and wrath. Then he goes on, and this is truly one of the most prophetic texts of the 20th century. At the end of the book at the end of the plague there's a festival in the town, and there are fireworks going off and people are very, very happy about the end of the plague, of course:

> And, indeed, as he listened to the cries of joy rising from the town, Rieux remembered that such joy is always impermanent. He knew what those jubilant crowds did not know but could have learned from books: that the plague bacillus never dies or disappears for

good; that it can lie dormant for years and years in furniture and linen-chests; that it bides its time in bedrooms, cellars, trunks, and bookshelves; and that perhaps the day would come when, for the bane and the enlightening of men, it would rouse up its rats again and send them forth to die in a happy city.

In the days after September 11th, actually, when in my world a lot of people were circulating a poem by W.H. Auden. It's a wonderful poem called "September 1, 1939," a poem he wrote about the beginning of the Second World War. I kept thinking about this passage in Camus's *Plague*. It was a lesson that we were going to have to learn again about evil and the various ways people try to resist it in all their best intention; some of them wise, some of them not wise, some of them successful, some of them not successful, not always the wise ways being successful ways. In all these ways, Camus strikes me as still someone of tremendous import for our world.

Interestingly, though, Camus, especially in *The Plague*, was criticized by his contemporaries—particularly on the Communist left in France; thinkers such as Sartre—for offering an essentially quietistic approach to evil. He depicted, they said, in *The Plague,* evil as a depoliticized, de-historicized, natural force; a plague, a bacilli, not at all the doing of actual human beings for real political motives. This is strange, they said, because Camus himself was so deeply politically engaged; and also because the world that they saw presented no such un-human natural force of evil. They weren't interested in the natural evils of earthquakes and things like that; that's a problem that in some ways we have to deal with but that's not the real problem, they said. World War II was not a natural evil; the malice that we see around us, Albert—they were saying to Camus—the malice we experience that you thought that was clearly human.

But you know Camus has a response, and if you understand his point the issue is there may be human malice, but it's not contingent in the sense that it will ever go away. The problem is that we have to learn how to address and confront evil. Yes, its configurations in the human world will differ from historical moment to historical moment, but evil will never go away, he thought. That's a very Augustinian point, and it's precisely because it's Augustinian in that way on the intractability of human evil that so many of the Communists in his world, who really were working out of a Marxist view where evil is fundamentally, essentially contingent, they couldn't stand that. Ironically, the debate between Camus and Sartre was really a debate between Augustine and Marx, but they didn't really realize it at the time (maybe Camus did a little bit.)

That's one novel of Camus's; but then eight years later he writes another, an equally interesting and in some ways far more troubling, far more ambiguous novel; one in which the human situation is more ambivalent where, in fact, there may not just be no saints ,but in some ways everyone might be a sinner. *The Fall, La Chute* in French, has the connotations of religious fall as well as the fall off of something—in this case, the fall off a bridge—and also the connotations of a moral collapse; so it's more like *The Collapse*, almost, in English, though it would have to include some sort of connotation of the fall. The narrator of the novel, Jean-Baptiste Clamence, is a human caught in the self-awareness of his own and his world's sin in a way that he recognizes but he cannot quite name nor can he escape. His name itself is really interesting: Jean-Baptiste Clamence. His name is "John the Baptist Clamence," "crying"; in Latin, the phrase is *vox clamans in deserta*, "a voice crying in the desert," "a voice crying in the wilderness." John the Baptist, the prophet. So on one level he's a prophet for telling a coming of a new order; but in another way he presents himself interestingly as at the center of the web. He lives in the innermost ring of the ring of canals in Amsterdam where he sits in a bar called the Mexico City. The innermost ring of a series of concentric canals: What does that make you think of? Satan in Dante's *Inferno*; another illusion that Jean-Baptiste Clamence himself understands and appreciates.

In the novel, he tells the story of his own collapse, but he does that in order convince the person he's talking to—it's a monologue, so he's trying to talk to the reader—that they are also unworthy, and by convincing them that they are unworthy, he will feel supreme above them. His picture, his strategy is, seduction by narcissism; and yet the seduction he employs is an incredibly self-conscious one, for he realizes that the narcissism that he deploys to seduce people actually governs his own life, even to the degree that his own confession of his sins is an attempt to make his audience admire him and respect him. This picture has never been equaled. The story Clamence tells of his own initial career as a great defense lawyer in Paris, particularly of widows and orphans, is a really interesting one. Initially he thought that he was a really noble person, but after a while he came to see that life as tremendously egotistical, all about promoting himself; and he came to see that life that way because of a series of events that happened.

One night, walking across a bridge in Paris after a successful not just court date but then assignation with a woman, he passes by a young woman leaning over the side of the bridge. Once he's is past, he hears a body plunge in the river and a series of cries as the person is carried downstream. He freezes. He could have run back, jumped in and saved her, but he doesn't. He calls this event his "baptism," and he makes it the focal point of a reconsideration of the whole shape of his life, discovering in it a history of selfishness and narcissism that he had kept from his own self-awareness. It is, then, an event that once it hits him in its reality is not just his baptism but also his "fall"; and it serves as a crucial moment in his moral collapse, and as well in the story he tells to try to shore up his ruins facing the recognition of that moral collapse.

Now he lives in Amsterdam and he defends criminals, and he hides in his apartment a panel of a stolen painting, "The Just Judges." It's an interesting one to hide; he cannot stand to have "The Just Judges" out there in public, he hides it in a closet in his room. Now he has a powerful aversion to thinking directly about justice and innocence because he believes that everyone is guilty. The task for humanity, he believes, has now become how to live with our guilt, for there is no way to escape it. As he says near the end of the novel, and really in reference to himself; this is in some ways the most sincere moment in the novel, the one sincere moment in the novel. He says, "But this is my life, this is who I am. I'm a wretched egotist who only feels good when I'm bringing other people down." But he says, but "what can one do to become another?" That simple question contains all the sincerity of a psychological anxiety that the rest of the prose of the novel refuses and obscures. Sin for Clamence, sin for this John the Baptist, is real; but grace is not. The character feels trapped in the Fall; hopeless, stuck in the bottom of Hell, in the middle of the concentric rings; trapped there in his own despair.

This novel as well ends with what actually has been, I think, an even more devastating peroration about what to think about life as a figure like Jean-

Baptiste Clamence when he finally finds out who the other person is, the person he's been talking to, in some ways the reader of the book. He says, "You, too, were once a lawyer; I knew it all along." And then he says this to his interlocutor:

> Please tell me what happened to you one night on the quays of the Seine and how you managed never to risk your life. You yourself utter the words that for years have never ceased echoing through my nights and that I shall at last say through your mouth says [These are words that Clamence has, he admits, wanted to say all the time since this night on the bridge; since his Fall. This is what he's always wanted to say.]: "O young woman, throw yourself into the water again so that I may a second time have the chance of saving both of us!" A second time, eh, what a risky suggestion! Just suppose, cher maitre, that we should be taken literally? We'd have to go through with it. Brr…! The water's so cold! But let's not worry! It's too late now. It will always be too late. Fortunately!

Just think about that end; that end kills me every time I read it. "It's too late now. It will always be too late. Fortunately!" There's a lot packed in there, right? First of all, the fundamental despair of Clamence at the recognition that he has this incredible longing that he wants things to be otherwise; he doesn't want to be damned, he doesn't want to be a sinner, he doesn't want to be a moral failure, he doesn't want to be in love with himself in this way. He wants to risk his life for something greater than himself, for another person. He had the chance once, and it's never come again. It couldn't come again, because in this life you only get that one chance. There is no grace, there are no second chances; it's always too late, we're always already trapped in sin. And then the devastating last word, "Fortunately!" Of course, Camus is playing on the joke of the Fortunate Fall, the *Felix Culpa*, here. In some fortunate way we are lucky, Jean-Paul Clamence says, that we cannot do anything here. But his notion of the *Felix Culpa* is both incredibly ironic and has at its heart a kind of utter despair of any hope. The reason this is fortunate is because we would just fail again. That's not the fortune of the traditional *Felix Culpa*; the reason the traditional *Felix Culpa* is fortunate is because our failure enables Christ to come and save people. Jean-Baptiste

Clamence, a voice crying in the wilderness, prophesies no Christ; he only prophesies our own fall.

Here, unlike in *The Plague*, recognition of evil seems to paralyze and corrupt, not to mobilize and purify. Are these two books' accounts of evil comparable, compatible? One thing they both have in common and that they share with Conrad and Freud, and distantly with someone like Nietzsche: Can we take the moral phenomena that we capture in the term "evil" seriously enough? Does our moral self-understanding—the way we picture the world as a whole, the shape of our lives within it—really help us come to grips with the realities that we call "evil?" This is one of Camus's most profound themes in all his writings. Is it possible, he worries, that there is something in human nature that makes it hard to take evil seriously enough?

Of all the lessons that Camus has, giving us that question and keeping it alive in our minds is perhaps the one that I'm most grateful for. We live in a world, he says, that has a hard time seeing evil, recognizing it for what it is. We'd rather avoid seeing it, in the world outside or in ourselves. We either make it into something that it's not—an ordinary natural illness; or maybe a vast metaphysical evil that is in some sense something we can never resist—when we actually ought to see it for what it actually is, which is a human corruption that perhaps, just perhaps, we may with some good fortune, or possibly some grace, be able to confront and resist. It's a moral victory just to see clearly for Camus; it's also a moral victory to be able to communicate that vision to others (this is something he shares very deeply with Joseph Conrad). And once we have seen evil for what it is, we must confront it, he thinks, knowing that there are no guarantees, no promises of victory, nor any consolations of an ultimate theological victory if we lose in the here and the now. All we have is the knowledge that evil is evil, and that we should not be evil, and so we owe it to ourselves, if we are the kind of beings we take ourselves to be, to fight it.

In our next lecture, I want to look at some religious thinkers, contemporaneous with Camus, who also responded to the various crises of the Second World War and tried very hard to take the evil that had reared its head in those events as seriously as it merited. We'll do that next.

Post-WWII Protestant Theology on Evil
Lecture 29

> For Tillich, as with Luther, the experience of evil is something that the devil seduces you into but does not compel you to do. There's a way that being "possessed" here gets at the genuinely *you* character of the evil act—the way that you are the one doing it—while also getting at the experience of this evil as something alien to your true being.

In thinking about evil, Christians face two important questions: First, can Christianity ever really take evil seriously enough? To many secular thinkers, the gospel can seem desperately optimistic, as if it's trying to overcompensate for the challenge of evil. Second, can Christianity take our age's evil seriously enough? In other words, do theologians manage to show how Christianity can grapple with the problems our world faces today?

Paul Tillich was a German Lutheran theologian who became an important philosophical voice in the years after World War I. In his essay on "the demonic," Tillich defines his subject as a perversion of creativity, a way in which the creativity that is the world's basic principle can go wrong. Sin is not sloth, or lassitude, or despair; it's an active energy. And evil is not simply an absence of good, but it has its own positive "givenness." The demonic exists as the most potent form of that givenness of evil as a tension between creative and destructive powers at the base of reality itself.

The demonic appears when the forms of reality are consumed by what Tillich calls the "transcendent depth of reality"; that is, when the forms in which we understand reality reveal themselves to be unable to fully contain the reality that they capture and deliver to us. If we think about all we can see in a beautifully crafted wooden chair, for example—its origin as a tree, the skill of its builder—we see that it is, in some sense, much more than a chair. And in trying to grasp that depth, Tillich says we begin to experience a vertigo about reality. It's this capacity of reality to overwhelm us, to threaten ordinary life, that for Tillich, is evidence of the demonic. It is especially visible in human personality, which can remain recognizably itself yet be "possessed" by a power beyond itself. For Tillich, grace is a healing of this bottomless character that we have discovered in our own existence.

While Tillich is useful for thinking about the positivity of evil, the Swiss Calvinist theologian Karl Barth explores the negativity of evil. Barth described evil and sin as grounded in "the nothing" that God has refused explicitly to create. This nothing is a genuine threat to everything that exists, it undergirds sin, and it is far more frightening than anything we can imagine. The nothing is a possibility that God might have created had God been different than the God we believe and confess God to be. Nonetheless, God allows a few tendrils of nothingness to creep into reality just so that humans know something of what we are not facing.

Barth described evil and sin as grounded in "the nothing" that God has refused explicitly to create.

For Barth, it is part of the mystery of God that evil exists at all. In some ways echoing the Book of Job, Barth believes that evil is related in a complicated way to the providence of God, and because of that, only the providence of God will be evil's final solution. Barth thinks that all of humanity is predestined to bliss and salvation from before the Fall, but he also tries to understand evil as something humans do as part of God's drama of creation. Thus, he emphasizes the profundity of evil within the context of the greater profundity of God's love for the world. Evil is only defeatable by God, and in fact, God uses it to demonstrate God's immeasurable love for humanity.

Reinhold Niebuhr is the most famous theological voice on evil in the 20th century. He offered an interpretation of traditional Christian visions of sin that reformulates the wisdom of that vision in a language suitable for modern people. According to Niebuhr, "sin presupposes itself"; it is intrinsic to the human condition, yet it is clear that humans should not be sinful. Sin is not necessary for humans, Niebuhr thinks, but it is an inevitable consequence of our current created condition. Humans are created as finite yet free, natural yet transcending nature. We recognize our hybrid constitution and are made anxious by it. It is that inevitable anxiety that induces us to indulge in pride—a denial of our createdness, our materiality—or sensuality—an embrace of materiality to the exclusion of the transcendent.

Grace, for Niebuhr, is the energy that allows us to go forward in our lives, knowing that our judgment is to come as sinners but also knowing that God has reservoirs of mercy meant to overcome our sin and heal our broken souls. The recognition of sin could be paralyzing, but it's not supposed to be, and God will not let us off the hook by claiming paralysis. Sin here is clearly a phenomenon of anthropology, a picture of the human; it is not a function of God's creative will. ■

Suggested Reading

Barth, *Karl Barth: Theologian of Freedom*, Green, ed.

Niebuhr, *The Children of Light and the Children of Darkness: A Vindication of Democracy and a Critique of Its Traditional Defense.*

Niebuhr, *The Nature and Destiny of Man*, vol. I, *Human Nature.*

Tillich, *Paul Tillich: Theologian of the Boundaries*, Taylor, ed.

Questions to Consider

1. What do you think are the most important similarities and differences among Tillich, Niebuhr, and Barth? What do they share that makes their accounts of evil similarly "Christian"? What important differences or disagreements exist among them?

2. Do you think Niebuhr is correct in claiming that sin is the only empirically verifiable doctrine? What role should experience play in judging our religious beliefs?

Post-WWII Protestant Theology on Evil
Lecture 29—Transcript

Welcome back. In this lecture, I want to look at three major Protestant theologians whose thought about evil was profoundly influenced by, but also in some important ways profoundly shaped the perception of, other people's thinking about World War II and the implications of World War II for thinking about the place of evil in the Christian narrative. For WWII did not only challenge non-theological thinkers and philosophers like Camus; if anything, its challenges to traditional religions were even more profound and the thinkers in those traditions did respond in profoundly creative and innovative ways. We'll see that in the next several lectures.

20th century Protestant thought on evil has been rich and diverse. In this lecture, I want to look at three particular versions of thinking about how to relate evil to Christian understandings of grace; for that's the big problem for all of them: how, that is, to relate a serious assessment of evil, especially in the wake of the Second World War, to the "good news" of the Christian Gospel, which seems to undermine the seriousness with which we ought to understand evil itself. The basic problem any Christian, especially Protestant thinker, faces in thinking about evil is pretty simple: If evil is something we can know and proclaim now—as the Gospel demands for Protestant Christians—is finally "overcome" by God, how can we take it seriously as a challenge we have to confront today? And does that message of the "good news" really seem plausible to us after all the evil we have confronted in the world in the past century or so, especially for these thinkers after all the evil that has just occurred in the Second World War?

This general field of uneasiness for Christian theology can be rendered more specific in two concrete questions. One is a challenge that pretty secular or even anti-theological thinkers like Marx, Nietzsche, Freud, maybe Conrad, maybe Camus can ask, and that is: Can Christianity ever really take evil seriously enough? That is, for thinkers such as these, a lot of Christian theology does not really confront the wholly abyssal character of evil, terrible bottomlessness of evil and the way it seems not to be framed by a good universe or a good God. The Christian gospel to these thinkers can seem simply to pour an oversweet syrup of how God is good and Jesus loves you over all the real, jagged, broken glass ugliness of our world. The gospel, to thinkers like this—these anti-theological or rigorously secular thinkers—can seem desperately optimistic, over-optimistic, as if it's trying to overcompensate for the challenge of evil.

The second kind of specific question to keep in mind as we're going through these guys is a more precise challenge, the challenge of the 20th century itself: Can Christianity take our age's evil seriously enough? Do the theologians of the age themselves manage to show how Christianity can grapple with the problems our world faced in that bloody century? Here we'll see the three thinkers we looked at answering this question in quite different ways, and in interesting ways they answer it because they work out of slightly different starting points to think about evil. Paul Tillich, as we'll see, starts to think about evil through thinking about the experience of aesthetic encounter; of encountering something and realizing there's more there than you initially thought. Karl Barth thinks about evil in light of God's salvific action to save the world and redeem the world, and in some ways thinks about evil in terms of God's providential sovereignty over the whole world; really, evil's a part of that story for Barth. Then Reinhold Niebuhr really thinks about evil as a kind of anthropological puzzle that has a bearing on our experience of things in the world—our aesthetic experience of beauty and things like that—has a bearing on God's plan for the world, but is really fundamentally a human phenomenon that we need to think about in human terms. Let me begin with Paul Tillich.

Tillich is a German Lutheran theologian who is trained in classical German style but who moves in surprising ways as a theologian once he reaches maturity. He was in World War I a chaplain in the Imperial German Army—a very academic chaplain, but nonetheless a chaplain still—and as effectively a 30 year old he survived the World War I battle of Verdun that was a charnel house, a battle in which roughly about a million Frenchmen and Germans were killed in a few square miles of mud over the course of about nine months. He came back to Berlin after the war and he began to be a very important theological and philosophical voice in the interwar years in Germany, but his opposition to the Nazis drove him out of Germany, from which he fled to the United States, and he taught basically from the 1930s to his death in 1965 in the U.S.

He wrote a number of very important works—he was a very influential thinker, both for academics and for the general public in the mid-part of our century—but for our purposes, the powerful essay he wrote on "the demonic" as a phenomenon of moral and religious life is really where we're going to look. This essay explores what he thinks of the experienced positivity of evil; the "positivity" there I mean the reality, the real presence of evil. The demonic is Tillich's way of talking about this positivity while he roots it in the fundamental facts of reality itself. Evil here, for Tillich, is not an accident introduced by the human fall in any way; in some important way, it's an intrinsic part of creation as such. It's a little bit like the combat myth, really. He wants to capture the experienced reality and presence and genuineness of evil that the combat myth captures so well, but he doesn't want to go all the way with that myth; he doesn't want to suggest that there's actually a demonic opposition to a divine God that is a rival to that God. That's not his point; his point is that the demonic is in some ways our recognition that reality itself has this dimension of overflowing that troubles and threatens us in powerful ways.

The demonic is, for Tillich, a perversion of creativity itself; that is, it's a way in which the creativity that is the world's basic principle in some way can, in fact, go wrong in threatening and terrifying ways. Sin, then, for Tillich, is not just a sloth or a lassitude or despair, or falling back into weakness, or anything like that; it's a real, active, dynamic, earnest energy. Evil is not simply an absence of good, it's not simply ignorance; it has its own positive "givenness." The demonic exists as the most potent form of that "givenness" of evil as a tension between creative and destructive powers at the base of reality itself. Tillich is German, he's trained in philosophy and theology, so he's going to go very abstract on you; we have to just expect that, have the right medicine, strap in the right way in the chair, and just get used to it. But what he does with this notion is really interesting, so just follow me here for a second.

All reality for Tillich has form; things manifest themselves to us, they give themselves to us in certain forms. This has the form of a tie, right? Before it's cut and shaped into the fabric of a tie, the tie looks just like a piece of fabric on a table or something, but it's given the form of a tie. The demonic appears when the forms of reality, each of them individually or one of them in particular, is consumed by what Tillich calls the "transcendent depth of reality"; that is, when the forms in which we understand reality, whereby through which we understand reality, reveal themselves to be unable fully to contain the reality that they capture and deliver to us. We see the object, but the object suddenly seems far more than just an object; more profound than that; something far more deep than the thing itself is that we had heretofore grasped it as being. Let me give you an example that's not a tie.

We sit on chairs all the time. But sometimes if you're in a store, or maybe better if you go to a woodworking shop, a place where there are carpenters working, and you see a chair that's just been finished—nicely sanded down, beautiful wood chair, maybe it's stained, so smooth; and it's just sitting there waiting to be delivered to some customer or something—sometimes you see more than an object to sit on, you see a beautiful thing. Quaker chairs are just lovely things; if you've ever seen a Quaker chair, a handmade wooden chair, just beautiful. It's a thing that's not just beautiful because of human artifice, but it's made of the wood from a tree that was living; a transformation of one thing into another reality. You see all the ways that nature, sunlight, water, brute muscle, and delicate surgical craft all went into making this beautiful chair, and how so much more than just a chair this actually is. Sometimes when I see a piece of beautiful wood furniture like that, it genuinely can look like it should be a piece of art, not a utilitarian device just for my butt. Tillich wants to say that in seeing all that, in apprehending it—not so much grasping it, but grasping how the chair is in some sense "ungraspable" as merely a chair; how much more it is than that—in seeing all that, we begin to experience a vertigo about reality, and about all the ordinary ways we rely on reality not to surprise us; to veil its full presence from us so as not to overwhelm us with its bare "thereness." It's that capacity of reality to overwhelm us that, for Tillich, is evidence of the demonic.

I can well remember one time when I was 15 or 16 and I was walking outside in a field. It was a field on a crisp New England day and I for some reason had to take off my glasses to wash them down, to rub them down; and as I took them down I looked up again and I realized that I wasn't seeing just within in the frame of my glasses, I was seeing the parts of my vision that normally my mind just didn't pay attention to, and suddenly the world appeared far vaster than it had ever appeared before to me (or at least recently, since I had glasses). I remember being overwhelmed by the width of the world in some way. That's sort of what Tillich is talking about, but not just the width of the world, the depth of the world; the idea that beneath everything there is still more. The thing about the demonic is that experience is given to us in the demonic as kind of threatening of our ordinary life.

The demonic here is especially visible—or experienced anyway—in human personality, which can remain recognizably itself yet be "possessed" by a power beyond itself. People talk about actors being "possessed" when they're doing things, or people talk about athletes being "possessed by the game" in some sense. The demonic here is a version of this kind of possession. It's experienced from the inside as a realization that I am far more than just the ordinary me I take myself for most of the time; that just as the chair speaks of depths of reality beyond an object suitable for merely sitting on, so much more do I contain depths of reality beyond what I ordinarily access of myself. I am, in some important way, far greater than He. That's a terrifying thought, or it can be; not just if you're playing soccer or something or football, but also if in some important way you discover that you have an ability to move crowds of people, or to convince students in your class of certain things, or to take control of a meeting and control the way that people understand what's going on in the meeting so that your will is done there.

These accounts of the demonic offer a theological picture of evil that acknowledges evil's reality for Tillich, but offers no immediate promise that humanity can triumph over it. For Tillich, the demonic is both sub-personal, and yet genuinely engaging of the personal, genuinely something that you do, both "you" and "not you." In a way, as I said, there's a way that the demonic is kind of structurally identical to the state of grace, to that state that the Ancient Greeks actually called the *daemonic*; that is, the state of being possessed by a *daemon* or a spirit. Here, what Tillich is trying to get at is the phenomenology of both being possessed or of seeing something that is itself and more than itself at the same time; of seeing a thing possessed. The aim is really just to express this experience of being recognizably one thing but also so much more than that.

For Tillich, if this is the demonic—this experience of not so much me going away but the trapdoor at the psychic base of me opening up to reveal the abyssal depths beneath me; if that is the experience of the demonic—for Tillich, grace is in some way, the response to evil is in some important way, the reconciliation of a healing of this abyssal character that we've discovered in our existence. It changes our visage of this, our experience of this, bottomless from one of terror and threat to one of comfort and assurance; it challenges us to see that what we thought of as terrifying is actually not terrifying but, in fact, a comfort that we are connected in profound ways to the infinite and ever-tumultuous, ever-burbling ground or foundations of our own being. For Tillich, famously, grace teaches that each person is accepted by this ground; that our experience of ourselves as "I" is but one manifestation of this larger force of being manifest in all things, and that as such we're a part of this greater cosmos, the great drama of being. This hopefully helps us understand ourselves not as needing to justify ourselves or prove our existence as real—a temptation that Tillich sees as lying at the base of our susceptibility to act out of our experience of the demonic in sin, this experience of our bottomlessness always threatens us and so we lash out in certain ways to convince ourselves we are one thing rather than another; this is the terrible prompting of evil for Tillich—instead, what grace gives us the ability to do in some sense is see not that we are bottomless, not that there's nothing below us, but that we are just the top of this larger structure of being that goes on beneath us infinitely. As Tillich's greatest theological sermon said: You have to come to see that "you are accepted"; that's Tillich's great line, "you are accepted."

Tillich offers a picture of evil as substantial, as the appropriation of the self, of its bottomlessness in a fearful way; but it's an appropriation that's positive. It's not a good thing, it's not positive in that way; but it's a genuine presence, not simply an absence. Mostly he does this in order to capture the experience of being "possessed" by positive power that he sees as part of what demonic reality is. Two things to remember here: First of all, remember that Tillich was a Lutheran theologian; for him, as with Luther, the experience of evil is something that the devil seduces you into, but does not compel you to do. There's a way that being "possessed" here gets at the genuinely you character of the evil act, the way that you are the one doing it, while also getting at the experience of this evil as something alien to your true being. That's one thing about Tillich; the other thing to remember is this is a guy who lived through infantry combat in the First World War, and there almost certainly were instances in assaulting a trench line or something like that where he probably felt or definitely saw people engaged in a kind of possession of themselves that struck him as profoundly demonic. Never forget the history of these people. Tillich is not talking in merely abstract ways, although he is very much an abstract German professor in his own relatively odd way (but we don't need to get into that). He's talking about experiences that were very close to him; he's not just making this stuff up.

To move to Tillich to Barth is really to change registers of thinking theologically. Tillich is a philosopher, a profoundly existential thinker, a brooding thinker in some ways; Barth is a Swiss Calvinist theologian whose first reflex is always to move very strictly to thinking about God, to thinking about theology. Barth is wonderful in terms of exploring how to think about the negativity of evil; Tillich is useful for thinking about the positivity of evil.

Barth's a Swiss Calvinist theologian. He was born in 1886, roughly Tillich's time; he dies in 1969, almost exactly contemporaneous with Tillich. Some consider Barth the greatest theologian since John Calvin, full stop; Catholic, Protestant, Eastern Orthodox, what have you. I'm actually among those who do. He worked a bit after World War II in Germany—he was a professor in Germany—but when the Nazis came to power he was a profound opponent of them and so he was kicked out of Germany and he went back to Switzerland, where he taught at the University of Basel for the rest of his life. He was one of the earliest opponents of the Nazis actually among religious folk, but almost entirely for theological reasons. Before he became a professor of theology, he was also a pastor with definite socialist leanings. He's famous for saying that pastors need to do theology with the Bible in one hand and the newspaper in the other.

When it comes to evil, Barth is a really strange character, and a lot of Barth's scholarship is still struggling to figure out what to do with his understanding of evil. He described evil and sin as grounded in "the nothing" that God has refused explicitly to create. That's very strange, and his vision of "the nothing" is profoundly obscure; people are still trying to figure out what exactly he means. In German, "the nothing," *Das Nichtige*, is not simply God turning away from, in metaphorical terms, an abyss of emptiness towards the creation that God will do, it's not like the backside of God in that way; it's more like this is something that God explicitly says "no" to in some important way. "The nothing" is something in excess, then, of human wrongdoing; "the nothing" is what God has said "no" to in order to say "yes" to creation. It is a genuine threat to everything that exists, and it undergirds sin; but more than sin, it is far more frightening than anything we can conjure up. "The nothing" is, in some sense, a possible non-creation that God might have created had God been different than the God we believe and confess God to be. In other words, God actively says "no" to "the nothing" precisely in positively creating the something that is creation, and creating the something that is creation as a gift to humanity of endless love in God. That's Barth's idea of what creation is: Creation is a theater in which the drama of God's affirmation of and love for humanity will play out. That's the positive story for Barth, and you always have to keep that positive story front and center; God's great plan for humanity and the world. But, he also says as a kind of appendix to that plan, you have God saying "no" to *Das Nichtige*, and also God allowing a few tendrils of *Das Nichtige* to enter into reality; God allows a few tendrils of nothingness, of "the nothing," to poke their heads into reality just so that we know something of what we are not facing; something of what God has chosen not to do.

Barth suggests, unlike Tillich, that the primary fact about evil is its fundamental irreality; in this way, he's kind of like Augustine, although there are big differences. He retains a Kantian sense of sin's inexplicability, its mysteriousness, but he radicalizes this inexplicability into more than a psychological problem; it becomes a problem for the cosmos, not just for our understanding. It's part of the mystery of God that evil exists at all. Barth is, in some ways here, going back to an echoing, that line of biblical thinking from the Book of Job forward: that in some sense, evil is related in some complicated way to the providence of God; and because of that, because evil is in some complicated way related to the providence of God, only the providence of God itself will be evil's final solution. Evil is so bad, Barth thinks, that only a truly extreme action on God's part, in Christ—in the second person of the Trinity; in the Son of God—is that which can guarantee the overcoming of evil and the gracious election of humankind.

Note here—this is interesting—for Barth, God's decision for humanity's election precedes the fall. Remember Calvin's supralapsarian double predestination; that is, humans are in some sense, for Calvin, predestined for Heaven or Hell before the fall, God has planned everything out in

God's absolute sovereignty. Barth also is a Calvinist, but he's a far more hopeful Calvinist than Calvin ever was. He actually thinks all of humanity is predestined to bliss and salvation from before the fall. But—and that's the way that Barth retains his notion of God's sovereignty but also tries to understand evil as not something humans do irrespective, independent of, or in rivalry to God but as part of God's whole drama of creation; God creates evil for humans to fall into in some sense but then will save them from that—but even though evil is bad and *Das Nichtige* is really terrible, Barth affirms that God is greater than it by far. So he tries to emphasize the profundity of evil only within the context of the greater, though admittedly harder to immediately perceive from time to time, profundity of God's love for and support of the world. The point for Barth, then, is just that evil is only defeated and defeatable by God, and in fact is used by God to demonstrate God's utterly gratuitous, absolutely immeasurable love for humanity; evil, that is, turns out to be God's "fall guy."

Our third theologian is Reinhold Niebuhr, a thinker who in important ways learned immensely from both Tillich and Barth, but also in interesting ways is both splitting the difference between them but also offering a third way altogether. Niebuhr is a very, very famous American Congregationalist theologian. He lived from 1892–1972, again pretty contemporaneous with both Barth and Tillich. He was enormously influential in the middle third of the 20th century. With his brother, H. Richard Niebuhr, he's the only American theologian who can stand in comparison with Tillich and Barth since Jonathan Edwards from the 18th century; and Niebuhr is without a doubt the most famous theological voice on evil in the 20th century. He offered an interpretation of traditional Christian visions of sin, one that reformulates the wisdom of that vision in a language suitable for modern people: people who are skeptical of the literal historicity of the Biblical narratives, dubious of the idea that there ever was an historical Adam and Eve, and scientifically literate in ways that make them doubt a lot of previous theological and religious teaching. He was so convincing in his reformulations of the doctrine of sin, for example, that there actually grew up a group of people called "atheists for Niebuhr"; people who didn't believe in God but agreed with his assessment of the human condition as trapped in sin. Niebuhr famously said that original sin is "the one Christian doctrine that is empirically verifiable"; if we look around in the world, we see that people are just not good. He said this is interesting because it tells us that we can actually learn something about the human condition from this doctrine itself irrespective of whether or not we buy into all of Christian theology, he thought.

Why does sin exist, Niebuhr wonders? He says "sin presupposes itself"; it's intrinsic to the human condition as we find it in the world, and yet it is clearly not something that is the way humans should be. Yet when we try to inquire as to its origins, we find that it is always already there before us in any moment of psychological excavation; when we look back down inside ourselves for some moment of innocence, we can never find it. For Niebuhr, that gets at this kind of originality of original sin. There's no way to be a human in this situation where sin is not involved.

Sin is not necessary for humans, Niebuhr things, but it is, in our current created condition, an inevitable consequence of our condition. Normally Niebuhr thinks sin is typically pride, it's an attempt to over-assert our will over reality because we deny our createdness, our finitude, our smallness, our materiality and imagine that we are essentially will, pure spirit, kind of something that is unbound by the material finitudes of our reality. That's the main theme for Niebuhr of sin; sin is primarily for him pride, the assertion of the self. But it doesn't have to be that; it can also be a form of what he calls sensuality, a way of only living in our finitude, in our material bodies without reference to our transcendent hopes and our transcendent longings. Either way, the basic story of sin is the same: Humans are created as finite and yet free, natural and yet also transcending nature. We recognize our hybrid constitution and are made anxious by it, we don't like being both matter and spirit; and it is that anxiety that inevitably arises in our situation that in turn (that anxiety) induces us in one way or the other to be either wholly fleshly and find our whole happiness in material goods (whether that's libertinism or Marxism), or to try to escape that material condition altogether and find our whole happiness in the ascetic escape from the self, denial of the flesh, and denial of finitude itself, as in some forms of religious extremism, some strands of technological utopianism, and Niebuhr thought, some kinds of democratic utopianism as well. Whether we sin via sensuality or pride, we are attempting most fundamentally to escape this hybrid condition, this condition of being in the tension of both matter and spirit, of being here and yet being able not to be here; and it is precisely that effort to escape that is in some sense inescapable to our world, to our condition, that is, in fact, sin.

Grace, for Niebuhr, is the merciful power and knowledge that lets people go forward in responsible moral action even as they know that such action inevitably stems from sinful persons, sinful characters. Grace is the energy, he thinks, that allows us to go forward in our lives in fear and trembling, knowing our judgment is to come as sinners but knowing also that God has reservoirs of mercy meant to overcome our sin and heal our broken souls. In other words, the recognition of sin could be paralyzing, Niebuhr thinks, but it's not supposed to be; and God will not let us get off the hook, he thinks, by recognizing and being paralyzed in our sin, like Jean-Baptiste Clamence, Camus's character was. Sin here is then very clearly a phenomenon of anthropology, a picture of the human. It relates first and foremost to our desire to escape our condition. Like Pascal, and possibly like Kant as well, sin here is in some sense always a temptation to escape. It's not as focused on the role of God in resolving this problem. For Niebuhr, then, evil, sin are anthropological categories first and foremost, part of our created makeup. Not a function not of God's creative will, as in Barth, but more a function of the human's creation; in some sense like Tillich, but not quite as natural, inevitable, and metaphysically necessary, cosmically necessary as in Tillich. Instead, there's still an insistence on the accidental nature of evil for Niebuhr, or at least an insistence on evil's accidental nature, even as he struggles to explain that.

Let me try to wrap this in here. This is a series of views on thinking about evil that have provided and continue to shape the way that many people, not only Protestant Christians, think and talk about evil today. In seeing this, we see a fairly broad range of ways to think about evil within the context of Christianity: a way related to Luther's insistence that the Devil works from within you, in the case of Tillich; a way related to Calvin's doctrine of divine predestination and divine sovereignty, as in Barth; and then Niebuhr's attempt to develop a picture of sin that seems fundamentally an anthropological doctrine, less related to doctrines of God.

Next we're going to turn to another major religious force shaping the way people talk about evil: Roman Catholic thought on evil in the 20th century.

Post-WWII Roman Catholic Theology on Evil
Lecture 30

Sin would have to be terrifically bad and God would have to be immeasurably loving for God to come down to earth, undergo a human death on the cross, and descend into hell all in order to overcome humanity's estrangement from God. For von Balthasar, that, in fact, is what happened.

In the 20th century, the Roman Catholic Church has made efforts to reach back into the tradition to uncover new resources to help people confront modern challenges. Evidence of these efforts is found in the theological reflections on hell by the Swiss theologian Hans Urs von Balthasar and in the mobilization of the category of "objectively evil acts" in papal teachings.

Von Balthasar was perhaps the most thoughtful and far-seeing Roman Catholic theologian of the 20th century. Most basically, he said that all Christians should pray that "all humans may be saved." According to von Balthasar, God clearly loves all humanity and wishes to save everyone from their own sin. Yet at the same time, God freely chooses to affirm human autonomy, especially the human's responsibility to accept salvation. Salvation encompasses the whole human, and thus, the whole human must participate in salvation. Those who do not make God's will for them their own will for themselves are destined to hell, defined as an utter separation from God.

Von Balthasar also said that we cannot know whether anyone—even Judas—has fully and finally rejected God. Because of this lack of knowledge on our part, we must acknowledge the real possibility of hell, especially for ourselves, but we are obligated by faith to hope that all may be saved. As evidence for this claim, von Balthasar points to two categories of scriptural passages in the New Testament that pertain to judgment and damnation. One of these speaks of individuals being condemned to eternal torment, and one expresses God's desire and ability to save all mankind. Our task is to acknowledge the tension between these two bodies of scriptural claims and hope, without presuming to know, that the claims that all can be saved theologically enframe the other claims about the potential for hell.

For von Balthasar, even sinners at the lowest depths of despair still find Christ with them and can walk out of hell with him, if only they will. The God who judges also accompanies the condemned to the seat of judgment and would stand in their stead to receive that judgment, again, if only the condemned will allow God to do so. It is a responsibility of everyone who properly thinks through the meaning of God's gift of salvation to humanity to understand that God's action is so powerful and so radical as to make salvation possible for every person. For von Balthasar, evil is an attempt to resist God's love, but we can hope that every being who is attempting to resist that love will one day give in, having realized that resistance is futile.

Killing even Hitler as a child to prevent the Holocaust and World War II would be evil because the actor would be taking the life of a small child.

In the 1990s, the language of intrinsic or objective evil began to appear in the discourse of the Catholic Church, particularly in the encyclicals of John Paul II. This pope was deeply concerned that the moral moorings of culture had been loosened in the late modern age, partially as a result of technology. Because humans can do so much more now than we used to be able to do, we increasingly bump up against the limits on what we ought to be able to do. John Paul saw the need to identify this temptation and resist it through the knowledge that certain things are intrinsically evil.

This language of objective moral evil focuses on the human capacity to engage in deliberate acts. In this understanding, acts are evil because of the circumstances surrounding them, because of the intention of the actor, or because an act is objectively evil. An act is objectively evil in one of two ways, the first of which is in its object, the most immediate result that the action seeks to achieve. Abortion is evil in the Catholic Church because the overt aim of the act is to end the life of a fetus. The second way in which an act can be intrinsically evil lies in the fact that its badness is wholly independent of the subjective attitude of the actor. Killing even Hitler as a child to prevent the Holocaust and World War II would be evil because the actor would be taking the life of a small child. In the language of the church, such an act "radically contradicts the good of the person made in God's image."

The language of an objectively evil act calls attention to increasingly powerful temptations in the modern world. Interestingly, this language has also moved from the realm of moral theology into that of social thought, that is, how the church speaks to society as a whole. Although it wasn't visible in much of the encyclical tradition before the 1980s, the language of intrinsic evil will likely be an important part of public discourse into the future. ∎

Suggested Reading

Von Balthasar, *Dare We Hope That "All Men Be Saved"? with A Short Discourse on Hell*, Kipp and Krauth, trans.

Questions to Consider

1. Von Balthasar's emphasis on God's enduring love and the hope of salvation offers a compelling Christian response to the problem of evil. Yet as noted in the lecture, critics worry that von Balthasar risks downplaying evil's significance. Is von Balthasar's hope for universal salvation overly speculative and "other-worldly" or compelling and powerful?

2. Are some acts objectively evil—always wrong, no matter the circumstance or intention? Does the Roman Catholic concept of objectively evil acts help to clarify our moral judgment, or does it obscure the complexity of moral decision-making?

Post-WWII Roman Catholic Theology on Evil
Lecture 30—Transcript

Hello again. In this lecture, I want to talk about the Roman Catholic Church's efforts in the 20th century to think about the problem of evil and focus especially on one very prominent thinker in the tradition, Hans Urs von Balthasar, and also focus on how a series of papal documents, statements by the Pope, encyclicals, things like that, have thought about exploiting the language of evil and the idea of objectively evil acts to talk about how to think about public life in the world today in a pluralistic context.

The Roman Catholic Church has emphasized, more explicitly than many Protestant churches, the need to retain a rich communion with the whole history of the tradition. But even in this church there have been interesting and powerful efforts to innovate by reaching back in the tradition in surprising ways to uncover new resources to help people confront new challenges. One important way of doing that is found in the theological reflections on Hell by the great Swiss Catholic theologian Hans Urs von Balthasar, and another way is the way that recent papal teachings have mobilized the category of "objectively evil acts" in the social encyclicals. Let me start with von Balthasar first.

Von Balthasar was born in 1905 and he died only in 1988. He's perhaps the greatest and most acute, most thoughtful and most far-seeing Roman Catholic theologian of the 20th century, probably in the last several centuries; most historically learned, most theologically wide-ranging, and generally recognized as a titan across the Christian world today and even beyond. In his eulogy for him, Cardinal Josef Ratzinger—now, of course, Pope Benedict XVI—called him "the most cultured man in Europe." He was an enormously spiritual person. Initially he was a Jesuit, but then he left the order to follow as a quasi-disciple of a controversial, very serious Catholic mystic, a woman named Adrienne von Speyr. Von Balthasar's theological work, he thought, was coupled with his own work in understanding and figuring out how she was a continuation of the very tradition of mystical teachings that he had found vital in the Roman Catholic tradition stretching all the way back to the 1st and 2nd centuries. His innovative thinking and his approach to thinking theologically not just on evil and Hell but also on the aesthetics of evil and God's response to it are, in fact, not only really profound and exciting for some people but served as quite controversial and tumultuous topics in his life, and they sometimes drew very disapproving looks from the magisterium, from the teaching authorities, of the Roman Catholic Church.

What's so audacious about what von Balthasar says? He says most basically that all Christians ought to pray that "all humans may be saved" and that all Christians ought to hope that all humans will be saved. It is the universalism of that account, the idea that everyone will be saved, which troubled the magisterium, which troubled the authorities of the Roman Catholic Church (at least some of them; clearly not the current Pope who thought of von Balthasar as a teacher and a mentor in important ways). But in opposition to the resistance he felt from the magisterium, here's how von Balthasar argued his case: God clearly loves all humanity, we know this, von Balthasar says, we know this from scripture, from the experience of the church, from our own experience, what have you; and God wishes to save everyone from their own sin. Jesus Christ's saving mission to the world is a mission for all humanity; no one is intended to be excluded from it. Von Balthasar thinks that salvation, Jesus's mission to the earth, is not an end zone touchdown dance where some are never meant to be part of the winning team. Jesus is not walking around the earth saving part of the people and saying to the others, "Ha, ha, you're not part of this team"; that's not what Jesus is doing. That would be a troubling notion of what God is about, because everyone needs God's efforts; why would God only select some to get those rather than everyone? That's von Balthasar's basic idea there.

Yet at the same time, God freely chooses to affirm human freedom, human autonomy, especially the human's responsibility to accept salvation. Just because it encompasses the whole human, the whole human has to participate in salvation for it to be genuine salvation; it can't be something imposed on humans for von Balthasar. The human will has to be engaged as well, and the human will can only be engaged if it will be engaged; it can't be forced by an external force. This is what is captured in scripture's continual insistence, for von Balthasar, that humanity must make God's will for them their own will for themselves; that is, they must affirm that their salvation is what they wish for. If they do not, they are destined to hell, which, for von Balthasar—and he explores the tradition of mystical reflection and experience in the church and also in his work; thinks about how people have imagined what Hell would be like (Dante, people like Saint John of the Cross, people like that)—he thinks that Hell is ultimately utter separation from God, a devastating thought for him.

So far so good, that's pretty much a standard exposition of salvation and damnation—God wants to save everybody but God respects people's freedom, and those who do not finally exercise that freedom go to Hell—but von Balthasar goes somewhere new next: He says that we do not know, and we cannot actually know, whether anyone has actually fully and finally rejected God. Even Judas—in Christian tradition, the one person who the tradition has been most confident in saying was in Hell; the person who it seems to be the case that Jesus says in scripture, "It would be better for him never to have been born"—may have had a final moment of repentance while he was hanging himself; von Balthasar notes that, scripture doesn't say it. His point is not that we know this; his point is that we can't know what happened. Because of this lack of knowledge on our part—and this is the key thing for him—for von Balthasar, while we must acknowledge the real possibility of Hell for all people, especially for ourselves because we know ourselves best of all, we are obligated, he thinks, by our faith and by our own hope for our salvation to hope that all may be saved.

Balthasar is not a believer in a sort of "final reconciliation of all things" that developed—heretically, for the Christian churches—out of the teachings of Irenaeus. He's not saying that everything finally will be brought together against those things' own will in some important way. He's not proclaiming this in any confidence. He's saying it as a mode of hope; as a way of living hopefully in the world. We don't know, he says, but we may hope that all may be saved and we should pray for it. He notes that scriptural passages, at least in the New Testament, that pertain to judgment and damnation are easily divided up into two groups. One series of passages speaks of individuals being condemned to eternal torment: the damned are those who have, in fact, rejected Christ, and they'll be cast into "the outer darkness" or "the eternal fire"; we all have heard those texts.

But there's a second set of texts as well; one that often doesn't go as well-noticed, von Balthasar thinks. These texts express God's desire and ability to save all mankind. For example, in John, as Jesus is anticipating his own suffering and death he proclaims, "Now is the judgment of this world ... when I am lifted up from the earth, I will draw all men to myself." For von Balthasar, that's a really crucial idea; all will come to Jesus. And Paul says in Romans: "God has consigned all men to disobedience that he [God] may have mercy upon all." This is important: Balthasar does not want to suggest that we should ignore the clear biblical themes of divine justice and God's righteous punishment of evildoers in order to affirm a more chipper view that takes damnation to be incompatible with God's nature as love, as groovy, or something like that. That's not von Balthasar's point; that would be insufferably shallow. Instead—and this is very, very important—he wants to inhabit the tension between these two bodies of scriptural claims and hope, without presuming to know, that, in fact, the claims that God will draw all to God's self are, in fact, theologically enframing the other claims about the potential for the lake of fire and Hell.

This is a theological and especially triune understanding of God and salvation. The depth of God's love for humanity, and the radicality of humanity's sin, its inexplicable self-alienation from God; these things are only truly known through appreciating the efforts and the process whereby God reveals that love, God's love, and in turn reveals—in revealing that love—reveals the depth of human sin. Sin would have to be terrifically bad and God would have to be immeasurably loving for God to come down to earth, undergo a human death on the Cross, and descend into Hell all in order to overcome humanity's estrangement from God. For von Balthasar, that, in fact, is what happened. Our condition is far more dire than we realize, but God's love is far more greater than we could ever imagine.

Furthermore, the nature of God's action here is really interesting too: God loves the world so much that God accepts the punishment due to humanity for our sin; this is von Balthasar, basic kind of Christian theology. God takes the place of the human of each of us. But—and again here, von Balthasar is a bit more radical than many—this also means that even sinners, in their sinning, even in the depths of their sinning all the way down into Hell, will find Jesus Christ, as the one who freely took the rejection due to humanity onto his own head, following with them, accompanying them all the way down to the lowest depths of despair. Even at the bottom, they still find

Christ with them, and they will take his hand and walk out of Hell with him, if only they will.

Recall the images of Dante here: Remember that after Christ, the gates of Hell in the *Inferno* had been busted open, and that the problem of the inmates was precisely that they didn't really want to leave; they kept trying to make excuses for themselves, excuses that really only convinced themselves, no one else. Von Balthasar knows his Dante very well, uses him thoroughly, and disagrees with the poet only in how von Balthasar simply thinks that at the bottom of despair, at the abyssal base of all hopelessness, there is reason to hope that the presence of Christ will finally be too seductive to resist, and so everyone finally will accept Christ's help.

The God who judges, and who will judge, also accompanies the condemned all the way to the seat of judgment, and would stand in their stead to receive that judgment, if only the condemned will let him. It's thus a responsibility incumbent upon everyone who properly thinks through the meaning of the Christian God's gift of salvation to humanity to understand that this God's action is so powerful and so radical as to make salvation quite possible for every person; and indeed, von Balthasar thinks, it's incumbent upon us to hope that this God is as good as we think, for if not, then we can have no confidence whatsoever that we ourselves are among the elect, as we are commanded to have that confidence. Again, von Balthasar does a lovely jujitsu here because the problem of Hell is by and large not a problem about "Why are we going to Hell?"; the problem of Hell for us is always a problem about "Why is anyone else going to Hell?" There are polls of Americans that frequently are taken about belief in Heaven, belief in Hell, and these sorts of things. Lots of people believe in Heaven; a significant number of people—not many, but still 20–30 percent—say they believe in Hell; but like 1 or 2 percent of the people believe they are going there. A lot of traditional Christian theology would have reversed those proportions, right? Most people are likely to go to Hell—that's the idea of a lot of traditional Christian theology—basically because most of us really suck (just to be honest). That's where Christianity comes out on that one.

But von Balthasar, in thinking about the nature of evil, turns the question of the mystery of evil into a larger evangelical opportunity, an opportunity he takes to sketch once again for all Christians the overall shape of their lives; lives lived, as he puts it, out of, and into, hope. The crucial thing about evil, for von Balthasar, is that we understand that evil is an attempt to resist God's love, but we can have hope that every being who is attempting to resist that love will one day give in, having realized that resistance is ultimately futile.

So that's one way that evil has been a major provocation in Roman Catholic theology in the last century or so. It really has served as a huge goad for the recovery through van Balthasar of the historical tradition of Christian theology and also a major rethinking of certain moments in the Christian message that other Catholic theologians continue to explore even today. But recently, another use of the language of evil has appeared in Roman Catholic Church discourse, and this is the language of intrinsic or objective evil; a language originally developed in moral theology, but now applied to large-scale public matters. This trend really started in the 1990s via papal encyclicals, particularly those of John Paul II, especially encyclicals like the "Evangelium vitae," "The Gospel of Life" and "veritatis splendor," "The Splendor of Truth." John Paul was deeply concerned that the moral bearings, the moral moorings of culture were getting loosened in the late modern age and he worried that people were finding it increasingly easy to leave their tradition moral convictions behind in the era of enormous technological power that we have now entered. Because the human will can do so much more than we used to be able to do, the limits on what humans ought to be able to do seem increasingly to be ones that we bump up against; and so lots of people—lots of scientists, ordinary people, politicians, leaders—all seem to want to explore doing things that maybe we used to think weren't so good (this is John Paul II's concern). So he begins in the 1980s and 90s to develop a language to identify this temptation and resist it by saying that some things are just intrinsically evil and can never be done.

This language of objective moral evil and objectively evil acts depends on a certain understanding of human acts, one that makes the human capacity to act a very distinctive and important characteristic of human beings. In some important way, the human capacity to act is perhaps the most distinctive thing about humans. Lower animals behave, lower animals do things, but they don't really act; only humans act, because to understand what a human is doing when she or he is acting, you have to comprehend what is going on in their heads, what they understand themselves to be doing. Eating a special holiday feast is a different thing than a dog eating out of its dish, and to deny the difference, even though both are forms of nutrition, will inevitably impair our understanding of what goes on in the feast. This is a profoundly anti-reductionist understanding of human behavior, one that emphasizes the unique status of human beings among all the creatures of the earth precisely because the stories human tell themselves about what they are doing and why they are doing it turn out to be intrinsic to the nature of the actions that they are performing.

This is an enormously philosophically complicated point, so let me just say one more thing about it, because it's both intrinsically interesting in itself and wonderful to think about and also really important for this. On this understanding of an act, if you were to film me with a video camera doing something—if there was a Nature Channel show or something that was filming humans—it wouldn't be able to understand what the humans were doing in the same way that the same Nature Channel camera, were it filming a pack of lions, would be able pretty well to describe what they were doing without accessing those lions' thoughts. But if you turn the camera on a bunch of humans, to know what they're doing, it matters enormously to figure out what they're doing inside their head. If you film me and two other people in a coffee shop sitting there drinking coffee and working on our computers or reading books or whatever, one of us—let's say me—is checking my email, reading an article, and writing some notes on the article on my computer; so I'm working in my role as a professor. Another of us is thinking about the enormous fight that she or he just had with their spouse and brooding over this and wondering whether this is the end of their relationship. The third of us is waiting anxiously to meet their mother who is just coming back from a troubling hospital procedure, and the mother will be able to tell them when they meet whether or not she in fact has cancer. All three of us might be sitting at the same darn table in the coffee shop, and we all three might be doing what look like the same things—one of us is reading a paper, one of us is simply drinking the coffee and looking around, one of us is typing away on a computer—but the three acts are very different, what we're doing when we're sitting there in the coffee shop: one of us is waiting for our mother, one of us is brooding over a fight, and one of us is kind of mundanely working on our job stuff. The difference in what goes on in our heads makes those acts very different. But if you see three lions lounging under a tree, what you're seeing are three lions lounging under a tree, full stop. That's this tradition's argument anyway.

On this tradition's account, acts are evil either because of the circumstances surrounding them, such as the naming of a person as a Jew when you are surrounded by Nazis looking for a Jew versus the naming of a person as a Jew when someone asks you who is interested in dating them, "Is that person a Jew, because my parents would like it if I also married within my own faith" and you're like, "Oh, sure, that's a Jewish guy." You can say those sorts of things in one context to a woman who's nervous about whether or not this is a guy who her parents will approve of or to a bunch of Nazis; and so in the second case the circumstances surrounding the act—the telling that, "Yes, this guy's a Jew"—make that act intrinsically evil; or, along with the circumstances around the act, an act can be made evil because of the intention of the actor (when you steal a book from a bookstore), or because an act is objectively evil (that's the third thing). So circumstances, the intention of the agent, or because an act is simply objectively evil; and that third one is the one we want to focus on here.

An act is objectively evil in one of two ways: First of all, in its object, in what it objectively is; that is, what's defined as "the proximate end [or the goal] of a deliberate decision," the most immediate thing that the action is trying to do. For example, consider the badness of abortion in the Roman Catholic Church: Abortion is an evil because the overt proximate aim of the act— that is, the aim that is most immediately intended, directly intended, by the doer—is, in fact, the ending of the fetus's life. Any number of other things can go on, but if the fetus' life ends, the procedure has been accomplished and is successful and if it does not end, the procedure has failed. Since the Roman Catholic Church understands the fetus to be a human person, that's why the Roman Catholic Church thinks is abortion is an intrinsically evil act, because it's killing a human being. That's one way, because of the proximate end.

The second way in which something can be an intrinsically evil act is in how its badness is wholly independent from the subjective attitude of the actor, the motive with which the agent believes him or herself to be undertaking it.

This is crucial, too. If you are trying intentionally to kill somebody because you're afraid of what they might do in the future—if you can go back and kill Hitler as a young boy—in that moment, even though what you want to do is not, in fact, just kill a young boy, you want to stop the Shoah, the Holocaust, you want to stop World War II, you're thinking, "I'm doing this to stop World War II," but, in fact, what's in your mind is not that important; what's really important is the objective act you're doing, and that is taking the life of a small child. The Church has said that an objectively evil act is—this is technical Church language—"incapable of being ordered to God" because it "radically contradicts the good of the person made in God's image"; radically, again, at its root, it contradicts the good of the person. Regardless of intention, regardless of consequence, that is, some acts, the tradition says, are simply intrinsically evil.

The basic principle behind this notion of objectively evil acts is a pretty old and long-standing one; the scriptural warrant for it: You may never say in the tradition, "let us do evil so that good may come of it." In other words, you cannot do, in the Roman Catholic tradition anyway, a necessary evil; there's no such thing as a necessary evil. The language of an objectively evil act, thus, is an attempt to identify an increasingly powerful temptation for some moderns, at least as the authorities of the Roman Catholic Church identify this temptation as increasingly powerful. I think it's pretty fair to say that many of us feel this temptation more than maybe people a century before did or something like that. That's not that controversial, I think. But the language has a real attention-grabbing character, and it focuses attention in a certain and important way. To call something objectively evil really stimulates the conscience; that is, it's a surprising term to hear in public discourse anyway, and it immediately calls our attention to something about the term that we might have passed over. If someone says, "I don't like that," we say, "Well, that's ok, that's your view"; if someone says, "That's bad," we're like, "Well, I mean I can understand that's your opinion"; but if someone says, "That's objectively evil," we're going to spend more time thinking about it, I think. The Church was thinking about this and they said, "This is a useful way of talking about it because it will bring into view more thoroughly how important this issue is for us." Also it makes us begin to consider this object in a more explicitly and overtly moral register; to say something's "bad" as not as strong as saying it's "evil." This goes back even to Nietzsche; Nietzsche would be rolling over in his grave at the language of the objectively evil act.

But note—and this is interesting—the language of objectively evil doesn't actually speak to the magnitude of the evil. The catechism of the Roman Catholic Church identifies both masturbation and homosexual acts as intrinsically evil acts, but the Church doesn't weigh both as equally evil. Nor is intrinsic evil a matter always to be legislated according to the church. Civil law is not designed to ensure moral perfection, to eliminate every objective evil out there; that would be far more invasive and probably demand too large and vast of a governing power for the Church. Rather, civil law, on the understanding of the Roman Catholic Church, is meant to secure the relatively well-functioning character of a social order. That's what it does.

Again, it's worth noting here also that this language is a relatively recent importation into Roman Catholic social thought from Roman Catholic moral theology. In other words—and this is important—the language develops in moral theology, in thinking about how to counsel individuals in guiding their moral lives, but it has been taken from that into the realm of social thought, into how the Church speaks to society as a whole, both to its faithful and to all of goodwill, including the pluralistic community it inhabits about what the Church's view is on certain things it at the society is considering. This language is not something that's actually visible much in the encyclical tradition really much before the 1980s. There's one paragraph actually in "Humanae Vitae," the 1968 encyclical that forbids birth control for Roman Catholics, but really that's about it. Before John Paul, there really wasn't much language of intrinsic evil or objectively evil acts. But nonetheless, it seems an important part of the public discourse of the Roman Catholic Church now and I think arguably probably into the future; so it's going to be an important part of the way people think about evil in coming decades.

Let me wrap this up a bit here. The two different uses of the language of "evil" that we've been looking at in the Roman Catholic Church show something of the power of the language and the range of temptations and the dangers to which it may be susceptible. On the one hand, von Balthasar's rigorous attempt to explore the way that God triumphs over evil by enduring it, by suffering it in our stead, and by showing us how evil is overcome in the theological realm generates a spirituality of hope and a practice of charity that is powerful and mobilizing; yet it's one that comes under theological and also non-theological complaint because people can worry that it doesn't take evil seriously enough, either on theological grounds by dismissing (this was some Roman Catholic authority's words) too quickly the possibility of Hell, and also on non-theological grounds by offering an apparently (or to critics apparently anyway) purely otherworldly response to evil. On the other hand, the Magisterium's attempt to develop and apply the language of "objectively evil acts" seems to identify and focus attention on a collection of acts the Church finds profoundly troubling and in need of explicit opposition; so it's a usefully mobilizing language. But on the other hand, some within and without the church have worried that this language may be too immediately demonizing of people and it may obscure the way that the moral experience of people is not ever as clean or as clear as this language suggests it should be, and so it suggests or implies a false clarity that may be more misleading than mobilizing.

Now I want turn to another religious tradition that has its own traumas with evil to confront, especially about the reality of evil in the 20th century: the Jewish tradition, and its confrontation with the catastrophe that befell the People Israel at the heart of the modern world and in the middle of the modern age.

Post-WWII Jewish Thought on Evil
Lecture 31

> The way we imagine the Shoah by and large today is that most people ... were killed in death camps and by industrial teams of the SS (the Nazi death guards). But this is, in fact, not true: Most of the victims— most of the Jews and other victims of the Shoah—were killed where they lived, almost at once by the German army when it came through.

At the end of the Second World War, the experience of the Shoah was one that most people simply could not process because they had no precedent for it. To think directly about the nature, meaning, and implications of this event has taken decades. In this lecture, we look at the work of four major Jewish thinkers on this issue: Richard Rubenstein, Arthur Cohen, Emil Fackenheim, and Emmanuel Levinas.

Richard Rubenstein is a living American philosopher and the author of the first book to explore the implications of the Shoah for Judaism from inside the Jewish faith (*After Auschwitz*). For traditional Rabbinic Judaism, Rubenstein argued, the Shoah must be understood either as a punishment or a complete mystery. He chooses the latter and claims that this mystery reveals the bankruptcy of some traditional Jewish understandings of God.

Rubenstein's argument is simple: to posit a just and omnipotent God who is in covenant with the people Israel and governing their fate and the fate of the world entails affirming that this God willed the murder of 12 million people. No one in his right mind would affirm that directly. Therefore, Rubenstein argues, the God of the traditional Jewish faith must be, effectively, dead. Furthermore, Rubenstein suggests that the Shoah reveals that the people Israel are not the chosen of God. Though Jewish rituals and practices have meaning and purpose, ultimately, the Shoah breaks apart any living relationship modern Jews could have with traditional Judaism. Jews should not, however, stop being Jews. Instead, they need to engage in a profound questioning of what God is doing now—if there is a God—and what the people Israel should do in the wake of Yahweh's demise. To reject the identity of the Jew is to continue the defeat that the Shoah represents of much of the people Israel.

One of the most interesting responses to Rubenstein was that of the American writer and philosopher Arthur Cohen. He saw the Nazi death camps as profane sites of anti-holiness, revealing a new kind of evil; this new evil is the *tremendum*, meaning both "the terror" and "the awesome." Cohen asserts that we must see the reality of the Shoah for what it represents, not simply treat it as continuous with other anti-Semitic pogroms. For Cohen, there is no "moral" to the story of the Shoah; it is an utter break with the past. He further believes that "God's silence is divine acquiescence in the work of murder and destruction." Because of this, Jews can break the bond with God; the *tremendum* has torn the covenant asunder. The God that the people Israel have worshiped is not the true Yahweh but an idol of their own fabrication.

For Cohen, the crucial thing to take from the Shoah is that we must see the reality of the camps for what they represent: a profound and profane series of sites of anti-holiness—a new kind of evil, the *tremendum*.

427

The God that Cohen wants the Jews to profess is more of a promise at present, not fully realized.

Emil Fackenheim, the third of our thinkers, experienced the Shoah firsthand. In his work *To Mend the World*, he asks what it means to be a Jew after the Holocaust. His answer is that the Jew is one who, without the historical accident of Hitler's losing the war, would be dead or would never have been born. In light of this new identity, Jews must undertake again the Jewish practice of *tikkun olam*, Hebrew words that mean "to mend the world." Among other things, the Jewish people must practice resistance to the aim of the Shoah, which was annihilation of the Jews. This annihilation would destroy the link between the God who will redeem the world through the Jewish people and a world that desperately needs redemption. To mend the world, Jews must recover the past of the Jewish tradition, recover from the trauma of the Shoah, and reconstitute their people. Fackenheim deems these obligations in the healing of the world the "614th commandment."

Emmanuel Levinas was another survivor of the Shoah and went on to become an incredible intellectual presence in the world. For Levinas, evil is suffering, and suffering is the transformation into passivity experienced by agents in the world through the actions of others. Evil affirms the presence of its victim no further than it needs the victim's existence in order to annihilate it. This kind of evil, Levinas thinks, is radically gratuitous, and the suffering it promotes is radically meaningless. Such suffering cannot be made useful for us. In fact, pain and suffering are, for Levinas, precisely the opposite of meaning; they are the annihilation of meaning. In the wake of Auschwitz, Levinas says that all people must care for one another. We must seek out those situations where people are being annihilated in this way and do what we can to stop it. It is only through that effort to stop suffering that any of our sufferings will ever have meaning. ■

Suggested Reading

Morgan, ed., *A Holocaust Reader: Responses to the Nazi Extermination.*

Roth and Berenbaum, *Holocaust: Religious and Philosophical Implications.*

1. Arthur Cohen stressed that the Shoah was a new kind of horror and not merely another expression of anti-Semitism. Do you think the Shoah is a totally unique experience of evil? Should the Shoah change fundamentally the way we view the problem of evil?

2. Does the Jewish experience of the Shoah offer a unique perspective for viewing the nature of evil? And might the particularity of this experience offer Judaism a particularly privileged view of evil?

Post-WWII Jewish Thought on Evil
Lecture 31—Transcript

Welcome back. In this lecture, I want to talk about a series of Jewish thinkers' attempts to come to grips with the enormous historical and theological trauma of what happened to the Jewish people in the 20th century, especially in the Shoah or the Holocaust. When I talk about this, I'll use this word "Shoah" a lot, and I do that on purpose. "Holocaust" is a word from Greek that means "burnt offering"; it's often used religiously as a sacrificial word. This is clearly not a good word to talk about the genocide that affected the Jewish people and many others in Central, Eastern, and Western Europe—all over Europe, really—in the middle of the 20th century. "Shoah" is a biblical Hebrew word that means "catastrophe."

There's an enormous debate about whether or not the Holocaust, the Shoah, is like other genocides. There are some important differences between the Shoah and other genocides that are worth noting. Other genocides—Rwanda, maybe Cambodia, maybe the suffering of the Armenians in Ottoman Turkey—seem localized to a people in one country; if the people weren't in that country, they would perhaps be safe. The Shoah exposed a Nazi plan to annihilate Jews around the world, it was a global ambition; plus, the Shoah was clearly part of the intrinsic war strategy of the Third Reich itself to the point where, in fact, important military costs were borne by the Third Reich so that they could kill more Jewish men, women, and children. And they killed a lot: In the course of the whole Shoah, which really gets going in a serious way in 1940–1941, more than six million Jewish men, women, and children—all of them, of course, civilians—are murdered. And also another six million other men, women, and children—again, all of them civilians—also died.

The way we imagine the Shoah by and large today is that most people we imagine are killed in death camps and by industrial teams of the SS (the Nazi death guards). But this is, in fact, not true: Most of the victims—most of the Jews and other victims of the Shoah—were killed where they lived, almost at once by the German Army when it came through. There were, of course, special units dedicated to killing; but sometimes normal army units just took it upon themselves to massacre whatever Jews they could find, especially on the Eastern Front. While the Holocaust, the Shoah, takes place across the whole scope of the Second World War, much of the orgy of killing actually happens in the 13 or 14 months between around September, 1941 and October and November, 1942; that's when most of what we know of the Holocaust actually happens.

At the end of the Second World War, the experience of the Shoah was one that most people simply had never had any precedent to understand; people couldn't process what had happened. When the first images were shown in a movie theater in London, Arthur Kazin, an American writer who was in the United States Army there, said that there were curious outbursts of laughter by people around him; not because people found it humorous at all, but because no one could process the information that their eyes were trying to convey to their brains. They looked at these images, they looked at these pictures of stick figures, and they just kind of burst out laughing like, "How … how can I … what do you do to that?"; that sort of laughter. It's hard for us now to imagine what it was like 60 years ago to live in a world where no one really had processed this thought of piles and piles of people, basically as thin as sticks, who had been turned into those victims on an intentional and industrial basis. Martha Gellhorn, a very hard-bitten war correspondent, was one of the first reporters to visit Dachau. When she was there, she went all through the camp—Dachau was one of the death camps—and she wrote after she came out an article that still is something I think that people should read now. At the end of the article about what she saw in Dachau she said:

> We have all seen a great deal now; we have seen too many wars and too much violent dying; we have seen hospitals, bloody and messy as butcher shops; we have seen the dead like bundles lying on all the roads of half the earth. But nowhere was there anything like this. Nothing about war was ever as insanely wicked as the starved and outraged, naked, nameless dead.

It took a long time, really genuinely a long time, for people to begin to process what the Holocaust, what the Shoah, meant. There's a wonderful book by a historian named Peter Novick entitled *The Holocaust in American Life*, which is a study of how it took decades for Americans to think in direct ways about the nature, meaning, and implications—religious, philosophical, moral, political—of this event. Nothing has so profoundly challenged, though, Jews in particular and the Jewish faith in general since the destruction of the Temple in Jerusalem by the Romans in 70 C.E. After the war, Jewish thinkers began slowly to try to come to terms with the challenge of the events and the implication they had for the basic principles of their faith. In this lecture, I want to look at how four people in particular, four major Jewish thinkers in particular, have thought about this issue: First I want to talk about Richard Rubenstein, then Arthur Cohen, Emil Fackenheim, and then Emmanuel Levinas. Let me talk about Rubenstein first.

Rubenstein is a living American Jewish philosopher at present, famous perhaps most for his book *After Auschwitz*, a book that was published in 1966 and is really the first book to argue from the inside of the Jewish faith about the implications of the Shoah for Judaism. For traditional rabbinic Judaism, Rubenstein argued, the Shoah must be understood either as a punishment or a complete mystery. He chooses the latter and says that this, in fact, shows the bankruptcy of some traditional Jewish understandings of theology; that is, some traditional Jewish understandings of the picture of God. Not the understanding of the people Israel in general, but their understanding of who God was, what God had covenanted to do, and what God was able to do now.

Rubenstein's argument was simple: to posit a just and omnipotent God who is in Covenant with the people Israel and directly providentially governing their fate and the fate of the world entails affirming that this God directly willed the murder of six million Jews and six million others. No one in their right mind would affirm that directly. Therefore, Rubenstein argues, we have to have a vision of God as effectively dead; for this God, the God of traditional Jewish faith, could not have allowed the Shoah, had this God been alive. Furthermore, Rubenstein wants to suggest that the Shoah shows that the people Israel are not in any important way the chosen of God; though their rituals have meaning and purpose, their practices, their forms of belief help them live and provide order to their lives, ultimately the Shoah breaks apart any living relationship we could have with traditional Judaism, he thinks. The Covenant made between Yahweh and the people Israel was broken in Auschwitz, he says: "the thread uniting God and man, heaven and earth, has been broken." He says whatever else you want to say, however else you want to start, you have to begin with that fact: Beyond all the actual, concrete human suffering, immeasurable human suffering, of the Shoah, there is the theological fact that all this means that this God is clearly not a God that we're dealing with now.

So what does that mean; should the Jews stop being Jews? No, he thinks. No; a more profound questioning should happen, a far more morally serious questioning, of what a God is doing now, if there is a God, and what the people Israel should do in the wake of the traditional Yahweh's demise. The insistence here is that the resistance to rejecting entirely the identity of the Jew is partially something really important; that resistance is something we need to keep alive—those of us who are Jews—precisely because to allow that to lapse is in some important way to continue the defeat that the Shoah represents of much of the people Israel. This was an astonishing book. It came almost out of nowhere, really, and it literally created the genre of post-Holocaust theology; that is, after Rubenstein had started writing, people began to imagine it's possible to think about Judaism in light of this. Before him, no one had the courage really, no one had the gumption to try to think about what it meant to be a Jew in the wake of this enormously annihilating event; and almost all the work that came after it felt compelled to respond to him.

One of the most interesting ones to respond was Arthur Cohen, who's an American Jewish thinker and writer, philosopher. He lived from 1928–1986. His book, *The Tremendum*, argued for a vision of the camps as a profound and profane series of sites of anti-holiness; a new kind of evil was revealed in the camps, the evil of the Tremendum. "Tremendum" is a Latin word that means "the terrible" or "the terror," but it also means "the awesome," "the thing that is amazing." He doesn't mean it to have the positive inflection there, but he does want to capture the negative inflection. For Cohen, what the Shoah teaches, the crucial thing he wants to take from this experience is that we must see the reality of the camps for what they represent, and the overall Shoah; not simply to treat them as continuous with other anti-Semitic pogroms that had come before—for after all, Jews have always suffered; historically, as we talked about in the rabbinic Judaism lecture, there had always been this history of Jewish suffering as part of the cost of bearing the sign of being the elect of God—but Cohen thinks this is a new kind of thing, this is the Tremendum; there's something new and troubling here. The

Holocaust is unique; it can't be grouped with other kinds of annihilationism. Nor is there any sort of "moral" to this story. The Shoah is the Tremendum, an utter break with all past events.

Given that, how should we think about God after the Shoah; how should we think about God in light of these events? Cohen is clear here, as clear as he thinks he can be, that "God's silence is divine acquiescence," he says, "in the work of murder and destruction." Because of this, the human can break the bond with God; the people Israel can break the Covenant; "the abyss of the historical" has torn asunder that Covenant; the Tremendum has ripped apart the garments that bonded the people Israel to their God. But, in fact, this just shows us that we—Cohen here is speaking of the Jewish people in general— had been worshipping an idol of our own fabrication. The Tremendum shows us that this god is not the real God, not the real Yahweh we should be following. A wonderful passage in Cohen here; he says:

> If we begin to see God less as an interferer whose insertion is welcome (when it accords with our needs) and more as the immensity whose reality is our prefiguration [in other words, the promise of what we will be; what we hope to become] ... we shall have won a sense of God whom we may love and honor, but whom we no longer fear and from whom we no longer demand.

What does this mean? It means that God—the God that Cohen wants the Jews to profess—is more of a promise at present, not fully realized; this God will be realized in the future, but not yet. This God is not here for us now.

Rubenstein and Cohen are both in important ways American Jews thinking seriously about the experience of the Shoah from an American context. Emil Fackenheim, the third of our thinkers, is someone who actually experienced it firsthand. He was born and raised in Germany, a promising young man, who was picked up with his family and sent with his family to the Sachsenhausen concentration camp by the Nazis when he was in his early 20s. He managed to escape from the camp, and with his younger brother made his way eventually to Canada. His parents eventually got out of the camp as well and made it to Canada also, but his older brother never managed to escape, and he was killed in the Shoah.

Fackenheim asks in his magisterial work—a very important work in post-Holocaust theology called *To Mend the World*—asks a basic question: After the Shoah, who is a Jew? What is a Jew? This is always a question for Jews: Who is a Jew? What does it mean to be a Jew? So Fackenheim says after the Shoah we ask it again: What does it mean? The Jew is one who, Fackenheim says, without the historical accident of Hitler's losing the war, would be dead or would have never been born. That's really important; think about that for a second. The new identity of the Jew is one who, absent the sheer historical luck of Hitler's defeat, would not be. The identity of the Jewish people, the identity of each individual Jew, has been profoundly transformed by Hitler's deeds and especially the Shoah. So Fackenheim brilliantly and famously argues that the Jews must refuse to give Hitler any "posthumous victories." The Jewish people must undertake again, Fackenheim thought, the Jewish practice of *tikkun olam*, Hebrew words that mean "to mend the world" (this is why the title of his book is *To Mend the World*). This is a general ethical obligation always for Jews, Fackenheim thinks; but after the Shoah, after the Holocaust, it takes on a new specificity as well: to heal the world is among other things simply to practice resistance to the evil aim of the Holocaust itself, and the evil aim of the Holocaust was to annihilate the Jewish people altogether.

Remember that in traditional Jewish theology, the Jewish people are not simply for themselves; the Jewish people are the elect of God not because God has chosen them and will take them away eventually, but because God is going to save the world through the Jews. To attack the Jews, from the Jews's own perspective, is to attack the whole world; to annihilate the very link between the God who will redeem the world and the world that desperately needs redemption. To heal the world, then, there must be a Jewish people; and the first obligation of the Jews for everybody, for everyone's sake, is to ensure that the people Israel continue. How do they continue? This is where Fackenheim offers some particular concrete suggestions.

Jews must recover. They must recover the past of the Jewish tradition; they must put themselves back in living continuity and living exchange with that tradition; they must begin to recover from the trauma of the Shoah itself; they must reconstitute their people, reconstitute their population, their communities; and they also recognize that both of these recoveries—

the recovery of the past and their recovery from the Shoah—in themselves and in their mutual interrelation will never be complete; they will always be incomplete. Furthermore, Fackenheim says, the name for all of these obligations, the names for this fundamental effort to mend the world, is something that Fackenheim proposes that we call the "614th commandment." Traditionally in rabbinic Judaism, people thought there were 613 *mitzvoth*, 613 laws, which Jews had to follow. Fackenheim wants to add just one, and it's a doozy; it's a wonderful, wonderful statement, and a relatively famous one:

> We are, first, commanded to survive as Jews, lest the Jewish people perish. We are commanded, secondly, to remember in our very guts and bones the martyrs of the Holocaust, lest their memory perish. [Already Fackenheim is saying this is about recovering the past.] We are forbidden, thirdly, to deny or despair of God, however much we may have to contend with him or with belief in him, lest Judaism perish. We are forbidden, finally, to despair of the world as the place which is to become the kingdom of God, lest we help make it a meaningless place in which God is dead or irrelevant and everything is permitted. To abandon any of these imperatives, in response to Hitler's victory at Auschwitz, would be to hand him yet other, posthumous victories.

To talk about this nest of practices he thinks is so important and compelling, Fackenheim uses a term, a very old and traditional term in Judaism, called "*teshuva*." *Teshuva* is a matter of turning—turning normally in terms of repentance—that Fackenheim means to turn to God; turning to God as human, so that God and human meet face to face. That, for him, is the core of Judaism, and what is called for after the Shoah is the rejuvenation of that encounter, the rejuvenation of *teshuva*.

To move from Fackenheim into Emmanuel Levinas is to move from someone writing in really fundamentally an American register—Fackenheim eventually becomes an American and Canadian scholar, a real import; someone who's writing in a very clear and public way—to talk about someone, with Emmanuel Levinas, who's an enormously philosophically complicated and ingrown intellectual thinker, intellectual presence in the world. Emmanuel Levinas is one of the most important postmodern philosophers and a thinker of real profundity. He was born in 1906 as a young Jewish Lithuanian, and he moved to Germany and studied with Husserl and Heidegger—two major, major philosophers; Husserl Jewish and Heidegger not, and eventually Heidegger siding with the Nazis—before he emigrates to France in the 1930s. While he survived World War II in a prison camp, and his wife and daughter survived hidden in a monastery, his father, his mother-in-law, and all his brothers were killed in the Shoah. After the war, he rebuilt his life, he rejoined his family, and he worked quietly for decades doing his own writing, engaging in intellectual debate, and only in the 1970s, 80s, and then 90s, as he became a very old man, was he recognized as an incredible intellectual, philosophical, and moral force, one of the people who redeemed Europe after the event of the Shoah.

At the center of a lot of his work is actually his notion of evil, and especially around the category of suffering. Evil, for Levinas, is fundamentally suffering. What does this mean? It means that evil is the experience of agents—active beings; you and I—being turned into something wholly, fundamentally passive; being turned into not agents, into what we are essentially not, by the action of another upon us. Levinas's sense of suffering in some sense then is of radical passivity; it's more radically passive than our senses, because the senses are modes of receptivity and thus welcome what they are given in the way of sense data. I said that relatively quickly, but let me say it again: Sense data—that is, the wavelengths of light or whatever—are welcomed by me and received by my eyes because my eyes are designed to receive them; in other words, it takes them and knows what to do with them in some important way. That's the part of me that's supposed to be receptive. Suffering is not that. Suffering is not me receiving things; suffering is just what happens.

It's through evil, in a way, that suffering is understood through the category of evil. Suffering is, in an important way, per se in itself is evil. Why is that? Because the activity of being caused to suffer means that I am no longer an actor, I am merely a passive recipient of something. But reception, again, sounds too much like it's something I'm collaborating in. I don't receive something like a gift; I don't ever receive it in that way, it just happens to me. Suffering in whatever form it is—mockery, physical violence, murder—

is always on a trajectory of turning humans into what they are essentially not; turning humans into corpses, or at least potential corpses. That's what suffering does for Levinas.

Evil, then, on this account, is radically negative. It affirms the presence of the victims only insofar as and no further than it needs the victim's existence in order to annihilate it. Evil, that is, only seeks out people as potential targets of its own malice. This kind of evil, Levinas thinks, is radically gratuitous, and in no good sense of the term "gratuitous." It is excessive, in a way, precisely because it seeks out being in the world and attempts to turn it into not being; attempts to turn it into what it is essentially not. Furthermore, this suffering is radically meaningless in itself, he thinks. The essay where he most famously talks about this is an essay called "Useless Suffering." So the suffering is radically meaningless in itself, and useless in itself; it cannot be intrinsically made useful for us. There is strictly no sense to be given to such suffering since precisely suffering is the annihilation of sense; the annihilation of those agents, who are in some sense the only creatures able to make sense. Pain, then, is not something that is intrinsically for our benefit or for our blessing; pain is, strictly speaking, non-sense: it has no meaning and offers no intelligibility. In fact, pain and suffering are, for Levinas, precisely the opposite of meaning; they are the annihilation of meaning, precisely because meaning is what is made by agents and they are the annihilation of agents.

Of course, suffering for me, when it's my suffering, can have meaning insofar as I choose to undergo this suffering in order to end someone else's suffering. If I see someone being assaulted and beaten within an inch of their life, I can run over and stop it, or at least try to interfere so that the attackers start beating me as well so I can drag the person away perhaps. In that activity, I suffer suffering; I suffer assaults on my being. Intrinsically, those assaults—those punches, those kicks—have no meaning; but in the narrative that I'm offering, they do have meaning because I suffered that senseless pain in order to stop another from suffering more senseless pain. But that is not to say that suffering itself can in itself be justified; no such justification exists. The pain of a suffering person at the hands of another is not warranted or merited by anything; it is just, strictly speaking, evil.

In a way, Levinas turns out to take Fackenheim's argument and universalize it in a certain sense. Fackenheim argued that you have to remain a Jew after Auschwitz; after Auschwitz, Levinas says, it's not Jews. All people must care for one another in a new way; they must care for one another to seek out those situations where people are being caused to suffer in this way, where people are being asked to disappear in their beings, to be annihilated. And now, the obligation to turn to God—which Fackenheim thinks is the fundamental obligation of all Jews after the Shoah—Levinas says the fundamental obligation of all people after the Shoah is to turn to one another; to turn to your fellow humans and see them, and see if you can stop whatever suffering is happening to them. It is only through that effort to stop suffering that any of our sufferings will ever have any meaning, will ever have any purpose. You can see how Levinas is simultaneously a Jewish thinker, but also one who takes a Jewish message—a kind of Jewish gospel of sorts—out to the world as a whole, universalizing the obligation to change your being after the experience of the Shoah.

All four of these thinkers are in complicated ways very seriously self-identifying themselves in their writing as essentially Jewish thinkers who are writing for others to hear but also importantly for the Jewish people. Levinas in his work is much vaguer on this, especially in the stuff we've been working on; but still, he thinks of himself as in some rich continuity with the Jewish tradition, and working out of that tradition in important ways. Next we turn to a Jewish thinker who is by no means less Jewish than they—no means less influenced, nor any less interested in Jewish themes—but whose views on the Holocaust and the Shoah were not centrally about its implications for Jewish tradition, but about its implications for the world as a whole, and who is unarguably still the most controversial thinker of the Shoah and arguably the greatest thinker of human genocide and mass political evil in the modern world: Hannah Arendt.

Arendt—The Banality of Evil
Lecture 32

> The dark discovery of the 20th century is that humans are far more plastic than we heretofore imagined. People in a totalitarian state are turned into zombies, again, or robots that annihilate themselves and one another, all in the interest of the abstract totalitarian state.

Hannah Arendt, one of the most innovative thinkers of the 20th century, gave us two concepts that are important for thinking about evil in its political dimensions: totalitarianism and the banality of evil. For Arendt, the dangerous innovation of evil in the 20th century is the capacity of states to make people who would never normally be capable of cruelty to others become actors who play significant roles in vast schemes of human annihilation.

In her book *The Origins of Totalitarianism*, Arendt argued that modern totalitarian states, such as Nazi Germany, effectively embody a new kind of radical evil. Arendt believed that the totalitarian state is aptly named because it demands the totality of all that is within its boundaries—the products, culture, bodies, and souls of its citizens. It seeks to control education, technology, media, and industry in order to directly shape humans. Ultimately, Arendt thinks, this means that the totalitarian state is hostile to the idiosyncratic individuality of human beings and to human freedom. Such a regime's project inevitably entails the destruction of the human's capacity to be genuinely human.

About 10 years after the publication of *The Origins of Totalitarianism*, Arendt attended the trial of Adolf Eichmann in Jerusalem; from this experience, she compiled her most controversial book, *Eichmann in Jerusalem: A Report on the Banality of Evil*. Where earlier Arendt had described totalitarian evil as radical, in the character of Eichmann, she saw it as banal. As savagely efficient as Eichmann was, there was nothing demonic about him. Further, Arendt challenged the moral and legal concepts that organized the war crimes trials. To judge evil at the level of the Holocaust on the old moral concepts of individual responsibility, personal integrity, and individual intents is cowardly and dangerous, and it avoids the fundamental philosophical challenges the Holocaust presented. Arendt saw the need for us to rethink our understanding of how individual moral awareness can be warped by a society-wide moral change and to realize that warping is possible only because of a certain superficiality to most people's moral character.

In other words, Eichmann retained the language of morality even while horribly misdirecting its aims.

In Arendt's view, Eichmann made the decision to continue shipping Jews to the death camps at the end of the war not because he was a demon, but because he believed himself to be doing his duty, which in his mind, went beyond mere obedience. In other words, Eichmann retained the language of morality even while horribly misdirecting its aims. Heinrich Himmler's 1943 speech to a group of SS leaders provides evidence for Arendt's view. Himmler assured his audience that despite what *they had gone through* in exterminating Jews, they had remained "decent" and had become "tough."

Arendt's point is that a society can experience not just a moral collapse but a kind of moral inversion, in which the form of morality—the language of duty, honor, conscience, right and wrong—is retained even as the content— the actual meaning of those terms—is utterly inverted. In her summary of what happened to morality in the Third Reich, Arendt says, "Evil in the Third Reich had lost the quality by which most people recognize it—the quality of temptation." In fact, Arendt suggests, temptation flipped its place in our moral experience of the world. The law told us to kill, so we began to experience the desire not to kill as a temptation, and temptations—from a moral standpoint—should always be resisted.

To call those who carried out the Holocaust demons is wrong because it both offers them an odd sort of compliment and provides us with a subtle form of consolation. It compliments participants by according them qualities of demonic magnificence that their characters do not evidence. And it consoles us by giving us a framework to comprehend figures like Eichmann, when in fact, that framework is shattered by the reality of who such people really were. The Holocaust was not just an example of people gone villainous;

it was, instead, a society lapsing into an insane form of moral stupor—the banality of evil. For Arendt, the Holocaust wasn't a conspiracy of satanic supermen; it was an essentially bureaucratic phenomenon, and this was the problem that wasn't addressed in the trial of Eichmann.

To call the totalitarian evil of the Nazi regime "banal" doesn't make it trivial; it brings to our attention the challenge of a new kind of evil in a world filled with totalitarian states—the kind of ordinary evil that Eichmann represented. Since the trial of Eichmann, history has shown that the lessons of Arendt have yet to be learned. ■

Name to Know

Arendt, Hannah (1906–1975 C.E.). Born to a Jewish family in Königsberg, the birthplace of Immanuel Kant. She studied philosophy with Martin Heidegger, with whom she had an affair, and Karl Jaspers.

Suggested Reading

Arendt, *The Origins of Totalitarianism*.

Browning, *Ordinary Men: Reserve Police Battalion 101 and the Final Solution in Poland*.

Questions to Consider

1. Arendt worried about the modern state's "totalitarian" demands and understood the threat of totalitarianism as the most important threat to human life in the modern world. Does totalitarianism continue to exist as the preeminent danger in our world, or have other dangers supplanted this one as the most significant threat to human flourishing?

2. Arendt's insights concerning the "banality of evil" in many ways echo earlier concerns over the camouflaged character of evil, though Arendt reformulates this worry in a distinctively modern way. Is our age, more than others, prone to camouflaging or overlooking evil through bureaucracy, duty, or avoidance? Is evil today truly banal?

Arendt—The Banality of Evil
Lecture 32—Transcript

Welcome back. In this lecture, I want to spend some time looking at the thought of Hannah Arendt, one of the most innovative and provocative political thinkers of the 20th century, and a person who gave us two concepts that are very important for thinking about evil in a political register, in its political dimensions, in the 20th and now the 21st centuries. These two concepts are, first of all, "totalitarianism," and second, "the banality of evil." We'll see that with these terms she has really set the terms literally of thinking about political evil, for better and worse, for all those who came after her.

Arendt's life is fantastic and rich, and I would urge you to read a biography of her life, it's really interesting. But generally, we can say this: She was herself both victim and theorist of the century's evils. Born in Germany in 1906, she was an astonishingly intelligent student, and studied with the philosophers Martin Heidegger and Karl Jaspers. She received her Ph.D. in 1929 at the age of 23—depressing for people like me—but then fled Nazi Germany for France in 1933, and finally reached America in 1941. She taught and wrote in America for the rest of her life, living in New York but travelling the world until she died in 1975. Arendt's thought in the period from 1945–1975, the last 30 years of her life, was really dedicated to making sense of the realities of the 20th century and the evil that riddled it. Her thought in these decades developed across the time she spent on it in an arc from totalitarianism to banality. Many think that these two concepts, for her, suggest two fundamentally opposed views of evil; but, in fact, I think that they cohere nicely together. The great and dangerous innovation of evil in the 20th century, on this reading of Arendt's work that I want to propose, is the capacity of states to make people who would never normally be capable of direct and massive cruelty to another person become actors who play quite significant roles in vast schemes of human annihilation. To see that, first I want to talk a bit about her first major work, *The Origins of Totalitarianism*, and then talk about her most controversial and probably famous book, *Eichmann in Jerusalem*. Let me start with *The Origins of Totalitarianism* first.

In this book, published in 1951, Arendt argued that modern totalitarian states like Nazi Germany and the Stalinist Soviet Union effectively embody a new kind of "radical evil." Particularly in the category of "totalitarianism" itself, Arendt thought she had identified a crucial political innovation of the modern world and named it for the monstrosity that it was. The totalitarian state is aptly named by her, because it demands the totality of all that is within its boundaries—the products of its citizens, the culture of its people, the very bodies and souls of its citizens, its own history—and it plans to do with all those things whatever it wishes. Control of the modern education, modern technology, modern media, modern industry, all these things; the totalitarian state wants control of everything, not simply for control's sake but actually in order to shape humans far more profoundly and directly than any political structure ever before ever could. Ultimately, Arendt thinks, this means the totalitarian state is set against human beings in their own idiosyncratic individuality; for humans are never so readily disposable as this totalitarianism state wants them to be. Human freedom, for her, can never be reduced to purely predictable-by-law behavior; in other words, it can never be properly understood in purely law-oriented terms. Because of that, totalitarianism has to be fundamentally hostile to human freedom; and because human freedom is essential to our understanding of human existence, Arendt thinks, this means that the totalitarian regime's project inevitably entails the destruction of the human's capacity to be not only a free actor, but to be a genuine human.

Humans are destroyed, she thinks, by the political system's relentless pressure on them, which creates instead of real humans, shells of human beings in their places. She famously says in the conclusion, the epilogue, to *The Origins of Totalitarianism*: "what totalitarian ideologies therefore aim at is not the transformation of the outside world ... but the transformation of human nature itself." This explains why, for her, she thinks it's important and useful to use the term "radical evil" to talk about totalitarian evil. Of course, this term hearkens back as you'll remember to Kant's discussion of "radical evil," especially in his *Religion within the Limits of Bare Reason*. For Kant, as you'll recall, radical evil is radical because it injects a principle of selfishness at the base of human agency, so that evil is finally a form of fundamental, radical selfishness for Kant.

That's not Arendt's views of the term "radical evil." For her, radical evil takes a more destructive and demonic form. It's radical because of its annihilating effects on political community and individuals. She says: The terrifying discovery, especially of the Second World War—this is one we'll come back to in a few lectures—is that "the psyche," the human individual, "can be destroyed" before their bodies are destroyed, and they can will their own annihilation in some important way; they can become, effectively, zombies. This is a reality that the 20th century has taught us in a far more profound way, she thinks, than any century before. The dark discovery of the 20th century is that humans are far more plastic than we heretofore imagined. People in a totalitarian state are turned into zombies, again, or robots that annihilate themselves and one another all in the interest of the abstract totalitarian state.

This was a remarkably controversial idea, and it gained a lot of traction in philosophy and politics in the years that came; but about 10 years after the first publications of *The Origins of Totalitarianism*, Arendt attended the trail of Adolf Eichmann in Jerusalem, an important German Holocaust agent, and she reported on it for the *New Yorker*. The articles that she wrote for the *New Yorker* became effectively the first draft of her most controversial book, *Eichmann in Jerusalem: A Report on the Banality of Evil*. What she saw in that trial, both in the way it was prosecuted and in the primary subject of the trial Eichmann himself, made her rethink—in some ways alter, in some ways deepen—much of what she had said 10 years before.

Eichmann is an interesting figure. He was, in many ways, the central bureaucrat of the Final Solution. Her story concerns Eichmann as an individual in the role he played, but also in what he suggests about the Holocaust as a whole. Of all the Nazi leadership caught and prosecuted after the war, Eichmann, she thinks, is in many ways the most interesting, if only because his case seems the most troubling for our received views of evil and wickedness. On many levels, Adolf Eichmann is a surprising figure to have risen so high in the Nazi hierarchy. He had been a vacuum oil salesman in the early 1930s, and then joined the Nazi Party and the SS in 1932 just before they took power, and began to ascend the ranks of the Nazis. If you'll recall Nietzsche's famous line: "Supposing truth were a woman, what then?" Here we can almost ask—Arendt almost explicitly asks— "Suppose evil is a vacuum oil salesman, what then?" In other words, if you think about how evil manifests itself in the 20th century, it doesn't manifest itself in Miltonic Satans; it manifests itself in these kinds of nebbishes, these figures like Eichmann.

Throughout the 1930s, his remarkable facility with bureaucratic matters and his unquestioning—literally unquestioning—devotion to work made him increasingly valuable. In 1942, he was given the job of "Transportation Administrator" for the Nazi genocide against the Jews, which put him in charge of managing a large part of the logistical bureaucracy of the Holocaust. He carried out his duties with relentless, unimaginative efficiency. His criminality as the central bureaucrat of the Final Solution would certainly be enough on its own to convict him of crimes against humanity, but his case is made more curious, and his soul seems all the more morally suspicious, because of a surprising event in the closing months of the war.

As it became clear that the war would be lost for the Nazis, Heinrich Himmler—Eichmann's superior and overall head of the SS—decided to stop shipping prisoners to the death camps. He ordered Eichmann to stop sending the trains there and keep the prisoners kind of as a bargaining chip for what Himmler hoped would be some kind of negotiated settlement with the Allies. Eichmann, however, disobeyed this direct order, and the trains kept running up to the end. Many thought that this showed Eichmann's utter savagery, his absolute evil; that even when Nazis like Himmler said, "Let's slow down on this," Eichmann said, "No, we've got to keep going." There's a lot of power to that idea, right? It makes sense. If Himmler says, "Don't kill Jews" and you keep killing Jews, there must be something really demonic about you, right? Arendt doesn't think so. Arendt says where once she had described totalitarian evil as "radical," now in the character of Adolf Eichmann she sees evil as "banal." In some sense, there was nothing demonic about him.

The story of Eichmann, though—and we'll explain why she thinks its "banal" in a second—is really just a frame that Arendt uses to hang her larger point on. She's worried about what the shape of the trial itself suggests; how, in fact, the trial is prosecuted, how Eichmann's case goes forward. The real question in the book, the one that took a little while for people to figure out she was asking, is simple but really quite disturbing: Do we have resources, she asks, in our ordinary moral vocabulary to help us to bring into view what the Holocaust really was and explain to us why it is justified to punish those who participated in it? She argues that no, in fact, importantly, we don't have quite all that we need; or rather, that we need to attend to the particularities of this experience in order better to be able to understand it, better to be able to judge those who did it, and—and this is very important for her—better to be able to respond to similar situations should they happen again. Arendt, that is, challenges the moral and legal concepts that organized the war crimes trials, and she argues that they need to be rethought. To judge the Holocaust on the old moral concepts of individual responsibility, personal integrity, individual intents she thinks, using these categories, is cowardly and dangerous and it avoids the really fundamental philosophical challenges that the Holocaust, the Shoah, presents to people today. She says in *Eichmann in Jerusalem*: "To fall back on an unequivocal voice of conscience"—suggesting that Eichmann had broken his conscience; he had violated his conscience in some sense, "not only begs the question, it signifies [this is really interesting] a deliberate refusal to take notice of the central moral, legal, and political phenomena of our century."

That's a devastating criticism. It sounds subdued; but to say that effectively these war crimes trials were deliberately designed—even if not consciously, she thinks—to avoid confronting the real challenges of the phenomena they tried to judge, that was what was so astounding, offensive, and insulting to many people about Arendt's assessment of the trial of Eichmann in Jerusalem. It sounded like she thought the prosecution was somehow wrong for judging him, and that was never her point. Her point, though, was that the prosecution's terms they used, the narrative they constructed of Eichmann, was flawed and allowed us to deflect our attention from what Eichmann really represented. There are two dimensions of these phenomena that Arendt wants us particularly to rethink: first, our understanding of how individual moral awareness can be warped by a society-wide moral change; and second, how that warping is itself possible only because of a certain superficiality to most people's moral character. Let me talk first about the question of the individual character's relationship to the larger social order, and this brings us back to Eichmann's decision to disobey Himmler's orders to stop shipping Jews to the camps.

Why did he do it? The obvious answer is in front of our faces, right? Surely he did it because he was a demon; because he was more evil, if it's possible to imagine, than the highest of the high Nazis. That's the prosecution's case: in some ways, Eichmann was more of a Nazi than the original Nazis. But that's not Arendt's point; she saw something else, something far more disquieting in Eichmann: Eichmann understood himself, first of all, not to be obeying orders but to be doing his duty, following the law. This is crucial, and Arendt built her argument around it. The language of morality in Eichmann's mind was retained even while its aims were horridly misdirected. There's an interesting moment in the trial, Arendt points out: Someone mentions Immanuel Kant and Eichmann happens to say, "Oh, yes, I've read Kant." One of the major bureaucrats of the Final Solution has read Kant and, in fact, he's read the *Critique of Practical Reason*, Kant's central ethical text. What's interesting about this—this is a classic German thing—is that Eichmann understood himself not simply to reject Kant, not at least at first, but instead alter Kant's view. He wants, he thinks—what he says—is to keep the intensity and the fervor of duty, of "doing one's duty," which goes beyond mere obedience. You do not only obey the law—whatever that law is—you must do so, if you are to be moral, with devotion to it.

This account of "doing one's duty" provides Arendt with an alternative account of why Eichmann sought until the end to carry out the transports to the camps. He did so not out of "fanaticism, his boundless hatred of Jews," in some sense, but out of duty; in Eichmann's own self-understanding, it was his conscience, Arendt thinks, that led him to do it. He thought it was his duty, under the law, to kill the Jews, and Himmler's order was illegal. That's an astonishing claim; but support for this view comes from a study of some of the things that Heinrich Himmler actually had said earlier in the war. There's an unbelievable speech—you can hear it on the web; you can hear Himmler's voice giving the speech—in Poznan, Poland, in 1943. He gave a speech to a group of SS leaders kind of at a conference of the SS ("The Holocaust: How It's Working So Far; What We Should Do from Here Out," something like that). The speech was one of the more remarkable events in the history of human morality. This is what he said in it:

> I want to tell you about a very grave matter in all frankness. We can talk about it quite openly here, but we must never talk about it publicly.

For all people who are Holocaust deniers, this speech is a devastating sign that, in fact, they're living in a fantasy world; because Himmler says here, "This is all something we can talk about here in secret, but we never want to admit it publically."

> I mean the evacuation of the Jews, the extermination of the Jewish people.

Think about this sentence: "

> Most of you will know what it means to see 100 corpses piled up, or 500 or 1000.

Imagine someone saying that: You know what this means; you know what it looks like. And then this; this is the abyssal sentence in some sense:

> To have gone through this [to have suffered this, he is saying to the SS officers who did it; who didn't suffer it, who did it] and, except for instances of human weakness, to have remained decent, that has made us tough. This is an unwritten, never to be written, glorious page of our history.

Think about that little excerpt there: What an unbelievable thing to say aloud; to form in your mind. There are many things to say about it; I won't have time for all of them, but one thing that's really interesting is that Himmler was right about one thing: There was enormous physical violence done to the people who perpetrated these crimes; their own bodies, in a way, revolted against them. Many of the people—many of the SS officers, the death camp guards, many of these people—suffered from ulcers, alcoholism, stress, and other bodily deformations; their very bodies revolted against the crimes that they committed. None of this is supposed to generate sympathy for the Nazis; but it's a sign of the monstrosity of their deeds that their very bodies rebelled against what they were doing. Arendt, then, is not arguing that the Nazis were morally well-formed agents; when Eichmann says he's doing his duty she has to believe him in some sense, but she's not saying she admires that or respects it, or that he understands his duty properly. What she is saying is that the Nazis in general, there were some sadists, some savage people—maybe a number of them—but they experienced their annihilationist practices as stemming from a command that seemed to them relevantly moral.

This is Arendt's crucial point: Arendt's point is that a society can experience not just a kind of moral collapse but a kind of moral inversion where the form of morality—the language of duty, honor, conscience, right and wrong—is retained even as the content, the actual meaning of those terms, is utterly inverted. We don't recognize this because we assume people do know somewhere deep down inside that they're bad; that they have a conscience that always tells them unerringly when they're right or when they're wrong. Perhaps, Arendt says, that's a mistake; perhaps when a moral transformation is broad enough and deep enough in a society—think about what a totalitarian state does to an entire nation—it is enormously difficult to resist this; not impossible for everybody, but difficult, so that almost everybody surrenders. As Arendt says, normally conscience motivates us to disobey orders only when they go against the law's normality. Normally, in our moral experience of the world, by and large morality and the law at least overlap significantly; there may be some tension, but normally what the culture as a whole says is right and wrong maps on pretty safely to what we think is right and wrong. But "in a criminal regime," she says, the "black flag" of conscience warning us that something is illegal "flies as manifestly above what normally is a lawful order—for instance, not to kill innocent people just because they happen to be Jews—as" that black flag "flies above a criminal order under normal circumstances"; I'm paraphrasing Arendt there. In other words, she says, in a criminal regime, the experience of when we are violating our conscience seems to map onto those situations that the law says are immoral even where the law itself is immoral; that is, those situations that the law lies to us about their immorality. In a criminal regime, the conscience tells us that morality itself is immoral.

Eichmann's experience, then, shows us what can happen when conscience exists within a framework of deep evil: We get not moral anarchy but moral inversion. Again, this is a passage from *Eichmann in Jerusalem*, one of the most devastating of passages, and her summary of what actually happened to morality in the Third Reich:

Just as the law in civilized countries assumes that the voice of conscience tells everybody "Thou shalt not kill," even though man's natural desires and inclinations may at times be murderous, so the law of Hitler's land demanded that the voice of conscience tell everybody: "Thou shalt kill," although the organizers of the massacres knew full well that murder is against the normal desires and inclinations of most people.

This is the important sentence:

Evil in the Third Reich had lost the quality by which most people recognize it—the quality of temptation.

Just think about that one sentence for a second. What she's saying is that in the Third Reich, evil no longer appeared to people as a temptation; it appeared to people as an order, an obligation, incumbent upon them from the law. She goes on: In fact, she suggests, temptation applied to goodness instead; it flipped its place in our moral experience of the world. The law told us to kill, so we began to experience the desire not to kill as a temptation; and temptations, we know morally, should always be resisted. So she goes on:

Many Germans and many Nazis, probably an overwhelming majority of them, must have been tempted not to murder, not to rob, not to let their neighbors go off to their doom [...], and not to become accomplices in all these crimes by benefiting from them. But, God knows, they had learned how to resist temptation.

In this context, Eichmann felt that the weight of morality, of respectable opinion, was all on the side of the Fuhrer's law, not Himmler's order. Therefore, Eichmann felt that Himmler's order was a temptation, Arendt is proposing, something he should not obey; not because he enjoyed killing Jews, but because he felt that he should always obey the law.

None of this is meant to exonerate or excuse anyone in Germany, least of all Eichmann; for after all, others in Germany in these years, even some on the front lines of the Holocaust, did know it was a tremendous evil and did try to fight it. But most didn't have that curious mix of strength of character and sheer dumb luck that enabled them to avoid it. Most of the people who participated in the Holocaust, though, were not devils. To call them "devils," for Arendt, is both offering them an odd sort of compliment and providing us with a subtle form of consolation. It compliments them because it suggests qualities of demonic magnificence that their actions do not evidence any character behind them of being. It consoles us because it means that we have a framework ready to comprehend who figures like Eichmann were and what he has done when, in fact, that framework is really shattered by the reality of what Eichmann really is. It seduces us into thinking that this is just another example of people gone villainous. But Arendt thinks that's not true; this is not about individual villains coordinating their work together. Instead, a society as whole went mad into a kind of moral stupor, and this is the term that Arendt characterizes as "the banality of evil," a term that because it is so common in our world we should seek to understand it.

The first thing to know about the banality of evil is that she doesn't think that every form of evil is banal; she wants to say that some kinds of evil—very important kinds—are banal. She thinks there are sadists, she thinks there are savage people, but that's not the issue; our normal morally categories can capture them. The problem is that we have a series of phenomena increasingly common in our world where individual villainy doesn't seem to capture the story. The Holocaust wasn't a conspiracy of satanic supermen, it was rather an essentially bureaucratic phenomenon, and it must be addressed as such. She thought that this was the problem, this is what wasn't addressed in the trial in Jerusalem: While the prosecution sought to portray Eichmann as a devil, he himself displayed none of the maliciousness attributed to him. He talked only in clichés, borrowed words and phrases from people who spoke to him and tried to just repeat what people said; he exhibited no ability to think on his own, nor any capacity for imagination. The disparity between the prosecution's portrayal of Eichmann as a kind of demonic villain and the uncomprehending, cliché-spouting, automatically unthinkingly mendacious idiot in the prisoner's dock was so great at times Arendt thought it threatened to turn the trial into a farce. The idea of attributing intention or motives to someone like Eichmann was almost out of place, she said. This is a classic line about Eichmann here; she says: "Except for an extraordinary diligence in looking out for his personal advancement, he had no motives at all … He merely, to put the matter colloquially, never realized what he was doing."

That's an interesting thought; how can the central bureaucrat of the Third Reich, of the Holocaust, of the Final Solution never realize what he's doing? A couple really interesting things to know about Eichmann: He only ever once saw the effects of massacre. Once, he was out in the field and he came across an "action," as they were called, where a bunch of people had just been shot and buried underground, and literally there was blood bubbling up from the ground. He described this in the trial and he said it made him very upset. The other instance is where one of the people, one of the Jewish council members he had been working with to organize the movement of the Jews, had been, from his perspective, accidentally picked up and taken to Auschwitz; and this guy got a note to Eichmann saying, "I'm in Auschwitz, can you help me?" So Eichmann—the only time he ever did—went to Auschwitz and he found this death camp prisoner and he said in the trail he put his arm around him and I said, "What a mess we've gotten ourselves into here!" Can you imagine this? An SS officer in Auschwitz going up to a person in the famous striped prisoner pajamas, putting his arm around him and saying, "Ja, my dear friend, how did this happen? This is terrible?" He couldn't get him out of Auschwitz, he said, that would have been against the rules—although Eichmann was the guy who ran the place; he was the boss of everybody—but he got the commandant to let this guy grate a gravel path. It turns out about six weeks later the guy was shot trying to escape anyway.

But think about the lack of reality Eichmann demonstrated in that event. Here he is in Auschwitz; he knows what goes on there, and he just won't even acknowledge it. He doesn't even realize, he doesn't seem to think of, anything that's actually before his eyes. That's what Arendt means. This is important; this suggests that calling totalitarian evil "banal" doesn't make it trivial. Arendt's point is not that Eichmann is an ordinary guy, that anyone would have done what he did; she simply claimed that Eichmann's evil doesn't require superhuman capacities on the one hand, or any kind of demonic-ness on the other.

Her claim is really that Eichmann's evil—his banality, his shallowness—is simply as deep as his evil could go. That's not to say that there aren't wicked people, again; but that the kind of evil we have to worry about politically in this world—the world filled with totalitarian states—is the kind of evil that Eichmann represents; that's the new challenge. We know about sadists, we know about tyrants; what we have to worry about now are bureaucrats. This suggests something of how she wants to condemn Eichmann as well; how she would write the trial. For her, the problem is not that Eichmann is a devil, a demonic person; the trial is not about his character, his soul; the problem is not who he is—at least that's not why he's on trial—he's on trial for what he did; he's on trial for his actions in the world and what they did to people in the world. The trial is a judicial and political act, not a moral assessment of Eichmann. She offers as moral assessment, but she wants to say that the judgment of the trail has to be about his actions; and the reason he needs to die—and she very clearly thinks that he needs to die, he needs to be hung—is precisely because of the actions he did, not because of the character he is.

Having said all that, let me wrap this up, because we'll see Arendt's thoughts coming back to us in future lectures. The lessons she offered are still yet to be learned. Many observers at the Yugoslavia War Crimes Trials in the Hague, trials of people implicated in the atrocities in the Balkans of all sides, many observers in the post-genocide Rwanda trials in Rwanda noted the incongruity of the prisoners' pre-war lives with their deeds; and many of the prosecution cases rely on trying to construct a prehistory of such people's sadism or cruelty. But often no such prehistory exists. The problem is, if we want to say that the reason that we can judge people as evil is because they are in some sense in their inner lives evil, we're going to misunderstand the character of modern political evil.

Arendt's study was a study done, in a way, from outside the experience of totalitarianism; but it's matched in certain ways by lessons from the inside as well, though here the work is presented by and large not as direct theoretical reflection, but instead as a series of literary reflections on the experiences of those who have suffered under totalitarian states. We'll see what to say about those things in the next lecture.

Life in Truth—20ᵗʰ-Century Poets on Evil
Lecture 33

That phrase—"*Hier is kein warum*," "Here is no why"—captures a certain kind of dimension of the death camps in a way that, for [Primo] Levi and for those who survived them, is essential to their experience, if not—if we can use the word—meaning.

The master genre of literary thinking about evil in the century or so before World War II was the novel, but since that time, more potent explorations of evil have been found in memoirs, essays, and lyric poetry. But such genres as these face two fundamental problems that complicate their success: the aesthetic problem that it is somehow improper to write poetry or seek beauty in the wake of the events of World War II and the more generic challenge of representation. How can the truth be told about such events when the reality of them seems to dwarf the human capacity to represent and comprehend the magnitude of what happened?

Paul Celan was a survivor of the Shoah who discounted the idea that the act of writing poetry after Auschwitz seemed somehow barbaric. In fact, Celan wrote poetry *about* Auschwitz and in German. For him, the point of poetry is to get at the truth of things, and if the truth is evil and suffering, even if it's in the voice of those who caused the suffering, it must be spoken. Perhaps the most powerful poetic representation of the Shoah is Celan's "*Todesfuge*," or "Death Fugue." Recall that a fugue is a musical piece that repeats itself cyclically before coming together in a resolution at the end. Celan's fugue, however, breaks apart at the end. The final stanza is composed almost entirely of fragments of earlier lines of the poem but now ominously enjambed and unable to communicate any coherent message. The experience of the camp, Celan suggests, is beyond time and beyond logic.

Czeslaw Milosz was a member of the Polish resistance army during the war and the cultural attaché for the new communist Polish government afterward. He later defected, lived in the United States for a time, and won the Nobel Prize for literature. Milosz believed strongly in the power of language to call our attention to facts and truths that we would rather not recognize. In such works as "A Poem for the End of the World" or "A Poor Christian Looks at the Ghetto," Milosz speaks with a profound directness about events taking place in front of his eyes.

In "A Poem for the End of the Century," Milosz seems to be troubled by the naivety of the postwar idea that evil has been vanquished. He suggests that his opinion is "a bit shameful," but he's compelled to think such thoughts and speak them by his own memories of suffering and death—both the suffering and death that he personally experienced and the suffering and death of Jesus. For Milosz, Jesus was both temporal and eternal, suggesting that the events of the 20th century spoke to something more perennial than just that time. Milosz says that at the heart of everything, perhaps, is a reality "of pain and also guilt / in the structure of the world." Given that, can we

> **[Zbigniew Herbert's] poems read like telegrams sent from some desperate city, fighting off an almost insuperable army.**

really believe that evil has been forever overcome? He ends the poem by saying that his concerns are "not for people" and that the postwar world is genuinely "blessed." The point seems to be that goodness is good in itself, even if not everyone can share in it.

In his poetry, Zbigniew Herbert is far more ironic, epigrammatic, and terse than his countryman Milosz. His poems read like telegrams sent from some desperate city, fighting off an almost insuperable army. Like Milosz, Herbert was a veteran of the Polish resistance army, and his poetry later became one of the inspirations for the Solidarity movement. Each word in Herbert's poems carries immense weight, but each also stands stripped of some essential ease about its meaning, lending his poems a sense of urgency. As he says in "The Envoy of Mr. Cogito," "you have little time you must give testimony." The overall impression of Herbert's poetry is one of ironic truth-telling against tremendous odds, offering us a powerful rhetoric by which to resist the attempt of the totalitarian state to lie to us constantly.

Probably Herbert's most directly relevant poem for us is one entitled "The Power of Taste." In it, he says that resisting totalitarian regimes "didn't require great character at all"; it required only taste. The ugliness of totalitarianism—"a home-brewed Mephisto in a Lenin jacket," "boys with potato faces"—could be resisted by someone with a proper sense of beauty. The ability to recognize beauty is a structure of the conscience that helps us sustain our moral stance in the world and, in the end, is the consummate way to resist evil. For Herbert, not to write poetry after Auschwitz would be to refuse to try to recover something of civilization and humanity in the wake of that horror. ■

Suggested Reading

Milosz, *The Captive Mind*, Zielonko, trans.

Weissbort, ed., *The Poetry of Survival: Post-War Poets of Central and Eastern Europe*.

Questions to Consider

1. In their own distinct ways, each of the authors in this lecture attempts to describe something of the nature of evil, yet each also suggests to us that the medium of poetry can help to illumine in ways that other kinds of words cannot. Does the medium matter when discussing the nature of evil? Are certain kinds of language (poetry or literature, for example) capable of revealing things that other mediums do not?

2. In what ways does the problem of evil reveal the limits of language? Can evil ever be adequately described or understood in human words?

Life in Truth—20th-Century Poets on Evil
Lecture 33—Transcript

Hello again. In this lecture, I want to talk about a series of Eastern European poets and some intellectuals as well in the way that they think about evil as a complement to what we've been talking about more theoretically with the work of Hannah Arendt and other philosophers and theologians.

If the master genre of literary thinking about evil in the century or so leading up to World War II was the novel—think about figures like Dostoevsky or Conrad; even a post-war figure like Camus, who has in some ways more to do with pre-war conceptions of how to think about evil—after World War II, the genre of the novel seems to be harder to sustain as a theoretical device, a generic device, to think about evil in. Novels capture large narrative forms and they offer large, kind of epic scopes for thinking about evil. A novel can make sense of a large social scene in that way. But since World War II, novels have seemed not as successful in capturing the human experience of evil. Instead, other genres—memoir, essay, and especially the genre of lyric poetry—have seemed more potent and offered more profound explorations of evil. But such genres as these face two fundamental problems that really complicate their success: one is an aesthetic problem, an aesthetic challenge; and one is a kind of more generic challenge about whether or not they can hear the truth they need to convey. Let me say something about both.

First, aesthetically: All poetry is haunted after World War II with the thought that it is somehow quite radically not just inadequate but actually improper to be writing poetry in the wake of these events. As the German thinker Theodor Adorno put it, a Marxist who had fled Nazi Germany, it may seem to us that "to write a poem after Auschwitz is barbaric"; that's his famous line, "to write poetry after Auschwitz is barbaric" (it's translated in different ways). Since World War II, in fact, there seems increasingly less and less confidence among many artists and intellectuals in general that beauty is something to be sought; that it's anything more than an escape from reality, a consolation for the true ugliness of reality. You may think I'm making too much of a few intellectuals, but I don't think I am; there are, in fact, powerful forces at work in our intellectual culture urging everybody to generate a kind of sheer ironic distance from all potential sources of inspiration in the world, and among those sources of inspiration, beauty is high on the list. Given that poetry is so much about beauty, poetry especially feels this challenge in profound ways.

Second, there's a second problem about the problem of representation itself; we saw some of this in Conrad. How can you actually tell the truth about what has happened? It seems at times that the realities can dwarf the human's imagination, its capacities to represent what has happened, to comprehend the full magnitude of it. In some ways here, irony is not the enemy; irony may be in some ways the ally. Consider the case of Primo Levi. He's a brilliant Italian chemist, and after the war a thinker and writer, who was also a survivor of Auschwitz. Here is the very first sentence of his memoir of survival from Auschwitz. In the American edition, it was translated *Survival in Auschwitz*, which sounds like a how-to guide; but in the original Italian and then in England, when it was translated into English in England, it was *If this be a Man*, because that's his question; is this human nature? This is the very first sentence:

> It was my good fortune to be deported to Auschwitz only in 1944, that is, after the German government had decided, owing to the growing scarcity of labor, to lengthen the average lifespan of the prisoners destined for elimination; it conceded noticeable improvements in the camp routine and temporarily suspended killings at the whim of individuals.

Think about that sentence; think about how it starts out. Unbelievable. "It was my good fortune to be deported to Auschwitz in 1944." Imagine the kind of irony of a sentence like that, and then, step back from it and imagine even more shockingly that Levi, in the rest of the sentence, unpacks how it's not ironic, how it's not sarcastic; how, in fact, the reality goes beyond irony because it was literally his good fortune that he was only sent to Auschwitz in 1944. When you see that, when you appreciate the magnitude of the irony in reality in a situation like that, you realize that irony is not only an optional source for thinking, it has to be concretely employed because reality is ironic already for us. So this tension between suspicion of beauty and endorsement of irony, and yet irony's corrosive effects on real beauty, this is a tension that all these artists, these poets and these thinkers, have to struggle with.

In this lecture, I want to look at three poets in particular who try to think about what it means toe experience evil in the 20ᵗʰ century and then what it means to try to resist it: First of all, Paul Celan, a survivor of the Shoah; second, Czeslaw Milosz; and third, Zbigniew Herbert. Milosz and Herbert are both Polish poets who were in the Polish resistance, though they did never end up in death camps. Let's start with Celan.

Celan lived from 1920–1970. He was a Romanian Jew who was picked up and sent to the death camps. He survived the Shoah, though his parents, who he deeply loved, did not. Eventually after the war he moved to Paris where he lived, growing increasingly known for his poetry; and yet over time, his post-war life, his survival of the death camps, became unendurable to him, and in 1970 he killed himself. As we saw, there is this famous line, "to write poetry after Auschwitz is audacious enough," it's barbaric, some people say; but what about writing poetry about Auschwitz? What about writing poetry about the death camps directly? And what about writing that poetry about the death camps in German? That's running straight into the wind. But that's just what Celan does, and he makes his case well: The deep point of poetry is getting at the deep truth of things, and if the deep truth is of evil and suffering, and is of evil and suffering in the voice of those who caused the evil and suffering as well as those who suffered it; even if the irony is too great for human minds to bear—and Celan excelled at offering a language in which irony could become too great for the human mind to bear—still, he thought, it must be spoken.

Perhaps the most powerful but still under-recognized, under-attended to, poetic representation of the Shoah, of the Holocaust, is Celan's own poem "Todesfuge," or "Death Fugue," which recounts one person's experience of the Holocaust, if you can call it that, although there's never an "I" in the poem, it's always a "we." This poem is unbelievably powerful and I would encourage everyone to try to read it. It's no more than a page or so, but it's visionary in its summary of the experience of the Holocaust.

A couple of elements in the poem are especially important, both for thinking about poetry and for thinking about Celan's approach to poetry. First of all, the poem starts with a couple very, very strange lines: "Black milk of daybreak we drink it at evening / we drink it at midday and morning we drink it at night." The collapse of the sequential character of human experience in the death camps is brought right to the fore there. First of all, bracketing the question of what the "black milk of daybreak" is; we drink this milk at evening, and then at midday, and then at morning, and then we drink it at night? For the inmates of these camps, as for the damned in Dante, there is no time anymore. There is no narrative structure to anything, just the endless deadly cyclical round of everyday, and eventually even the pieces of those days break apart. Remember, this is a fugue, it's a death fugue. A fugue is a musical piece that repeats itself cyclically in complicated ways before coming together in a resolution at the end. His fugue breaks apart at the end. As the poem comes to whatever conclusion it can manage, these words keep repeating, but the final stanza itself is composed almost entirely of fragments of earlier lines of the poem, but now enjambed together in ways that bear an ominousness but seem to resist communicating any coherent message. In a way, Celan is suggesting, the experience of the camp is outside of time, it's outside of history; and the collapse of narrative structure that the poem represents, the poem gives to you if you try to read it, it's not only beyond time in a way, but by being beyond time, by being beyond temporal structure, by being beyond storytelling it's beyond sense-making, it's beyond logic.

Here as well, a fantastic story from Primo Levi's *If This Be a Man* can be quite pertinent. Levy at one point, early in his time at Auschwitz, is doing something and he sees some guards, I think, hurting somebody else for what seems no reason to him, and he wonders what's going on and he asks them, "*Warum?*" "Why? Why is this happening?" The guard turns to him and strikes him very hard and knocks Levi down, and the guard says, "*Hier is kein warum!*" "Here, there is no why!" In other words, here, you don't get to ask these questions of why; for you, there is no reason for anything. Everything that happens, happens because of causes far beyond your understanding. Do not attempt to understand. That phrase *hier is kein warum*, here is no why, captures a certain kind of dimension of the death camps in a way that, for Levi and for those who survived them, is essential to their experience if not, if we can't use the word, meaning.

Secondly, about Celan's poem: In a complicated way, the inmates of the camp are implicated in the instruments of their own destruction just because the poem itself is in German. Famously this poem says, one of its lines repeated several times is, "der Tod ist ein Meister aus Deutschland"—that is, "Death is a Master from Germany"—and in the poem, the only named character is named Margarete and Shulamith. It's a non-Jewish name and then a Jewish name, a hybrid of German and Jew. The idea here seems to be that part of the trauma of this evil is that it is so deeply intimate to the inmate's own ordinary experience. There is some way that for Celan it mattered very much that his poetry was written in German about the experience of what happened to a people who were German, but also not German, not allowed to be German; who were going to be exterminated precisely because of their difference from what their exterminator saw as true "Germanness." Celan, that is, wants to think about how it is possible to go on being who you were before the death camps, if you were a German Jew, if you were from a family that spoke German; how it is possible to go on in some continuity from what happened before to what happens afterwards.

The analogy here is famously at the end of Elie Wiesel's *Night*. At the end of *Night*, Wiesel, for the first time in years—he survived Auschwitz—he looks at himself in the mirror and he sees a figure there that bears no resemblance to any understanding of himself, and that's the way that *Night* ends, if you have ever read the memoir *Night*. He says, "I looked into the eyes of someone entirely different from me, entirely strange to me." That moment is intention for Wiesel in the same way that Celan's use of German is intentional. How do you connect who you are, who you thought you are, with who you have become, what has happened to you? What kind of continuity is available to people after these events. That's a profound question, and Celan's use of German itself as a poetic language asks that question. But there's a terrible, stubborn—one can't say insistence—but a quiet pulse in Celan's writings; a pulse of something almost too weak to be called a "minority report" or a minor theme, but a faint quavering sense of hope, even if the hope is in some sense superhuman.

To move from Celan to Czeslaw Milosz is to move from someone who suffered from the Nazis as an inmate to someone who suffered from the Nazis as a subject and then also as a resistor to the Polish army. Milosz was born in 1911 and he only died in 2004. He was actually a secret resistor during the war, and then after the war he was initially the cultural attaché for the new communist Polish government in their Paris embassy. But as the government became more and more under the thumb of the Soviet Union, he became less and less enamored of it. He defects in 1951 and in 1953 he publishes his book *The Captive Mind*, one of the moral great works of the 20th century, of intellectual free thought in the 20th century, against his friends', his fellow intellectuals' romance, with communism and communist ideology, before the Second World War and then after the Second World War. He befriended Camus in Paris, and became a kind of marginal figure on the French scene precisely because he was an anti-communist when most of the French intellectuals, with Camus as an exception and a few others, were not anti-communist; Camus and the others were anti-communist, but the others were mostly communist.

He ended up emigrating to the U.S. in 1960. He taught at the University of California in Berkeley from 1961–1998, when he retired and went back to Poland. He won the Nobel Prize for literature. In contrast to Celan, Milosz's poetic voice developed before World War II and so was not forged in the crucible of that event, but it was profoundly shaped by it. But he never thought, in all of his poetry even to the end, that it was impossible to ask direct questions about reality using plain and straightforward language. In a way, he always believed in language's power—he was troubled in his belief, but he believed in its power—not so much to represent reality as a whole, but rather to call our attention to facts and truths we would rather not recognize, or at least rather not admit to ourselves that we know. In poems like "A Poem for the End of the World" or "A Poor Christian Looks at the Ghetto," a poem about the Warsaw ghetto in Warsaw in 1942, I believe, in the middle of World War II, in those poems he speaks with a profound directness, although a philosophical depth, about what's going on in front of his eyes. He retained a complicated, combative, disputatious faith in the Roman Catholicism of his youth, though he was always tempted by darker interpretations of reality than mainstream Roman Catholicism allowed. If von Balthazar is an optimistic Roman Catholic thinker, Milosz, insofar as he is a Roman Catholic thinker, is in some ways the opposite. But nonetheless, in the end, he found in the image of the crucified Christ—in God dying on the Cross—a powerful image through which to meditate on the mysteries of human providence, suffering, and iniquity in this world:

One poem in particular he wrote, called "A Poem for the End of The Century," written in 1991, has always, for me anyway, stuck with me as speaking of these themes with special clarity and intensity. As he says at the beginning of this poem, he writes it in a time of triumph, when, as he says, "the notion of sin had vanished." Those of us who remember the immediate post-Cold War years, there was a sense—you know, the famous book about the end of history—that somehow maybe things might be getting better now; maybe a certain kind of dramatic evil could not come back and haunt us again. Milosz finds, though, that he is troubled by the idea that evil has been vanquished; he thinks that that belief is naïve. But he suggests also that his belief is "shameful"—he says "shameful"—in this situation, but that he's compelled to think these thoughts and speak them, at least in the poem, by his own memories of suffering and death; not just the sufferings and death of those he knew personally in his life, though he knew both suffering and death and was well-acquainted with those who experienced both, but also with the suffering and death of Jesus Christ, a figure for Milosz who was both temporal and eternal, suggesting both that the events of the 20th century were events of that century, but also spoke to something more profound, something more perennial. He says that at the heart of everything perhaps is a reality "of pain and also guilt / in the structure of the world." Given that, he says, can we really believe evil has been forever overcome? (Remember his old friendship with Camus.)

He ends the poem, interestingly, by saying that his concerns, his thoughts, the dark brooding that he undertakes, "is not for people"; and he says the world now, after the end of the Cold War, is genuinely "blessed"—he says, "Blessed be harvests, vintages, and celebrations even if not everyone is granted serenity." It's a wonderful poem. It's a poem of someone from the 20th century thinking about what has happened in the century, and how at the end of the century somehow all of that experience seems to have been rendered lost, disconnected from the future in some way.

Think about what he says, though; he says this wonderful line: "This language is not for people." What does that mean? Not for others to hear? Not for humans in general? That he should try to unlearn the memories he's had? It's unclear what he actually wants to say there. And then consider the line, blessed be all these things, "Even if not everyone / Is granted serenity."

Goodness is good in itself, even if not everyone can share in it; even if some people's experience makes it impossible for them to appreciate it; even if the people whose own experiences of evil, suffering, and horror are the experiences that make it possible for other people to have the blessedness and the happiness they have. Their experiences of suffering and evil cannot be considered to count against the blessing and the joy of the people who experience the fruits of their suffering. For Milosz, that is, innocence is real, and it's a good thing. But innocence and experience coexist in the world, and there is no way, it seems—at least this poem suggests there's no way—for experience to help innocence learn what it doesn't know. All it can do is wait to see what happens. So Milosz helps us think about how we might be vexed in passing on the lessons gained by hard-won experience to those who do not have those experiences; and yet, the experience is there, and in no way is Milosz himself doubtful that it's true or important. In a way, the question is how that language—that language that is not for people—can be made suitable for people; and the answer to that question is precisely the body of Milosz's own poetry, for he wrote to show that a language of real horror, real suffering could be glimpsed and appreciated by those blessedly ignorant of those phenomena at first-hand.

To turn from Milosz to his countryman Zbigniew Herbert is to turn from someone with a romantic and philosophical expansiveness in his poetry to someone far more ironic, epigrammatic, and terse. Reading Herbert's poetry, it feels as if these poems were really telegrams sent from some desperate city fighting off an almost insuperable army; and, in fact, one of his greatest books, and one of his greatest poems, is entitled *Report from the Besieged City*. Herbert was born in 1924, and he died in 1998. Like Milosz, he was a veteran of the Polish Resistance Army against the Nazis, but unlike Milosz he spent most of the rest of his life in communist Poland, not as a supporter of the regime but as a resistor and a dissident. Never a favorite of the Communists, for a while he was actually completely suppressed and unpublished. At one point he was reduced to having to donate his own blood to get a little money; for six months, the only work he could do was donating pints of blood to get money. Nonetheless, he persevered in his writings and his convictions, and by the 1980s his poetry was one of the main inspirations for the resistance movement Solidarity; in fact, his poem "The Envoy of Mr. Cogito" is considered by many Poles the anthem of Solidarity itself.

Herbert's poetry is profoundly curtailed, terse; each word carrying immense weight but each one also standing stripped of some essential ease about its meaning so that the sense of urgency from line to line in his poems is tremendous. As he says in "The Envoy of Mr. Cogito": "you have little time you must give testimony"; the sense of the need to get going on sharing these thoughts with people, and yet the obscurity of what the thoughts are that are to be shared is very important to him. His poetry completely lacks punctuation; there are no commas, no periods, no semicolons, none of that. This lack of punctuation increases their sense of desperate urgency, but also strips them of one aid for comprehending their full meaning, so that we have the experience in reading him of something momentous being pressed on us violently, but also vaguely, as if the poems seem to have suffered some kind of grammatical trauma; these poems have stumbled out of a terrible plane crash that there were lucky to keep their own skin from. In general, the overall impression of Herbert's poetry is one of ironic truth-telling against tremendous odds, offering us—and this is, I think, his really important thing—one powerful rhetoric by which to resist the attempt of the totalitarian state to lie to us constantly.

For our purposes, probably his most directly relevant poem is one entitled "The Power of Taste." In that poem, he says that resisting totalitarian regimes (as he did) " didn't require great character at all," it only required taste, he said; taste, an aesthetic sense, that the terrors of totalitarianism were pressed home in so ugly a form that they could be resisted. He describes them as "a home-brewed Mephisto in a Lenin jacket"; "boys with potato faces"; rhetoric that was "made of cheap sacking." In other words, he thinks, it was the ugliness of totalitarianism that someone with a proper sense of beauty could, in fact, resist. In taste, then, he thinks, "there are fibers of soul the cartilage of conscience" (that's a line of his). It's an interesting claim: that in some ways, in our ability to know what beauty is, we seem some kind of stiffness—cartilage, not bone; not totally rigid, but some kind of structure of the conscience—that helps us sustain our larger moral stance in the world. Knowing what beauty is, is connected, he thinks, to knowing what ethics is. And so, he argues, in confronting political dangers or forces that would demand your obedience, Herbert says, "Before we declare our consent we must carefully examine / the shape of the architecture the rhythm of the drums and pipes."

Here the idea is that poetry, and aesthetic work more generally, is not simply one way that such evil may be described and then resisted, it is in fact for Herbert the consummate way to resist such evil; to fight against the fundamental ugliness of totalitarianism just is to fight against its most profound instrument of darkness. If that is true, then Herbert actually has a charge, a response to Adorno's charge—Adorno's charge that to write poetry after Auschwitz is barbaric—and his response is: No, no, no; it is not to write poetry after Auschwitz that is barbaric. That would be to refuse to attempt to recover something of the civilization and the humanity—not that those two are the same things for Herbert; he's not that foolish—in the wake of these horrors.

Let's conclude on this. The visions of evil that these poets represent are diverse, but in each case the experience of the subject before the challenge of evil is directly thematized and explored. For Celan, the problem was how to represent an evil that broke apart normal human experience itself. For Milosz, the problem was how to attempt to communicate such untimely thoughts in a time of universal utopia and happiness. For Herbert, the challenge is to make plausible the idea that totalitarian evil's great vulnerability—one of its great vulnerabilities anyway—is precisely its ugliness, and that the work of poetry and of beauty just is the work of resisting those evils.

Given those insights, what can we do? What about positive guidance? What advice or lessons did these poets have for us? Much of that depends on which one you ask, of course. Milosz and Herbert in particular seem to point to the possibility that life in Totalitarian societies, outside of death camps, can teach us some new insight into the nature of evil in our world; and in this their lessons are fleshed out and unpacked a bit by their less poetic, but no less deep thinking, fellow intellectuals: people like Adam Michnik in Poland, Gyorgi Konrad in Hungary, Václav Havel in Czechoslovakia (these are the great leaders of the Eastern European resistance against totalitarianism). These thinkers diagnosed their situation in terms that oftentimes drew from, and always resonated with, these poets and thinkers like Arendt: They all saw the basic problem they faced as how to live an honest life when the whole world around you wants to live in a lie. As Havel put it, the power of ideology is the way it convinces people that reality is as the ideology, the totalitarian state, says it is; but it does so through terror and the threat of terror, which eventually convinces all of us to live in this lie.

For thinkers like Havel, Konrad, and Michnik, we must instead live "in the truth," and this will eventuate in a certain kind of rival life against the totalitarian state, the creation of cells of resistance within this state. This rival community survives not by a mass movement, not by any kind of large-scale structures or sheer force, but rather by expressing and sharing a certain quality of truth-telling. This truth-telling couldn't be denied or annihilated, not exactly, by ideology; all it could try to do was compel us not to believe in it. But if it were denied—as by the authorities it so often was denied—still, even in the effort to deny it, the truth called attention to itself and some people would notice. That was why, amidst all the sordidness of the 20th century, the world was so blessed to have a number of these resistance movements that finally were able to show the crucial weakness of totalitarianism and its crucial vulnerability simply to the sheer fact of telling the truth.

In the next lecture, I do want to move to another genre, another approach, altogether: I want to think now not so much about poets and writers and intellectuals and artists, but now about a series of scientists and their own recent troubling discoveries about our propensities towards something that looks a lot like evil.

Science and the Empirical Study of Evil
Lecture 34

The [Good Samaritan] study uses the biblical story perhaps most profoundly anathema to its findings as a core component of its experiment—it's almost as if these psychologists were guided by Satan or something. It's just such a perfect example of why exactly the Good Samaritan story needs to be still listened to by many Christians.

Since World War II, social scientists have developed various experiments to attempt to measure the human's tendencies toward blind obedience or willful engagement in inflicting cruelty on others. In this lecture, we'll look at three such experiments: the famous Milgram experiments on obedience to authority, Philip Zimbardo's notorious Stanford prison experiment, and the disturbing series of Good Samaritan studies run at Princeton Theological Seminary.

In 1961, Stanley Milgram, a psychologist at Yale University, conducted a series of experiments designed to highlight the power of authority. Subjects were recruited to administer a series of electric shocks of escalating voltage to victims strapped to a chair in another room, out of sight but not out of hearing. As the subjects thought they were giving the victims increasingly powerful shocks, a tape recorder in the other room played a series of desperate cries while an actor banged on a wall, then fell ominously silent as the shocks rose above a certain level. Ultimately, the subjects were directed to give three 450-volt shocks in succession to the now-silent victim.

In Milgram's first set of experiments, 65 percent of participants delivered the final series of shocks, though many were very uncomfortable doing so. At some point, every participant paused and questioned the experiment. Only 1 participant out of 40 steadfastly refused to administer shocks above the 300-volt level. Later studies showed that roughly two-thirds of all participants inflicted what they thought to be fatal voltages under orders from the experimenter. Although Milgram's experiment is contested, it points to a disquieting aspect of the behavior of ordinary people in modern industrial society.

Another psychology professor, Philip Zimbardo of Stanford, explored humans' tendencies toward brutality in the Stanford prison experiment. Here, 21 undergraduates deemed psychologically stable were chosen to act as guards and prisoners in a mock prison. The guards were given uniforms, mirrored sunglasses, and wooden batons, meant to be worn only to signify that they were guards. The prisoners were given ill-fitting smocks and stocking caps, were called by assigned numbers, and wore chains around their ankles. All participants understood that they were taking part in an experiment.

The prisoners were "arrested" at their homes, then brought to the mock prison, where the guards quickly lived into their roles to a much greater degree than was anticipated. From the first day, they enjoyed demonstrating their status to the prisoners and, by the end of the experiment, roughly one-third of them showed clear sadistic tendencies; that is, they clearly enjoyed inflicting pain and got pleasure from the infliction of pain itself, no matter that it led to other benefits for them.

Zimbardo and others have argued that the experiment suggests not a "lord of the flies" mentality among humans but the malleability of the human personality, that is, how readily we inhabit a role when we are provided with a rationale for it and a suitable set of surrounding social structures. Zimbardo and his

Dover Pictorial Archive Series.

Studies, including those based on the Good Samaritan parable, have drawn some scientists to the situational attribution theory, which says people are much more determined by their surrounding context than their innate character.

team believed the experiment revealed that people are inherently creatures of context, even if that context is temporary and, perhaps, implausible.

Zimbardo's experiment showed how easy it is for humans to slip into the grip of sadism; equally troubling, the Good Samaritan studies, conducted by John Darley and Daniel Batson at Princeton University, showed how easy it is for people to be lured away from goodness by even trivial circumstances. These studies involved groups of seminary students asked to give a talk either about the parable of the Good Samaritan or about job opportunities in a seminary. Some were told that they had to hurry across campus to give the talk, while others were not told to hurry. On the way to the lecture site, all the students passed by a person slumped in an alleyway, obviously in need of help. As you might guess, the depressing conclusion was that the students who had been studying the Good Samaritan story did not stop any more often than the ones preparing for a speech on job opportunities. If they were in a hurry, only about 10 percent would stop to give aid, even when they were on their way to deliver a sermon about the Good Samaritan.

All these studies point to the conclusions of situational attribution theory, according to which people's behavior is more determined by their surrounding context than their innate character. Character, as an innate moral quality we possess, is not so important as we might think; perhaps it's not even real. However, it's also true that in the right context, people can be better than we anticipate; they can possibly find the resources within themselves to be moral. Perhaps in coming decades, psychologists will find ways to explore how people can learn to help one another and to resist evil. ■

Suggested Reading

Milgram, *Obedience to Authority*.

1. Modern experimentation has suggested that context is key in guiding human behavior, toward both good and evil acts. How might this suggestion change our conception of the relation between evil and human character? Is context the key to improving an evil character or corrupting a good one?

2. What is the usefulness of science in understanding evil? Can science play a role in helping us to combat or control evil, or is evil something that lies somehow beyond the realm of science?

Science and the Empirical Study of Evil
Lecture 34—Transcript

Welcome back. In this lecture, I want to turn from the thinking of philosophers and theologians, and the poetry and prose of writers to consider several disturbing experiments that psychologists have performed in recent decades that suggest a set of disquieting insights about human nature and its susceptibility to what we want to call "evil."

Can evil be understood, can it be studied in a scientific manner in the way that we study plants or rats or neutrons or atoms? People have tried to do this for some time. But since World War II, this pressure has become greater because of worries that many have—we saw this most prominently formulated by the thinker Hannah Arendt—that the evils of the 20th century are in some sense unprecedented and need new thinking, not just the repetition of old traditional ways of thinking, but genuinely new thinking to figure out what evil is in its essence and what to do about its challenge. And so, since World War II—and in some ways prompted by the events of World War II—a number of social scientists, and especially social psychologists, have begun to develop experiments; experiments that are sometimes of questionable moral status themselves (we'll hear about that in a minute), but experiments that attempt to get at measuring the human's tendencies towards blind obedience or willful engagement sometimes in inflicting cruelty and suffering on other humans. Just as an interesting side note, it's worth nothing that there have actually been significantly fewer studies from the opposite side, from the side of victims, what it is like to be a victim in these situations. Why that is, I won't speculate here.

I have very good friends in the social sciences who are involved in this work. I think that sometimes they are a bit too confident about their findings—both in terms of the lessons they take away from them and the novelty that they ascribe to those lessons—but nonetheless these studies, these experiments, are really quite revealing and not as well known as I think they should be. Most generally, these studies suggest that, in a way that few philosophers and theologians have seemed fully to appreciate, who you are and how you behave is significantly dependent on where you are, on your context, on your setting. People's character is, in other words, interestingly and significantly context-specific. If you are in a setting where conditions are conducive to being a good person, you are more likely to be a good person; if you are in a setting where that is not the case, the opposite outcome can be anticipated.

As I said, these are interesting and thought-provoking experiments; and I suspect we'll have more of them in coming years. One of the most burgeoning fields in psychology right now a field called "positive psychology"; that is, a study of not so much how humans go wrong, as psychology is traditionally been in the 20th century anyways—a study of human pathologies—positive psychology wants to study: What are the conditions that make humans go right? Whether on the negative or the positive side these psychological studies will actually answer conclusively any of the questions we have been asking, and the questions that we actually want answers to about evil, wickedness, and cruelty, is another question; but nonetheless, I think these are very interesting and important studies.

In this lecture, I want to look at three experiments in particular, each of which has troubled those who engaged in them and those who reflect on them in important and profound ways. In wide-ranging discussions of thinking about evil, these experiments come up again and again, and so it's worth your while to hear about them and to consider their implications. They are: the famous Milgram experiments on obedience to authority; Philip Zimbardo's notorious "Stanford Prison Experiment"; and the disturbing series of "Good Samaritan" studies run at Princeton Theological Seminary.

First, consider the famous "Milgram Experiment." Stanley Milgram, a psychologist at Yale University, began in 1961 a series of experiments that were prompted by his reflections on the trial of Adolf Eichmann, the same trial that Arendt reported on. His question was: Were those who perpetrated the Holocaust individually motivated to do so, or were they really, as many of them said, "just following orders"? I don't want to confuse the arguments of Arendt and Milgram here, so don't think that they're saying the same thing; consider each of the arguments separately. Here, let's just focus on Milgram. The experiment he designed was designed to highlight the power of authority for humans by showing the power that concrete authorities could have over ordinary people. People were recruited in these studies, unknowingly, for the experiment in which they were ordered by an experimenter—dressed as a scientist in a white coat—to inflict a series of electric shocks of escalating, and finally clearly deadly, voltage upon a victim strapped to a chair in another room, out of sight but not, unfortunately for the subjects, out of hearing.

As the subjects thought they were giving the victims increasingly more powerful shocks, a tape recorder in the other room played a series of increasingly desperate cries while an actor banged on a wall, then fell ominously silent as the shock levels rose above a certain level. Throughout the screams, some subjects exhibited clear signs of what psychologists call "dissonance"—nervous laughter, sweating, shaking—but reliably when asked they would continue and they would escalate the pain. At the point where the victim stopped making any noise, many subjects asked to stop and see if the victim was ok. But the "scientist" induced them to keep going with a series of four increasingly stern commands to continue, culminating in the final verbal command if they kept saying, "Will you check on this person?" The final thing they would say is, "You have no other choice; you must go on." If they still wanted to stop after the fourth command, the experiment would stop; otherwise they continued giving these shocks until they had given three 450-volt shocks in succession to the now-silent victim, at which point the experiment was considered complete.

In Milgram's first set of experiments, fully 65 percent of the participants delivered these experiments' final series of shocks, though many were very uncomfortable doing so. Remember, this is an experiment, there are no real people being shocked here; no one is actually being hurt. There's a tape recorder, there are actors banging on the walls; this is all fabricated by Milgram, though the subjects don't know it's being fabricated. At some point, every participant in the experiment, every subject, paused and questioned the experiment. Some said they would refund the money, they'd give it back (they were paid for participating in the experiment). Interestingly, though, only 1 participant out of 40 steadfastly refused to administer shocks at the 300-volt level or above, at which point it was unmissably clear that the shocks were profoundly painful, agonizing, for the subjects involved.

A later study of the Milgram experiment and similar experiments that were carried out like the Milgram experiment, that were carried out in future years, found that, across all of the experiments summed up and averaged, the percentage of participants who are prepared to inflict under orders fatal voltages remained remarkably constant at roughly two-thirds of all participants. Here we actually have some numbers, some relatively disquieting numbers, to put on the propensity of humans to be wicked. Milgram's experiment is enormously contested, but in this way it seems very important that we pay attention to it: for what it shows is that ordinary people in modern industrial society—at least as ordinary as college undergraduates can be; and that's one of the challenges to Milgram: whether or not the test subjects he was working with are actually a reliable body to generalize across the society—but given the range of subjects and the range of experiments that were carried on in the years following Milgram's pioneering experiments, to find again and again that roughly two-thirds of participants in all of these experiments are willing to obey the orders of the experimenter, the scientist, and cause unbearable, quite literally unbearable, pain they think to people who are suffering in a room a little bit away from them is an astonishing, and I would say extremely interesting and disquieting, fact about human nature.

Milgram's study was famous for talking about obedience to authority; but was there another way of thinking about human wickedness, one that talked more about humans' tendencies to become willingly quite brutal. Another psychology professor, Philip Zimbardo of Stanford—who actually was a high school classmate of Milgram's, by the way—thought that he could explore this phenomenon as well. Zimbardo undertook what came to be known as the famous "Stanford Prison Experiment." In 1971, Zimbardo ran this experiment and had findings interestingly consonant with Milgram's. He and his team picked 21 Stanford undergraduates whom they deemed the most psychologically stable and healthy of the group that they had assembled from more than 75 that they had initially assembled, and these people were put in distinct roles, they played distinct roles, in a mock "prison" built in the basement of the Stanford psychology building. Some were called prisoners, others were called guards, and the selection process between these two groups was random. The guards were given weapons, they were given clothes, mirrored sunglasses, and wooden batons not to be used in violent ways—the batons were not to be used to beat anybody—but merely to be worn to signify that they were guards. The prisoners were given ill-fitting smocks and stocking caps that rendered them constantly uncomfortable. They were called by assigned numbers, sewn on their uniforms, instead of by their names. A chain around their ankles reminded them that they were, in fact, the prisoners in this experiment.

From the beginning, everybody knew this was a psychology experiment, a study, hypothetical; this wasn't meant to be the real thing. The participants chosen to play the part of prisoners were then "arrested" at their homes and "charged" with armed robbery. The local Palo Alto police department helped by making the arrests and conducting full booking procedures on the prisoners, including fingerprinting them and taking mug shots; if any of you have done any experimentation in the social sciences in the past couple decades, you'll realize that this was truly another era. The degree to which the psychology experiment was run entirely on its own irrespective of any standards of conduct or anything like that is really amazing, and it's caused a great deal of criticism for Zimbardo; but nonetheless, I think the findings of his project still stand.

At the police station—once they were there; once they had been photographed and fingerprinted—they were transported to the mock prison, where they were strip-searched and given their new identities. Things quickly got out of hand. The guards clearly so to speak "lived into" their roles more than was anticipated, and from the beginning they enjoyed demonstrating their status to the prisoners. On day two of the experiment, the prisoners revolted, and the guards, acting entirely on their own, used fire extinguishers to scuttle the revolt. As the days grew on, the guards grew increasingly sadistic, humiliating the prisoners whenever possible. Roughly one-third of the guards showed clear sadistic tendencies as psychologically defined; that is, they clearly and demonstrably enjoyed inflicting pain and getting pleasure from the infliction of pain itself, no matter that the pain infliction led to other benefits for them, such as increased power over the inmates, getting to do what they wanted, whatever. It was clear that these guards enjoyed the infliction of pain itself, not its benefits pragmatically for them.

For a second here, just think about that: Zimbardo chooses these people precisely because they are the most stable of the people he's assembled, the 75 people; and these are Stanford undergrads, these are pretty emotionally well put together people. Even in the early 1970s, Stanford's still a pretty good school. These are some pretty well-disciplined, well-organized human beings; and a third of them, probably much to their own surprise after the experiment's over, discover that they actually enjoy inflicting pain. That's a thought to ponder.

On the third day of the experiment, the prison was moved, as the guards began to worry that a prisoner released on the second day because he was clearly undergoing psychological stress would come back to break up the "prison," no longer, for those on the inside, both prisoners and guards, merely considered an experiment. The experiment got ever more brutal. Finally, on the sixth day, an external observer—a grad student brought in to interview subjects—was so troubled by the conditions and the behavior that she witnessed that she demanded that the experiment be stopped.

Zimbardo and others have argued that the experiment suggests not a kind of "lord of the flies" mentality among humans, but rather instead how malleable human personality is; how readily we inhabit a role when we are provided with a kind of rationale for it and a suitable set of surrounding social structures in our immediate surroundings that allow us to inhabit this role properly. Note how unimportant the ultimately "fictional" character of the experiment was to the participants. Every one of them knew from the beginning that this was entirely a psychological experiment; it was a camp, it was a study, it was something with a finite beginning and a finite ending. The crucial thing, though, it turned out for everybody—guards and prisoners alike—was that there were immediate "props" around the world that could sustain the illusion from moment to moment that this was a real situation. The guards, once they put on their uniforms, their sunglasses, and held their batons, began to really live into that role in astonishing ways. The prisoners, once they had been picked up by the police and transported to the prison, clearly felt like they were in some sense prisoners. Zimbardo and his team thought that this suggested—maybe evidenced quite conclusively for them—that people are inherently creatures of context, and the context doesn't have to be in place for all that long; doesn't even have to be all that enduring, or stable, or even ultimately plausible for us to have it be sufficiently powerful in order to organize our behavior by means of it. Even a make believe context, as children will play, turns out to have all the reality we need to become, for fully one-third of us, one-third of the most stable of us, to become sadists.

Zimbardo's experiment was controversial for a number of reasons, and Doctor Zimbardo himself is has never been a slouch at self-promotion; but it's self-promotion, I think, for a very good cause. His studies, especially the prison experiment, show how easy it is for humans to slip into the grip of domination and sadism. What's equally troubling, though, is other studies that suggest how un-easy, how difficult, people find it to be kind at times; how easy it is for people to be lured away from goodness, or even decency, by circumstances that seem trivial at best. That is the perhaps depressing lesson of the so-called "Good Samaritan" studies, the third set of studies I want to look at in this lecture. Let's turn to those now.

John Darley and Daniel Batson were two psychologists at Princeton University, and they decided to run a study to figure out when people would help other people. They took as their subjects a group of seminary students, assuming that people who were in seminary—they hadn't been drafted into seminary; they wanted to go there—they felt some kind of vocation to care for other people in some sense. Half the students were given the parable of the Good Samaritan, asked to read it, and then told to go to another building across campus and give a sermon about that parable. The other half were asked to give a sermon about job opportunities in a seminary. So there are two sets of people: one set given the parable of the Good Samaritan and told to give a sermon; another told to give another kind of sermon that's maybe a little more self-interested. Some of each group were told they had to hurry to give their sermon; others in each group were not told that. So you actually had four different sets of people: the hurrying Good Samaritans, the not-hurrying Good Samaritans, the hurrying business opportunities or job opportunities in the seminary, and the not-hurrying job opportunities in the seminary. On the way to the building where they would each give the sermons, subjects passed by a person slumped in an alleyway; possibly the victim of a violent attack, but in any event, someone who looked to be in need of real help. It was ensured that the people going on the way to give the sermon were each able to see and perceive and apprehend what was going on with this person; they couldn't just walk by unseeing, they saw what was going on. The question that the psychologist asked was: Would these people stop to help the person?

As you might guess, the depressing conclusion was that the people who had been studying the Good Samaritan story did not stop any more often than the ones preparing for a speech on job opportunities. The factor that really seemed to make a difference was how much of a hurry the students were in. If they were in a hurry, only about 10 percent would stop to give aid, even when they were on their way to deliver a sermon about the Good Samaritan; that is, a story about how all the people should stop and give aid. The ironies of this experiment are manifold. Most profound is the fact that the study uses the Biblical story perhaps most profoundly anathema to its findings as a core component of its experiment; it's almost as if these psychologists were guided by Satan or something, it's just such a perfect example of why exactly the Good Samaritan story needs to be still listened to by many Christians. For what does the Good Samaritan story tell you but that context should never matter?

After all, in the story of the Good Samaritans, the point of the story is that the Samaritan—the person who does stop and help the person on the side of the road—were considered outcasts in the Judaism of Jesus's Palestinian world. People thought that Samaritans were unlikely to be moral in any situation, much less in a situation dealing with a victimized stranger. The closest stereotype in the modern world would be the way that gypsies were stereotyped a hundred years ago; a Samaritan would be more likely to rob the beaten and bleeding victim again than to help him; that would be the expectation. So Jesus's parable tells you that what matters is not the outward appearance of the person—the priest and the Levite in the story pass the victim by, though they have all the outward trappings of those who should help—instead the story is supposed to say that it is the despised Samaritan who helps because he's good on the inside, as it were; because the Samaritan is, in some sense, a person whose inner character is so strong as to make him stop. What the psychologists found out, though, is that hardly anybody actually operates under those assumptions. Ten percent of the people who listened to the story of the Good Samaritan but were in a hurry stopped to help.

The lesson we can draw from all of these stories, the scientists say, is a lesson contained in what they call the "situational attribution" theory. This theory says that people are much more determined by their surrounding context than their innate character. Situations cause behavior; behavior, character, does not drive situations. That's the idea. This fact, for the psychologists, entails good news and bad news. Bad news first: The bad news is that "character," as an innate moral quality we possess, is not so important as we might think; perhaps it's not actually even real. Perhaps we are always just a step or two away from indifference, obedience for cruelty, or outright sadism. On the other hand, there is in some ways some good news about this story: In the right context, given the right circumstances, people can be better than we anticipate. People are possibly going to be able to find resources within themselves if they're in a context, or if they have the time, to let themselves be moral. This is a sign of some hope.

Is either of these points really "news?" That is, someone might say to the psychologist, don't we already know these insights from the history we've been studying all along? Don't we know from Arendt that people will obey mindless? Don't we know that many people will turn out to be sadists even if we don't see them being sadists in ordinary life? Don't we know that most of us don't care? The point of the Good Samaritan story is that everyone should care, but the fact that the story is there suggests that Jesus thought it was important for people to know that many of them didn't care, and that they should. In other words, whether or not the novelty of these experiments is as novel as they thought it was is an open question. But I still think, even if you don't think they're all that novel—I think they're pretty novel, I think they're pretty interesting; even if you don't think that—they're still profoundly interesting and sobering studies. In different ways, they seem to suggest that, in fact, these are not just hypothetical situations where people might become wicked; we have some confirmable evidence outside of the actual reality of history itself but in somewhat more controlled experimental environments of what actually could happen to people. I would hope that in coming decades psychologists, maybe especially in the positive psychology movement, may find ways to explore how people can learn to help each other or to resist such evils as well. But this set of very depressing experiments is at least a good start.

Next, we're going to return to our track of asking about the way that thinkers have dealt not so scientifically but more in terms of journalism and thinking, philosophy and religion, with the history of evil since the Shoah in the litany of genocides and atrocities that we've seen happen in the world since 1945.

The "Unnaming" of Evil
Lecture 35

> After 9/11, ... we seemed forced to choose between either a language
> of evil that provides a kind of inadvertent metaphysical compliment
> to bad people by calling them "evil" (in a way that makes Osama bin
> Laden sound like Darth Vader) or a language of intelligible or at least
> explainable motivations that forbids [us] from talking about bad people
> as bad, ... but just misunderstood.

A general theme for these lectures, especially the ones covering the 20th century, has been a deepening sense of the disparity between our thinking about evil, historically and today, and the realities that that thinking is meant to represent and help us respond to. From Joseph Conrad to Freud to Hannah Arendt, we've seen a growing unease in these lectures about our capacity to grasp and communicate the reality of evil. It's also true that this is, in some ways, an old theme, stretching back to the *Epic of Gilgamesh* and Genesis. Nonetheless, contemporary thinkers seem to be explicitly concerned with whether or not our power has outstripped our wisdom.

The philosopher Michel Foucault said, "For centuries, humanity had been what Aristotle had said we were: a natural animal with a political situation that it had to work out. But now we are an animal whose politics put our very natural survival into question." That fact is new in the past century or so and gives rise to a cluster of anxieties: about genocide, scientific and technological developments, and the changing nature of culture and society in general. The question we face today is whether our new situation is really amenable to treatment and understanding by the traditional resources we use to understand and respond to evil.

One dimension of this question is seen in the concerns of scientists, from those associated with the Manhattan Project forward. J. Robert Oppenheimer, technical director of the Manhattan Project, made an exemplary statement about science struggling with its moral implications in the wake of World War II: "In some sort of crude sense, which no vulgarity, no humor, no overstatement can quite extinguish, the physicists have known sin; and this is a knowledge which they cannot lose." The knowledge these scientists used had been meant for healing and improvement of life, but it had now been turned to purposes of annihilation. In the past 50 years or so, with germlines, DNA modifications, and other "advancements," the potential exists for science to be even more destructive than it was with the development of nuclear weapons.

We are a nation that seems serially to obliterate the dark lessons of the past, and this does not seem to be our problem alone.

Another body of thinkers and writers, especially journalists, who wonder whether we have learned anything about evil since World War II is those who have dealt with the history of genocide. Arendt had warned that the techniques of terror pioneered by the Nazis would be taken up and improved by others, and she has been proved right in such places as Cambodia, the former Yugoslavia, Rwanda, and the Sudan. Such genocidal events seem to explode into our consciousness as if they had come out of nowhere, but in retrospect, we discover similar patterns. Why is it so hard for us to name these realities and figure out how to stop them?

Over the past 20 years or so, a number of journalists have thought about this question and tried to come up with a template for identifying and resisting events of mass genocide. First, we must understand the reality of the situation as clearly as possible and resist the temptation to immediately fit it into received moral patterns. Then, we must communicate the facts we have discerned in a vivid and powerful way, although it may be difficult to convince others of the reality we have witnessed.

These two areas of concern—those about science and those about uncovering the realities of evil—reemerged after the events of September 11, 2001. In the aftermath of 9/11, many spoke of the loss of innocence for the United States, the loss of a naïve belief that the world was good. In thinking back over our history, however—the Civil War, the genocide against Native Americans, two world wars, Vietnam—one wonders how many times the United States can lose its innocence. We are a nation that seems serially to obliterate the dark lessons of the past, and this does not seem to be our problem alone. The crux of the problem in modern cultures seems to be that we lack both the language and the imagination to respond usefully to the challenge evil presents to our moral self-understanding.

Today, we imagine the world and people as basically ordered. This means that we imagine evil as the sudden and inexplicable eruption of malice and madness in an otherwise harmonious world. But genocide and other events of mass evil will always surprise us as long as we think that humans cannot be bad. This is not so much an understanding of evil as a failure to understand it. One solution to this failing is to explore humanity's thinking about evil in the past and to look for echoes that can be useful to our thinking in the modern world. ■

Suggested Reading

Mills and Brunner, eds., *The New Killing Fields: Massacre and the Politics of Invention.*

VanDeMark, Brian. *Pandora's Keepers: Nine Men and the Atomic Bomb.*

Questions to Consider

1. Oppenheimer noted that physicists had "known sin" in the creation of the atomic bomb. Have our other current technologies known sin in the same way? How has our growing knowledge and technical sophistication been complicit in evil, and how important is this complicity?

2. What conclusions ought we to draw from the persistence of genocide throughout the 20th century? Is genocide a particularly modern expression of evil? How should we situate these crimes in relation to others throughout history?

3. Do we have the resources to understand and respond to evil in the modern world? If so, what are these resources and how ought we to use them? If not, why not?

The "Unnaming" of Evil
Lecture 35—Transcript

Welcome back. In this lecture, I want to extend our selections on how people have thought about evil from the period immediately following the end of the Holocaust, or the Shoah, through the rest of the 20th century, through 9/11, and up until today.

A general theme for these lectures, especially the ones covering the 20th century, has been a deepening sense of the disparity between our thinking about evil, historically and today, and the realities that that thinking is meant to represent and help us respond to. While the scientists have been growing more confident perhaps—as we saw in the lecture on some experiments on evil—in their ability to understand evil, those who do not use scientific methods (journalists, intellectuals, philosophers, theologians, writers) have been growing more uncertain of our ability to talk about evil; and even some scientists, those most immediately and intimately involved in the development of new technologies in the past 100 years or so, have their doubts about the degree to which science itself can help us think about evil. Perhaps their worry is science is exactly exacerbating our struggles with evil.

To see this, consider some of the stories we've been telling. From Conrad forward, we've seen a growing unease about the fundamental disparity in our readiness and perhaps our capacity to understand or grasp the reality of evil. Let's recap some of this development here: In very different ways, in both Nietzsche and Conrad, we see a story being told of a witness of extremity, a veteran, a survivor; someone who has seen something real—unable to get a hearing when they "come back" to everyday civilization, to our ordinary life of today, because of the nearly unbridgeable distance of their experience from our common reality. For Nietzsche, it was figures like the madman who proclaims "God is dead," or in another book of his, the prophet Zarathustra; figures like this who are impossible to understand as inhabiting civilization in the same way that the people they are trying to speak to inhabit that world. For Conrad, it was Marlow, struggling with the impossibility of attempting to communicate and succeeding in communicating to the refined, civilized people he circulates around in Europe his own experiences of the heart of darkness and the bestiality of human beings in the far reaches of the Congo.

For a thinker like Freud, he points out in his own work—especially as we saw in his discussion of his self-understood discovery of the death drive—how what he thinks of as unpleasant scientific discoveries, discoveries that uncover unpleasant facts that are undigestible by our ordinary human life; our regular, everyday, civilized experience—these unpleasant, undigestible discoveries are met with hostility and resistance. A thinker like Albert Camus, who in *The Plague* tells a story of how deeply hostile and skeptical people were to admitting the possibility that the plague was among them, and how quickly after the plague had passed that they go back to their ordinary everyday lives as if no lessons needed to be learned from the trauma they had just survived. Then, in my view, consummately in the work of Hannah Arendt, who really does suggest that the political developments of the 20th century are in some ways far more terrifying than the technological developments. The political reality of totalitarianism for Arendt, and what it means about both the plasticity, the malleability of human character and also the kind of ultimately futile effort to make people better by directing moral language at them if they are under conditions of totalitarian terror. For Arendt, these facts mean that we have to think anew, as she says at one point think "without a banister," about how to understand our world and how to respond to the challenges within in it in order to accommodate, again, what she called, "the central political phenomena of our century."

This is a powerful and new theme developing in the 20th century, whether the resources we have from the past are able to help us or not. But in some ways, this is an old theme, and it can be a mistake to think that these worries, these concerns, are altogether new; they go very deep in human history. Remember that wonderful beginning, one of the alternate beginnings, to the *Epic of Gilgamesh*: "It is an old story, but one that can still be told." The word "still" there speaks importantly of how insistent even 4,500 years ago, maybe more, people understood that knowledge from the past stood in some complicated, tentative, possibly superfluous relationship to the conditions of the present. Consider also, even in Genesis, the tree of the knowledge of good and evil; the idea that knowledge is somehow only apprehensible for what it is once it is acquired, and that the apprehension of that knowledge, the knowledge itself, brings with it a certain kind of regret about acquiring that knowledge in the first place; a certain kind of ambivalence about it. Maybe the knowledge isn't as useful as we thought it was. Maybe our concerns are new now; what we thought would help us is now seen to hurt us in some way. The old Roman myth of Pandora's Box is often used as a good example of this. Remember, if you will, Pandora finds in her house a box that says, "Do not open; all the furies and all the terrible negative emotions, all the things that will pollute human life, are contained in here. Don't open it." But, of course, she can't help but do so; and by opening the box, all knowledge is released, but all trauma follows with it as well. The knowledge we maybe gain perhaps may be something that is useful, but we often find that we have regretted gaining it; and also that once gained, it is impossible to lose again.

Nonetheless, contemporary thinkers do seem to repeatedly worry about this in a way that genuinely is new; a way that is explicitly concerned with whether our power has outstripped our wisdom in a fundamentally new way. Remember that quotation of Michel Foucault that I gave several lectures ago:

> For centuries [he says], humanity had been what Aristotle had said we were: a natural animal with a political situation that it had to work out. But now we are an animal whose politics put our very natural survival into question.

That fact, it seems to me, is new about the past 100–150 years or so; and again and again, this cluster of themes repeats. You can see it in our anxieties about genocide; in our anxieties about scientific and technological developments; even in our anxieties about the changing nature of culture and society in general. The deep question that we are facing increasingly today, and have faced increasingly since the end of World War II, is whether our new situation is really amenable to, suitable to, treatment and understanding by the traditional resources to understand and respond to evil.

Here I want to talk about several different dimensions, several different genres, of this concern. First, I want to talk about a series of scientists' concerns, particularly founded in the development of nuclear weapons; about what they had done and whether it could ever be undone. Then I want to talk about a series of questions and concerns repeatedly raised in different settings by journalists and intellectuals about whether or not we have learned anything from the genocidal violence of World War II. Then finally, I want to talk about how both of these sets of questions have been raised anew again—

especially in the United States, but actually around the world as well—in the wake of the terrorist attacks in the U.S. on September 11, 2001, and in the discussions and actions that came after those attacks.

Let me start with the physicists, the scientists. The story of the Manhattan Project is well known, and even the moral story of the project is well known. In the late 1930s, a number of scientists began to be terribly worried that Nazi Germany was using its scientific ability—which was in many ways preeminent in the world at that time—to develop a new kind of terrible weapon: a nuclear weapon. One of them convinced Albert Einstein to write a letter to Franklin Roosevelt explaining what all this meant—because Einstein was already recognized as a public figure, a genius who Roosevelt might listen to—and saying that unless the United States began research to develop its own nuclear weapon, the day might come when Nazi Germany had a nuclear bomb that could annihilate a city in an instant. So the physicists, out of fear for what was happening, were actually able to provoke America into producing a nuclear weapon.

In a way, they are the ultimate 20th century representation of the myth of Pandora's Box; the self-destructive power we gain that we can never put back. These scientists, all of whom had started off their scientific careers in the hope of improving the human condition, gaining a kind of sheer speculative knowledge about the structure of the universe, none of them wanted to be creating infernal weapons. These scientists created the conditions for the world's annihilation, vastly expanding humanity's capacity to destroy itself. The scientists were unprepared for this. J. Robert Oppenheimer is really exemplary of this. His work in leading the Manhattan Project's scientific research division, which designed and built the atomic bomb, is well known. People were as eager to work on this as they were on anything in their lives, precisely because they were terrified that the Germans would get the bomb first. But as it became clear that they wouldn't, the scientists began to have concerns about what they were involved in, what they were doing; but by then it was too late.

Oppenheimer, after the war, brooded about this in powerful and far-reaching ways; and he gave a wonderful speech in which he said, in 1946: "In some sort of crude sense, which no vulgarity, no humor, no overstatement can quite extinguish, the physicists have known sin; and this is a knowledge which they cannot lose." This statement, that "the physicists have known sin," was an exemplary statement of science struggling with its moral implications in the wake of World War II. The knowledge that scientists had used had been meant for healing and improvement of life, but now had been turned to self-destructive, annihilating purposes. Oppenheimer was speaking really of nuclear weapons, relatively—as these things go—crude technologies of destruction. Science in the past 50–60 years has now managed to work at the sub-molecular level, with germlines and DNA modifications that are far more potentially pervasive and destructive. Computer technology has developed to such a degree that now computer viruses, a reality that would have been undreamed of even 40 years ago, a kind of danger that no one even imagined, can now actually destroy or at least paralyze civilization. Just consider in the past 10–15 years the growth of the word in English, "weaponized"; science itself has become weaponized. That's one kind of set of examples; a set of examples about worries about whether or not science itself is something that was supposed to fight evil but now has come to signify a kind of destructive agglomeration of people's powers. Have we learned anything since World War II? The scientists wonder if we have.

Another body of thinkers who worry about this is those who have dealt with the long and dark history of genocide since 1945. Their perpetual worry is that "We thought we had learned some lessons, but it seems that we have either unlearned them, or never learned them in the first place." Evil is still hard to believe. Remember that in writing *Eichmann in Jerusalem*, Arendt had warned that the techniques, political and murderous, that the Nazis pioneered would be taken up and improved, in some sense perfected, by others. She says in that book, "Look, it's important for us to get this trial right; not just for the importance of making sure we understand why we are condemning Eichmann—that's important in itself—but also because whether or not we like it, these things are going to happen again." Once a political event like this has happened, it is much easier for it to happen again. Once the strategy, the devices, the techniques of terror are used, others will learn of them and employ them in their own settings. We have to know how to deal with them when they appear again.

This has become a deep question for thinkers—intellectuals, political thinkers, journalists, sometimes especially journalists—since 1945, because again and again these events have slowly emerged to explode into our consciousness as if somehow they had come out of nowhere, where we are astonished by them. But afterwards, in historical retrospect, we discover again and again some of the same patterns happening. You have Cambodia, the former Yugoslavia, Rwanda, the Sudan; these are the most widely recognized post-1945 genocides. What do we do about these realities? How do we confront them? How do we understand them? Furthermore, given that sometimes we know they're actually happening, why do we find it so hard to name them for what they are and to discern how to resist them, how to stop them?

Over time, over the past 20 years or so actually, a number of journalists have thought a lot about this and tried to come up with some way of offering a template for identifying and resisting events of mass genocide. The first thing they say we need to do is know the facts; get as clear as possible on the realities. Again, think about Arendt here: The first thing you need to do is be clear about what actually is going on, and resist the temptation to offer immediately a moral template kind of fitting over the situation so that it appears in received moral patterns. If we had offered a moral template on Eichmann, we would have thought of Eichmann as a devil, she thinks. That's not actually what's going on. At times during the Yugoslav conflict, people talked about Yugoslavia as riven by ancient tribal wounds. The argument about the Tutsi and the Hutu in Rwanda was also one about primeval historical enmities between these peoples. But as we go on to understand the history of these conflicts, it turns out that these rivalries, these conflicts, are not always primeval; and even if they are of long-standing duration, as they were in the former Yugoslavia, for a long time people of different ethnic and religious identities are able to live in harmony and then suddenly someday snap, they're not. Why? It's easy to think in terms of evil as the primitive, the age-old ethnic tensions or tribal enmities or whatever, but that's never quite right; there's always some instigating force that creates the conditions, because there are long-ago ethnic oppositions throughout the world that never quite explode into genocide, do they? That's the first thing; get the facts right.

The second thing: Communicate those facts in a vivid and powerful way. A lot of what happened in the former Yugoslavia managed to stop when a few very brave journalists managed to get into Bosnia and find various killing fields in Bosnia where Bosnian civilians had died. When that happened, finally, provocations forced the United States' and Western powers' hands into getting force used in order to stop certain genocidal activity from happening. But the important thing there for journalists is they have to be able to give vivid images of what happened in these holocausts, in these events. The fundamental difficulty for a lot of these writers, a lot of the journalists and thinkers who were talking about this, is of trying to bring to people's attention in a good way; what they are actually seeing, what is there to be seen on the ground. If you read reports of Bosnia or if you read reports of Rwanda, one of the themes that's perpetually there is always the theme of, "I saw this, but I didn't believe it; and then when I tried to report it back home, people found it incredible that this was happening." It's hard to imagine that in Rwanda in about 100 days 800,000 people were killed; and not in death camps, not often with guns, not often with explosives, often with machetes. In 100 days, 800,000 people were hacked to death. Of course that's going to be hard to understand, but that's the fundamental job of a journalist who is covering these events: to bring home to people the reality of what is going on; getting people to see what is out there to be seen. That, of course, goes back to Conrad's idea that in some sense we need to use words to make people see.

These two bodies of literature—concerns about science, concerns about technology—and then concerns about how to bring into view the realities of the evil around us both reemerged for us really after the events of September 11th in the United States and also in global discourse, really. On the one hand, the events of 9/11 produced an enormous amount of fellow-feeling, an enormous amount of community in the United States and around the world for the United States. Seeing 3,000 civilians reduced to ashes in a matter of minutes meant a lot to everybody in the world, and there was a positive sense of hope and camaraderie that came out of that. But on the other, as the days went on, a repeated language came up again and again of the U.S.'s loss of its innocence; the U.S.'s loss of a naïve belief that the world had been always good, or was fundamentally good, or after the Cold War had been good. Again and again, when I heard this rhetoric on the radio or on TV or what have you, I kept wondering: How many losses of innocence can the United States survive? Think of it: You could consider the American Civil War a loss of innocence; the Indian Wars, the genocidal Indian Wars, a loss of innocence; World War I; the Great Depression; World War II; Vietnam. How many times can we lose our innocence? The 1940s and 50s actor and writer Oscar Levant once said a wonderful line about the 50s movie star Doris Day, the epitome of wholesomeness in the 1950s. Levant said of her, "I actually knew her before she was a virgin."

In a way, the United States is a nation that seems serially to forget that it knew itself before it was innocent; it seems serially to obliterate the dark lessons of its past. Maybe this is, in fact, though, a general lesson about humans in the modern world. That's what Albert Camus said, right? Remember the end of the play where he says that Rieux recalls that the jubilant crowds do not know what they could have learned in books; that the plague bacillus—and I'm just paraphrasing here—lurks in corners, and cupboards, and crannies, and nooks in their houses; but that one day, for the bane and enlightening of humanity, the plague would send forth its rats again to die in a happy city. Camus's thought there, that in some sense the world needs to be remaindered but perpetually forgets to remember the fact of these evils, suggests that this story goes pretty far back into history.

As I said to you in one of the lectures, a poem that circulated pretty quickly after 9/11, a famous poem by W.H. Auden, the English and American poet, a poem entitled "September 1, 1939," suggests something of this weariness as well. He says—thinking about the beginning of World War II but it really was an appropriate way to begin the decade—in his poem:

> the enlightenment driven away,
> the habit-forming pain,
> mismanagement and grief
> we must suffer them all again."

And sure enough, after the attacks of 9/11, a few days, a few weeks, a few months went by and there was an increasing rhetoric of fear and terror of enemies that began to pervade the American political scene. It was something that could have been foreseen, and surprisingly wasn't foreseen very much.

There's something fundamental about the U.S. that believes in its optimism, in an optimism that's close to naïve, and perpetually forgets the lessons of the past; the kind of perpetual amnesia machine that lets the U.S. not remember what it has done, what we have done, here in the United States. But as I said, this is not a problem unique to the United States; there is something deeply modern about our ability to forget evil, something from the Enlightenment perhaps, something from the optimism of the will that the Enlightenment promotes. After 9/11, it seemed, we discovered, that if we had a language of evil to use but if we wanted to use it we seemed forced to choose between either a language of evil that provides a kind of inadvertent metaphysical compliment to bad people by calling them "evil" in a way that makes Osama bin Laden sound like Darth Vader, or a language of intelligible or at least explainable motivations that forbids from talking about bad people as bad, as malicious, but just misunderstood, amenable to being talked out of their future aggression.

In the 1990s the famous cannibal criminal in America, Jeffery Dahmer, who I think killed and ate something like 20 young men, famously said when he was arrested, "All along, I knew I was either evil or sick; and now, thank God, I know I was sick." I just think the self-consciousness of Dahmer in that moment is a self-consciousness that is far more cultural than personal; he's offering the two options that the culture provides: either demonic magnificence or simple insanity. I don't think that works for much of our world. We don't, I think, really understand the grammar of evil; and that's what these thinkers worry about, the thinkers since 1945.

The imagination has very little capacity to comprehend, nor really any language, any power, to represent the horrors of our world. That's why so much of the 20th century's literature, from Conrad's *Heart of Darkness* forward, has been dedicated to the impossibility of representing the extreme experiences most distinctive of our age. Those fortunate enough to resist a numbing cynicism about our world inhabit a state of perpetual and repeated moral astonishment. Yet we're always able to forget that we were once not virgins.

Not only has there been precious little serious sustained reflection on the problem of evil, despite what all of our thinkers have said, what's worse is that we rarely even realize this; indeed, our intellectual energies often seem as cultures, as modern cultures, to have been spent more on avoiding thinking about evil than on thinking about it. We've largely forgone attempting to comprehend evil, and choose instead to try to ignore or dismiss evil through some form of ironic alienation, muscular moralism, or, if you can imagine it, some combination of both. This is the crux of our problem: Modern cultures seem to lack the ability, and more particularly the moral imagination, to respond usefully to the challenge evil presents to our moral self-understanding.

The contemporary literary critic Andrew Delbanco puts it well:

> A gap has opened up [he says] between our awareness of evil and the intellectual resources we have for handling it ...

Sound familiar? Sound like anyone else we've heard? Sounds like Hannah Arendt to me.

> [t]he [reality] of evil [he says] has never been richer. Yet never have our responses been so weak. We have no language for connecting our inner lives with the horrors that pass before our eyes in the outer world.

In Delbanco's view, we have undergone a process of "unnaming evil" in the past century or so. This is the story of our growing incomprehension of evil, despite thinkers like Arendt, despite thinkers like Conrad, Nietzsche, Freud, the Christian theologians, the Jewish theologians, the political thinkers, the poets, the novelists. We have grown increasingly unable adequately to understand both the evils we mean to oppose, and those evils in which we may from time to time occasionally—just throwing this out there—those evils that we may find ourselves implicated in. This is the story that our thinkers from Nietzsche forward have found themselves worrying about and attempting to resist.

Today, perhaps, our culture is too optimistic; today we imagine the world as basically ordered, and people as basically ordered as well. When they're not, there's something medically wrong with them, and so we can treat them medically; and this means that we have to imagine evil as the sudden and wholly inexplicable eruption of malice and madness in an otherwise harmonious world. Genocide, events of mass evil, will always surprise us as long as we think that humans cannot be bad. That is not so much an understanding of evil as a failure to understand it, and it reflects the fact that our culture's essentially optimistic vision of human beings as basically good and intelligible leaves no space for people who do apparently unintelligible, and certainly horrific, deeds. All we can do then is imagine the people who do these deeds are either subhuman or superhuman in some sense; either superhuman in their malevolence and give their wickedness a monstrous, supernatural cast, or somehow they're not fully mature humans, they're more like beasts, monkeys, or dogs. Neither of these, it seems to me, is fully adequate.

How do we do better than this? In a way, that's why I'm giving this whole lecture series. We need to know more about the past, and we need to know how almost everything we think about evil today, when we occasionally think about it, has an echo in that past. Even if the echo is different from where we are now, nonetheless, learning about the history of thinking about why evil exists will hopefully provide us with some resources for thinking in the future. Exploring some answers to those questions is the point of our next, and last, lecture.

Where Can Hope Be Found?
Lecture 36

One of the things that [entertainment] is most interested in is criminality, evil, malice, these sorts of things. The reason why? Because for us especially as moderns, as people here in the 21st century, it's hard for us to imagine a world where evil of our sort exists; we don't know what to do.

A s we've seen throughout these lectures, evil is truly what Zbigniew Herbert called the "dense and dark material" of history, and to shed light on it requires many consciousnesses. But the fact that evil is a difficult problem doesn't mean that we can't wrestle some comprehension out of its mystery. The approaches we have explored to thinking about evil offer us a good place to begin.

Over the course of these lectures, we've seen the manifold attempts by thinkers and writers of diverse beliefs to represent and anatomize evil, diagnose its challenges, and formulate responses, and certain themes appear in this thinking repeatedly. Such thinkers as Plato, Augustine, and Pascal believed that evil suggests a kind of nihilism—nothingness—in the world, while Aristotle, Nietzsche, and Freud viewed evil as a natural component of the world. Irenaeus, Hegel, and many contemporary thinkers imagine evil as an inevitable step in the process of maturation for human beings and, perhaps, the cosmos as a whole. We've also seen a longstanding debate between thinkers about evil: Again, such thinkers as Plato, Augustine, and Pascal see evil as the refusal to be properly extreme in the pursuit of virtue, while others, such as Aristotle, Montaigne, and Hume, see a danger in the expression of extremity.

The debates we've seen related to theodicy raised questions about the implications of our understanding of evil for our understanding of the universe and the reverse, that is, the implications of our understanding of the universe for our understanding of evil. Another issue we've explored is the relationship between civilization and barbarism. In the 20th century, Arendt and others have argued that modernity itself is complicit in creating new kinds of evil. The literature we've read—the work of Dante, Milton, Camus, and others—vividly captures the question that perhaps lies at the heart of thinking about evil: What is its fundamental character? Is it banal, empty, demonic? Is it unnatural to our cosmos or part of the world's essence?

The extent of malice in the 20th and 21st centuries has been truly remarkable, yet we generally think of ourselves as somehow in a better moral situation than people in previous centuries. Something like the Holocaust, for example, would have been unimaginable in the 18th century. The problem seems to be, as Andrew Delbanco said, that "a gap has opened up between our awareness of evil and the intellectual resources we have for handling it." Because we don't understand evil, we don't know how to resist it. Evil bewilders us, and our typical response to it is often a theatricalization that masks our incomprehension.

A more poignant, ironic joke on the part of whatever God may be is hard to imagine: that Western civilization has returned to fight in its birthplace.

It's stunning to think that American troops are now fighting in places that the Greeks and Romans fought 2,500 years ago. For some time in the last decade, the ruins of the ancient city of Babylon were within the perimeter of an American military base. A more poignant, ironic joke on the part of whatever God may be is hard to imagine: that Western civilization has returned to fight in its birthplace. It may be that the challenge of evil is just too hard for us, but we can't stop asking the questions. We know that evil isn't likely to go away, and even if we try to avoid it, it will loom on the edge of our consciousness and eventually intrude into our lives again.

We need a way of thinking about evil that will avoid two significant pitfalls: the attempt to demonize people who are unlike us and the temptation to internalize evil and paralyze us with guilt. These lectures have suggested several routes to a workable language of evil. Still, there is a latent time bomb here: Does the knowledge or insight we might gain about the problem produce anything like hope? Any answer to the problem of evil must recognize the thought that we may not be able, finally, to gain any useful insights about it.

It seems that all the evidence of evil, suffering, and cruelty in the world would not provoke us unless we felt that they were, in some fundamental way, wrong. The fact that evil is so puzzling and the fact that humans have persisted in our questioning of it seem themselves signs of hope. But we should not be self-congratulatory about our stubbornness in this arena. It's not a form of moral courage but a form of what we might call moral acknowledgment, of giving witness to what we see. Our reflection on evil doesn't begin from theoretical presuppositions or armchair philosophizing but by attending to our "pre-theoretical" responses to evil. We naturally resist evil—intellectually and practically—and in that resistance, we manifest some sense of goodness and justice. Perhaps a truly useful response to evil can be found in this practical resistance. ■

Questions to Consider

1. Can you identify one aspect of the course or one insight into the nature of evil that you found especially compelling? What about this insight is significant for you and why?

2. What do you think Leonard Wolf was trying to say when he observed, "I'm planting iris and they will be flowering long after [Hitler] is dead"? What hopes are capable of sustaining us against evil, and how can we cultivate these?

Where Can Hope Be Found?
Lecture 36—Transcript

Welcome back. It's time to end these lectures on the history of human attempts to discern why evil exists and how we should live in its shadow. I want to end now by looking back on all these lectures and suggesting some lessons that we can draw from them for our own lives, both today and going forward.

It is truly, in the words of the Gilgamesh scribe, "an old story, / but one that can still be told." It is what in our very first lecture we heard Zbigniew Herbert call history's "dense and dark material," which will require many consciousnesses to shed light upon it. You might think from this that evil has no solution; that there is nothing to do but bear it as best we can without hope of any intellectual advance in comprehending it, any insights that we can gain from this struggle. But I don't want to end with so completely a pessimistic note; for pessimism is its own kind of consolation, isn't it? To despair of a solution, to drop our tools and just walk away, is so much more easy than struggling with the idea that the answers won't come easily, if at all. No, our problem is simply that the challenge is genuinely, genuinely hard; it's something we've been struggling with ever since the first pages of recorded history. It probably will be something we continue to wrestle with until the sun burns out, or we do. But that it is difficult does not mean that we cannot wrestle some deeper comprehension, some richer apprehension, out of the mystery; and I submit that a number of the ways of looking at evil that we have talked about in these lectures offer us good places to begin in this project.

Let me begin just by recapitulating something of the journey we've been on here. Over the course of these many lectures, we've seen the manifold attempts by thinkers and writers of diverse beliefs to represent and anatomize evil, diagnose its challenges, and formulate a range of responses. There are, of course, severe limits to what we've studied; most obviously, we've only studied what can broadly be called Western conceptions of evil. But, in fact, there have been, over the course of human history, and are currently, several major civilizational ways of being human, distinct ways of understanding the cosmos and the humans' place within in it: China, Mesoamerica, Ancient

Near East, South Asia, Sub-Saharan Africa—in Sub-Saharan Africa there might have been several distinct ways of being human—and then Europe. In these lectures, we've really only been studying the European and a few Ancient Near Eastern approaches to these things. Others with other skills with other forms of learning can talk in an educated way about those other forms of being human; but not I. Nor even within this Western tradition have we studied everyone that we could have studied. We've not addressed some really major thinkers such as Kierkegaard, Abelard, Seneca, Cicero, Carl Jung, Karl Rahner, Zoroaster, Locke, Burke, Tocqueville, Foucault, Montesquieu; there are thousands of people we could have talked about. All of them have much to say about evil that would be good for us to hear; that we could learn much from.

But within the confines of these lectures, we've done enough, I think, to give us some basis on which to form some thoughts about how people in the West have thought about these matters for the last 4,000–5,000 years; that's a fair range, I think it's reasonable to say. What these lectures teach us is the intractability of the challenge of evil for humanity, and humanity's ceaseless efforts to confront that challenge. In this way, Rousseau was right: You'll recall that he said that we cannot help but ask these questions, we cannot help but struggle with them, precisely because the reservoir of hope in our beings is such that it can never be fully quenched; we always ask these very abstract questions of why there is evil. It's not simply a matter of putting a Band-Aid on the immediate problems that evil presents to us: the wounds, the damages, the evils, the malices, the vindictiveness of our moment. All of those events, all those phenomenon make us step back from them in some part of our brain, in some part of our soul, and say: How does this world hang together if these kinds of questions, if these kinds of realities are there?

In all these, certain themes and issues have appeared again and again. We've uncovered what we could call different layers, different strata of thinking about evil. Most basically, as we saw from the first lecture forward, there are three large families in the people we've looked at, three large families of thinking about evil, understanding it. On the one hand, you have pictures of evil represented as in some sense about folly, stupidity, and about nothingness; the people like Plato on the one hand, Augustine, Pascal, people who think that in some important way evil suggests a kind of nihilism that is available to use in the world. A second family of theories talks about evil in terms of a natural component of our world, a part of our world that is in some important ways inexpugnable from it, a consequence of just the kinds of creatures we are and the kind of world this is. In this sense, thinkers in different ways such as Nietzsche and Freud, Aristotle, possibly even someone like Thucydides could be here; suffering and malice are simply part of the world we live in. Then in the third category of theories about this, we saw thinkers like Irenaeus and Hegel and, as I suggested, much of our contemporary thinking imagines evil as a kind of inevitable step on the process of maturation, for human beings, perhaps for the cosmos as a whole. In some important way in this family's view, evil is an estrangement that is necessary for us to become mature, to become properly self-conscious about who we are and our place in the cosmos. All of these accounts, all of these families, are in important ways significant, valuable, and they're important testimony and insights that it's worth our hearing.

Another layer is the question of whether—and this is, I think, really interesting to me, because before I had worked out these lectures I hadn't actually seen this—but there is a longstanding debate between those who see evil as in some important way the refusal to be properly extreme in the pursuit of virtue; the refusal to see that sometimes virtue requires a real zealotry. In a way, Plato, Augustine, Pascal all line up on this side that evil turns out to be a kind of mediocrity in the face of a situation where extreme effort is required. But on the other side, there's another body of scholars, another collection, who say, "You know, there's something there, but the danger is that, in fact, evil is exactly the expression of an extremity, an extreme zealotry, where moderation is the better course: thinkers like Aristotle, arguing against Plato; Montaigne, arguing against Pascal; Hume, arguing against any number of people. This tension between "Is evil something that is a manifestation of our failure to be properly committed to the world, or to the cause of the good, or God?" versus a construal that says, "Evil is in some ways an overcommitment, a hyper-commitment, to a narrow range of ends that when we are committed to them fail to make us see the full range, the full spectrum, of human being and human goods." That's another layer.

A third layer would be the questions of the implications of our understanding of evil for our understanding of the universe as a whole, and of our understanding of the universe in turn for our understanding of evil. All the debates around theodicy, all the debates around whether or not increased knowledge of the cosmos is going to help us master the propensity we have to evil; these debates are all informing this level of the question of evil. Another one is the question of the relationship between civilization and barbarism, and even the debate that emerges in the 19th century and then grows in importance in the 20th: the debate about whether or not modernity itself is in some ways complicit for creating new kinds of evil. Remember Hannah Arendt saying that the problem with totalitarian evil in the 20th century is it creates a new kind of political evil that we never had imagined could exist before; the kind that shows us that humans can actually be turned into kind of robots or zombies. Connected to this: themes of technology and scientific advance; the dangers of knowledge and experience; the possibly novel challenges of modern politics, especially the totalitarian states, as Arendt says; even the hegemony of a particular kind of "scientific rationality" or a way of thinking about life itself as potentially too restrictive to contain the full spectrum, again, of human life. These sorts of what you can call "dimensions" of how evil can affect our thinking, the mode of intellectual engagement with the world, that's another dimension of evil that we've tried to bring to our attention, highlight and focus on in an explicit way.

Last, but certainly not least, the question that, for me anyway, lies at the heart of a lot of these issues, and that is, again for me, captured most vividly in a few very intense, very powerful pieces of art by Dante, Milton, Conrad, possibly Camus's *The Fall*, with Jean-Baptiste Clamence: the question of the deep, fundamental character of evil. Is it banal? Is it empty? Is it demonic? Is it vacuous? Is it positive? Is it ultimately unnatural to our cosmos, to us, or is it fundamentally part of the world's essence? All these are questions that we've been trying to get at in these lectures.

One problem that we face with evil today is just that we don't know how to handle it. When we think about, outside of the scope of these lectures, people today, ordinary, everyday people, all of us together, we seem not to be able to understand the problems we confront when we confront evil. If you think about the 20th and 21st centuries' horrors, the extent of suffering and human malice in these centuries has truly been remarkable; and yet often we think about ourselves as somehow in a better moral situation than people in previous centuries. Whatever you say about the 18th century, something like the Holocaust was unimaginable in it. The invention of modern terrorism is, in fact, a modern invention. The intentional attempt to destroy human civilians with bombs itself is a relatively modern invention. Why do we continue to insist that somehow we are morally superior to people three or four centuries ago, if we're doing this and they wouldn't have even found it thinkable? Again, think about Andrew Delbanco's line, the line I gave you in the last lecture, the previous lecture: "a gap has opened up between our awareness of evil and the intellectual resources we have for handling it."

That might be the problem here: Increasingly, we know neither how to resist nor how to suffer evil, most basically because we don't understand it. Evil bewilders us, and our typical response to it is really more of a theatricalization of a response; it's kind of a histrionic that reveals not any real horror at the reality and danger of evil, but rather our fear of admitting our incomprehension of what it is we confront, what it is we are called to respond to, when we encounter evil. Much of our current entertainment—movies, TV, what have you—is fascinated by evil, but that's partially because, importantly because, we don't understand it. Entertainment returns us to the puzzles of our lives in interesting ways and offers us short-term solutions, like snack food, like junk food, to dealing with that. One of the things that it most is interesting in is criminality, evil, malice, these sorts of things. The reason why? Because for us especially as moderns, as people here in the 21st century, it's hard for us to make sense of a world where evil of our sort exists; we don't know what to do.

To see what I mean about this, just witness the confusion that people felt, again, after 9/11. Everyone used the language of "evil"; pretty much everybody talked about it incessantly for a few weeks, but it was a fairly brittle language we used. Some people thought that this was a direct attack by evil incarnate in some sense, and others reacted against that, resisting any use of the discourse of evil. Few imagined that there could be a place to stand between a kind of furious demonization of people who are not like us and an abject self-recrimination, blaming us and us alone for what had happened. Since then, the historical depth of our problems has grown even more immense.

I remember in the 1990s opening up a magazine once in the early 90s and seeing a wonderful cartoon. It had these two old men sitting in an old men's club and they're sitting there, it looks like they're just staring off into space astonished by the history of the world, what current events were taking them to be. This is 1992–1993, when the collapse of the former Yugoslavia was underway; and these old men, you can imagine them having been born around the beginning of the First World War, are sitting there and one of them says to the other, "The Balkans, this is where I came in." The idea of the cartoon being that in some sense we've had a whole century and look, we're back where we started again. But as I give these lectures now, American troops, my country's troops, are fighting in places that the Romans and the Greeks and Alexander the Great fought in 2,500 years ago. For a long time in this last decade, American troops actually had the ancient city of Babylon within one of their military bases; the ruins of the city were within the perimeter of the base. A more poignant, ironic joke on the part of whatever God may be is hard to come by; that somehow Babylon, this is where Western civilization came in, and look, we're back there at it again. Maybe these questions are just too hard for us; maybe the problems are simply intractable.

But why not, then, simply punt on asking them? Why not just avert our eyes from these questions? Why not just eat, drink, and be merry? For me, there are two basic reasons: First, evil hasn't gone away, nor is it likely to. As the contemporary American poet Charles Simic says, "God's refuted but the devil's not"; and insofar as it's not, it will continue to be a puzzle for us. That's the second point: We can't avoid thinking about evil. If we try to avoid it, it looms over the horizon as what remains un-thought for us; and so all our thinking knows of its presence just over the edge of our vision, and eventually it will intrude again into our lives, and into our minds, as it did for many of us on one beautiful, crystal-clear, late summer day in 2001.

But even if know why, we still have to think about how to think about evil. We need a way of thinking about it that will avoid the two sorts of pitfalls that I mentioned earlier, the two sorts of pitfalls that thinking about evil is especially prone to stumble into: on the one hand, the attempt to demonize other people, people who are unlike us; on the other hand, the temptation to internalize evil, to render it entirely a phenomenon that makes us worried about gaining and accruing guilt in our souls in some way. If we can find a language of evil that neither, first of all, affixes too quickly and easily the title of "evil" to people or to groups who are unlike us in some fundamental way; and also, second of all, does not paralyze us with guilt and drag us down into despair; if we can find a language of evil that does neither of those things, avoids those problems, then we have something that's possibly workable.

I've suggested in these lectures that there are several different routes to such a possibly workable language; which one you think is best is in some ways a matter of your own judgment. But there's another question behind the problem of evil, and this is a kind of little latent time bomb in the question, laid down at least as early as the tree of the fruit of the knowledge of good and evil; and that's the question of whether or not the knowledge that we could gain, the theoretical insight we would gain, does it produce anything like hope? Many thinkers, ancient and modern, would suggest it doesn't. Consider the Book of Ecclesiastes: "In much wisdom is much grief; and he that increaseth knowledge, increaseth sorrow" Or, as T.S. Eliot put it: "After such knowledge, what forgiveness?" These are real questions, and we cannot avoid them. We cannot deny their concerns. Any answer to the problem of evil must recognize the profoundly sober thought that we may not be able finally to gain any useful insights; not just insights that are interesting and illuminating about evil, but insights of the sort that might provide us with hope, that might provide us with knowledge not just about evil but how to go on from our encounters, concrete and otherwise abstract, with evil.

But you know, all the evidences of evil, suffering, and cruelty in the world are not the only thing about our world; they would not provoke us unless we felt that they were in some fundamental way wrong; exceptional, curious, anomalous, problems that require explanation. If the world was organized in such a way that evil was truly naturally a part of it, so that it fit smoothly into the world, we wouldn't find it so puzzling. The bare fact, that is, that evil is so puzzling is itself, I think, a sign of hope. And not the only sign of hope it seems to me, at least not for me. Here at the end, consider the witness of Leonard Woolf, a great English writer, intellectual, political activist, and husband and savior sometimes of Virginia Woolf; I'll let him attest to what I mean here. I take this account from his autobiography of the years leading up to World War II, an autobiography that he wrote in the 1960s. In that, he recounts at the end (and I'm quoting him now):

A little scene which took place in the last months of peace. They were the most terrible months of my life, for, helplessly and hopelessly, one watched the inevitable approach of war. One of the most horrible things at that time was to listen on the wireless to the speeches of Hitler, the savage and insane ravings of a vindictive underdog who suddenly saw himself to be all-powerful. We were in Rodmell [that's their country house] during the late summer of 1939, and I used to listen to those ranting, raving speeches. One afternoon I was planting in the orchard under an apple tree "iris reticula," those lovely violet flowers which, like the daffodils, "come before the swallow dares and take the winds of March with beauty" [he loves poetry; great guy]. Suddenly I heard Virginia's voice calling to me from the sitting room window: "Hitler is making a speech." I shouted back: "I shan't come. I'm planting iris and they will be flowering long after he is dead." Last March [this is March of 1966 now, he's writing about recent events], 21 years after Hitler committed suicide in the bunker, a few of those violet flowers still flowered under the apple-tree in the orchard.

It's the bold resilience of those flowers and the hope they represent that the world is fundamentally a good place, that it is something that's worth saving, worth living in, that serves to enable a rejuvenated belief, a resuscitated belief, both in the idea of evil and in the idea of an evil enframed by goodness; in the idea that humans have standards against which they may willfully revolt, and that in so doing they are violating the order of nature itself. And it is in those flowers that we have seen imitated throughout these lectures in human beings stubbornly persisting in the face of great pressures never to surrender to despair.

But more than this, we can say here at the end, that in fact the stubborn persistence of those flowers speaks of another kind of persistence: namely, our own. Our own persisting to ask the question of evil, to continue to be puzzled at it, not just to be resist it but to be puzzled by it, to find evil a mystery, something that needs an explanation, something that raises question of meaning for us. It's a fact not often taken enough notice of, and less still taken enough account of, that this puzzlement is itself a sign of tremendous hope about our condition. If, for example, we were to consider the pessimistic argument that the reality of evil should teach us that our world is not fundamentally morally ordered, then it seems that our continually asking of this question is a problem for us. As the great English Christian apologist and novelist-writer C.S. Lewis has put it in terms of people's stubborn belief in religion in the face of pessimism (and I read from Lewis here):

> The very strength and facility of the pessimists' case at once poses us a problem. If the universe is so bad, or even half so bad, how on earth did human beings ever come to attribute it to the activity of a wise and good Creator? Men are fools, perhaps; but hardly so foolish as that.

Lewis wants to say here: If the evidence is so strong against goodness, how did people ever come to imagine that there was a good Creator, a good God, a good moral order?

> The direct inference from black to white, from evil flower to virtuous root, from senseless work to a workman infinitely wise, staggers belief. The spectacle of the universe as revealed by experience can never have been the ground of religion: it must always have been something in spite of which religion, acquired from a different source, was held.

So much Lewis. Think about that phrase, "In spite of which." In that phrase, we perceive something remarkable: namely the fact of our stubbornness in insisting that the basic truth about the world is its goodness. But we should not be self-congratulatory about this stubbornness; it's not something we seem to will consciously to affirm; it's not, that is, most basically a form of moral courage but rather a form of what we might call "moral acknowledgment," of confessing, giving witness to what people simply see. This isn't really a theoretical insight; this is fundamentally a practical insight. Our reflection on evil doesn't begin from distanciated theoretical presuppositions or from an armchair philosophizing situation, but by attending to and reflecting on our "pre-theoretical" responses to conflict, suffering, and evil. Humans naturally resist evil; they resist evil both practically in their bodies by fighting it, they resist it cognitively and intellectually in their minds by refusing to accept the picture of the world that evil would press upon us. They even, in part, resist not only evil from the outside but their own evil, their own sinful deeds, their conscience often attests against this; and they should do so—this is Lewis's argument, and I think it's mine, too—for evil is inherently evil, and in their very resistance, cognitive and practical, theoretical and muscular, they manifest some sense of goodness and justice; an intuition that seems a providential, provisional witness of some basic goodness present in the world.

This explains part of the difficulty that we have found humans to have in thinking about evil. For while we might think about it as a speculative matter, a theoretical matter, perhaps the origins of a truly useful response to evil, those origins are found in our practical resistance to evil itself; to the bare fact that what we call evil we call "evil" and not just "the way things are," or "how the world is organized," or "just part of the deal." Our practical astonishment at, our puzzlement at, and our resistance to evil may be more useful for thinking about a proper overall understanding of what evil is and why it exists than we might at first give it credit for; we might want to look more to our practical reactions to evil than our theoretical speculations. Perhaps, that is, more deeply than the details of their various answers to the question "why evil exists," the thinkers and the texts that we have looked at in this lecture series help us come to a better understanding of evil simply by the bare fact that they all found it a puzzle of one sort or another. Perhaps that is the crucial clue we have been stalking all along. It may well be that, in the bare experience of mystery at the puzzle of evil, we see the secret to the answer to that mystery; not in any theoretical resolution, not in any psychological consolation, but simply in the fact that in our minds, in our hearts, in our souls, in our spirits, and with our hands, we are opposed to evil and we struggle with it every day, and the struggle goes on.

I think that's where we'll end this. Thank you for spending this time with me. These lectures have been a pleasure for me, and I hope they have been for you as well.

Timeline

c. 200–500 .... Formation of the Talmud.

324 .... Constantine Christianizes
the Roman Empire.

354–430 .... Augustine of Hippo.

410 .... Rome sacked by Visigoths.

c. 570–632 .... Muhammad.

c. 644–652 .... Uthman, the third caliph,
canonizes the written Qu'ran.

1033–1109 .... Anselm of Canterbury.

1224–1275 .... St. Thomas Aquinas.

1265 .... Aquinas begins writing the
Summa Theologiae.

1265–1321 .... Dante Alighieri.

1308–1321 .... Dante writes his *Commedia*
(the "Divine Comedy").

1348 .... Black Death ravages Europe.

1453 .... Constantinople falls to the Ottomans.

1517 .... Martin Luther publishes his 95 theses;
Protestant Reformation begins.

1532 .... Machiavelli's *The Prince* is
published posthumously.

1588–1679 .... Thomas Hobbes.

1608–1674 .... John Milton.

1623–1662 .... Blaise Pascal.

1642–1651 .... English Civil War.

1651.. Hobbes publishes *Leviathan*.

1667.. Milton publishes *Paradise Lost*.

1670.. Pascal's *Pensées* published.

1710.. Gottfried Wilhelm Leibniz publishes *Theodicy*.

1724–1804 .... Immanuel Kant.

1755.. Earthquake devastates Lisbon.

1770–1831 .... G. W. F. Hegel.

1775–1783 .... American Revolutionary War.

1793.. Kant writes *Religion within the Boundaries of Mere Reason*.

1815.. Napoleon defeated at the Battle of Waterloo.

1835–1910 .... Mark Twain (Samuel Clemens).

1844–1900 .... Friedrich Nietzsche.

1848.. Karl Marx publishes the *Communist Manifesto*.

1856–1939 .... Sigmund Freud.

1861–1865 .... American Civil War.

1865 .... Lincoln's Second Inaugural Address.

1884 .... Mark Twain publishes *The Adventures of Huckleberry Finn.*

1886 .... Nietzsche's *Beyond Good and Evil* appears.

1906–1975 .... Hannah Arendt.

1913–1960 .... Albert Camus.

1914–1918 .... First World War.

1917 .... Bolshevik Revolution establishes communism in Russia.

1929 .... Freud writes *Civilization and Its Discontents.*

1939–1945 .... Nazis invade Poland, World War II.

1943 .... Heinrich Himmler delivers speech to his soldiers in Pozan.

1945 .... Auschwitz liberated by Soviet troops.

1945 .... The United States drops the first atomic bomb on Hiroshima.

1948 .... Albert Camus' *The Plague* appears.

1961 .... Trial of Adolph Eichmann in Jerusalem.

2001 .... Terrorists attack the World Trade Center.

Glossary

Abraham: Early patriarch of Israel whose story is recounted in Genesis. He makes a covenant with God and obediently follows God's command to sacrifice his son, Isaac, though God intervenes at the final moment.

akedah: Hebrew word meaning "binding," associated with the story of Abraham's obedient willingness to sacrifice Isaac and God's deliverance.

akrasia: An ancient Greek term that Aristotle uses for "weakness of will." Suggests an explanation for evil as a pathology of moral motivation, a divided, incoherent, or "weak" will.

Babel: In the book of Genesis, the site where humanity attempts to construct a tower to heaven; often associated with Mesopotamian Babylon. The story describes evil as overt rebellion against God and suggests a link between evil and "empire" that carries over into the Christian New Testament.

Cain and **Abel**: Sons of Adam and Eve in Genesis. The story recounts the murder of Abel by his brother, Cain, after God shows favor to Abel. Suggests that evil is now a permanent feature of human life that must be struggled against.

contrapasso: Theme in Dante's *Inferno* that emphasizes the continuity between sin and punishment in hell. Suggests a notion of hell as intrinsic punishment, in which punishment is a constitutive part of the nature of evil.

das Nichtige: Karl Barth's term to describe "the nothing," a force in excess of human wrongdoing that threatens everything that exists and undergirds sin. Barth uses the term to stress evil's unreality but also its profundity and depth.

death drive: Term used by Sigmund Freud to describe the instinct opposite to Eros in the human psyche that seeks to dissolve the world back into a primeval, inorganic state. The concept denies that evil can be explained rationally and introduces guilt into the human psyche.

divertissements: Term meaning "diversions" used by Blaise Pascal to describe a way of being in the world aimed at avoiding the facts of one's existence, especially the fact of death.

Enuma Elish: Babylonian creation myth, in which the god Marduk establishes himself as king over the gods by defeating Tiamat, the chaos monster.

Genesis: First book of the Jewish and Christian Scriptures, which tells the story of God's creation of the world, the origin of evil, and the development of the people Israel. Includes the stories of Adam and Eve, Cain and Abel, and Abraham and Isaac.

Gilgamesh: Important surviving work from Mesopotamia in the 3rd millennium B.C.E., in which the hero, Gilgamesh, suffers as he searches for immortality and founds a city. An important early text to understand a world where suffering occurs.

Hinneni: Hebrew word often translated "Here I am." Appears throughout the Hebrew Bible and Old Testament to denote a posture of attentiveness and obedience. Used by both Abraham and Samuel when each receives a call from God.

Iblis: Rebellious angel in the Qur'an, later associated with Satan. Refuses to obey God's command to "bow down" before Adam, and from this refusal, all evil proceeds. His story displays a connection between evil and moral rectitude; in the Sufi tradition, evil grows out of Iblis's scrupulous monotheism. Later characterizations of Iblis stress both evil's personal and impersonal character.

Job: Book of the Hebrew Bible and Old Testament that recounts the story of Job, a righteous man who is tested by God. The text is famous for its focus on the non-explicability of evil and suffering.

Oedipus Rex: Greek tragedy written by Sophocles, an Athenian tragedian. The drama tells the story of Oedipus, the king of Thebes, who unknowingly murders his father, Laius, and sleeps with his mother, Jocasta. Highlights the relationship between evil and tragedy in Greek thought.

original sin: Christian doctrine that stresses evil as dramatic, powerful, and endemic to the human condition. Presented in limited form in the New Testament and later developed by such Christian theologians as Augustine of Hippo.

Paradise Lost: Epic poem composed by John Milton, an English poet in the 17th century. The poem tells the story of the Fall of Adam and Eve; it is especially famous for its compelling treatment of Satan.

The Peloponnesian War: A historical work written by Thucydides, recounting the war between the Greek city-state of Athens and its rival, Sparta. Includes the story of Athens' turn of fortunes following its cruelty to the Melians and suggests the lack of straightforward moral order in the world.

pleasure principle: Term coined by Sigmund Freud to describe our desire to be happy and feel pleasure, while acknowledging that happiness is not a normal state of human life. The pleasure principle leads to the sublimation of our desires in order to achieve relative happiness.

Qur'an: Sacred text of Islam, literally meaning the "recitation." Contains the revelation according to Muhammad, transmitted to him by Gabriel.

Rabbinic Judaism: Form of Jewish faith and practice that flourished from the 3rd century C.E., the era of the composition of the Talmud, to the present. It takes Talmud to be an authority in interpretation of the Torah. This tradition offers a picture of evil in mundane terms.

radical evil: The term used by Immanuel Kant to describe the fundamental disposition of the will to privilege itself over the general good. The term stresses the idea that evil's resolution must go beyond cognition to a transformation of character itself.

Revelation: Apocalyptic text contained in the New Testament that describes the final cosmic battle between God and the forces of evil. Stresses the conception of evil as a cosmic struggle that must be patiently endured until conquered by God.

Shoah: Hebrew word meaning "catastrophe," now often used to describe the Holocaust.

yetzer ha ra: Hebrew term meaning "evil impulse." Key term in discussions of evil by Rabbinic Judaism; stresses evil as a part of humanity's created nature and rooted in self-interest. Leads to a vision of evil as less a cosmic struggle than a practical challenge.

Biographical Notes

Alighieri, Dante (c. 1265–1321 C.E.). Born in Florence, Italy, to a prominent family. Like many of his contemporaries, Dante was thoroughly involved in the controversy between the Guelphs and the Ghibellines, two factions associated with the papacy and the Holy Roman Empire in a struggle for political prominence. Dante was a moderate member of the Guelph party; after the triumph of his political enemies among the more extreme Guelphs, Dante was exiled from Florence for life while he was in Rome on an embassy. He never saw Florence again. Afterward, he began to write the *Commedia*, a poem that recounts Dante's journey through heaven, hell, and purgatory. *The Inferno*, one section of the *Commedia*, became one of the most important depictions of hell in the Western imagination. Dante's body still rests in Ravenna, in exile from the Florence that he loved; the sentence of death the Florence City Council had laid down upon him during his life was at last revoked by that Council, by a vote of 19 to 5, in 2008.

Aquinas, Thomas (1225–1274 C.E.). Born to a prominent family in Aquino in southern Italy. At the age of 19, Aquinas expressed a desire to join the monastic order of the Dominicans, but his family opposed this decision and locked him in a castle for two years. During this time, his family made every attempt to dissuade him from his decision, at one point even hiring a prostitute to convince Aquinas to renounce his celibacy. Eventually, however, his family relented and Aquinas joined the Dominican order. He moved to Paris, where he became a professor of theology. He eventually moved to Rome, where he began work on his *Summa Theologiae*, arguably the most important work in medieval theology and one of the most important in the history of Western Christianity. Near the end of his life, Aquinas had a series of experiences that made him stop writing; when asked why he had stopped, he replied that, compared to what he had now experienced, "all I have written is straw." Having written more than 10,000 pages, he died when he was not yet 50.

Arendt, Hannah (1906–1975 C.E.). Born to a Jewish family in Königsberg, the birthplace of Immanuel Kant. She studied philosophy with Martin Heidegger, with whom she had an affair, and Karl Jaspers. Arendt completed a dissertation on Augustine but was prevented from continuing in academia because she was Jewish. To escape Nazi persecution, in 1933, Arendt fled to France, then in 1940, to America, where she became a prominent intellectual in New York City. She published *On the Origins of Totalitarianism*, a famous work analyzing the nature of totalitarian regimes. She also reported on the trial of Adolf Eichmann for the *New Yorker*, later transforming her work into *Eichmann in Jerusalem: A Study on the Banality of Evil*. Arendt had a distinguished academic career and taught at numerous institutions before becoming the first female professor to teach at Princeton University. She is now recognized as one of the most important philosophers of the 20th century.

Aristotle (384–322 B.C.E.). Born in Stageira as a member of the aristocracy. Eventually, Aristotle made his way to Athens, became a disciple of Plato, and studied at Plato's Academy for almost 20 years. Following his departure from the Academy, he was invited by Philip II of Macedon to become the tutor of Philip's son, Alexander the Great. Aristotle later returned to Athens to found his own school, the Lyceum. Like Plato, Aristotle wrote dialogues, but none has survived. Many of Aristotle's most important works are thought to be lecture notes taken by his students.

Augustine of Hippo (354–430 C.E.). Sometimes called the "second founder of the faith," Augustine is commonly recognized as one of the most important figures in Western Christianity. He was born in Thagasate, a Roman city in North Africa. He studied rhetoric and eventually moved to Carthage. There, he began to live an increasingly hedonistic lifestyle and became involved with the Manicheans, a religious sect that divided the world dualistically into good and evil. At the age of 30, Augustine moved to Milan to occupy a prestigious chair in rhetoric. During this period, he moved away from Manicheanism and eventually converted to Christianity. With his conversion, Augustine gave up his career in rhetoric and later returned to Africa, where he founded a semi-formal monastery with friends. On a visit to Hippo, he was forced to become a priest and bishop-in-waiting of the town. He wrote a large number of highly influential works, including *Confessions* and *The City of God*.

Calvin, Jean (1509–1564 C.E.). Calvin was born in France and studied philosophy and law. He was strongly influenced by French humanism and was eventually forced to flee France because of his call for Catholic reforms. In 1536, Calvin published the first edition of *Institutes of the Christian Religion*, a key text of the Protestant Reformation, and eventually made Geneva a center of the movement. Historically, Calvin's reforms and the community in Geneva are the origin of the Presbyterian Church. Calvin outlived his wife and all his children, and—to protect against people seeking relics—he was buried in an unmarked grave in the Geneva cemetery.

Conrad, Joseph (1857–1924 C.E.). Born to a noble Polish family under the name of Józef Teodor Konrad Korzeniowsk. Conrad was orphaned at the age of 11, after his mother and father died of sickness. He became a seaman at the age of 16 and spent several years sailing around the world on both legal and illegal ventures. He eventually assumed the position of captain aboard a steamship in the Congo, and this experience became the basis of *Heart of Darkness*. Owing to failing health and the desire to write, Conrad settled in Essex, England, where he became one of the great modern novelists and a narrator of stories hard to tell over high tea.

Dostoevsky, Fyodor (1821–1881 C.E.). The son of a violent alcoholic, a former military surgeon who practiced at a hospital for the poor in Moscow. His mother died when he was 16, and his father died two years later, possibly murdered by his serfs. Dostoevsky was subject to epilepsy fits from the age of 9, but he attended military school despite his ailments. He soon began to write but was imprisoned and sentenced to death for his involvement with Petrashevsky Circle, a radical literary group. He endured a mock execution before a firing squad and was sent to a prison camp in Siberia. Following his release, Dostoevsky was forced to serve several years in a Siberian military regiment. He wrote prolifically for the remainder of his life, and his works are commonly recognized as masterpieces of Russian and world literature.

Freud, Sigmund (1856–1939 C.E.). Born in Píbor, a village in the Austro-Hungarian Empire, to poor Jewish parents, who sacrificed to provide their son with an excellent education. The family eventually moved to Vienna, where Freud studied and, later, joined the medical faculty at the University of Vienna. He began to experiment with hypnosis but soon abandoned this method in favor of discussions meant to unlock the unconscious. Freud began to publish his ideas in the 1900s and soon developed a following in psychological circles. His fame continued to spread through and after the First World War. In 1932, he received the prestigious Goethe prize for his contributions to German culture, but in 1933, the Nazis took control of Germany and designated Freud's books to be banned and burned. Freud and his family went into hiding and eventually escaped to England; four of Freud's sisters, however, died in concentration camps. He himself died in September of 1939, worried that, in the struggle through world history of the titans—the death drive and the love drive—the death drive had finally won.

Hegel, G. W. F. (1770–1831 C.E.). Born in Stuttgart, Germany. When he was 13, his mother died of fever, which Hegel and his father both caught and barely survived. After completing his early education, Hegel enrolled at the seminary in Tübingen, where he became friends with Friedrich Schelling, later a well-known philosopher. Hegel worked as a private tutor before becoming a professor at the university in Jena, where he witnessed Napoleon Bonaparte, after a battle, cantering through the streets on horseback. Eventually, Hegel became widely recognized for his work *The Phenomenology of Spirit* and was appointed to the prestigious chair in philosophy at the University of Berlin. Hegel is best known as a key figure in German idealism, a movement that stressed the importance of ideas and the mind as driving forces in history. Hegel's philosophy is also known as one of the most important reactions to Immanuel Kant and was highly influential on Karl Marx.

Hobbes, Thomas (1588–1679 C.E.). Born in Wiltshire, England—supposedly when his mother heard news of the first sighting of the Spanish Armada—and educated at Oxford. He began his academic career by translating Thucydides's *The Peloponnesian War*, the first translation of that work ever attempted in English. During the English Civil War, Hobbes moved to France and composed *Leviathan*, a political treatise that argued for the legitimacy of governments on the basis of social contract and the supremacy of sovereign authority.

Irenaeus of Lyon (c. 150–c. 202 C.E.). Irenaeus was probably born in Smyrna and raised by Christian parents. During the persecution of Christians by Marcus Aurelius, Irenaeus was imprisoned for his faith, and he eventually became the second bishop of Lyon. During his tenure as a bishop, Irenaeus composed "Against Heresies," a famous Christian apologetic work against Gnosticism. He was also the first church father to attest to the validity of the four Gospels that later became part of the New Testament.

Kant, Immanuel (1724–1804 C.E.). Born in Königsberg, Prussia, where he lived all his life. A student at the University of Königsberg, Kant made several important contributions to astronomy in his early career before turning increasingly to philosophy. In 1781, after almost a decade of silence since becoming a professor at the university, Kant published the *Critique of Pure Reason*, a work widely regarded as one of the most important in the history of philosophy. He went on, over the next 20 years, to revolutionize philosophy in many ways. Kant is most famous for arguing that causality, time, and space are not the products of empirical observation; rather, he said, they are structures built into the nature of reason itself. Likewise, Kant's moral philosophy, especially his *Groundwork for the Metaphysics of Morals*, has been highly influential in Western thought. Kant died in Königsberg, having never traveled more than 100 miles from that city.

Luther, Martin (1483–1546 C.E.). Born in Eisleben, Germany, a city that was then part of the Holy Roman Empire. Luther briefly studied law but became a monk in the Augustinian order after making a vow during a lightning storm. Eventually, Luther began to teach theology at the University of Wittenberg, where he famously published his 95 Theses protesting the church's sale of indulgences in 1517. His dispute with Pope Leo X resulted in Luther's excommunication and the beginning of the Protestant Reformation. Theologically, Luther's most important claim was his emphasis on justification by faith—the insistence that human beings are saved by God on the basis of grace alone, apart from any righteous works.

Machiavelli, Niccolo (1469–1527 C.E.). Born in Florence, Italy, where he received a classical education and training in service to the Florentine state. Machiavelli became Second Chancellor of the Republic of Florence, in charge of managing foreign affairs and the militia. With the triumph of his political enemies, he was tortured and exiled from Florence. He was the author of *The Prince*, a political treatise for rulers that argued that moral perfection cannot govern the world, especially in politics. Machiavelli is considered by many to be the first political "realist."

Marx, Karl (1818–1883 C.E.). Born and educated in Trier, Germany. He enrolled at the University of Bonn but later transferred to the University of Berlin. There, Marx encountered the Young Hegelians, a group of thinkers who advocated for radical political proposals in conversation with Hegelian philosophy. Marx was influenced by this movement, though he also began to develop his own account of "dialectical materialism." He soon traveled to Paris, where he met his lifelong friend, Friedrich Engels. Eventually, Marx and Engels published *The Communist Manifesto*, a radical political tract that attacked capitalism and characterized history as the development of class struggle. Following its publication, Marx moved to London, where he remained until his death, struggling with ill health and in conditions of near poverty for himself and his family. He never stopped predicting the eventual communist revolution, which he was convinced would begin in either England or Germany.

Milton, John (1608–1674 C.E.). Born in London and received an elite education with help from his wealthy father. Milton enrolled at Christ's College, Cambridge, where he received his M.A. but continued his learning far beyond his university education. He traveled extensively before returning to England, where he began to write tracts supporting the Puritan and Parliamentary factions of the English Civil War and played various roles in the Commonwealth government of Oliver Cromwell. After Cromwell's death and the restoration of the monarchy, Milton went into hiding, was arrested, and was briefly imprisoned. Upon his release, he lived quietly in London for the remainder of his life, gradually going blind. At this late stage in his life, Milton published *Paradise Lost*, an epic poem recounting the Fall of Adam and Eve.

Nietzsche, Friedrich (1844–1900 C.E.). Born and raised in Röcken, a small town near Leipzig, the son of a Lutheran minister who died when he was 5. Nietzsche enrolled at the University of Bonn to study theology but turned to philology after losing his faith. He was considered the most brilliant and promising of scholars and became professor at the University of Basel at age 24—still a near-record in classical studies. He served as a medical orderly in the Franco-Prussian War, confronting the horrors of that conflict and suffering a series of ailments as a result. Nietzsche returned to Switzerland, where he became increasingly disillusioned with German culture and academia. He eventually gave up his position in Basel and lived the life of a wandering writer. His writing became increasingly provocative, and he continued to write prolifically until a mental collapse in January 1889, when he was 44. His many books were all written between 1872 and 1889, and most of them in his last few years of sanity.

Plato (428–347 B.C.E.). Born in Athens, the son of Ariston, a prominent aristocrat. As a young man, Plato seems to have traveled extensively before returning to Athens, with ambitions to be a poet; there, he became a disciple of Socrates. He wrote philosophical dialogues, almost all of which feature Socrates as the main character, and eventually founded his own school, the Academy, where he later became the teacher of Aristotle, among others. Alfred North Whitehead once said that all of philosophy is but a series of footnotes to Plato.

Bibliography

Adams, Marilyn McCord, and Robert Merrihew Adams, eds. *The Problem of Evil*. Oxford Readings in Philosophy Series. New York: Oxford University Press, 1990.

Anderson, Gary. *The Genesis of Perfection: Adam and Eve in Jewish and Christian Imagination*. Louisville, KY: Westminster/John Knox, 2001. A vivid study of how Jews and Christians understood the story of Adam and Eve in the four or five centuries after Jesus.

————. *Sin: A History*. New Haven: Yale University Press, 2009. Just what the title says: a history of Christian (and some Jewish) thought about sin.

Anselm. *Anselm of Canterbury: The Major Works*. Edited by Brian Davies and G. R. Evans. New York: Oxford University Press, 1998. A great collection of Anselm's philosophical and theological treatises. "On the Fall of the Devil" is here, in about as clear a translation as one can hope for, which doesn't mean it is easy reading.

Antognazza, M. R. *Leibniz: An Intellectual Biography*. New York: Cambridge University Press, 2008.

Aquinas, Thomas. *On Evil*. Edited by Brian Davies. Translated by Richard Regan. New York: Oxford University Press, 2003.

————. *Summa Theologiae*. Translated by the Fathers of the American Dominican Province. Notre Dame, IN: Christian Classics, 1981.

Arendt, Hannah. *The Origins of Totalitarianism*. Rev. ed. New York: Harcourt Brace Jovanovich, 1968 (1951).

Aristotle. *Nichomachean Ethics*. Translated by Terence Irwin. Indianapolis: Hackett, 1985.

————. *Poetics*. Translated by Richard Janko. Indianapolis: Hackett, 1987.

Augustine. *City of God*. Edited and translated by R. W. Dyson. New York: Cambridge University Press, 1998. A magisterial retranslation of the whole of this massive book, this translation of the *City of God* should last English-speaking readers for another 50 years or so.

————. *Confessions*. Translated by Maria Boulding, O.S.B. Hyde Park, NY: New City Press, 1997. There are many translations of the *Confessions*, and many of them are good for different reasons (who can resist a translation by someone named Pine-Coffin?), but this is perhaps the clearest.

Awn, Peter J. *Satan's Tragedy and Redemption: Iblis in Sufi Psychology*. Leiden: E.J. Brill, 1983.

Barth, Karl. *Karl Barth: Theologian of Freedom*. Edited by Clifford Green. Minneapolis: Fortress Press, 1991.

Beer, Anna. *Milton: Poet, Pamphleteer, and Patriot*. London: Bloomsbury, 2008.

Bouchard, Larry D. *Tragic Method and Tragic Theology*. University Park, PA: Pennsylvania State University Press, 1989.

Bowker, John. *Problems of Suffering in Religions of the World*. Cambridge: Cambridge University Press, 1970.

Brown, Peter. *Augustine of Hippo: A Biography*. 2nd ed. Berkeley: University of California Press, 2000. A great biography of Saint Augustine and a remarkably good read; Brown is a legend among scholars and a terrifyingly erudite person. He wrote this work in his 20s but revised it almost 40 years later, adding two new chapters that are well worth reading. Other biographies exist and are worth reading—those of Lancel, O'Donnell, Chadwick—but Brown's is on another plane altogether.

Browning, Christopher. *Ordinary Men: Reserve Police Battalion 101 and the Final Solution in Poland*. New York: Harper Perennial, 1993.

Brueggeman, Walter. *The Prophetic Imagination*. 2nd ed. Minneapolis: Fortress Press, 2001. A clear, brief, but profound study of the nature of prophecy in ancient Israel and up to the time of Jesus.

Calvin, John. *Institutes of the Christian Religion*. Edited by John T. McNeill. Translated by Ford Lewis Battles. Louisville, KY: Westminster/John Knox, 1960. One of the great works of the human mind and one of the truly systematic visions of the Christian faith available. Powerful and searching, perhaps nowhere more searching and ruthless than in the discussion of the absolute sovereignty of God.

Camus, Albert. *The Fall*. Translated by Justin O'Brien. New York: Alfred A. Knopf, 1956.

———. *The Plague*. Translated by Stuart Gilbert. New York: Alfred A. Knopf, 1948.

Connor, James A. *Pascal's Wager: The Man Who Played Dice with God*. San Francisco: HarperOne, 2006. A fine and vivid biography of Pascal, paying attention both to his scientific and mathematical work and his religious thought.

Conrad, Joseph. *Heart of Darkness*. Edited by Paul Armstrong. Norton Critical Editions. New York: W.W. Norton and Co., 2005.

———. *The Secret Agent: A Simple Tale*. New York: Oxford University Press, 2008.

Dalley, Stephanie. *Myths from Mesopotamia: Creation, the Flood, Gilgamesh, and Others*. Oxford World's Classics. New York: Oxford University Press, 2009.

Damrosch, David. *The Buried Book: The Loss and Rediscovery of the Great Epic of Gilgamesh*. New York: Henry Holt, 2007. The great story of how the *Gilgamesh* epic was discovered by a self-educated, working-class Englishman.

Dante, Alighieri. *Inferno*. Translated by Robert Hollander and Jean Hollander. New York: Anchor, 2002. The first part of the *Commedia*, this is the section on hell. This translation is good, although there are others. My recommendation is to check out several at your library and see which you think best gets at the Italian.

Dostoevsky, Fyodor. *Crime and Punishment*. Translated by Richard Pevear and Larissa Volkhonsky. New York: Vintage, 1993.

———. *Demons*. Translated by Richard Pevear and Larissa Volkhonsky. New York: Knopf, 1994. There are many translations of Dostoevsky, but this one stands out. Pevear and Volkhonsky are a husband-and-wife team of translators, apparently retranslating all the great works of 19th-century Russian literature in a new and powerfully vibrant (and apparently more accurate) prose. Were there a charity given to supporting artists, I would urge you to donate to it in the hopes that some money would go to Pevear and Volkhonsky. May all the gods smile on them.

Evans, G. R. *Augustine on Evil*. New York: Cambridge University Press, 1990. A classic account of Augustine's thinking on evil. Clear and acute.

Forsyth, Neil. *The Old Enemy: Satan and the Combat Myth*. Princeton: Princeton University Press, 1989. A fantastic work of scholarship that is part detective story, part archaeology: a study of the traces of the ancient Near Eastern combat myth in scriptures, literature, and writing from before the Hebrew Bible through the thought of Saint Augustine. Fascinating and a source for many screenplay ideas for those with eyes to see.

Foster, Benjamin R. *The Epic of Gilgamesh*. Norton Critical Editions. New York: W.W. Norton and Co., 2001. A good translation of *Gilgamesh* that also has a number of useful secondary sources attached.

Frank, Joseph. *Dostoevsky: A Writer in His Time*. Princeton: Princeton University Press, 2009. For those of you who are *really* interested in Dostoevsky, this almost-1,000-page abridgement of Frank's monumental five-volume biography should be enough. For those of you still hungry for more, adjourn to the steppes with some vodka, black bread, butter, and salt and enjoy the five volumes over a long Russian winter. Birch branches and steambath optional.

Freud, Sigmund. *Civilization and Its Discontents*. Translated by James Strachey. New York: W.W. Norton and Co., 2010. Not a perfect translation. Strachey was quite interested in making psychoanalysis into a science; thus, he translated a number of terms into technical jargon when Freud's German was quite colloquial (ego for *ich* ["I"], superego for *uber-ich* ["over-I"], id for *es* ["it"], and so on). But until we have a better one, this is the translation to use.

Friedrich, Hugo. *Montaigne*. Translated by Dawn Eng. Edited by Philippe Desan. Berkeley: University of California Press, 1967. The classic study, biographical and literary, on Montaigne. A great read, too.

Gordon, Bruce. *Calvin*. New Haven: Yale University Press, 2009. A rich and powerful biography of John Calvin, with a wealth of insight about his world, so deceptively unlike ours.

Grene, David, and Richard Lattimore, trans. and eds. *The Complete Greek Tragedies*. 4 vols. Chicago: University of Chicago Press, 1992. Collecting all we have left of Aeschylus, Sophocles, and Euripides, in translations that are both faithful and vivid, this is the foundational resource for reading the tragedies for those without a working knowledge of ancient Greek.

Hawkins, Peter. *Dante: A Brief History*. Cambridge, MA: Wiley-Blackwell, 2006. A nice introduction to Dante; highly recommended.

Hegel, G. W. F. *Phenomenology of Spirit*. Translated by A. V. Miller. New York: Oxford University Press, 1977.

Heschel, Abraham Joshua. *The Prophets*. New York: Harper Perennial Modern Classics, 2001.

Hick, John. *Evil and the God of Love*. Rev. ed. San Francisco: Harper and Row, 1978. An "Irenaean" theodicy, updated for the modern age, Hick's work was fundamental in bringing Irenaeus back into the conversation. Reasonably clearly written.

Hobbes, Thomas. *Leviathan*. Edited by Richard Tuck. New York: Cambridge University Press, 1996. Many editions of *Leviathan* exist, but this is my favorite. Great introduction by Richard Tuck.

————, trans. *The Peloponnesian War*. Edited by David Grene. Chicago: University of Chicago Press, 1989. A wonderful resource for *two* major thinkers: Thucydides and Hobbes. Not just in language but in argument, someone who has read Hobbes's *Leviathan* will see in this translation powerful echoes of the lessons Hobbes tried to teach in his philosophy.

Hume, David. *Dialogues Concerning Natural Religion*. Indianapolis: Hackett, 1998. Hume's classic attack on proofs of the existence of God and of a rational basis for theism. A great read.

Irenaeus. "Against Heresies," in *Ante-Nicene Fathers,* vol. 1, *Apostolic Fathers, Justin Martyr, Irenaeus*. Edited by Alexander Roberts and James Donaldson. Revised by A. Cleveland Coxe. Peabody, MA: Hendrickson Publishers, 1995. The most physically accessible translation of Irenaeus, this is a 19th-century work, but it includes all that remains of Irenaeus's writings in one volume.

Kant, Immanuel. *Religion within the Boundaries of Mere Reason and Other Writings*. Translated by Allen Wood and George di Giovanni. New York: Cambridge University Press, 1999.

Kierkegaard, Søren. *Fear and Trembling*. Edited and translated, with introduction and notes, by Howard V. Hong and Edna H. Hong. Princeton: Princeton University Press, 1983. A powerful discussion of Abraham and Isaac but really about Kierkegaard. Good stuff.

Kovacs, Judith, and Christopher Rowland. *Revelation: The Apocalypse of Jesus Christ.* Cambridge, MA: Wiley-Blackwell, 2004. A fantastic exploration of the meaning and history of the book of Revelation from its composition to today. Readable but also deeply historically researched, this is a tremendously interesting work.

Kramer, Samuel Noah. *The Sumerians: Their History, Culture, and Character*. Chicago: University of Chicago Press, 1971.

Larrimore, Mark. *The Problem of Evil: A Reader*. Cambridge, MA: Blackwell, 2001. A tremendously rich collection of works of all sorts, from antiquity to the 20th century, dealing with the problem of evil. Most excerpts are brief enough to read in a sitting but profound enough to return to again and again.

Lear, Jonathan. *Freud*. New York: Routledge, 2005. Lear is one of the best philosophers working today and a trained psychoanalyst. This is his most mature statement of his philosophical engagement with Freud—yet formulated in a remarkably clear and accessible prose.

Leibniz, G. W. *Theodicy: Essays on the Goodness of God, the Freedom of Man, and the Origin of Evil*. Translated by E. M. Huggard. Chicago: Open Court, 1998. The classic philosophical work on evil by Leibniz. Surprisingly clear reading—just hard thinking.

Levenson, Jon D. *Creation and the Persistence of Evil*. San Francisco: Harper and Row, 1989. A powerful dismantling of Christian presuppositions about the God of Abraham, Isaac, and Jacob by a prickly minded professor. Fun times.

Luther, Martin. *Basic Theological Writings*. Edited by Timothy Lull, William Russell, and Jaroslav Pelikan. Minneapolis: Augsburg Fortress Press, 2005. As good a collection of Luther's work as you could hope for.

Machiavelli, Niccolo. *The Portable Machiavelli*. Edited by Peter Bonadella and Mark Musa. New York: Penguin, 1979. There are many good collections and editions of Machiavelli's works; I suggest this one only because of the breadth of the selections.

Martinich, A. P. *Hobbes: A Biography*. New York: Cambridge University Press, 1999. A great, thick biography. As with Captain Willard's mission in *Apocalypse Now*, read this biography and you'll never want another.

Marx, Karl. *The Marx-Engels Reader*. 2nd ed. Also with writings by Friedrich Engels. Edited by Robert C. Tucker. New York: W.W. Norton and Co., 1978. Contains choice selections from a number of Marx's greatest writings. Perhaps my favorite piece here is a letter he wrote to a friend, given the title "For a Ruthless Criticism of Everything Existing."

Mason, Herbert. *Gilgamesh: A Verse Translation*. London: Penguin, 2003 (1970).

Meyers, Jeffrey. *Joseph Conrad: A Biography*. New York: Scribner, 1991. Several biographies are available of Conrad, but no one has "done" Conrad as Joseph Frank has "done" Dostoevsky (or Leon Edel has done Henry James). Nonetheless, this is perhaps the best "brief" (400 pages!) biography out there. A more remarkable life in its overall shape—yet uneventful in its day-to-day experience—is hard to imagine.

Midgley, Mary. *Wickedness: A Philosophical Essay*. New York: ARK Paperbacks, 1986.

Milgram, Stanley. *Obedience to Authority*. New York: Harper Torchbooks, 1974.

Mills, Nicholaus, and Kira Brunner, eds. *The New Killing Fields: Massacre and the Politics of Invention*. New York: Basic Books, 2002. A powerful collection of journalism and reflections on journalism of the era from the fall of the Berlin Wall in 1989 until September 11, 2001. Focuses on Yugoslavia, Rwanda, and East Timor.

Milosz, Czeslaw. *The Captive Mind*. Translated from Polish by Jane Zielonko. New York: Vintage International, 1981 (1953).

Milton, John. *Paradise Lost*. Edited by Gordon Teskey. Norton Critical Editions. New York: W.W. Norton and Co., 2004. The Norton Critical

Editions are student editions, filled with historical and biographical backgrounds to the text, as well as a number of important critical essays from the text's publication to today. This is an especially wonderful one.

Mitchell, Stephen. *The Book of Job*. New York: Harper, 1992. A modern commentary on Job, which looks like a translation.

Montaigne, Michel de. *The Complete Essays*. Edited and translated by M. A. Screech. New York: Penguin, 1993. A fine edition of the *Essais*, ably edited and translated.

Morgan, Michael L., ed. *A Holocaust Reader: Responses to the Nazi Extermination*. New York: Oxford University Press, 2000. Complementing the Roth and Berenbaum collection (below), an excellent collection of writings from Jewish thinkers and beyond about the Shoah/Holocaust.

Nehamas, Alexander. *Nietzsche: Life as Literature*. Cambridge, MA: Harvard University Press, 1997. An exploration of Nietzsche's philosophy, focusing on his aesthetic view of human life.

Neiman, Susan. *Evil in Modern Thought: An Alternative History of Philosophy*. Princeton: Princeton University Press, 2004. A great history of modern thought from the perspective of the problem of evil. Both gripping reading and profound thinking.

Newsom, Carol. *The Book of Job: A Contest of Moral Imaginations*. New York: Oxford University Press 2003. A vivid discussion of Job, with real attention to the inner logic of the book as a whole.

Niebuhr, Reinhold. *The Children of Light and the Children of Darkness: A Vindication of Democracy and a Critique of Its Traditional Defense*. New York: Charles Scribers' Sons, 1960. A classic and powerful statement of the political implications of Niebuhr's theology.

———. *The Nature and Destiny of Man*, vol. I, *Human Nature*. Louisville, KY: Westminster/John Knox, 1996. Almost anything of Niebuhr's would be good to read, but this might be the best. A clear and succinct picture of human nature and the character of sin, displayed in its systematic and theological character.

Nietzsche, Friedrich. *Beyond Good and Evil*. Translated by Walter Kaufmann. New York: Vintage, 1989.

———. *On the Genealogy of Morality: A Polemic*. Translated by Maudemarie Clark and Alan J. Swensen. Indianapolis: Hackett, 1998.

Noll, Mark. *America's God: Jonathan Edwards to Abraham Lincoln*. New York: Oxford University Press, 2002. A study of American religion, culminating in the conflagration of the Civil War, and a careful discussion of Abraham Lincoln's attempts to understand that war in theological terms.

Nussbaum, Martha. *The Fragility of Goodness: Moral Luck in Greek Tragedy and Philosophy*. New York: Cambridge University Press, 1986. A powerful description of the way that Plato and Aristotle thought about the tradition of Greek tragedy, one arguing that Aristotle can accommodate the sort of "moral luck" to which the tragedies call our attention, while Plato cannot.

Obermann, Heiko. *Luther: Man between God and the Devil*. Translated by Eileen Walliser-Schwarzbart. New Haven: Yale University Press, 1992. A great biography of Luther by his greatest modern student.

Padel, Ruth. *In and Out of Mind: Greek Images of the Tragic Self*. Princeton: Princeton University Press, 1992.

Pascal, Blaise. *Pensées and Other Writings*. Edited and translated by A. J. Krailsheimer. New York: Penguin, 1995.

Pinkard, Terry. *Hegel: A Biography*. New York: Cambridge University Press, 2001. As befitting a scholar as dense as Hegel, this is a long biography of a relatively uneventful life. But Pinkard—a philosopher as well as a biographer—does a wonderful job of explaining Hegel's work through his life (a very Hegelian thing to do). Worth reading for many reasons.

Plato. *Gorgias, Menexenus, Protagoras.* Edited by Malcolm Schofield. Translated by Tom Griffith. New York: Cambridge University Press, 2009. A clear translation of the *Protagoras* with several other dialogues. A nice collection.

———. *The Republic.* Translated by G. M. A. Grube and C. D. C. Reeve. Indianapolis: Hackett, 1992. For my money, one of the best works of philosophical translation of the past century. Grube's edition, revised by Reeve, is easily accessible yet sacrifices nothing of the depth of the philosophy.

Ricoeur, Paul. *The Symbolism of Evil.* New York: Harper and Row, 1967.

Roth, John K., and Michael Berenbaum. *Holocaust: Religious and Philosophical Implications.* New York: Paragon House, 1989. Along with the Morgan collection (above), an excellent collection of writings from Jewish thinkers and beyond about the Shoah/Holocaust.

Russell, Jeffrey Burton. *The Prince of Darkness: Radical Evil and the Power of Good in History.* Ithaca: Cornell University Press, 1988.

Scheindlin, Raymond. *The Book of Job.* New York: W.W. Norton and Co., 1999. A modern translation and commentary on Job.

Skinner, Quentin. *Machiavelli: A Very Brief Introduction.* New York: Oxford University Press, 2000. Skinner is a tremendous scholar who has revolutionized our thinking on Renaissance philosophy and political thought; this is a lovely gem of a book exploring Machiavelli's life and work.

Thucydides. *The Landmark Thucydides.* Edited by Robert B. Strassler. Translated by Richard Crawley. New York: Free Press, 1998. Modifying a 19th-century translation, this copy of Thucydides's *Peloponnesian War* is especially useful for understanding the context, the geography, and the physical reality of the history. Often used in teaching Thucydides to military officers.

————. *The Peloponnesian War*. Translated by Stephen Lattimore. Indianapolis: Hackett, 1998. For my money, the best translation of Thucydides's Greek; the simple, straightforward prose captures more of the power of the Greek and the ruthlessness of the realities than other more ornate or antique translations.

Tillich, Paul. *Paul Tillich: Theologian of the Boundaries*. Edited by Mark Kline Taylor. Minneapolis: Fortress Press, 1991.

Todd, Olivier. *Camus: A Life*. Translated by Benjamin Irvy. New York: Alfred A. Knopf, 1997.

Twain, Mark. *The Adventures of Huckleberry Finn*. Edited by Tom Cooley. Norton Critical Editions. New York: W.W. Norton and Co., 1998.

Urbach, Ephraim E. *The Sages: The World and Wisdom of the Rabbis of the Talmud*. Translated by Israel Abrahams. Cambridge, MA: Harvard University Press, 1987. A wonderful tour through Rabbinic Judaism, with a substantial discussion of the "evil impulse."

VanDeMark, Brian. *Pandora's Keepers: Nine Men and the Atomic Bomb*. New York: Back Bay Books, 2005. A wonderful study of nine scientists who were most responsible for the atomic bomb and how they dealt with its consequences.

Von Balthasar, Hans Urs. *Dare We Hope That "All Men Be Saved"? with A Short Discourse on Hell*. Translated by David Kipp and Rev. Lothar Krauth. San Francisco: Ignatius Press, 1988.

Weissbort, Daniel, ed. *The Poetry of Survival: Post-War Poets of Central and Eastern Europe*. New York: St. Martin's Press, 1991. Just what it says: a wonderful collection of such poets as Paul Celan, Czeslaw Milosz, and Zbigniew Herbert. A great introduction.

Williams, Bernard. *Shame and Necessity*. 2nd ed. Berkeley: University of California Press, 2008. One of the greatest philosophers of the second half of the 20th century was also one of the last philosophers properly educated in "the classics." Coincidence? Not to hear Williams tell it; this book explores the implications of the worldview expressed by the Greek tragedians and Thucydides in a way that is philosophically demanding, deeply disturbing, and existentially exhilarating. A book whose vision (it was first published in 1993) is still in the process of affecting contemporary philosophy.

Notes

Notes

Notes

Notes

Notes

Notes

Notes